BONNIE-SUE

A Marine Corps
Helicopter Squadron
in
Vietnam

BONNIE-SUE

A Marine Corps
Helicopter Squadron
in
Vietnam

Marion F. Sturkey

Heritage Press International
Plum Branch, South Carolina

BONNIE-SUE: A Marine Corps Helicopter Squadron in Vietnam

Library of Congress Catalogue Card Number: 96-75261

International Standard Book Number: 0-9650814-2-7

First Edition: {First printing - April 1996
                {Second printing - March 1997
                {Third printing - January 1999

Published by
HERITAGE PRESS INTERNATIONAL
204 Jefferson Street
P. O. Box 333
Plum Branch, South Carolina 29845

Manufactured in the United States of America

Grateful acknowledgement is extended to the staff members of
the Marine Corps Historical Center. They provided assistance and
access to their holdings and reference material. Also, **grateful
acknowledgement** is extended to hundreds of Vietnam War-era
Marine Corps helicopter pilots, aircrewmen, and infantrymen.
They volunteered their time, personal records, and recollections in
the furtherance of this project.

In Memoriam

The following 28 Marines from HMM-265 made the Supreme Sacrifice in the noble cause of freedom during the course of the Vietnam War. They are among the 58,132 American Servicemen who selflessly laid upon their country's altar a life full of the highest promise, in hope of a brighter world.

William E. Johnson	Captain, USMC
Ronald E. Pfeifer	First Lieutenant, USMC
Robert R. Telfer	Sergeant, USMC
Howard D. Strouse	Gunnery Sergeant, USMC
David L. G. Moser	Staff Sergeant, USMC
Herbert S. Murff ***	Sergeant, USMC
Curtis R. Bolscheid	Captain, USMC
John S. Oldham	Major, USMC
Thomas M. Hanratty	Private First Class, USMC
Jose J. Gonzales	Lance Corporal, USMC
John A. House II	Captain, USMC
H. H. Fleming III	First Lieutenant, USMC
William T. Hale	First Lieutenant, USMC
Jeffery W. Rainaud	First Lieutenant, USMC
Gary D. Kemski	Corporal, USMC
Marvin Wesley Jr.	Corporal, USMC
William Emerson	Captain, USMC
John R. Harrell	First Lieutenant, USMC
Peter R. Bossman	HM3-USN
Ramond E. Glover	First Lieutenant, USMC
John A. Prombo	First Lieutenant, USMC
Wallace C. Bergstrom	Gunnery Sergeant, USMC
Jack E. Muisener	Sergeant Major, USMC
Howard E. Morse	Corporal, USMC
Jose R. Bernal	Sergeant, USMC
Robert J. Himler	First Lieutenant, USMC
Donald G. Lammers	First Lieutenant, USMC
Michael Alberici	Lance Corporal, USMC

*** (Returned to United States; died from wounds)

Table of Contents

List of Maps and Photographs

But we know we can no longer find security and
well-being in defenses and policies that are confined
to North America, or the Western Hemisphere, or
the North Atlantic Community. This has become a
very small planet.

-- (Dean Rusk; April 23, 1965)

Prologue

Messenger: **Prepare you, generals:**
The enemy comes on in gallant show;
Their bloody sign of battle is hung out,
And something to be done immediately.
-- (William Shakespeare; in *Julius Caesar*)

On the vast Asian continent, south of China and east of India, lies a mysterious land generally known today as Indochina. According to legend, the people of this huge story-book tropical peninsula were descended from the union of a dragon and a fairy. However, history tells us that Mongols from the north, and Thais and Indians from the west, migrated into this region of southeast Asia during the first millennium B.C. They intermarried with local Indonesian natives and created a distinct new culture. These people eventually named their new country Viet Nam -- The Home of the Southern Viet People -- and they gradually became known to the outside world as the Vietnamese. Their land extends 1200 miles south from China to the Gulf of Thailand.

In the third century B.C., China invaded and conquered Vietnam. The Chinese Han emperors established colonial rule and imposed their religion, social customs, and technical skills on the Vietnamese people. Although the Vietnamese repeatedly attempted to militarily oust the Chinese, they actually benefited from the stability of over 1000 years of foreign occupation. Colonial Chinese governors used Vietnamese laborers to build roads, and they established an advanced agricultural system of canals and dikes. New schools were founded to teach Chinese language, arts, and history.

The first major Vietnamese rebellion against Chinese occupation began in 39 A.D. Over the next 800 years there were many such rebellions, and the Vietnamese heroes and martyrs of legend were always those who rose up against the despised oppressors from the north. The greatest martyr was Ly Bon, a Sino-Vietnamese noble who led a 20,000 man military revolt in 544 A.D. Ly Bon enjoyed great initial success, but he was eventually defeated and beheaded by the victorious Chinese Army.

Notwithstanding such revolts, Chinese rule remained firm until the fall of the powerful T'ang Dynasty. Taking advantage of Chinese instability, the Vietnamese rose up and drove out the hated Northerners. The crucial battle at Bach Dang in 938 A.D. is as famous in Vietnamese history as the epic Battle of Yorktown in American history.

All warfare is based on deception.
-- (Sun Tzu; in *The Art of War*)

At Bach Dang the Vietnamese troops drove hundreds of iron-tipped pilings into the river bottom, just below water level. Then they lured the Chinese Navy into their trap. The Chinese ships were heavily damaged, the Vietnamese Army routed the Chinese Army, and Vietnam became an independent state at last.

Vietnam has always been a land of militarily powerful and culturally advanced civilizations. The great Khmer Kingdom had been founded in the ninth century in what is now Cambodia, and the navigable Mekong River connected its capital to the South China Sea. With slave labor the Khmers built reservoirs, canals, and roads. Angkor Vat, their great temple built as a burial vault for their king, is more elaborate than anything left to the world by the Greeks, Romans, or Egyptians. This great temple-tomb still stands as mute witness to the glory and power of the Khmer society. Meanwhile, on the eastern coast of Vietnam the seafaring kingdom of Champa had been established by pirates, wanderers, merchantmen, and local Vietnamese adventurers. During a series of wars lasting over 400 years, the Khmers finally defeated the Chams in 1471 A.D., executed the Cham King, and militarily unified all of Vietnam.

During the past 1000 years, Vietnam has been in continual military and social turmoil. On various occasions, most notably in the thirteenth century, China again invaded Vietnam and was defeated only after inflicting great damage and loss of life. The two main religious and political groups, the Buddhists and the Confucians, constantly bickered and vied for power. The savage Montagnard mountain tribesmen often raided and sacked the coastal villages of the more civilized Vietnamese farmers. However, European influence gradually became a stabilizing factor. Marco Polo had come to Vietnam in 1280 A.D., and over the next 500 years he had been followed by Portuguese, Dutch, and French traders who sought silk, cinnamon, spices, and tea.

Nguyen Anh became Emperor of Vietnam in 1802. He built the Great Mandarin Road from Saigon, in the south, about 900 miles north to the rice-rich Red River Delta. From their regal Imperial Capitol inside the citadel in the city of Hue (pronounced, *Whay*), later Nguyen emperors began land reforms to benefit the Vietnamese farmers. Still, regional strife lasted until the mid-1800s, when the French stabilized Vietnam and imposed a semblance of social order. During the past two centuries the United States often came to the aid of the French colonial government in Vietnam. The famous *USS Constitution* sailed into Tourane Bay in 1845 and shelled the city of Tourane (later to be renamed Da Nang) in a vain effort to force the release of a jailed French missionary.

European nations vied for economic and military control of Vietnam during the latter half of the 1800s. In 1859 the French Army attacked and seized the Vietnamese military citadel in the southern city of Saigon, and by 1883 the French completed their military occupation of Vietnam. Within several years roughly 15,000 French colonialists ruled about 16 million Vietnamese. The colonial government imprisoned 20,000 suspected opponents of French authority, and over 700 were guillotined without benefit of trial. In the remote countryside and the small villages, insurgents were collectively labeled "bandits," and the French Army beheaded thousands of presumed bandits who were caught.

> Emperor Tu Duc . . . passed away with curses against the invader [the hated French Army] on his lips.
> -- (Edward Doyle et al; in *Setting The Stage*)

French became the second language of the Vietnamese. Farmers grew rice for shipment to Europe, rubber tree plantations covered the highlands, and opium was sold to Chinese dealers for foreign export. Although the peasants' lot in life improved little, by the early 1900s the major cities had adapted to the French colonization. Saigon, often called the "Paris of the East" and the "Pearl of the Orient," evolved into a bustling center of commerce. The citizens of the historic city of Hue, on the banks of the River of Perfumes, could justifiably boast of the unparalleled beauty of the former Imperial Capital of Vietnam. In Hue the sacred tombs of the emperors and the Imperial Palace, modeled after the Chinese palace in Peking, were unique to all of southeast Asia. Hanoi, the new French capital of Vietnam, became the cultural center of Indochina. With its wide avenues, university, and famed Temple of Literature, it was indeed the showplace of the French Foreign Empire.

European France fell to the German Army in June 1940 during the early days of World War II. Soon the potent Japanese war machine rolled south into Vietnam, and the French Vichy government turned over control of Indochina to the Japanese Imperial Army. The United States, by then at war with Japan, joined the local Viet Minh communist guerrillas in an effort to harass and defeat the Japanese occupation force. The Japanese finally capitulated in 1945. The president of the new provisional government of the Democratic Republic of Vietnam, Ho Chi Minh, borrowed language from the United States Constitution and declared absolute Vietnamese independence.

The new Vietnamese independence would prove to be short-lived, because the French Army again seized control of Vietnam. Financially aided by the United States, the French began an eight year battle to defeat the now formidable nationalist Viet Minh communist army. Finally, deep in the mountains at remote Dien Bien Phu, 6200 French paratroopers, indigenous soldiers, and foreign mercenaries faced 49,500 Viet Minh troops under the command of General Vo Nguyen Giap. The Viet Minh Army surrounded Dien Bien Phu Valley with Russian-built heavy artillery that they had disassembled and hauled hundreds of miles through the mountains. The Viet Minh began their siege on March 13, 1954. Outnumbered, outgunned, and surrounded, the French still fought bravely and tenaciously, but without relief or resupply they were doomed from the outset. Viet Minh loudspeakers blared "Surrender or die!" in French, German, and Vietnamese.

By early May, desperation gripped the surviving bone-weary French, but still they fought on. Their was no more food, medical supplies were running out, and the French defenders were almost out of ammunition. Sixty-two helicopters, fighters, and transport aircraft had been shot down by the Viet Minh antiaircraft (AAA) batteries that ringed Dien Bien Phu Valley. The constant Viet Minh artillery barrages had pounded the once proud French fortress into a muddy, bloody, and burning shambles. At 1700 Hours on May 6, the French commander, General Christian de Castries, radioed Hanoi for the last time: "Au revoir, mon general; au revoir, mes camarades." Minutes later hundreds of Viet Minh soldiers swarmed over the French command bunker and raised the flag of the Democratic Republic of Vietnam.

"C'est fini?"

"Oui, c'est fini!"

The French Army still occupied most of Vietnam, including all of the major cities. However, after the fall of Dien Bien Phu the French politicians simply lost the *will* to continue the struggle in Indochina. At the Geneva Conference it was agreed that the French Army would withdraw all of its combat troops and that Vietnam would be divided at the 17th parallel.

> The conference takes note of the agreements ending hostilities in Laos, Cambodia, and Vietnam . . . .
> -- (from *Final Declaration of the Geneva Conference*)

The communist Viet Minh, under the leadership of Ho Chi Minh, would control the north. President Ngo Dinh Diem would remain in power in the south until free nationwide elections could be held to unify all of Vietnam. Unfortunately, it was not to be. In the north, Ho Chi Minh formed the National Liberation Front for the purpose of taking military control of the Vietnamese southerners, who now relied on the United States for economic aid.

North Vietnamese Army (NVA) "political advisors" infiltrated into South Vietnam and organized sympathetic peasants into military units. These local Vietnamese guerrillas would eventually become known as Viet Cong (slang for *Vietnamese Communist*) or simply "VC." They got Russian and Chinese weapons from their North Vietnamese supporters and began attacking South Vietnamese troops of the new Army of the Republic of Vietnam (ARVN). When these attacks met with little initial success, North Vietnamese Army units marched south across the 17th parallel and orchestrated their own attacks on South Vietnamese military and government targets. In the late 1950s the United States began rushing military arms, aircraft, supplies, and military advisors to assist the South Vietnamese. Once again, Vietnam was at war.

In the south, Diem proclaimed that his Republic of Vietnam would remain an independent nation. Diem was backed by the United States, which, in the wake of the Korean War, relied on a free and democratic South Vietnam to block further Russian and Chinese military expansion in Indochina. Dwight D. Eisenhower, President of the United States, was faced with communist military advances in Europe and throughout Africa and South America, so he challenged his military Joint Chiefs of Staff: "My God, we *must* not lose Asia! We've got to look this thing right in the face!"

The United States inaugurated John F. Kennedy as president in 1961, and he cautioned the Soviets and Chinese that the American people would "pay any price and bear any burden to ensure the survival of liberty." At that time there were less than 900 United States military advisors in South Vietnam. However, Kennedy and his successor, Lyndon B. Johnson, both vowed to take any and all necessary steps to thwart the communist attacks.

South China Sea, April 15, 1962 (Palm Sunday): The metallic ear-shattering growl of supercharged R-1820 Wright engines reverberated across the flight deck. Viewed from Pri-Fly high above, the *USS Princeton* (LPH-5) had become a living kaleidoscope of whirling rotors and flashing red anticollision lights. In the cockpits of the drab green Sikorsky H-34 helicopters, United States Marine Corps pilots warmed their nine-cylinder radial engines at 2000 RPM. Two sets of wary eyes scanned each instrument panel as the temperature and pressure needles slowly settled into the green arcs on the gauges. Then a quick radio check-in confirmed that each H-34 was loaded, warmed up, and ready to launch. The helicopters and the men of Marine Medium Helicopter Squadron 362 (HMM-362) were headed for war in South Vietnam.

Lieutenant Colonel Archie J. Clapp, the squadron commanding officer, manned the right seat in the cockpit of Number One. With his left arm he slowly pulled in collective pitch. Below the metal firewall in front of the cockpit, his engine hammered out 1525 horsepower to counter the aerodynamic drag as his rotors bit into the crisp morning air. The H-34 rose and then accelerated forward and upward, shuddering through translational lift. Behind Colonel Clapp, the remaining Marine Corps helicopter pilots cranked in full power. They clawed their way skyward behind Colonel Clapp as he turned toward the Vietnamese coastline, 16 miles to the west.

The United States, as a leader of the free world, cannot afford further retreat in Asia.
-- (Richard M. Nixon; April 1954)

The Marine Corps helicopters flew over the mouth of the Mekong River on the aerial trip to their new home, the old World War II Japanese fighter airstrip at Soc Trang. Here the Marines of HMM-362 landed, 85 miles south of the South Vietnamese capital city of Saigon. They set up a helicopter base virtually overnight. All pilots and aircrewmen (*aircrewmen* are helicopter crew chiefs and helicopter gunners) had exchanged their bright international-orange flight suits for tan colored attire in order to make themselves less conspicuous targets. They had come to South Vietnam to fly combat support missions for the ARVN soldiers. Soon their air-portable Tactical Airfield Fuel Dispensing System (TAFDS) was in working order. The Marines set up billeting and helicopter maintenance tents, and they launched their first combat mission three days later on April 18.

From this modest beginning, code named Operation Shu-Fly, the Marines learned much about flying helicopters in a combat environment. At the outset the Sikorsky H-34 helicopters were totally unarmed, but soon the helicopter copilots and crew chiefs began using the old reliable "grease-gun" to cover their helicopter while on the ground and under fire. Quickly seeing the need for more firepower, the Marines discarded the grease-gun in favor of a pair of hatch-mounted M-60 machineguns.

By September of 1962 the Marines of Operation Shu-Fly were ordered to leave Soc Trang. They moved north to Da Nang, the new name for the old French colonial city of Tourane. Here at Da Nang, in the shadow of Monkey Mountain and lofty Dong Den Mountain, the helicopter squadron began flight operations at the main airport just west of the city. During the next two years the Marine Corps rotated several H-34 squadrons into the Shu-Fly role: HMM-163, HMM-261, HMM-364, and HMM-365. The Shu-Fly name was soon dropped in favor of the more functional "Marine Unit Vietnam." But although the name had changed, the job remained the same -- fly combat support missions for the South Vietnamese Army soldiers.

> The Marines are here to help you. Do not run from them! If you run, they may mistake you for a Viet Cong and shoot you. Stand still and the Marines will not harm you. Tell this to your friends.
> -- (English translation; text of an aerial-drop pamphlet)

But the war was rapidly changing. North Vietnam stepped up its rate of support to the Viet Cong, and the North Vietnamese Army began sending entire battalions of its own troops into the fighting in South Vietnam. Below the 17th parallel the North Vietnamese built underground barracks, workshops, hospitals, and fuel depots. In response, the United States poured in military supplies to the embattled South Vietnamese. Still, although the Americans provided the helicopters, pilots, and aircrewmen, South Vietnam provided the infantrymen to fight the communist invaders from the north.

By early 1965 the government of South Vietnam teetered on the brink of total military collapse. The North Vietnamese funnelled munitions, men, and all of the tools of war into the fight. Without massive military intervention, the outmanned and outgunned South Vietnamese faced certain defeat.

<u>Da Nang, March 8, 1965, 0803 Hours</u>: The first wave of the 3rd Battalion, 9th Marines, sloshed across the beach north of Da

Nang, just south of the Nam-O Bridge on Colonial Route 1, the former Great Mandarin Road. Later that same day another battalion from the Third Marines swooped down from Okinawa on C-130 turboprop transports. With the H-34 helicopters of HMM-162 for logistical support, these Marines formed the 9th Marine Expeditionary Brigade. They had come to Vietnam to protect the city of Da Nang and its large airbase from further Viet Cong and North Vietnamese attacks.

Our Country! In her intercourse with foreign nations, may she always be in the right. But, Our Country, right or wrong!
-- (Stephen Decatur; 1779-1820)

Soon more Marine Infantry, the "Grunts," and more helicopter squadrons arrived. They set up an enclave at Phu Bai, seven miles south of Hue. More Grunts and yet another helicopter squadron built a camp at Ky Ha on the seacoast south of Tam Ky. The Marines began aggressively patrolling the Vietnamese countryside to track down the elusive enemy, who had been wrecking havoc in his raids on the cities. For the Marine Corps the "Dirty Little War" had started. Men fought and died, but 14,000 miles away in the United States, the public knew little of what was going on in Vietnam. However, that was about to change.

Da Nang, March 31, 1965: The morning sun had burned away the night mist as Larry Burrows, a photographer and correspondent for *Life Magazine*, ambled out to the flight line. There the Marine H-34s of HMM-163 were getting last minute checks by their crew chiefs. Today the pilots and aircrewmen of HMM-163 would pick up an assault force of ARVN soldiers and fly them into an enemy infested area in the flatlands near Da Nang. Burrows would tag along to see if there might be a newsworthy story that he could forward to his editors in the United States.

Burrows would ride in the helicopter designated YP-13 (spoken, *Yankee-Papa thirteen*). He found the right helicopter by checking the faded white lettering on the tail of each H-34. Burrows briefly chatted with the Marine Corps pilot, Captain Peter Vogel. Then he met his host and unofficial narrator for the flight, the 21 year old helicopter crew chief, Lance Corporal James C. Farley. Soon they picked up their cargo of nine frightened ARVNs, and they were on their way. In addition to YP-13, sixteen more H-34s from HMM-163 bored their way through the sky toward the drop point.

Burrows wondered if there would be a salable story here. He watched as the helicopter gunner, Private First Class Wayne Hoilien from Viroqua, Wisconsin, snapped a serpentine linked belt of ammunition into the M-60 machinegun mounted in the open hatch. Then Hoilien reached up, twisted the friction lock on the front of his flight helmet, and lowered the dark protective visor down over his face. To Burrows, Hoilien looked like a medieval warrior dressed for battle.

The 17 helicopters roared down with the sun at their backs and headed toward a series of flooded rice paddies. Enemy soldiers, entrenched along a treeline, opened fire on the H-34s as they flared to land. Rounds ripped through the thin aluminum skins of the helicopters. The Marine gunners answered the incoming enemy fire with their M-60s.

As the wide-eyed ARVNs leaped out and scrambled for cover, Captain Vogel saw a helicopter in trouble. Enemy machinegun fire had downed YP-3. The helicopter was stranded in the paddy with its engine still running and its rotors still turning. Vogel could see the pilot of YP-3 slumped forward in his seat, either unconscious or dead. Farley fired another M-60 burst at the muzzle flashes in the treeline. Then he jumped out of his helicopter and splashed across the rice paddy to try to aid his downed squadronmates.

> Marines never left a dead colleague on the battlefield if they could find enough of him to bring back, and sometimes this wasn't much.
> -- (Jon Boulle; quoted by author Philip D. Chinnery in *Life on the Line*)

The hapless pilot of YP-3 had taken an enemy round through the neck. He hung forward in his seat in the cockpit, restrained only by his lap belt and shoulder harness. After clambering up the side of the fuselage on the outside of the cockpit, Farley reached inside and killed the Wright R-1820 engine with the magneto switch. He grabbed the unconscious pilot around the shoulders, but he did not have the needed leverage to lift him up and over the lip of the escape hatch (a sliding window) on the side of the cockpit.

The YP-3 copilot, First Lieutenant James E. Magel, had been shot below his right armpit. The gunner, Sergeant Billie Owens, had caught a round in his shoulder. Farley half dragged and half carried them out of their downed helicopter. He helped the two wounded men as they sloshed and staggered back across the paddy to YP-13. As they crawled inside, Hoilien traded long bursts with an enemy machinegunner in a nearby treeline.

Vogel cranked on full power, snatched the collective pitch lever upward, and jammed the cyclic control forward. YP-13 started clawing for airspeed, altitude, and relative safety. As they climbed through 500 feet of altitude, Farley and Hoilien turned away from their M-60s and tried to help the wounded men.

Burrow's photographs would later depict the desperate race against time as they sped back toward the field hospital near Da Nang. Sergeant Owens sat slumped back in a web troop seat with his eyes closed and his face contorted by pain. Lieutenant Magel, still conscious and still wearing his flight helmet with the visor down over his eyes, lay bleeding on the aluminum floor of the helicopter cabin. Farley knelt by the prone copilot and frantically tried to stem the steady flow of blood. Despite Farley's efforts, Magel's lifeblood slowly oozed away. He died on the aluminum cabin floor of YP-13 before they landed at the field hospital.

After the mission, Burrows counted eleven bullet holes in the fuselage of YP-13. His black and white photographs captured the stark anguish on the face of the young crew chief. Farley emotionally related his vain effort to pull the pilot out of the cockpit of the downed helicopter in the paddy. He told Burrows how he had tried to help Lieutenant Magel, how he had tried to stem the loss of blood. But despite his desperate efforts to save the pilot, Magel had died in his arms.

Burrows had been on the helicopter ride of his life. Yes, he indeed had a salable story. His vivid photographs and his lengthy feature article, "One Ride with Yankee-Papa 13," would later begin on page 24 of the April 16, 1965, issue of *Life Magazine*.

Gradually the Marine Grunts replaced the ARVN soldiers in northern South Vietnam. The Grunts fanned out into the villages and hamlets, where they started medical assistance and civic action programs. They built schools, dug wells, repaired bridges, and their corpsmen provided the only medical treatment that many of the villagers had ever known.

The Marine Corps and the United States Air Force brought in their attack and fighter aircraft to the main airport at Da Nang. The Marine helicopter squadrons left the main airport to the jets, and they built their own new base three miles to the east. They called their new home "Marble Mountain" because of the nearby volcanic rock mountain that bore the same name. Here on the east side of the Cau Do River, right on the beach by the South China Sea, the Marine helicopter pilots and aircrewmen settled into their daily routine. The Marines also set up a smaller helicopter base at Ky Ha, far to the south. In addition, they based a single squadron of H-34s at Phu Bai, about seven miles south of Hue.

Lean and lanky Second Lieutenant William T. "Tee" Holmes Jr. was a typical Marine Corps helicopter pilot. His father had been killed-in-action on Okinawa in April 1945, so Tee had grown up in rural Dublin, Georgia, under his mother's guiding hand. With a slow and nasal southern drawl, like hand rubbed hickory, no one would ever mistake Tee for a New York Yankee.

Tee had blazed through basic flight school Marine Aviation Cadet (MARCAD) Class 42-63 in Pensacola, Florida, one week ahead of me. The following year we had roomed together at Whiting Field during T-28 flight training. Still later in mid-1965, we had shared an off-base apartment near the Marine Corps Air Facility at New River, North Carolina. Tee loved to party, and he loved to play his guitar and sing. In times of real or perceived crisis, he always wore his perpetual and impish Georgia grin.

Ky Ha, December 7, 1965: Tee arrived in Vietnam and got assigned to HMM-364, an H-34 squadron at Ky Ha. The squadron administrative officer told Tee that he would "replace Lieutenant Johnson." Tee and Johnson were friends. They had been together in the United States only eight days before, but then Johnson had gotten his Official Orders and had caught an immediate flight to Vietnam. "He's transferred *again*?" Tee wondered. But before he could ask where Johnson had gone after only a week in Vietnam, the administrative officer added: "He already got himself killed. You'll sleep in his cot."

> Johnson, S G -- 1Lt USMC -- Nov 11 40 - Dec 3 65 -- Applegate, CA -- MIA.
> -- (from casualty listings in *Vietnam KIAs & MIAs*)

Tee walked from the HMM-364 flight line up to tent city. Ky Ha was a primitive base, and rain had turned the red laterite clay into a slick and gooey soup. Boards and mats had been laid on the ground inside of the tents, and they helped Tee keep his feet out of the mud. Inside of his tent, Tee stowed his flight gear in a wooden box that was propped up six inches off of the mud in order to keep the contents as dry as practical. He noted that Johnson's spare set of mud-caked boots was still under his canvas cot. Eight days before, Tee and Johnson had parted in the United States. Now, Johnson was gone forever.

> Life really is a fragile thing. And in most cases, when one's life is cut short, the cause can be traced back to some seemingly insignificant quirk of fate.
> -- (William T. "Tee" Holmes; years later)

Tee got his first flight assignment the next morning, December 8. He would be the copilot for Captain Jim Givan in Bureau Number 145768 (the *Bureau Number* is the military serial number of a Marine Corps helicopter). They would fly a logistics mission 47 miles straight up the coast to Da Nang, nothing more than a "milk run," Tee was told. This was the standard way to break in a new pilot in Vietnam, allowing Tee to get familiar with the maps, radio frequencies, and flight procedures before flying on real combat missions.

The miserable rain and fog left them with two choices. They could fly under Visual Flight Rules (VFR), do a little nifty scud running, and zip right up the coastline. They would have to fly low over the seacoast to stay under the clouds. But they could probably remain far enough out over the ocean to avoid possible ground fire, Tee reasoned. On the other hand, they could climb up into the clouds and fly under Instrument Flight Rules (IFR). Either way they should encounter no problem, Givan told Tee.

Tee and Givan piloted the last helicopter in the flight of three H-34s. They took off from Ky Ha, flew over the steep cliff at the seashore, and then rotored northward toward Da Nang. The weather quickly turned rotten. A gale was brewing, and the wind swept in from the open sea at about 35 knots. Visibility fell to a couple of miles in the rain, and there was a hard overcast about 500 feet above the surface of the ocean. Yet, except for the lousy weather the flight to Da Nang proved to be uneventful.

The three helicopters landed at the depot at Da Nang, shut down their engines, and the crew chiefs and gunners started loading supplies. Tee helped them load about 80 cases of beer, plus helicopter spare parts and a variety of helicopter maintenance equipment. Then they fired up their radial engines, engaged their rotors, and took off for home.

As they flew out over the sea, Tee saw that the weather had really turned sour. Forward visibility had decreased to about a mile in the rain, and the cloud ceiling had dropped. Still, the three helicopters managed to stay VFR as they skimmed along about 200 feet above the waves. Tee felt no cause for alarm. Nothing could go wrong, he reasoned. On the helicopter ICS system the four man crew of Tee's H-34 kept up a sarcastic running chatter about the "beautiful" weather. Also, since this was Tee's first mission in Vietnam, he busied himself with his maps. Peering through the rain and fog, he tried to see recognizable landmarks on the beach, now partially obscured about 500 feet off to his right. This was really exciting flying!

The TACAN (a bearing and distance navigation radio) picked up mileage and heading to Chu Lai. By Tee's calculations they were somewhere near Tam Ky, and in roughly eight minutes they would be back on the ground at Ky Ha, he figured. But unfortunately, Tee would be wrong. His flight logbook would later be inscribed by the dutiful HMM-364 operations clerk: "8 Dec 65 - BuNo. 145768 - Ky Ha to Da Nang - CRASH AT SEA."

The FM radio rasped: "Takin' fire from the beach!"

Instantly, Tee's buttocks puckered shut.

Exactly where the fatal round struck the helicopter, no one knows. The H-34 engine suddenly died. No warning, no cough, no sputter; it just quit. The abrupt and unexpected silence seemed almost deafening.

Givan keyed the FM radio: "MAYDAY! MAYDAY!"

A military helicopter without engine power glides only slightly better than a falling anvil. And with only 200 feet of altitude, Tee and Givan had just a few precious seconds until impact with the water down below. Down collective! Full right rudder! Harness locked! Jam the cockpit escape hatches open! Here comes the water -- Flare! -- Flare! -- Flare!

One HMM-364 aircraft, participating in a three aircraft administrative flight from Da Nang to Chu Lai . . . made an autorotation into the surf. The gunner was not seen again. During the entire rescue operation, enemy small arms fire was received from a nearby treeline.

-- (*MAG-36 Command Chronology*; December 8, 1965)

The Sikorsky helicopter hit the water hard, rolled inverted, and began sinking toward the bottom of the sea. Under water in the upside-down cockpit, Tee remembered his dilbert-dunker training from flight school at Pensacola. He yanked his radio cords loose from his hardhat. For a second or so, Tee struggled to get out of his seat, then realized that he was still strapped in. He felt for the quick-release arm, hit it, and he was free.

Tee squeezed through the escape hatch and started swimming up toward the surface. When his head shot out of the water, he saw that the waves were about eight feet high. Tee squirmed out of his flak jacket and could stay afloat pretty easily after that. The stinging wind whipped the blinding salt spray across his face. Each time Tee topped a wave he could hear and see the enemy firing at him from the treeline on the beach.

Fortunately the other two H-34s had heard Givan's "Mayday." They circled back, their gunners firing at the enemy muzzle flashes on the beach. Tee did not know which threat was the greatest. If he started waving his arms, he would attract more enemy fire from the beach. But if he did not wave, his squadronmates might not see him. Tee would explain to me many years later that it became an easy choice: "I waved and splashed like a maniac!"

As the two H-34s bored in, their crew chiefs kicked out case after case of beer to lighten the load for the rescue. They reeled

Givan up on the hoist. By now Tee's crew chief had rolled ashore in the surf. Both helicopters landed on the beach, picked up the crew chief under fire, and then returned to rescue Tee. Fighting against the rotorwash, Tee threw his arms through the horse-collar. He was hoisted aboard, and he belly-flopped into the cabin.

Tee thought: "My gunner, Corporal Corle -- where's Corle?" The two remaining H-34s repeatedly circled and searched in vain, but they never found the missing helicopter gunner. The wind-swept ocean had swallowed Corporal Corle.

CORLE J T -- CPL USMC -- Dec 29 41 - Dec 8 65 -- Pitcairn PA -- MIA
-- (from casualty listings in *Vietnam KIAs & MIAs*)

The two remaining helicopters veered away from the shore and headed for the safety of the open sea. Tee sat upright on the aluminum floor and turned to face the gunner, who was firing a long burst at the treeline. An empty cartridge from the machinegun struck Tee squarely in the forehead.

"I'M SHOT! I'M SHOT!" Tee wailed as he collapsed back onto the floor of the cabin. He frantically felt his forehead and then examined his hand -- no blood! Tee gradually realized that he had been hit by a hot empty brass cartridge, not by a bullet.

Lying on the metal cabin floor, Tee ripped off his hardhat. The engine roar was almost unbearable without it as the H-34 sped down the coastline toward Ky Ha. Tee had swallowed a lot of seawater, and the nausea swept over him without warning. He crawled to a rear hatch, hung his head out into the slipstream, and vomited over and over. Yet, something was amiss. Twice when Tee was not even retching, he got splattered by windblown vomit. Was the rotorwash somehow sucking it back up on him? How could that be? Years later, Tee would explain how he soon solved the riddle:

Finally I looked forward. There was Givan, hanging out of the forward hatch and vomiting into the slipstream. Each time he vomited, I got plastered with it.

The two H-34s landed at Ky Ha. Following standard procedure,

Tee spent the night in the hospital tent, but sleep would not come. It was mind-boggling. Tee had gotten to Vietnam the day before, and already he had replaced Johnson, his good friend. Johnson was missing-in-action and presumed dead, and Tee would be sleeping in Johnson's old cot. Now Tee had been shot down, shot at, scared to death, and he almost drowned. And his gunner, Corporal Corle, a 23 year old native of Pitcairn, Pennsylvania, was missing-in-action. Maybe he got shot, maybe he just drowned, but in any event he was dead and gone. And all of this had happened within one day, on Tee's *very first mission*, a simple logistics flight. "I'll never survive this war!" Tee thought to himself.

By the spring of 1966 the Marines had largely gained military control of the coastal plain stretching from Chu Lai up to Hue. Slowly they rooted out the enemy units, village by village. But their Dirty Little War would soon change forever. North Vietnam began throwing mechanized regiments of its army into the struggle for control of South Vietnam. North Vietnamese engineers built a network of concealed jungle roads, known as the Ho Chi Minh Trail, to funnel men and munitions into the fight. The NVA set up underground hospitals, fuel depots, and supply caches to support their growing army in South Vietnam.

Marine helicopter pilots found that they faced an enemy who grew stronger with each passing month. Back in the Shu-Fly days they had contended only with local insurgents, but now they battled heavily armed North Vietnamese soldiers. Yet, the helicopter pilots still had not faced off against heavy antiaircraft batteries. Could they pass such a trial by fire? The answer would come deep in the jungle at the remote camp at A-Shau.

West of the city of Hue, buried deep in the inhospitable Annamese Cordillera, lies the beautiful and mysterious A-Shau Valley. Running 15 miles northwest to southeast, the valley parallels the Laotian border about two miles inside of South Vietnam. In the spring of 1966 the North Vietnamese began preparations for their summer offensive against Hue, the former Imperial City of Vietnam. They planned to use the heavily jungled A-Shau Valley as a munitions depot and staging area. Their only military obstacle was the small ARVN outpost in the valley.

By March 1966 the ARVN camp at A-Shau had been beefed up. It was manned by 380 indigenous Civilian Irregular Defense Group (CIDG) soldiers. These local soldiers -- "Ruff-Puffs," we called them -- were commanded by a small team of Special Forces advisors from the United States Army. There were no passable roads through the mountains, and A-Shau lay far beyond the range of friendly artillery. The monsoon now shrouded the valley in heavy fog and continuous drizzle, making relief or resupply by air almost impossible. Further, there was no reasonable expectation of air support against an attacking force. Pilots would look down upon a solid sea of fog and clouds. A pilot's first attempt to dive down through the layer of clouds, guessing where the mountains might be, was likely to be his last.

[A deceased] pilot had committed the unforgivable error of flying his aircraft into a cloud with a mountain hidden inside. -- (H. Lee Bell; in *1369*)

A-Shau Valley, March 9, 1966, 0300 Hours: The North Vietnamese soldiers of the 95th Regiment, 325th NVA Division, crept into prepared assault positions. Then they began a three hour mortar barrage against A-Shau. At dawn two NVA companies attacked the south wall of the ARVN camp, but the Ruff-Puffs fought back and held their positions. The NVA soldiers pulled back, manned their AAA batteries around the camp, and waited.

Alerted by radio, the Marines at Phu Bai readied two companies from the 1st Battalion, 1st Marines, to fly into the besieged camp by helicopter. But it could not be done. The helicopters could fly IFR through the clouds to the skies over the A-Shau Valley, but they could not find their way down to the camp on the valley floor. The lethal cloud layer over the valley had mountains for teeth, and there were no electronic navigation aids at the camp. The Marine H-34s had radar altimeters, but it does a pilot no good to know that he is 300 feet vertically above the ground if he is flying straight toward the side of a sheer cliff.

However, two Marine helicopters would manage to reach the valley. HMM-263, based at Marble Mountain, had two helicopters standing Search and Rescue (SAR) duty at Quang Tri. They both launched, climbed IFR up through the opaque skies in their

"Powerglide" H-34s, and headed for A-Shau, hoping to evacuate some of the wounded defenders. Navigation toward A-Shau posed no problem. They simply tracked outbound on the Phu Bai TACAN for 33 miles. However, getting down through the clouds upon arrival was another matter, so they circled around, looking in vain for a hole in the overcast. Finally, through a small break in the clouds they glimpsed the jungle below, and down they went.

In the lead H-34, First Lieutenant Richard A. Vas Dias zipped down and skimmed under the overcast toward the camp. The North Vietnamese AAA batteries opened fire. Vas Dias was hit repeatedly, and he crashed. His wingman, First Lieutenant David E. Burst, ignored the tracers reaching up for him and roared down for the rescue. He landed, picked up the downed Powerglide crew, and hightailed it for home.

Back at Phu Bai, Lieutenant Colonel Charles A. "Chuck" House, the commanding officer of HMM-163 (the two helicopters on SAR duty at Quang Tri had been from HMM-263, a different squadron), could do nothing but sit and wait. He periodically sent out an H-34 to check on the weather over A-Shau, but the overcast remained solid. Night came, and all that the "Superchief" pilots of HMM-163 could do was sit around and listen to plaintive radio transmissions from the besieged camp.

March 10, 1966, 0530 Hours: Just before dawn the NVA again opened up with mortars and recoilless rifles. They followed this barrage with a ground assault that breached the south wall of the camp. For the defenders the situation became desperate. At daybreak fixed-wing support stacked up over A-Shau, trying to find a way down through the layer of clouds. Some pilots succeeded, but others were not so lucky.

High above A-Shau, First Lieutenant Augusto M. Xavier pointed the snout of his Marine Corps A-4 Skyhawk attack jet at a small hole in the clouds. He screamed down, got under the overcast, and made a low-level bombing run. Desperately trying to stay VFR, tracers arcing up at him, Xavier horsed the VMA-311 Skyhawk around and made another pass. Then he zoomed up into the clouds, clawing for altitude. No one ever saw him again:

Died 10 Mar 66 approximately 55 miles west of Da Nang, Republic of Vietnam, while on a close air support mission,

either shot down by enemy ground fire or crashed into the mountains surrounding A-Shau during pullout.
-- (from Casualty Card; First Lieutenant Augusto M. Xavier)

Luck smiled on others. Two Air Force piston-powered A-1 Skyraiders also made it down through the clouds. One of the Skyraiders, piloted by Major Dafford W. Myers, took hits from heavy North Vietnamese AAA fire and crash-landed on the primitive A-Shau airstrip. Myers leaped from his burning Skyraider, ran 80 meters, and hid in a ditch. Circling above, his wingman, Major Bernard F. Fisher, watched the NVA soldiers swarm over the airstrip and surround the burning Skyraider. They had not yet found Myers in the ditch.

Fisher, a devout Mormon, would not abandon his friend. Incredibly, Fisher swooped down and landed right on the NVA-controlled airstrip. He dodged shell craters and debris and scattered the NVA soldiers, who initially thought he was crash-landing also, and held their fire. Fisher braked and skidded to a stop by Myer's hiding place. Myers dashed to Fisher's plane, clambered up onto the wing, and dove inside.

Now the NVA realized what was happening. As they opened fire, Fisher rammed the Skyraider's throttle to the firewall. His aircraft was riddled with bullets from the incredulous NVA soldiers. Still, he made it out alive. (Fisher would later receive his country's greatest military tribute, the Medal of Honor.)

One man with courage is a majority.
-- (Thomas Jefferson; 1743-1826)

By late afternoon on March 10, the remaining defenders at A-Shau were holed up in bunkers along the north wall of the camp. It was now too late for reinforcements, and there was no safe place for helicopters to land. Time had almost run out. If the Americans and Ruff-Puffs could survive until dark, perhaps they could make a break for the surrounding jungle.

The impending fall of the camp at A-Shau was acknowledged by "The Highest Possible Authority" in the United States chain of command in Vietnam. Military reinforcement or rescue clearly was out of the question. Now, even if they got through the overcast without crashing into the mountains, it would be suicidal -- absolutely suicidal -- to send Marine H-34s into the teeth of the battle, into the NVA controlled camp. But this would not be a military decision. "The Highest Possible Authority" decreed that there would be a *gesture*, a symbol of *good faith* to the South Vietnamese people. Forget reason! Forget the cost! There would be no debate: "Order the Marine Corps to fly to A-Shau!"

<u>March 10, 1966, 1630 Hours</u>: Colonel House got his orders: "Launch immediately. Evacuate any survivors left at A-Shau." Marines at war do not question direct orders. Colonel House launched from Phu Bai and led his flight of 16 helicopters toward the mountains and jungles to the west.

The Superchief H-34s arrived over the valley and found a hole in the cloud cover. Escorted by Huey gunships from VMO-2, the H-34s thundered down toward the ground. The enemy AAA batteries belched orange flame, gray smoke, and hot steel. Flying through a hail of groundfire, House landed in a clear and flat area near the north wall of the camp.

Sheer pandemonium broke out -- bedlam!

NVA soldiers fired at the helicopters. The helicopter gunners fired back at the muzzle flashes. The helicopter pilots, crew chiefs, and gunners could not hear the individual weapons firing. Instead, they heard only a continuous deafening and horrible roar.

The Special Forces advisors lost control of the terrified Ruff-Puffs. In panic, the Ruff-Puffs abandoned their wounded compatriots. They threw down their weapons and stampeded and trampled over each other in a wild and mindless rush for the helicopters. They dove inside and packed the H-34 cabins. Outside of the helicopters, other Ruff-Puffs clung to the struts, the hoists, and the wheels. Much too heavily loaded now, the H-34s did not have enough engine power to take off. The Special Forces men screamed at the Ruff-Puffs, pulled at them, beat them, clubbed them with rifle butts, but the Ruff-Puffs still clung to the helicopters. Numbed and frozen by fear, they would not budge. There was only one rational choice left to be made.

The Americans fired into the hysterical men.

-- (Jack Shulimson; in *U.S. Marines in Vietnam: An Expanding War, 1966*)

The Special Forces men began shooting the Ruff-Puffs and dragging their bodies out of the helicopters. His H-34 now lightened, Colonel House took off. As he accelerated skyward he got blasted by a recoilless rifle, and he crashed. His wingman, First Lieutenant William A. Gregory, met the same fate. So did several others. Still, many of the Superchief helicopters survived the firestorm at A-Shau, and they snatched 69 Ruff-Puffs and four Special Forces advisors out of the hail of enemy fire.

Mercifully, darkness came. The camp was now completely in the hands of the NVA. Many of the Ruff-Puffs, American advisors, and downed Marine helicopter crewmen fought their way into the jungle, and those who survived fell under the command of Colonel House.

March 11, 1966: At first light the Superchief pilots launched for A-Shau to search for their squadronmates. Around noon they spotted one group of them in a clearing two miles northwest of the camp. The H-34s roared down, the NVA opened fire, and the same sad story repeated itself. Once again the terror-stricken Ruff-Puffs threw down their rifles and swarmed into the helicopters. There was no viable choice. Many Ruff-Puffs had to be shot.

> It was a hell of a thing to have to do. Some of them had to be shot in order to maintain control. It was either that, or sacrifice everybody.
> -- (an A-Shau survivor, in a television interview)

Colonel House and six more Marine crewmen from the H-34s shot down the previous day were picked up, along with 60 more Ruff-Puffs. A few Special Forces advisors clambered aboard too, and the Superchief pilots flew them all back to Phu Bai.

March 12, 1966: Marines were still missing. At daylight on March 12 the HMM-163 pilots launched again to continue the search. They spotted another group and zipped down for the pick-up. For some senseless reason the Ruff-Puffs panicked and began fighting among themselves, shooting each other, shooting their own comrades. It seemed hopeless. Yet, the helicopters rescued 34 more survivors, including two more Marines and a handful of Special Forces advisors. When he landed back at Phu Bai, Captain Wilbur C. McMinn Jr. had an incredible 126 bullet holes in his H-

34. The evacuation of A-Shaw was over.

The miracle of A-Shau was that so many Marine helicopters, pilots, gunners, and crew chiefs survived. But of the 24 helicopters assigned to HMM-163, a staggering 21 of them had suffered "major damage," including the ones that were shot down and lost.

Colonel House had followed orders. It had not been his decision to fly into the very face of the NVA batteries, nearly within spitting distance of their heavy weapons. Colonel House had not made the decision to swoop down into the grazing and interlocking fields of automatic weapons fire that the NVA had arrayed against anything moving above ground at A-Shau. Colonel House and his Marines had known the odds against them. And they had known that while a helicopter is a wonderful machine that can do many wonderful things, it is not a battleship. But knowing this, the pilots, gunners, and crew chiefs still had flown into A-Shau. That was their job. They were Marines.

Meanwhile in Quang Tri Province, the northernmost province of South Vietnam, all had been relatively quiet. There was little reason for conflict here. On the fertile coastal plain, fishermen daily plied their trade, and rice farmers subsisted by cultivating the earth as their fathers and forefathers had done. The rugged mountains and dense jungles to the west were almost totally uninhabited. True, there were small South Vietnamese military outposts at Dong Ha and at Khe Sanh, just below the demilitarized zone. And true, the coastal plain comprised the infamous "Street Without Joy" chronicled by the eminent French historian and writer, Bernard B. Fall.

From their base at Phu Bai, 40 miles to the south, the Marine Grunts often sent out platoon sized patrols into the sleepy rice paddies and hamlets. Still, the Marines in Quang Tri Province had encountered only local Viet Cong insurgents, not North Vietnamese Army soldiers. Real warfare, siege warfare, 24 hour artillery duels, World War I style trench warfare, regimental attacks pitting thousands of Marines against the North Vietnamese Army had not come to Quang Tri Province -- not until the terrible and brutal summer of 1966.

Then, down from the north . . . .

Demilitarized Zone, May 17, 1966, 0045 Hours: The major halted his troops when they reached the riverbank shortly after midnight on May 17. He turned and looked at the 174 officers and men assigned to him. In the moonlight their khaki twill uniforms and soft pith helmets immediately identified them as soldiers of -- the *North Vietnamese Army*.

Although they all carried AK-47 assault rifles, they otherwise were lightly armed. On this secret mission they had come not to fight, but instead to reconnoiter the defenses of the "imperialist" American Marines and their South Vietnamese "puppets." In front of the major lay the Ben Hai River in the Demilitarized Zone (DMZ) separating North Vietnam from South Vietnam.

> Compatriots! Rise up! The hour for national salvation has struck! We must sacrifice even our last drop of blood to safeguard our country. Even if we have to endure hardships in the Resistance War, with the determination to make sacrifices, victory will surely be ours. Long live an independent and unified Vietnam! Long live the victorious Resistance!
> -- (Ho Chi Minh; December 20, 1946)

On the northern riverbank the major rested his men and rechecked his field map. They had marched for four hours to reach this shallow point on the river where they could wade into South Vietnam. His comrades deserved this rest, the major thought to himself. Their reconnaissance mission was crucial to the success of the coming invasion. Although personally dedicated to the selfless principles of the People's Army, the major was still immensely proud that he had been personally chosen to lead this mission.

Of course, the major mused, he was indeed highly qualified. The son of a prominent family in Vinh, his father had been martyred earlier in the revolution in an obscure battle against the French. After his father's death the major had vowed to continue the fight. He had excelled in school, studied at the university in Hanoi, received his commission in the army, and had been promoted three times. Yes, the major thought, he was the one for the assignment at hand. He and his 174 comrades had been training specifically for this vital mission for many months. Now, finally the hour had arrived, and they were ready.

The longer the struggle lasts, the more your enemy's position deteriorates, both diplomatically and psychologically. Time is on your side, not on the side of the imperialists.
-- (Mao Tse-tung)

The major watched his troops resting and quietly talking among themselves. Theirs would not be an easy task, he knew. They had to enter South Vietnam and remain undetected while gathering information on the positions, capability, and defenses of the imperialist American Marines.

These Americans were hard to figure out. The major knew from his studies in Hanoi and from his military training that the imperialist Marines, with their proud tradition, would be fierce fighters. On the other hand, the Americans were foolish, maybe even a little crazy. They did not keep their military plans secret. Each week Hanoi got imperialist magazines such as *Time* and *Newsweek*. These publications outlined the plans and goals of American military commanders, and these capitalist magazines even offered a forum for some American politicians to openly criticize the American war effort. How could the Americans expect to wage a war that way? Crazy! It did not make sense! Privately, the major suspected that it all might be an elaborate imperialist plot designed to mislead the North Vietnamese Army.

Well, it now mattered little what the politicians did, said, or thought. Now the issue would be decided on the battlefield, the major knew. The 10,500 troops of the North Vietnamese Army 324-B Division, backed up by 11,000 more men from the 341st Division, were waiting. They were poised just north of the DMZ, ready to follow him south and invade South Vietnam. They would bypass the provincial capital of Quang Tri and capture the city of Hue, the former Vietnamese Imperial Capital.

Of course, the South Vietnamese puppets would not pose a military problem for the potent North Vietnamese Army, but the imperialist American Marines would be different. The Marines would fight! However, the major was well aware that he and his 174 comrades could do much to negate the threat from the American Marines.

Available intelligence showed that the Marines had either one or two infantry battalions based somewhere at Phu Bai, seven miles south of Hue. At Phu Bai the Marines also had an undetermined number of H-34 helicopters. Perhaps the Marines had an infantry platoon or two at Quang Tri or Dong Ha. No one really knew for sure, but it was the major's job to find out. Did the Marines at Phu Bai have artillery support? Where were the bulk fuel tanks for their helicopters? The Marines recently had begun using the old French dirt airstrip at Dong Ha. What were they up to? From revolutionary sympathizers and spies, it had been learned that most of the Marine helicopters were based at Marble Mountain, far to the south. Did the imperialists have the men, the fuel, and the necessary supplies to relocate and sustain helicopter operations at Phu Bai, Quang Tri, or Dong Ha?

Crucial questions! The major realized just how important a task he and his comrades faced. In large part, the success of the coming invasion hinged on the major's ability to document the military and logistic capability of the imperialist American Marines.

What the bourgeoisie, therefore, produces, above all, is its own grave-diggers. Its fall and the victory of the proletariat are equally inevitable.
-- (Karl Marx and Friedrich Engels; in *The Communist Manifesto*)

The coming maelstrom would be a costly battle for both sides, the major knew. The imperialist Marines would not give up without a fight, and they were well armed and trained. They doubtless would try to use their helicopters to remain mobile, in an attempt to compensate for their numerical disadvantage. Therefore, it would be imperative for the North Vietnamese to move their 12.7mm, 23mm, and 37mm AAA batteries onto the battlefield. The imperialist helicopters *must* be neutralized. Then the North Vietnamese would use their superior heavy artillery and manpower advantage to bleed the Marines, wear them down, destroy them. In the long run his army could not lose, the major had been told.

North Vietnam had the fourth largest standing army in the world. Only China, the Soviet Union, and the imperialist Americans had more men in uniform, and the American politicians dared not wage full-scale war so far from home. Here in Vietnam, the major's dedicated "People's Army" was commanded by General Vo Nguyen Giap, the architect of the great victory over the French at Dien Bien Phu in 1954. Many of the major's comrades might be martyred, but in the end his army would prevail.

In the moonlight the major gathered his men around him for a final briefing. He had lived and trained with them, and now they were ready. He thought of his wife and children back in Vinh. He had only been authorized to tell them that he was embarking on a special mission. The major knew the many dangers of his assignment, and he realized he might join his father in death as a hero of the Revolution.

From his studies at the university, the major recalled how Julius Caesar had thrown down the gauntlet to his enemies by crossing the Rubicon River in 49 B.C. Now the major had his own Rubicon to cross. "How glorious!" he thought. Then, with the North Vietnamese National Anthem, Tien Quan Ca (translation: *Forward, Soldiers*) on his lips, the major waded across the Ben Hai River and proudly marched into South Vietnam.

Naturally the common people don't want war. . . . But voice or no voice, the people can always be brought to the bidding of the leaders. All you have to do is tell them they are being attacked and denounce the pacifists for lack of patriotism.
-- (Herman Goering; 1893-1946)

BONNIE-SUE

A Marine Corps
Helicopter Squadron
in
Vietnam

-- Helicopter Valley --

We do not want an expanding struggle with consequences that no one can foresee, nor will we bluster or bully or flaunt our power. But we will not surrender, and we will not retreat.
-- (Lyndon B. Johnson; July 28, 1965)

<u>Marble Mountain, July 14, 1966, 1500 Hours</u>: The stifling heat and humidity of the Indochinese afternoon hung over our makeshift ready-room like an oppressive wet blanket. Like most of our squadron's helicopter pilots, I had sought refuge here in the shade under the drab olive-green General Purpose tent. All of the exterior canvas tent flaps had been rolled up to allow a slight cooling breeze to drift through our primitive flight briefing area. I idly watched as several Marines thumbed through the worn pages of some of the magazines that always seemed to litter our ready-room. Two nearby pilots silently matched wits with a disoriented sand crab by herding it back and forth across the marston-matting floor with the butts of their survival knives. Most of the others napped or daydreamed as the hot afternoon slowly slipped away.

Twelve feet in front of me, Major Eugene W. "Dud" Gilbert, our squadron operations officer, slid back in his squeaky wooden chair. He stood, paused, and drawled: "Listen up! Listen up!"

Spellbound, I listened as Major Gilbert ordered most of us to straggle up to the mess hall for a special briefing. The next morning we would launch before daylight as part of a huge and secret multi-squadron mission, he soberly intoned. Major Gilbert read the names of the pilots and copilots from our flight schedule: "Colonel Mendenhall and Dooley, McAllister and Richey, Maxwell and Johnson, Harper and Diacont . . . ." The list seemed to be endless, but I finally heard my own name called: "Roberts and

Fracker, Rolfe and *Sturkey* . . . ."

Our squadron, HMM-265 (a military acronym meaning *Heli-copter, Marine, Medium, arbitrary designation number 265*), had flown ashore in Vietnam on May 22, 1966, almost two months earlier. So far our hardback tent had served us well as a squadron ready-room and flight briefing area. The wooden benches were a little short on comfort, but we felt right at home with steel matting covering our dirt floor, a dilapidated wooden desk for Major Gilbert, and our Acey-Deucey board in the corner. Why go the mess hall? And why were so many pilots needed? I had never heard of a combat mission that required 28 pilots and 14 helicopters, over half of our squadron. Further, Major Gilbert had told us, other squadrons also would take part in this clandestine endeavor.

In groups of two's and four's with bulging map bags in hand, we shuffled off toward the mess hall. I tagged along with Captain Brian W. "Moose" Rolfe. He would fly as my Helicopter Aircraft Commander, my "HAC," and I would handle the copilot's chores.

To be a Marine pilot is to be the chosen of the chosen.
-- (Jon Boulle; quoted by author Philip D. Chinnery in *Life on the Line*)

As we ambled up the sandy road, the blinding and hot midday sun glistened on the steel matting of the flight line at Marble Mountain. Our helicopter base lay on the sandy seacoast just east of the city of Da Nang, right on the beach by the South China Sea. Moose and I walked past rows of drab green Sikorsky H-34 helicopters, and on the north side of the flight line we glanced at the menacing Huey gunships of VMO-2. Then we plodded on through the sweltering afternoon heat to the mess hall, the pride and joy of Marble Mountain.

Able to seat roughly 200 Marines, the new mess hall was a relatively modern wooden building. It sported a genuine galvan-ized tin roof -- rare at Marble Mountain where canvas tents were the norm. From shoulder height to the ceiling, screen wire allowed a cooling breeze to enter. Moose and I sauntered in, found a vacant spot, and plopped down on a bench to wait. We watched as helicopter crews from other squadrons wandered inside and found seats. In addition to our 28 pilots from HMM-265, roughly

30 more pilots from our sister squadron, HMM-164, soon arrived. As we waited, 25 or more H-34 pilots and 22 Huey gunship pilots walked into the mess hall. Even the pilots from the giant H-37 "Deuce" contingent were present. All in all, over 100 Marine Corps helicopter pilots filled the mess hall, and Moose and I definitely knew that something big lay in store for us.

As we waited, I looked at some of the other H-46 pilots from my squadron. My peers were the junior first lieutenants, and we hailed from cities and towns all across the United States. Huey Walsh had been born and raised in Pensacola, Florida. James H. "Jim" Hodgson III called Valley Forge, Pennsylvania, his home. Lynn M. LaPointe came from Huntsville, Alabama. Glancing down at my NATOPS checklist, I saw my own name and rank stamped on the cover: "Marion F. Sturkey, First Lieutenant, USMC." I was a fiercely proud native of the tiny town of Plum Branch, a sleepy little crossroads of 96 souls tucked far back in the rural pine forests of western South Carolina.

Yet, regardless of our place of birth, we pilots shared a common bond. We all had graduated from military flight training as Naval Aviators, and we all wore the coveted Golden Wings. After joining HMM-265, we had trained for another year in North Carolina and the Caribbean. Aboard the helicopter carrier USS Boxer (LPH-4), we then had sailed across the Atlantic Ocean, cruised through the Mediterranean Sea, the Suez Canal, the Red Sea, and entered the Indian Ocean. The Boxer had rounded the Malay Peninsula at Singapore and steamed northward. We had flown our helicopters ashore at Marble Mountain, just east of the bustling city of Da Nang, the new name for the colonial French seaport of Tourane. Our mission was daunting but easily defined: "Provide logistical air support for the Third Marine Division."

> Those who expect to reap the blessings of freedom must, like men, undergo the fatigue of supporting it.
> -- (Thomas Paine; 1737-1809)

Recognized by our radio call-sign, "Bonnie-Sue," we flew the huge CH-46A helicopter. In abbreviated military lingo, the full CH-46A designation was shortened to simply H-46, and pilots just spoke of it as the "forty-six." We had been chosen to pilot a state-of-the-art flying machine, a Boeing Vertol tandem-rotor helicopter with true all-weather capability. The H-46 had dual hydraulic systems, dual Stability Argumentation Systems (SAS), and dual electrical systems. Our helicopters had protective armored seats for the two pilots, plus armor plate that covered the twin General Electric T-58 jet turbines. Back in the cabin we had room to carry 22 combat-loaded Marines, although for tactical reasons we generally carried only about 14 to 16. For defense there were gunmounts on each side of the cabin, and we could mount either M-60 machineguns or the heavier and deadly .50 caliber weapons. And compared to other helicopters, we were *fast*. The H-46 cruised at 120 to 130 knots, 133 to 150 miles per hour, and could quickly leave the lumbering H-34s and Hueys far behind. With a maximum gross weight of 21,400 pounds, over ten tons, we also could carry a much heavier load than the smaller helicopters.

Waiting for the briefing to begin, my mind wandered back over the previous two months. We had been busy flying medical evacuations (medevacs), combat assaults (strikes), and resupply missions during which we transported troops, food, ammunition, water, and all of the other necessities of warfare. True, we had taken a few casualties. Within two weeks of our arrival, we had lost one of our helicopters. Bureau Number 152510 had crashed on Dong Den Mountain while flying supplies to the Marine observation post on that 2847 foot high craggy peak. The copilot, First Lieutenant Arnold "Arnie" Reiner, had later mused that his overturned helicopter would have rolled all the way down the mountain if it had not been impaled by jagged tree stumps. And on a personal note, I remembered that on July 4, Staff Sergeant N. L. Perry, one of our crew chiefs, had been shot in the back during a *hairy* night helicopter extraction from a hot landing zone. Still, we had done well. With our 22 helicopters and 41 pilots, we maintained an aerial lifeline to the Marine Infantry in the field.

I idly pulled out some of my 1:50,000 scale maps that we used for day-to-day flying. When we had first arrived in Vietnam, most of our missions had been flown from Marble Mountain, home of Marine Air Group 16 (MAG-16), of which HMM-265 was a part. South of Marble Mountain lay the rice-rich coastal flatlands that were infested with Viet Cong. For the Marine Infantry, the "Grunts," the forward command post south of Da Nang sat atop

Hill 55, named like all hills or mountains for its height in meters above sea level. The Grunts considered Hill 55 to be a natural spot for such a base of operations. The French had used it during the previous decade, but their Foreign Legion had lost a battalion -- an entire infantry battalion! -- there one dark night.

Farther to the south lay Ky Ha, the home base for MAG-36 and four more squadrons of Marine Corps helicopters. Looking at the dark green area on my map directly west of Da Nang, I saw the wild and rugged, inhospitable, and largely uninhabited mountains, the Annamese Cordillera. Years later, writer Donald Wharton would describe this hostile and forbidding terrain:

> Most of the region consisted of rugged mountains covered with a thick, multitiered 80 to 100 foot high jungle canopy.

North of Da Nang on the coastal plain was Phu Bai, the Marine base camp with a single supporting squadron of H-34s. Farther to the north past the city of Hue was the small outpost at Dong Ha, with its quaint old French barracks and hard-packed dirt airstrip. And west of Dong Ha, buried deep in the heavily jungled mountains, was a breathtakingly beautiful, mysterious, and dreamlike place. This modern day Shangri-La was the small outpost at Khe Sanh. But unlike the populated coastal areas, Khe Sanh was so remote and so peaceful that there should never be any fighting there, I naively reasoned.

Putting my maps away and looking around, I realized that the mess hall had filled up. Pilots were engaging in the usual jovial banter, but this time it was different. There obviously were enough crews here to man over 50 helicopters. What was going on? Whatever it was, it did not take a genius to figure out *where* the action would be.

For the past few weeks we had spent most of our time flying combat missions out of Dong Ha, about ten miles below the DMZ. We had flown Marine reconnaissance teams from Recon Group Bravo into the mountains northwest of Dong Ha. These five to eight man Recon (military slang for *Reconnaissance*) teams formed the eyes and ears of the Third Marine Division. They were not supposed to fight. Their hazardous job required them to avoid detection by the enemy. The Recons would silently and stealthily probe through the jungle and report by PRC-25 radio on enemy troop presence and movement.

The Recons had plenty to report. They had found camouflaged North Vietnamese Army (NVA) field hospitals, rice stockpiles, troop concentrations, mortar pits, and fortifications. The NVA was there, almost everywhere. Of 18 Recon teams that we had inserted by helicopter, 14 of them had quickly radioed us for a helicopter extraction because of inadvertent contact with the enemy. Flying back down to pick up the Recons, often under fire, had really kept our adrenaline pumping. On the other hand, we did not have to fly back down to rescue the Chinese Nung mercenaries that we sometimes used instead of the Marine Recons. With the Nungs we simply had flown to the designated spot on the map, "coordinates classified." The Nungs would jump out of our helicopter and vanish into the jungle. They were on their own with no questions asked, and those who returned would be paid "by the ear."

1545 Hours: "Attention on deck!" We stood in unison.

"As you were."

The MAG-16 Commanding Officer, Colonel Richard M. Hunt, had walked into the mess hall. He was followed by several of his official functionaries that I did not recognize. My own commanding officer, Lieutenant Colonel Herbert E. Mendenhall, had arrived with the commanding officers from VMO-2, HMM-164, and HMM-163. Moose elbowed me, and we shared innocent but eager grins. Whatever was in the works far exceeded anything we ever had been involved in before, and we both were proud to be a part of the coming mission. Colonel Hunt faced us and wasted no time in getting to the point: "Gentlemen, at zero-eight-hundred tomorrow morning, the Division will begin an assault against the North Vietnamese Army."

A briefing officer laid out the tactical situation for us. The coming Marine Corps offensive had been named Operation Hastings. The briefing officer explained that the North Vietnamese Army had marched south across the DMZ and had encamped in the mountains west of Dong Ha. Intelligence reported that there were "many hoofprints going in, but none coming out." The NVA planned a lightning strike southward over the flatlands, we pilots were told, to capture the city of Hue.

The intelligence was fascinating. The 324th Division of the North Vietnamese Army had crossed the border, it said, and had massed in Quang Tri Province next to the 17th parallel's demilitarized zone.
-- (*Time Magazine*; July 29, 1966)

The fortified enemy command post had been spotted on the top of Hill 208, only twelve miles west of Dong Ha. Now the headquarters of the 324-B North Vietnamese Army Division, 10,500 men strong, was *inside* of South Vietnam. Further, the 90th NVA Regiment, with 1500 men, was entrenched and waiting in the rugged Song Ngan Valley. Roughly three miles to the southwest, the 812th and 803rd NVA Regiments were encamped near the "Rockpile," a jagged 700 foot high granite outcropping on the northern bank of the Cam Lo River. Other enemy battalions were strung out just below the DMZ from the mountains toward the sea. But even more sobering was the revelation that another 11,500 men of the 341st NVA Division were staged along the northern border of the DMZ, poised for the attack on Hue.

The military and political implications of the loss of Hue were unthinkable. Hue, the former Vietnamese Imperial Capital, could not be allowed to fall to the North Vietnamese. But the out-numbered Marines did not have the manpower to form a defensive line in hope of stopping the mechanized North Vietnamese Army, and our artillery was no match for theirs. There was only one viable option remaining, we were told. Before the enemy could begin an offensive toward Hue, we must *attack*.

Our coming "spoiling attack" in the mountains was designed to throw the enemy off stride. We would stage massive surprise helicopter assaults. Our helicopters would fly the 3rd Battalion, 4th Marines, into the western maw of the Song Ngan Valley at map coordinates YD-038649, code named Landing Zone (LZ) Crow. The Third Battalion would set up a blocking position at the western end of the valley. Then helicopters would fly the 2nd Battalion, 4th Marines, to the eastern end of the valley at map coordinates YD-085655, code named LZ Dove. The Second Battalion would then attack to the west. Flanked and possibly confused by Marines on both the east and west of them, the enemy would hopefully retreat northward across the DMZ.

The 1st Battalion, 3rd Marines, would travel by truck to Cam Lo, seven miles to the west of Dong Ha. There they would set up a defensive perimeter around the Marine 105mm and 155mm howitzer batteries. Meanwhile, the Battalion Landing Team (BLT), comprised of the 3rd Battalion, 5th Marines, would storm ashore just below the DMZ and push westward toward the mountains. Security for the vital dirt airstrip at Dong Ha would be handled by the 2nd Battalion, 1st Marines. The only reserve unit available was the 1st Battalion, 1st Marines. Initially it would be held in the rear at Dong Ha, but it would be thrown into the fray as the fighting progressed.

"Your helicopters are the key!" Colonel Hunt repeatedly warned us. Our few battalions of Marine Grunts would be vastly outmanned by the huge North Vietnamese divisions and regiments. We would use our helicopters to remain mobile in an attempt to compensate for our numerical disadvantage.

We must substitute *esprit* for numbers!
-- (General J. E. B. "Jeb" Stuart, Confederate States Army)

Our newer and larger H-46 helicopters would be the primary troop carriers, backed up by the smaller and slower H-34s. Nimble Huey gunships would fly cover for us. Medevacs would be handled by H-34s, with a gunship flying chase on each mission. This multi-squadron assault would require all of the helicopter squadrons to abandon their normal squadron radio call-signs and use the MAG-16 call-sign, "Rose-Ann." Moose and I, designated as Rose-Ann 1-15 (spoken, "Rose-Ann one-dash-fifteen") would fly our H-46 in the initial aerial assault into the western mouth of the enemy controlled valley.

From aerial photographs, LZ Crow looked big enough for four H-46s to land at one time, we were told. We would pick up the Grunts -- no South Vietnamese ARVN soldiers, this attack was a Marine Corps show -- at Dong Ha and fly westward along the Cam Lo River. North of the Rockpile our flight would make a gradual 180 degree descending turn to the right and approach LZ Crow from the west. Artillery at Cam Lo, augmented by fixed-wing airstrikes, would hammer the landing area for 20 minutes preceding our helicopter landing.

We worked out scores of details during the two hour briefing: radio frequencies, multi-squadron coordination, radio call-signs, ground-to-air coordination, crew assignments, troop loading plans, artillery fire zones, and known enemy AAA sites. Moose and I scribbled the required facts and figures on our kneeboard pads and marked our maps as necessary.

Finally: "O. K., that's it. Any questions?"

A hand shot up: "Sir, what about the wind?"

"What about it?"

"Well, sir, we're committed to land to the east. We're gonna' be heavy. It's gonna' be hot. Aaaahhh -- what if the wind is -- you know -- *wrong*?"

A moment of dead silence followed. Moose elbowed me again and grinned, for no pilot present needed any explanation. The wind direction the next morning would be crucial. In a fixed-wing airplane you can land with your engines throttled back to idle. But in a fully loaded helicopter you often need almost full engine power to land. You can land a helicopter into a headwind. You can land with a crosswind. You can land with no wind at all. But in a heavily loaded helicopter, a *downwind* landing invites disaster.

If the wind blew in from the west, and we landed downwind to the east, we could find ourselves in serious trouble. We would scream down over the trees toward LZ Crow, turbines spooled down, with the noses of our helicopters pulled high in the air to bleed off airspeed. In the last 15 seconds or so, if we landed downwind, we would be out of translational lift. Then, when we tried to pull in maximum power to land, the helicopter rotors would be clawing and scratching for clean air and getting nothing but downwash. Bad news!

"We've taken that into account." The briefing officer told us that the following morning in the landing zone, the weather forecast predicted no wind at all. Should there be any wind, it would blow in from the east, naturally. The basic meteorological explanation followed. The morning sun would cause the air to warm and rise over the mountains. Cooler air from offshore would move inland to fill the resulting low pressure void. Therefore, any possible wind the next morning would blow in from the east.

This textbook answer sounded good, and I had to admit that it made sense. Moreover, with scores of helicopters swooping down to land, I guessed that you could not delay the landing direction decision until the last minute. Still, I harbored a tiny kernel of doubt, and I was not alone. Just suppose -- not that it would happen, but just suppose -- that the wind direction changed. Suppose we came roaring into that jungle valley the next morning, hot and heavy, and had to land downwind. I did not want to dwell on the many potential pitfalls in such a course of action.

"Any more questions?" There were none. Moose and I gathered up our maps and stuffed away our kneeboard pads. We followed the other pilots outside into the blistering and suffocating heat from the late afternoon sun.

July 15, 1966, 0445 Hours: The next morning in the dark in our hardback tents, we pulled on our flight suits, gathered our gear, and headed for the mess hall. Breakfast consisted mainly of coffee and quiet conversation. Then we trudged down through the soft sand, walked across the steel matting on the flight line, and shuffled into the HMM-265 ready-room tent.

As we covered last minute details, the mechanics outside swarmed over our helicopters. Among them was Bureau Number 152498, which Moose and I would fly. The mechanics checked out each H-46 under the watchful fatherly eye of its crew chief. Meanwhile, the gunners lugged their machineguns from the armory tent out to the helicopters, mounted them in the gunmounts, and returned to the armory for load after load of ammunition.

After our briefing I left the ready-room and headed for my waiting H-46, taking care not to slip on the dew that covered the metal marston-matting. I watched the older and smaller H-34s taxiing out to the runway, their red rotating beacons casting eerie shadows in the darkness. The lethal Huey gunships had already gone. After a quick pre-flight with flashlights, Moose and I crawled aboard, strapped in, and fired up our twin turbines. Within minutes we arced out into the pitch black eastern sky over the South China Sea.

Following Colonel Mendenhall, we headed north. Monkey Mountain fell behind us, then lofty Hai Van Pass. At 3000 feet above the water we paralleled the coastline as the eastern sky gradually brightened. Our flight overtook a squadron of slower H-

34s, and they soundlessly floated behind us as we bored on northward. Off to our left, sparkling in the first rays of the morning sun, lay the placid Lagune De L'ouest and its dozens of arrowhead shaped fishtraps. On up the Vietnamese coastline, past the provincial capital of Quang Tri, Colonel Mendenhall led our flight of 14 helicopters. Then he turned inland, and we followed him as he began a gradual descent. Then I spotted our destination straight ahead of us, the red laterite dirt airstrip at Dong Ha.

Dong Ha, July 15, 1966, 0710 Hours: Marines and helicopters! Marines and helicopters everywhere! All around the Dong Ha airstrip, Marines and helicopters covered the terrain.

From the two H-46 squadrons then in Vietnam, HMM-164 and HMM-265, a total of 27 helicopters had arrived and refueled. The Huey gunships of VMO-2 were already there, armed to the teeth. Nearby, row after row of the older H-34s squatted in the grass, ready for duty. To the east the "Barrelhouse" H-34s from HMM-161 filled the sky as they roared in to join the helicopter armada. Even the venerable Deuce, the giant and maligned H-37, was represented. Four of the drab green twin-engine monsters were being serviced and refueled over by the dirt runway. Years later my Marble Mountain tentmate Huey Walsh would reminisce and muse: "We could almost hear the bugles blowing!"

> The marching columns extended back as far as the eye could see in the distance. It was a grand and glorious spectacle, and it was impossible to look at it without the utmost admiration.
> -- (General Daniel H. Hill, Confederate States Army; on the morning of September 14, 1862)

Dong Ha looked like a primitive and Godforsaken place back in July 1966. Named after the Vietnamese village a half mile to the north, Dong Ha was the northernmost military outpost in South Vietnam. Actually, except for the Marines, there was little else here. The airstrip was the only tangible asset at hand. Still, Dong Ha now formed the nucleus of the Marine staging area for the assault on the North Vietnamese Army. The sun, a half hour up into the eastern sky, had already begun heating up the Vietnamese landscape. It was hot and getting hotter by the minute. The usual cooling sea-breeze, blowing in from the coast eight miles to the east, had not yet materialized.

One by one the helicopter pilots shut down their engines and crawled out to stretch their legs and wait. Meanwhile, the Marine crew chiefs stayed busy. Marines by profession, mechanics by trade, they each stuck with their assigned helicopter. Each crew chief did treble duty as a mechanic, a loadmaster, and as a door gunner in the air. Now they all carefully checked their helicopters again: fluid levels O. K., hydraulics O. K., avionics O. K., all mechanical systems properly working. With their tasks completed, the crew chiefs congregated with the gunners for quiet conversation and, for most, a quick smoke.

Many of the pilots wandered over to what The Command had officially and grandiosely termed Air Operations North. We pilots had a much more simple name for it: "Op's North." Only three short days before, Op's North had been nothing more than a makeshift tent, a tarpaulin stretched over poles. It had been valued more for its ability to block out the blinding sun than for its possible use as a shelter from the rain. But now Op's North was a full General Purpose Tent complete with status boards and electronic radio wizardry.

Op's North was home-away-from-home for Major Frederick "Fred" Seitz and Captain Harry R. "Bob" Mills. On paper, both were members of my squadron, but since May they had been on temporary loan to MAG-16 Headquarters ("Group") at Dong Ha. Major Seitz and Bob had pretty much been cut from the same cloth. Redheaded, mustached, and built like a miniature fireplug, Major Seitz was the head-honcho for Marine Air at Dong Ha. Bob Mills, always Gung-Ho, a veteran of the old Shu-Fly days, was now on his second combat tour in Vietnam.

Well, I guess you can just call me an American Patriot.
-- (Harry R. "Bob" Mills; years later)

Between tours in Vietnam, Bob had taught newer pilots how to fly with the now obsolete grease-gun strapped around their necks. He offered them words of wisdom about not shooting holes in their own rotor blades or shooting down their own wingman. At

Dong Ha, Bob had become the MAG-16 Helicopter Fragger ("frag" is Marine Corps aviation slang for *fragmentary order*, a flight assignment), and he reported directly to Major Seitz.

The Marine Infantry, the Grunts, straggled up behind their assigned helicopters. Here they dropped their gear, their rifles, and sat down on the grass to wait. Each Grunt was totally silent, I noted. None of them laughed, joked, or even spoke. None visibly evidenced fear, but each of them seemed lost in his own private thoughts. I saw that most of the Grunts were just 18 to 20 years of age, perhaps a year or so removed from high school. A disproportionate percentage of them came from the rural bible-belt southern states, and they already were veterans at their military profession. The Grunts had become trained killers. The huge red and gold sign at the Marine Corps Recruit Depot at Parris Island, South Carolina, was no joking matter: "THE DEADLIEST WEAPON IN THE WORLD -- A MARINE AND HIS RIFLE."

Each Grunt carried the M-14 rifle (the new M-16 had not yet become available), deadly at short distances, yet accurate up to about 600 meters. Most had taped their M-14 magazines together, back to back, allowing them to fire two magazines with only a flick of their experienced wrists. Seven grenades hung from each belt, two smoke grenades and five "baseballs" with a killing radius of 20 meters. More ammunition, three canteens of water, an entrenching tool (a small folding shovel), a machete, first aid kit, flak jacket, steel helmet, and a full field pack completed their gear, over 80 pounds per man.

A few Grunts wandered over by the runway where a military chaplain, a Catholic Priest decked out in his flowing white robe, had set up an altar atop a stack of ammunition crates. Covered with red laterite dust, he was saying Mass and giving the Holy Communion to those few who were inclined to participate. First Lieutenant George H. Diacont Jr., one of our Bonnie-Sue pilots, pulled out his 8mm movie camera and captured the priest on film behind his makeshift altar, with three Grunts kneeling in front of it. Years later after his 8mm film had been transferred to VHS videotape, George would give me a copy.

The Grunts knew full well what lay in store for them that hot

Indochinese morning. Dong Ha was near the coast in the flatlands. The coming battle, however, would be fought on terrain that is maddening, worse than any the Marine Corps had ever encountered, even worse than Guadalcanal. The mountains west of Dong Ha are cloaked in 100 foot high jungle canopy. Beneath that dense foliage lies a tangled and nearly impenetrable mass of vines and undergrowth so thick that machetes are needed to hack through it. The jungle vegetation is so dense that at midday it appears almost as dark as at midnight. There would be no breeze to ease the stifling and suffocating heat, no relief from the constant swarms of stinging insects that make days miserable and nights unbearable. The jagged and jungled Cordillera is a wild and uninhabited wilderness. It is spooky beyond mortal belief, a foreign land where demons, trolls, and evil spirits might live and roam the earth.

It is terrible terrain for fighting.
-- (*Newsweek Magazine*; August 8, 1966)

The Grunts knew this. And they also knew that lurking in that murky and foreboding jungle, dug in, camouflaged, concealed, well armed and trained, were Giap's Finest, 10,500 soldiers of the North Vietnamese Army 324-B Division.

The NVA would be ready. Commanded by General Nguyen Vang, the enemy soldiers of 324-B were dedicated to their cause. Their command post on Hill 208 lay just twelve miles west-northwest of Dong Ha and only five miles northwest of the Marine artillery batteries at Cam Lo. From their vantage points high in the mountains, the NVA spotters doubtless had watched the Marine build-up at Dong Ha and Cam Lo. They were not blind to the clouds of red dust that billowed skyward as flights of Marine transports shuttled in and out of the Dong Ha airstrip. The NVA spotters could easily watch the Marine truck convoys rolling into Cam Lo on old Colonial Route 9, now a one-lane-wide dirt road. The NVA had a grandstand seat from their mountaintop command post. Without question the NVA knew of the Marine build-up, and they knew that the Marines had come to fight.

So the NVA knew the Marine Corps plan, and the Marine Corps knew the NVA plan. The waiting game had ended.

Dong Ha, 0740 Hours: Brimming with enthusiasm, Moose

came running back to our waiting H-46 and shouted: "Let's go!" We clambered aboard Bureau Number 152498. I crawled into the cockpit and eased into the armored left seat while Moose took his place on the right. Back in the cabin our crew chief began shepherding 14 Grunts aboard. They entered through the rear ramp and, like the proverbial herd of elephants, stomped their way up into the helicopter. Each took his assigned place in one of the web troop seats that line each side of the H-46 cabin. The Grunts strapped in, and then there was nothing for them to do but wait, perhaps their hardest task of all.

Our automatic ritual unfolded up in the cockpit: strap in, plug in, check your flight gear, check your .38 caliber service revolver, start the check-list. In addition to our standard ammunition, a few pilots carried what we all called a "silver bullet." This single hollow-point cartridge was reserved as a final and ultimate defense, a guarantee of instant painless death. I never carried a silver bullet, trusting that I would never have a need for it. Moose and I started going through the pre-start, engine start, and rotor start check-lists. There are 66 separate items on these H-46 checklists, but we had them all memorized:

```
. . . Engine Fire Control Handles  . . . . . . . . . . . . . . . . . IN
Engine Fire Extinguisher Switches  . . . . . . . .  NORMAL
Hydraulic Isolation Switch . . . . . . . . . . . . .  NORMAL
Master Caution Panel  . . . . . . . . . . . . . . . . . . .  TEST
ATS . . . . . . . . . . . . . . . . . . . . . . . . . . . . . . . . . OFF
Altitude Hold . . . . . . . . . . . . . . . . . . . . . . . . . . OFF
Speed Trim  . . . . . . . . . . . . . . . . . . . . . . . .  AUTO
SAS . . . . . . . . . . . . . . . . . . . . . . . . . . . . . . . . OFF
Stick Position Trim . . . . . . . . . . . . . . . . . . . . . ON
```

We came to checklist item number 35. I pushed the spring-loaded Auxiliary Power Plant (APP) switch to "Start," and we instantly heard the familiar shrill whine as the small auxiliary turbine accelerated. Fifteen seconds later I flipped the Power Control Master Switch forward, and our electrical and hydraulics systems sprang to life. We quickly ran through the rest of the check-list. I fired up the Number One Engine, then the Number Two Engine, then engaged our massive rotor system. All of our temperature and pressure needles soon settled "in the green."

Our flight leader radioed: "This is Rose-Ann one-dash-one,

radio check."

"Rose-Ann one-dash-two."

"Uuuuuhhh, Rose-Ann one-dash-three."

"Rose-Ann one-dash-four."

"Rose-Ann one-dash-five . . . ."

So it went, and then finally it was our turn. Moose keyed the UHF radio mike switch on the cyclic control. His radio transmission bled back into the earphones built into my flight helmet, my hardhat: "Rose-Ann one-dash-fifteen."

"Aaaaahhh, Rose-Ann one-dash-sixteen."

"Rose-Ann one-dash-seventeen . . . ."

After the radio check-in had been completed, Rose-Ann 1-1 sucked in full power. He briefly hovered in a cloud of red dust, then took off westward. He was followed by the other three helicopters in the first division (a *division* is a flight of four aircraft). After a 15 second wait, Rose-Ann 1-5 and the rest of the second division followed suit. Next the third division took to the air, and soon it became our turn.

Moose and I piloted Rose-Ann 1-15, the third helicopter in the fourth division. Moose slowly pulled in collective pitch, and we shuddered into the air behind our division leader. In addition to our crew chief and gunner, riding in the cabin behind us were 14 helpless and trusting Grunts whose immediate future and fate lay solely in our hands.

Once airborne, each division leader climbed -- how cool and fresh the air felt -- to 3000 feet and gently banked left, turning in a two mile diameter circle. The trailing helicopters slipped inside of their leader's turn radius, leveled, and let geometric and aeronautical theory become reality. One by one, as if riding on invisible steel rails in the sky, we glided toward our flight leader. Each H-46 slipped over to the proper "step-up" position, banked, stabilized, and joined up in loose division formation.

Another radio check confirmed that everyone was airborne and joined up. We headed westward through a brilliant blue sky, following the Cam Lo River. At a slow cruise speed of 115 knots, we covered the six miles to Cam Lo in three minutes. Below lay the Marine artillery batteries, the last friendly position. In front of us were the mountains and jungles: "Indian Country."

Up ahead of us, Huey gunships from VMO-2 led the way as

usual. Behind the Hueys came the main troop carriers, our H-46s, 20 of them in this initial flight. Our 20 helicopters carried Grunts of the 3rd Battalion, 4th Marines. The rest of the Third Battalion, plus the other Grunt battalions, still waited back at Dong Ha for us to return. It promised to be a long day.

Meanwhile, five miles ahead of us two Huey gunships had been coordinating an airstrike around our destination, LZ Crow. Six Marine Corps F-8 Crusader ground-attack jets from Da Nang, radio call-sign "Oxwood," blasted the surrounding jungle with 500 pound bombs, napalm, and 20mm cannon fire. Then, their ordnance gone, the F-8s headed for home. Now the Marine howitzers at Cam Lo opened up and sent dozens of high-explosive 105mm and 155mm shells whistling down into the landing area.

In choosing LZ Crow, the MAG-16 Staff had wisely relied on aerial photographs and eyeball aerial reconnaissance from 2000 feet. Had they gone down for a closer look, they would have drawn more enemy attention.

Yet, the enemy 324-B Division commander, General Vang, was not stupid. There were only a few clear landing areas in the valley. Would General Vang anticipate a helicopter assault? The Marine Command hoped not. After all, the NVA was preparing for an offensive against Hue, not for a defensive struggle in the mountains. Still, what lay ahead was largely unknown. Perhaps the NVA had filled all potential landing areas with anti-helicopter stakes, 20 foot tall posts designed to strike and destroy the rotors of the landing helicopters. Maybe the NVA had stretched steel cables across the landing sites. Pressure-sensitive mines? Punji stakes? Worse yet, perhaps the NVA had surrounded the few potential landing zones with a thousand or so soldiers, all armed and ready, just waiting for the helicopters to swoop down and land.

But no matter what lay in store, there was now no turning back. Our helicopter assault was irrevocably committed to LZ Crow, for there was no alternate landing area. Hopefully we would zip down into the valley, land, offload the Grunts, and hightail it out of there without a shot being fired. If not . . . .

I could see the guns swivel and I could hear the steady pop of
.50 caliber rounds, and I suddenly realized we were under fire.
-- (Lewis B. Puller Jr.; in *Fortunate Son*)

When under fire on the ground, Grunts can dive for cover.
Helicopter pilots can not. For a helicopter pilot on the ground in
a hot landing zone, there is no place to hide. All you can do is sit
there, just sit there and take it. There was not an NVA soldier in
324-B who would not relish a good, clean, close range shot at a
Marine Corps helicopter on the ground.

Loading or unloading, a helicopter on the ground in a firefight
is a big green bull's-eye. Sure, the H-46 engine armor plate helps.
But if you do happen to lose one of your engines on the ground,
you are there to stay. And true, the H-46 pilot's armored seat can
be a real lifesaver, because it can stop a .30 caliber round at point
blank range. The armored seat provides protection under you,
protection behind you, and protection on both sides of you. But
your feet, arms, and head stick out. And from the front the seat
offers the pilot no protection at all. Our only protection from
frontal fire was the flak jacket that we wore over our flight suits.
It would stop most shrapnel, but not a high velocity bullet. The
new and protective Pilot's Armored Chest Protector (initially called
a "chicken plate" and later dubbed a "bullet bouncer") would not be
available to us until the following month.

In the cabin behind the pilots, there was no protective armor
for the crew chief, gunner, and Grunts. They each had flak jackets,
of course. But instead of *wearing* their flak jacket, many elected
to fold it up to double thickness and *sit* on it. When questioned
about this seemingly odd habit, they invariably responded with a
nervous laugh and the now familiar cliche: "Take my arms, take
my eyes, take my feet, take my legs, but don't take my [testicles]!"

Grunts always view helicopter pilots with a liberal dose of
apprehension. Under even the best of conditions, most Grunts look
upon transportation by helicopter as an evil omen, an occupational
hazard, a mode of travel to be avoided if humanly possible. For
these Grunts, a helicopter assault into a hot landing zone can be
terrifying. While in the helicopter in the air, they have no control
over their destiny. Strapped into the web troop seats, they are
buffeted by the wild vibration of a twisting high-speed autorotative

descent. The shrill metallic whine of the aft transmission drowns out the wail of the turbines. Battered by the tooth jarring shudders from flying through the invisible rotor-wash of a preceding helicopter, hearing the crackle of small arms fire below, the Grunts are powerless to respond. Swept along by unseen aerodynamic and mechanical forces beyond their control and understanding, they pray for the relative safety of a firefight on solid ground.

Song Ngan Valley, July 15, 1966, 0755 Hours: Our flight of helicopters swept westward toward the Rockpile, then turned to the north. Below us was the jungle, an unbroken sea of green. Off to my left, the volcanic black wall of the massive Razorback glistened like a mirror in the early morning sunlight.

Up ahead in a Huey, the Tactical Air Controller, Airborne (TACA), verified that the F-8s had headed back toward Da Nang and that the Marine artillery had ceased fire. Our flight leader, Rose-Ann 1-1, was Lieutenant Colonel Warren C. Watson. He commanded HMM-164, the only other H-46 squadron then in Vietnam. Colonel Watson had the honor of leading the assault because HMM-164 had been in Vietnam longer than my squadron. With his first division tucked in behind him, Colonel Watson turned to the right and screamed down into the jungle valley below.

Into the valley of Death / Rode the six-hundred.
-- (Alfred Tennyson; in "The Charge of the Light Brigade")

The four helicopters in the first division, Rose-Ann 1-1 through Rose-Ann 1-4, zipped down on a southeasterly heading. They landed in LZ Crow, dropped their ramps, and the Grunts charged out into the landing zone. Not a shot was fired. As the pilots sucked in power and lurched skyward, my FM radio crackled: "Zone secure. Zone secure."

The second division, led by Colonel Mendenhall and consisting entirely of HMM-265 helicopters and crews, turned onto final approach as the first division took off from the landing area. This second division lined up in the following order:

	No. 1	No. 2	No. 3	No. 4
Pilot:	Mendenhall	McAllister	Maxwell	Cumpston
Copilot:	Dooley	Richey	Johnson	LaPointe
Rose-Ann:	1-5	1-6	1-7	1-8

Emboldened by the "zone secure" report, meaning that no enemy fire had been received, Colonel Mendenhall kept his airspeed up as he raced toward the valley floor. This looked easy enough. However, something was terribly wrong. Through the plexiglass windshield the "picture" looked correct. Airspeed, height above ground, closure rate, and descent angle all looked good. Unfortunately, things were not as they appeared.

The terrain sloped downhill ahead of them, creating a cruel optical illusion. Further, the wind had begun whipping through the valley from the west, not from the east as forecast. Although their airspeed, rate of descent, and angle of descent *looked* good, the helicopters were actually too high and too fast, a potentially deadly combination. To compound the problem, the air temperature -- hot air is an anathema to jet engines -- had soared. Worse yet, each helicopter still had roughly 2200 pounds of fuel on board, and each was heavily laden with Grunts and equipment.

For the helicopter pilots, all of the ingredients for disaster suddenly combined and surfaced. It was *hot*, the helicopters were *heavily loaded*, they were flying *too high* and *too fast*, they were landing *downwind*, and they were landing *downslope*.

An approach over downhill sloping terrain creates the *optical illusion* [emphasis added] of aircraft to ground separation less than the actual aircraft to [level] ground separation.
-- (from MAG-16 Accident Board Report)

Downwind and downslope! Colonel Mendenhall and Gerry Dooley both saw their peril at the same time. With the nose of their H-46 pointed skyward, collective pitch bottomed, cyclic back, they frantically tried to bleed off their groundspeed. Then, still 50 feet in the air and just when they needed it most, they ran out of vital translational lift because of the downwind landing.

The two pilots jointly sucked in collective pitch, but their powerful General Electric turbines had to spool up from flight idle.

For a helicopter pilot, there is no more horrible and helpless feeling in the world. You do not need to look at your Triple Tachometer. You can *hear* your lifesaving rotor RPM, your "turns," winding down. Shuddering, losing turns, Colonel Mendenhall and Dooley mushed over the trees and fell into the landing zone.

Behind Colonel Mendenhall, the next two helicopters veered away from their division leader. Captain Thomas C. "Tee-Cee" McAllister and First Lieutenant George G. Richey Jr., flying Number Two, safely landed in the southern corner of the landing area. Number Three, piloted by Captain John T. Maxwell Jr. and First Lieutenant Kenneth H. "Chuck" Johnson, swung left, almost in front of Number Four. In the left seat, Johnson saw Number Four hurtling toward him. He jammed the cyclic to the right and somehow managed to reach the extreme edge of the landing area.

For Number Four, flown by Captain George W. Cumpston and First Lieutenant Lynn M. LaPointe, there seemed to be no place to land. They still had plenty of groundspeed, but they ran out of forward airspeed because of the downwind landing. Without forward airspeed their helicopter rotors lacked the desired clean *bite* of air that all helicopter pilots call translational lift. And without translational lift the powerful turbine engines could not offset the tremendous aerodynamic drag on the rotor blades. On the ICS, LaPointe helplessly warned his HAC: "Turns! Turns! Turns!" Wallowing forward past the other helicopters, Number Four dropped to the ground amid a thicket of 12 to 18 foot high trees.

The Grunts charged out of the first three helicopters. Aided by 3000 psi hydraulic fingers, the pilots raised their ramps, and the three H-46s took off in a whirlwind of dust and vegetation.

Still on the ground in the thicket, Cumpston and LaPointe were in trouble. Their heavy 50 foot diameter rotors had sawed off the tops of the small trees. The rotor blades were not damaged, but the helicopter rear ramp hung down over a small creek. The Grunts crawled down directly into the water below. The helicopter crew chief quickly lowered the front door, thus enabling the cabin to be more rapidly evacuated. Then, ramp up, door closed, Cumpston pulled in power and lurched skyward.

The third division, Rose-Ann 1-9 through Rose-Ann 1-12, consisted entirely of H-46s and crews from HMM-164. Somehow they all made it into the landing zone, although Number Four ran out of power and turns and fell into the bushes, just like Cumpston and LaPointe. Still, the Grunts charged out into the landing zone without incident, and the four helicopters clawed their way up and out of LZ Crow. So far no hostile fire had been encountered, but that was about to change. On climbout one of the HMM-164 pilots laconically radioed in the blind: "Takin' fire from the ridge."

"O. K. You hear that?" Moose asked on our ICS. The crew chief, gunner, and I all rogered the report. Moose turned to me, gave me a nervous laugh, and then keyed the ICS mike: "Sturk, stay with me 'till we're down."

I knew exactly what Moose meant. For the record, he was flying our helicopter, but in a combat environment I was expected to *ride* the controls with him. If he got hit, I could instantly take over. However, once we landed I had to get our ramp down -- fast -- and then get it back up as soon as the last Grunt was out. Every second I delayed was another second of vulnerability that we had to spend sitting there in the landing zone.

Ahead of us, Major Gilbert led our division toward LZ Crow. Our four helicopters lined up in a standard division formation:

	No. 1	No. 2	No. 3	No. 4
Pilot:	Gilbert	Roberts	Rolfe	(unknown)
Copilot:	(unknown)	Fracker	Sturkey	(unknown)
Rose-Ann:	1-13	1-14	1-15	1-16

Tucked in behind Major Gilbert on the right in the number two slot were First Lieutenant Joseph T. "Joe" Roberts and his copilot, First Lieutenant Frederick C. "Chick" Fracker Jr. Moose and I followed in a loose trail position on Major Gilbert's left. Number Four followed behind and to our left. Down below, disaster waited for one of our four helicopters.

Delayed by the division in front of us, Major Gilbert now turned right onto final approach and bottomed his collective pitch lever. In the number two position, Joe and Chick found themselves in an aerodynamic trap. They were caught on the inside of Major Gilbert's turn radius.

As Joe would later explain, he did everything he could do to slow down. He could have slipped over to his left, on the outside of his leader's turn radius, but that would have boxed out the two following helicopters. So, Joe hung tight on the right, above and behind his division leader.

Zooming down toward the landing area, Major Gilbert could not see Joe and Chick above and behind him. Unfortunately he had to slip to the right to avoid a helicopter from the departing third division, and that unavoidable move put Joe and Chick in deep, deep trouble. They hauled the cyclic back into their laps. No good! Hearts pounding, they sucked in full collective pitch and tried to wave off. Not enough power!

"Watch the turns! Watch the turns!"

Rose-Ann 1-14 was heading for the ground.

Too many cards were stacked against them. Blind fate had dealt a losing hand to Joe and Chick. Through no fault of their own, they had simultaneously run out of airspeed, altitude, rotor RPM, engine power, and luck.

Floundering, overloaded, and sinking toward Major Gilbert's whirling rotors directly below them, Joe and Chick tried the only possible option left to them. They threw their heavily loaded helicopter to the right. They almost made it; they *would* have made it. But unfortunately they hit a tree, a *big* tree.

EP-155 was lost in a small downhill zone with tall trees on the approach end.
-- (*HMM-265 Command Chronology*; July 15, 1966)

Joe's rotor blades ripped into the trunk of the tree, and the rotor blades came out second-best. Limbs flew; pieces of rotor blade flew. The H-46 slammed to the ground, and the aft rotor head went into a ground resonance condition. In less than two seconds the centrifugal force of the unbalanced rotor system literally tore the helicopter apart.

The entire aft pylon -- transmission, rotors, and all -- ripped off of the fuselage. The helicopter (EP-155, Bureau Number 151961) was destroyed.

Meanwhile, Moose and I barreled down toward the left side of the landing zone. Luckier than Joe and Chick, we had been on the outside of Major Gilbert's turn radius. Yet, we barely got our helicopter stopped. The cyclic kept coming back, back, as we pointed the H-46 nose at the sky. All I could see was blue sky above me and huge trees on my left. Then, like the others, we managed to mush into the landing zone with the sickening sound of our dying rotor RPM in our ears.

Strapped into my armored seat on the left, I had been intent on keeping us out of the trees. I had not seen Joe and Chick when they crashed off to our right. Number Four suddenly zoomed by overhead. He had been far enough behind us, had seen Joe and Chick hit the tree, and had been able to wave off.

"Get 'em out!" I urged the crew chief on the ICS.

"All clear."

"Ramp coming up."

Still turned around in my seat and looking back into the cabin, I watched as the powerful twin hydraulic pistons sucked the ramp upward. Suddenly, over the metallic whine of the engines I heard a series of rapid-fire snapping and popping noises.

Moose keyed the ICS: "LOOK AT THAT!"

I looked up and saw nothing amiss.

Moose, again: "LOOK AT THAT!"

"What? . . . What?"

"THERE! THERE! THERE!" Moose jabbed with his index finger and pointed to our two o'clock position.

Eighty feet in front of us sat an H-46 in a clump of bushes. Something had gone terribly wrong, I knew, but for a full two or three seconds I could not comprehend what my eyes were telling me. My mind would not accept it.

Then it hit me. The helicopter had only about ten feet worth of rotor blades left on the aft rotor head. Almost hidden in a cloud of dust and debris, I noted that the aft pylon tilted absurdly rearward. The green fuselage was twisted and broken.

And yet another one! Forty feet farther away in another cloud of dust lay the remains of another H-46. The crooked spar of what had once been a rotor blade stuck straight up into the air. The rear half of the helicopter was a crumpled mass of smoking metal.

Two HMM-164 aircraft slightly overshot the zone, landed in close proximity to one another, intermeshed aft rotor blades, and suffered strike damage.

-- (*HMM-164 Command Chronology*; July 15, 1966)

From our training, Moose and I instantly knew what we had to do. We could not delay. In an assault the landing area must be kept cleared to allow the remaining helicopters to land. Moose pulled in collective pitch, hovered, nosed over, and we were on our way out of the valley and headed back toward Dong Ha.

Not until much later did we find out what really had happened to the three H-46s that crashed in LZ Crow that morning. Flying in EP-155, Joe and Chick had hit a tree; that was simple enough. But while I had been busy eyeing the Grunts as they ran out of the cabin of our helicopter, the fifth division had been roaring down to land behind us. With two helicopters from HMM-265 and two more from HMM-164, the fifth division had lined up as follows:

	No. 1	No. 2	No. 3	No. 4
Pilot:	Reap	Sellers	Harper	Farrell
Copilot:	Partington	Brown	Diacont	Leer
Rose-Ann:	1-17	1-18	1-19	1-20

In Rose-Ann 1-17, Major Thomas S. Reap led the fifth division down toward LZ Crow. My good friend, former MARCAD Roger D. Partington, was Reap's copilot. Flying the number two H-46 were Captain Wiley J. Sellers and his copilot, First Lieutenant C. D. Brown. Bringing up the rear were two HMM-265 helicopters. Captain Richard O. "Harpo" Harper and First Lieutenant George Diacont flew Number Three. Captain Leo J. "Crazy-Leo" Farrell and First Lieutenant Gerard R. "Gerry" Lear manned Number Four, tail-end-Charlie.

Major Reap wisely elected to "land long" to make the downwind landing easier on the helicopters behind him. He touched down in the bushy area just beyond the designated landing zone. In Number Two, Sellers and Brown had their landing spot picked out. But they were overloaded, out of translational lift, losing turns, and dropping toward the ground. Still, they would have safely made it, but about 30 feet above the ground they saw Marine Grunts right under their sinking helicopter, trying to scramble away to safety. Full power could not slow the descent of the H-46, so Sellers and Brown threw their helicopter to the side, away from the Grunts below. As they fell to the ground, their spinning rotors intermeshed with the rotors of Number One. Major Reap would later recall: "Suddenly the aircraft disintegrated."

> Parts began to fly in all directions and in the next instant both aircraft rotor systems contacted each other . . . breaking both fuselages in several places. At this point both my co-pilot and myself were not sure if they had hit each other or if they had landed on mines or received mortar fire.
> -- (Captain Richard O. Harper; in his written statement filed with the MAG-16 Accident Board Report)

On final approach, Harpo and Diacont saw the two helicopters crash and tried to wave off. They ran out of power and turns, and their H-46 mushed to the ground behind the three downed Marine helicopters. The last H-46 in their division, Rose-Ann 1-20, managed to wave off. He made a quick 360 degree turn and then returned and landed without incident. The last of the 20 helicopters had now touched down in LZ Crow.

After his Grunts debarked, Harpo stayed in the landing area to evacuate the crews from the downed helicopters, plus the casualties from the crashes. In the left seat across from Harpo, George Diacont picked up his 8mm movie camera, pointed it at the carnage in front of him, and began filming. Years later, viewing his film is reminiscent of the historic film of the John F. Kennedy assassination in Dallas, Texas. Grunts ran back and forth across the landing zone, trying to link up with their platoons, trying to help the injured. Some Grunts still crawled out of the broken hulks of the three ill-fated helicopters.

> Two Marines had been killed and seven injured. Some of the casualties were the result of men being hit by the still-whirring rotor blades of the downed choppers.
> -- (Donald Wharton; in "Invasion Repelled")

George Diacont, like me, sat in the copilot's seat on the left side of his helicopter. Like me, he had not seen Rose-Ann 1-14, the first of the three H-46s that crashed. But then George panned his movie camera to his right and suddenly, there it was, or what was left of it. George panned back to the left. There were Crazy-Leo and Gerry, identified by the faded white EP-174 lettering on the fuselage of their H-46. George zoomed his camera in on the two helicopters that had struck each other. Rose-Ann 1-17 (Bureau Number 151930, YT-15) and Rose-Ann 1-18 (Bureau Number 151936, YT-18) lay twisted and broken and would never fly again.

Sitting in the cockpit, George kept his camera rolling. In front of him, Grunts carried the injured men to the waiting helicopters as sniper fire started singing across the landing zone. Harpo's crew chief, Lance Corporal Elmer F. Durbin, ran over to each crash site to make sure that all helicopter crewmembers were accounted for. He enlisted the aid of the Grunts and moved the stranded H-46 crewmen and the casualties from the crashes back into his helicopter. Then he returned to the wrecks to salvage the machineguns.

Durbin spotted an injured Grunt. Motionless, the man was only visible from the chest up, and Durbin thought that the Grunt had stumbled into a deep hole. Durbin ran over to help, but he discovered that there was no hole. A flying piece of rotor blade, a literal scythe of death, had cleanly severed the Grunt's body at chest level. The Grunt's erect upper torso, his head, and parts of his arms were all that was left of him.

Oblivious to the increasing enemy fire that now whipped across LZ Crow, Durbin stuck to his task. The machineguns and crews from the three downed H-46s were finally carried aboard Rose-Ann 1-19 and Rose-Ann 1-20, along with seven Grunts who had been injured in the crashes. Also loaded were the lifeless bodies of two more Grunts who had been killed by the mangled rotor blades.

The two H-46s took to the air, scratching for altitude and safety. Riding in the cabin of Harpo's helicopter, Major Reap's crew chief got wounded by North Vietnamese small arms fire during the climbout. Durbin and the gunner, Lance Corporal George C. Delanoy, returned the enemy fire until they climbed through 800 feet. Harpo then pointed his helicopter nose eastward and sped toward the field hospital that had been set up in the former French barracks at Dong Ha.

HMM-164 lost another H-46. Two of their helicopters took off after another trip to LZ Crow, and at about 500 feet they began to draw heavy fire from the NVA on Hill 208. Both H-46s took a few hits, their gunners returned the fire, and for a few moments there was no further cause for alarm. But one of the two H-46s, piloted by Captain Robert E. Johnson, was in trouble. An enemy round had holed the aft transmission. The bullet hole allowed the transmission fluid to dribble down onto the hot turbine engines. In the cockpit the amber Master Caution Panel warning light winked on. The transmission temperature climbed, while the transmission pressure fluctuated and then dropped to zero. Dense white smoke, caused by the transmission fluid vaporizing on the hot engines, poured out of the engine compartment and into the cabin.

Thinking that he was on fire and, worse yet, faced with imminent transmission seizure, Johnson dove for the ground. The hasty forced landing at YD-097635, three miles northwest of Cam Lo, sheared the left main landing gear. Johnson's H-46 was out of action. HMM-164 had started the day with 13 helicopters, and already they were down to only ten.

The rest of the morning passed in a whirlwind of flights. We flew the 2nd Battalion, 4th Marines, into LZ Dove at map coordinates YD-085655. Next, the remainder of the 3rd Battalion, 4th Marines, crawled aboard our H-46s, and we flew them westward to LZ Crow to join their comrades. The day stretched on, and Moose and I made two flights to Khe Sanh, 28 miles to the west, to drop off a radio communications team. Many flights down to Phu Bai followed in order to ferry reinforcements up to Cam Lo and Dong Ha. We flew more sorties to LZ Crow, more sorties to LZ Dove, more Recon inserts deep in the hills. The cycle became routine: load, launch, deliver the goods, return, refuel, check for bullet holes and battle damage, and start all over again.

The VMO-2 After Action Report for July 15 details one of their quick Recon insertions and extractions on July 15. Two of the "Deadlock" Huey gunship pilots had flown cover for a lone Recon-carrying H-34 helicopter from HMM-161:

Two UH1Es . . . escorted Barrelhouse 2-1 [the H-34] on a Recon insertion at YD-049610. The [radio] call for extraction came almost immediately as the Recon team made contact with the enemy. The Hueys covered the extraction, firing suppressive fire into and around the LZ. They expended three thousand rounds of 7.62 [mm] ammunition and twenty-eight 2.75 inch rockets in covering the successful extraction by the Barrelhouse [helicopter].

To the west the ground action had heated up. Hueys and H-34s took most of the ground fire now. They stayed busy shuffling small Grunt units around and hauling the wounded out of the hills. One of my former MARCAD buddies, First Lieutenant Otto H. Fritz, flew H-34s for HMM-161, and he made trip after trip into LZ Crow. For the H-46 pilots, much of the time was spent on Recon inserts deep in the mountains to the west. Most of these went smoothly, at least mine did, but other H-46 crews were not as fortunate. One of our HMM-265 helicopters traded fire with an NVA heavy machinegun on the southern side of Lu Bu Mountain, near the headwaters of the Cam Lo River.

Received heavy fire 50 cal. or above [near] YD-835640.
-- (*HMM-265 Command Chronology*; July 15, 1966)

Many of the small Recon teams, four or five men apiece, were inserted by the H-34s. With a pair of VMO-2 Huey gunships flying cover, an H-34 dropped off a Recon team at YD-049610, two miles east of the peak of Hill 549. Contact with the enemy was almost immediate.

The size of the reconnaissance force varied with the location and purpose of the mission. Sometimes just a few Recons were needed to man an observation point high atop a ridge or mountain that was virtually inaccessible except by helicopter. In the valleys a reinforced platoon often was required. Bonnie-Sue pilots flew one such reinforced team of 35 Recons into the lush river valley at YD-085486, six miles southwest of Cam Lo.

The afternoon wore on, and it seemed to me that the tactical news from the Song Ngan Valley sounded encouraging. Although the 3rd Battalion, 4th Marines, was having trouble in their push to the east from LZ Crow, the other Marine ground units fought their way to their objectives.

Late in the day, HMM-164 got some good news. Their

wounded dove H-46 with the sheared landing gear had been repaired by helicopter mechanics, fired up, and safely flown back to Dong Ha. The downed helicopter had been guarded by a Sparrowhawk reaction team. Now, HMM-265 got the frag to fly to the former forced landing site and bring back the 18 Grunts who had guarded the helicopter.

Two Huey gunships would fly cover, and two H-46s would make the pick-up. Captains John Maxwell and Richard H. "Rollo" Langenfeld were our two HACs who drew the mission. Five minutes after takeoff from Dong Ha, Maxwell and Langenfeld arrived over YD-097635 and made radio contact with the Sparrowhawk radioman down below. He reported that the Grunts were taking occasional fire from NVA snipers, nothing more.

Covered by the gunships, Rollo and John zipped down and landed without any problem. The Grunts jumped out of their freshly dug fighting holes and from concealed locations in the nearby brush and dashed toward the helicopters. With the Grunts aboard and their ramps up, the H-46s powered skyward. Just as he shuddered through translational lift, John caught a fleeting glimpse of what he thought might be a Grunt lying behind a log. John continued his climbout, but on the ICS he told his crew chief to question the Grunts. Were they all aboard? The confused Grunts did not know for sure, because about half of them were on each of the two helicopters.

John radioed to the gunships for help. Yes, John was told, one of the gunships would fly down for a final look just to make certain, because Marines do not leave their comrades behind in combat. As the first gunship screamed down, a human form stood up and waved his arms in the landing area -- friend or foe? The gunship's boresighted M-60s were ready, just in case, but the man turned out to be a Marine Grunt. This time he did not hesitate. He dashed to the gunship, dove inside, and the Huey headed up toward the other three helicopters that were orbiting above.

Thoroughly cursed by the gunship crew chief, the unnerved Grunt tried to explain: "But we wuz takin' fire!" So, he said, he had decided to hunker down behind the log to "wait it out." Fortunately for him, fool's luck had prevailed. But had it not been for the sharp eye of John Maxwell, the Grunt would not have been discovered missing until after the Sparrowhawk team had landed and regrouped at Dong Ha. The folly of the Grunt's decision to remain in the LZ alone was vividly and vehemently explained to him in explicit language that he could clearly understand.

By late afternoon on July 15, we got a lull in the stream of frags that had kept us in the air most of the day. Moose and I shut down Bureau Number 152498 on the grass south of the Dong Ha airstrip and crawled out to stretch our legs and quench our thirst. Soon I strolled over to chat with a group of my peers who were lying on the grass in the shade under one of our helicopters. All of us already had our share of "War Stories" to tell about our first day of flying in Operation Hastings. We took turns, each hanging onto every word that was spoken, but often butting in when we had some tidbit of information to add. We flew with our hands as we described the flying and fighting. I recounted my first landing in LZ Crow, and I took perverse delight in detailing what little I had seen of the death of Rose-Ann 1-17 and Rose-Ann 1-18. Lynn LaPointe rolled in laughter as I confessed that I had failed to see the two H-46s when they crashed less than 100 feet in front of me.

First Lieutenant Huey C. Walsh, one of my five tentmates back at Marble Mountain, dropped down on the grass with us. We bled each other for the latest news, but none of us really had much of a grasp on the overall progress of the fighting to the west. Consequently, we lounged around and began to retell some of the older War Stories from our two months of flying in Vietnam. Some of us added several verbal degrees of embellishment to our tales. The old universal military axiom is correct: "The farther from the battle, the thicker the flak." But Huey had the best War Story of all, totally true, well documented in writing and with a photograph, and more hilarious with each retelling. None of us ever tired of hearing Huey recount his now infamous *snake story*. As we lay on the grass, Huey once again began explaining his dubious claim to fame.

On July 6, nine days earlier, Huey had crawled into Bureau Number 152501. His mission: fly to Khe Sanh for Search and Rescue North (SAR North) duty. With Captain Duane S. Jensen as his HAC, Huey had left Marble Mountain, picked up the special maps, radio frequencies, and codes from the Air Force at Da Nang, and rotored his way northward.

This had been Huey's first combat mission with Duane, and it would turn out to be unforgettable. Huey was flying the helicopter as they cruised toward Khe Sanh at 3000 feet. Suddenly, just north of Hai Van Pass, Duane screamed:

"AAARRRUUGGHH!"

"Whaaa . . . what?" Huey stammered.

"SNNAAAKKKEE!"

A greenish-brown snake slowly slithered through their cockpit! Duane had encountered the serpent as it crept past his right elbow on the narrow aluminum ledge below his sliding window.

In horror, Huey watched as Duane threw off his shoulder harness, grabbed his survival knife, and began madly thrashing away at the right side of the cockpit. Faced with Duane's maniacal assault with the knife, the snake dropped from the ledge, slithered between Duane's rudder pedals, and vanished behind the instrument panel. Ever so slowly, Duane got back into his seat.

The rest of the flight to Khe Sanh turned out to be uneventful. After they landed, needless to say, Duane, Huey, their crew chief, and their gunner conducted a meticulous search for the snake. They failed to find the serpent. The crew chief volunteered that his H-46 had been used to fly a group of ARVNs to An Hoa the previous day. Could the snake have been carried aboard in one of the chicken crates? In any event there was "no joy" (military pilot's parlance that means *no visual contact*) with the snake.

Once during the day Duane and Huey launched, but their assigned rescue sortie soon was aborted. They flew back to Khe Sanh, and the snake was nowhere to be seen on this short flight. Perhaps it had wormed its way out of the helicopter and back into the jungle, they reasoned, or *hoped*. Control scrubbed the mission late in the afternoon, so Duane and Huey fired up their engines and headed south toward Marble Mountain and a possible hot supper. All at once by Duane's right knee, the serpent reappeared:

Maybe the previous episode had me keyed up, or perhaps the stress of the day's events contributed, but I really came unglued this time.

-- (Duane S. Jensen; years later)

Once again: "SNNAAAKKKEE!"

This time, Duane elected not to fight the unwelcome stowaway. He threw off his shoulder harness, clambered out of his armored seat, crawled out of the cockpit, and retreated to the relative safety of the helicopter cabin.

From his childhood, Huey had always feared snakes. Now he had been left alone with the scaly nemesis in the H-46 cockpit. From his left seat he kept a wary eye on the reptile. Fortunately the snake soon did an about face and slipped back behind the instrument panel. In an unconvincing and high-pitched voice, Huey told Duane that the crisis had ended. Duane eventually crept back into the cockpit and gingerly eased into his seat.

By this time Walsh was getting quite a kick watching Jensen trying to evade the persistent snake. His laughs didn't last long. Ten minutes later the viper came out on the other side of the [H-46 instrument] panel, only a few inches from Walsh. -- (from article in *Navy Times*)

Huey did not even try to put up a fight. He bailed out of his seat and left the cockpit to Duane. Safely back in the cabin, Huey announced his intention to remain there. Meanwhile, the crew chief and gunner nervously prayed that when their pilots evacuated the cockpit, they both would not do so at the same time.

Finally the snake returned to its hiding spot behind the instrument panel, and Huey cautiously crawled back into his seat and strapped himself in. They made it back to Marble Mountain without further contact with the serpent, and Duane immediately *downed* the H-46. His single entry on the maintenance yellow-sheet said it all: "SNAKE IN THE COCKPIT!!!"

The maintenance crew had to tear out the aluminum floor panels, but they finally found it: a Bamboo Viper, a genuine "six-stepper," smaller than a Cobra but venomous and deadly. They promptly decapitated the sinister stowaway. The crisis finally was over.

Under the headline, "Snake Livens Up Routine Mission," *Navy Times* later printed a feature article on what Huey called his "most exciting flight." The accompanying photograph showed Duane and

Huey, both wearing silly grins, gingerly holding the headless carcass of the serpent.

The sun gradually dipped down toward the crests of the hills west of Dong Ha, but the new frag brought us to our feet. Water and ammunition, in that order, were the most important commodities to be delivered. The Grunts needed ammunition, but they needed water even more. All day long they had battled the North Vietnamese soldiers in the stifling hot valley under a cloudless sky. The heat, humidity, terrain, and their exertion had taken the expected toll and had sapped their strength. Drinking water, precious drinking water, was their most critical need.

The heat with no breeze and unlimited humidity was devastating.
-- (Captain Robert Modrzejewski; quoted by Timothy S. Lowry in *And Brave Men, Too*)

I was among the designated pilots, and we quickly gathered for the briefing. We would load up with drinking water, ammunition, and Grunt reinforcements at Dong Ha. Our helicopters would make the short flight to LZ Crow, where we would drop off the reinforcements and cargo. Then we would pick up the Grunt casualties waiting there for us and fly them back to the field hospital at Dong Ha. It sounded simple enough. We had been flying in and out of LZ Crow more or less all day now, so we no longer needed our maps to find our way there. Eight H-46s were needed, and all of them would come from HMM-265, with Colonel Mendenhall as our flight leader.

Moose and I walked around Bureau Number 152498, just checking, and things seemed to be more or less in order. The crew chief already had escorted the Grunts into our H-46 cabin, along with 25 to 30 five gallon water cans and several crates of ammunition. We ran through our checklist, fired up, and launched. Quickly we rendezvoused with an H-46 ahead of us flown by Major Gilbert. Our flight of eight helicopters climbed on course to 2000 feet and circled just north of Cam Lo. There was a ten minute delay because the Grunts up ahead in the Song Ngan Valley had monitored the wrong radio frequency. Soon we sorted out the problem, and the questions began: How is the zone marked? Wind condition? Where are the good guys? Where are the bad guys? How close? Would we likely take fire on approach? From where? On and on it went, and finally we were ready.

This promised to be a short hop. We were all full of fuel, so Gerry Dooley, the copilot in the first helicopter, reached to his right and flipped the Fuel Jettison toggle switches for both of his fuel tanks. I always loved to watch an H-46 jettisoning fuel in flight. Twin trails of JP-4 fuel gushed rearward into the slipstream from the tanks in the stub-wings, and it made the H-46 look like an air-show aircraft trailing twin white and wispy contrails. At a rate of 600 pounds per minute, the helicopter was lightened. Dooley flipped the jettison switches back to the "Normal" position after dumping about 1000 pounds of jet fuel. We all did likewise, for the memory of the three crashes earlier in the day was fresh in our minds. It was hot, we were heavily loaded, and there was no sense in tempting fate. We still had enough fuel left to fly for at least an hour, but in 15 to 20 minutes we probably would be back on the ground at Dong Ha.

This time our approach into LZ Crow would be from the east. The best intelligence available indicated that our biggest threat would be from the heavily wooded ridge south of the landing area. Consequently, we would make a high speed descent into the valley well to the north of that ridge.

Colonel Mendenhall and Dooley started their approach, swooping down north of Hill 208. Right behind them came their wingman, EP-171, flown by Tee-Cee McAllister and George Richey. About 400 meters farther back were the next two helicopters. John Maxwell and Chuck Johnson piloted the first, while George Cumpston and Lynn LaPointe flew the second. Three-hundred meters behind those four H-46s, Moose and I followed Major Gilbert. We watched the first two helicopters race down between the green hills. Then our radio crackled with the rasping voice of Colonel Mendenhall's warning:

"TRIPLE-A! TRIPLE-A! -- ABORT! ABORT!"

Colonel Mendenhall saw the tracer rounds reaching up for him. Then he spotted the NVA crew-served gun. He jammed his cyclic forward and sucked in all of the power that his two turbine engines could muster.

To Gerry Dooley, the enemy tracers looked exactly like "tremendous orange beer cans" as they zoomed by his cockpit. He instantly rode the cyclic and collective with Colonel Mendenhall. They evaded the enemy fire and then climbed up out of the valley.

Tucked in tight behind their flight leader, McAllister and Richey saw the tracers. They heard Colonel Mendenhall's radio warning. Then one of their machineguns began firing back in the cabin. They pulled in full collective pitch to abort the approach, but it was too late. Their luck had run out.

WHHAAAMM! WHHAAAMM! WHHAAAMM!

Tremendous blows against the fuselage!

The 12.7mm NVA antiaircraft gun, deadly against helicopters, had found its mark. Exactly where the lethal rounds struck the doomed H-46, no one will ever know. But somehow a pressurized fuel line had been hit, and the highly flammable and volatile jet fuel created an instant inferno.

1815H: A CH46-A of HMM-265 was hit at 1500 feet and commenced burning. The aircraft exploded after hitting the ground and the fate of the crew and 12 troops aboard is unknown . . . .
-- (from MAG-16 SITREP [situation report] 142101H to 152100H July [July 14, 2101 Hours to July 15, 2100 Hours] 1966)

From roughly 800 meters behind the stricken H-46, I saw the flames. It looked like just a small sheet of flame at first. Then it grew and grew, trailing back from the left side of the Bonnie-Sue helicopter. "Get it down! Get it on the ground!" I thought.

I watched, Moose watched. There was nothing that we could do. Number Two headed for the valley floor, trailing black smoke and orange flames. He turned slightly to the left, still descending, and the ugly ebony trail of smoke grew thicker, steadily thicker.

Moose keyed the mike: "Come on, Tee-Cee. Come on!" Moose and Tee-Cee were close friends, and in anguish Moose again implored: "Come on, baby. Come on, baby!"

Wordlessly, I watched. It was surreal, unbelievable, macabre, horrible. Angry orange flames and jet black smoke now billowed out behind the doomed helicopter as it headed for the valley floor. Moose banked left, putting the valley on the right side of our cockpit. I could no longer see the burning H-46, but I listened as Moose continued to transmit in the blind. He was pleading now: "Come on, Tee-Cee! Come on! Get it down . . . ."

> TC's craft was in flames as it descended through about 800 feet. [It] rolled over and exploded on impact and there was no doubt in my mind there would be no survivors.
> -- (John T. Maxwell; years later)

Moose relinquished the cyclic and collective to me and slumped back in his armored seat, looking straight ahead. I wrapped our H-46 around hard to the left and got a fresh view of the valley down below. A boiling pillar of dense black smoke had mushroomed skyward. From the ground, wicked-looking orange flames rolled upward into the rising column of smoke. Colonel Mendenhall would later describe it as a "burning mass." The helicopter, or whatever might have been left of it, was not visible, only the flames and the boiling column of smoke.

I had seen an aircraft burn like this in November 1964 at South Whiting Field near Milton, Florida. At 1200 feet in the flight-of-four ahead of me, a MARCAD flight student had gotten the tail of his T-28 sawed off by the propeller of another aircraft. He had vertically plunged down into the pines. I had seen his funeral pyre, the jet-black column of smoke from the burning 115/145 gasoline, and no one had to explain to me what it meant.

Now I watched an identical column of smoke as we circled southeast of the Song Ngan Valley. Colonel Mendenhall and Dooley made a high speed pass over the crash site. Major Gilbert made a pass right behind them. Dooley insisted that they try to land, but his idea got vetoed. There was nothing that they could do to help. The H-46 had crashed in a rugged area, and there was no nearby place to land. Even if Colonel Mendenhall and Dooley could have landed, they could not have done anything to help their squadronmates.

We got sketchy details from the Grunts in the valley on our FM radio. The Grunts had initially rushed toward the burning wreckage to try to help, but they were soon driven back by the intense heat and a chain of explosions from the grenades and ammunition "cooking off" in the fire. Two weeks later the August 1, 1966, issue of *Newsweek Magazine* would note:

A Communist incendiary bullet . . . sent the chopper flaming into the hills . . . and crashing almost on top of one of the Marine units on the ground to produce one of the war's most spectacular sequences of battle photos.

Huey Walsh was flying as copilot in tail-end-Charlie, Number Eight, and he looked down at the grim scene below. He saw what he would later call the "orange explosion" when the burning H-46 slammed into the trees. Mere happenstance had apparently saved Huey's life. He had been scheduled to fly in the ill-fated number two position, but a last minute change had reshuffled the flight line-up. Like all combat helicopter pilots, Huey knew that there was no safe position flying into a hot landing zone. Sometimes the guys up front would take the rounds, and at other times they just stirred up trouble for the guys in the rear. Now, viewing the crash site and fire from 2000 feet, Huey thought out loud: "Somebody Up There must be looking out for me."

Back in the pack, above and behind us, George Diacont again had been busy with his movie camera. With a zoom lens, he captured the shoot-down and fiery crash. Many years later, George would give me a VHS videotape copy of his original 8mm film.

We all knew that there had been four of our Bonnie-Sue squadronmates aboard the burning H-46. In addition to McAllister and Richey, there had been the crew chief, Sergeant Robert R. Telfer, and the gunner, Sergeant Gary A. Lucus. And strapped into the web troop seats in the cabin had been twelve trusting and totally helpless Marine Grunts.

The enemy antiaircraft guns would have to be located and silenced before we would make another attempt to resupply LZ Crow. Colonel Mendenhall scrubbed the mission, and our seven remaining helicopters flew back to Dong Ha. After landing I wandered over and found Huey Walsh and George Diacont, and we sat down in the late afternoon shade under one of our helicopters. Huey, George, and I quietly and academically debated the chance of rain that night, but our hearts and minds were elsewhere.

Eventually we walked up to Op's North to see if the Grunts in the valley had radioed back any news about our missing squadronmates. No, there was no news at all, we were told.

Marine Air had started the day with 27 new H-46s, and we had planted five of them in the Song Ngan Valley. One of those five (Bureau Number 151599, the *wounded dove* from HMM-164 with the sheared landing gear) had been recovered, of course. But the other four (EP-155 and EP-171 from HMM-265, and YT-15 and YT-18 from HMM-164) had taken their last flights.

No one knows who first coined the new name. The "Song Ngan Valley" had previously sufficed. In the Vietnamese language, *song* means *river*, and the Ngan River did flow through the valley. But the valley got a new name on July 15. The Grunts liked the new name and thereafter used it exclusively. Marine Air quickly accepted the new name, and the Marine Command, Task Force Delta, also began using it. Next, the media picked it up. The new name was descriptive, it fit. The new name eventually would be used in military reports, newspapers, and books -- universally used. It would become a part of Marine Corps lore and stand along with other time-tested names such as Bloody Nose Ridge, Mount Suribachi, and Chosin Reservoir. The Marines had renamed the Song Ngan Valley on July 15. It became "Helicopter Valley."

The sun slowly sank below the rim of the hills in the west. Roughly a third of the helicopters remained at Dong Ha on standby for night medevacs and emergency ammunition resupply missions. Before the so-called *day* ended, Harpo would log 13.6 hours of flight time, representing about 16 hours in his H-46 cockpit. Emergency night medevacs would account for 3.2 hours of his total time in the air.

The rest of us launched into the night sky and headed south toward Marble Mountain. We landed, taxied in, refueled, and turned our helicopters over to Maintenance for the night. Captain Joseph G. "Joe" Roman was our squadron duty officer that evening, and he stayed in radio contact with the command post for Marine Air at Dong Ha. One by one we straggled over and quietly asked Joe the obvious question. No, he told us, there was no new information about our lost squadronmates in Helicopter Valley.

The Marble Mountain mess hall was still open and waiting for us, so we walked inside and filled our empty stomachs. Then we shuffled up the sandy road to our tents to get some rest:

> . . . after the longest day I ever hope to spend. We were so sure T.C. [Captain Thomas C. "Tee-Cee" McAllister] was a goner that we drank all his booze, toasting him.
> -- (John T. Maxwell; years later)

I had logged 8.2 hours of flight time on Operation Hastings that day. Moreover, I knew that the next day many of us would be going back up north to Dong Ha and Helicopter Valley. Totally exhausted, I pulled off my flight suit and boots, collapsed onto my canvas cot, and immediately fell into a deep and dreamless sleep.

Marble Mountain, July 16, 1966: I did not go back up north on July 16. By chance, Moose and I teamed up again in a different helicopter, Bureau Number 152498. We spent our day flying short frags in the flatlands below Marble Mountain, and we incurred 2.2 hours of flight time, according to my logbook. Most details of that day have long ago faded from my memory, but there is one event that I can never forget.

I met a *ghost*.

I came face-to-face with a dead man.

I squinted my eyes against the blinding glare of the sun as I walked from the tent area down toward the HMM-265 flight line. I vaguely became aware of a Marine in a flight suit stumbling toward me, headed up toward tent city. The tall black-headed Marine turned and ran over to me, wearing a tired but wide ear-to-ear grin. My feet suddenly stopped working.

> The pilots and one crew member of the CH-46A from HMM-265 which exploded at 1815H, 15 July, escaped with burns. All other[s] in the aircraft are presumed dead.
> -- (from MAG-16 SITREP [situation report] 152101H to 162100H July 1966)

Could it be . . . RICHEY! GEORGE RICHEY! Yes, George

was alive! Covered with black soot, dirt, and grime, he easily could have been mistaken for a chimney sweep. It seemed like eternity before I was able to speak.

"We thought -- I thought you were dead!" I finally stammered.

"I thought so too," George softly replied.

Rapidly, George told me what had happened. Flying as Colonel Mendenhall's wingman the previous afternoon, he and Tee-Cee had roared down into Helicopter Valley. Yes, they had seen the tracers, but it was too late. They took hits from the North Vietnamese antiaircraft gun, and one of their fuel lines must have ruptured. Flaming pressurized fuel gushed into the cabin behind them, and thick, choking black smoke totally filled their cockpit.

George continued his story. They lost an engine right at the outset, but it did not matter. They were in a full autorotation. Unable to see the instrument panel, unable to see out of the cockpit, they jettisoned the cockpit emergency escape hatches. Still unable to see the ground below, they yawed the helicopter, trying to clear the smoke. Tee-Cee suddenly glimpsed the ground below and flared.

They really did not hit too hard, George explained. But they struck the trees on the side of a hill, and the H-46 rolled over and beat itself to death. From the raging fire in the cabin behind them, searing flames roared into the cockpit. Unable to see, George felt his way out of the hatch and fell to the earth. Tee-Cee, badly burned, tumbled out after him within a few moments. Blinded and unable to see at all, they could do nothing to help anyone else. They crawled away from the intense heat and the noise of the fire.

George explained that the Grunts finally found him and Tee-Cee and took them to a company command post, where corpsmen bandaged their burns and poured water into their eyes. There they remained until nightfall. The NVA repeatedly tried to overrun the Grunts during the night, but the Grunts held. Throughout the long night, George related, H-34s managed to fly into LZ Crow to haul out some of the wounded Grunts. George was offered a ride out, but hearing the constant rattle of small arms fire, he refused and elected to wait until morning. He and Tee-Cee were medevaced out shortly after daybreak and flown to the field hospital at Dong Ha. Later they were packed onto a C-130 with other casualties for the airplane trip to Charlie-Med at Da Nang.

George was singed, bruised, and shaken, but basically O. K. Tee-Cee would be in the hospital for a few more days, I was told. Tee-Cee had been banged up and burned a lot worse than George.

LUCUS, Gary Alan, 1859141, Sgt USMC, WIA Quang Tri [Province], Republic of Vietnam, Second and Third Degree Burns, Face and Arms . . . .
-- (Casualty Card; Sergeant Gary A. Lucus)

George explained to me that his gunner, Sergeant Gary A. Lucus, had been *horribly* burned, but that he had lived through the night of July 15. George had no idea how Sergeant Lucus had gotten out of their burning and overturned H-46. The Grunts had found Lucus huddled in the jungle, in shock and unable to speak, 50 meters from the fire. His fire-resistant flight suit, although burned through in places, had saved his life. But it had not saved his face, hands, and arms. The skin had burned off of his hands, and remnants of his flesh dangled down spaghetti-like from his fingers. His entire face was charred and blackened. Yet, he was still alive when he was medevaced to the field hospital Dong Ha.

TELFER, Robert Ray, 1877872, Sgt USMC, KIA, Died 15 Jul 66 vicinity of Quang Tri Province . . . . Aircraft was hit by heavy weapons fire and exploded after impact with ground. BODY NOT RECOVERED.
-- (Casualty Card; Sergeant Robert R. Telfer)

George dropped his head: "Telfer -- aaahhh -- Telfer didn't make it." Sergeant Robert R. Telfer, the young crew chief, had died and burned up in his helicopter. George really did not know what had happened to Telfer back in the flaming cabin during their fiery descent. Maybe he got shot, maybe the impact killed him, or maybe the fire just incapacitated him. Originally from Fonda, New York, Sergeant Telfer had celebrated his 24th birthday on July 14. He had died the following day, 10,400 miles from home.
"What about all the Grunts in the cabin?" I softly asked.
"Uuuuuhhh -- all dead."
"What got 'em, the fire?"
"We'll never know."

Although cruelly burned, Sergeant Lucus had survived and would later be medevaced to the United States Naval Hospital in Yokosuka, Japan. Two months later when he regained partial use of his hands, he would peck out a three page typewritten letter to his erstwhile HAC, Tee-Cee McAllister. Many years later I would acquire a copy of that letter. In a subsequent exchange of correspondence, Gary Lucus would authorize me to republish a transcript of it. However, many parts of the 1966-vintage letter are too personal, too private, better left unsaid. The emotional and lengthy letter dated September 5, 1966, would begin as follows:

Dear Capt. McAllister,

It sure was good to hear that you and Lt. Richey got out [of the burning helicopter] and are in good shape and was also glad to get your letter.

As to my going to the states. Well, I'll be leaving here in a week or so and as it stands I'll be going to either Camp Pendleton or San Diego.

The reason for me going to the states is because of my left hand. I have feeling in it, but it doesn't seem to want to do what I tell it. It is real stiff but the Dr. says it will come along in time. My skin graphs are doing wonderful and in a year or so they should be so smooth that no one will ever be able to tell I've had them.

In his letter, Lucus began explaining what had happened back in the H-46 cabin as they had roared down into Helicopter Valley. The crew chief, Sergeant Telfer, spotted the enemy gunners. Telfer then leaned into his M-60, ripping off long bursts at the antiaircraft gun in a jungle clearing down below. Then Lucus described the heavy blows as the NVA rounds tore through the fuselage of his H-46. He said that it sounded exactly "like some-one out on the stub-wing with a ball bat" beating on the side of the helicopter.

Lucus detailed how flames suddenly enveloped the rear of the cabin around the overhead engine compartment doors. He said that in a few seconds the whole rear half of the cabin turned into a cauldron of fire. Lucus grabbed the fire bottle, but Telfer snatched it from him and ran aft to battle the flames. Lucus then wrote:

My eyes started to burn. Sgt. Telfer wasn't able to get all the way aft to use the extinguisher because the flames were half way forward and the heat to[o] intense.

Dense black smoke filled the cabin, and it boiled up into the cockpit. On the ICS, Lucus heard the pilots exclaim that they could not see. Lucus unstrapped and wedged his huge body into the opening leading to the cockpit. He desperately tried to block out the blinding smoke so that McAllister and Richey could see to fly them to the ground. Lucus felt the "intense heat," and he turned to try to look aft into the burning cabin. In his letter he explained: "I couldn't see anything."

Then the helicopter slammed into the trees. Lucus evidently lost consciousness, and when he regained his senses most of the fire had burned itself out. He could see green bushes through the remaining smoke and flames. Lucus saw two other men in the burning helicopter cabin who were still alive. One of those men was his friend, the helicopter crew chief, Sergeant Telfer:

His right leg, from above the knee, was on the outside of the plane and was pinned there. He hollered for me to pull him out, but [his leg] wouldn't budge. He then told me to break it off, God how I tried to pull it out but it just had to[o] much weight on it.

Lucus yelled to Telfer to hold on; Lucus would get someone to help pull him out. Then Lucus crawled to a Grunt who was still alive and started dragging him forward through the cabin. But there was another explosion, and the Grunt fell on top of Lucus and lay motionless, no longer breathing. Lucus then crawled to another Grunt and pushed him upright. The man was dead, and Lucus wrote: "I can still see his burning hair."

Unable to get help, Lucus crawled back to Sergeant Telfer as more ammunition cooked off all around them. Grabbing Telfer's flak jacket through the arm holes, Lucus tugged with all of his might, but it was no use. Telfer was now limp and lifeless -- gone. The back of Telfer's flight suit had been burned away, and Lucus saw a huge hole in his friend's back. Lucus felt for a pulse and found none. In his letter he wrote: "He was dead, I couldn't believe it."

Lucus crawled up into the cockpit and squeezed out of the helicopter through the copilot's escape hatch. The Grunts later found him, and they took him to their corpsman. Lucus lived through the night, and he was medevaced to Dong Ha after daylight the next morning in an H-34. He eventually ended up in the hospital at Yokosuka. Lucus noted in his letter:

> Their [sic] are two men here in the hospital that were on the hill when we hit and they said that one man ran out of the back [ramp of the helicopter and fell to his death] when we were about half way down and that another man jumped out just before we hit and the plane landed on him. They also said that there was an explosion and screams just after we hit but I don't remember them, maybe I was knocked out. I don't know. I imagine this seems like a long letter but these are the things that I remember and, in time, hope to forget. I haven't slept a nite since it happened because I keep thinking I could have helped someone besides myself.

Gary Lucus would slowly recover from his severe burns. As his body healed, the doctors at Yokosuka also would find that Lucus had been shot in the buttocks. Perhaps the bullet came from the ammunition cooking off in the fire, or maybe it came from the attacking NVA during the night in LZ Crow. Lucus had never realized that he had been shot.

I had no way to know it in July 1966, but fate would bring Gary Lucus and me together in the hospital at Yokosuka two months later.

After his recovery, Lucus would elect to remain in the Marine Corps. He would receive his commission and return for a total of four combat tours in Vietnam. Lucus eventually would retire with his family in Lakeside, California. Whenever I think of him and of the horror and agony he endured, the final line from Rudyard Kipling's tribute always comes to mind: "You're a better man than I am, Gunga Din!"

Hard Days,
-- Hard Nights --

✓ **Helicopters! And the valor and skill of the pilots has outrun the book. The stars on their Air Medals are matched only by the stars in their crowns!**
-- (Lieutenant General Victor H. Krulak, Commanding General, Fleet Marine Force, Pacific; July 11, 1967)

When the Marines charged into Helicopter Valley, their world changed forever. For the helicopter crews, days become a nonstop ballet of troop lifts, strikes and assaults, Recon inserts, resupply missions, and medevac flights to recover the dead and wounded. Nights were a time to regroup, rest, service the helicopters, and prepare for the next day of combat flying. For the Marines who battled the NVA, the world ceased to exist beyond the confines of northern First Corps (written, *I-Corps*; pronounced, *eye-core*), the northernmost military region in South Vietnam.

Of course, there was *another* world thousands of miles away. In that other world in July 1966, the French joined the atomic club by detonating their first nuclear bomb. At Wimbledon, an American tennis player named Billie Jean King triumphed over Maria Bueno of Brazil. Flamboyant labor leader Jimmy Hoffa voted to give himself a hefty $25,000 pay raise. And a disillusioned loner, Richard B. Speck, silently crept into a nurse's dormitory in the city of Chicago.

The other world offered a new Ford Galaxie automobile for $2699. Sirloin steak cost just 88 cents per pound, turkey could be bought for 39 cents per pound, and a pound of sugar sold for a meager eight cents. Newspapers contained comic strips featuring Little Orphan Annie, Rip Kirby, and Steve Canyon. The tongues of social gossipers were fueled by the Las Vegas marriage of 50 year old Frank Sinatra to 21 year old Mia Farrow. And a fanatical 24 year old ex-Marine rifle sharpshooter, Charles J. Whitman, barricaded himself atop the lofty belltower at the University of Texas -- with his rifle.

But life in this other world held no meaning at all for the Marines who battled the North Vietnamese soldiers in Helicopter Valley. The other world was foreign, totally forgotten. It might as well have been on another planet.

Joe Roberts and Chick Fracker would soon be back in the cockpit. They had been bruised and battered in the crash that destroyed EP-155, but physically they suffered no lasting ill effects. For the crew of the ill-fated EP-171, it was a different story. The H-46 crew chief, Robert Telfer, was dead. His body had burned to ashes in the fire that had totally consumed the helicopter. The pilots, Tee-Cee McAllister and George Richey, were burned but would soon recover. However, for their gunner, Gary Lucus, the night of July 15 had been filled with unending agony and terror.

Lucus had been horribly burned in the crash. Third degree burns had melted away the flesh from his hands and from much of his arms. His face had been charred, and the skin had fallen away. The corpsmen had done their best to comfort Lucus, but nothing could eliminate his excruciating pain. When night fell the corpsmen had carried Lucus to a thickly wooded area near the battalion command post at LZ Crow. Here they had laid him between two logs. The Grunts planned to medevac him to Dong Ha by helicopter if he lived through the night. "Hang on, just hang on!" they had urged him.

No moonlight had filtered down through the thick foliage. Out of the misty blackness the NVA came -- mortar attacks followed by ground assaults. Firefights had raged throughout the night. The combatants, almost invisible to each other in the darkness, had fired at muzzle flashes. Tracers, green for the NVA and red for the Marine Grunts, arced through the night. Lying between the logs and writhing in agony, Lucus had been defenseless.

After a brief respite the NVA had swarmed forward in force, and they charged through the Marine perimeter. In hand-to-hand fighting the Marine Grunts had thrown themselves at the onrushing enemy soldiers. In the jungle undergrowth the crackle of M-14 and AK-47 rifle fire had been broken by the dull thud of rifle butts striking the enemy. Shouts, screams, and the moans of the dying had pierced the night as the combatants drove their bayonets home.

Get the blade into the enemy. This is the main principle in bayonet fighting. It is the blade that kills.
-- (from *Guidebook for Marines*)

During a lull in the fighting, the battalion chaplain had crawled over to the spot where Lucus lay concealed between the logs. Lucus would never forget the chaplain's whispered promise: "Son, I won't leave you."

Again the NVA had swarmed forward out of the night. Again they had rammed their way through the Marine lines, but the Grunts had finally thrown the enemy back each time. Lucus and the chaplain had watched the NVA soldiers repeatedly charge and then fall back, jumping over the logs that formed their hiding place. Finally the chaplain had unholstered his .45 caliber pistol, and he prayed aloud. The chaplain had not been afraid, Lucus would tell me many years later. He had just been beseeching his God to forgive him for "shooting other human beings." The chaplain had kept his promise; he never left Lucus, and the Grunts at LZ Crow had held throughout the night.

Meanwhile, McAllister and Richey had been placed in another area with the majority of the Marine wounded. Although injured and burned, they had been far better off than Lucus. They had been able to defend themselves, but they were woefully short on ammunition for their .38 caliber service revolvers. Several hours before dawn during a lull in the battle, an H-34 medevac helicopter had swooped down out of the night into LZ Crow. Some of the critically wounded Grunts had been thrown aboard and flown to safety. Another H-34 had landed, and more "priority one" medevacs were evacuated. When yet another H-34 had managed to slip down and land in the embattled valley, the Grunts yelled to McAllister and Richey to climb aboard. Both pilots had refused. Under even the best of conditions, Marine Corps helicopter pilots do not want to *ride* in a helicopter cabin. They want to be in control of their destiny in the cockpit with cyclic and collective in hand. Further, McAllister and Richey had been shot down just nine hours earlier. A perilous night medevac flight out of the valley under enemy fire had not sounded attractive. They had elected to take their chances on solid ground with the Grunts until daylight.

Dawn had finally come, and the rising sun soon burned away the night fog that had shrouded the Cordillera. More H-34s had zipped down and landed with ammunition and drinking water. With gunships from VMO-2 buzzing overhead, McAllister and Richey had jumped aboard for the seven minute flight to the field hospital at Dong Ha. One by one the heavily loaded H-34s had cranked in power and clawed their way up over the trees. Skirting Hill 200 to the south, which had been fortified by the enemy, the helicopters had climbed eastward over the ridge toward the Cam Lo River and safety.

In delirium and strapped to a makeshift litter, Lucus had been pulled up through the trees on the hoist of a hovering H-34. Helped by the gunner, the H-34 crew chief had pulled Lucus inside. For Sergeant Gary Lucus the long night had ended, but his battle for life had just begun.

USS Princeton, July 16, 1966, 0640 Hours: The dim grey light of dawn revealed 16 green H-34 helicopters spotted on the flight deck of the helicopter carrier *USS Princeton* (LPH-5). The *Princeton* slowly cruised parallel to the Vietnamese shoreline roughly twelve miles off the beach. Below decks the last elements of the Battalion Landing Team (BLT) were saddling up. One company of Grunts was to fly ashore by helicopter, and two more companies were already packed into amphibious landing craft and ready to storm the beach.

0730 Hours: The armored amphibians churned ashore two miles north of the mouth of the Cua Viet River. India and Kilo Companies, 3rd Battalion, 5th Marines, slogged inland near the hamlet of Giem Ha Trung. Simultaneously the Grunts of Lima Company flew toward the shoreline in the H-34s. Eight minutes after takeoff from the *Princeton*, the flight leader radioed, "Feet dry." The helicopters flew over the beach, and the flight pressed on westward past the Grunts on the ground. As usual the Grunts in the helicopter cabin silently endured the ride, because conversation above the deafening roar of the radial engine was impossible. Eyed with apprehension by their Grunt passengers, the H-34 gunners hunched over their M-60s and intently scanned the terrain below.

Over the landing areas, the H-34s spiraled earthward. One group landed at YD-261710, a series of flooded rice paddies on the eastern bank of a small stream. Another contingent landed two miles to the southeast near the western edge of the coastal two mile wide sand dune area. As the morning progressed, additional units of the Third Battalion flew ashore by helicopter, and by midday the entire BLT would be on the beach. Their mission was to block off the coastal lowlands to keep the NVA from marching farther south.

Dong Ha, July 16, 1966, 0800 Hours: As the sun inched higher above the eastern horizon, the airfield at Dong Ha bustled with activity. Another helicopter assault was in the making. To the casual observer the activity at the dirt airstrip mirrored the events of the previous morning. Helicopters refueled, crew chiefs made final checks of their flying machines, Grunts wordlessly waited at their embarkation points, and pilots gathered at Op's North for last minute briefings.

Four squadrons of helicopters were fragged to carry the 2nd Battalion, 1st Marines, to YD-073664. Code-named LZ Robin, the landing area lay just under a mile northwest of LZ Dove at the eastern end of Helicopter Valley. The terrain here featured rolling hills covered with chest-high elephant grass. Gunship support for the transport helicopters would be provided by "Klondike" Huey gunships from VMO-6, based at Ky Ha, and from VMO-2, which operated out of Marble Mountain. Today the helicopter assault would be led by H-34s from HMM-163, based at Phu Bai. Commanded by Lieutenant Colonel Charles A. "Chuck" House, HMM-163 was an experienced squadron. There was not a Marine helicopter pilot in Vietnam who had not heard of the incredible helicopter rescue mission in the A-Shau Valley four months earlier. And we all knew that it had been the helicopter crews of HMM-163 who had flown their H-34s into the North Vietnamese firestorm at A-Shau.

By 0815 Hours the Grunts had all boarded their assigned helicopters. The terrain south of the airstrip came to life with spinning rotors and flashing red anticollision lights. One by one the H-34s lifted and spawned blinding clouds of red laterite dust. They took off toward the west, followed by the larger H-46s. The *HMM-163 Command Chronology* contains a Special Operations Narrative on the tactical aspects of this helicopter assault:

> Briefing of the pilots was conducted by Rose-Ann [a MAG-16 Operations Officer]. A multi-squadron flight made up of planes from HMM-161, HMM-164, and HMM-165, led by HMM-163, were [sic] to lift the Second Battalion, First Marines. Gunship support was provided by Klondike aircraft from VMO-6, TACA provided by Deadlock Playboy, with Rose-Ann 6 observing the entire show. Due to the abundance of plotted .50 caliber MG [enemy antiaircraft machineguns] positions located throughout the operating area, a specific approach and retirement route was plotted. . . . Climb on course to Cam Lo where [a] right turn to a heading of 350 degrees was initiated and maintained for 4 miles. This led to the I. P. which was located 300 degrees at 8 miles from Dong Ha TACAN. Here a left turn to a new heading of 260 degrees took place and after traveling this heading for 3 miles [it] placed you at the landing zone. The LZ consisted of a large flat area of burned off grass. One area was completely free of obstacles while another smaller area to the south was littered with burned trees. . . . the Superchief aircraft landed, successfully evading the obstacles. Weather conditions for the mission were excellent. A stiff west wind combined with [an] early morning H-Hour allowed for a straight in approach to be made with the sun to our back. Two complete waves of aircraft, plus a third wave of . . . Superchief aircraft, completed the lift . . . .

After the morning assault into LZ Robin, helicopter crews settled into a predictable routine of Recon inserts, resupply hops, and medevacs. HMM-161 had stationed one of its H-34s in continuous orbit at 3000 feet high over Cam Lo. This helicopter served as an airborne radio relay between the Marine command post at Cam Lo and the two battalions already in Helicopter Valley. Without this lofty radio relay, communications would have been partially blocked by the mountains.

Flying west from Cam Lo along the river, helicopters pass Dong Ha Mountain, Hill 549, on the north side of the river. A series of unnamed mountains lie to the south. Eight miles west of Cam Lo, a pilot suddenly breaks out into a beautiful, lush, tropical, and green valley. Flying into this misty valley for the first time, I recall being totally awed by the sheer beauty of the terrain. To a pilot the Cam Lo River is a silver ribbon far below, sparkling in the sunlight as it meanders through the valley. The surrounding mountains seem like an impenetrable barrier to the outside world. The view stuns the senses.

Two jagged and rocky promontories dominate the valley floor. At XD-979558 on the north bank of the river, a gnarled granite mass juts over 700 feet (much higher than the Washington Monument) straight up into the sky. On our maps this craggy peak had a name, Thon Khe Tri, but we immediately came up with a more descriptive and pronounceable name, the "Rockpile." The Rockpile offered an unparalleled observation point. It commanded the valley and was almost inaccessible from the ground because of its height and steep sides.

Beginning a mile northwest of the Rockpile was a three mile long ridge of solid rock. The volcanic sides of the jagged and rugged ridge ran almost vertically to the valley floor and consequently were not covered with vegetation. The ridge jutted up over 1000 feet into the air and was honeycombed with caves, as the Grunts would soon learn. Pilots immediately dubbed the volcanic ridge the "Razorback," and the enormous valley became "Razorback Valley."

HMM-265 got fragged to fly a Recon team to the top of the Rockpile. Eighteen Recons loaded themselves down with food and water in addition to their combat gear and radio equipment. The Marine Corps "eyes and ears" were headed for a lookout post in the clouds. There was no level place to land on top of the craggy Rockpile, so the H-46s hovered above it while the crew chiefs used their cargo hoists to reel the Recons down to the rocks below.

Two of our CH-46A [helicopters] lifted 18 Marines of First Force Recon from Dong Ha to XD-979558 where these troops were inserted atop a 1000' hill. The aircraft were unable to land and the troops were discharged from a hover.
-- (*HMM-265 Command Chronology*; July 16, 1966)

Like all Recon teams, the Marines on top of the Rockpile hoped to avoid contact with the enemy. Their sole propose was to secretly watch North Vietnamese Army activity in Razorback Valley and report enemy troop movements to Cam Lo by radio. When possible, from their lofty perch they would call in artillery strikes on the North Vietnamese troops and equipment.

While the Recon insert on the pinnacle of the Rockpile provided a dose of danger, another Recon insert deteriorated into a comedy of errors. Major Ray F. Smith hailed from my native state, for he had grown up in the small rural town of Pelion, South Carolina. He was a combat veteran who had flown Marine A-1 Skyraiders in Korea. Major Smith was one of the few so-called Bonnie-Sue super-HACs in our squadron who were designated to pilot the specially prepared H-46 slicks, the heavy-haulers. On the morning of July 16 he flew a slick, Bureau Number 152513, and most of his missions proved to be short hops. He would log only 2.3 hours of flight time that day. However, one of his Recon insert frags turned out to be memorable and hilarious.

Task Force Delta wanted to put a Recon team into the DMZ. Officially, of course, this could not be done. In theory, the DMZ was truly "demilitarized" and off limits to both the Marines and the NVA. Unofficially, both the Marines and the NVA put their troops wherever they wished. In fact, we routinely flew SOG teams deep into Laos. So, Major Smith got a briefing that included a 1:50,000 scale map with a large penciled dot on it. The indicated location was deep inside of the DMZ: "Major, this is your drop point."

In time of war, the first casualty is truth.
-- (Boake Carter; in *Reader's Digest*, January 1938)

In order to conform to official policy, Major Smith was given a separate set of "official" map coordinates that corresponded to a different location several miles farther south below the DMZ. The

Recons were supposed to get the same briefing. However, Murphy's Law prevailed, and the naive Recons somehow trusted the "official" map coordinates.

Major Smith and his copilot, my tentmate Huey Walsh, launched from Dong Ha and headed north. At 130 knots they arrived over the drop point in eight minutes. They zipped down, dropped off the Recons in the DMZ, and flew back to home plate at Dong Ha.

Several hours later the Recons spotted an NVA troop column. The Recons were deep in the bush, and each tree and rolling hill looked just like the next. On their map they quickly plotted the enemy position relative to their "official" map coordinates. By radio the Recon team leader contacted Cam Lo and asked Marine Artillery to fire on the North Vietnamese. The procedure was routine: authenticate, friendly coordinates, target coordinates, read back, verify, and fire a white phosphorus marking round. Within a minute a 105mm howitzer at Cam Lo belched fire and smoke, a "Willie Pete" shell arced northward, and Artillery radioed to the Recons: "Call the smoke."

Far to the north, the Recons waited . . . and waited . . . .

The round had probably been a dud, they assumed. At their request another Willie Pete shell was soon blasted skyward from Cam Lo . . . still nothing. A third attempt produced the same negative results.

What could possibly be wrong? The Recons were *sure* of their position, and Marine Artillery knew exactly where its rounds should be impacting. The Recons tried to help. They could see smoke from another fire mission several miles to the south of them, they radioed. After several more marking rounds were fired in vain, the Artillery Officer and Force Recon liaison finally figured out the problem -- "Where are you guys?"

The Recon mission had to be aborted because the Marine howitzers did not have the range to fire on a target that far north of Cam Lo. Major Smith launched from Dong Ha, flew to the *real* Recon team location in the DMZ, picked up the Recons, and flew the sheepish team members back to Dong Ha.

The helicopters of MAG-16, augmented by others from MAG-

36, stayed busy. At Dong Ha a continuing chain of helicopters used the Tactical Airfield Fuel Dispensing System (TAFDS), commonly called the fuel pits. At Dong Ha, 20,000 gallons of JP-4 jet fuel for the turbine powered helicopters had been stored in huge collapsible rubber bladders. The fuel pits also held more bladders full of almost 28,000 gallons of high octane 115/145 aviation gasoline for the reciprocating engine aircraft and helicopters. Every drop of fuel was needed.

Helicopters of MAG-16 flew round-the-clock in support of Operation Hastings.
-- (*1st Marine Air Wing Command Chronology*; July 17,1966)

The Grunt battalions north and west of Dong Ha depended on helicopters as their only means of resupply, their lifeline. West and north of Cam Lo there were no usable roads to the troops in the field, so ammunition, food, water, and reinforcements all were flown to the Grunts by helicopter.

Some helicopter crews flew special missions, and even the Special Landing Force (SLF) squadron aboard the *USS Princeton* (LPH-5) got into the act. On July 17 the SLF helicopters launched and headed up the coastline to a point six miles north of the DMZ, one mile off the beach. Well within range of the NVA shore batteries, they plucked two downed Air Force F-4C crewmen out of the sea and flew them to safety aboard the *Princeton*. Two H-34s from HMM-163 flew into North Vietnam to pick up two more downed Air Force pilots. Heavy antiaircraft fire met them within five miles of the crash site. Still, the "Superchief" H-34s landed, picked up the grateful and unhurt pilots, and raced back to the field hospital at Dong Ha.

In one way or another the HMM-265 helicopter crews stayed busy, and routine resupply hops accounted for a fair share of our H-46 flights. Many other missions were medevac frags, but not all Grunt casualties in the field were due to wounds received in combat. Heat exhaustion and heat stroke were common from around midday to late afternoon. Immersion foot, falls, burns, snakebites, and a variety of non-combat related maladies all took their toll on the Grunts. During the daytime in relatively secure landing zones, helicopters hauled injured Grunts out of the hills on request. At night or at times when the Grunts were under fire, helicopter medevac missions were flown only when the injury or wound was potentially life-threatening.

When not flying, helicopter crews led a fairly comfortable life at the Dong Ha airstrip. Hot food was served once a day. For the other meals we had all the C-Rations that we could eat, and they were filling if not appetizing. Between flights we lounged in the shade, napped, played cards, or swapped good-natured lies and War Stories about our missions. With a laugh, we usually remarked that it sure would be great when we finally got home to Marble Mountain, back to the relative luxury and comfort of our own tent.

Don't think a pilot's life is one of endless flying and glory. You will spend lots of time sitting on your backsides.
-- (Commander Fred Sowrey, Royal Air Force; June 1940)

At night at Dong Ha, we H-46 pilots often had time on our hands. H-34s and Hueys usually flew the majority of the emergency medevacs and emergency ammunition resupply frags at night. Unless the casualties in the field got pretty heavy, or unless high altitude or heavy lift capability was needed, the H-46s stayed on the ground at night. Pilots and aircrewmen stayed with their helicopters, pulled out their inflatable air mattresses (commonly called, *rubber ladies*) and slept on them inside of the H-46 cabins. Depending upon which way the night wind was blowing, we often could hear the Marine and NVA artillery duels in the mountains to the northwest. Major Fred Seitz and Bob Mills officially were still members of HMM-265, but they were assigned full time duty at Op's North. They kept us abreast of the tactical news from the ongoing fighting in Helicopter Valley.

Helicopter Valley: By the second day of Operation Hastings, the 2nd Battalion, 4th Marines, had pushed westward to LZ Crow. Here they had linked up with the 3rd Battalion, 4th Marines. Although there had been sharp firefights, the larger NVA units had not yet been committed to battle, and fighting had been mainly confined to small clashes.

The North Vietnamese were in the valley in great strength, no question about it. On the first day in the valley, the Third Battalion had overrun an NVA field hospital with 200 beds, all perfectly concealed beneath the dense jungle canopy. The hospital had been constructed of bamboo and wood, but except for four NVA guards it had been totally unoccupied. The Grunts shot the four enemy guards and destroyed the hospital and an enormous ammunition cache of antitank mines and antiaircraft ammunition. But where were the main force NVA units? The Marine Command did not know for sure, but all signs indicated that the NVA command post was still atop Hill 208. Intelligence and aerial reconnaissance confirmed that it was heavily fortified.

Commanded by Captain Robert J. Modrzejewski, Kilo Company from the Third Battalion had maneuvered south to try to cross the Song Ngan River. From the southern riverbank, Kilo Company planned to probe the NVA defenses on Hill 208. However, thus far the company had been unable to cross the river. The entrenched NVA on the south bank repulsed the Grunts each time they tried to cross, and the Grunts had suffered many casualties in their attempts. In the late afternoon on July 16, Kilo Company dug in for the night. The Grunts hoped to find a more lightly defended spot where they could cross over to the southern riverbank early the next morning.

1900 Hours: Just before dark the North Vietnamese stormed all sides of the Kilo Company perimeter. First, NVA mortars rained down from the sky, and then the enemy infantrymen charged forward. Most of the Grunt casualties came from hand grenades. The battle raged until just before midnight, when the NVA withdrew toward Hill 208. One Grunt would later explain: "We could hear bodies being dragged through the jungle for hours after the shooting stopped."

July 17, 1966, 0730 Hours: Daylight revealed 79 more NVA bodies that had not been dragged away. Many of them lay within ten feet of the Marine lines. Miraculously, only one Grunt had been killed, but almost 40 had been wounded during the three and a half hour fight.

More Grunts poured into the jungle south of Helicopter Valley. The Recons high atop the Rockpile, slightly under six miles southwest of LZ Crow, had a spectacular and almost impregnable vantage point from which to observe the surrounding valley. They radioed many reports of NVA troop movements, so a swarm of MAG-16 helicopters roared into the valley east of the Rockpile. In flight after flight they moved the 2nd Battalion, 1st Marines, from their reserve location at LZ Robin to the Rockpile area. The hunt for the main force NVA units now shifted into high gear.

By nightfall on July 17, a major confrontation was brewing. Thus far the NVA had tenaciously resisted all of the Grunt efforts to cross to the southern side of the Song Ngan River. The NVA had dug in, fortified their positions, and defended the likely avenues of attack on their fortress on top of Hill 208. Both sides lobbed mortars down on their opponents. The North Vietnamese and the Grunts obviously knew that a major battle was inevitable.

Helicopter Valley, July 18, 1966, 1400 Hours: Task Force Delta was led by Brigadier General Lowell E. English. From his forward command post at Cam Lo, he worked out a plan to outflank the North Vietnamese. The two Grunt battalions near LZ Crow would sweep northeast along the northern bank of the river. At a lightly defended point they would cross to the southern bank, and then they would attack southeast along the high ground. The objective still remained Hill 208, only the tactics had changed.

The 3rd Battalion, 5th Marines, was helicoptered in to help, and the Grunts attacked to the northeast according to plan. Modrzejewski's Kilo Company remained behind near LZ Crow to destroy captured ammunition, and demolitions specialists planned to destroy the three downed H-46s that were still in LZ Crow. However, at 1400 Hours the NVA attacked.

The North Vietnamese poured out of the surrounding jungle. The Grunts of Kilo Company, roughly 170 men, faced an entire NVA regiment. The bloody battle would rage for hours on level terrain covered by thick elephant grass.

They were blowing bugles and we could see them waving flags
. . . . We were being attacked by a thousand men. We just couldn't kill them fast enough.
-- (John J. McGinty III; years later)

Hardest hit was the 32 man First Platoon commanded by Staff

Sergeant John J. McGinty III. First Platoon quickly got cut off and separated from the rest of Kilo Company. Fixed-wing Marine air support was already on station overhead, so their napalm canisters and 500 pounders soon rained down on the attacking horde. Marine Artillery pounded the surrounding jungle, but for the Grunts of First Platoon, it was not enough.

The NVA relentlessly charged forward, and there were just too many of them. Fighting against overwhelming odds, First Platoon was being ripped to pieces. Now the NVA soldiers rammed their way between the individual squads of the Grunt platoon. The overwhelming sensation was that of deafening noise and bedlam. No one could hear the individual weapons firing, the bombs exploding, the shouts and screams. There was only a continuous cacophony, a horrible roar.

Sergeant McGinty was hit, then hit again. Still, he stayed on his feet and shouted above the din to encourage his men as the NVA charged one of his remaining fire teams. Armed only with a .45 caliber pistol now, McGinty killed five of the onrushing enemy soldiers at point-blank range.

Sheer desperation gripped the remaining Grunts of First Platoon. Their only corpsman had been killed, ammunition was running out, the NVA swarmed toward them in human waves, and most of the Grunts who were still alive were wounded.

There is many a boy here today who looks on war as all glory. But boys, war is *Hell*!
-- (General William Tecumseh Sherman; August 12, 1880)

Bleeding and now on his knees, McGinty crawled from man to man, helping the wounded reload their weapons, shouting encouragement, directing rifle fire. NVA bodies covered the battlefield, but the enemy still charged forward against the Grunts of First Platoon.

The rest of Kilo Company fared somewhat better. Captain Modrzejewski had been wounded the night before, but he had refused evacuation so that he could stay in the valley with his men. Now he manned the radio and calmly directed the airstrikes and artillery. Many of his Grunts were almost out of ammunition. Dropping his radio, Modrzejewski grabbed ammunition boxes and ran from squad to squad to make sure that his men could keep on putting rounds into the ranks of the attackers. Running upright in the chest high grass, he presented the NVA with a perfect target, but he seemed to have a charmed life.

Often the combatants could not determine friend from foe. On the northern riverbank one group of Grunts formed a tight perimeter. They watched as a group of 20 to 30 NVA soldiers ran toward them. Apparently the enemy soldiers initially thought they were running toward their own comrades. They realized their mistake about 20 meters away. Finding themselves in an open area with no cover, the enemy soldiers leaped into the nearby river and swam toward the NVA-controlled south bank. One Grunt later explained: "All we could see was their heads and rifles above water. It was like shooting pumpkins."

Dong Ha, July 18, 1966, 1400 Hours: I manned the copilot's seat in Bureau Number 152515, and my HAC was one of the more flamboyant aviators ever to strap on an H-46, Captain Richard H. "Rollo" Langenfeld. Rollo never walked, he strutted. One sensed that he looked upon the entire world as his private domain. Tall and muscular, Rollo lived on the razor's edge, and he flew the same way. Described by Colonel Mendenhall as an outstanding pilot, Rollo was convinced that no enemy gunner alive could blast him out of the sky.

We had made a few short flights, but the morning had passed rather uneventfully. We lounged and laid in the shade for the most part, napping, trying to stay out of the blinding glare and heat of the sun. Nine miles to the west of us, Kilo Company battled for its life, but we knew nothing of it. For us it promised to be just a hot but uneventful afternoon. There did appear to be a lot of activity over at Op's North, but unless we got the word to saddle up, we would just let the afternoon slip away.

The shrill whine of T-53 Lycoming turbines shattered the relative quiet. One after another the Deadlock gunships of VMO-2 launched and headed toward the hills to the west. Leading the gunship flight was Lieutenant Colonel Arnold W. Barden, the commanding officer of VMO-2. He had been given a rapid briefing: "Launch immediately, fly to YD-041649, support a Marine Infantry Company under attack by the NVA."

Armed, airborne, and heading through a cloudless sky, the

gunship pilots checked the newly penciled dot that represented YD-041649 on their maps. They were heading for Helicopter Valley again. The target map coordinates lay right on the eastern edge of the now familiar LZ Crow, close to the Song Ngan River. Up front, Colonel Barden switched his radio selector switch to the FM position, keyed the cyclic mike switch, and radioed the Grunts. He only knew them by their call-sign and radio frequency. Colonel Barden did not know it, but he was on his way to the besieged Grunts of Kilo Company.

The roar of rifle fire punctuated the Grunt radio transmissions. The Marines were cut off, swarms of NVA bore down on them, casualties lay everywhere, and they were vastly outnumbered and outgunned. The enemy attacked from the north, west, and south, a Grunt officer radioed above the din of battle. He wanted to conduct a fighting withdrawal to the east. But one of his platoons was cut off, and he would not abandon his trapped men.

Helicopter Valley, July 18, 1966, 1440 Hours: Colonel Barden dumped collective pitch and started down for a strafing run. The NVA infantry was there, almost everywhere. The North Vietnamese were fighting their way across what earlier had been the command post for the Third Battalion. As would later be documented in the VMO-2 After Action Report for that day, July 18, the gunships "attacked 500 NVA near YD-041649." And those 500 enemy soldiers were just the ones that the pilots could see.

Colonel Barden: "Deadlock's rolling in hot."

Firing their guns and rockets, the gunships bored in and made pass after pass. Targeting the NVA was difficult, because the North Vietnamese could crouch down in the chest-high elephant grass or take cover in the trees along the river. After the gunships passed over them, they would stand up to fire. However, other NVA soldiers elected to stay in the open where they stood, fought, and openly challenged the gunships.

The aerial assault by the gunships became a pure Wild-West shootout. Both sides fought with tenacity, but the gunships slowly gained the upper hand. The AK-47s of the enemy soldiers proved to be no match for the boresighted machineguns and rockets of the gunships. Also, despite being badly mauled and outnumbered roughly seven-to-one, Kilo Company doggedly fought on.

Although bloodied, the NVA still presented a formidable force to be reckoned with. They set up machineguns and waited for the gunships to circle around and make another strafing pass, and then it became gun against gun.

Helicopters are not tanks. Those windshields are not jet-age plastic that bullets bounce off of.
-- (Captain J.W. Rider; in *Marine Corps Gazette*, October 1967)

The Hueys dished it out, but not with impunity. Colonel Barden's helicopter repeatedly took hits. He managed to limp back to Cam Lo where he made a precautionary landing. Yet, in the end the combination of aerial helicopter firepower and the grit of Kilo Company blunted the NVA assault.

The tide of battle slowly turned. Reinforcements trickled in, and the Grunts of Kilo Company fought their way to what was left of First Platoon. Sergeant McGinty, bleeding and battered but still alive, and his remaining Grunts linked up with the main body of Kilo Company. Then the entire company withdrew while still under intense small arms and automatic weapons fire. They left no wounded Grunts on the battlefield, but they had to leave their dead.

Dong Ha, July 18, 1966, 1600 Hours: Meanwhile, unaware of the fighting that raged nine miles to the west, Rollo and I lay in the shade of our helicopter at Dong Ha, half asleep. A kick in the buttocks jolted me back to reality: "Get up! Emergency medevac!"

Rollo and I pulled the plugs on our rubber ladies and stowed them behind our seats in the cockpit. Rollo then shuffled off to the briefing while I preflighted our H-46. Everything looked to be in order, so the crew chief locked the clamshell doors topside, buttoned up the two interior engine access doors, and rechecked our machineguns and ammunition.

Waiting for Rollo to return, I guessed that we probably had a 30 to 40 minute flight ahead of us. It would likely take about ten minutes of flying time to our target, some loiter time while we radioed the Grunts and figured out where the good guys and bad guys were located, a quick landing, and then a ten minute hop back to Dong Ha. As far as I knew, this would be just another routine medevac frag. But unaware of the fierce fighting going on in Helicopter Valley, I fortunately had no idea what actually lay in store for us. In reality, before the day ended I would log 8.4 hours in the air, and 2.6 hours of that total would be after nightfall.

Helicopter Valley, July 18, 1966, 1625 Hours: Our first frag turned out to be an emergency ammunition resupply mission. Loaded with grenades and 7.62mm ammunition, we rotored our way toward the eastern end of Helicopter Valley. Radio transmissions jammed our FM frequency. Fixed-wing support zoomed around high overhead while the helicopter gunships darted over the treetops in the valley. Several resupply helicopters were trying to locate the proper drop points, and the tactical situation on the ground was mass confusion. Firefights raged all up and down the floor of the valley.

The Grunts were spread out in various locations and concealed from aerial view by the jungle. A Forward Air Controller (FAC) had direct radio contact with Tactical Air, but logistical support requests were handled in another manner. The Grunt commander who needed a helicopter radioed Battalion, and the request was passed to Air Liaison and then routed to "Group" at Dong Ha. Group fragged an appropriate type and number of helicopters for the mission and briefed the crews. Our helicopters then carried troops, food, ammunition, or whatever was needed toward the map coordinates where the designated ground unit was supposed to be waiting. Flying toward the Grunts at 3000 feet above the terrain, our flight leader would contact the Grunt radioman on the specified FM frequency. Then the questions would begin.

Where was a suitable landing area? Where were the Grunts? Where were the enemy troops? How far away? Were the Grunts taking fire? From where? Where were the other friendlies (we did not want to accidentally fire on them)? On and on it went. With experience, we learned to judge the urgency of the situation on the ground in part by the pitch of the Grunt radioman's voice. And under fire, the Grunts often radioed that they were taking incoming "off to our flank" or "right in front of us." To a pilot such verbiage is meaningless. We needed direction and distance: north, south, east, or west, and how far away?

When all the details were settled, the Grunts would pull the pin on a smoke grenade, releasing a billowing cloud of bright green, yellow, or red smoke. Now, from our aerial perch over a half mile above, we could finally see where the Grunts were located. Still, caution prevailed because the NVA could monitor our radios, and they had their own smoke grenades. As a precaution against flying into an enemy helicopter trap, we always made the Grunts verbally verify the color of the smoke that we saw.

The afternoon wore on, and Rollo and I got no respite. For hours we shuttled Grunts and supplies in and out of Helicopter Valley. Many of our missions carried us into the rolling hills northwest of Dong Ha and east of LZ Dove, and into the Division Command Post at Cam Lo. During the rest of the long afternoon we stayed in the air almost constantly, pausing to refuel whenever we had only about 1000 pounds of JP-4 fuel remaining in our stub-wing tanks.

Skirmishes flared along the length of the valley. Soon the field hospital at Dong Ha was full of wounded, and MAG-16 squadrons were hard pressed to keep up with logistical requirements. HMM-161 alone hauled 120 medevacs out of the hills, and their After Action Report would dryly note: "All aircraft took fire." Most of the MAG-16 helicopters were in action, and 24 additional H-34s and four "Klondike" gunships from VMO-6 at Ky Ha flew to Dong Ha to assist MAG-16. Scores of helicopters swarmed in and out of the dirt airstrip, half shrouding the airfield in a choking cloud of thick red dust.

1900 Hours: The firing and fighting in Helicopter Valley gradually died out. The 170 Grunts of Kilo Company had opposed an entire NVA regiment. Retreating to the northeast, the Grunt survivors straggled to a point a mile from LZ Crow, and there they dug in. Throughout the long afternoon, helicopters flew in to bring more ammunition and haul out the casualties. The hours seemed to crawl by. Rollo and I were now caked with sweat and grime, but there was no slackening of the pace. The sun gradually descended toward the mountains in the west, and we eagerly looked forward to the coming night.

That terrible autumn day had been a long one, but the late afternoon seemed even longer. The sun seemed almost to go backwards in the sky. I thought that night would never come!
-- (Lieutenant James A. Graham, Confederate States Army; in reference to the battle at Sharpsburg [known in the northern United States as *Antietam*], Maryland, September 17, 1862)

Darkness gradually enveloped man and machine, but it did nothing to slow the pace of our helicopter missions. We still made flight after flight to support the Grunts in Helicopter Valley. Trying to find the Grunts in the dark, I grimly remembered the black gallows humor voiced by one of my friends during our MARCAD days: "Flying at night is just like flying in the daytime -- but you can't see where you're going!"

Under enemy fire, flying into small remote landing zones surrounded by tall trees could be difficult enough during the day. At night such flying demanded all of the skills we could bring to bear. The hardest task was *finding* the Grunts. In lieu of a smoke grenade, the Grunts signaled us with a flashlight at night, a mere pinpoint of light far below. A cautious power-on approach was the only way to descend. We had to almost *feel* our way down, and we never knew for sure if the landing area was suitable until we got down to it. To avoid giving the NVA a visible target, we kept our red rotating anticollision lights and our running lights turned off. The hover lights were not used for the same reason, and only a complete idiot would switch on the controllable searchlight. The tension became alive and tangible. I stayed dripping wet with sweat, and it was not due to the heat. The exhortation of the King in Shakespeare's *Henry V* came to mind: "Once more unto the breach, dear friends, once more . . . ."

Lieutenant Colonel Arnold E. Bench was in the valley with his command, the 2nd Battalion, 4th Marines, that deadly July night. He watched as the helicopters repeatedly swooped down out of the night sky and shuttled in and out of the landing zone, and he marveled at the persistence and courage of the helicopter crews. Writing of the helicopter pilots years later, Colonel Bench noted:

On a pitch-black night they descended into an unlighted gorge, talked in by their exhaust glow, to have a flare popped when they were only a few feet off the landing zone.

To the Grunts on the ground, our helicopters seemed to possess some unearthly and mystical power at night. Descending without lights, we were invisible. The Grunts could talk to us on the radio, they could hear us coming, but they could not see us. As we neared the ground the silhouette of our helicopter, a ghostly apparition, would materialize out of the night. When we pulled in more power to cushion our landing, we blinded the Grunts with the man-made windstorm created by our rotor system. As we sat in the landing zone, we could watch the nightmarish and shadowy ballet of war as the Grunts rushed to unload our H-46 cabins. A helicopter sitting in a landing zone is always an enemy "mortar magnet," so both the Grunts and our helicopter crews wanted to spend as little time on the ground as possible.

Our squadron did not lose a helicopter that night, but we had more than a few close calls. The nearest brush with tragedy came on Frag Number 1401. Piloting the Bonnie-Sue H-46, Bureau Number 152496, was our squadron commanding officer, Colonel Mendenhall. Gerry Dooley, a veteran of the original Shu-Fly squadron, manned the copilot's seat on the left. If ever there had been a highly qualified helicopter cockpit duo, this was it.

However, Colonel Mendenhall had been getting by on two hours of sleep each night since July 15. Gerry had been flying each day and spending his nights supervising and encouraging the maintenance crews. Colonel Mendenhall and Gerry had been in the air most of the previous day, and now it was after midnight. For hours they had been slipping in and out of Helicopter Valley, trying to squeeze down into bomb crater landing zones, trying to keep their rotor blades out of the trees. The tension had become almost unbearable, and they were soaked with perspiration and grime. Both pilots were now completely exhausted and physically drained. Bone-deep fatigue numbed them and hung over them like a heavy wet blanket. Then they drew Frag Number 1401, and they flew back to Helicopter Valley and picked up a load of casualties.

Safely airborne with 16 critical medevacs in the cabin, Colonel Mendenhall pointed the nose of his H-46 toward Dong Ha. On the FM radio, Rose-Ann Operations reported that the field hospital at Dong Ha was jammed with casualties, and it could handle no more. Divert south toward Charlie-Med at Da Nang, Colonel Mendenhall and Gerry were told. But the hospital at Da Nang lay 80 long miles to the south, so Gerry keyed the mike and radioed Op's North: "We can't, they [the wounded Grunts] won't live that long."

The hospital ship, *USS Repose*, was much closer and only about

25 miles off the coast. So, Colonel Mendenhall and Gerry flew out into the ebony void over the South China Sea and homed in on the electronic signature of the *Repose*. There was no moonlight, no starlight, no light at all. They flew eastward into the folds of the giant black pit that now had totally swallowed them alive. There was no sensation of motion for the pilots as they languished in the red glow of the instrument panel lights. The world beyond the confines of their aluminum cockpit was unseen and foreign. Fighting against fatigue, the two pilots concentrated on their IFR scan as the Distance Measuring Equipment cockpit display (DME) rolled along at two miles per minute. On that pitch black night over the ocean, their eyes stayed glued to the instrument panel. The electronic magic of the TACAN guided them toward the unseen *Repose*. The Bonnie-Sue pilots did not know it, but fate had set the stage for aeronautical disaster.

> DISORIENTATION, SPATIAL: A condition in which a pilot or other crew member is unable to determine accurately his spatial attitude in relation the surface of the earth; it occurs only in conditions of poor visibility or when vision is otherwise restricted, and results from vestibular illusions. Called also *Pilot's Vertigo*.
> -- (from *Dorlands Medical Dictionary*, 26th Edition)

Blindfolded, a man can still place his forefinger on the tip of his nose. He can do this because his muscle and nerve fibers tell him, without benefit of sight, the positions of his legs, arms, and fingers. However, equilibrium is an entirely different matter. It is controlled by the labyrinthine and vestibular apparatus of the inner ear. The human brain coordinates sensory data from the inner ear, aided by optical data from the eyes, and this enables man to achieve position sense. With his eyes closed, he can stand erect without falling down.

Yet, from childhood games we know that our usually reliable sense of equilibrium can be fooled. If we spin around six or seven times and then suddenly stand still, the inertia of the fluid in our inner ear causes a false sense that we are still spinning. If this is done with the eyes closed, the brain is robbed of vital optical input, and it is hard to keep from falling to the ground.

For pilots, however, the issue is much more complex. In a strictly aerodynamic environment, direction means nothing, *up* and *down* have no significance. Without benefit of eyesight or visual reference to the ground, a pilot can not tell the difference between level flight, a coordinated turn, or inverted flight as long as the wings or rotors are pulling one "G." The aircraft may be upside down, climbing, descending, or turning, but there is no indication that all is not well if the cockpit needle-and-ball are centered.

On a totally black night with no visual reference points outside of the cockpit, a pilot's only hope of survival lies in total reliance on his flight instruments. They do not lie. Somewhere ahead of the aircraft in the black void, a light appears to move upward and to the right. Is the light really moving, or is the aircraft descending and turning left? The answer lies in the instrument panel. Outside of the cockpit, visual depth perception is lost, relative motion sense is blocked, and closure rate means nothing. Throw in chronic pilot fatigue, and all of the ingredients for tragedy are present.

South China Sea, July 19, 1966, 0050 Hours: The *USS Repose* slowly came into view, a shapeless mass of bright lights ahead of the H-46. Only the lights were visible, nothing else. Closing in on the lights, the pilots could not see the ocean below or the ship itself -- only the lights. Colonel Mendenhall set up a turning descent and eyeballed his cockpit Artificial Horizon and Vertical Speed Indicator. Closer and closer, lower and lower they flew. Both pilots strained their eyes and peered into the bright lights in an effort to see the outline of the hospital ship and find the elevated helicopter landing pad.

A large red cross slowly materialized amid the lights. Transitioning from an instrument approach to a heads-up visual approach, the pilots headed for it. Nothing but the red cross and the lights were visible, nothing else mattered, they were almost there . . . looking good . . . closing in . . . not quite right . . . maybe a little fast . . . slip it . . . a little more . . . a little . . . .

Gerry suddenly screamed: "PULL UP! PULL UP!"

"Whhaaa . . . AARRUUUUGGHH!"

Full up collective!

Back cyclic!

The fuselage shuddered in protest. The whirling rotors clawed at the air. Only a few precious feet above the waves, the helicopter stabilized and then started scratching for altitude and airspeed. Within 15 seconds the H-46 pilots had regained vital forward airspeed and established a safe climb. Hearts pounding, hyperventilating, they tried to figure out what had gone wrong.

Colonel Mendenhall and Gerry had not been headed for the helicopter landing pad at all. Instead, numbed by fatigue, they had mentally and visually zeroed in on the first thing they could see, the red cross on the side of the ship. With depth perception and closure rate visually blocked, with night vision destroyed by the bright lights, with no visual reference to the hull of the ship or the surface of the water, the only thing visible had been the bright red cross. With the H-46 banked to the left in a turn, the red cross had looked like it was on a horizontal surface. Instead, it was painted on the side of the ship. Sinister vertigo had seized control, and Colonel Mendenhall and Gerry had shot a blind approach toward the *vertical side* of the ship. They almost dove straight into the sea. Their crew chief, their gunner, and the 16 wounded Grunts would have perished with them.

The two pilots carefully circled around for another approach, and this time they visually located the elevated helicopter landing pad. Colonel Mendenhall made a cautious approach while Gerry kept his eyeballs glued to the instrument panel. They landed without incident.

The NVA paid a terrible and prohibitive price for their human wave assault on Kilo Company. Although they fought bravely, the NVA died by the hundreds. After that bloody day the NVA largely abandoned their mass formation and human wave assault tactics in favor of hit-and-run ambushes. They fought in strength only when defending well fortified positions.

The Marine Grunts also paid a high price. Of the 32 men in McGinty's understrength First Platoon, 26 were dead or seriously wounded. Only six of McGinty's Grunts were still left to fight. All of Kilo Company had been decimated down to only 80 remaining men, and most of them had been seriously wounded. Speaking of those 80 Grunts who were still alive, Modrzejewski would later recall: "I had kids who were hit in five or six places."

Older men declare war. But it is youth that must fight and die.
-- (Herbert Hoover; June 27, 1944)

The bitter fighting on July 18 had been the most brutal thus far
in the campaign. The Grunts had taken on the best soldiers that the
North Vietnamese Army had to offer. Many months later,
Modrzejewski and McGinty would both receive the Medal Of
Honor for valor "above and beyond the call" in Helicopter Valley
that day. They would be among only six Marines who would
receive the Medal Of Honor during all of 1966.

July 19 became a day of regrouping by both sides in preparation
for another clash. On the morning of July 20, Grunts from 2nd
Battalion, 4th Marines, stormed Hill 208 after it had been plastered
by Air and Artillery. The Grunts finally broke through the heavy
NVA fortifications.

Dong Ha, July 20, 1966: With Hill 208 now in Marine hands,
another helicopter assault was readied. Twelve H-34s from HMM-
363, twelve more from HMM-163, and another five from HMM-
161 prepared to carry the 1st Battalion, 1st Marines, into battle.
The "Superchief" H-34 helicopters of HMM-163 led the flight,
escorted by Deadlock gunships from VMO-2. The landing area lay
a mere three miles almost due west of Cam Lo in a half mile wide
valley at YD-073613, east of Dong Ha Mountain and one mountain
ridge south of Helicopter Valley.

With the sun at their backs, 29 helicopters in the first wave
swooped in for an unopposed landing. Two more waves were
needed to bring all of the battalion into the valley. Once they were
all on the ground, the Grunts pushed westward and swept through
the valley toward the Razorback, located six miles to the west.

The Grunts ran into North Vietnamese patrols in the valley, and
skirmishes flared off and on throughout the day. Captain Robert
E. Johnson, flying an H-46 from HMM-164 in support of the First
Battalion, went down for the second time within a week. This
time, however, NVA fire was not the culprit. At cruising altitude
the compressor on one of his turbines suddenly seized. Johnson
was more fortunate than he had been six days earlier, and he flew
back to Cam Lo on his remaining engine. His helicopter was
repaired and would be flown back to Dong Ha the next day.

Other helicopters had to dodge heavy ground fire. First

Lieutenant Ron Critser, orbiting at 3000 feet in his H-46 from HMM-164, got holed by an NVA antiaircraft battery. On another risky mission YR-18, an H-34 from HMM-161, flew down into a hot landing zone.

CRRUUUMMPP! CRRUUUMMPP!

North Vietnamese mortars bracketed the helicopter. The entire crew -- pilot, copilot, crew chief, and gunner -- was hit by flying shrapnel. Although wounded, the two pilots managed to take off and flounder through the air to a safe landing area.

Other helicopter crewmen were luckier than those aboard YR-18. On the night of July 20, Captain John Leighton slipped down out of the dark sky and intended to land at Dong Ha in his H-46. Fifty feet above the ground he lost one of his engines. With no airspeed or altitude to spare, Leighton's rotor RPM decayed below the magic number, 88 percent, and the inevitable chain reaction started. The generators kicked off-line: no instrument panel lights, no trim system, no SAS. The H-46 crashed and suffered strike damage, but Leighton and his crew from HMM-164 escaped serious injury.

Dong Ha, July 21, 1966: Helicopter crews busily prepared for another day in the air. Ten miles to the west the Marine offensive had rolled into high gear. The surprised North Vietnamese saw their positions fall, one after another, in the face of the relentless Grunt onslaught.

I teamed up with Captain Joseph G. "Joe" Roman in Bureau Number 152515 for another day of flying. Along with other HMM-265 crews and four crews from HMM-164, we carried another Grunt assault force into the hills. This time the landing zone was in a new area of operations in the narrow Khe Da Bong Valley at XD-976520, two miles due south of the Rockpile. From the landing area the Grunts planned to push northward toward the Rockpile and the Cam Lo River. Throughout the day, Joe and I slipped in and out of the valley and kept the Grunts supplied with the tools of their trade. According to my logbook, Frag Number 1549 accounted for all of my 5.3 hours of flight time that day, and it was mostly routine resupply hops. Some of the more glamorous missions fell to others, but it was simply the luck of the draw:

The jet pilot had ejected over water and was reported downed [in the ocean in his survival raft] on the 340 degree radial, thirty-six miles from the Dong Ha TACAN.
-- (*HMM-163 Command Chronology*; July 21, 1966)

Hit and crippled by antiaircraft fire over North Vietnam, the A-4D Skyhawk pilot had made it to the coast before ejecting. He safely parachuted into the sea, but now the race was on. Who would get him first, the North Vietnamese patrol boats or a United States helicopter?

Six helicopters raced northward to try to rescue the downed airman. Major Joe P. Beno and his wingman, on Search and Rescue (SAR) and medevac standby at Dong Ha, launched in their Superchief H-34s. Another section (two aircraft constitute a *section*) of H-34s led by Captain F. E. Walker also launched and raced north past the DMZ into North Vietnamese territorial waters. At the same time, two long-range United States Air Force helicopters churned northward from their SAR North base at Quang Tri. All six helicopters reached the downed pilot at about the same time.

A military pilot's greatest fear is that he will be shot down behind enemy lines and abandoned. By tradition, Marine Corps pilots have been indoctrinated never to allow their comrades to be taken captive. Ignoring the shells from the North Vietnamese shore batteries, Major Beno took over as the on-scene commander and dove down toward the water. Until then the erstwhile Skyhawk driver had kept as low in his raft and as inconspicuous as possible in order to make himself a more difficult target for the enemy batteries on the coast. However, as Major Beno's H-34 approached the downed pilot, he "popped smoke" and began flailing the air with his arms. Major Beno hovered, lowered the horse-collar, and reeled the Skyhawk pilot up on the electric hoist.

The two Air Force helicopters returned to Quang Tri. Major Beno cranked in full power and flew directly to the *USS Princeton* (LPH-5), where the grateful Skyhawk pilot was dropped off for a medical examination and debriefing. The Marine H-34s then bored their way back to Dong Ha, landed, refueled, and waited for the next call for their services.

My squadron lost another helicopter. This time the cause was
not hostile enemy fire, not mechanical failure, not bad weather, but
instead a combination of circumstances that snared the pilots in a
web of confusion.

I vividly recall the unfortunate chain of events, since I had
listened and watched from about 100 meters away while the drama
unfolded. Late in the afternoon at Dong Ha, several H-46s from
HMM-265 were preparing to launch. My helicopter was already
refueled and ready to go, so we started our engines and engaged
our rotors in the grassy area south of the dirt runway. Still, one
helicopter was not quite ready to depart. Captain William E.
"Pappy" Johnson had taxied over to the hot-point TAFDS refueling
spot right by the dirt runway. With his engines running and rotors
turning at 100 percent, he was topping off his tanks with JP-4 fuel.
Following normal procedure, Pappy's crew chief stood outside of
the helicopter to monitor the refueling process. He stayed in ICS
contact with Pappy via the electrical "long-cord" attached to his
flight helmet.

Aircraft were landing, aircraft were taking off. Dong Ha
Tower, a wooden shack manned by a Marine Air Controller, was
attempting to insure that no two aircraft tried to occupy the same
spot in the sky or on the ground at the same time. I remember that
the radio chatter on our UHF was almost constant and non-stop.
For Pappy while he was refueling, the radio babble was a
secondary consideration to his ICS contact with his crew chief.
When hot-point refueling, one simple mistake could cause his H-46
to explode and turn 2400 pounds of JP-4 jet fuel, essentially
kerosene, into a gigantic orange fireball. Pappy was bone-weary
like the rest of us, and somehow the accident just happened.

> Pappy probably realized that his rotors wouldn't clear the Cee-
> one-thirty's wing.
> -- (Harry R. "Bob" Mills; years later)

An inbound C-130 four-engine turboprop transport plane was
cleared to land. The pilot radioed to Dong Ha Tower that he was
on short final approach. What Pappy and his copilot heard and
what they understood, no one knows. Furthermore, it would soon
be too late to ask (Pappy died in a crash three months later on

October 6, 1966). Evidently, Pappy at first thought that his crew chief was back inside of their H-46, but one thing is clear. Pappy knew that he had to move his helicopter in a hurry to get out of the way of the speeding C-130.

I watched the mishap in living color, almost like a patron in a motion picture theater. Pappy's helicopter lifted directly from the fuel pits and started to air-taxi. But the crew chief was still standing outside on the ground, tied to the moving helicopter by his helmet and long-cord. Suddenly the pilots realized the danger, and Pappy's helicopter slammed to the ground.

Whhaaaamm!

"Look! Look! Did you see that?" my HAC exclaimed.

Yes, I had seen it. A few seconds later Pappy's nasal but calm radio voice crackled over the UHF. He was going to shut down, he said. There was no cause for alarm, but he wanted to get out and check his helicopter. The rest of us also shut down, crawled out of our cockpits, and ran over to take a look.

Pappy's H-46 would not fly again. From a distance it looked undamaged, but up close we could see the wrinkled fuselage and popped rivets. Scratch another H-46. Still, no one got hurt, although the crew chief came close to having his head jerked off by the long-cord.

In many other instances we were lucky. On July 22 another HMM-265 helicopter got totally riddled with ground fire at AT-824606 on top of Nui Dong Lam Mountain, southwest of Da Nang. No one aboard even got a scratch out of the incident. And the next day, July 23, the crewmen of a "Millpoint" H-34 from HMM-363 became innocent victims of a pilot's worse possible nightmare, a midair collision. Near XD-980640, an unlucky Air Force pilot had his eyes on the terrain below and accidentally flew his light L-19 observation plane right into the tail rotor of the much heavier Millpoint helicopter. The hapless L-19 pilot was dead before he hit the ground, of course. The H-34 lost its tail cone and crashed, but the Millpoint crew survived with fairly minor injuries.

First Lieutenant Noel S. Salmon returned to Dong Ha from Okinawa. Noel, a good friend of mine and an H-34 pilot in HMM-263, arrived several days after the rest of his squadron. When he finally got to Op's North, Noel was assigned to man a radio as a Group Liaison with the Grunts. Actually, it was pretty boring work. Most of the time he slouched on the ground under the shade of a tarpaulin and tried to stay out of the blinding glare of the sun.

Noel idly chatted with First Lieutenant Ray Ramsburg, another H-34 pilot in HMM-263. There was little action on the radio, and the only excitement that day involved wagering on which way the red laterite dust would blow when the C-130s and C-123s landed. Noel and Ray wordlessly prodded a centipede through the grass with the points of their kneeboard pencils. There was nothing else to do, and they listlessly endured the hot and humid summer day.

Nearby was a platoon of Grunts that had just been flown back to Dong Ha from the battlefields in the hills to the west. The Grunts were too exhausted to speak. Their filthy and unshaven faces bore no trace of emotion. Their hollow and vacant eyes all embodied that thousand-yard-stare that said more than any words ever written. Each Grunt evidenced a physical and mental fatigue of the body and soul that no amount of rest ever could erase. Most of them had collapsed onto the ground in the bright sunshine and had fallen into a deep sleep.

Soldier, rest! Thy warfare o'er, Dream of fighting fields no more.
-- (Sir Walter Scott; in "Soldier, Rest! Thy Warfare O'er")

One Grunt got out his sterno pot and began warming up a C-Ration can of ham and lima beans. Half asleep and staring straight ahead like a zombie, he made a mistake. He forgot to punch a hole in the top of the can. The beans soon reached the boiling point, and the usual laws of physics prevailed. The can exploded like a miniature 105mm howitzer. It momentarily deafened everyone and covered the Grunt with scalding lima beans. He fell over backwards and screamed: "CORPSMAN! I'M HIT! I'M HIT!"

Looking at the dazed and disoriented Grunt covered with beans, Ray and Noel realized that they were fortunate. Helicopter pilots flew high above the suffocating muck and mire of the jungle, while the Grunts had to slog through it on foot each day. Between flights in the daytime, we pilots stayed dry in the helicopters when it rained. On hot sunny days we put our rubber ladies on the ground under the fuselage and lounged in the shade between missions. We usually had plenty to eat and drink. If a pilot could avoid getting shot down and killed, this was not a bad way to fight a war.

Lying in the shade of my helicopter at Dong Ha, I listened as one of my peers recounted a hilarious War Story that had involved two friends of mine. By now we all had heard the tale many times. But no matter who retold the story, it invariably started out the same way: "MAYDAY! CHOPPER ON FIRE!"

Five months earlier in February 1966, two HMM-263 pilots, Ed "Easy-Ed" Sieffert and William T. "Tee" Holmes, had drawn the mission: "Spray for mosquitoes today." Although the mosquito spraying operation had been assigned to the pilots of HMM-263 at Marble Mountain, the actual spraying was to be done on the coastal plain south of Ky Ha.

An H-34 could be outfitted with either of two separate spray rigs. One set-up involved spray booms on both sides of the helicopter, and the slipstream powered small propellers that operated the spray mechanism. The other system used the ram air from the H-34 exhaust stack, below and to the left of the cockpit, to power the sprayer. In flight both systems put out a billowing trail of white mosquito spray. It made an H-34 look exactly like the Blue Angels during an airshow, we claimed with a moderate dose of exaggeration.

On the early February 1966 morning, Easy-Ed had crawled into the HAC's seat. Absolutely nothing bothered Easy-Ed, for he took combat flying in stride and never got rattled. Eventually, when his 13 month combat tour in Vietnam was completed, he would routinely be taken off of flight status while waiting for orders to return to the United States. However, Easy-Ed would be unable to tolerate the sheer *boredom* of not flying combat missions, and he would demand his share of the perilous medevac flights.

Tee Holmes, my former MARCAD roommate, had clambered into the copilot's seat. Tee hailed from the rural town of Dublin, Georgia, and he shared a dubious claim to fame that only a handful of surviving Marine Corps helicopter pilots could match. He had been shot down on his first -- *his very first* -- flight in Vietnam back on December 8, 1965. If a crisis existed anywhere at all, Tee was often right in the middle of it.

Twenty minutes later, Easy-Ed and Tee zipped along at 200 feet over the paddies in their sprayer-equipped H-34. Their exhaust driven sprayer trailed a thick white cloud of insecticide behind them. Their map had been marked with the designated spray area, so they flew a grid pattern back and forth. In the bulbous H-34 nose the radial Wright R-1820 supercharged engine hammered out the horses needed to turn the 56 foot diameter main rotor, and Easy Ed and Tee bored holes in a cloudless sky on a perfect day for flying. Even the enemy cooperated, because the H-34 had not yet taken sniper fire.

Meanwhile, climbing through 8000 feet high overhead, a Marine jet pilot, radio call-sign Condole 3-1, had just taken off from nearby Chu Lai. Scanning the terrain below, he spotted a helicopter in the worse possible kind of distress. The Condole pilot quickly snapped his aircraft into a steep diving turn and cranked in 243.0 megacycles on his UHF radio:

"Mayday! Mayday on Guard! Chopper on fire!"

Chu Lai Tower heard the urgent distress call. So had all aircraft within radio range, including Tee and Easy-Ed. The burning helicopter was about eight miles south of Chu Lai, the excited Condole pilot soon radioed. He had the helicopter in sight, and it was "still airborne, still burning!"

Easy-Ed and Tee already had Chu Lai, Channel 50, tuned in on their TACAN. They were ten miles south of Chu Lai, so the burning helicopter had to be somewhere near them and easily within sight. They searched the sky in vain. Where could it be?

Tee dialed in Guard Channel while Easy-Ed wrapped the H-34 into a tight 360 degree turn. Easy-Ed keyed the mike and drawled: "Aircraft transmitting on Guard, this is Powerglide two-dash-two, over."

"Powerglide, this is Condole, go ahead!" the jet pilot replied.

"Say-again location."

"Aaaaahhh -- about, uuhhh -- nine miles south of Chu Lai!"

Easy-Ed and Tee again searched the sky and saw nothing. They radioed to Condole that they were right in that same area, but that they did not see a burning helicopter. Both H-34 pilots knew that the smoke trail from any burning aircraft in flight always makes it easy to spot. Easy Ed and Tee circled and kept their eyes peeled for the telltale trail of smoke.

"Powerglide, this is Condole; he's turning, still burning, the smoke's pouring out!"

"No joy."

Ten long seconds passed, then: "Powerglide, Condole, over!"

"Condole, go ahead."

"Powerglide, this is Condole three-dash-one. He's still burning, still burning and pouring out smoke -- still in a right turn -- it's gotta' be bad!"

"Roger, Condole, still no joy."

"He's just north of the river!"

"Condole, we're lookin', we're lookin'."

Easy-Ed and Tee quizzed each other on their ICS. Where? Where? They were within a mile of the location the excited Condole pilot was describing to them. And since they were only 200 feet or so above the ground, the burning helicopter and its trail of smoke should be perfectly silhouetted against the sky. Where could it be? Where could the . . . .

Bingo! It finally hit them!

Easy-Ed and Tee trailed a billowing cloud of white insecticide, obviously *smoke* to the Condole driver. Just to make sure, Easy-Ed banked left and radioed a query to Condole.

"AFFIRMATIVE! YOU GOT HIM!"

Easy-Ed, Tee, and their crew chief all rolled in laughter. Easy Ed then switched off the H-34 sprayer and laconically radioed Condole. The crisis was over, nothing more than a false alarm. Easy-Ed radioed that he sometimes flew around trailing smoke that way. Sometimes flames too, he added. Then, after getting over the giggles, he explained his trail of *smoke* to Condole.

Humiliated, the jet pilot firewalled his fast-mover and headed for home. Helicopter pilots! All the ready-room tales and all the horror stories that he had ever heard obviously were true. "Powerglide, you guys are *crazy*!" he radioed. Then he climbed up toward the wispy clouds high above and vanished in the bright eastern sky, far out over the shimmering South China Sea.

Marble Mountain, July 23, 1966, 2005 Hours: Shortly after nightfall I had congregated with most of the other off duty pilots in the Marble Mountain O'Club. Located just north of the pilots' tents, the O'Club was pretty basic: wooden floor, wooden walls, and a canvas tent for a roof.

Alcoholic refreshment and warfare have gone hand-in-hand since time immemorial. The Roman Legions of Julius Caesar, 2000 years before, had been appropriately wined the night before battle so that they would sleep well and be ready for combat. Here at Marble Mountain with the Marines in 1966, it was no different. The O'Club opened only at night, and alcohol fired the spirit and deadened the senses, leading to a restful night of sleep. Without the O'Club, many a pilot would have to spend his nights soberly contemplating the next day's perils and hazards -- not a good idea. So the O'Club offered nickel beer in exchange for "funny money," Military Payment Certificates (MPCs). I planned to anesthetize myself on nickel beer and have a good time since I was not on the standby flight schedule that night.

> Happy hour with alcohol was a means to dilute the days of boredom and to temporarily erase the moments of screaming sounds of human agony, to wash away the residual visions of the pieces of smoking or burned flesh torn apart -- the hidden truths of real war.
> -- (H. Lee Bell; in *1369*)

I sat on a bench with other junior lieutenants in the north corner of the O'Club, laughing and joking. As the alcohol began to take its toll, we broke into impromptu song after song. We sang our crude and obscene version of "Let Me Call You Sweetheart!" to the old familiar tune, but the wording of our stanzas bore little resemblance to the bittersweet romantic ballad after which our song was named. Most of our songs were characterized by gallows humor and references to the perils of combat flying. "Call out the [expletive deleted] Reserves!" had an almost infinite number of verses, and I invariably got the words to them mixed up. Still, I struggled along at the top of my voice and then revelled in the singing of the loud and blasphemous refrain.

By now we all had friends who had been shot down and killed. Holding a beer aloft, someone often stood in tribute to one of our many fallen comrades. Surprisingly, a brief moment of silence always followed. Then we would sing our special song in honor of the deceased pilot. Although there were at least a dozen verses, the popular refrain never changed:

So take down his medals, dear Mother!
Dear Mother, put them away!
He was a daring copilot!
But he died in a whore-house in Hue [pronounced, *Whay*]!

No one that I knew had ever seen a house of prostitution in Hue or anywhere else in Vietnam. Perhaps the sheltered REMFs in Da Nang frequented such establishments, but we did not. We had a war to fight. Nonetheless, the words to the song rhymed, they sounded great, and we loved it.

This banality would go on for several hours, I knew. Perhaps a few of the participants would become so inebriated that they would begin *lighting farts* for the benefit of the rest of us. A man's life could never get any better than this, I reasoned. The alcohol had temporarily blocked out our recollection of the daily death and destruction to which we had been exposed a few hours earlier. I planned to revel in the camaraderie until the O'Club closed, stagger back to my tent, and get a restful night of sleep.

CCRRUUUMMPP!

For a full two seconds, everyone froze in place.

CCRRUUUMMPP! CCRRUUUMMPP!

Mortars! Incoming mortars!

Instantly we knew what was happening. The enemy was attacking Marble Mountain. I leaped to my feet and dashed for the door like the 50 or so other helicopter pilots present.

CCRRUUUMMPP! CCRRUUUMMPP! CCRRUUUMMPP!

I ran as fast as I could through the soft sand and reached my tent. In the dark I grabbed my flak jacket, my cartridge belt, and my .38 caliber service revolver. Almost stumbling over Huey Walsh in the dark, I ran back outside and dove into our bunker.

The Marble Mountain Air Facility, Republic of Vietnam, was taken under mortar attack . . . . Approximately 50, 81mm mortar rounds detonated over and on the [base] . . . .
-- (*MAG-16 Command Chronology*; July 23, 1966)

The mortars were impacting to the south of us near the flight line. For some strange and unrealistic reason I felt no fear, but the sound of the explosions fascinated me. The sucking and crunching blasts were followed by an eerie, shrill, metallic, rasping noise. I would later learn that most of the incoming rounds were air-bursts. The shrapnel shower on the steel marston-matting of the flight line caused the unique sound.

We hunkered down in the bunker and peered out into the night. When the mortars stopped, would a ground attack follow? If so, the regular perimeter guard would be our first line of defense.

Major John L. Driefer shared a nearby bunker with several HMM-265 pilots. One of those pilots was Captain Duncan B. McLaurin, a native of the small rural farming community of Dillon, South Carolina. Years later, Major Driefer would fondly recall Duncan's nasal drawl during the mortar attack: "I sure wish I was back home right now, wiggling my bare toes in cow manure."

In the night sky above, Deadlock 16-0, Deadlock 16-2, and Deadlock 16-4 were returning to Marble Mountain from Dong Ha. The three gunships were just about to land when the fireworks began. Seeing their home airfield under attack, the gunships quickly targeted the mortar tubes, located about 2600 meters southwest of the flight line. Deadlock's guns and rockets soon silenced the mortars, or perhaps the enemy simply ran out of mortar rounds.

Within five minutes it was all over. But several hours later when I laid down for the night on my cot, I was still wearing my flak jacket. I slept in it that night, just in case.

The next morning I checked out the enemy's nighttime handiwork on the flight line. Several helicopters had been peppered with shrapnel holes, and a Huey had taken a direct hit on its rotor blade. HMM-265 had suffered almost no battle damage, although one high explosive round had impacted on top of the sandbag wall that surrounded our armory. The canvas tent that covered our armory had a lot of holes in it, but that was about the extent of the damage.

Back up near the DMZ on July 24, the Grunts began a two day assault on Hill 362. The NVA and the Marine Grunts fought savagely and brutally on the steep promontory on the northeastern slope of Dong Ha Mountain about five miles west of Cam Lo. During the struggle a young Lance Corporal, Richard A. Pittman, posthumously earned his place in Marine Corps history books. After being driven off of the hill, the NVA pulled back to regroup. The larger North Vietnamese units melted away toward the DMZ to the north or into the wild and inaccessible jungle to the west.

Now the Marine Command concentrated on locating and eliminating the smaller enemy units left behind. For the helicopter crews the daily routine changed little. Our H-46 was a flying truck, and we used it to keep the Grunts supplied with the necessities of warfare. The days rolled by and the only things that changed were the LZ map coordinates. On paper, Operation Hastings officially ended on August 3, 1966. The North Vietnamese 324-B Division had been bloodied and thwarted by the surprise Marine offensive.

However, ominous intelligence revealed that two more NVA Divisions, the 304th and the 341st, were massing on the edge of the DMZ. So as Operation Hastings ended, Task Force Delta set into motion a new plan that very day, Operation Prairie. In fact, nothing had changed but the name.

I started keeping a diary in a hardbound Federal Supply Service ledger-book. This practice was officially forbidden, since any diaries that might fall into NVA hands could provide the enemy with valuable intelligence. Still, the prohibition was unofficially overlooked, so I took pen in hand and made my first rambling diary entry on August 5, 1966:

5 August 66, Friday: Very little activity today; most of our few hops were [post maintenance] test hops. I got Huey Walsh to sign for all of the tools in the metal & hydraulics shops. Capt. Dooley took custody of the TBA gear . . . .

From somewhere in my schoolboy background, I had always remembered the infamous retort of Adolf Hitler: "Who says I am not under the special protection of God?" As for myself, I had never believed that I enjoyed Divine Protection. Still, I naively considered myself to be immune to the perils of warfare. Youth and ignorance usually walk hand-in-hand. However, perhaps I simply placed innocent faith in the spiritual assurance found in the Book of Psalms, Chapter 91, Verses 5 through 7:

> (5) Thou shalt not be afraid for the terror by night; nor for the arrow that flieth by day; (6) Nor for the pestilence that walketh in darkness; nor the destruction that wasteth at noonday. (7) A thousand shall fall at thy side, and ten thousand at thy right hand; but it shall not come nigh thee.

Not having clairvoyant power, I had no way to know that I would only get to make one more handwritten entry in my new diary. *The Odds*, every civil or military pilot's nemesis, were about to catch up with me. My good luck was about to run out. I had no way to know it in advance, but I would draw a frag for an emergency night medevac into Razorback Valley on August 8. It would prove to be the longest night of my life.

We flattened plenty of cities in Germany and Japan in World War II. I don't know what's so sacred about Hanoi. Let world opinion go fly a kite!
-- (Mendel Rivers)

The Eighth
-- Night of August --

**Don't worry! They couldn't hit an elephant at this distance.
-- (The last words of General John Sedgwick, U. S. Army,
just before he was shot and killed by a Confederate States
Army sniper near Spotsylvania on May 8, 1864)**

Few pilots *really* thought about getting shot. As for me, at only
24 years of age I had innocent and ignorant confidence in my
personal immortality. Like most of my friends, I saw myself as a
part of a noble crusade, a just cause that was destined to triumph
over the perceived evils of communism. John F. Kennedy had told
us so, and we all shared his vision of an enlightened and
democratic world. By now Kennedy had been dead for almost
three years, gunned down on November 22, 1963, by a leftist
assassin, but his charismatic vision and his Camelot lived on after
his death. The United States would prevail, my squadron would
prevail, and I would surely prevail.

Kennedy's successor, Lyndon B. Johnson, had carefully spelled
out the formula for American Foreign Policy in his speech at Johns
Hopkins University. My squadron and I made up an integral part
of that formula, and we had no misgivings about the danger of the
job at hand. But we were trained, we were ready. Moreover, to
a man we shared that unique camaraderie that only Marines in
combat will ever know. We lived and flew in the company of
death, but we shared an unspoken bond, a blind trust, an
unquestioned loyalty to each other.

Thinking back, I could still remember my last night in the
United States before HMM-265 left for Vietnam. Captain Charles
E. Sturkey, my older first cousin, commanded a Marine infantry

company at Camp LeJeune, and we had socialized late into the evening. Neither of us had dwelled on the possible danger, for we had been too engrossed in the great adventure of it all. Ever since the American Civil War in the previous century, our family had maintained a tradition of military service to our country in wartime. Punctuated with a laugh, my cousin's parting retort had expressed our sentiment: "Remember, the gook ain't been born who can put lead in a Sturkey boy!"

Naturally, in the back of my mind I understood the grim realities of warfare. My buttocks always puckered shut whenever we took fire. And I knew that my best friend from my MARCAD days at Pensacola, First Lieutenant William T. "Tee" Holmes Jr., had been shot down into the sea on his very first helicopter mission in Vietnam. Further, I had to admit that HMM-265 had suffered its fair share of casualties in the fighting so far.

In modern war . . . you will die like a dog for no good reason.
-- (Ernest Hemingway)

I remembered that on July 4 my own gunner, right behind my cockpit, had been shot during a risky Sparrowhawk insertion near Hoi An, south of Da Nang. And I had helplessly watched from high above while Tee-Cee McAllister and George Richey had gone down in flames on July 15.

Still, I rationalized that misfortune would always plague others, but never me. Tee Holmes was a good pilot, but ever since the Training Command he had been cursed with bad luck, just like my wounded gunner, I reasoned. Bad luck had snared McAllister and Richey too, because a last minute schedule change had put them in the ill-fated number two slot the day they got shot down.

On the other hand, fate and good luck had smiled on me. I remembered July 11, the day that Captain James M. Schmidt and I had teamed up in Bureau Number 151960 down in "Arizona Territory" near An Hoa. We had logged 4.1 hours in the air that day, and on one mission we had flown SAR for an H-34 that tried to extract some Grunts from a hot landing zone. The H-34 had zipped down to hover height, promptly got shot full of holes, and was downed in the zone. On our radio, Schmidt and I heard the Grunts and the downed helicopter crew pleading for help as several

M-14s kept up a steady chatter in the background. In our H-46 cockpit we each took several deep breaths, then dumped collective pitch, roared down, landed, picked up everybody, and hightailed it out of there without taking a single hit. Schmidt and I later had gotten the Boeing Rescue Award certificate for that chancy mission, but we both knew that the fancy document meant little. We had just been lucky.

My good luck had continued to hold. On August 3, Gerry Dooley and I had manned the Sparrowhawk standby helicopter at Phu Bai. At 1230 Hours we launched and sped to YD-762092, only six minutes away on a hill overlooking the Ta Trach River. A Recon team was under heavy attack and about to be overrun. Captain Joseph G. "Joe" Roman and Huey Walsh, orbiting above us, had laid down suppressing .50 caliber fire as Gerry and I swooped down for the rescue. One of the Recons took a round in the head while boarding our H-46, but we got them all inside, took off, and headed for Phu Bai. After we had dropped off the casualty at Alpha-Med, Barrelhouse Base called for help. Nine more Recons were besieged at YD-788073. No problem; we had rescued them too. Gerry and I attracted a lot of enemy fire, but our helicopter weathered the storm and our entire crew had come through unscathed. We had good luck, nothing more, but in my naive mind I had become invincible. No premonition warned me that I was destined to be among the wounded pilots referenced in a MAG-16 Situation Report (SITREP) that would be issued at 2100 Hours on August 8, 1966:

> During the afternoon and evening of 8 August on a routine Recon retraction in the area of XD-989600, the following took place. During the course of the retraction, 7 UH-34Ds of HMM-161, 4 CH-46As of HMM-265, and 8 UH-1Es of VMO-2 received damage from small arms fire. . . . Of the 7 UH-34Ds, 3 are still flyable; of the 4 CH-46As, 2 are still flyable; of the 8 UH-1Es, 6 are still flyable. HMM-161 had one gunner KIA, and HMM-265 had 6 [sic, should be *seven*] WIA, of which 3 were pilots and 3 [sic, should be *four*] crewmembers.

The basic rules for flying helicopters in combat are rather

simple. We all heeded the standard admonitions about not getting caught "low and slow" and keeping our "turns" up. I vowed to myself that I would never allow my helicopter to get trapped in a deadly Triple-H combination (high, hot, and heavy). I would not be among those hapless pilots who were destined to run out of altitude, airspeed, engine power, and bright ideas all at the same time. Of course, as a realist I knew that a combat pilot always needs lots of pure *luck* on his side, and so far my good luck had held. Full of youthful enthusiasm, I assumed that my good fortune would last forever. Unfortunately, it would not.

Phu Bai, August 6, 1966, 0800 Hours: Marine helicopters lined the asphalt runway at Phu Bai, eight miles south of the former Imperial Capital at Hue. Phu Bai served as the Marine staging area for an offensive thrust into the coastal flatlands between Hue and Quang Tri, 31 miles farther north. Code-named Operation Colorado, the helicopter assault was designed to drive the enemy out of the infamous "Street Without Joy."

First Lieutenant Wayne A. "Vic" Vecchitto and I flew in Bureau Number 152517, and we had plenty of company. Three separate squadrons took part in the helicopter mission that would fly the Grunts into battle. Sixteen H-34s from HMM-263 spearheaded the assault, and their squadron commanding officer, Lieutenant Colonel Jerome L. Goebel, led the entire strike force. We all took off from Phu Bai and headed northeast. Behind the H-34s were ten H-46s from HMM-164, followed by ten more from HMM-265. Vic and I flew as a part of the latter group, and the helicopters ahead of us filled the air as we cruised through a clear blue sky.

Gunships and artillery prepped the landing zones, and then we all landed and dropped off the Grunts. Initially the offensive met little resistance, but by noon both the Grunts and the helicopter crews discovered that the assault would not be a cakewalk. The 16 slower H-34s took a total of 19 hits. Also, one of the faster H-46s from HMM-164 caught a round that severed a transmission oil line, and the tandem-rotor helicopter had to shut down in the landing zone. Other helicopters quickly flew a maintenance team to the site, hasty repairs were made, and the damaged H-46 was flown back to Phu Bai. My squadron fared better, because only four of our ten H-46s took hits.

By the early afternoon a large contingent of the helicopter strike force was no longer needed. Vic and I flew back to Marble Mountain, and later that afternoon he and I teamed up again on a post-maintenance test hop. I followed that short flight with a quick frag with Major Frank B. Ellis. That completed my flying for the day, and I looked forward to a relaxing night.

Northern Quang Tri Province, August 6, 1966: Meanwhile, far to the north just below the DMZ, the valley east of the Razorback was still infested with company-size NVA units. The Marine Command now elected to stand back and use artillery to whittle away at the North Vietnamese, a less costly tactic than frontal assaults by the Grunts. The only problem with artillery fire alone was that the exact locations of the mobile NVA units often could not be determined. To assist their artillery, the Marines needed their "eyes and ears" in the valley.

Small Recon teams, four or five men per team, were routinely inserted by helicopter into enemy territory. These men hoped that they would not have to fight. Instead, they would clandestinely set up hidden observation posts and pinpoint enemy activity. Talking by battery powered radios with their artillery liaison at Cam Lo, the Recons would then direct the fire of Marine howitzers.

> MISSION: Observe and maintain surveillance of main valley running east-west through area of operation; capture one prisoner; be prepared to call supporting arms on enemy targets of opportunity.
> -- (Patrol Report; Team 61, 1st Force Recon, August 6, 1966)

The four Recon Marines of Team 61, 6th Platoon, prepared to leave Dong Ha for a helicopter ride twelve miles to the west. Led by Staff Sergeant Billy M. Donaldson, the small Recon Team was known as "Groucho Marx" because of their radio call-sign. They carried two radios, a PRC-25 and a PRC-10, in addition to their weapons. Their only other special equipment was a set of vital 7 x 50 power binoculars.

The four Recons of Groucho Marx were accustomed to contact with the enemy. Just three days earlier they had been extracted by a Huey from VMO-2 while under heavy NVA fire. One of the Deadlock pilots, First Lieutenant Richard L. Drury, almost got his arm blown off by an NVA .50 caliber machinegun during the extraction, but he had survived. Now, just 72 hours later, Groucho Marx was headed back into the field. With enough C-Rations and water to last three days, the four Recons crawled into the Huey.

Razorback Valley, August 6, 1966, 1900 Hours: The Huey spiraled down and dropped off the Recons in a lush and subtropical valley twelve miles west of Dong Ha. Had the Recons been geologists or botanists, they would have been awed by the sheer beauty and ruggedness of the land. To the west lay the gnarled black granite cliffs that formed the eastern wall of the Razorback. Directly to the south, three miles away, the Rockpile jutted 700 feet straight up into the sky. To the east lay Dong Ha Mountain, Hill 549 on our maps, and the heavily jungled Nui Cay Tre Ridgeline walled in the valley on the north.

However, the Recons were not interested in the scenery. They had come into Razorback Valley to hunt men. They moved easily through the chest-high elephant grass to an isolated observation point at XD-998597, where they planned to spend the night. Here the Recons waited, motionless and silent.

2300 Hours: An NVA troop column slowly snaked along the stream-bed below the Recons in the darkness. The sound of the enemy soldiers talking and moving through the thick undergrowth continued for roughly an hour until around midnight. Then all was quiet and still again.

August 7, 1966, 1100 Hours: An hour before noon the next day, the Recons of Groucho Marx again detected other men in the valley. Thin trails of smoke from small cooking fires drifted up through the treetops 500 meters to the northwest, along the stream-bed. Periodically the Recons could hear the NVA soldiers talking and laughing. Unlike their encounter the previous night, the visual sighting of smoke now enabled the Recons to pinpoint the enemy.

071100H [August 7 at 1100 Hours at]/XD-988597: The patrol heard talking and saw smoke [in the] vicinity [of] XD-982599. -- (Patrol Report; Team 61, 1st Force Recon, August 7, 1966)

Quietly speaking into his microphone, Sergeant Donaldson radioed the NVA position to Cam Lo. Minutes later Marine artillery shells rained down on the enemy, and Groucho Marx radioed "good coverage" of the target back to artillery liaison at Cam Lo. When the howitzers ceased firing, VMO-2 Deadlock gunships took up the slack and strafed the stream-bed where the campfires had been spotted. After making several passes over the target, the gunship pilots turned to the east and headed back toward Dong Ha to rearm and refuel.

The Recons of Groucho Marx quietly congratulated themselves. They had located the enemy and had called in artillery fire and gunships on him. But now, the Recons realized, the NVA commanders obviously knew that the American Marine spotters were in the valley with them, somewhere nearby.

Dong Ha, August 7, 1966: Meanwhile, helicopter operations at Dong Ha continued. Armed gunships squatted in the grass south of the airstrip, ready to escort medevac helicopters or lend fire support to the Grunts in the field. There was no major fighting going on west of Dong Ha now, so most of the action was taking place in Operation Colorado far to the south. Still, Grunt patrols west of Dong Ha bumped into small NVA units now and then, and helicopter crews could count on periodic radio calls for help.

Captain William Buchanan and First Lieutenant Robert Bailey piloted a pair of gunships on a medevac escort. The H-34 medevac helicopter took fire in the landing zone, and the gunships dove down to target the enemy gunners. Bailey's gunship took two hits, but its covering fire enabled the H-34 to successfully pick up and evacuate the wounded Grunt.

This sort of small unit action characterized MAG-16 helicopter flights in the mountains west of Dong Ha. Both combatants periodically probed the positions of their adversary, but there were no major troop movements and no major ground battles. Helicopter crews at Dong Ha consequently sat around with a great deal of idle time on their hands, so Task Force Delta dispatched most of the helicopters back to Marble Mountain and Phu Bai.

Razorback Valley, August 7, 1966, 1600 Hours: The Groucho Marx patrol slowly crept to a better vantage point roughly 100 meters from their old position. Now they could hear NVA soldiers, hidden by the vegetation, talking to the east and to the north of them. The NVA apparently used water buffalo to transport their food and munitions, because the Recons smelled what they called a "distinct odor of livestock." Secure in their new position at XD-988598, the four men of Groucho Marx prepared for their second night in the valley.

The NVA knew the Recons were out there, somewhere, and they sent out their own patrols to scour the valley for them. The Recons could not see the North Vietnamese in the dark, but they sometimes could hear them talking and moving through the undergrowth. Several times the enemy soldiers passed within 100 feet of the concealed Recons. No one slept that night.

August 8, 1966, 0900 Hours: Daylight prompted an increased NVA effort to locate the Recons. However, the men of Groucho Marx were not overly concerned quite yet. The valley was huge, and they were well hidden by the thick vegetation. Unless the NVA happened to stumble right on top of them, their position would not be compromised. Meanwhile, they could plot NVA locations and call in more artillery or gunship missions, they reasoned. Also, they knew that helicopters were standing by at Dong Ha to fly out and extract them if they needed to leave the hostile valley.

However, by 0900 Hours it became obvious that the NVA soldiers were conducting an on-line search for the Marine patrol. One such sweep came within 50 meters of Groucho Marx. Sergeant Donaldson called in more artillery fire on an enemy position 300 meters to the east of the team. Judging from the screams of the wounded North Vietnamese soldiers, the high-explosive rounds had impacted right on target. But the Recons knew that the North Vietnamese would now intensify the search, so it was time to radio for help from the gunships.

Dong Ha, August 8, 1966, 1000 Hours: Major Fred Seitz manned the MAG-16 Op's North tent just south of the airstrip. He got the request from the Grunts: launch gunships to support Groucho Marx. Within five minutes a pair of Hueys was airborne and headed westward. The Deadlock helicopters made radio contact with Groucho Marx, concealed in the broad valley below. The Recons explained that the NVA soldiers were mainly to the west and north of them. This information was of no value to the gunship pilots because they could not see where the Recons were located, and the Recons dared not "pop smoke" for fear of giving away their hiding spot to the NVA. Finally the Recons took a calculated risk. They fired white phosphorus marking grenades toward the enemy soldiers. Now the gunships had something to shoot at, so they flipped their arming switches and rolled in hot.

Concern was growing at Op's North. Groucho Marx was under pressure, so perhaps it was time to extract the patrol. Not yet, the Recons radioed, because there was a suitable helicopter landing area only 150 meters away. If Grunt reinforcements were flown to the valley, they might be able to capture an NVA prisoner, one of the original objectives of the Recon mission. The Grunt Command mulled it over and passed another request to Major Seitz. A reaction force would be helicoptered into the valley. Upon their arrival a decision would be made to either reinforce or extract Groucho Marx.

Four Bonnie-Sue H-46s from HMM-265 loaded up with 40 Grunts from Echo Company, 2nd Battalion, 4th Marines. Escorted by Deadlock gunships, the H-46s launched from Dong Ha and headed west toward Razorback Valley.

Razorback Valley, August 8, 1966, 1215 Hours: The four H-46s flew down, landed, and dropped off the Grunts without incident. Not a shot was fired. The Bonnie-Sue pilots sucked in collective pitch, and the camouflage-green helicopters headed east, their job now over. The two Deadlock helicopters stayed in a racetrack orbit over the valley and waited to see if the Grunts needed help from the gunships' machineguns and 2.75 inch rockets.

1215-1310H [1215 Hours until 1310 Hours]. Mission 8-7001I. Two UH-1Es flew SAR for retraction of "Groucho Marx," did not make pickup, put in reaction force [the reinforcement force of 40 Grunts from Echo Company] instead.
-- (*VMO-2 After Action Report*; August 8, 1966)

Second Lieutenant Andrew W. Sherman commanded the Grunt reaction force, and his men quickly linked up with Groucho Marx on top of a small knoll at XD-986599. Sherman wisely set up a defensive perimeter and had his men dig fighting holes, just in case. Then he sent a contingent down to check out the small stream-bed where the NVA had been sighted earlier in the day.

The NVA soldiers had vanished. For several hours the Grunts cautiously poked and probed through the thick undergrowth within 200 meters of the knoll. They found plenty of freshly dug fighting holes and other evidence that the North Vietnamese had been there, but the enemy had now slipped away into the surrounding jungle. "How far away?" the Grunts wondered.

By now it was midafternoon, and a command decision was made. The entire 44 man force would be extracted from the valley. The H-46s had already left Dong Ha to return to Marble Mountain, so eight "Barrelhouse" H-34s from HMM-161 got the frag. Escorted by Deadlock gunships, the H-34s arrived over the original landing area, to which all of Lieutenant Sherman's Grunts had now returned. The small landing zone was supposedly secure, but the lead H-34 went down alone as a precautionary measure. The helicopter landed, loaded up, and the pilots pulled in collective pitch and headed skyward. As the Sikorsky helicopter cleared the treetops, an enemy machinegunner opened fire.

The chopper received heavy automatic weapons fire . . . .
-- (Patrol Report, Team 61, 1st Force Recon, August 8, 1966)

Four more H-34s swooped down, but now the NVA opened up from the ridgeline north of the landing zone. Rounds whipped through the air and tore through the aluminum skins of the H-34s. Twenty Grunts made it into the helicopters. The Barrelhouse pilots cranked on full power and clawed their way over the treetops, heading for Dong Ha.

Twenty-two year old Corporal Ronald L. Belknap, from Daly City, California, was the crew chief aboard YR-22, one of the H-34s. He hunched over his door-mounted M-60 machinegun and searched the ground below for a target. Down below an NVA heavy machinegunner aimed upward at YR-22 and squeezed the trigger. One of his 12.7mm rounds slammed through the fuselage and struck Corporal Belknap squarely in the back of his head. Belknap died instantly, and his lifeless body crumpled to the aluminum floor of the helicopter cabin.

Aircraft received a .50 caliber hit, killing the crew chief.
-- (*MAG-16 Command Chronology*; August 8, 1966)

On the ground the rate of incoming fire intensified. The remaining H-34s started down to pick up the rest of the Grunts, but Lieutenant Sherman waved them off. He and his remaining 23 men made a hasty withdrawal back toward the knoll, where their freshly dug fighting holes waited for them. Over two hours of daylight were still left, and Sherman believed that the small and steep knoll would be easily defensible. He had plenty of ammunition, so he and his men reoccupied the knoll and waited for the NVA to make the next move.

The Grunts occupied classic defensive terrain: a small and steep knoll with clear fields of fire on all sides. Also, they had the protection of their fighting holes. Any attacking force would surely suffer horrible casualties. But the North Vietnamese commanders now knew exactly where the Grunts were located. For an hour the NVA marshaled their forces and massed in the rugged ravines and gullies to the north and east of the knoll. Then they stormed forward toward the Grunts on the top of the knoll.

The enemy, in company strength, tried to assault the Marine position.
-- (Jack Shulimson; in *U.S. Marines in Vietnam: An Expanding War, 1966*)

Almost 200 enemy soldiers charged the 23 Marines. The NVA poured out of the surrounding jungle and ran up the sides of the knoll. Everyone was firing, yelling, screaming. The almost overwhelming noise of battle rose to a deafening crescendo. One Grunt would later explain: "They were screaming bloody murder during the first charge, like they were crazy drunk or something."

The Grunts fought back with M-14s, M-60s, M-79s, pistols and grenades, everything they had. Private First Class Robert Callaway watched the onrushing tan-uniformed soldiers as they threw themselves against the tiny perimeter on the knoll. Callaway would later be quoted in *Pacific Stars & Stripes*:

> They hit us all of a sudden. I saw this one guy yelling and waving his arms around. He looked like a squad leader or platoon commander. I shot him. We were shooting them with pistols and throwing grenades like they were going out of style.

The NVA attack faltered, and the survivors ran back into the surrounding jungle. They regrouped, waited for reinforcements, and then charged again.

The Grunts also beat back the second attack, but not without cost. Lieutenant Sherman had been shot and killed. Many other Grunts had been hit, some by rifle fire, others by shrapnel from enemy grenades. Command passed to an Echo Company platoon sergeant, Robert L. Pace.

Reinforced again, the NVA soon rushed up the sides of the knoll for the third time. Again the Grunts threw the enemy back, but Sergeant Pace had been shot in the head during the assault. Command of the beleaguered Grunts and Recons now fell into the hands of Sergeant Donaldson, the leader of the original Groucho Marx patrol.

Ammunition was running out. Daylight was running out, because the sun would set in little more than an hour. Worse yet, as the minutes ticked away, more North Vietnamese reinforcements arrived to join their comrades in the dense jungle surrounding the small knoll. The NVA now had taken up positions on the east, west, and south of the embattled hill. The Grunts were truly desperate. On their radio they pleaded for help from Dong Ha. "You better *hurry!*" they radioed.

Dong Ha, August 8, 1966, 1800 Hours: Pilots and aircrewmen from HMM-161 volunteered to try to fly reinforcements and ammunition to their fellow Marines in the embattled valley. With their H-34 cabins loaded with Grunts, they flew to the Rockpile, turned north, and then screamed down toward the knoll. But the NVA soldiers were waiting for them, and sheets of withering fire drove the helicopters away.

At his command post at Dong Ha, the Echo Company commander, Captain Howard V. Lee, a New York native, knew what had to be done. Without ammunition his trapped men on the knoll were doomed. There was no place for helicopters to land, but he had to try. Lee asked for six volunteers to fly with him to Razorback Valley. The sudden response almost brought tears to the eyes of many. To a man, the Grunts of Echo Company all volunteered.

Two H-34s from HMM-161 got the frag for the hazardous attempt. Loaded down with all the ammunition crates and grenades they could carry, Captain Lee and three of his men clambered aboard one of the helicopters. The three other Grunts crawled into the other Sikorsky warhorse, and the H-34s launched and headed westward in the company of a pair of Deadlock gunships.

The success or failure of this desperate late-afternoon resupply attempt could not be predicted in advance, of course, and the dwindling hour of daylight remaining was crucial. Consequently, MAG-16 Operations elected to prepare for the worst. Op's North flashed an urgent radio message to Marble Mountain: "Emergency medevac. Fly four H-46s to Dong Ha."

Razorback Valley, August 8, 1966, 1900 Hours: The two H-34s carrying Captain Lee and his six volunteers radioed the gunship pilots, trying to figure out a place where they could land. The NVA had everything zeroed in on the knoll, so to try to land there would be akin to suicide. After getting radio advice from the Grunts on the ground, the pilots made their best guess and zipped down toward the battle below.

The first H-34 swooped down and landed in a flat and clear area between the knoll and the NVA soldiers. Captain Lee and his three men leaped out and ran toward the Grunt perimeter, lugging their ammunition crates with them. There was a lot of firing going on, Lee would later recall. Just as he reached the perimeter, he saw the Grunt radio operator take a round in the arm. Sergeant Pace staggered by, spewing blood from his head wound. Captain Lee and his three men dove into nearby fighting holes.

The other H-34 landed on a narrow saddleback about 100 meters away. The three Grunts piled out and found themselves stranded. The North Vietnamese soldiers were between them and the Grunts on the knoll.

Both H-34s took hits, but they managed to claw their way skyward and out of the valley. The pilots had done their jobs. Now they pointed the bulbous noses of their helicopters eastward and raced back toward Dong Ha.

However, the three Grunts on the saddleback were still cut off, and they had no radio. Captain Lee had seen where the helicopter dropped the stranded men. When they failed to reach the perimeter, he called on Deadlock for assistance. High overhead, Major Vincil W. Hazelbaker piloted one of the two VMO-2 gunships circling the valley. Talking to the Grunts on his FM radio, he learned of the three stranded men from Echo Company. Deep and dark shadows slowly settled over the valley. Where were the stranded Grunts? Major Hazelbaker talked it over with his copilot, First Lieutenant Antony B. Costa, but they could not spot the trapped men. Suddenly they saw green smoke on the saddleback -- a smoke grenade! Major Hazelbaker dumped collective pitch, jammed the cyclic forward, and the Huey gunship dove down toward the valley floor.

We made two passes, and our door gunners were busy [firing].
-- (Vincil W. Hazelbaker; years later)

On the third pass the gunship flared and landed. The three stranded Grunts rushed to the helicopter and dove into the cabin. Major Hazelbaker snatched the gunship into the air, then dove behind the saddleback so that he was protected from further fire by the steep terrain. He and his wingman then sped to Dong Ha, where they deposited the three shaken Grunts into friendly hands.

<u>Marble Mountain, August 8, 1966, 1915 Hours</u>: Eighty miles to the south at Marble Mountain, unaware of the fighting in Razorback Valley, I lounged on my canvass cot in my tent. The O'Club was not in my plans that evening since I was still on standby status for nighttime missions. Yet, I knew the chance of a frag at this late hour was pretty slim. I had just finished a big supper, and I looked forward to an uneventful and restful night.

My plans got interrupted when our duty officer banged on the side of the tent: "Sturkey! Medevac at Dong Ha!"

I quickly gathered my flight gear and prepared to trudge down to the HMM-265 ready-room tent by the flight line. First Lieutenant Ronald E. "Ron" Pfeifer, one of my tentmates, lazily propped his head on one elbow on his cot five feet away. Ron, often called the Gentle Giant because of his soft-spoken demeanor and huge size, casually wished me good luck on the medevac flight. It would probably be nothing more than routine, he volunteered. Ron and I exchanged animated grins, but then, for some reason, he turned deadly serious. Years later, I would wonder if Ron somehow had a premonition of things to come:

"You be *careful* up there."

"See ya' in the morning!" I quipped with a laugh.

What is the matter? What is wrong? Do you think that perhaps I will not return?
-- (Manfred von Richthofen [the Red Baron]; to the German mechanic who asked for Richthofen's autograph before his final and fatal combat mission on April 21, 1918)

Although I had no way to predict it at the time, I would not see Ron the next morning. In fact, I would *never* see him again. Misfortune in Razorback Valley would delay my return to Marble Mountain for 116 days, over four months. And by the date of my return to my squadron, Ron would be dead.

<u>Dong Ha, August 8, 1966, 2005 Hours</u>: Fifty minutes later, strapped into the copilot's left seat in Bureau Number 152498, I squinted through the swirling laterite dust and dim twilight as we landed at Dong Ha. Captain Richard O. "Harpo" Harper manned

the HAC's seat on my right. Back in the cabin behind us, we had two veteran crewmen. Sergeant Herbert S. Murff, our crew chief, had been with the Marine Corps H-46 program almost since its inception. Originally from Caruthersville, Missouri, the soft-spoken Murff was a skilled mechanic and a gutty career Marine. Back at New River, just before we had left for Vietnam, Murff had suffered a concussion when he fell from atop the open forward transmission clamshell doors of an H-46. From his hospital bed, Murff had called Colonel Mendenhall and insisted that his squadron not leave for Vietnam without him (he got his wish). Lance Corporal Luke A. Stephen, a relative newcomer, rounded out our four man crew, but already he had proved his mettle as a door gunner.

Harpo and I piloted the number three helicopter, Bonnie-Sue 9-3, in the flight of four H-46s. We lined up in the following order:

Helicopter:	EP-166	EP-170	EP-163	EP-164
Bonnie-Sue:	9-1	9-2	9-3	9-4
Pilot:	Tinsley	Richey	Harper	Farrell
Copilot:	Roberts	Albano	Sturkey	Joyner
Crew Chief:	Hedger	(unknown)	Murff	(unknown)
Gunner:	Dusman	(unknown)	Stephen	(unknown)

In the Dong Ha fuel pits we topped off our tanks with JP-4 fuel and then hovered over to a vacant spot south of the dirt runway. Harpo crawled out to go to a quick briefing. Like the other copilots, I stayed strapped in my seat and kept our engines running and rotors engaged at the radioed request of MAG-16 Operations. Time had become critical, for it was almost dark.

Harpo returned within a few minutes, crawled into our cockpit, strapped in, and filled me in on the briefing while I scribbled the details on my kneeboard pad. Years later, I would *find* that faded and long-lost kneeboard pad sheet with its details of our frag:

Mission:	Frag Number 591
Radio contact, MAG-16:	Rose-Ann Alpha, 42.3 FM
Radio contact, VMO-2:	Deadlock, 49.6 FM
Radio contact, Grunts:	(same)
Running lights:	Steady-dim
Map Coordinates:	10 mile fix, 280 radial, Dong Ha
Notes:	"20 Grunts surrounded on hill"

Harpo explained that a "skinny platoon" of about 20 Grunts was surrounded on a small and steep hill. Some were dead, others were wounded, and they had fought off several attacks. The smaller H-34s earlier had tried to extract the Grunts, but had been driven away by ground fire. In our larger and more powerful H-46s, we were going to land on the hill and snatch all of the Grunts out before complete darkness set in.

Bonnie-Sue 9-1, our lead helicopter, was loading up with twelve Grunt reinforcements. Nine-dash-one would try to find a place to land on or near the hill. According to our plan, the twelve Grunt reinforcements would charge out of nine-dash-one and fight off the North Vietnamese. Meanwhile, the dead and wounded would be loaded aboard nine-dash-one, which would take off with the casualties and head straight for the field hospital. Then our remaining three helicopters would swoop down and land. All remaining Grunts would clamber aboard, and we would fly them back to Dong Ha.

In the fading twilight, I could see the whirling rotors and green fuselage of EP-166, our flight leader. "Let's go!" I thought to myself. It was almost dark.

Suddenly, Major Fred Seitz ran to our helicopter and grabbed the external troop commander's ICS set. His voice remained steady, but the tension came through loud and clear: "Get 'em out, Harpo! You *gotta'* get 'em out!"

"We'll get them," Harpo calmly replied.

In nine-dash-one, Captain Dale L. "Papa-Bear" Tinsley and First Lieutenant Joseph T. "Joe" Roberts had been downed by a hydraulics malfunction. Their helicopter could not take part in the rescue attempt. Pilots never leave their wingman, so nine-dash-two, flown by First Lieutenants George G. Richey Jr. and Paul J. Albano, would stay with nine-dash-one while mechanics tried to repair the problem. These first two helicopters would have to remain at Dong Ha.

We could wait no longer. Harpo and I had been Number Three in the original lineup of four helicopters. With Number One and Number Two grounded, we now took the lead.

The twelve Grunt reinforcements got out of nine-dash-one, piled aboard our H-46, and strapped themselves into the web troop seats in the cabin. We sucked in full power, launched, and headed into the western sky. Trailing behind us was EP-164, flown by Captain Leo J. "Crazy-Leo" Farrell and Charles D. "Buzz" Joyner. I reached down to my right and cranked in 49.6 on the FM radio so that we could talk to the gunships and the Grunts on the knoll.

"You're gonna' take fire," Deadlock warned us, and we would not be able to land on top of the knoll because it was too small and too steep. But there was a relatively clear bombed-out area just to the south-southwest. We probably would be able to squeeze down into it and land, Deadlock informed us.

The heaviest enemy fire would come from the west, north, and northeast, according to Deadlock. Whether or not the NVA were also in the bombed-out area was not known. The two Deadlock gunships would stick with us and cover us on our approach, they radioed, but then we were on our own.

Razorback Valley, August 8, 1966, 2020 Hours: Our two H-46s flew westward past the Rockpile, then turned north and slowed to 100 knots. The two gunships slipped in to join us, one on each side of us and slightly behind our H-46. Looking over my left shoulder, I could see one of them, and in the faint twilight it looked sinister and menacing while silhouetted against the sky.

It had become too dark to pick out terrain features. The gunships and the Grunts would have to talk us down. On the ICS, Harpo gave a final briefing to Sergeant Murff, manning the starboard machinegun, and to Lance Corporal Stephen, manning the machinegun on the other side of our H-46. Our greatest concern was that they might accidentally fire on the Grunts in the darkness. And after we landed, Murff was responsible for getting our twelve reinforcements out in a hurry. Then we had to sit there -- just sit there and take the heat -- until the dead and wounded Grunts were all loaded aboard.

We verbally rehearsed our plan on the ICS. Strange, but I remember that our voices were calm and steady, and none of us had any reservations despite the perils of our task. We had to succeed. Our only fear was the fear of possible failure, the fear of making some dumb mistake, the fear that we might somehow let our fellow Marines down. The Grunts down below depended on us. They relied on us in a way that no men can understand unless they have endured the volatile crucible of warfare together. We could not -- *must* not -- fail them.

"Sturk, get on here with me."

I rogered Harpo's request. For the record, he was flying our helicopter. But flying down into the hot landing zone below, I would ride the cyclic and collective with him, just in case.

Guided by the gunships, we turned eastward and started down. This would be a power-on approach all the way, since we could not yet see where we might land. Deadlock hung with us, radioing verbal guidance. Down below the Grunt radioman chimed in and tried to help. I could tell that he was scared. His whispering voice sounded squeaky and several octaves too high. From experience I knew why he was whispering -- not a good omen for us.

We slowed to about 70 knots as we passed through 300 feet of altitude. Peering through the darkness, I could now see the ground below me. The faint light remaining revealed deep gullies and ravines all around the small knoll. Where could we land? Where?

Buurrrrrppp! Buurrrrrppp!

The gunships opened fire. Their tracers, beautiful at night, ripped downward and then seemed to slow, fade, and instantly vanish as soon as they struck the ground. Now I could see the bomb crater, our intended landing area. The gunships kept firing hundreds of orange tracer rounds into it. So far nothing was coming back up at us.

From one of the gunships: "Straight ahead, Bonnie-Sue."

"Roger."

Passing through 150 feet and 40 knots, the gunships could no longer maintain their nose-down firing attitude. They pulled in power, accelerated, and veered away from us. Now, Harpo and I were all alone.

Below lay a mass of gullies and stumps. In the faint twilight I could easily have seen enemy muzzle flashes, but there were none. Sixty feet away at my ten o'clock position near the top of the knoll, I glimpsed a man as he jumped into a fighting hole. I hoped he was a Marine, and I saw no one else. Down we went, lower and lower. Now I saw that tree trunks littered the ground all around the bomb crater, but I figured we had just enough room to squeeze down into it.

We had it made now. Twenty-five feet above the crater, we

killed our forward groundspeed. Harpo and I started to ease our helicopter down, taking care to avoid hitting the surrounding trees with our whirling rotor blades. However, the next eight or nine seconds seemed like an eternity.

We were twenty feet above the ground when the firing started.
-- (Richard O. Harper; years later)

POP! POP! POP-POP-POP-POP!
Enemy rounds whipped through our cockpit! We were landing right among the North Vietnamese soldiers. They were under us, all around us -- everywhere!
POP-POP-POP! POP! POP! POP-POP-POP!
Suddenly a violent shudder wracked our H-46. An invisible giant hand, it seemed, had grabbed the fuselage. The collective dropped, the cyclic shook. I did not know it then, but Harpo had just been shot in the chest.
With strength born of raw fear, my right hand clamped down on the cyclic. The terrible shaking stopped. I instinctively pulled in almost full collective pitch. Then I felt Harpo on the cyclic with me, jamming it forward.
"TURNS! TURNS! WATCH THE TURNS!"
CLLAAANNGG! CLLAAANNGG!
Several bullets ricocheted off of the sides of our armored seats.
Power! Power! The overhead forward transmission groaned in protest as our rotors bit into the night air. Our helicopter leaped upward and forward as we struggled to steady the controls. Mere words could not help us now, and neither of us spoke. We knew what we had to do. I thought to myself: "Go, baby!"
Without warning: WHHAAAAMM!
A horrible blow to my right foot!
Someone had taken a baseball bat -- at least it *felt* like a baseball bat -- and had swung with all of their might against the heel of my flight boot. The impact knocked my whole leg upward. My right shin slammed against the sharp bottom edge of the instrument panel, and the inertia spun my whole body around sideways in my armored seat.
"I'M HIT! I'M HIT!"
Instantly, I was ashamed. My voice on the ICS side-tone in my

flight helmet had sounded shrill and childlike. I made no further needless exclamations and instead concentrated on maintaining control of our helicopter: engines O. K., turns O. K., still at full power, still flying. We floundered through translational lift and accelerated upward and forward.

The shooting abruptly stopped. I reached up to the overhead console and flipped off all of our external lights. There was no sense in making ourselves a more visible target. We sped over the treetops, then climbed, and there was no more enemy fire. Our entire nightmare had lasted less than ten seconds.

CAPT Richard O HARPER 071918/7335 HOSTILE wound missile penetrating left chest through and through . . . .

1stLT Marion F STURKEY 091161/7335 HOSTILE wound missile right foot . . . .

SGT Herbert S MURFF 1607851/6418 HOSTILE wound missile penetrating abdomen . . . .

LCPL Luke A STEPHEN 2037354/6611 HOSTILE wound missile lacerating right forearm . . . .

-- (MAG-16 Casualty List; August 8, 1966)

Our helicopter swiftly gathered speed and altitude as we drooped the turns down to 94 percent. On the instrument panel in front of me, the Master Caution Panel light flashed on, and several individual caution lights winked at us. But we were still flying. I scanned the black and white gauges that relayed to the cockpit the mechanical health of our H-46. Everything looked "in the green."

Back in the cabin behind us, Stephen keyed his ICS mike. He had been shot in the arm, he told Harpo and me, but he could still man his machinegun. Murff was hit too, Stephen continued, and it looked bad. Murff was writhing on the cabin floor and unable to speak. Our twelve Grunt passengers appeared to be unhurt. Two of them were trying to aid Murff, who was bleeding from the mouth and a from a wound in his stomach.

Incredible! In a span of less than ten seconds, 34 enemy rounds, fired at an almost point-blank range of 20 to 50 feet, had ripped into our helicopter. The trained NVA soldiers had aimed at our cockpit, and all of their rounds had struck the forward fourth of the fuselage. Our entire crew had been wounded.

"Sturk, where're you hit?" Harpo asked.

"My foot."

A full 30 seconds passed without further comment while we fought to gain altitude and clear the ridge to the south. Then I asked Harpo if he was O. K. In his nasal yet somehow subdued voice, Harpo told me that he had been shot twice, once in the right hand, and once in the chest.

"Jesus!" I thought. Unlike me, Harpo had not worn his recently issued Pilot's Armored Chest Protector, his "bullet-bouncer" (later to be sarcastically nicknamed a *chicken-plate*), the combat helicopter pilot's equivalent of the medieval knight's breastplate. The enemy round had torn through his flak jacket and had ripped completely through his chest, three inches below his heart.

We climbed up over Hill 549, reached the Cam Lo River Valley, and headed east toward Dong Ha. My right foot felt totally numb. I only felt pain just below my knee where my shin had been slammed up against the bottom edge of the instrument panel. I knew the enemy bullet had come up through the helicopter floor because it had knocked the rock-hard leather heel of my boot straight upward. Sheepishly, I now wondered if perhaps the round had simply lodged in the heel of my boot. Maybe I was not really hit after all.

Flexing my ankle, I wiggled my right foot around inside of my boot. My exploratory effort was rewarded by a wet, warm, squishy feeling. Now I knew.

Our H-46 seemed to be airworthy. The Automatic Trim System (ATS) had been shot out, and the SAS control felt sloppy. One by one I checked each of the rectangular amber warning lights on the Master Caution Panel, and it looked like there were no problems that we could not handle.

But the large Master Caution Panel light kept flashing. Harpo was the first to spot our problem, our Number One Boost system. We helplessly watched the gauge as the hydraulic pressure slowly dropped toward zero.

Our H-46 could fly on either one of our two 3000 psi hydraulic boost systems. But without at least one operative boost system, without its powerful hydraulic fingers to control the massive rotor head swashplates, our helicopter would literally rip itself apart in the air. It would take on the aerodynamic characteristics of a falling brick. If we lost both of our engines, we could still autorotate down to the ground, hoping to end up in an area free of trees. But we knew that if we lost both of our boost systems, we would all be dead.

Our vital Number One Boost slowly died, and soon we could hear the empty pump cavitating. Now we were flying on the Number Two Boost alone. Harpo and I knew that all of the actuators and SAS links were hydraulicly separate, but mechanically common. How badly were we damaged? Would our helicopter hold together until we reached Dong Ha?

Neither of us spoke; there was no need for conversation. We rotored eastward through the night at 1500 feet, almost abeam of Cam Lo. We could make an emergency landing there, we knew. Our wingman, EP-164, was behind us in a loose trail position, and he could pick us up and carry us on to the field hospital. On the other hand, each passing minute was precious. Stephen and I did not have life threatening injuries, but Harpo had a bullet hole in his chest. Murff was lying in a growing pool of his own blood back in the cabin.

Harpo and I looked at each other in the eerie red glow from our instrument panel lights. He did not have to ask, for I knew what his yet unspoken question would be. And I knew that we were a team. We might succeed, or we might fail, but we would have to succeed or fail *together*. There was no other Marine Corps way. I realized that I really had no choice at all, so I took a deep breath and keyed the ICS: "Let's try to make it to Dong Ha."

Dong Ha, August 8, 1966, 2025 Hours: Deadlock radioed ahead to Fred Seitz and Bob Mills at Op's North. Our reinforcement and extraction attempt had failed. Hearing this news at Dong Ha, Papa-Bear Tinsley knew that he and his wingman were the last hope for the surrounded Grunts on the knoll. He knew that he also might fail, but he at least had to try.

Bourbon: The Devil take order now! I'll to the throng;
Let life be short, else shame will be too long.
-- (William Shakespeare; in *Henry V*)

Ignoring his hydraulics malady, Papa-Bear took off and headed westward into the night, followed by EP-170, his wingman. By now complete darkness had set in. Papa-Bear would have to attempt a landing right on top of the knoll.

Meanwhile, Harpo and I raced eastward through the night toward the safety of Dong Ha. Harpo suddenly jerked sideways in his seat. At first I thought he had gone into convulsions because of his chest wound, but I was wrong. Harpo excitedly yelled to me: "You got it!"

Scalding hot liquid, either leaking hydraulic fluid or transmission fluid (we would later learn that the forward transmission, right above our cockpit, had three bullet holes in it) was dripping down on Harpo. Soon I also got covered with the steaming and sticky mess. But the forward transmission temperature and pressure gauges stayed within the prescribed green arcs, so we forged ahead.

I reached to my right and tuned in Dong Ha Tower on our UHF radio. Harpo radioed ahead, and his steady voice did not betray our distress. Our informal UHF radio transmissions with Dong Ha Tower were documented:

"Dong Ha, Bonnie-Sue nine-dash-three."

"Bonnie-Sue, this is Dong Ha, go ahead."

"Dong Ha, Bonnie-Sue is four miles west -- uuuhh -- we're inbound with wounded, we want the runway."

Under routine conditions, helicopters did not take off or land on the dirt runway at Dong Ha. Instead, they used the grassy area on the south side of the dirt airstrip to allow the runway to be readily available for fixed-wing aircraft. Only in a dire emergency would a helicopter pilot need the added safety of a run-on runway landing. To the Dong Ha Tower controller, Harpo had sounded like an inbound pilot on a routine medevac flight.

"Bonnie-Sue, cleared to land, use the grass, sir."

Harpo dryly retorted: "We want the runway."

"Bonnie-Sue, use the grass, we've got fixed-wing holding."

"Dong Ha, this is Bonnie-Sue -- we're all hit."

"Say again?"

"We're all hit, all of us -- the pilot, copilot, crew chief, and gunner -- we want the runway!"

"Aaaaahhh, roger, Bonnie-Sue -- your discretion, sir."

Spurred onward through the night by a mixture of both hope and fear, we sped toward Dong Ha and safety. My heart pounded furiously in my chest, but we almost had it made now. We swooped down out of the western sky and raced toward the parallel runway lights. Almost there! Then in the center of the instrument panel, our dreaded Master Caution Panel light winked on again. I scanned the panel. Oh, no! The Number Two Boost!

The rectangular warning light flashed out its message of impending doom. Immediately we riveted our eyeballs to the small round pressure gauge above the center console. Before our eyes, our last remaining boost system began to die. The needle danced wildly in the gauge . . . 2800 . . . 2400 . . . 1900 . . . .

But disaster would be a few moments to late to snare us. The runway lights flashed past under our helicopter. With the collective bottomed and the nose of our H-46 pulled high in the air, we bled off our airspeed as we skimmed along five feet above the airstrip. Then Harpo veered off to the right and softly settled onto the grass. As our nosewheel hit the ground, I grabbed both Engine Condition Levers and yanked them all the way back to the "Stop" position. Harpo reached up to the overhead console and flipped the electric Rotor Brake toggle switch. We had made it home alive!

Razorback Valley, August 8, 1966, 2035 Hours: EP-166 and EP-170 arrived over the valley and found that total darkness now shrouded the terrain. Papa-Bear Tinsley orbited in his lead H-46 while talking on the radio with the Grunt commander, Captain Lee, in the black void somewhere down below. Yes, Papa-Bear radioed, he was willing to attempt a landing on the knoll.

From below ground level in a fighting hole so the NVA could not see it, the Grunts switched on a flashlight and pointed it skyward. Papa-Bear spotted the light and slowly and cautiously started down into the dark valley below him. Guided only by the pinpoint of light and Captain Lee's voice on the FM radio, he headed for the knoll. However, Papa-Bear's effort was destined to fail. Ten feet above the ground, enemy fire raked his helicopter.

CAPT Joseph T ROBERTS 084240/7335 HOSTILE wound missile lacerating left forearm . . . .

SSGT Edward R DUSMAN 1555282/6615 HOSTILE wound missile lacerating face . . . .

CPL John A HEDGER 20433471/6418 HOSTILE wound missile right and left thigh . . . .

-- (MAG-16 Casualty List; August 8, 1966)

North Vietnamese rifle and machinegun fire ripped through the aluminum fuselage of EP-166. Papa-Bear remembers overreacting by pulling in too much collective pitch. His copilot, Joe Roberts, kept the turns under control. Badly damaged, EP-166 shuddered and then started scratching for altitude and airspeed. Joe took "just shrapnel" in his left arm, he later would modestly claim. But back in the cabin the gunner, Staff Sergeant Edward R. Dusman, got staggered by a round that slammed through his flight helmet and ripped into his face.

The crew chief, Corporal John A. Hedger, fared worse. An enemy .50 caliber round shattered both of his legs above the knee. Hedger never lost consciousness, but he crumpled to the cabin floor. Dusman knelt by his friend and desperately tried to stem the massive loss of blood.

> Mission 8-6001B: Two UH-1Es flew SAR for emergency extraction. Extraction incomplete. Attempted resupply of E-2 [the Grunts on the knoll from Echo Company] and Groucho Marx. Attempt unsuccessful.
> -- (*VMO-2 After Action Report*; August 8, 1966)

Papa-Bear and Joe hung on as their H-46 vibrated eastward through the night sky. They had their hands full since both SAS systems had been shot out. Hedger needed medical aid in a hurry, the two pilots knew. Escorted by Deadlock, Papa-Bear and Joe wallowed back toward the Marine base at Dong Ha.

Dong Ha, August 8, 1966, 2035 Hours: After I had stopped the engines, Harpo had wasted no time in evacuating our cockpit. Instead of making a normal exit through the cabin, he had reached to his right, hit the emergency escape hatch handle, and lowered himself to the ground. I had always harbored a secret and childish urge to jettison my own escape hatch, and now I had my chance. I twisted the yellow lever, easily snapped the safety wire, and watched the hatch fall to the ground with an embarrassingly loud clatter. I swung my feet and body through the opening and gingerly eased down to the ground.

I saw that Bob Mills and others were carrying Murff out of the cabin. Harpo, Murff, Stephen, and I were loaded aboard two mighty-mites and driven to a shabby old masonry French barracks north of the runway. On stretchers we were carried into the barracks, commonly called the Dong Ha field hospital.

I watched a whirlwind of activity while lying on the concrete floor. Three or four corpsmen were present, along with an older man who I assumed was a doctor. All clad in dirty field utility uniforms, they busied themselves treating Murff, Harpo, and another wounded Marine that I did not recognize. I noted that Murff's face had turned ashen and blue-gray. "So this is what dying men look like," I thought to myself. Looking across the small masonry room, I saw Harpo sitting on the floor and leaning back against the wall. His chest was being wrapped with multiple layers of compress bandages, and Harpo watched the corpsmen with a surreal air of apparent detachment.

After the life-threatening wounds had been treated, it became my turn. A sweat-soaked corpsman turned to me and saw me holding my right leg up off of the floor. He looked at my right boot, but I elected not to follow his gaze.

"You hit anywhere else, Lieutenant?"

"No."

"That boot's gonna' have to come off -- you in pain?"

"Yeah," I lied, apprehensive now for the first time.

A shot of morphine gave me a warm and comfortable rush, sort of a cozy and intoxicating high. Using scissors, the corpsman snipped my boot laces, pulled off my boot, and started wrapping my bleeding right foot with layers of gauze and tape. I still felt numb, no pain at all.

Sitting on the floor while the corpsman plied his trade on my foot, I looked over at my discarded boot and picked it up. Right in the bottom of the heel I saw a small hole. "Not bad," I thought to myself. It looked like a pencil had somehow been pushed through the leather heel. But then I saw the large, jagged, and bloody exit hole in the back of my boot, two inches above the heel. It looked as though a twelve-gauge shotgun had somehow been fired from somewhere inside of my boot. I instantly turned my eyes away, and no amount of money could have enticed me to look at my boot again.

Minutes later we were all driven back to the runway, carried aboard a waiting C-130, and placed in litters that were stacked three-high along each side of the cargo hold. Directly across from me lay Harpo. Right under him, Murff filled the lower litter. We waited in the soft shadowy red glow of the C-130 cargo hold lights. I would later learn that we were waiting for Corporal Hedger, who was by then being treated at the aid station. Finally when all were aboard, we roared down the runway and headed for Da Nang, 80 miles to the south.

Murff lay in his litter ten feet across from me. He did not speak, although I could see that he was alive and semiconscious. Twice during the 20 minute flight he rolled his head to the side and vomited an evil crimson liquid onto the metal floor of the C-130. From the litter above, Harpo reached down, grasped Murff's hand, and tenderly held it -- all the way to Da Nang.

Razorback Valley, August 8, 1966, 2100 Hours: On the knoll, Captain Lee radioed that he had only 16 men, including the wounded, who were still able to fire and fight. Ammunition had run low again, and Lee himself was now seriously wounded. In a telephone call to me many years later, Lee would explain: "The grenade that wounded me hit about two feet away. It exploded, but there was no pain."

The grenade had blown jagged shrapnel into Lee's right eye, right arm, and lower body. One piece of steel tore into his buttocks and exited on the inside of his thigh. The sheer force of the grenade blast blew off his .45 caliber pistol belt and canteen. Nonetheless, although maimed and blinded in one eye, Lee remained in command.

2130 Hours: The NVA made another mass attack against the Grunts. Screaming and swarming up the sides of the knoll, the North Vietnamese soldiers fired and hurled grenades as they charged the tiny Grunt perimeter. The Recon team Patrol Report would later note the attack:

> 082130H [August 8, 2130 Hours]: [The NVA attacked] up 3
> sides of the hill. They threw grenades and tried to penetrate the
> perimeter but were repelled by Marine rifle fire. Ammunition
> supply at this time was critically low.

Two more H-34s from HMM-161, with all volunteer crews,
flew to the valley, but they could not even find the knoll in the
dark. Overhead in his gunship, Major Hazelbaker heard the
plaintive radio transmissions from the Grunts. They desperately
needed more 7.62mm ammunition. Major Hazelbaker decided to
try to sneak his gunship to the Grunt perimeter by flying low along
a steep ravine on the southeast of the knoll. The walls of the
ravine and the nearby saddleback would shield him from enemy
fire, he hoped. With the aid of a flareship and a little luck, he
might make it to the edge of the perimeter and drop off his linked
machinegun ammunition. The daring plan worked, and Major
Hazelbaker would later modestly explain to me:

> With the light from a flareship, Costa [his copilot] and I
> slipped our gunbird up the backside of the small hill and
> passed our remaining ammo into a foxhole. The last flare
> went out just as we were making our departure and turning
> into the uphill drainage -- really one of the more exciting
> moments.

Emboldened by his success, Major Hazelbaker decided to try
again. To him it seemed logical that a Huey slick could slip up the
ravine, unload crates of sorely needed ammunition, and evacuate
some of the critically wounded men. He termed the risk factor
"acceptable." Years later when I asked him to define *acceptable*,
he would muse: "Don't ask what that is, I don't know."

Dong Ha, August 8, 1966, 2200 Hours: Major Hazelbaker flew
back to Dong Ha and exchanged his Huey gunship for a Huey
slick, a cargo hauler. The slick was then loaded down with crates
of 7.62mm ammunition, M-79 rounds, and grenades. The risky

plan now called for flying back to Razorback Valley, sneaking up the ravine in the dark, and kicking out the ammunition to the Grunts on the knoll. Hopefully the Grunts would then load their most critical casualties aboard, and Major Hazelbaker would fly them back to Dong Ha. For this perilous task an all volunteer crew was requested.

Major Hazelbaker and Costa would go, of course, since they had discovered the hidden route to the knoll. There was no shortage of VMO-2 volunteers to fly as gunners, but the first two Marines to step forward were Corporal Eppie Ortiz and Lance Corporal James E. "Jim" McKay.

Jim McKay: The fact that he volunteered to fly to the knoll with Major Hazelbaker defies logic, almost defies belief. You see, earlier that day, McKay had flown as a gunner aboard another Huey gunship from VMO-2. That flight had been McKay's last scheduled combat mission. His combat tour in Vietnam had come to an end, and he was supposed to return to the United States.

A short, slightly built, and soft-spoken Marine, Jim McKay had joined the Marine Corps in June 1964. In early 1965 he had arrived in Vietnam with the Third Shore-Party Battalion. That duty had proved to be too tame, so in December 1965 he had made a special request to transfer to Force Recon. McKay, an armorer by trade, spent the next couple of months in the field on patrol with the Recons. However, by February 1966 he had less than a month remaining on his standard 13 month tour in Vietnam. McKay wanted more.

From the ground, McKay had watched the gunships dart and swoop around. Yes, that was just the role he wanted, and it would allow him to stay in Vietnam. So, McKay arranged a deal with the Marine Corps. He volunteered to extend his combat tour for six more months in exchange for reassignment as a helicopter gunner in a VMO-2 gunship. The Marine Corps granted the unusual request in March 1966. For the following six months, McKay had daily lugged his M-60 machinegun and ammunition to the designated Huey and served as a gunner when airborne and as a loadmaster while on the ground. He had his share of narrow escapes. Most recently, on August 3 he had been manning his M-60 right behind First Lieutenant Richard L. Drury when an NVA .50 caliber round nearly severed the lieutenant's arm.

Now it was August 8, 1966, McKay's last scheduled day for combat missions. After his afternoon flight he had been scheduled to turn in his gear and catch the first available helicopter to Da Nang. He would then get a ten day R&R in Singapore as a reward for volunteering for the six month extension. Then he would be flown directly back to the United States.

But after turning in his gear at Dong Ha, McKay refused to catch one of the many available flights to the safety of Da Nang. He knew that some of his Recon buddies were in the Groucho Marx patrol. McKay's friends were surrounded on the knoll in Razorback Valley, vastly outnumbered by the enemy, and fighting for their lives in the dark.

I did only what my duty demanded. I could have taken no other course without dishonor.
-- (General Robert E. Lee, Confederate States Army)

McKay was supposed to go home that hot summer evening of August 8, but he refused to leave Dong Ha. He would not abandon his friends, his comrades. As soon as he got the chance, he volunteered to fly with Major Hazelbaker. McKay and the other three Marines piled into the Huey slick, fired up the powerful T-53 Lycoming turbine, and launched into the August night toward Razorback Valley.

Razorback Valley, August 8, 1966, 2240 Hours: The Huey slick arrived over the valley, and Major Hazelbaker made radio contact with the Grunts on the knoll. He had done almost the same thing before in the gunship. Now he planned to fly down the ravine in the slick, reach the knoll, unload the ammunition, and evacuate some of the casualties.

As the flareship dropped a flare, the Huey slick dove down into the shadows and entered the safety of the ravine southeast of the knoll. Slipping up the ravine, Major Hazelbaker put his right skid next to the ground and eased his Huey up the side of the knoll, shielded from NVA fire. Near the top, he put the right skid on the ground next to a Grunt fighting hole and hovered with the other skid over the ravine. Ortiz and McKay threw out the ammunition crates. However, neither they nor the Grunts ever got the chance to load any of the wounded Marines into the helicopter.

Received intense small arms, automatic weapon, and .50 cal[iber] fire from all around the zone. Wingman [Major Hazelbaker] made resupply [but] was shot down in the LZ.
-- (*VMO-2 After Action Report*; August 8, 1966)

BBLLAAAAMM!
An enemy rocket struck the hovering helicopter! The impact, high atop the rotor mast, blew off the pitch control rods. The concussion from the blast knocked McKay up onto the console between the two pilots. Stunned, Ortiz fell back onto the web seats, his flight helmet shattered.

Up in the cockpit, Costa had shrapnel in his leg. Although dazed, Major Hazelbaker hit the rotor brake and shut down the wildly vibrating and bucking Huey. Years later he would explain to me: "I still don't know why we didn't roll down the hill."

McKay (who should have been safe in Da Nang by now) had three holes in his back. The hot steel had ripped completely through his protective flak jacket, but he crawled out of the helicopter and started toward two Grunts in a nearby fighting hole. From somewhere down below the enemy began firing. McKay felt no impact or pain, but he inexplicably fell down. He got up, then fell again. "What's wrong with my legs?" McKay wondered. Trying to get back on his feet, he tumbled down the side of the ravine and lost consciousness.

When he regained his senses, McKay found that everything around him was quiet. Why had he fallen? What was wrong?

LCPL James E McKay 2095581/2111 HOSTILE missile wounds left knee and back right side.
-- (MAG-16 Casualty List; August 8, 1966)

Almost a quarter century later, McKay would explain to me: "I ran my hands down my leg and located the injury, then understood what my problem was." McKay had been shot in the left knee. The bullet had severed the tendons, and his lower leg flopped around like a loose hinge. McKay could not walk or stand up.

McKay heard Vietnamese voices farther down below him, so he pulled out his pistol and started crawling up the hill. One of the Grunts had seen him tumble down, and the Grunt low-crawled down to meet McKay. They both made it back up to the perimeter and dropped into a fighting hole. After a brief exchange of rifle fire with the NVA down in the ravine, all was quiet.

2250 Hours: The Marines on the knoll breathed a little easier for the first time in several hours. The resupply helicopter had been shot down, but now they had crates of sorely needed ammunition and grenades, plus the two M-60 machineguns from the Huey. Captain Lee, his strength ebbing, still crawled among his men, encouraging them and calming them.

Major Hazelbaker and his copilot joined the fight on the ground.
-- (Jack Shulimson; in *U.S. Marines in Vietnam: An Expanding War, 1966*)

The two downed Huey pilots helped the Grunts man the perimeter. Major Hazelbaker initially wondered why there was no constant shooting going on. The black Grunt in his fighting hole explained that the Grunts would not fire unless they could see their target; otherwise, the NVA would fire back at the muzzle flashes. That made sense, so Major Hazelbaker waited and listened. He took over the ground-to-air FM radio and contacted the escort gunship circling overhead, piloted by Captain Jack Nolan. Major Hazelbaker then coordinated all of the air support and artillery missions for the rest of the night.

Ortiz, the Huey crew chief, was in bad shape. Shrapnel had penetrated his flight helmet and his skull, and he alternated between listlessness and unconsciousness. McKay took his defensive place in the Marine perimeter despite the severity of his wounds.

There would be no more mass assaults against the knoll during the night. Still, all night the NVA probed the Marine perimeter.

You could hear [the NVA] dragging off the bodies. Every time we shot at them, another grenade would come in.
-- (Grunt corpsman on the knoll, name unknown)

Captain Lee, now sightless in one eye, continued to lose blood and strength. He would later recall that Costa stayed with him and helped him throughout the night, and he remembers Costa's calm voice: "Captain, le'me see if I can plug up your holes."

Soon the Grunts got a new weapon: Spooky, the magic dragon in the sky. The venerable old World War II-vintage Douglas C-47 had found a new role. Fitted with three hatch-mounted General Electric SUU-11 7.62mm miniguns, Spooky could lay down an incredible 6000 rounds per minute. Major Hazelbaker got a flashlight and, from the bottom of his hole, aimed it skyward at Spooky. Yes, the C-47 pilot radioed, he saw their light, and he knew their position. Major Hazelbaker requested a fire mission.

> A long wide undulating ribbon of fire appeared from the sky.
> I knew we were dead.
> -- (Vincil W. Hazelbaker; years later)

Spooky's miniguns belched fire and emitted an unearthly and horrible moan. The Grunts and stranded helicopter crewmen on the knoll could not see the individual tracers, just a solid finger of fire, a blinding shaft of light slicing down from the sky. One can only imagine what it was like for the enemy soldiers who were targeted by Spooky. For the Grunts on top of the small knoll 50 meters away, it looked too terrifying, too close.

<u>Marble Mountain, August 9, 1966, 0200 Hours</u>: For the Grunts trapped in Razorback Valley, help was on the way. Two hours after midnight, far to the south at Marble Mountain, First Lieutenant William T. "Tee" Holmes, my former MARCAD roommate, was quietly shaken awake by his squadron duty officer: "Holmes, get up, emergency medevac." Originally in HMM-364, Tee now flew H-34s in HMM-263, the "Powerglide" squadron.

Frag number 736 put Tee in Bureau Number 149318 as part of a six helicopter mission. At the Marble Mountain briefing there was not much information available. Tee and the other H-34 pilots were told that a reinforced Recon team was surrounded, a Huey had been shot down, and several H-34s and H-46s had been riddled by enemy ground fire. Replacement helicopters and pilots were needed at Dong Ha.

<u>0225 Hours</u>: The flight of six H-34s launched from Marble Mountain, headed out over the sea, and then turned north. There was no moonlight, no light at all. Following IFR procedures, the pilots tracked outbound on the Da Nang TACAN, Channel 37. They switched to 278.4 on the UHF radio and called "Panama" for radar vectors past the invisible 3907 foot peak of the mountain at Hai Van Pass. Once vectored past the unseen mountain, the pilots all switched to Phu Bai Approach Control and continued northward while tracking inbound on the Dong Ha TACAN, Channel 46.

In the left seat of his H-34, Tee peered ahead into the darkness but could see nothing. There were no lights below, and the world outside of his cockpit consisted of a dimensionless ebony void. Tee could not see the land, the sea, the moon or stars; he saw nothing except the endless pit of darkness. Exclusive of the steady roll of the digital DME indicator on his instrument panel, Tee had no sensation of speed or motion.

Off to his left where the mountains should be, Tee suddenly saw a brilliant beam, a bright shaft of light. Obviously originating from some type of aircraft, the beam flickered on and off. Tee and his HAC watched in fascination. What could it be? Tee would later learn that they had been watching the faraway deadly finger of fire from Spooky's miniguns in Razorback Valley.

Tee landed at Dong Ha, but there was nothing that could be done until daylight. The H-34 pilots sat around the operations tent, drank black coffee, and waited. From time to time, Tee wandered inside to listen to the radio contacts with the gunships and the Grunts on the knoll. However, that soon proved to be too nerve-wracking. Tee crawled back into his H-34, curled up on the troop seats, and unsuccessfully tried to get some sleep.

<u>Razorback Valley, August 9, 1966, 0400 Hours</u>: Captain Lee finally relinquished command. All night he had moved among his men to encourage them, but now he lay slumped against the side of his fighting hole. The slow but steady loss of blood had sapped his strength, and he no longer had the ability to crawl from position to position. Lee now turned his Grunts over to a new commander, Major Hazelbaker.

Dawn was still over two hours away. If they could hold out

until dawn, helicopter pilots from Dong Ha could see to land nearby with reinforcements, Major Hazelbaker knew. The NVA were no longer making frontal assaults, and instead they seemed content to probe the perimeter with grenades and small arms fire. The Grunts had gotten a Huey full of ammunition when Major Hazelbaker had been shot down before midnight, but now most of it had been expended. Could they hang on until daylight?

Down in the dark ravines below the knoll, the North Vietnamese soldiers kept as close to the Grunt perimeter as possible. The closer they got to the Grunts, the safer they were from Spooky and the gunships circling high above. Earlier in the night they had repeatedly tried human wave attacks up the steep sides of the knoll, but the entrenched Grunts had clear fields of fire and had thrown back each assault. Consequently, the NVA now were content to creep within throwing distance, lob in a grenade or two, and then spray the knoll with AK-47 fire before scurrying for cover.

0615 Hours: The eastern sky beyond Hill 549 grayed and then brightened, and soon the first faint rays of dawn slowly illuminated Razorback Valley. Now Major Hazelbaker busied himself on his radio. Two Deadlock gunships buzzed overhead, and fixed-wing support from Oxwood 63 and Oxwood 67, plus Condole 55 and Condole 56, was on call over the valley.

The Marine pilots overflying the valley could now see the knoll, and they wasted no time in pounding the surrounding terrain. The Grunts, perilously low on ammunition, now had help from above. As the minutes ticked by, the enemy probes against the small perimeter faded away. The NVA soldiers fell back and withdrew toward the heavily jungled Nui Cay Tre Ridgeline to the north.

0710 Hours: A silver-gray Marine Corps A-4 Skyhawk sliced down out of the sky and leveled, heading up the valley. The A-4 pilot laid down a phosphorus smoke-screen between the Grunts on the knoll and the enemy on the ridgeline to the north. Then a flight of blunt-nosed H-34s from HMM-263 spiraled down and landed 200 meters to the west, bringing in the first wave of the Foxtrot Company relief force. More helicopters soon flew in and landed with the remainder of Foxtrot Company plus a contingent from Echo Company. The men of the relief force linked up with the exhausted Grunts on the knoll. The helicopters met no enemy fire. The "Groucho Marx Battle," as the Marine Corps history books would later call it, had come to an end.

Now the H-34s returned to pick up the casualties, and this time they landed right on top of the knoll itself. They had to land one at a time because the knoll was so small and steep. In the second H-34, Tee Holmes made a careful power-on approach. The knoll appeared only about 30 feet high, he estimated, and in his recorded verbal narrative years later, he explained to me:

> It had been hand-to-hand during the night. When we [landed] you could see all of the bodies, all in tan uniforms, the dead North Vietnamese. Man, the dead guys were lying all over, all over the hill. It was hard to find a place to put the [helicopter] landing gear down without putting it on top of one of them.

The H-34s first picked up the most seriously wounded Marines, the priority one medevacs, and flew them to Dong Ha. Then they returned to evacuate the walking wounded. On their last trip to the knoll they would pick up the dead Marines, for whom time no longer mattered.

Costa had an ugly shrapnel wound in his leg, but he insisted on sticking with his erstwhile HAC, Major Hazelbaker. They crawled into one of the rickety H-34s for the eight minute ride to the field hospital. As their helicopter climbed eastward, Costa unholstered his .38 caliber revolver, aimed out of the left hatch at the NVA-held ridge to the north, and cranked off a single round. Perhaps he just wanted to make sure that he got to take the final shot.

> The Marines lost five killed and 27 wounded. Four of the dead Marines were from Company E, while one was a UH-34 gunner. Of the wounded, 15 were from Company E, one from the 1st Force Reconnaissance Company, and the remainder [eleven] from the MAG-16 helicopter crews.
> -- (Jack Shulimson; in *U.S. Marines in Vietnam: An Expanding War, 1966*)

The Grunts fanned out and searched the ravines and jungle below the knoll, but the NVA had melted away. The North Vietnamese had fought fiercely and bravely, for they were disciplined and hardened soldiers. They loyally had carried most of their dead comrades away with them, and the Marine Grunts found no NVA bodies left in the gullies far down below the knoll. But the NVA had wisely been unwilling to risk crawling up the steep slope toward the Grunts in the dark to retrieve their dead who had fallen atop the knoll. There, 37 dead North Vietnamese soldiers lay sprawled around the tiny Grunt perimeter.

> No tongue can tell, no mind [can] conceive, no pen [can] portray the horrible sights I witnessed this morning.
> -- (Captain John Taggert, U. S. Army; at Sharpsburg [known in the northern United States as *Antietam*], Maryland, on September 17, 1862)

The last of the Grunts on the knoll boarded the helicopters and headed for Dong Ha. As they left they saw that thousands of huge black ants and swarms of flies had descended on the bodies of the dead enemy soldiers. Already bloating in the morning sun, the NVA bodies would be left where they had fallen. The heat and the scavengers would take their toll by early afternoon.

Dong Ha, August 9, 1966, 1120 Hours: Somewhat surprised that he was still alive, Major Hazelbaker crawled out of an H-34 cabin at Dong Ha. Caked with filth and grime, he wandered into the Op's North tent and found that the VMO-2 relief detachment had not yet arrived at Dong Ha. Major Hazelbaker began wondering how he was going to get back to Marble Mountain. Then Costa hobbled in and reported that he had arranged for the two of them to be flown home in an H-46. Major Hazelbaker had never before ridden in an H-46, and he explained that the prospect of the novel flight was "exciting."

Maintenance crews set to work repairing the helicopters that had suffered battle damage during the previous night. Only three of the seven H-34s from HMM-161 were still flyable. In addition, two Hueys plus the two H-46s from HMM-265 would be unable to fly again until extensive repairs were completed.

Bureau Number 152498, the H-46 that Harpo and I had flown, still squatted in the grass where we had left it. The warhorse had taken 34 hits. Incredibly, all of the 34 hits had been in our cockpit and gunner's station areas. The forward transmission had been holed, and major structural, electrical, and hydraulic repairs would be needed. Even the crucial sync-shaft between the forward transmission and aft transmission, the H-46 equivalent of the proverbial "Jesus-nut," had a jagged bullet hole through it. But although crippled, our helicopter still had gotten us home.

> His clothes were mud caked, and the telltale signs of war reflected in his eyes.
> -- (*Pacific Stars & Stripes*; describing one of the E Company survivors of the "Groucho Marx Battle")

Tee Holmes wandered over to a Grunt who had been flown back from the knoll in an H-34. Sitting on the ground, Tee and the young Grunt struck up a conversation, and Tee asked the teenage Marine what had happened during the long night on the knoll. Years later in a recorded narrative, Tee told me:

> One Marine got out [of the helicopter], about eighteen [years old], covered with dirt and gunpowder, black under the eyes. They were glassy. He was exhausted. Man, he looked bad, real bad. He said he had his bayonet fixed all night. I asked if he had been scared, and he said, "Yeah!" [He said that] right before daylight he had one bullet left. *One* bullet, just *one* bullet! So he started throwing rocks at the NVA in the dark -- you know -- tryin' to make 'em think the rocks were grenades. Only *one* bullet left! He was saving it for the final [enemy] charge. He told me he realized he was gonna' die. Then, once he accepted that, he wasn't scared anymore.

Charlie-Med, August 9, 1966, 1330 Hours: At Charlie-Med, the field hospital near Da Nang, Harpo and I lay in adjacent bunks. Our ward housed roughly 18 other new casualties. The screen wire walls, which could be covered with roll-down canvas during inclement weather, allowed a cooling breeze to enter. After surgery the previous night, my right foot had been swathed in fresh gauze and tape. It looked mummified, but I felt no discomfort except for my sore right shin. Harpo had been heavily bandaged like me, but he also appeared to be in good spirits.

Major General Lewis W. Walt, the Third Marine Amphibious Force commander, walked into our ward. From an accompanying aide, General Walt got the name of each Marine, and he spoke quietly and personally with each man who was not too heavily sedated. The general briefly stopped and talked with Harpo and me, but I now recall nothing of the content of our conversation.

General Walt finally stopped by a bunk where a muscular black Marine lay with his upper torso covered in bandages. With tubes in his nose and mouth, the Marine could not have spoken even if he had been conscious. I watched General Walt quietly confer with his aide, who shuffled through some documents. Then with an almost inaudible comment, General Walt leaned over, grasped the young Marine's limp hand, and held it tightly for several moments.

1500 Hours: The time had come for me to go. The doctors told me that I would be medevaced from Vietnam to the United States Naval Hospital in Yokosuka, Japan. My right foot needed reconstructive surgery in Japan, I was informed. Harpo would stay at Charlie-Med awhile, but he would later continue his recuperation at the main NSA hospital near Da Nang.

Harpo and I shared an emotional parting handshake. Then the corpsmen loaded me onto a litter and carried me into an ambulance with other casualties for the five minute ride to the Da Nang Airport. Within the hour I was aboard a silver C-130 turboprop aircraft, arcing up eastward over the South China Sea.

The lesson of all history warns us that we should negotiate only when our military superiority is so convincing that we can achieve our objectives at the conference table, and deny the aggressor theirs.
-- (Richard M. Nixon)

-- Mutter Ridge --

Only the dead have seen the end of war.
-- (Plato; 428-347 B.C.)

Yokosuka, Japan, late August 1966: The United States Naval Hospital at Yokosuka, Japan, had geared up to handle many of the most severe American casualties from the fighting in Vietnam. Wounded men who were treated at Yokosuka got medical care unsurpassed anywhere in the world.

By the last week of August, I was headed down the pathway to recovery. No period of hospitalization can be expected to be pleasant, but I was afforded the very best in medical care and personal consideration. With my right leg in a jack-knife position, my injured right foot had been grafted to the calf of my left leg, a *cross-leg-flap* in medical parlance. A single cast totally immobilized both of my legs to allow the left leg "flap" to take root in my right foot. I got generous injections of Demerol every three hours, 24 hours per day, and the pain-killer wrapped me in a soft anesthetic blanket that made days bearable and nights restful. All in all, I considered myself to be a lucky man.

> The medical personnel . . . in Yokosuka were dedicated professionals who worked tirelessly every day in a world of blood and gore that would have broken men and women of lesser statue.
> -- (Lewis B. Puller Jr.; in *Fortunate Son*)

The officers' ward at Yokosuka was now a temporary home for many wounded helicopter pilots from Vietnam. Yokosuka handled the special cases, the cases requiring unique medical treatment. We often joked among ourselves that we had been secreted away here in Japan in order to keep us from offending the sensibilities of society in the United States.

First Lieutenant Hugh A. "Bear" Wilson deserved his nickname, because he really looked like a bear. Tall, big-boned, and barrel-chested, Bear shared a hospital room with me and two other wounded pilots in early September 1966. Bear had been wounded twice, but the first incident had been minor. Back on August 21, Bear had been flying his HMM-263 "Powerglide" H-34 near the Rockpile when a North Vietnamese rifle round ricocheted through his cockpit. Bear caught light shrapnel in his right calf, but he had been treated and returned to duty. However, disaster had caught up with him only eight days later.

> 1stLt Hugh A. Wilson, HMM-263, HOSTILE, 29 Aug 66, 1/2 mi[le] SE [southeast of] Hill 55, wound missile through left popliteal space, evacuated to "C" Med, ...
> -- (MAG-16 Casualty List; August 29, 1966)

As a copilot in an H-34 on the night of August 29, Bear had flown from Marble Mountain down to Hill 55 to pick up medevacs. Enemy fire had found its mark, and one round hit Bear in the left knee. The round had torn completely through his knee joint just under his kneecap, and Bear's HAC had flown the H-34 straight back to Charlie-Med. Within a matter of days, Bear had found himself in the hospital at Yokosuka. One might think that Bear would never walk again, but the surgeons and orthopedic specialists plied their professional magic on his left knee. It took three separate surgical procedures to repair the damage, but Bear finally would walk out of the military hospital in Japan. After a long period of further recuperation, he eventually would fly Marine Corps helicopters again.

One day a nurse rolled a wheelchair into my room, and I got a welcome surprise. Sitting in that wheelchair and clad in a floppy hospital gown was, believe it or not, Sergeant Gary A. Lucus. Oh, what a sight he was! Lucus had baby-soft pink hands and a pink face from the horrible burns that he had suffered when his helicopter had been shot down six weeks earlier on July 15. Lucus had been our HMM-265 supply sergeant, and I knew him well. We both stared at each other and laughed aloud at the obvious visible evidence of our medical predicaments. It thrilled me to see Lucus again.

Lucus and I talked for an hour or so like young schoolboys in a show-and-tell class. He told me about his fiery crash in Helicopter Valley on July 15, and he explained to me how his friend, Robert Telfer, had died. Then Lucus got a small Polaroid camera and snapped a photograph of me lying in my hospital bed. He handed me the picture and quipped that it would make a good souvenir from Japan. Then a nurse came and wheeled Lucus away. He later would be medevaced to the United States, where he would complete his recovery.

Later when I became ambulatory, I met a Marine pilot who had been *shot right between the eyes*. A week earlier, Major Fred D. "Pat" Patterson Jr. and his copilot, First Lieutenant "Tony" Perez, had climbed aboard their HMM-361 helicopter at Ky Ha and had headed for a landing zone near Quang Ngai. On final approach an enemy round shattered their cockpit windshield, smashed through Major Patterson's helmet visor, and struck him right at the top of the bridge of his nose -- right between the eyes! The round had passed through his brain and had cleanly exited his skull above and behind his right ear.

Adrenalin pumping and heart pounding, Perez had pulled in full power and had flown the H-34 back to Ky Ha. Major Patterson had been limp and unconscious but still alive when they landed, so he got medevaced to the NSA hospital up at Da Nang for neurosurgery. Wonder of wonders, he had survived. He eventually had been flown to the hospital at Yokosuka where his wife, Carol Patterson, a Navy nurse (the officers' ward evening charge nurse), was stationed.

Visiting in Major Patterson's hospital room always awed me. He retained all of his mental and physical faculties except for the eyesight in his right eye. There was a neat little bullet hole between his eyes, and an only slightly larger exit hole in the back of his head. These two holes were connected by an incision scar extending up over the top of his shaved head, where the surgeon had gone in to tidy-up the damage. It never ceased to amaze me that I could sit there and hold a normal conversation with a man who had -- *really* -- been shot right between the eyes.

In the future no one wins a war. It is true, there are degrees of loss. But no one wins.
-- (Brock Chisholm)

Yet, as miraculous as Major Patterson's survival seemed, it was at least equalled by the good fortune of an ARVN soldier, Private First Class Nguyen Van Luong (in Vietnam, not at Yokosuka). The young ARVN soldier had been rushed into the NSA hospital at Da Nang where Harpo was recuperating. The exact nature and extent of Luong's injury was not initially known. He had a gaping hole, a massive wound, on the top of his shoulder. Also, for some undetermined reason his lower rib cage and stomach were abnormally extended. Captain Harry Dinsmore, the attending surgeon, ordered x-rays on the unconscious Vietnamese soldier to determine the extent of his skeletal injury.

When he viewed the x-ray film, Captain Dinsmore first assumed that his grim-faced assistants were playing a practical joke on him. The x-rays seemed to show the gigantic silhouette of a *mortar round* totally embedded in Luong's chest and abdomen. But it turned out to be no joke.

During a mortar attack the 60mm mortar round had ripped down into Luong's body through the top of his shoulder. The first two miracles were that it did not detonate, and that Luong had thus far survived the trauma of the massive wound. The high explosive round, 60 millimeters in diameter and about a foot and a half long, was lodged inside of Luong's lower chest cavity just under his rib cage. Twin layers of sandbags were quickly stacked chest-high around the operating room, and Captain Dinsmore then carefully cut open Luong's chest and abdomen. Aided by demolitions experts, he gingerly removed the live mortar round. It was hastily carried away and detonated in a remote area west of the hospital.

Luong made a complete recovery. Over a month later the October 14, 1966, issue of *Life Magazine* would feature Luong's incredible brush with death on pages 98-A and 98-B. One photograph would show the hospital x-ray, which clearly depicted the huge mortar round inside of Luong's chest. Another would show an unsmiling and post-operative Luong wrapped in bandages from his waist to his neck. The accompanying narrative would provide the fascinating details of Luong's never-before-heard-of injury and survival.

Razorback Valley, late August 1966: The Marines gradually consolidated their hold on Razorback Valley. The eleven Recons high atop the Rockpile watched the valley floor and reported NVA troop movements to the Marine Command by radio. Helicopters hovering with one wheel on the rocky peak and the other two wheels dangling over the cliffs kept the small team on the Rockpile supplied with C-Rations and water.

During the last week of August a savage battle raged for control of the Razorback. North Vietnamese heavy machineguns on the Razorback threatened the helicopter lifeline to the Rockpile, and the Marine Command tried to eliminate the threat. VMO-2 Huey gunships and artillery blasted the black granite walls of the Razorback. However, the NVA soldiers simply pulled back into the protective caves that honeycombed the volcanic rock. The Grunts eventually had to scale the lofty Razorback on foot, and they attacked the enemy in caves described as "large enough to drive two trucks through, side by side." It proved to be bloody work, but by the end of August the Grunts controlled the Razorback. Captured North Vietnamese soldiers from the 803rd NVA Regiment reported that their ultimate mission would have been an attack on the vital Marine artillery base at Cam Lo.

Con Thien, September 7, 1966: MAG-16 helicopters ferried an assault force from 2nd Battalion, 4th Marines, into the Con Thien area nine miles northwest of Dong Ha. The next day the Second Battalion, reinforced with gunships and tanks, attacked the 90th NVA Regiment just south of the DMZ near the village of Gia Binh. The North Vietnamese had posted a sign printed in English on the outskirts of the village: "We will fight to the last man." The NVA defenders were dug in, and it took a week of heavy fighting to drive them back north into the DMZ. Without question the North Vietnamese were intent on pushing southward as soon as the winter monsoon began.

Marine helicopter pilots are a gregarious and strange lot. Grim and fatalistic humor is a way of life. Jokes about all manner of in-flight emergencies and combat hazards are part of the game. The NATOPS Manual for the H-46 is full of proven procedures that will enable a pilot to deal with almost any foreseeable emergency: Dual SAS failure, Compressor stall, Engine compartment fire, Autorotative landings, Engine control system failure, and so forth. These procedures are committed to memory and rehearsed over and over. The desired corrective action becomes automatic, a professional response to deal with the problem at hand. No matter how major the malfunction, there is always a way out, a way to survive, a way to live to fly and fight again another day.

In mental self-defense, helicopter pilots resort to joking about the dangers of their chosen trade. They shrug off most thoughts of possible mechanical failures, system failures, and wartime perils -- all except one. No sane pilot ever jokes about the ultimate H-46 systems failure, the curse too terrible even to be *mentioned* in the NATOPS Manual. No one jokes about an H-46 helicopter pilot's terminal nightmare: In-flight Control System Failure.

> A helicopter does not want to fly. It is maintained in the air by a variety of forces and controls, working in opposition to each other. And if there is a disturbance in the delicate balance, the helicopter stops flying immediately and disastrously. This is why . . . all helicopter pilots are brooders, introspective anticipators of trouble. They know that if anything bad has not happened -- it is about to.
> -- (Harry Reasoner; on *ABC News,* February 16, 1971)

In cruising flight in an H-46 helicopter, if you lose control over the rotor head swashplates, you die. It is as simple as that. There is no parallel in fixed-wing aircraft. No matter how dire the emergency, no matter how much battle damage his airplane might have suffered, the fixed-wing jet pilot still has a *chance* to eject, parachute down to the earth, and survive.

However, in an H-46 helicopter, loss of control over the massive swashplates will cause the rotor system to slam to full pitch or flat pitch, full left or full right, full forward or full aft. Down you will go in a violent and uncontrolled spinning and tumbling fall that literally will tear the airframe apart. The six-blade tandem-rotor system, 83 feet and 4 inches from the front to the rear, will allow no escape. The tons of inertia in the whirling rotor blades will chop and chew the fuselage and the hapless crew into spaghetti. There is no way out and no way to escape. If you suffer an In-flight Control System Failure in an H-46, you are a dead man.

Yet, three Bonnie-Sue helicopter crewmen from HMM-265 somehow managed to snub their noses at certain death one sunny September morning at Marble Mountain. The word *miracle* does not even apply.

<u>Marble Mountain, September 14, 1966</u>: Captain Joseph G. "Joe" Roman chanced to draw the HAC's assignment. Second Lieutenant Richard T. "R-Tee" Harry got assigned to handle the copilot's chores. Corporal W. L. Diehl would naturally go along because he was the loyal crew chief for the helicopter. The H-46 bearing Bureau Number 152506 and designated as EP-165 had been flown over to dispersal pad number seven the previous afternoon. Now the three man crew prepared to shuttle the helicopter back to the HMM-265 flight line. No gunner was necessary for this brief and simple assignment.

Joe and R-Tee conducted the routine pre-flight inspection. Joe crawled on top of the fuselage, mounted the open clamshell door steps, and checked the transmissions and rotor heads. Meanwhile, R-Tee checked the cabin and engines. All appeared to be in order, so while Diehl secured the clamshell doors, Joe and R-Tee climbed into the cockpit. They strapped in, plugged in, and brought the 21,400 pound gross weight H-46 to life. They saw no logic in air-taxiing over to the flight line and blowing sand over everything within 200 feet. Consequently, Joe planned to take off and shoot a couple of touch-and-go landings on the marston-matting of the Marble Mountain runway. After that he would ground-taxi back across the steel matting to the flight line.

Joe challenged R-Tee to a sporting contest to see who could make the smoothest run-on landing. An experienced and skilled pilot with a feather-touch on the cyclic could glide down at 50 knots and grease the main landing gear on the runway without so much as a bump or shudder. Joe talked with R-Tee and Diehl on the ICS and briefed them on the plan. Diehl plugged in his "short-cord" and sat on the console in the rear of the cockpit behind and between the two pilots. He would judge the finesse and smoothness of the two landings and decide which pilot would be the winner.

Laid-back R-Tee literally oozed calm self-confidence. He took off southward and climbed, then made a 180 degree turn to the left out over the ocean and paralleled the beach on his down-wind leg. Abeam the approach end of Runway 17, R-Tee lowered the collective, turned left, and slipped down toward the runway. His touch-and-go landing turned out to be a genuine greaser, and he knew that it would be hard to beat. Turning to Diehl and grinning, R-Tee relinquished the cockpit controls to Joe.

In sharp contrast to R-Tee's laid-back style, Joe was always full of energy and enthusiasm, always Gung-Ho, an aggressive professional. He turned down-wind at 700 feet above the ocean and called the tower prior to beginning his approach. Then a Bird Dog (a Cessna O-1 light observation airplane) pilot unexpectedly radioed the tower; he was on a short final approach, he reported.

Joe extended his downwind leg while he and R-Tee tried in vain to visually spot the small Bird Dog that was supposedly flying somewhere below and to the left of them. They searched the sky, but neither of them could see the Bird Dog. Where could it be?

With no warning: BBLLAAAAMMM!

A tooth-jarring impact!

The cyclic ripped out of Joe's grasp. His feet were knocked from the rudder pedals. The H-46 snapped, twisted, and rolled. Up and down, around and around they tumbled. Visually, everything turned into a swirling blur of motion. Plummeting earthward, Joe saw blue sky through the plexiglass in front of him in one instant, then land, then water, then sky again. He remembers screaming incoherently, because he knew that he was going to die.

Neither pilot could even get his hands back on the cyclic. It snapped and banged insanely from side to side, forward and backward. Rolling, falling end over end earthward, R-Tee thought that perhaps the SAS had somehow gone berserk. "THE SAS! CUT OFF THE SAS!" he thought. In sheer desperation he tried, but the violent vibrations and the tumbling helicopter prevented him from even moving his arms toward the SAS switch.

I looked out of the north side of the tent and saw a CH-46A starting to disintegrate.
-- (First Lieutenant Robert W. Forsyth; Accident Board witness)

Plunging earthward, the helicopter could have impacted at any location and in any direction: forward, backward, inverted, or vertically. Plummeting out of control, the H-46 momentarily pitched up to an almost vertical attitude. The spinning rotors acted like a giant air brake and reduced some of the forward groundspeed. Then the inevitable structural disintegration began.

The tortured fuselage at last surrendered and broke into two halves. The rear half, shredded by the whirling rotors and now aflame, dropped straight back into the sea. The front half contained Roman, Harry, and Diehl. It rolled inverted and plunged down into the ocean. The spinning rotor blades somehow spared the battered but still intact cockpit. JP-4 fuel, which is essentially kerosene, gushed from the ruptured fuel cells and sent an ugly pillar of orange flames and black smoke high into the sky.

The aircraft pitched nose up to an estimated 70 degrees nose high, shearing the aft rotor blades. The forward section of the airframe folded up, backwards, and appeared to land in an inverted attitude in the water, alongside the aft portion.
-- (Major George N. Holstead; Accident Board witness)

The two separate halves of the H-46 had crashed into the sea about 50 meters from the beach at Marble Mountain. The burning and twisted wreckage lay strewn in the rolling surf right in front of the O'Club tent, just beyond the bunkers manned by the Marble Mountain perimeter guard.

In the flooded cockpit the three Marines were still alive! True, they were bloody, battered, and dazed, but they still lived. They had crashed inverted into the sea in water only five feet deep.

The waves washed Diehl out of the remnants of the forward section of the fuselage and into the surf. R-Tee unstrapped and intended to crawl out of the cockpit and into the cabin. However, at the rear of the cockpit he managed to swim clear of the wreckage through the gaping hole where the rest of the fuselage should have been.

Seawater now had filled the shattered cockpit. Joe kicked his emergency exit open, shimmied through, and began swimming for his life. Within moments his strength was gone, and he could go no farther. His legs failed him, sank, and immediately touched the sandy sea-bottom. Joe then realized that he was in water only waist deep.

The perimeter guard Marines abandoned their bunkers, raced to the beach, and helped the three erstwhile aviators crawl ashore to safety. Meanwhile, off-duty pilots in the nearby tents ran toward the beach. Bob Mills sped to the waist-high concertina wire and stopped while he tried to figure out how to get around it. He watched as Pappy Johnson ran past him and leaped over the tangled concertina on a dead run.

Another HMM-265 helicopter, EP-159, landed on the beach, and the crew rushed out to aid their squadronmates. Tom Shea, Billy Collins, Bob, Pappy, and others helped the three injured men get into the cabin of EP-159. Each was so debilitated that he had to be *carried* aboard. An awed crowd of onlookers quickly gathered, but it had to move back when the fire offshore began cooking-off the ammunition in the aft section of the downed H-46.

I thought we'd been hit by a missile.
-- (Richard T. "R-Tee" Harry; years later)

I thought we had a midair collision with the Bird Dog.
-- (Joseph G. "Joe" Roman; years later)

The flight to Charlie-Med at Da Nang took only three minutes. Once there, a Catholic Priest took a cursory look at the bleeding and battered Joe Roman and began administering the Last Rites. He stopped when Joe sat up, unaided. R-Tee had been brutally hammered and beaten in the crash, but he had suffered no serious internal injuries. Diehl also had escaped with his life.

Captain Dale L. "Papa-Bear" Tinsley rushed into Charlie-Med to check on the condition of Roman, Harry, and Diehl. Still erroneously thinking that he had been in a midair collision with the small observation airplane, Joe anxiously tugged on the sleeve of Papa-Bear's flight suit: "What about the Bird Dog?"

"What?"

"The Bird Dog, we never saw him!" Joe exclaimed.

"Whhaaaa . . . .?"

"The Bird Dog we hit -- what happened to the pilot?"

Later in the day the remains of the doomed H-46 were fished out of the surf. Subsequent examination of the wreckage quickly revealed the problem. A giant bolt had failed. This put additional stress on two additional bolts that held the aft yoke support assembly to the airframe. When these two remaining bolts suddenly sheared, all control over the aft rotor head was lost:

> (1) Investigation revealed the bolt NAS1308-23, item 82 of reference (c) was in place, partially backed out of support 107C1714, item 86 with nut missing and bolt t[h]reads intact. Bolts NAS1306-27W, item NR 83, were torn out of supporting nuts and airframe. Bolts NAS 1306-25W, item NR 77, were also torn out . . . . These circumstances deprived the pilot of control over the aft rotor head.
> -- (from *HMM-265 Aircraft Accident Board Report*)

Quickly the *what ifs* set in. What if the nose had not pitched up in the last seconds before impact? What if control had been lost at normal cruising altitude of 3000 feet? Or what if control had been lost at only 100 feet, and the helicopter had impacted the ground or water at 120 knots? What if they had crashed on land with no water to cushion the impact, or far out at sea where they surely would have drowned? What if Diehl had not been up in the cockpit and out of reach of the out-of-control aft rotor blades that severed the fuselage?

The questions continued on and on. What if they had crashed at night? -- Or in the jungle? -- Or alone? What if they had carried a full load of Grunts in the cabin, ready to be thrown out when the fuselage broke into. Or what if the fuselage had not broken into, and the cockpit had fallen into the sea with the rest of the burning airframe and the ruptured fuel tanks?

We had no control over the aircraft. God was the pilot.
-- (Richard T. "R-Tee" Harry; years later)

The Lord was there.
-- (Joseph G. "Joe" Roman; years later)

In aviation folklore, a *good landing* is humorously defined as "any landing that you can walk away from." This was the stuff from which aviation legends are born, and Joe and R-Tee became instant heroes, living legends. It seemed that if you knew them, talked with them, touched them, or later flew with them that it was a good omen, and somehow their incredible luck might rub off onto you. They were bigger than life and truly immortal, it seemed. Nobody could have survived a complete In-flight Control System Failure in cruising flight. Yet, somehow the Bonnie-Sue crewmen had walked away from certain death. Among H-46 pilots, their incredible War Story never dies:

"Hey, remember the crash at the Marble Mountain O'Club?"

"Yeah [always accompanied by a throaty laugh], right by the beach."

"Joe and R-Tee -- remember?"

"*Crazy*! Those *crazy* guys!"

"One-in-a-million."

"Right. It could *never* happen again. I mean, the whole -- you know -- the whole thing just -- ripped apart in the air -- broke into pieces, crashed and burned right there. Right by the O'Club! Right there! Right out there in front of everybody!"

"Never again."

"Roger that."

"Never -- not in a million years!"

Special Landing Force, September 15, 1966, 0700 Hours: At dawn eleven amphibious LVTs from the *USS Vancouver* (LPD-2) churned through the South China Sea toward the shore. Inside of the LVTs, Grunts from 1st Battalion, 26th Marines, were ready to set up blocking positions along the coast. The LVTs lumbered ashore on Blue Beach midway between the DMZ and the mouth of the Cua Viet River. The Grunts ran out of the landing craft and stormed across the beach, and the empty amphibians headed back to sea toward the *Vancouver*.

0720 Hours: Viewed from Pri-Fly aboard the *USS Iwo Jima*

(LPH-2), the flight deck was alive with swirling helicopter rotors. The "Millpoint" H-34s of Colonel James D. McGough's HMM-363 had fired up in preparation for an aerial assault six miles inland from Blue Beach. The Grunts climbed aboard and the H-34s took off, circled, joined up, and headed to the west.

At 0740 Hours the first wave of Millpoint helicopters touched down and discharged the Grunts in the flatlands west of old Colonial Route 1. There was no opposition to the helicopter landing, so the H-34s sped back toward the *Iwo Jima* for another load of Grunts. As the morning progressed, the Grunts of the First Battalion reached their assigned objectives with almost no resistance other than the terrain and the oppressive heat.

The H-34 helicopters of HMM-363, the Special Landing Force (SLF) squadron, were joined by ten more H-34s from HMM-161. They all stayed busy shuttling the Grunts around, and heavy-lift helicopters moved Marine howitzers from Blue Beach to locations farther inland and west of Route 1. For the pilots, crew chiefs, and gunners, the morning had passed without incident. Yet, the coming sweltering afternoon would bring the first armed encounters with the North Vietnamese Army units.

Shortly after noon a Marine Recon team silently eased single file along a trail through the undergrowth. Visibility through the tangled vegetation along the sides of the foot path was limited to little more than an arm's length. As they rounded a bend in the trail, the Recons were suddenly surprised to find themselves face-to-face with an equally surprised group of NVA soldiers. For an agonizing several seconds, the stunned adversaries froze in place, only 15 feet apart. Then both sides opened fire, and Grunts and North Vietnamese alike dove for cover in the thickets lining both sides of the trail.

The sound of the gunfire rapidly attracted both Marine and NVA reinforcements, and soon a full platoon of Recons was engaged in a firefight with an NVA company. Helicopter gunships and fixed-wing support arrived and ran into fierce enemy fire. Five helicopters took hits, and two crewmen were wounded before enemy contact was finally broken later that afternoon.

For the helicopter crews, the following days provided more of the same. Most of the heavy fighting centered around the Con Thien and Gio Linh areas north of Dong Ha. However, the most bitter battles in the fall of 1966 would be fought in the mountains to the west. There the Marines and NVA would initially clash in Razorback Valley, which was by now familiar territory to the helicopter pilots. Later the combatants would engage in a bloody two-week battle for control of the rugged three mile long ridgeline that walls in Razorback Valley on the north. Yet, as late as mid-September it was unlikely that many of the Grunts or helicopter crewmen knew the name of this rugged and jungled ridgeline where so many men, both Asian and American, would perish in the weeks to come. Only a few Marine patrols had yet tried to probe the forbidding and steep southern slope of the ridge. But within only 15 short days, by the first week of October, Marines everywhere would recognize the name of this newest and bloodiest battleground in all of Vietnam -- Nui Cay Tre Ridge.

Viewed from the Rockpile three miles to the south, Nui Cay Tre Ridge looked beautiful on those autumn mornings in 1966. By around 0900 Hours each day the sun would burn off the night fog that had half shrouded the peaks of the ridge in a shimmering blanket of white mist. Helicopter pilots had not yet tried to drop Recon teams there because the ridge was densely wooded, and aerial reconnaissance had failed to reveal any area where a helicopter might land. Besides, Marine Intelligence had learned that Nui Cay Tre Ridge had been heavily fortified by the NVA.

However, military control of Nui Cay Tre Ridge was a part of the Task Force Delta plan to thwart the expected NVA monsoon offensive. The Marine Command knew that it could not allow the ridge to remain an enemy fortress. The Command detached Colonel Mendenhall from HMM-265 and transferred him to Dong Ha as commander of Marine Air for the coming assault.

Razorback Valley, September 15, 1966: MAG-16 helicopters made last minute trips to fly supplies from Dong Ha to the 1st Battalion, 4th Marines, encamped near the base of the Rockpile. Ten extra H-34s from HMM-161 flew to Dong Ha to complement the many H-46s and H-34s already there and waiting. Then two companies of Grunts from First Battalion cautiously swept northward from the Rockpile and headed toward the southern slope of Nui Cay Tre Ridge. The first day passed uneventfully as the

Grunts used machetes to hack their way across the valley floor. The helicopter crews lounged around in the shade back at Dong Ha and waited for frags that never came.

September 16, 1966, 1200 Hours: Bravo and Delta Companies pushed forward in column and reached the southern slope of the ridge. Here they encountered North Vietnamese who had fortified themselves inside a series of trenchlines and bunkers. The Grunts engaged in a series of fierce firefights with the entrenched NVA soldiers. Quickly the Marines radioed a request back to Op's North at Dong Ha: "Launch the gunships."

VMO-2 Hueys took off and headed for the valley 14 miles to the west. The pilots by now had become so accustomed to Razorback Valley that maps were needed only when the destination was given as numerical map coordinates. Upon arrival the gunship pilots and their gunners found plenty of targets, because the enemy was trying to flank the two Grunt companies. The fierce fighting would last over two days.

YR-1, a "Barrelhouse" H-34 from HMM-161, headed toward a landing area hastily chopped out of the undergrowth one mile northeast of the Razorback. Right at the base of Nui Cay Tre Ridge, the speeding helicopter came under intense enemy fire and was hit repeatedly with near disastrous results. The *HMM-161 Command Chronology* would later explain:

> On a medevac to XD-973604, YR-1 took intense fire resulting in many hits. The throttle control box was hit causing the [engine] controls to go to full power. A climb was initiated and the plane returned to Dong Ha airstrip while IFR in the clouds. At 7000 feet the mixture was secured and a full autorotation was made into a rice paddy. An overcast from 1500-2000 feet upwards made this feat extremely hazardous.

YR-1 suffered a near mortal hit, and the Wright R-1820 engine roared to full power. To the non-flying layman this might sound like a minor problem, but the two H-34 pilots knew that rotor system disintegration was a split second away. They snatched in full collective pitch to add aerodynamic drag from the rotors and counter the torque from the engine. The two pilots knew that they had no choice. They could either climb, or die. The H-34

NATOPS Manual dryly notes the proper emergency procedure in Section 5-4: "The excess power should be absorbed by climbing."

Climbing through 2000 feet, the stricken Barrelhouse helicopter entered a solid cloud layer, and the pilots lost all visual contact with the ground below. Their functional electrical system still powered all of their electronic equipment, so they headed back toward Dong Ha, guided only by a nervous faith in the H-34 TACAN and their Artificial Horizon in the instrument panel. By the time the TACAN showed station passage at Dong Ha, the H-34 had reached 7000 feet. The helicopter was still in the clouds and still climbing. As the copilot cautiously pulled the red fuel Mixture Control knob rearward, the engine coughed and then stopped. Down collective! Full right rudder! With the rotors now at flat pitch, the H-34 spiraled down through the clouds toward the ground like an iron sled on rails, an IFR autorotation.

YR-1 broke out of the clouds at 1700 feet, and the pilots autorotated down and landed in a flat area that fortunately was clear of trees. Their wingman, YR-21, landed and picked up the downed crew. The YR-1 gunner had been shot through his knee, but the crew chief and the two pilots escaped with only frazzled nerves to bear witness to their harrowing flight.

Because of the heavy fighting at the base of Nui Cay Tre Ridge, VMO-2 Hueys helped the H-34s haul wounded Grunts out of the valley. Two Deadlock helicopters took a total of nine hits, but the pilots and aircrewmen came through unscathed. The H-46s of HMM-265 contributed by handling the missions requiring heavy lifting capability. The tandem-rotor Boeing helicopters rushed more ammunition to the Grunts and dropped off reinforcements at YD-188555. Back at Op's North, Colonel Mendenhall had a busy day keeping tabs on the scores of helicopter frags needed to support the Grunts in the field.

September 17, 1966: The following day, September 17, proved to be another mission-filled day for MAG-16 helicopters. A detailed diary entry in the After Action Report for HMM-161 highlights the day's combat action for the Barrelhouse squadron at Dong Ha. It summarizes the many frags for only *one* squadron on just *one* day during the battle for control of Nui Cay Tre Ridge:

Operation Prairie saw a hectic day. Eighteen medevacs, 32 passengers, and 6850 pounds [of cargo] were carried. In the morning, YR-21 was approaching a landing zone at XD-967595 for a medevac and drew automatic weapons fire. The appro[a]ch was waved off and no hits were received. At approximately 1630 [Hours] YR-4 was sitting in Permission [sic, should be *Persimmon*] CP at XD-975565 and came under mortar attack. Three rounds exploded within 20 meters of the aircraft. Over 400 hits were sustained, but the plane was airworthy and was flown to Dong Ha. The crew chief and gunner were wounded with small bits of shrapnel in the face, arms, and legs. Neither pilot was injured. At approximately 1910 [Hours] YR-17 was on an emergency ammo resupply to XD-956592. There was no landing zone, so a hover delivery was employed. Heavy fire was encountered, driving YR-17 into the trees, damaging the rotor tips. The aircraft was flown to Dong Ha with extensive small arms damage.

Nui Cay Tre Ridge, the northern border of Razorback Valley, runs three miles east to west. It is dominated by two peaks, Hill 400 to the east and Hill 484 to the west, slightly under two miles apart. The contour lines on our 1:50,000 scale maps almost merged to reflect the steepness of the slopes on Hill 400 and Hill 484. Military logic and Marine Intelligence indicated that these two peaks would be the most heavily fortified parts of the ridge.

September 18, 1966: HMM-263 and its H-34s had also joined the struggle. Many of my old Training Command buddies flew for HMM-263, and four of their helicopters got drilled by ground fire on trips to aid the Grunts. Yet, by the afternoon of September 18, the Grunts had broken out of the NVA encirclement at the base of the ridge. The North Vietnamese had been dug in and waiting in their log and concrete reinforced bunkers, and they appeared determined to hold their fortified positions at all costs. Discretion is truly the better part of valor, so the Marine Command wisely decided to forego another frontal assault on the south slope where NVA mines, mortars, and heavy fire had met the attack. Task Force Delta planned to pull back and attack the exposed eastern flank of the entrenched North Vietnamese.

HMM-265 got its roughest assignment on the night of September 18. The enemy mounted sharp counterattacks that continued throughout the afternoon and night. Before midnight the Grunts ran low on ammunition, so the Bonnie-Sue pilots drew the new frag: Emergency night resupply.

During the daytime, flying a helicopter down to support Grunts in a firefight involves acceptable risks under certain circumstances. At night, however, such a flight brings additional hazards to bear. The main difficulty is that the pilots simply can not see where they are going, can not see obstacles, and often can not tell the difference between friend and foe. Orbiting high overhead at night and talking to the Grunts down below by radio, pilots can see the muzzle flashes and watch the tracers fired by the opposing forces.

If the enemy shoots at you, the tracers appear to float up slowly at first. Then they seem to speed up and curve away as they whiz past (and generally behind) your helicopter. Actually, it is all an optical illusion. The tracers initially appear to move slowly because they are headed directly toward the helicopter -- right at you -- and there is no visual indication of relative motion. But as your helicopter moves forward, the tracer bullets continue upward in a straight line. To a pilot, it looks like the tracers are curving behind him and speeding up. Cutting off all external lights and starting to spiral down into all of that, the tension becomes almost tangible, almost alive, almost sexual.

From 3000 feet of altitude, as you flip off your lights and start to spiral earthward through the night sky, the incoming tracers stop. Without any external lights, your helicopter suddenly has become invisible to the enemy gunners. From inside of your cockpit, the fuzzy red glow from the instrument panel lights protects your night vision. Peering ahead through the plexiglass windshield, your only visible reference to the landing area is a pinpoint of light from a flashlight, or perhaps from a Zippo cigarette lighter. You can see the light from 3000 feet above, but vital distance sense, depth perception, and closure rate mean nothing in the sea of darkness. Hopefully the light you see is the right one, but you never know for sure until you near the ground. Then if your world suddenly lights up with incoming tracers, you know that you guessed wrong.

HMM-265 pilots and aircrewmen repeatedly took their Bonnie-Sue helicopters into Razorback Valley on the night of September

18. The Grunts got the essentials of warfare, 13,300 pounds of ammunition and supplies according to squadron records. Nearby, HMM-263 stayed busy hauling out First Battalion casualties. Two Deadlock gunships made a strafing run on NVA positions, and their M-60 machineguns set off a huge secondary explosion that showered debris over the jungle. All of the gunships, H-34s, and H-46s eventually made a safe return to Dong Ha that night.

HMM-265 now had a permanent detachment of four Bonnie-Sue H-46s at Dong Ha, reinforced by two more down at Phu Bai. HMM-164 kicked in another half dozen, giving Colonel Mendenhall twelve H-46s available for daily frags. VMO-2 maintained its own rotating detachment at Dong Ha, and a mixed bag of waiting H-34s always sat in the grass south of the airstrip. Naturally, whenever an emergency popped up, more helicopters always could be dispatched from Marble Mountain to Dong Ha, and they would arrive within the hour.

Air Force B-52 bombers winged in from Guam and pounded the North Vietnamese staging areas in the DMZ. These Arc-Light missions were designed to interdict the southerly flow of NVA soldiers and supplies toward Nui Cay Tre Ridge. Meanwhile, 1950s-vintage Air Force C-123s, radio call-sign "Ranch-Hand," rained defoliant onto the enemy supply trails north of the ridge. The unfortunate Ranch-Hand pilots were the most shot-at pilots in the war. They had to fly low and slow on their unarmed spray runs. They borrowed a slogan from the old Smokey-the-Bear forest-fire-control campaign to come up with their own catchy squadron motto: "Remember, only we can prevent forests."

The United States Air Force had begun Operation Ranch-Hand over four years earlier on January 12, 1962. This controversial project had been approved after bitter debate, at the *highest* levels of the United States Government, over whether the United States would be criticized for using chemical warfare in Vietnam. During the next nine years over 19 million gallons of defoliating herbicides would be sprayed on Vietnam and parts of Laos in an effort to kill jungle vegetation and expose enemy supply trails.

While Bonnie-Sue aircrews flew their H-46s in Vietnam in the latter half of the 1960s decade, no one had yet coined the term

Agent Orange. Actually, the defoliant looked *white*, not *orange*, whenever we helicopter pilots watched from above while the C-123s made their risky low-level spray runs. To me the white spray trailing back from a trio of C-123s always looked beautiful when silhouetted against the vivid green jungle below. No pilot that I knew ever hesitated to fly through the spray trails and inhale the vapor. At night we did not worry about sleeping in our helicopter cabins, which had become filthy with the jellied jungle-rot and grime from our daily chain of Grunt passengers. In 1966 and 1967 we assumed that the defoliant only killed trees. The term Agent Orange would eventually be derived from the bright orange-colored steel barrels in which the defoliant had been shipped to our airstrips so that it could be pumped into the C-123 spray tanks.

> It was chemical warfare pure and simple. Its defenders had the arrogance to maintain that what would kill trees would not hurt people, or American people anyway. We knew it was dirty work from the beginning.
> -- (Morley Safer; in *Flashbacks: On Returning to Vietnam*)

Ironically, the defoliant proved to be a cruel time bomb that would maim and kill Marines for decades to come. Slowly the story would unfold. The defoliant contained the highly toxic carcinogen, *dioxin*.

In the 1970s a flood of former Vietnam servicemen would begin seeking treatment at Veterans Administration hospitals in the United States. They would suffer from a variety of medical, genetic, and psychological illness attributed to their exposure to Agent Orange. On May 7, 1984, a Federal Judge would announce a $180 million out-of-court settlement against seven chemical companies in connection with the lethal carcinogen. At the time of that settlement, over 40,000 servicemen would have initiated claims against the chemical manufacturers. However, the dioxin time bomb would continue to take its deadly toll. By the 1990s the Veterans Administration would be treating hundreds of thousands of Vietnam-era serviceman for a variety of debilitating illnesses -- mainly cancer -- attributed to Agent Orange.

<u>Nui Cay Tre Ridge, September 22, 1966</u>:   The long-awaited Marine flanking attack began. First, Marine artillery pounded away at the fortified southern slope of Nui Cay Tre Ridge. Next, VMO-2 gunships buzzed down to rocket and strafe the NVA fortifications. Within minutes a gray pall of smoke and dust half shrouded the center of the southern avenue of approach to the ridge. But it was only a diversion, a ruse as old as time itself.

Mystify! Mislead! Surprise!
-- (General T. J. "Stonewall" Jackson, Confederate States Army)

A flight of H-46s swooped down and landed a half mile from the eastern end of the ridge. Grunts charged down the ramps and took cover in the surrounding vegetation, but they met no enemy resistance. More flights brought in the remainder of Lieutenant Colonel William J. Masterpool's 3rd Battalion, 4th Marines, radio call-sign "Mutter." The Marine plan called for a three mile assault westward along the spine of the ridge. By evening the battalion had pushed almost a half mile up the eastern end of the ridge without meeting any opposition, so they dug in for the night.

Meanwhile, at Dong Ha the helicopter crews mostly sat and waited. General William C. Westmoreland, the Army MACV (Military Assistance Command, Vietnam) commander, suddenly arrived and boarded a VMO-2 Huey for a personal visit to Khe Sanh and Lang Vei. Two of our Bonnie-Sue helicopters took fire during a routine logistical troop transfer, but there was no significant ground contact with the enemy during the day.

<u>September 23, 1966</u>: Inching westward up Nui Cay Tre Ridge on September 23, the Grunts had little trouble with the North Vietnamese, whose main defenses lay farther ahead.   The mountainous terrain and jungle undergrowth, however, proved to be an enemy more formidable than the Grunts had ever faced before. Two weeks later on October 7, *Time Magazine* would describe the fighting and the tropical battleground: "It combined the horror of a Guadalcanal jungle with the exhausting steepness of the slopes at Chapultepec."

That terrain! The bloody maddening uncanniness of it!
-- (Michael Herr; in *Dispatches*)

A gnarled and tangled mass of vines, brush, and bamboo covered the jungle floor to a height of nine to ten feet. The Grunts could not see through it, walk through it, or crawl through it. They had to hack their way through the jungle with machetes, propelled as much by their arms as by their feet. Above this nearly impenetrable undergrowth, deciduous trees up to eight feet in diameter at their base towered to a height of 90 feet. Their lush canopy blocked out the sun. On the ground the Grunts stayed in single file in the shadowy darkness and suffocating heat, and anyone who fell behind might be lost forever.

H-34s got the frags to resupply the Grunts on the jungled slope of the ridge. The Grunts carried only their weapons, ammunition, two canteens, and two socks stuffed with C-Rations. They tried to hack out makeshift landing areas with machetes, explosives, or anything else they had. They failed, and there was no place for the helicopters to land. Consequently, the pilots resorted to using their hoists to lower supplies while hovering over the treetops. Then any casualties would be hoisted up into the helicopter for the flight back to the field hospital at Dong Ha.

HMM-263 drew most of the frags for resupply and medevac missions for the "Mutter" Battalion. The two H-46 squadrons mainly stayed on standby for heavy lift assignments, although two H-46s now stayed in the air 24 hours a day for radio relay purposes. VMO-2 pilots kept busy as medevac escorts for HMM-161 and HMM-263, and the Deadlock pilots also worked as aerial spotters for the Marine artillery batteries at Cam Lo.

Cam Lo River Valley, September 25, 1966, 1915 Hours: Prior to each mission, part of our briefing consisted of Artillery (called, *Arty*) Fire Zones to be avoided. Even while in flight, we monitored our radios for new Arty fire missions. Pilots took this precaution in order to avoid the possibility of flying through the path of the Marine Corps 105mm and 155mm howitzer shells. Even the giant B-52 Arc-Light bombing missions got included in these Arty briefings, and Operations always referred to these heavy carpet bombing flights as "heavy artillery." Still, no precautionary system can be totally infallible, and on September 25 the system somehow broke down. No one knows why.

At 1915 [Hours] on the 265 degree radial at 12 miles from Dong Ha TACAN, YR-3 was hit by friendly artillery. . . . The four crewmen were killed, together with a corpsman from HMM-265.

-- (*HMM-161 Command Chronology*; September 25, 1966)

The helicopter flew westward on a routine frag to pick up a medevac. Suddenly an orange explosion blasted the flying machine apart. The H-34 disintegrated, and flaming wreckage rained down from the sky. The pilots and crew members undoubtedly never even felt the blast that killed them. Remnants of the helicopter fell into the inaccessible jungle below, and it was not possible to recover the remains of the crew. All five men were initially listed as missing-in-action, but eventually they were declared to be dead. The Casualty Card for each member of the crew begins with the same words: "Died 25 Sep 66 vicinity of Quang Tri Province, Republic of Vietnam . . . ."

Capt	Phillip A. DUCAT	086222	Fort Wayne, Indiana
1Lt	Dean W. REITER	090724	Manchester, Missouri
Cpl	Vernon H. PARKER	2023506	Secane, Pennsylvania
LCpl	Arthur W. GREENE	2149931	Chicago, Illinois
HM-3	Peter R. BOSSMAN	(unknown)	(unknown)

Considering the different altitudes possible, different locations, different routes, different times, and the precautionary measures taken, it seemed almost impossible that a helicopter had been hit by friendly artillery. Still, it happened. This is the only documented instance that I know of where a Marine helicopter in flight was blasted out of the sky by our own ground-to-ground artillery.

YR-3 was gone now, but the mission remained. Shaking off the bad news, other HMM-161 helicopters cranked up to complete the medevac frag. Before the afternoon ended, the H-34s hauled 25 Grunt casualties from the jungle to the field hospital. Sleeping in their cold H-34 cabins that night, HMM-161 pilots and aircrewmen silently mourned the loss of their squadronmates who had taken YR-3 on its last flight.

<u>Nui Cay Tre Ridge, September 27, 1966, 0730 Hours:</u> ı.. Grunts of the Third Battalion began the final push toward the top of Hill 400. So far the Grunts had fought only the terrain and small NVA patrols, but the real battle lay just ahead. For the next two days the Grunts would go head to head with hordes of North Vietnamese defenders. Helicopter crews would do what they could to help, but the brunt of the battle would be borne by the Grunts on the ground. Fixed-wing support helped, helicopter support helped, and artillery support helped. However, the outcome of the brutal battle for Hill 400 would hinge on the most basic tenet of Marine Corps doctrine, the Marine Infantryman.

> As we got close to [Hill] 400 . . . we saw more and more enemy positions, including enough huts in the ravines to harbor a regiment, and piles . . . of ammunition.
> -- (Captain Roger K. Ryman; later speaking of the prelude to the struggle for Hill 400)

As the Grunts pressed forward and upward, three civilians went with them: Derek Taylor, a British reporter; John Schneider, a UPI photographer; and Arnaud de Borchgrave, *Newsweek Magazine* Senior Editor and Chief European Correspondent. During the next two days the three civilians would get much more than they had bargained for.

Arnaud de Borchgrave was no naive journalistic rookie or stranger to war. He had parachuted into Dien Bien Phu in 1954, and he had gone to the Belgian Congo in 1960. Now the *Newsweek Magazine* editor would be on hand to witness the battle for Hill 400 and the rest of Nui Cay Tre Ridge. In the coming hours he would be wounded, and he would see the real war, the dirty war fought by the Grunts and the helicopter crews. Arnaud de Borchgrave would survive, and he would be medevaced to safety by a Marine Corps H-34 on the afternoon of September 28. From his handwritten notes would come the most riveting, compelling, and compassionate first-hand account of the Vietnam War, or of *any* war. The notes scribbled by Arnaud de Borchgrave on the slopes of Hill 400 would first be published in *Newsweek Magazine* on October 10, 1966. With the written consent of *Newsweek,* a transcript of that article is reprinted below:

THE CRUCIAL TEST: Just south of the Demilitarized Zone (DMZ) that runs along the border between North and South Vietnam, U. S. Marines and North Vietnamese regulars are now locked in one of the most crucial campaigns of the Vietnam war. For more than a month, units of North Vietnam's crack 324B Division have been seeking to seize control of "the Rockpile" -- a rugged 700-foot-high-outcropping which dominates the main valley approaches to northern South Vietnam. By last week the fight for the Rockpile had become the focal point of Operation Prairie, a Marine spoiling attack against North Vietnamese penetration from the DMZ. At stake in Operation Prairie is nothing less than a decisive test of whether the U. S. can defeat the North Vietnamese in their own backyard . . . . As a result, the fighting has grown so fierce that two weeks ago American casualties soared to a record 142 killed and 825 wounded. In the midst of the swirling battle last week was *Newsweek* Senior Editor Arnaud de Borchgrave, who was slightly wounded. Below is his report.

THE BATTLE FOR HILL 400

"I hope to occupy that hill by tonight," says Col. William Masterpool, the soft-spoken commander of the Third Battalion of the Fourth Marine Regiment. It is the morning of Sept. 27 and we are standing on the top of "Hill 363" (so designated because of its altitude in meters). The colonel is pointing to "Hill 400" -- control of which is vital to control of the Rockpile itself.

Eight hundred yards of jungle separate us from the objective. Everyone already had a three-day beard. We are handed a C-ration pack and rationed to one canteen of water each. Here is the record of the next 31 hours:

0930 [Hours, September 27, 1966] -- As we thread our way along the ridgeline between the two hills, I notice a few bone fragments on the trail. Then dried, bloodstained Marine flak jackets and fatigues. "What's this?" I whisper to the man behind me. The answer chills me. This was where a Marine company took 60 percent casualties during an earlier operation.

0940 -- We pass a skull on a stake at the side of the trail. A few yards further a crudely penned note on a branch says in English: "We come back kill marines." K for Kilo Company is ahead of us.

1005 -- After an exhausting climb, we reach the top of Hill 400. Point man stumbles over bamboo pole. It triggers claymore mine 3 yards back of him as well as several grenades strung from branches. Four casualties. Suddenly, machine gun fire opens up. Impossible to see where it is coming from. Marines return fire forward and on both flanks. Shouts of "Corpsman (medic)!"

1020 -- As I emerge in a small clearing, there's deafening explosion followed by shouts of "Incoming mortar!" I run a few feet, see old artillery hole and fall in. Five Marines land on top of me. Mortar shells impact all around us. I can't move and have trouble breathing. Mercifully, shelling stops after four minutes. One Marine is lying with his head half severed 3 feet from a hole he didn't quite make. Everyone seems to be shouting at once: "Quick! More ammo forward!" "Corpsman!" and "John's got his foot blown off." "Where's Mathews?" someone calls -- and is answered by "He's KIA (killed in action), sir."

1025 -- Capt. "Jay-Jay" Carroll of Miami, commander of Kilo company, sees me without a helmet. He says he never wears one, unhooks his own from his belt and throws it to me. I also pick up a flak jacket from a KIA.

1030 -- Casualties stagger back across small clearing where Marines have set up a 20-yard wide perimeter on both sides of trail. Marine gives me two hand grenades, saying "You may need these soon." Single rounds coming in from three sides of perimeter. Some Marines digging furiously while others provide covering fire. I peer over my hole and spot four NVAs crawling past no more than 50 feet below. I yell to Captain Carroll who is standing up ramrod straight under heavy fire a few feet away, giving orders to his radioman. Carroll pulls the pin from a grenade and hurls it over my head, throws three more before going back to his radio. I toss another one for good measure. A Marine shouts at me: "Release the spoon or the gooks may have time to toss it back."

1035 -- The chaplain, Capt. Stanley J. Beach of Sass City, Mich., stumbles by with wounded man slung around his shoulders. Marine in nearby hole shouts to a buddy: "I got a feeling they don't like us."

"Personality conflict," says the other.

1040 -- Lead squad falling back on perimeter. Carroll leads reinforcements forward -- forward being less than 100 yards away. Two machine guns keep up intense fire. NVA now have us almost surrounded. I have a terrible feeling I will never see my family again.

1043 -- First air strike. Two Phantoms scream in at treetop level, dropping napalm, then, on their second pass, 500 pound bombs. Fragments fly over our holes, thudding into trees. Two men get hit by shrapnel. "Not close enough," says Captain Carroll to the FAC (Forward Air Controller). I feel if it's any closer, we'll all get killed. But Carroll says the ordnance fell 200 meters away and he wants it 100 meters closer. Next strike comes in at 75 meters. This must be what an earthquake feels like.

1050 -- Captain Carroll leads his men forward again. We have a whole company, but only a few men can go forward at a time single file. Almost sure death for the point man. No sooner out of the perimeter than NVA machine gun fire starts up again. NVA still clinging to our positions. The closer they stick, the safer they feel from air strikes. More bombs and napalm.

1105 -- Second mortar attack. I crawl out of my hole to the rear of perimeter, hoping to be closer to the battalion CP (Command Post) if and when lull in fighting comes. I dive under thick tree trunk that was blown down by artillery. Nine more terrifying mortar explosions followed by the sickening cries of "Corpsman, over here." Chaplain Beach is still carrying wounded back to a bomb crater where we have requested a hoist lift by basket for the critical cases as soon as the choppers can make it in. Carroll says to one wounded man: "Nice going, Marine. Sure appreciate what you did up there."

1115 -- More air strikes, still just 100 meters away. I am going deaf. I can't hear what wounded Marine is asking me. Water, I think. He has a stomach wound so I just give him a few drops to wet his lips. Another Marine tells me NVA bodies are stacked up waist-deep on the trail, but no one can get near them because of automatic crossfire from both sides of jungle. He could see NVA dragging bodies away with vines tied to their ankles.

1130 -- Grenade rolls down to where Derek Taylor, the correspondent for Britain's *Guardian*, is crouching. Taylor, quick as lightning, grabs it, throws it downhill and flips back into his hole. It explodes a second later and doesn't so much as scratch him.

1145 -- Two MIA (missing in action) just outside the perimeter. Five volunteers go forward to look for them. One gets cut down by automatic fire. Carroll hurls a smoke bomb, tells FAC to drop ordnance 50 yards beyond where bomb lands, then takes cover. More air strikes.

1215 -- Finally, thank the Lord, a brief respite. Just occasional incoming sniper rounds. Keeping my head down, I make my way back to the bomb crater where emergency cases are waiting in the broiling sun. My remaining canteen is shared among the wounded. Most of the men from Kilo company, who left Hill 363 before me, have not had food or water in 24 hours.

1310 -- First chopper tries to hover overhead while basket is lowered. He is driven away by ground fire. On second try, pilot radios air too thin to hover and drops back into valley. On third try, one man is hoisted. Corpsman tells me he has about 30 minutes to live. Pilot radios he died in chopper on way to hospital at Dong Ha. Ten minutes later, two more are taken out. Rest must be carried back along trail to headquarters. NVA ground fire getting heavy.

1430 -- Arrive at Colonel Masterpool's CP. Engineers are carving an LZ (landing zone) out of the jungle with twenty-pound charges of high explosive. Every few minutes an engineer yells "Fire in the hole" and everyone scrambles for cover as another charge of TNT rattles your teeth and covers you in dust and tree bark. Colonel Masterpool is lying on the ground studying his map, quietly giving orders to artillery, air, and his company commanders. His calm voice restores my confidence, by now badly shaken. I catch his eye. "Do you think you've got a story yet?" he wisecracks.

1500 -- Fierce fighting again at Kilo which is taking place on the lip of Hill 400. All hell seems to be breaking loose 200 yards away in straight line (about 400 yards by trail). Sniper rounds begin whistling across the CP. Once again the NVA appears to be working around our flanks. Marines spray bushes below the CP. Wounded still coming. After blasting some 250 pounds of TNT the LZ still looks depressingly small. I figure that it won't be completed before sundown and begin digging my own hole.

1630 -- After 90 minutes of intermittent digging, my hole also looks depressingly small. I lie in it to try it out, but it's a foot and a half short and only 2 feet deep. Blisters on both hands are open and bleeding. Six feet from my hole, UPI photographer John Schneider has found an NVA hole with log roofing. I am envious.

1700 -- Hungry, nothing to eat or drink. Schneider shares his last sip of water with me. We agree mortar attack is coming as the enemy can pinpoint our position from all the LZ blasting that is still going on. Schneider goes forward and I crawl into my hole and wait. Sniper fire continues, punctuated with the chatter of Marine machine guns. Still rough at Kilo. Air strikes almost continuous. Word is that the fighting is still seesawing across 100 yards of terrain. Marine bodies are being laid out just behind our holes.

0220 [five hours before dawn on the morning of September 28] -- Beautiful cloudless night but cold (low 50s). Smell from decomposing bodies makes me nauseated and I pull my poncho over my face. Now immune to sound of gunfire and confident will pull through and get out by chopper tomorrow. Then, I think that it won't be possible because there are too many wounded to go first.

0230 -- Musings interrupted by first shattering mortar blast. It knocks me out of my hole. I quickly roll back in as second, third and fourth -- all the way up to twelve -- impact in CP area. Again heart-rending shouts of "Corpsman!" Twenty feet below my hole six Marines are wounded -- six men of a seven-man squad knocked out of action.

0820 -- Fourth mortar attack. I lose count of number of rounds. Fear is a hard thing to dominate. Wounded hobbling in from bushes. I figure it won't be long before my number comes up. Terry Sicilia of Pasco, Wash., bleeding and waiting for corpsman, tells me it's his third Purple Heart in six months. "I guess it's home for me."

0900 -- Artillery now whistling in just ahead of us. One of our own 105-mm shells falls short -- smack into CP perimeter, 4 yards from Chaplain Beach's hole. Five more wounded. Beach's left leg shattered. He's also bleeding from the stomach. All he says is: "My God, I hope the choppers make it today." One Marine begins crying when his buddy dies. Artillery is instantly called off. Air strikes ordered instead. FAC reports enemy mortar position spotted. In minutes direct hits are reported.

1010 -- Fifth mortar attack catches me some 50 yards from my hole. I zigzag back and literally throw myself into my hole. A Marine lands on top of me and is hit in the back with the third burst. I push the Marine off me and lift up the top of his fatigues. A piece of shrapnel is sticking out of his back. Someone says my arm is bleeding. I don't feel anything, but there are three small holes in a neat little row just below my elbow. Mortar fragments. My helmet, already peppered with dents when I got it from a KIA (I had returned my first one to Captain Carroll), now has a few more holes in it. James Bourgoin of Great Falls, Mont., is the wounded Marine next to me. He is 19. He tells me that he and the chaplain were going to have a long chat soon about a personal problem; his fiancee is Catholic and he is Protestant.

1045 -- UPI's John Schneider brings good news from Kilo where he had gone for the third time (I would like to believe he doesn't know what fear means, but know I am wrong). The Marines have overrun several NVA machine gun nests and captured a Chinese gun mounted on wheels. Intelligence also reports we have forced the CP of the 42nd NVA Regiment off Hill 426 -- the lip that protrudes from Hill 400.

1205 -- LZ is getting bigger -- 450 pounds of dynamite have gone into it by now. Chopper should be coming in soon. Barely have time to sigh in relief.

1210 -- Sixth mortar attack. Back in my hole. It's now almost routine and I am no longer quite as scared. Nearest one this time landed 20 feet away. I am now convinced that one can survive anything but a direct mortar hit.

1355 -- The worse yet. NVA have infiltrated back. Firing breaks out on all sides. "Quick! All ammo forward!" yells a sergeant. Kilo is being battered again. "All corpsmen to Kilo," comes another order. The ground-air liaison team at Kilo -- three men -- has just been wiped out by a mortar hit. Someone shouts, "We've run out of battle dressings." I hand over my first-aid kit.

1440 -- "Every available man in the line," shouts a lieutenant. Grenades are issued to the correspondents. Another voice says: "We need more men to hump ammo over to Kilo." A wounded man tears off his WIA (wounded in action) tag and lifts two boxes of ammo in each hand. As he passes the CP on his way to Kilo, Colonel Masterpool calls out: "What's your name, son?" I can't hear the man's answer, but I see Colonel Masterpool pat him gently on the back. Several shrapnel casualties are now moving into the firing line.

1445 -- Air strikes coming every 30 seconds. The ground trembles continuously. Once again, I feel the end is near -- at least for me. I get an uncontrollable case of shakes. I wonder if I ever had what it takes to be a Marine and conclude that I never did and don't now.

1500 -- Miraculously, the firing dies down. Choppers are ordered in -- fast. They had been hovering one mountain range away. The first one is once again driven away by ground fire. Rocket-firing Hueys silence the fire. Then the choppers begin coming every two minutes, dumping ammo and water -- the first water in 48 hours for most Marines -- and taking out the casualties.

1600 -- The KIA are now being loaded. The rotor downdraft blows the ponchos off the bodies. There is one man without a head.

<u>1612</u> -- Schneider and I jump into a chopper with two new casualties just up from Kilo. Schneider only leaving because he has run out of film. He plans to return tomorrow morning.

HMM-265 gradually increased its share of the perilous medical evacuation flights. Major John L. Driefer recalls the hazards involved in hovering over the trees while trying to reel the casualties up on the hoist. He never knew for sure where the NVA soldiers were or whether or not they would open fire. On one mission he carefully hovered his H-46 over the trees and lowered a wire litter in an effort to pick up a serious casualty. Buffeted by the rotor downwash, the Grunts got the wounded man strapped into the litter. However, the litter had been rigged for a Huey, not for an H-46. There was no way to get the litter up through the belly "hell-hole" hatch and into the cabin. Stymied, the crew chief winched the litter up snug against the bottom of the fuselage of the H-46. Then Major Driefer flew to a secure area where they landed and carried the injured Grunt safely inside of the helicopter cabin.

The H-34s were a better choice for up-through-the-trees medevacs because the hoist on an H-34 is mounted outside of the fuselage above the cabin door. When a casualty was hoisted up by an H-34, the crew chief and gunner reached out, grabbed the steel cable, and swung the injured man inside. This process undoubtedly terrified many wounded Grunts, but it saved a lot of lives.

<u>September 28, 1966, 1800 Hours</u>: By the late afternoon on September 28, the Grunts finally drove the NVA off of Hill 400. The fighting had been some of the most savage of the war to date. Hill 400 had been an NVA fortress, and the North Vietnamese had not given it up without a fight. *Time Magazine* would chronicle the fierce battle in its October 7, 1966, issue. The *Time* writers reported that the victorious Marine Grunts "found a Communist regimental command post replete with underground rooms and trenches."

Hill 400 was now in Marine hands, but the *Time* article pointed out that farther down the Nui Cay Tre Ridge, "there were plenty of Reds left." That was true, and in fact their numbers were being replenished from the jigsaw trenches and concrete bunkers in the

DMZ only two and a half miles to the north. Also, a third North Vietnamese Army Division, the 341st, was massing just north of the DMZ near the coast. As soon as the monsoon rains began, it could drive southward along the flatlands toward Dong Ha, Quang Tri, and Hue.

News of the brutal and horrible fighting for Hill 400 received world-wide notice. Addressing 150,000 worshipers in Saint Peter's Square, Pope Paul VI called for negotiations in order to stop the carnage. *Krasnaya Zuezda*, the Soviet Defense Ministry newspaper, complained that "Russian military experts" assisting the North Vietnamese with their antiaircraft missiles had been endangered. That same day as if on cue, Soviet Deputy Premier Vladimir Novikov publicly announced that the Soviet Union would provide further economic and military aid to North Vietnam. But to the Marines on Nui Cay Tre Ridge, all of this hand-wringing and communist-bloc sabre-rattling meant nothing.

> Victory at all costs, victory in spite of all terror, victory however hard and long the road may be; for without victory there is no survival!
> -- (Winston Churchill; in the House of Commons, May 1940)

Neither papal pleas from Rome nor Russian and Chinese threats of military intervention concerned the Marines in South Vietnam. The Marines had a more immediate problem to contend with, the entrenched North Vietnamese soldiers remaining on the western end of Nui Cay Tre Ridge. From their lofty perch on top of Hill 400, the Grunts could see their final objective, Hill 484, one and a half miles farther west along the ridge. Slowly and methodically they began to work their way toward it.

HMM-263 got a new commanding officer, Lieutenant Colonel M. T. Jannell, on October 1. He quickly dove into his new role. The NVA began employing recoilless rifles against the Barrelhouse H-34s, but the durable helicopters escaped without damage. Meanwhile, General English left Dong Ha and used a VMO-2 slick to make courtesy calls on the various battalion command posts so that he could spend time with the Grunts in the field.

October 2, 1966: The Grunts still fought their way westward along the crest of the ridge, and the Bonnie-Sue helicopters from HMM-265 often got the frags to keep them supplied. A new helicopter assault into the flat and lush valley just east of Dong Ha Mountain at YD-081614 also involved my squadron. One of the landings was aborted at the last minute due to an artillery fire mission. Fortunately there was no repetition of the artillery shoot-down disaster that had plagued HMM-161 in September.

First Lieutenant Arnold "Arnie" Reiner had arrived in Vietnam with me in May 1966. However, Arnie was in the first group of our HMM-265 pilots who had transferred to HMM-164 in order to diversify the squadron tour rotation dates. Arnie was a free spirit who heard and heeded the unique sound of the proverbial different drumbeat. He did things his own way. Arnie even had his nickname, instead of his surname, stenciled on the standard pilot's nametag on his flight suits. This departure from normal military protocol would later cause him to be erroneously identified in writing by the Grunts as "Captain Arnie."

Arnie and his HAC, James A. "Shakey" Hollis, got fragged for an emergency extraction on the late afternoon of October 2. West of Quang Tri, a Recon team had come under attack by a larger NVA force, and reinforcement of the team did not appear to be possible. The Recons were holding the top of a steep and heavily wooded hill, and there was no place for a helicopter to land nearby. Fixed-wing aircraft, gunships, and an H-34 had tried to help, but the H-34 had gotten shot up and had to head for home.

Arnie and Shakey realized that the Recons were defending rough terrain. A helicopter pilot's only option was to hover over the trees and try to hoist the team members aboard. Slipping down toward the hill in a power-on approach, they waved off when an NVA machinegun opened fire on their H-46. Years later, Arnie would still recall the Recon radioman's pleading request, "Come back! Don't Leave!" or words to that effect.

The pilots were down to around 800 pounds of fuel, but they decided to try again and come in from a different direction. With Shakey flying the helicopter, they approached, stabilized in a hover, and got ready to reel down the hoist cable. Then the shooting started: POP! POP! POP-POP-POP-POP!

To Arnie the gunfire was so loud and so close that he first

thought it was his own gunners firing. But then his helicopter gunners *really did* start shooting, and they blasted away at the enemy with their .50 caliber guns, right behind Arnie's cockpit.

Lt. A. Reiner, a copilot, was wounded in the action.
-- (*HMM-164 Command Chronology*; October 2, 1966)

Enemy rounds smashed up through the floor and into the cockpit. The large Master Caution Panel light opened its dreaded amber eye. The fuselage shuddered under the barrage of gunfire, and Arnie felt a shower of flying plexiglass and hot shrapnel dig into his arm. Shakey yanked the collective up and dove over the side of the hill. Enemy fire had shot out the ICS, so the pilots resorted to screaming at each other in an effort to communicate.

Arnie felt sure they were going to crash. He yelled at the top of his voice to Shakey: "THE RIDGE! THE RIDGE!" Arnie's hands were glued to the collective and cyclic, and he dared not release the controls to point at the peak and cliffs just ahead of them. Shakey understood. If they could clear the ridge before mushing into the trees, the high terrain would protect them from North Vietnamese rifle fire.

But the helicopter did not crash. The sturdy H-46 held together, and within minutes Arnie and Shakey landed at the Citadel in Hue. As it turned out, other helicopters soon ferried reinforcements to a suitable landing area, and the four-man Recon team got reinforced.

Inside of the Alpha-Med field hospital at Phu Bai, a corpsman used a scalpel and tweezers to laboriously pick shrapnel out of Arnie's anesthetized arms and elbow. The corpsman finally finished his task and told Arnie that he was medically free to return to his squadron.

Wondering what time it was, Arnie pulled his wrist-watch from the zippered left-breast pocket of his flight suit, where he always kept it while flying. While in the H-46 cockpit there is no need to look at one's wrist-watch, because the instrument panel clock glares at both pilots. To a pilot in flight, minutes of fuel remaining and elapsed time are crucial, but time of day means little or nothing. Now, outside of Alpha-Med, Arnie saw that his watch had stopped keeping time three hours earlier. A sliver of steel shrapnell had impaled the crystal and metal watch case. "Close!" Arnie thought.

He wandered toward the airstrip and tried to figure out how he could find a helicopter ride back to his squadron.

October 3, 1966: HMM-265 flew over 800 ARVN soldiers into the coastal flatlands so that they could mill around in relative safety. Meanwhile, on Nui Cay Tre Ridge the Marine Grunts fought their way toward Hill 484. Two of the supporting H-46s from HMM-164 got hit going into Razorback Valley, but the crews escaped injury in their lightly damaged helicopters.

First Lieutenant Otto H. Fritz, a friend of mine from MARCAD Class 42-63, had been an H-34 pilot in HMM-161. He had arrived in Vietnam in March 1966, but after six months of flying H-34s he had taken his last flight on August 11. Otto then got the closest thing to the kiss of death for a helicopter pilot in Vietnam. He had gotten reassigned as a FAC for the Third Marines.

Otto learned first-hand what Nui Cay Tre Ridge was like. Where there were trails, the NVA had camouflaged fighting holes scattered along likely avenues of approach. The enemy had cut log-reinforced steps into the sides of the steep hills. Forward visibility through the dense jungle undergrowth could be as little as five feet ahead of you. After a firefight at night, Otto would lie prone on the ground and listen for movement in the jungle, where the NVA dead often lay only ten to twelve feet away. There was no sleep at all for days at a time. Otto remembers watching one of his friends, a Grunt sergeant, desperately trying to save some of his wounded men during a firefight:

He charged a machinegun bunker with hand grenades, trying to save some guys. He didn't have to do it. He got slaughtered. He had two kids.

Otto and the Grunts lived together and fought together. In addition to the North Vietnamese, filth and vermin were their constant enemies. Land-leaches, similar in appearance to inchworms, infested the ground and quickly attached themselves to exposed human flesh. Crawling along the ground each day, digging in, unable to bathe for weeks at a time, the Grunts stayed caked with a repugnant oily combination of perspiration and grime.

They wore no underclothing, no type of skivvies or tee-shirts. Underwear of any kind would have been unbearably hot, and it would have quickly rotted away in the putrid wet environment. In general, Otto and the Grunts went without water, went hungry, went without sleep, and lived under the threat of imminent death from mortars, artillery, and bullets. During the night they often curled up in their fighting holes and listened to the constant moans and screams of the wounded men, both Asian and American, lying around them. Often during their daytime prowls through the jungle, some exhausted Grunts would pray for a firefight just so they could stop and rest for a while.

Many academicians and schoolboys naively believe that the worst part of war is merely getting shot at. Yet, that is only a small fraction of the horror of war. In his riveting work, *NAM*, Mark Baker captured the true essence of warfare and explained: "War is not killing. Killing is the easiest part of the whole thing." Over the centuries the weapons and tools of war have changed greatly, but the lot of the infantryman has changed little.

> If a man had told me 12 months ago that men could stand such hardships, I would have called him a fool!
> -- (Lieutenant James H. Langhorne, Stonewall Brigade, Confederate States Army; on January 8, 1862)

Many helicopter pilots who had been converted into FACs would survive their tour with the Grunts and eventually return to the cockpit. Otto would turn out to be one of the fortunate FACs who would live to fly helicopters again, but he would never forget his six months with the Grunts of the Third Marines. But unlike Otto, many other FACs never left Vietnam alive. One of my friends, Captain Gary W. Hoglund, got converted from a Marine Corps pilot into a FAC. His life would instantly be snuffed out by an exploding artillery shell on May 17 of the following year.

<u>Nui Cay Tre Ridge, October 4, 1966, 0930 Hours</u>: First Platoon, Mike Company, crawled up the steep slope toward the peak of Hill 484. Machinegun fire and a shower of grenades from above drove the Grunts back. A movement around the NVA flank

also failed, so the Grunts hunkered down and called in Marine Air. Throughout the rest of the day the log and concrete bunkers on the crest of the ridge got pounded by fixed-wing and artillery. HMM-265 flew over 5000 pounds of supplies, ammunition, and water to the Grunts on the slopes of the ridge. The Bonnie-Sue helicopters also rescued one Recon who had somehow gotten detached from his unit and lost in the hills.

October 5, 1966, 1000 Hours: Mike Company again assaulted the hilltop in the face of almost point-blank machinegun fire. This time the Grunts would not be denied, and they shot and bayoneted their way through the enemy fortifications. By 1330 Hours the NVA soldiers who were still alive had abandoned their bunkers and trenches and fled westward into the jungle. The battle for Nui Cay Tre Ridge slowly sputtered to an end. MAG-16 helicopters quickly flew to Hill 484 to bring water to the fatigued Grunts and to evacuate the casualties. Most of the work fell to the H-46 crews because of the high altitude and the heavy lifting capability required.

Colonel Masterpool's Third Battalion had driven the entrenched NVA out of their fortress on the crest of the ridge. Thereafter, for the duration of the war, Nui Cay Tre Ridge was universally known as "Mutter Ridge" because of the radio call-sign of the victorious 3rd Battalion, 4th Marines.

Of course, Marine casualties had not been light. One of the dead was the 29 year old commander of Kilo Company, the leader so frequently mentioned in the *Newsweek Magazine* article, Captain James J. "Jay-Jay" Carroll. He had not taken part in the final assault on Hill 484, but instead had remained on Hill 400 to help coordinate helicopter missions and direct artillery fire. He died there when an artillery shell slammed into the Grunt command post. Later he would be posthumously awarded the Navy Cross for valor in combat on Hill 400. Also, the Marine artillery base at Cam Lo would be renamed Camp Carroll in honor of this former charismatic commander of Kilo Company.

Dong Ha, October 6, 1966: MAG-16 helicopter crews began a gradual stand-down now that Mutter Ridge was held by the Grunts. HMM-265 had two H-46s grounded at Dong Ha due to battle damage, but the flying in the mountains was not completely over yet. One of our H-46s came under heavy fire at YD-998587 in the valley right at the base of the western slope of Dong Ha Mountain. And one of my peers was about to get the scare of his life. He was about to get shot in the right heel, just like me.

Captain Gerard R. "Gerry" Lear and First Lieutenant Lynn M. LaPointe had both been with HMM-265 since their arrival in Vietnam in May. On October 6 they drew what sounded like a routine medevac frag, but as they zipped down just to the west of the Razorback, rifle fire repeatedly holed their H-46. Gerry got shrapnel in his arms, and Lynn took a round squarely in his right heel. But Lynn proved to be luckier than I had been in August.

Capt Gerard R. LEAR 087582/7335 HOSTILE, Shrapnel wounds caused by small arms . . . .

1stLt Lynn M. LaPOINTE 091221 HOSTILE, Wound in right heel from small arms fire. Two days confined to quarters.

-- (MAG-16 Casualty List; October 6, 1966)

The enemy round ripped through structural braces in the fuselage and had partially spent its inertia before striking the thick heel of Lynn's boot. It penetrated all the way through the heavy leather heel, but there it stopped, barely nicking through the skin of Lynn's foot. When he got to the field hospital, Lynn got antiseptic and a small bandage for his heel. He retained his perforated flight boot as a unique and personal souvenir from Vietnam. (Ironically, although Lynn would survive his combat tour in Vietnam, he would die in an automobile accident shortly after his return to the United States.)

USS Vancouver, in the South China Sea: Nine miles east of Dong Ha the Cua Viet River empties into the South China Sea. Twelve miles offshore the Marines of the Special Landing Force (SLF) slowly sailed back and forth parallel to the coast of South Vietnam just below the DMZ. Aboard the _USS Iwo Jima_ (LPH-2) and its escort ships, the Grunts of the SLF, 1st Battalion, 26th Marines, deserved the rest. They had battled the NVA from July 16 through September 25, over two months. Every day they had slugged it out with the enemy infantry in the hostile flatlands around Con Thien and Gio Linh. The SLF helicopter squadron, HMM-363, had flown ashore and operated under the control of MAG-16 during the worst of the fighting. Now everyone was back aboard ship for some badly needed rest and regrouping.

Aboard one of the escort ships, the *USS Vancouver* (LPD-2), was the only officer in the United States Navy that I personally knew, my younger brother, Ensign O. Lee Sturkey Jr. My brother, one of the 26 officers in ship's company, was engrossed in the floating poker game in one of the vacant troop officer staterooms. Empty coffee cups and cigarette butts littered the table, and several paperback novels, magazines, and graphic *skin* books were available for leisurely reading. The Marine Corps combat cargo officer, Major Fred Houle, was in the game, along with several junior Navy officers.

Since there was no medical emergency aboard ship at the moment, the ship's doctor, Lieutenant Samuel D'Amato, also participated in the nickel-dime-quarter game. Now slouched back in his chair, Sam hailed from West Chester, Pennsylvania, a town of about 15,000 souls located roughly 25 miles west of Philadelphia. As usual, Sam was dressed for the occasion: baseball cap, tee-shirt, khaki trousers, black shoes, no socks, and no belt. The war? It might as well have been a thousand miles away. But then the squawk box came alive with a metallic rasp: "Mister D'Amato, please lay to the flight deck."

Another interruption! At least once a day, Sam's professional medical services were needed. Some bumbling sailor had probably cut himself in the machine shop, burned himself in the galley, or smashed his finger with a hammer while chipping paint on the hull of the ship, they surmised. Sam tossed his cards on the table, slid back in his chair, rose, and shuffled his way toward the door.

"Hurry back, Sam."

"Yeah -- we need your money."

The poker game continued. As usual they would deal Sam back in as soon as he returned from wherever he was going. He would be gone for 30 minutes at the most, they knew from months of experience.

A Marine Corps H-34 was sitting on the *Vancouver* flight deck with its engine running and rotors turning when Sam arrived. "Oh, no!" Sam thought to himself. Once a week or so he had to do this. The Marine helicopter would fly him over to one of the other escort ships where a doctor was needed. Maybe to the *Thomaston*, but certainly not to the *Iwo Jima*, Sam hoped. The high-ranking "brass" aboard the large helicopter carrier would frown on his casual attire. But it was too late to go get dressed, so Sam took the familiar black medical field bag that a corpsman handed to him and crawled aboard the H-34.

Sam settled into a web troop seat on the left side of the helicopter, away from the open door to avoid the slipstream. He always hated riding in Marine Corps H-34s. They were filthy dirty, the engine noise was deafening, they rattled in flight, and Sam had never put a great deal of faith in their mechanical reliability. But it would be only a two minute flight to any of the ships near the *Vancouver*. Even in a rickety old H-34, a two minute ride could not be too bad, Sam reasoned.

The radial Wright engine roared to full power, the helicopter shook and rattled, and they took off and headed skyward. A full minute later, Sam noted that they were still climbing. With surprise and a tinge of disgust, he wondered how high the pilots intended to climb during a half mile flight to another ship. But the helicopter continued to climb, and Sam looked out of the hatch and saw the afternoon sun at their ten o'clock position. To his surprise, he saw that the Marine helicopter was boring its way westward toward the coast of Vietnam.

Rescue the perishing, care for the dying,
Snatch them in pity from sin and the grave;
-- (Fanny J. Crosby; in "Rescue the Perishing")

After ten minutes the H-34 flew over the beach, far below. Sam watched the Marine crew chief and gunner clearing their M-60 machineguns and straightening out their linked ammunition belts. The crew chief donned his flak jacket and pulled down his protective helmet visor, covering his entire face above his mouth. To Sam, he looked like a medieval knight preparing for battle.

"Where're we going?" Sam yelled.

The crew chief could not hear him.

Sam unstrapped, grabbed the sleeve of the crew chief's flight suit, and screamed above the deafening noise of the engine and rotors: "WHERE'RE WE GOING?" The crew chief raised his helmet visor, pointed his gloved right forefinger to the west, and shouted an unintelligible answer to Sam.

The H-34 bored due west for 30 to 40 minutes. The gunner and crew chief ignored Sam and intently scanned the terrain below. Sam could not hear them, but he could see their lips moving as they talked into their helmet microphones while speaking to each other and to the pilots on the ICS. Then the crew chief bent over, raised his helmet visor, put his face right in front of Sam's face, and bellowed: "Get Ready!"

"Ready for what?" Sam wondered. Then the bottom fell out, it seemed. Down they went, shuddering, shaking, and spiraling earthward. Sam kept a death-grip on the metal tubing of the web seat and watched the green earth coming closer and closer. Green trees flashed by the open hatch, and then the helicopter slammed to the ground.

"GET OUT! GET OUT!"

Sam leaped out of the hatch with his medical bag in hand. He had no idea where he was or where he was supposed to go. Instinctively he crouched down in the chest-high grass to wait until the helicopter rotors stopped. But to his abject horror, the pilots cranked in full power and took off. All alone now, Sam watched in disbelief as the H-34 headed for the clouds. "This really can't be happening," Sam thought as the roar of the helicopter engine and the popping of the rotors slowly faded away.

Then Sam heard men yelling and hollering, and he turned and saw the Marine Grunts. There were about 15 of them on top of a steep wooded hill about 125 yards or more away. Between Sam and the Marines on the hill lay a tangled mass of jagged rocks, tree stumps, and sharp-edged high grass -- elephant grass, he later would be told.

The animated Marines were waving and yelling something, so Sam began climbing and crawling uphill toward them. Up the slope he went, slipping, stumbling, and sliding. He was almost halfway there now. As Sam got closer he could see the Marines more clearly. They were all jumping around and yelling to him. What were they trying to say? . . . What? . . . .

Sam pressed ahead, exhausted and drained. Not much farther

to go now, he thought. But the Marines ahead now screamed at him. What were they yelling? What was it? "My? . . . Mine? . . . MINES! MINES!"

Sam ignored the warning. With all logic and reason cast aside, he crawled the last 20 yards into the Marine perimeter. It felt great just to be alive!

As it turned out, one of the Marines had suffered a serious head injury. Their corpsman had radioed to base and asked that a *real* doctor be flown to the hill to treat the injured man before he was helicoptered to a field hospital. Why the helicopter had not landed him on top of the hill, Sam never knew. Maybe it had been the mines, or perhaps it had something to do with the nearby trees.

Sam patched up the injured Marine as best he could. The helicopter returned, landed, and Sam crawled inside with the casualty. They flew to a primitive field hospital somewhere, and the Grunt was carried away. Then the H-34 flew Sam back to the *Vancouver*, back to civilization and sanity.

Sam stumbled back into the stateroom and found the poker game still in progress. Everything was as it had been when he had left, and for a brief moment Sam trifled with the notion that perhaps he had hallucinated the events of the past two hours. Could it really have happened? Could he have been caught up in some type of time-warp? Then one of the poker players noticed Sam's arrival. Sam looked disheveled, ashen, almost catatonic; his treasured baseball cap had been lost, and his khaki trousers were ripped and covered with dirt. Ever so slowly, Sam told his shipmates his harrowing tale.

Dong Ha, October 6, 1966, 2030 Hours: Now that the fighting in the mountains had entered a lull, many of the helicopters began to leave Dong Ha and straggle back toward home plate at Marble Mountain and Phu Bai. However, one ill-fated Bonnie-Sue crew from my squadron would never arrive home alive.

I did not mean to be killed today.
-- (Vicomte de Turenne, a French soldier; as he lay dying at the battle of Salzbach in 1675)

A cold rain and low clouds descended on northern I-Corps in Vietnam by nightfall on October 6. Nonetheless, the crew of EP-154 welcomed the news that they were to leave Dong Ha and head for home. Days and nights of primitive living and cold food would be behind them as soon as they reached the relative comfort of their tents at Marble Mountain. The four man crew quickly readied their H-46 for the 45 minute flight.

Up in the cockpit the pilot, Captain William E. "Pappy" Johnson, whose hometown was Tallahassee, Florida, got ready to launch. He knew that except for the rotten weather it should be a routine IFR flight. They would climb up into the rainy night sky and radio the controller at Phu Bai Approach Control on 315.5 megacycles while they tracked inbound on the Phu Bai TACAN. The coastal plain was totally flat between Dong Ha and Phu Bai, so there should be no radio navigation problems or obstacles to avoid. Ronald E. "Ron" Pfeifer, the Gentle Giant who had been one of my five tentmates, settled into the copilot's spot on the left and strapped himself into his armored seat. Gunnery Sergeant Howard D. Strouse and Staff Sergeant David L. Moser took their places back in the cabin, and one passenger bound for Phu Bai also crawled inside.

Bob Mills was still the MAG-16 helicopter fragger at Dong Ha, and he recalls his squadronmates saying goodbye. Then he watched them take off and saw their flashing red anticollision lights slowly disappear into the gloomy night sky. The 43 mile flight down to Phu Bai took slightly over 20 minutes. Pappy and Ron dropped off their passenger there, and then they took off again and headed south toward Marble Mountain and home. But they never arrived; they vanished.

For some reason the four HMM-265 crewmen and their Bonnie-Sue H-46 got swallowed up by the dark Indochinese night. No one would *ever* solve the riddle. Speaking of Pappy years later, Bob Mills summed it up: "He flew to Phu Bai, took off for Marble Mountain, and was never heard from again."

6 Oct 66: Two pilots and two crewmen in EP-154 missing in action enroute [from] Phu Bai to Marble Mountain Air Facility. -- (*HMM-265 Command Chronology*; October 6, 1966)

EP-154 departed IFR from Phu Bai and never made the expected radio vector contact with either "Panama" or "Waterboy" on Monkey Mountain near Da Nang. It was only 39 direct air miles from Phu Bai down to Marble Mountain, but helicopters normally flew a circuitous route far out over the ocean before turning south. The 3907 foot high peak of the mountain at Hai Van Pass was nothing to be trifled with when flying IFR at night in the rain and clouds.

An unofficial IFR approach into either Marble Mountain or Da Nang was available to all pilots. To land at Marble Mountain, pilots simply tuned in Channel 62 on the TACAN and intercepted the 088 degree radial at the eleven mile DME fix. This put the helicopter about ten and a half miles out over the sea, since the transmitter was less than a mile inland from the beach. From the eleven mile fix, you just tracked westward toward the beach while dropping down to 500 feet for a downwind entry into the traffic pattern to land at Marble Mountain. However, since there was no radio contact with EP-154 after it left Phu Bai, it is doubtful that the Bonnie-Sue H-46 ever got past the many towering and mist-shrouded mountains between Phu Bai and Da Nang.

Flying in the night rain with fog was a death warrant.
-- (H. Lee Bell; in *1369*)

What happened? Most pilots voice a distaste for IFR flying at night in the mountains, but Pappy and Ron had flown from Dong Ha to Phu Bai without difficulty. If they had been worried about the last half of their trip, they could have stayed at Phu Bai overnight. If their UHF communications had failed after takeoff, a flight without radar vectors still should not have posed a major problem. Their TACAN would have given them both distance and bearing, and it would have enabled them to navigate their way out over the sea and around the mountains. If both the TACAN and the UHF had failed, they still could have found their way by using the low frequency Automatic Direction Finder (ADF) beacon at Da Nang. Dual engine failure? Failure of both electrical generators? Probably not. The chances of such simultaneous failures were astronomically remote. Sudden flight control failure? Spatial disorientation? Or, could a rare and sinister TACAN forty-degree-lock-on malfunction have lured them into the side of a mountain? No one knows.

By 0930 Hours the next morning, MAG-16 knew that the H-46 was missing. Search aircraft launched, but they were hampered by poor visibility and rain that still shrouded the huge mountains north of Da Nang. Two days later on October 9, a Navy S-2F airplane with Magnetic Anomaly Detection Gear assisted in the hunt for EP-154. The search area was eventually widened to cover vast areas of the South China Sea where floating wreckage might have been carried by the ocean current, but the search teams found nothing at all. On the afternoon of October 10, the hunt for the missing Bonnie-Sue helicopter was officially abandoned.

USMC and USAF SAR Facilities terminated search at 1345 [Hours] 10 Oct 66.
-- (*MAG-16 Command Chronology*; October 10, 1966)

Ten months older than me, Ron had been a soft-spoken and courteous 25 year old native of Bellerose, New York. Thinking back, I never recall hearing Ron utter an unkind word about anyone. That was not his manner. Ron had been one of my five tentmates, and he was the first one of us to die.

Captain Richard O. "Harpo" Harper: In a combat environment he was called "Harpo" by those both above and beneath him in rank. In addition to his pilot's duties, Harpo had been the squadron S-4 officer (logistics and supply), but he made his greatest contribution to HMM-265 from the HAC's seat in the H-46 cockpit. A fearless pilot, an admired administrator, and a professional Marine, Harpo simply got the job done.

Harpo and I had flown EP-163, Bonnie-Sue nine-dash-three, two months earlier on the fateful eighth night of August. Escorted by Huey gunships, we had descended into the dark valley 1200 meters east of Razorback Ridge. Twenty feet above the ground we suddenly had been drilled by enemy fire, and our entire crew got hit. Harpo had taken a round in his right hand and another in his chest, but he hung on and saved the day. He had kept us flying, and we had limped back to Dong Ha and safety.

Capt Richard O, HARPER 071918/7335 HMM-265, HOSTILE, 8 Aug 66, 8 1/2 miles WNW of Dong Ha; wound, missile; penetrating left chest through and through . . . .
-- (MAG-16 Casualty List; August 8, 1966)

After leaving Charlie-Med, Harpo convalesced at the NSA hospital at Da Nang. Harpo initially felt somewhat sorry for himself, but he quickly got jolted back to reality by a young wounded corpsman lying in the bunk next to him. The corpsman was a big and lanky black lad who was partially mummified in bandages. He had suffered multiple wounds and was getting stiff injections of Demerol on a regular basis to suppress the pain. Being pretty well immobilized and anesthetized, the corpsman drifted in and out of consciousness. When he could speak, the young man kept mumbling over and over: "I was *beautiful* -- I was *beautiful*." With his eyes closed and his lips curled up into a secret and knowing smile, he kept repeating: "*Beautiful -- beautiful -- I was beautiful*."

The young black corpsman had lived in the Watts section of Los Angeles, California. Harpo never learned his name, but when the Demerol was not working its magic, Harpo engaged the lad in conversation. The young man had always wanted to be a Marine, he murmured, but he could not enlist in the Marine Corps because he had "lifted some hub caps" while in high school. He settled for the Navy, became a corpsman, and managed to get assigned to a Marine Rifle Company. Not quite a Marine, but the next best thing, he said.

Then came the ambush and firefight. Harpo learned that the corpsman had repeatedly ignored his own safety to run forward and drag wounded Marines back out of the line of enemy fire. But now, when he was conscious in the hospital ward, the wounded lad would accept no credit for bravery under fire. However, he confided to Harpo that he got the chance to do a little free-lance fighting on his own. He even "gave orders to the lieutenant," he whispered.

Lying next to Harpo in the ward, the wounded corpsman seemed oblivious to those caring for him. Through the sedatives he smiled that terrible and secret survivor's smile. Time after time, Harpo could hear him softly mouthing the same words: "*Beautiful*

-- man, I was really *beautiful* . . . ."

General Walt made his daily trip through the ward, and Harpo watched him when he stopped by the young corpsman's bunk. The wounded corpsman lay unconscious while wrapped in an artificial anesthetic blanket. General Walt quietly leaned over and pinned the Silver Star on the white sheets. To Harpo, the black lad truly was *beautiful*. Many years later, Harpo would tell me that he had been proud and honored to be lying next to the young corpsman.

The wound in Harpo's chest slowly healed. The entry wound in the left side of his chest and the exit wound in his back had been enlarged by the surgeon, who had snipped away the surrounding flesh. I looked worse than it really was, Harpo would later recall, almost like he had been shot through the chest with a cannon. But now the scar tissue had formed into ugly bluish-black depressions streaked with red -- bullet holes.

Harpo finally became fully ambulatory and was medically released to return to HMM-265. Although able to walk unaided, the weeks of lying in bed had taken a heavy toll on his strength and stamina. Consequently, Colonel Mendenhall put him on administrative leave and sent him to Subic Bay in the Philippines. There, Harpo was to rest, regain his strength, and complete his recovery.

Several days after arriving in the Philippines, Harpo walked into the Cubi Point BOQ bar one evening -- Navy Country. He sat alone and drank bourbon at a table in the corner. The bar was empty except for Harpo and eight to ten Navy A-4 Skyhawk pilots who were on shore liberty from one of the aircraft carriers that had just returned from Yankee Station.

From his table in the corner, Harpo quietly watched the Navy pilots. They were flying with their hands, winging their way toward their targets deep inside of North Vietnam. They skillfully evaded imaginary MIG-21s and batteries of antiaircraft guns. Drinking, laughing, talking all at once, they were really into it, hip to it. They repeatedly toasted their survival which, Harpo noted, was becoming more and more miraculous with each fresh round of drinks.

And yes, the Navy lieutenants vocally assured each other, they were the bravest of the brave, the best of the best. They were the fearless defenders of freedom, the cream of America's manhood.

Unlike the pilots of F-4 Phantoms and A-6 Intruders, they needed no navigator, radar intercept officer, or copilot. In their single-seat and single-engine jet Skyhawks, they flew alone into the teeth of the radar controlled 87mm and 57mm North Vietnamese antiaircraft fire. Then they fearlessly dove toward their targets and flew into the range of the 37mm and 23mm guns below 10,000 feet. While diving down on Haiphong Harbor and Thanh Hoa Bridge, they skillfully managed to evade the heat-seeking Atoll missiles fired by pursuing MIGs. Then they sped back toward their carrier in jets riddled with scores of bullet holes.

It was mostly the liquor talking, of course. A few more drinks and they would inevitably gather at the end of the bar for *carrier landings*. First, they would line up five or six tables and then dowse the tabletops with beer to make them slippery -- the flight deck would then be ready. One by one the Navy pilots then would run at full speed, leap, belly-flop onto the slick tabletops, and skid to a stop on their stomachs. Naturally, each of them would claim to have snagged the "number three wire," the third and desired arresting gear cable for fixed-wing carrier landings.

Finally the A-4 pilots noticed Harpo, who was still drinking alone in the corner of the barroom. They saw the Golden Wings pinned above the left breast pocket of his summer khakis. Harpo's post-hospital pallor stood out in stark contrast to their suntanned faces. With a grin, one lieutenant looked Harpo's way, slowly bowed to the waist, and then remarked, "Good evening, *sir*!" with a sarcastic emphasis on the last word.

Without a doubt, the Navy pilots had mentally pegged Harpo. Pale and alone, he obviously was nothing more than an armchair pilot, a desk jockey. Harpo looked like a genuine REMF (spoken, *re-miff*; an acronym derived from *Rear-Echelon-Mother-Fu* . . . [expletive deleted], a contemptuous term used by combat pilots and infantrymen to describe military personnel in safe locations far from the battlefields, especially those in administrative roles). Looking at Harpo, the Navy pilots thought they saw nothing more than a washed-up aviator hiding in a paper-pushing job to avoid the hostile skies over Vietnam. Conversely, the A-4 pilots were the Bronze Gods Off To War.

"Let's hear it for the Marines!" one of their number mockingly implored. There was total silence for a couple of seconds. Then they all broke into spasms of laughter. This was their show now, and it was all for Harpo's benefit.

"LET'S HEAR IT FOR THE NAVY!" another shouted at the top of his voice. They all erupted into wild shouts, cheers, and laughter and ordered yet another round of drinks.

The A-4 pilots soon returned to their vocal flying. It sure was tough, one of them remarked, having to miss out on the real war up north when they sometimes flew down to support the Marines in I-Corps. Of course, another lieutenant loudly suggested, "that Marine in the corner" would not know what they were talking about, because he was pretty safe here in the bar.

We are all here for a spell, so get all the good laughs you can.
-- (Will Rogers; 1879-1935)

The Navy revelry continued for another half hour, and the alcohol took its inevitable toll. The slurred versions of daily escapes in the flak-filled skies over North Vietnam became increasingly harrowing, and bombing accuracy improved with each fresh round of drinks.

Finally, enough was enough. Harpo pushed back his chair, rose, and slowly walked over to the Navy pilots. They instantly fell silent and leaned back against the bar, drunkenly grinning at Harpo and checking him out.

"You guys really take a lot of hits?" Harpo ventured.

For a moment the jet pilots were confused. Was this Marine serious? Then they all tried to answer at once: "Oh, yeah! Oh, yeah!" Trying to act solemn now, the Navy lieutenants eagerly explained that they took hits on every mission -- well, *almost* every mission, several added. The North Vietnamese threw up a murderous barrage of antiaircraft fire at them, but they always ignored it and bored in on their targets. Of course they did! Each of them was lucky to still be alive. Further, one lieutenant continued, as soon as they went back on Yankee Station they would doubtless be flying north of the Red River. They might die there, but they would do their duty. Of course they took hits, plenty of hits, scores of hits! Their A-4s were riddled with bullet holes. Then the lieutenants fell silent and waited for Harpo to respond.

"Well, I did a little helicopter flying in Vietnam," Harpo said.

Then he softly continued: "You know, Marines don't count bullet holes in the *aircraft* -- Marines only count *real* bullet holes."

No response, just quizzical stares.

"You guys ever see a *real* bullet hole?" Harpo asked.

Still no response.

Harpo ripped off his shirt. Contrasted against his pale chest, the ugly bluish-black and red scar tissue glistened in the harsh white light from the bar. The Navy pilots just stared -- stunned, speechless, and suddenly stone sober. Harpo pointed his forefinger at the entrance wound in his lower chest. Then he turned around and showed the Navy pilots the ragged exit wound in his back.

In the quiet of the barroom, Harpo spoke almost in a whisper: "*Real* bullet holes -- they look like this going in -- and like that going out."

Without saying another word, Harpo picked up his shirt and walked back to his table in the corner. The lieutenants silently turned back to the bar. There were no more swirling battles with MIGs, no more SAMs and missiles to evade. The enemy AAA batteries had ceased fire. There would be no more harrowing escapes that night. Carrier landings on the tabletops in the bar were forgotten.

After finishing their drinks, the Navy pilots shuffled toward the door. The last lieutenant stopped, walked straight over to Harpo's table, and thrust out his hand. Harpo stood up and accepted the sincere handshake.

"Have a good evening, sir!" the Navy lieutenant said, and this time there was no hint of sarcasm in his voice. Then he left Harpo alone in the bar and followed his squadronmates out into hot and humid Philippine night.

What counts is not necessarily the size of the dog in the fight. Instead, it's the size of the fight in the dog.
-- (Dwight D. Eisenhower)

Into the
-- New Year --

The psychological and political consequences of a United States defeat in Vietnam . . . would be disastrous in much of Asia.
-- (Hanson W. Baldwin; in the *New York Times Magazine*; February 21, 1965)

October 24, 1966: As the fighting raged in Vietnam, Lyndon B. Johnson, President of the United States, met in Manila with the leaders of South Korea, Thailand, the Philippines, New Zealand, Australia, and South Vietnam. They met to plot strategy to thwart the North Vietnamese military machine. But in reality, thwarting only the North Vietnamese would have taken precious little effort. True, North Vietnam had the fourth largest standing army in the world, but the North Vietnamese provided only the human fodder in support of the war against South Vietnam. The North Vietnamese had a simple agricultural economy, and they lacked the heavy industry and technology needed to manufacture the required tools of modern warfare.

The Soviet Union and China gave North Vietnam all of its radar systems, antiaircraft batteries, surface-to-air missile systems, jet fighters, mines, mortars, and artillery for the war. Russian instructors trained the North Vietnamese pilots, while Chinese advisors trained the NVA infantry. Each day long military supply trains rumbled down the winding railroad from China into Hanoi, and Russian cargo ships docked at Haiphong to deliver the war material needed each week to keep the North Vietnamese Army supplied. International military experts figured that 6000 tons of munitions and food per day poured into North Vietnam from its powerful communist neighbors to the north.

> The Soviet People . . . regard it as their sacred duty to give
> support to the people fighting for their independence.
> -- (from *PRAVDA*; the Soviet Union government newspaper)

Heavy 122mm Soviet D-74 field guns and huge 155mm howitzers enabled the NVA to engage the Marines in set artillery duels. Mach-2 Soviet MIG-21 fighters defended the skies over North Vietnamese military bases. The Soviets even provided all 36 of the MI-4 Hound and the KA-25 Hormone helicopters flown by the North Vietnamese Air Force. NVA infantrymen carried the Chinese AK-47 assault rifle, and their 7.62mm ammunition came from both Russia and China. The hand grenades of choice were the Chinese RG-Y2 or the RGD-5. China also supplied most of the NVA trucks, but the North Vietnamese PT-76 tanks came directly from the Kirov Factory in Leningrad, deep in the heartland of Soviet Russia. In the final analysis, North Vietnam provided nothing but the men to fight and die.

On paper, no country ever issued a formal declaration of war during the battle for South Vietnam. Officially the conflict was an internal struggle between the South Vietnamese government and the insurgents in the countryside. A few naive politicians believed that the fighting simply pitted the South Vietnamese against the invading North Vietnamese. Yet, knowledgeable historians and military strategists knew the truth. In reality the Vietnamese people, both in the north and in the south, merely provided the battleground for a military confrontation between the United States and the two Asian communist giants, Russia and China.

Consequently, when President Johnson sat down with the leaders of the six other allied countries in Manila, he knew the real enemy. He had detailed the root of the problem in his landmark foreign policy address at Johns Hopkins University: "Over this war, and all of Asia, is another reality -- the deepening shadow of Communist China."

That same day, October 24, the same communist shadow caught up with a former MARCAD who was a friend of mine. First Lieutenant Joseph G. "Joe" Healy, a Deadlock pilot in VMO-2, flew out to do battle with the Russian and Chinese pawns. His

Huey went down nine miles north of Dong Ha, but Joe survived and got medevaced to the *USS Repose*. Doctors treated him for a broken leg, a dislocated shoulder, and multiple lacerations and wounds. Joe eventually would recover and return to the cockpit.

Marine helicopter pilots now found that they had to battle an additional enemy, the Northeast Monsoon. November brought the onset of the dreaded monsoon with its months of heavy daily rains. Beginning around a month later in December and lasting through March, pilots faced the miserable weather phenomena called the *Crachin*. Between periods of heavy monsoon rain, the *Crachin* was characterized by a constant drizzle and widespread fog that usually kept ceilings below 1000 feet. As a general rule, helicopter pilots would postpone routine resupply missions if 1000 feet of terrain clearance could not be maintained. Flying much lower than 1000 feet above the ground invited enemy fire, and there was no reason to needlessly risk a helicopter and crew. However, emergency ammunition resupply missions, medevacs, or troop extractions under fire were a different matter. Regardless of the weather, these critical missions had to be flown in order to support the Grunts who depended on us.

Captain Dale L. "Papa-Bear" Tinsley remembers getting a frag to launch on an emergency medevac just prior to midnight one dark and rainy night. He knew that he would be flying blind toward a landing area he could not see. Hopefully he could find his way close enough to spot the Grunt radioman's flashlight in the darkness below. If he could avoid the mountain peaks, he could home in on the flashlight beam while the radioman tried to talk him down to a safe landing. Realizing what lay in store for him, Papa-Bear paused beside his waiting H-46 and vomited onto the marston-matting before climbing into the helicopter cockpit.

The foul flying weather forced helicopter pilots to alter their tactics, but some things never changed. When HMM-263 Captain James E. VanGorder took a round in his left leg on November 14, the location and circumstances had been heard many times before: "Two miles SE Hill 55 on medevac . . . ."

Marble Mountain, December 3, 1966: Three days earlier I had been discharged from the United States Naval Hospital at

Yokosuka, Japan. Now, after a brief stopover in Okinawa, I found myself back in Vietnam. I got reassigned to my old squadron again, and I even got quartered in my former tent. With one exception I still had the same tentmates, pilots Huey Walsh and Jim Hodgson and also our squadron supply officer, Warrant Officer Sidney M. Wire. My only tentmate who was absent was Ron Pfeifer. He had been listed as missing-in-action since October 6, the rainy night when his H-46 had disappeared during a flight from Dong Ha to Marble Mountain.

I dug out my two Nomex flight suits from my footlocker that my squadron had stored for me. Months before I had carefully stenciled a large, sinister, and evil-looking black bat on them, and I was glad to see that my artwork had been preserved. Jim Hodgson began calling me Bat-Pole, a reference to my tailored *batsuits* and my thin beanpole appearance, he chuckled.

I went back to flying. I was crazy.
-- (Mark Baker; in *NAM*)

I got back into an H-46 cockpit on December 4 for the first time since August. Vic Vecchitto and I flew a 0.6 hour post-maintenance test hop in Bureau Number 152505. The following day, Operations assigned me to three more test hops plus an administrative flight with First Lieutenant Robert D. "Bob" Porter. These easy flights were designed to strip away the mental and physical rust that I had accumulated during my 116 day absence.

<u>December 7, 1966</u>: With George Richey as my HAC, I strapped myself into Bureau Number 152517 for my first combat mission. By the end of the day we had logged 3.5 hours in the air, according to my logbook. The specific details of that day have long been forgotten. It was a routine mission down south of Marble Mountain, as I vaguely recall. But on that mission I found that I now confronted a new enemy, one that I had not previously faced in Vietnam. I never verbally acknowledged the existence of my new adversary to anyone, not then, and not in the years to follow. But my newfound enemy was real and formidable, and he had a shameful name -- Fear.

I did my best to conceal my new enemy from friends, but my invisible nemesis rode with me in the cockpit for almost a month.

Funny, but although the prospect of dying did not scare me, I was *terrified* of getting wounded again and returning to the hospital. On any given mission I knew that my chance of getting hit again was pretty slim, but still I had to *force* myself to go through the motions. During a briefing in our ready-room tent for a hot Sparrow-Hawk mission, I remember that I had to squeeze my legs together so that my friends would not notice my trembling knees. I did my best to exhibit a calm facade, and I prayed that my voice would not betray the truth. We launched, took hits at BT-017606, and our gunner caught a round in the shoulder. The elephant, as they say, instantly sat on my chest, and I could not breathe for 15 seconds. However, over an agonizing period of several weeks my unreasonable fear gradually faded away, and I recalled a parallel situation from my childhood.

Panic: A sudden unreasonable and overwhelming fear that can paralyze those faced with real or imagined danger.
-- (from the *Red Cross Lifeguard Manual*)

Back in May 1953 as an eleven year old boy, I had been playing in the woods near my home in the rural community of Plum Branch, South Carolina. Walking barefooted near the former site of my late grandfather's ferry across the Savannah River, I had stumbled into an unplanned encounter with a deadly Cottonmouth Moccasin. The serpent struck, his fangs found their mark in my left foot, and the venom put me in the sickbed for over a week. After I recovered I initially had been terrified of going back to play in the woods. There were snakes lurking everywhere, my irrational imagination had told me. The fear of getting bitten again overwhelmed me, consumed me, petrified me. However, my mindless panic had gradually subsided, and by the mid-summer of 1953 I had put snakes back into their proper perspective.

Now, 13 years later, I faced the same mental dilemma in Vietnam. Yet, as the December days passed my mind slowly replaced fearful imagination with a more realistic view of the potential danger. My odds of getting hit again were no worse than those of anyone else, I reasoned. Moreover, I knew that my best defense lay in aggressively doing my job. Slowly my unreasonable childish fear dwindled away, and within a month the problem was all but forgotten.

The Vietnam to which I returned had changed during my four month absence. We still called our living quarters *tents,* but the former canvas roofs had been replaced with galvanized tin roofing during November. Just north of our living area a new system had been set up to heat the water tank where we bathed. Each afternoon a kerosene heater raised the water temperature so that nighttime showers were more comfortable. Even our daytime "house-mouses," our Vietnamese maids, benefited from the change because they now could wash our filthy flight suits in warm water. After two or three days we got accustomed to sauntering to the water tank in the nude and taking a shower among them as they washed our clothes. However, all of the rumors about porcelain commodes proved to be unfounded, and we continued to use the officers' six-hole outhouse on the northern edge of our tent area. Scattered elsewhere around Marble Mountain were crude urinals, 55 gallon drums with the top and bottom cut out and half buried in the sand. Wire mesh covering the open top of each urinal kept the scorpions and insects out.

Up north near the DMZ, Dong Ha had been transformed into a major Marine Corps base. A new wooden mess hall had sprung up, and it served hot meals 16 hours each day. Steel marston-matting now covered the former dirt runway in order to accommodate heavy fixed-wing C-123 and C-130 transports during the monsoon season. Radar at Dong Ha searched the northern sky for the telltale electronic echoes that would signal the approach of attacking North Vietnamese MIG-21s. Quad-fifty AAA batteries now stood ready to repulse enemy aircraft, but one thing had not changed for the Marine helicopter pilots. Our basic mission still remained the same -- support the Grunts.

The monsoon rain and drizzle made a pilot's life miserable. At 1500 Hours one rainy afternoon, two HMM-265 helicopters were assigned Frag 1563-B to resupply two Grunt companies west of An Hoa. The two H-46s were crewed by the following Marines:

	Bonnie-Sue 3-1	Bonnie-Sue 3-2
Pilot:	Maj. Richard O. Harper	Maj. John T. Maxwell

Copilot:	Capt. Leo J. Farrell	1Lt. F. C. Fracker
Crew Chief:	SSgt. Cecil H. Dickey	Cpl. Schwartzenberger
Gunner:	Cpl. Jimmy A. Zerelli	Cpl. Joel M. Zerns

A Deadlock gunship from VMO-2, flown by Captain Alan H. "Al" Barbour and First Lieutenant Mike H. Clemens, escorted the two larger helicopters. In the lead H-46, Major Richard O. "Harpo" Harper headed south toward An Hoa and tried to stay VFR under the cloud layer. The weather erroneously had been reported as 1500 feet broken, but Harpo was forced down to around 400 feet. His flight drew automatic weapons fire all the way from Hill 55 to the An Hoa runway. After landing, Harpo was told that his mission had been upgraded to an *emergency* medevac and resupply.

In the landing zone to the west the Grunt radioman, "Pygmalion one-four," reported that the cloud ceiling was 200 to 500 feet above ground, with only a half mile visibility. Even worse, Harpo's map showed that a 1200 foot high ridge lay between An Hoa and the Grunts. There was no way to get over it or around it without going IFR, so the three helicopters shut down at An Hoa and waited for a break in the weather. Darkness soon came, and the helicopters remained on five minute standby for a launch. However, heavy rain and fog continued throughout the night, and the Huey and H-46 crews had to remain on the ground at An Hoa. In their wet flight gear -- clothes never really dry out during the rainy season -- they curled up in their helicopter cabins and tried to get some sleep.

Daylight brought no immediate break in the rain and clouds. At 1100 Hours, Pygmalion radioed that the Grunts desperately needed small arms ammunition, and they had wounded men to be medevaced at the earliest opportunity. The weather seemed to be clearing, the radioman added, so Captain Barbour fired up his gunship to check the cloud ceiling over the landing area. Yes, he soon radioed, the H-46s could give it a try now.

The two transport helicopters launched, but before they reached the ridge the clouds closed in again. Harpo turned back and returned to An Hoa. Now Barbour's gunship was trapped below the clouds in the valley to the west, so he landed at the Grunt command post. Waiting there until the clouds momentarily parted, Barbour launched with the most critically wounded men aboard, and he successfully made it out of the valley.

An hour later the rain slackened, and the cloud base seemed a little higher. The three helicopters launched from An Hoa, skimmed over the ridge, and found their way into the valley. All three landed, and the Grunts rushed to unload ammunition and food from the two H-46s. Struggling through waist deep water in the flooded rice paddies, they began loading their casualties into the helicopters. The enemy was believed to be mainly to the east and southeast, Pygmalion radioed. Taking that information into account, Barbour's gunship hovered and then accelerated skyward.

[Barbour's gunship] was hit by automatic weapons fire from the northeast . . . which did severe damage to the aircraft and wounded the crew chief.
-- (Major Richard O. Harper; in the After Action Report)

Several NVA bullets ripped through the aluminum skin of the Huey, and one hit Sergeant J. F. Odgen, the gunship crew chief. He slumped into a web seat in the cabin as the gunship sped out of range of the enemy below. The Huey had been riddled, but it would safely make it back to An Hoa.

Meanwhile in the landing zone, Harpo's H-46 was mired up to its stub-wings in the paddy. The huge crew chief, Sergeant Cecil H. Dickey, helped the Grunts muscle the casualties aboard. Loaded at last, Harpo rocked the H-46 to get the landing gear unstuck from the mud. Once free, he headed up out of the zone to circle and wait for his wingman.

Grunt KIAs and more wounded were still being loaded aboard Number Two, flown by Major John Maxwell and "Chick" Fracker. Noting that the lone H-46 was still not airborne, the NVA resorted to their most effective weapon against helicopters.

"MORTARS! MORTARS!"

The Grunt radioman screamed into his microphone as he sloshed for cover behind a paddy dike. The NVA were walking the high-explosive rounds toward the landing zone. Safely circling high overhead, Harpo saw the eruptions of grey smoke with deadly orange hearts as the mortar rounds exploded. He radioed to his wingman to take off at once. Pygmalion repeated his frantic warning too, but Major Maxwell still stubbornly refused to budge.

Pygmalion 14 . . . advised Major Maxwell to expedite his take-off to save his aircraft.
-- (Major Richard O. Harpo; in the After Action Report)

Grunts still struggled through the water to drag WIAs into the H-46 cabin. Major Maxwell knew that a hasty takeoff might be the death sentence for any severely wounded Marines left behind. If he left without them, the rain and clouds could close in at any minute, and it might be many hours before another helicopter could grope its way through the fog into the valley. Consequently, Major Maxwell sat there as the mortar rounds came closer and closer. Ignoring the frantic warning from Pygmalion and ignoring Harpo yelling at him on the radio, he crouched back in his protective armored seat. It was now or never.

Finally the crew chief keyed his mike: "All aboard, sir!"

Chick: "Ramp up."

Major Maxwell snatched up the collective pitch lever, and the loaded H-46 struggled for altitude and flying speed. As they cleared the tops of the trees, the NVA machineguns opened up on them. Back in the cabin the crew chief, Corporal G. J. Schwartzenberger, and the gunner, Corporal Joel M. Zerns, manned their guns and fired back through the rain at the enemy gunners.

He took off, and another mortar [round] hit right there, you know, right where he had been.
-- (Richard O. Harper; years later)

Both H-46s evaded the groundfire and headed north. Critically low on fuel now, they sped straight for the G-4 NSA hospital at Da Nang instead of taking the longer trip to Charlie-Med. They dropped off the casualties at the hospital landing pad, and then the two helicopters flew home to Marble Mountain. The pilots and aircrewmen refueled their helicopters, feasted on C-Rations, and then set out in search of dry flight suits.

The North Vietnamese kept up their forays into Razorback Valley. From their outpost at the base of the Rockpile, the Grunts sent out company size patrols to try to rid the valley of the enemy soldiers. The Grunts on patrol needed a FAC to talk "pilot talk" to Marine Air. Mike Company, 3rd Battalion, 3rd Marines, had one of the best, First Lieutenant Otto H. Fritz.

Three years earlier, Otto had been drawn to the Marine Corps by the lure of flying helicopters. Tall, blond-headed, and armed with a perpetual smile, Otto had left Texas A&M and had headed for Pensacola, Florida. He had been one of the twelve Marines who entered MARCAD Class 42-63 one week ahead of me. Four months of academic, military, and physical training quickly passed, and then flight training began. Otto had progressed rapidly, but near disaster caught up with him one year later.

Otto had completed his solo night navigation syllabus, but his roommate at Whiting Field, NAVCAD David "Dave" Jorges, had not. No problem, they figured; they would sneak out and fly the "solo" night flight together. Under cover of darkness that November night in 1964, Otto had dashed to Dave's waiting T-28, clambered aboard, strapped in, and off they went. Unfortunately, they got caught. There had been no dilly-dallying around, because the dreaded Speedy Board had convened the very next morning. Otto had broken the rules, and he knew that by noon he most likely would be on a Greyhound bus headed back home to Texas. There was only one slim chance at salvation -- play dumb.

"Sir, we didn't know!"

. . .

"Prohibited?"

. . .

"Yes, sir -- yes, sir! -- I agree, sir."

. . .

"No, we just want to fly and serve our country, sir!"

. . .

"Well, sir -- aaaaahhhh -- we room together and study together. I guess we sort of assumed we could -- aahh -- fly together."

Notwithstanding their flagrant disregard for regulations, Otto and Dave at least had initiative and guts, the Speedy Board officers had realized. So, miracle of miracles, the Speedy Board had accepted (but not *believed*) the explanation offered by Otto and his friend for their unique "solo" night training flight. Thereafter, Otto had lived at the proverbial foot of the cross until he completed flight training. Finally in the late spring of 1965 the big day had arrived. Otto mastered his E-13 check flight at Ellyson Field, and the Marine Corps had designated him a Naval Aviator.

Otto had gotten to Vietnam in January 1966, and he joined HMM-161. He flew H-34s with the "Barrelhouse" squadron for six months, and his days and nights soon had become predictable: medevacs and resupply flights, with a few strikes thrown in now and then for good measure. Otto had developed into an aerial artist in the H-34, a skilled combat pilot. Then to his utter dismay, the Marine Corps had decided to reassign him as a Forward Air Controller, a FAC.

Razorback Valley, early December 1966: As the FAC for Mike Company, Otto humped through the thick vegetation with the Grunts in the heavily jungled Razorback Valley in search of the elusive enemy. Mike Company set up ambushes, dug fighting holes, set up interlocking fields of fire, and set out their claymore mines. Motionless and soundless in the stifling heat with a thousand Asian bugs and insects feeding on their bodies, they waited for the NVA to blunder into the killing zone. The Grunts tried to ambush the NVA, and the NVA simultaneously tried to ambush the Grunts. Sometimes the Grunts got lucky, and sometimes luck smiled on the enemy.

> We set up ambushes. The NVA set up ambushes. It was just a matter of who would walk into an ambush first.
> -- (Otto H. Fritz; years later)

December 9, 1966: Mike Company, now down to about 120 men, had been in heavy contact most of the day. Down in the valley between the Razorback and Mutter Ridge, the Grunts were locked in a fierce firefight with the NVA. For the Grunts who had been killed, time no longer mattered, but time was critical for the wounded. Mike Company needed medevac helicopters in a hurry, and Otto saw that there was no place for the helicopters to land nearby. He started working his way back toward a bomb crater where he could talk the helicopter pilots down to a safe landing.

With his radio operator, "Frenchie," and his 3.5 inch "Rocket-Man," Otto crawled down the hillside and then dashed across a clear area where he was exposed to enemy fire. He then worked his way up a hill to a 1000 pound bomb crater where one Grunt platoon had left its field packs. Many of the Grunt KIAs also had been left here, and their rapidly bloating bodies lay sprawled out in the afternoon sun. Otto planned to wait here for the rest of Mike Company to climb up and join him, and then he would radio for the helicopters. But the firefight raged on, and the Grunts in the valley below could not break contact.

The late afternoon sun dipped below the rim of the Razorback. Otto, Frenchie, and Rocket-Man were stranded and cut off from the rest of their company in the dark. An elephant trail passed below them, down in the edge of the trees, but their position at the bomb crater seemed secure for the night. The enemy did not know where they were, Otto reasoned. Cautioning his two companions to stay quiet, Otto positioned Rocket-Man 50 to 60 feet away behind a boulder on the opposite side of the crater. Then Otto and Frenchie back-crawled under a tangled bush where they planned to spend the night. Frenchie and Rocket-Man were gutty Marines, but like Otto they were exhausted, bone tired, and worn out. Rocket-Man had not slept at all in two days. Otto pulled out his Colt .45 caliber semiautomatic pistol, rested it on his chest, and waited.

Just before midnight, Otto heard the distinctive and dreaded bird-cadence, the chirping whistle. The NVA soldiers were coming along the elephant trail 100 feet below Rocket-Man, down in the trees. "Don't move, stay quiet!" Otto thought to himself. For 20 minutes, groups of enemy soldiers walked single file along the trail down below Otto in separate groups of perhaps 30 men each. Otto's heart pounded, and he fought to keep his breathing quiet. As long as he and his two men stayed quiet, they would be safe, he knew. The enemy had no way to know that the three Marines were on the hillside.

Then the snoring started.

"Oh, no! Rocket-Man!" Otto thought.

It was now too late. Otto could not risk crawling 50 feet across the crater to awaken and silence Rocket-Man. Even if he could sneak over to Rocket-Man, the sleeping Marine would likely cause an audible commotion when Otto tried to quiet him or wake him. What could Otto do? There were about 25 to 30 enemy soldiers on the trail below the bomb crater. Surely they must hear the loud snoring by now, Otto thought.

The bird-cadence abruptly stopped. Otto's heart also seemed to stop. All was quiet, all except for Rocket-Man, sound asleep and snoring behind the boulder on the edge of the bomb crater.

Frenchie and Otto lay motionless on their backs under the bush in the dark. There was nothing that they could do, and the minutes crept by with agonizing slowness. At least a half hour passed, and then Otto saw the enemy soldiers. Silhouetted against the terrain in the moonlight, three NVA infantrymen stealthily slipped up the hill, one careful step at a time. Soundlessly, like ghosts, they eased up toward the bomb crater. They slipped right up to the sleeping and snoring Rocket-Man. Wordlessly, they now motioned to each other with their hands in the moonlight.

"This is it!" Otto knew. At least the element of surprise would be on his side. He could probably kill these three NVA soldiers, but then their comrades would charge up the hill. He and Frenchie would not stand a chance, he realized, but they would sell their lives as dearly as possible. Otto tightened his grip on the butt of his pistol. He would have to fire quickly.

However, now the three enemy soldiers hesitated. They looked down at Rocket-Man, sleeping and snoring. But they also saw the Grunt field packs, enough packs for at least a platoon. They noticed the Grunt KIAs in the bomb crater, and it did not make sense. Otto could almost see their mental questions.

The three NVA soldiers did not know what to make of what they saw. They could not solve the puzzle. There were many packs and many dead men, but where were the other Marines? The NVA knew that the Marines would not abandon their dead, and what about this lone sleeping and snoring Marine? Why was he alone? Could this be some kind of a trap, an ambush, and was the sleeping man the bait that would ensnare them? If they killed him, would he die quietly, or would his screams alert other Marines lurking somewhere nearby?

Ever so slowly and silently, the three NVA soldiers turned, stole away, and evaporated into the darkness. Rocket-Man peacefully slept on. He would live to fight again another day, and so would Otto and Frenchie.

December 10, 1966, 0300 Hours: Three hours after midnight the Grunts in the valley headed up the hill toward the bomb crater. There were a lot more bad guys than good guys in the valley, and the Marines figured they might get overrun before dawn if they stayed on the valley floor. They came crashing up the hill -- like a herd of elephants, Otto would later tell me -- and making plenty of noise and yelling so that Otto would not mistake them for the NVA. Otto and the Grunts formed a perimeter and held in place until daylight. Then they started down the hill again. On a whim, Otto stripped the flak jacket off of one of the Grunt KIAs and put it on. He had no way to know it, but that extra flak jacket would save his life before the end of the day.

If I should come out of this war alive, I will have more luck than brains.
-- (Manfred von Richthofen [the Red Baron]; September 1914)

For five hours the Grunts hacked their way through the vines and undergrowth in the valley. Overhead was a solid canopy of foliage that rendered the sky totally invisible. Otto kept talking on his radio to an orbiting Bird Dog pilot who was coordinating an airstrike by F-4 Phantoms. The jets were swooping down and attacking North Vietnamese positions on the Razorback. The 1000 foot high Razorback was honeycombed with caves that had been dug either by the Japanese during World War II or by the Viet Minh during their war with the French. The NVA were now holed up in these caves, deep inside of the almost impregnable Razorback. Regular dive bombing had no effect, so the F-4s were making low-level runs in an effort to lob 500 pound bombs straight into the mouths of the caves.

From the jungle floor, Otto could not see the F-4s, but he could hear them. Either on run-in or run-out they were overflying Mike Company, and premature or late bomb release could be disastrous. Otto radioed the Bird Dog pilot and told him to change the run-in heading for the F-4s. The pilot rogered the request, but he had a lot going on, he was almost bingo on fuel, and he was taking fire. Somehow the F-4 pilots never understood the danger.

Otto and the Grunts reached the river just north of the Razorback and strung out single file to cross it. The water was about armpit deep and the going was slow, but about 20 Marines made it to the other side. The company executive officer, First Lieutenant Steve Sayer, was next in line to start across. He suddenly just froze in place. Then he turned and faced Otto.

I can't explain it, but Steve somehow knew that he was about to die. He had a *premonition*, no doubt about it.
-- (Otto H. Fritz; speaking of Steve Sayer years later)

Steve blurted out: "I can't go!"
Otto urged his friend to start across the river.
Steve's reply: "Otto, you go ahead -- I'm a dead man."
Otto had never seen fear in the young lieutenant, but now it was etched all over his face. Steve would not budge. Totally shaken by this strange reaction, Otto climbed down the riverbank into the water and started across the river. It was slow going, but he made it about halfway across. Otto looked back over his shoulder and saw that Steve was still standing on the riverbank and staring at him. "What's wrong?" Otto wondered . . . .

Meanwhile, to the F-4 pilot high above the valley, it looked like another routine bomb run. He rolled in hot, lined up on the glistening black granite wall of the Razorback . . . 385 knots . . . straight and level . . . right over the trees . . . steady . . . steady. The pilot pickled a 500 pound bomb, pulled back on the stick, and the twin-jet Phantom soared skyward toward the clouds. Tragically, the pilot had released the bomb a split second too late. The bomb sailed all the way over the crest of the Razorback and gracefully arced down toward the river.

Otto had no warning. He did not see the impact. There was just a violent concussion and a tremendous blow against his back. The blast knocked Otto flat in the water.

"MORTARS!" Otto thought. Out in the river in the open, he was totally exposed. Otto grabbed a quick breath of air and then stayed underwater as long as he could. Then, regaining his footing in the riverbed, he saw his blood in the water -- no pain -- and he knew that he had been hit. Fighting the current, Otto struggled back to the riverbank.

The jagged steel shrapnel had hit Otto in the back. His spare flak jacket that he had taken from a Grunt KIA only hours before had deflected the shrapnel, slowed it down a little, and saved his life. However, the bomb had killed eleven Marines. Thirteen more, including Otto, were wounded.

Otto radioed for medevacs, and H-46s and H-34s flew out from Dong Ha, 17 miles to the east. There was no place for the helicopters to land, so they hovered over the river while the dead and wounded were dragged aboard. The unwounded Grunts of Mike Company helped Otto into the last H-34, and after a ten minute flight to Dong Ha he was rushed into the field hospital.

> He responded to Humanity's clear call, And knew the Voice Divine; He gave his all.
> -- (The epitaph of Joseph Preston Strom; killed-in-action in World War I at Brest, France, on October 8, 1918)

Steve Sayer, a native of Watertown, New York, had been 24 years old. The bomb had impacted right by him, and all that was left intact was part of his upper torso and one arm. The rest was simply blown away. Steve and Otto had shared that unique camaraderie, that special trust and loyalty that only Marines in combat will ever know. Steve had stayed on the riverbank, and he had died there. Over a quarter century later, Otto would remain absolutely certain that Steve somehow had known that he was about to die. Years after the war, Otto would explain to me that he can never erase the memory of the last words softly spoken to him by his friend: "Otto, you go ahead -- I'm a dead man."

As the December days passed, Marines and helicopters from HMM-265 became increasingly caught up in the secret "Project Delta" missions at Khe Sanh. Located in the mountainous northwest corner of South Vietnam, Khe Sanh was the perfect spot from which to launch clandestine cross-border flights into Laos. By early December my squadron maintained two helicopters at Khe Sanh specifically for these hush-hush assignments. On many of the Project Delta missions, our helicopters ferried indigenous Montagnards or Chinese Nung mercenaries deep into Laos. Their job called for hit and run raids and ambushes against the NVA units and supply bases hidden in the Laotian jungle.

> Another good thing we've done is insert mercenaries into Laos. There are some weird things going on over here. The poor folks back home have no idea.
> -- (Captain Joseph D. Snyder; in March 1969)

There had been 28 cross-border missions during the previous month. Officially, no American ever flew into Laos. If anyone turned up dead or missing in that forbidden neverland, the casualty was simply coded to Project Delta with no further explanation. On my birthday, November 9, one of our FACs had been shot down in Laos. The *HMM-265 Command Chronology* noted the Project Delta loss and described the location in two words, "Coordinates classified." Some of our Project Delta missions had involved North Vietnam itself. Back on November 11, Harpo and his copilot, First Lieutenant Paul J. Albano, had flown 4.9 hours in Bureau Number 152501. During the day they made four separate forays north of the DMZ in their H-46.

My Project Delta frags never required me to fly north of the DMZ, and my only two flights into North Vietnam took place on SAR North assignments. All of my Project Delta missions took me into Laos, directly west of Khe Sanh. On one flight we landed in the flat Laotian valley at XD-641372, the site of the abandoned French airstrip, Ban Houei Sane North, and there we dropped off a team of Chinese Nungs. The Laotian village a mile to the south on the Se Pone River looked just like the Vietnamese villages on the other side of the border. Yet, on these secret flights into Laos, we all knew that we were playing a deadly game without any rules.

On paper, these missions never existed. Washington had proclaimed that no American servicemen were fighting in Cambodia, North Vietnam, or Laos. If we got shot down, our wingman would try to swoop in and pick us up. If that failed, we would try to "escape and evade" (E&E) on foot and make our way back to an American outpost in South Vietnam. In theory, some of the Laotian villagers might assist us. On the other hand, they might kill us, so our E&E plans called for avoiding them if at all possible. To be ready for a worse case scenario, we each carried a standard plastic "Blood Chit" with which we might be able to barter our way into friendly hands:

I am an American. I do not speak your language. Misfortune forces me to seek your assistance in obtaining food, shelter, and protection. Please take me to someone who will provide for my safety and see that I am returned to my people. I will

do my best to see that no harm comes to you. My government will reward you.
-- (English translation; wording on the Blood Chit)

A shadowy Studies and Observation Group (SOG) had been organized almost three years earlier on January 24, 1964. In this clandestine and secret program, North Vietnam was called *New York*, and Cambodia was known as *Arizona*. The SOG command directed all of our Project Delta and SOG flights into Laos. Shining Brass was the official code-name given to some of the operations, but we helicopter pilots normally referred to the whole endeavor as Project Delta. When I got the chance to fly on these missions, I knew that I had really gotten in on something special. Further, at Khe Sanh I was able to watch the Central Intelligence Agency (CIA) mercenaries, the famous Air America pilots and cargo kickers with their gold bracelets and their legendary aura of romance and intrigue. All of their fixed-wing C-46 transports were meticulously maintained, and they each had "Air America" stenciled in small black letters on their vertical stabilizers.

Captain Gerald F. "Gerry" Dooley was a stocky cigar chewing pilot in HMM-265. Gerry had been with the Marine Corps H-46 program since its inception, and had consequently been designated as the maintenance officer for our squadron. However, when that duty detracted from his flying time, he requested reassignment to the secret SOG team at Khe Sanh: There he would spend the better part of four months working with not only the Marines and Nungs, but also with elements of the Army Special Forces Group. At Khe Sanh, Gerry made life-long friends with men like Lieutenant Colonel John Hayes, who had his deltoid blown off and yet refused evacuation. But the most unique men at Khe Sanh were not Americans; instead, they were the Chinese Nung mercenaries hired by the CIA to do the killing and the dirty work. Bob Mills would sum it up years later in a conversation with me:

Gerry Dooley was working with SOG at Khe Sanh, carrying Nungs into Laos. They were mercenaries, you know, *paid by the ear* by the CIA. The Nungs were bad, man, really bad dudes. They were the kind of guys you would see in *Apocalypse Now*. Dooley volunteered for this assignment.

My tentmate Huey Walsh also got in on some of the SOG flights deep into Laos. Flying to a prearranged spot, Huey landed and dropped off a band of Nungs who carried tiny battery powered homing transmitters. The Nungs would slip down to the Ho Chi Minh Trail under cover of darkness and attach the transmitters to the underside of NVA trucks. Two days later, Air Force bombers would home in on the transmitters.

The Army had 70 Special Forces men who routinely flew into Laos with both Chinese Nungs and Vietnamese Montagnards. On many of their larger operations, HMM-265 crews were called upon to resupply the ground force several days after insertion. Major Maxwell recalls that many of these missions became highly sophisticated. Ammunition and food were pre-packaged in aerodynamic M-24 canisters which were designed to be dropped from A-1 "Sandy" Skyraiders. Since the H-46 is not a dive bomber, the canisters to be delivered by the Bonnie-Sue helicopters were simply stacked on the rear ramp. On one mission, Major Maxwell flew to the designated map coordinates and spotted a loincloth-clad native waving a red bandanna from his perch in a tall tree. The H-46 ramp was then lowered in flight, and the canisters were rolled overboard during a low speed 40 knot pass. HMM-265 eventually was commissioned to make a special report on this novel aerial delivery technique. The final report stated in part that the canisters proved to be ". . . capable of penetrating dense jungle canopies, which made them particularly adaptable for clandestine/reconnaissance resupply operations."

First Lieutenant Kenneth H. Johnson (his nickname, while appropriate in Vietnam, is now entrusted to those of us with whom he served) and Harpo flew on what became known as the Body Snatch mission. President Lyndon Johnson was still publicly claiming that no American military men had set foot in Laos or Cambodia (he *had* acknowledged that we had flown into North Vietnam, but only to rescue downed airmen, he claimed). However, the North Vietnamese Army in Laos had spread-eagled a captured Special Forces soldier on top of a cleared hill. The man was dead, of course, but the Project Delta coordinator back at Phu Bai insisted that the body be recovered.

The NVA had set up the body as a helicopter trap. Harpo and Johnson launched in two H-46s, accompanied by four gunships and two Sandy Skyraiders. Arriving over the hill, the gunship pilots could clearly see the body on the ground. It looked too obvious. Sensing the danger, a single gunship made a high speed pass to see what reaction there might be. As the helicopter zipped down, the North Vietnamese opened up with 12.7mm machineguns.

The pilot dove for the deck and escaped.
-- (Richard O. Harper; years later)

Angry orange tracers reached up for the gunship. Orbiting overhead, the H-46 pilots watched the muzzle flashes from the deadly NVA crew served guns on the slopes of the hill. One Huey had been lost earlier in the same area, and the wreckage was still visible. To Harpo it all seemed like a further waste of American lives. He radioed Sandy and asked that 500 pounders be dropped on both the wreckage and the body. Control nixed that plan, but at least Harpo's insistence prompted Control to scrub the mission. All helicopters made it back to base without loss of life.

Laos, December 10, 1966: The Army had used one of its own Hueys in Laos, and it had been shot down. A cross-border mission was quickly thrown together to recover the wreckage and rescue the helicopter crewmen, who still were believed to be alive. Long after the mission a Distinguished Flying Cross recommendation would contain the following explanatory narrative:

On December 10, 1966, Captain DOOLEY was the Flight Leader of a four plane CH-46A detachment from Marine Medium Helicopter Squadron 265 assigned to Project "Delta" (classified Top Secret) at Khe Sanh, Republic of Vietnam. Captain DOOLEY was launched on a mission in connection with Project "Shining Brass" (classified Top Secret). The assets of Projects "Delta" and "Shining Brass" were pooled for this mission which included an Air Force FAC, three (3) Army UH-1E gunships, six (6) CH-46A helicopters, four (4) from HMM-265 and two (2) from HMM-164, numerous fixed-wing aircraft and elements of the 5th Special Forces Group. The mission of this tri-service team was to (1) insert members of the 5th Special Forces Group into an area northwest of Khe Sanh, (2) secure an area which held the wreckage of a United

States Army UH-1E helicopter, (3) retrieve the helicopter and crew and (4) extract the landing force. The eighty (80) man insert was made by Captain DOOLEY and two (2) HMM-164 helicopters at dawn . . . .

As the morning sun crested Dong Chio Mountain east of Khe Sanh, the helicopters joined their fixed-wing escort and headed west into Laos. There were four Bonnie-Sue H-46 helicopters from HMM-265 involved. The names of the crewmen in one helicopter are unknown, but the other Marines are listed below:

	No. 1	No. 2	No. 3
Pilot:	Dooley	Shea	Rolfe
Copilot:	Clark	Hodgson	Dremann
Crew chief:	Violissi	Gamble	McCosar
Gunner:	Rivas	Sherrill	(none, a "slick")

The helicopters flew to the crash site in Laos. There they dropped off the 80 man reaction force on a ridge that was covered with six to eight foot tall elephant grass. This was typical vegetation for the Laotian high-country, and men standing erect usually were totally concealed by the thick saw-toothed elephant grass. The insertion came off without a hitch, and the transport helicopters headed back to Khe Sanh to refuel and wait.

The reaction force radioed Khe Sanh in the early afternoon. The downed Huey, its crew, and the reaction force itself were all ready to be extracted. "Moose" Rolfe, the HAC, and Captain Timothy R. "Tim" Dremann, the copilot, headed back to Laos. They flew an H-46 heavy-hauler, a "slick" that had been stripped of all non-essential weight. Even the pilot's armored seats had been removed, and no machineguns or gunner were carried. With their belly-mounted external cargo hook and the proper sling, these specially prepared H-46s, two to a squadron, could easily lift the weight of a downed Huey.

Captain Harold C. Clark manned the copilot's seat in Gerry Dooley's H-46. He would later provide a written statement that included the initial mention of NVA fire: "The slick received ground fire, from one or two positions near the pickup site, which [sic] was suppressed by the gunships." Ignoring the threat, Moose hovered over the downed Huey while a ground crew attached the sling to the cargo hook. He then took off with the Huey dangling below him on the sling and flew directly back to Khe Sanh.

The plan now called for extraction of the reaction force and the downed Huey crew. They were all on the same ridgeline, but they were in two separate defensive positions about 200 meters apart. Down in the shallow valley below the ridge, the NVA had watched the whole show. Now the North Vietnamese knew what the Americans planned to do, so they started working their way up the side of the ridge toward the reaction force.

The two HMM-164 helicopters roared down and picked up one of the two groups on the ridge. As they sucked in power and headed skyward, they got into a gunfight with the advancing enemy. With their gunners ripping off long bursts, the H-46s climbed up out of harm's way and orbited to wait for the second group of men on the ridge to be extracted.

Gerry Dooley radioed for the gunships to cover him. He bottomed his collective and wrapped the H-46 into a diving and spiraling turn down toward the ridge.

The aircraft received hits although "S" turns at about 120 knots were made . . . .
-- (Captain Harold C. Clark; in a written statement)

Back in the cabin the crew chief, Sergeant Theodore J. Violissi, and the gunner, Staff Sergeant Frankie Rivas, answered the NVA guns with their own .50 caliber weapons. Rivas would later explain in a written account of the mission: "On our way into the zone we were receiving heavy machinegun fire . . . ." Hearing the enemy rounds ripping through the fuselage behind him, Gerry jammed the cyclic forward, sucked in full power, and aborted the landing attempt.

Reinforcement was out of the question, so the men still on the ridge had to be extracted. Gerry circled around for another try and used the terrain for cover. Coming in low and fast, he got supporting fire from the gunships and from the other H-46s circling above. But again the NVA targeted his speeding helicopter.

This approach was made through a hail of small arms fire.
-- (from Distinguished Flying Cross recommendation)

Gerry plopped his H-46 down in the tall grass between the advancing enemy and the Special Forces men. With all candor, it was probably the tall elephant grass that saved the day. The enemy soldiers could look upward and see the helicopters circling high overhead. However, they could not see Gerry's helicopter on the ground because the thick grass was taller than they were, so they resorted to blindly firing toward the sound of the turbines and whirling rotors 80 meters ahead of them.

All 30 Americans on the ridge rushed inside of the cabin of Gerry's H-46, and the helicopter could not get airborne with that heavy a load. Gerry called for his wingman to land, and Sergeant Violissi ordered ten of his passengers to get out. The number two H-46, flown by Captain Roger T. "Tom" Shea and my tentmate Jim Hodgson, landed nearby. The ten excess men ran aboard, and both H-46s then clawed their way upward into translational lift.

As the helicopters came into view above the tall grass, the NVA gunners began blasting away at them. Now, however, the odds definitely favored the gunships and the H-46 gunners. With no friendly troops on the ground to worry about, everyone on the ridge was fair game. Sergeant Rivas, the gunner in the lead Bonnie-Sue H-46, later wrote: "The pilot maneuvered the [helicopter] to give the gunners a good angle of fire . . . ."

All of the H-46 gunners were firing now, and they were joined by the potent M-60s and 2.75 inch rockets from the gunships. Although the NVA fired back, they were firing at swiftly moving targets. Conversely, the helicopter gunners were shooting at stationary targets on the ground. The collective firepower of the helicopters suppressed the ground fire, and the flight turned east and headed for home. Darkness was settling in on the elevated Khe Sanh Plateau when the pilots touched down at the Marine outpost. They had done their job, and no men or helicopters were left behind in Laos.

I do not remember all of my Project Delta flights from Khe Sanh, although a few of the missions are forever stamped in my memory. But while my recollection may be fallible with respect to dates, other images will never fade away. Back in those December days of 1966 before the coming battles in 1967 for the hills to the north, before the horrible siege in 1968, Khe Sanh was beautiful. The outpost was so remote, so distant from the outside world, and it was cut off and surrounded by rugged mountains. Time meant nothing here.

I remember peacefully napping on the soft grass under my H-46. Not a sound broke the absolute silence on the plateau. To the northwest, slightly under three miles away, Hill 861 dominated the landscape. Less than two miles farther north, the twin peaks of Hill 881 North and Hill 881 South jutted over a half mile into the air, and a misty haze always seemed to shroud the mountaintops. We sometimes saw the mystical "six shades of green" when the sun broke through the clouds and bathed the jungle with its light. It reminded me of the Great Smokey Mountains in the Appalachian chain back in western North Carolina -- simply beautiful! In this fairy-tale land surrounded by a vast wilderness, warfare somehow seemed out of place. "Who would ever want to *fight* here?" I often wondered.

The Nungs would fight, I soon learned. And, experience proved, they would fight for the highest bidder. Fortunately, at the time the CIA was willing to cough up more money for their services than anyone else, and in return the CIA got a savage and soulless mercenary.

The Nungs that I encountered did not speak English. Communication between we pilots and the Nungs was not necessary anyway. A simple "Number one!" or "Number ten!" and a smile adequately conveyed any message that I had to deliver. The Chinese people are traditionally wagerers and gamblers, and the Nungs that I met at Khe Sanh were no exception to that rule. I remember often watching them engage in their daily sport, and we cruelly called it a rat-roast.

The Nungs trapped the huge two pound wharf rats that thrived around the Khe Sanh garbage dump. In the early afternoon they would gather together, drink an intoxicating brew of their own making, and then get down to business. First, a designated Nung would select two rats and place them in a wire cage about five feet square. Then amid much shouting and revelry, each Nung would place his bet. They each wagered on the rat which they hoped would be the last one to die.

When all bets were in, the two rats in the cage were thoroughly doused with kerosene. A thrown torch would then set both rats ablaze, and the almost instant putrid stench of burning flesh was overwhelming and nauseous. The last charred rat to stop squealing, kicking, and twitching was declared the winner. Amid much more revelry and glee, the appropriate monetary awards were distributed to the Nungs who had bet on the winning rat.

I soon tired of watching the daily rat-roast. However, the Nungs relished this afternoon diversion from their mercenary chores, and I realized that they were ideally suited for the job for which they were paid. I was thankful that they were fighting on our side, not for the North Vietnamese. The Nungs were nothing more than hired guns, merciless and savage killers in a savage land.

Dong Ha, Christmas Day, December 25, 1966: The Marines had been battling the NVA all week long. In theory there was a Christmas truce in effect, but someone obviously forgot to inform the Grunts and the North Vietnamese. The sun was rapidly sinking below the hills in the west, but I got fragged for another mission.

My HAC, Captain Leo J. "Crazy-Leo" Farrell, and I piled into our H-46, Bureau Number 152503. We fired up the turbines while the ammunition and C-Rations were loaded. When everything was aboard we launched from Dong Ha and headed toward an LZ at the base of the Rockpile, 14 miles to the west. Darkness was settling in, and the air was glassy smooth and free of the usual daytime thermal turbulence. Crazy-Leo propped one foot on the edge of the instrument panel and feigned absolute boredom as I flew westward. About two miles from the Rockpile, I radioed the Grunts on the ground. They popped green smoke that I had to strain to see in the dim twilight. I dumped collective pitch, spiraled down, landed, dropped the ramp, and our crew chief helped the Grunts offload the cargo in our cabin.

Leo intoned: "I'll take us home. Get the ramp, Sturk."

"I've got the ramp."

"Ramp up," our crew chief confirmed on the ICS.

Crazy-Leo pulled in collective, hovered, and then sucked in full topping power. We were homeward bound. "Let's try the scenic route," Crazy-Leo snickered as he raced eastward at 130 knots, just 50 feet over the treetops. We sped through the winding valley along the Cam Lo River, and the southern slope of Hill 549 presented only a dark green blur on my left.

Normally we would not have done this, for we were still in Indian Country. Although the Marines pretty well controlled it now, you never could tell when the NVA might reappear. But by now it was almost totally dark, and at our speed and treetop height it would be hard for the enemy to get off a clean shot at us. We rotored through the valley just south of Hill 328 as we headed for the flatlands and Dong Ha. If we were lucky there might be hot food for our Christmas supper, I hoped. Our rotor system was in perfect track, no vibration at all. The air was silky smooth, a perfect end to an uneventful Christmas Day.

Flying consists of hours and hours of boredom, interrupted by brief moments of stark terror.
-- (anonymous; old aviator's axiom)

Suddenly, without warning: WHAAAAMMMM!
A powerful blow against our fuselage!
Crazy-Leo and I heard the heavy thump, and we felt the airframe shudder. We had been hit -- bad! Instinctively my buttocks puckered shut, and I glued my eyeballs to the instrument panel in front of me. Down collective, back cyclic! Torquemeters O. K., engines O. K., all gauges in the green, and the dreaded amber Master Caution Panel eye was not winking at us. I searched the instrument panel and saw nothing amiss. But what had hit us? Or what had we hit? "Altitude, Leo!" I nervously urged my HAC.

Crazy-Leo had already started a cyclic climb, because we would have had fewer options if we had kept flying just above the treetops. All systems looked functional. For a brief moment I almost believed I had hallucinated the heavy blow against our H-46. Crazy-Leo also was stumped. We looked at each other and exchanged blank questioning stares, then nervous giggles.

Our crew chief stuck his head into the cockpit and gave us a condescending look as if to ask: "What have you silly pilots done to my helicopter?" We did not know, but we knew that something a lot bigger than a 12.7mm round had hit us. We had actually felt the whole airframe shudder. "Flight control damage?" we both wondered.

We safely made it to Dong Ha and landed about 100 meters south of the runway. After climbing out of the cockpit, we got our flashlights and set out to examine the helicopter. We quickly solved the mystery when we saw irrefutable proof that a large nocturnal Asian vulture had taken his last flight. At a closure rate of 130 knots, it had slammed into the avionics compartment in the nose of the helicopter, right in front of our cockpit. Remnants of the carcass of the vulture were still partially embedded in the ruptured metal skin of the avionics bay door. What a mess!

Crazy-Leo erupted into hysterical laughter. After partially recovering, he started making disparaging quips about the presumed stupidity of the deceased vulture. "No! No! No!" the crew chief shouted in gleeful disagreement. He opined that the vulture, with fornication probably on his mind, had been lustily winging his way in hot pursuit of a female buzzard when we heartlessly blasted him out of the sky. Other pilots and aircrewmen wandered over to see what all of the commotion was about, and they soon joined in the verbal jousting.

Well, the fun was now over, so Crazy-Leo began to complete the paperwork required after all flights. When he listed the mechanical problems with the helicopter, he made only one entry on the yellow-sheet: "BLOOD, FLESH, AND FEATHERS IN HELICOPTER." Then we all sauntered off in search of some hot food and a warm beer for our Christmas supper.

January 1, 1967, New Year's Day: In a faraway world in January 1967, a former actor, Ronald Reagan, took the oath of office as Governor of California (he would later become President of the United States). Lester G. Maddox, a balding restaurateur with a penchant for oak axe handles and selective seating, got sworn in as Governor of Georgia. Jack Ruby, a hero to some and a fool to others, died of cancer in prison.

Herb Albert headed the popular instrumental musical group, The Tijuana Brass, and he outsold The Beetles two-to-one worldwide. A motion picture fairy-tale for adults, *The Sound of Music*, was destined to become an ageless classic. Paul "Bear" Bryant and his beloved Alabama Crimson Tide rolled over the Nebraska Cornhuskers 34 to 7 in the Sugar Bowl. And the very first Super-Bowl featured most valuable player Bart Starr, who quarterbacked the Green Bay Packers to a 35 to 10 romp over the Kansas City Chiefs. But none of this mattered to the Marines who fought in Vietnam. Their only concern was the massive threat posed by the North Vietnamese Army.

The North Vietnamese 320th Division, composed of two NVA Regiments and one Viet Cong Regiment, and the NVA Third Division, identically composed, operated in the mountains of southern and central I-Corps. The biggest threat to the Marines, however, lay in the far north. Four entire NVA Divisions -- almost unbelievable! -- were encamped along the DMZ. All under the command of North Vietnam's Military Region Four, the NVA 320th, 304th, 324-B, and 325-C Divisions were strung out from the mountains to the South China Sea. Near to their supply bases and supported by heavy ground-to-ground artillery, the mechanized and potent NVA war machine was preparing for a monsoon offensive. Marine Air, the NVA commanders knew, would be hamstrung by the foul monsoon weather.

Below the DMZ the Marines prepared for the inevitable onslaught. The First Marine Division, headquartered at Da Nang, had taken charge of all military operations in I-Corps south of Hai Van Pass. The Third Marine Division had moved north to Phu Bai, and its forward command post at Dong Ha was headed by Brigadier General Lowell E. English. He spread his seven understrength infantry battalions out below the DMZ to counter the massive threat from the north. Seven skinny battalions were not enough, he knew, but no additional forces were available.

The Marines are stretched as taunt as a bowstring.
-- (General Vo Nguyen Giap)

The largest Marine combat base, naturally, was Dong Ha. Just below the DMZ and north of Dong Ha, Marine infantry and artillery had established strongpoints at Gio Linh, named after the nearby village, and at Con Thien, a barren hill overlooking the coastal plain. The old artillery base at Cam Lo was still in operation. Farther west at the base of the Rockpile, more artillery was hauled in and readied. And at remote and westernmost Khe Sanh, sometimes called "The End of the Line," artillery and infantry were positioned to block the NVA mountain infiltration routes into South Vietnam.

Major Frank B. Ellis, the "Silver-Fox," now commanded HMM-265. A future Lieutenant General, Major Charles A. "Chuck" Pitman, had recently joined our squadron and had taken over maintenance officer responsibilities. As a relatively lowly first lieutenant, I had a few collateral duties, but my main job was still to be found in the H-46 cockpit.

On January 1, 1967, there were 65,789 Marines in all of Vietnam. Of these, 12,910 were pilots, aircrewmen, mechanics, or technicians attached to the First Marine Air Wing. Most of these Marines were assigned to the fixed-wing squadrons or support units. Only 3758 Marines flew and fought in the helicopter squadrons based at Ky Ha, Marble Mountain, and Phu Bai.

The past year had ushered in big changes for Marine helicopter operations. Most notable had been the arrival of the first two H-46 squadrons, HMM-164 and HMM-265, in the late spring. By the end of the year two more H-46 squadrons, HMM-165 and HMM-262, had landed in Vietnam and were now located at Ky Ha. Counting the Hueys, the H-34s, the H-46s, and even the eight giant H-37 Deuces still on hand, the Marine Corps had eleven helicopter squadrons in Vietnam. These eleven squadrons had a total of 234 helicopters, although 52 others had been destroyed in crashes or shoot-downs during the past twelve months. All of the Marine helicopters were based at either Ky Ha, Marble Mountain, or Phu Bai, where relatively secure maintenance facilities had been set up. From the two northernmost bases, Marble Mountain and Phu Bai, rotating detachments of Hueys, H-46s, and H-34s shuttled back and forth for temporary duty at Dong Ha and Khe Sanh.

At the northernmost Marine helicopter base at Phu Bai, the "Superchief" pilots of HMM-163 considered themselves to be the elite of Marine Aviation. These were the famous men who had flown on the incredible rescue attempt at A-Shau nine months earlier. Isolated at Phu Bai and far from the watchful eye of MAG-16 brass, the Superchief pilots and aircrewmen enjoyed a devil-may-care life. In reality the HMM-163 crews were a somewhat rag-tag band, but they relished their role as the northernmost helicopter squadron in Vietnam. Even their squadron ready-room tent possessed a casually aristocratic flair. A large handpainted wooden sign over the ready-room door proudly identified the squadron as "T. W. A." Underneath in very small letters and enclosed in parenthesis was the explanation: "Teeny Weeny Airlines."

The dash of the HMM-163 pilots did not stop there. They had adopted the world famous beagle, Snoopy, as their mascot, and another elaborately painted sign inside of their ready-room featured a grinning and sneering Snoopy piloting a Superchief H-34. The enemy soldiers down below were drawn as little stick-men sloshing through the mud, and Snoopy's gunners were mowing them down. With one paw out of the cockpit, Snoopy prepared to drop an 81mm mortar round earthward. He held a glass of champagne aloft with his other paw, and his red scarf trailed back into the slipstream as he flew his helicopter over the battlefield. But the crowning touch to the sign was not Snoopy or the artwork, but instead the caption: "MARINE AVIATION LENDS DIGNITY TO WHAT WOULD OTHERWISE BE A DIRTY BRAWL."

January 4, 1967: Four months earlier a freak set of circumstances had spelled near disaster for an H-34 from HMM-161. Now the same kind of lightning was about to strike an H-34 from a different squadron, HMM-263 at Marble Mountain. First Lieutenants William G. "Bill" Barnes and James H. "Jim" Street, both friends of mine, flew their Powerglide H-34 down into the rice basin south of Da Nang. They landed, loaded up with Grunt casualties, and took off again. From the nearby riverbank an enemy gunner opened fire, and one round smashed into the R-1820 Wright engine throttle control box. The impact shattered the fuel control arm, and the engine roared out of control to full power.

Bill snatched in collective pitch to keep the rotor system from overspeeding and disintegrating. Just like the hapless HMM-161 crew, Bill and Jim had no viable options available to them. They could climb, or die.

At 500 feet above the ground the damaged H-34 with the runaway engine entered the cloud base. The pilots had no alternative. The *MAG-16 Command Chronology* would later make note of their perilous IFR flight back toward Da Nang. Bill, the HAC, chose to home in on the Da Nang TACAN, Channel 37, rather than head back toward nearby Marble Mountain. The secure area surrounding the huge Da Nang airfield was much larger, and better crash and rescue facilities were also located at Da Nang.

By the time the digital DME mileage gauge rolled down to zero, Bill and Jim were at 8500 feet and still in the clouds. Carefully they verbally rehearsed their plan on the ICS, because they would not get a second chance. Jim would pull the Mixture Control all the way back to Idle-Cut-Off. When the engine sputtered and died, Bill would jam the collective down and kick in right rudder. Then they would autorotate down through the clouds. If they were lucky, they would break out of the overcast over a suitable landing area.

Jim, a former Class 29-63 MARCAD from Atlanta, Georgia, grabbed the red Mixture Control Lever in his right hand. He took a deep nervous breath and then pulled the lever rearward.

Jim pulled the mixture back -- but nothing happened!
-- (William G. "Bill" Barnes; years later)

The engine kept on hammering away at full power. They would later find out that the enemy bullet had disabled both the mixture control and throttle control linkage arms.

"Kill it with the mags!"

Unable to shut off the flow of fuel into his runaway engine, Jim reached for the magneto switch and twisted it all the way to the left. The engine coughed, then stopped.

With his heart in his throat, Bill slammed the collective down and kicked in full right rudder. He would only get this one chance, he knew, as he blindly spiraled down through the clouds. His eyes stayed glued to the Artificial Horizon and the Airspeed Indicator as he held the damaged H-34 in a 15 degree right bank. Right under his Airspeed Indicator, the Dual Tachometer needles had split, and the only force keeping the rotors turning was the upward flow of air through the unpowered rotor system. Bill milked the collective to keep the lifesaving rotor RPM within the prescribed limits.

Da Nang Tower had halted all inbound and outbound traffic.

The crippled H-34 broke out of the clouds right over the north-south runway. Bill autorotated down, flared, and cushioned the touchdown with collective pitch and the stored inertia in the main rotor system. They landed right on the runway, and the H-34 even had enough ground roll to coast off onto an adjacent taxiway. (Bill had no way to know it then, but fate would once again give him a brush with disaster before the end of January.)

Two days later HMM-362, flying with the SLF aboard the *USS Iwo Jima* (LPH-2), *USS Vancouver* (LPD-2), and the *USS Thomaston* (LSD-28), kicked off an operation far to the south. A mixed bag of H-34s and H-46s began ferrying the 1st Battalion, 9th Marines, into the flooded rice paddies along the coastal plain. This action marked the last time the SLF was used below I-Corps in Vietnam. The SLF offensive, called Operation Deckhouse V, accomplished little. The Grunts sloshed through waist deep water and found few signs of the enemy. On the second day of the operation a Grunt passenger accidentally dropped an armed grenade in one of the helicopters. The blast killed both the Grunt who erred and the helicopter gunner, who dove for the loose grenade and tried to toss it out of the H-46. The sturdy helicopter, YL-45, did not crash, and it limped back to a safe landing on the *Iwo Jima*.

Back in I-Corps the helicopter squadrons carried on business as usual. On January 6 while Operation Deckhouse V was cranking up, HMM-265 got the chance to help out a Marine fixed-wing pilot. The A-4 Skyhawk driver had ejected in hostile territory south of Hill 55, and he immediately pulled out his battery powered emergency radio. Transmitting on Guard Channel, he pleaded for help. His distress call caught the ear of two HMM-265 pilots.

Put your beeper on the air,
There's a rescue chopper near.
Oh, Hallelujah! Oh, Hallelujah!
Put your beeper on the air, and you'll be saved.
-- (anonymous; refrain from helicopter pilots' barroom ballad)

An H-46 zoomed down and picked up the unhurt but shaken Skyhawk pilot, and within 15 minutes he was deposited at Charlie-

Med at Da Nang. Several days later he sent the customary bottles of liquor to all four members of the Bonnie-Sue helicopter crew.

Marble Mountain, January 8, 1967: Until January 8, Marble Mountain had been home to only four types of Marine helicopters: the venerable H-34, the huge but cantankerous H-37 "Deuce," the Huey, and the H-46. Now a brand new helicopter came on the scene, and we all dubbed it the Super-Bird. The giant Sikorsky H-53 had finally arrived in Vietnam.

As far back as the mid-1950s, the Marine Corps planners had dreamed of a helicopter that could lift 20 tons, a helicopter that could lift its own weight. As early as March 1959, Sikorsky had modified a single H-37 into a Flying Crane and had designated it the S-60. Yet, twin supercharged Pratt & Whitney radial engines could produce only 4200 shaft horsepower, and the ungainly Flying Crane never entered the Marine Corps inventory. Undaunted, in 1962 the Sikorsky engineers had mated powerful twin turbines to the S-60 and had redesignated it the S-64. The Marine Corps had then expressed genuine interest, but funding problems doomed the project. Although the S-64 became a civilian success, it never wore Marine Corps green.

Sikorsky had started anew. The military version of the S-64 was scrapped, and a brand new design evolved. A massive 72 foot diameter main rotor topped the fuselage, and it was powered by two General Electric T64-GE-413 turbines that produced 7900 shaft horsepower. The new helicopter first flew in October 1964. Months of research and flight testing followed, and Sikorsky engineers made the necessary modifications to prepare the new helicopter for military duty. In September 1966 the Marine Corps had taken possession of the first four new helicopters, and the huge H-53 Sea Stallion entered active duty.

In Santa Ana, California, the four H-53s had gotten protective armor for the pilots and engines, and machinegun mounts were installed on each side of the cabin. By early December new sand filters had been fitted on the turbine air intakes. The four H-53s were then loaded aboard the USS Croatan (TAKV-43) for the long trip across the Pacific Ocean to Vietnam. Finally on January 8, 1967, the four new helicopters were unloaded onto the dock at Da

Nang and then towed overland to nearby Marble Mountain. The new H-53 squadron, HMH-463 (meaning, *Helicopter, Marine, Heavy, arbitrary designation number 463*), began preparing the new arrivals for combat duty. Recognized by their radio call-sign, "Dimmer," the H-53s would provide the true heavy-lift capability so desperately needed by the Marines. The H-53 packed the lifting power to retrieve any downed helicopter except another H-53.

Low clouds and poor visibility continued to hamper our flight operations. Routine resupply missions were scheduled to fit in with breaks in the weather to the extent possible, but emergency missions were another matter. Captains George W. Cumpston and Billy D. "Mad-Dog" Collins, both HACs, got fragged to launch from Dong Ha. There were three Marine patrols in separate locations below the DMZ and north of Con Thien, and they were out of C-Rations, the Grunts reported. Colonel Mendenhall, the officer in charge of Marine Air at Dong Ha, fought the frag as best he could. He knew there was little hope that the helicopters could locate the Grunts in the torrential rain, and he also knew that two H-46s and their crews would be endangered. Finally faced with a direct order from Task Force Delta, he had no choice. The frag would require two HMM-265 helicopters: "Launch the forty-sixes."

On one terrible day with heavy rain, fog, and a ceiling of about 200 feet . . . .
-- (Herbert E. Mendenhall; years later)

Collins and Cumpston loaded up, fired up, engaged their rotors, and cautiously took off northward. If they got over 200 feet above the ground, they would be swallowed up by the clouds. If that happened they could pull in power and execute an immediate IFR climb. Then a GCA instrument approach back to Dong Ha, or to Phu Bai 40 miles to the south, would be their only option.

The two helicopters cautiously eased northward under the clouds. In the pouring rain, forward visibility was almost nothing at all, so the pilots air-taxied at 50 knots and groped their way over the terrain. On the FM radio they contacted the Grunts as they maneuvered by dead reckoning toward the charted landing areas.

Viewed through the plexiglass windshields, the ground below was a soggy gray tangle of undergrowth. Terrain features meant nothing. They stowed their maps and tried to get the Grunts to direct them aurally toward the landing areas that were obscured by the torrential rains.

"We hear you," one Grunt radioman reported. That was encouraging, for the H-46s must have been within a mile or so for the Grunts to hear the sound of the rotors. For 20 minutes the Grunts tried to direct the helicopters, but their efforts turned out to be futile. Just before aborting the mission, Cumpston and Collins happened to overfly one Grunt patrol at a height of about 40 feet. The helicopters dropped down and landed, and the Grunts unloaded the cargo while the pilots pondered their next move. They elected to scrub the rest of the mission before they flew into the ground or stumbled into an NVA bivouac area and got everyone killed. Pulling in power and turning southward, the two HACs headed back to Dong Ha. They would return when the weather improved to the extent that they could see where they were going.

Foul flying weather and ground fire were not the only hazards. The Night-Striker Recon team boarded an HMM-265 helicopter on January 11, and their stay in the field would be three to five days if everything went according to plan. However, the NVA routinely booby-trapped likely helicopter landing zones, and on this occasion the NVA had guessed correctly. The H-46 landed, the ramp dropped, and the Recons ran for cover in the surrounding brush. Ten feet from the H-46, one of them snagged the enemy trip wire. The blast downed three men, and the unwounded Recons helped their injured comrades back into the helicopter. The H-46 headed for the field hospital, and the crew would later muse that they had made the quickest Recon extraction in Marine Corps history.

Ban Lanh Village, January 14, 1967: Although most of the fighting raged in the north, the rice basin south of Da Nang remained a lethal cauldron of enemy activity. On January 14 the two H-46 squadrons at Marble Mountain put together a total of twelve H-46 helicopters for what would become known as the River Raid. Roughly seven miles west of Hoi An, about halfway upriver toward An Hoa, lies the village of Ban Lanh. Although it bears only one name, there are really two separate villages about 1000 meters apart, one at BT-010541 and the other at BT-014548. The two collections of thatched hootches are separated by rice paddies, and these paddies had been flooded by the January rains.

The Marine Grunts patrolled the area from the river northward to Da Nang, 13 miles away. However, the land south of the river remained completely hostile Indian Country. A network of enemy trenches and bunkers ringed the twin villages at Ban Lanh. A blue and red National Liberation Front flag, emblazoned with a bright yellow star, defiantly fluttered in the breeze from the top of a flagpole in the easternmost village.

The Marine plan called for a company of Grunts, about 180 men, to fly in by helicopter and destroy the fortifications. There was to be no attempt to occupy or control the villages. This would be just a raid, nothing more, and the enemy was expected to put up stiff resistance.

I did not fly in the morning assault, but the pilots involved reported only light ground fire on the initial troop lift. The twelve helicopters, each carrying about 15 Grunts, flew in, dropped off the troops, and departed without much of a problem. But the Grunts ran into a veritable hornet's nest as they worked their way toward the enemy defenses. It did not take long for them to radio for artillery support and medevac helicopters.

Two Bonnie-Sue H-46s from HMM-265 clawed their way skyward from Marble Mountain and headed south toward Ban Lanh. The second H-46 was piloted by two of the most colorful aviators in the entire Marine Corps, Captain Harry R. "Bob" Mills and First Lieutenant Emmitt E. "Fat-Jack" Exum Jr.

Bob Mills had been in the original Shu-Fly squadron down at Soc Trang. Now he was back as an experienced HAC for his second combat tour in Vietnam. Bob and his filthy red bandanna had become a familiar sight at Marble Mountain, and you could always count on Bob to be pretty close to the action. He had already completed his stint as the MAG-16 helicopter fragger at Dong Ha. Now he devoted all of his time to his true love, flying as a HAC in one of our Bonnie-Sue H-46s.

Fat-Jack, Bob's copilot on this medevac mission, was a flamboyant flyer from MARCAD Class 29-63. During basic flight training, Fat-Jack had marched into Naval Aviation history -- also *worldwide* aviation history -- when he established an infamous aeronautical record that still stands a quarter-century later. Fat-Jack is the only known pilot in the world who has survived a midair collision on his very first solo flight.

Way back on February 13 (his birthday), 1964, Fat-Jack had taken off from Saufley Field north of Pensacola in his T-34, radio call-sign Sioux-Falls 128. This had been Fat-Jack's first solo flight. He had completed his prescribed maneuvers and then had headed back toward Saufley Field, overflying Barron Field at 1400 feet. Down below a flight of five T-28C Trojans had inadvertently broken their 800 foot altitude cap while climbing for a flight out to the *USS Lexington* for carrier landings. At a head-on speed of about 300 knots, both pilots had glimpsed each other just a split second before the impact.

WHHAAAACCKK!

A glancing blow to Fat-Jack's right wing!

The impact broke Fat-Jack's wing spar. His aileron ripped completely off of the T-34, and part of his flaps had followed suit. Initially unable to pull his wounded airplane out of a steep right spiral, Fat-Jack had repressed the temptation to bail out. With full power, full left rudder, and full left aileron -- but still in a right spiral -- he slowly had managed to climb to 4000 feet. Then he had gradually made his way back toward Saufley Field by flying a series of elongated right-turn circles in the sky. Alerted by radio, the crash crew, the meat wagon, and hundreds of spectators had gathered at home plate to watch the impending crash.

Fat-Jack had disappointed them all. Aided by a combination of dumb luck and flying skill, he had correctly timed his circling descent and had landed right on the Saufley Field runway. To this day, Fat-Jack remains the only known *surviving* pilot in the world who has logged both his first solo, and a midair collision, on the same flight.

Now, three years later, Fat-Jack and Bob were flying together in Vietnam. Following Number One, they landed in a flooded rice paddy just outside of the village of Ban Lanh. Sitting in the paddy like a big green bull's-eye, they waited while the Grunts dragged the casualties toward the helicopter.

Enemy fire raked the landing zone. Hit repeatedly, unwilling to sit there and take the heat, Number One sucked in power and took off, trailing water and mud from his landing gear and stub-wings. Bob and Fat-Jack ignored the incoming fire, because the Grunt casualties had to be evacuated. Bob would describe the dangerous mission to me many years later:

> Huey gunships were making head-on strafing runs on each side of the LZ. Small arms fire and the gunship's rockets were making geysers in the rice paddies in front of us. The Grunts were screaming at us [on the radio] to hold our fire because they didn't know the positions of all the friendlies. Our own crewmen were screaming [on the ICS] for permission to fire because of the incoming. It was as hot a zone as I'd ever seen. It was absolutely chaotic.

The sharp crackle of rifle fire swept across the paddy. Frantic FM, UHF, and ICS transmissions blurred together. Back in the H-46 cabin the crew chief and gunner opened fire, adding to the bedlam. Gunsmoke drifted across the landing zone and partially obscured the view of the combatants. Bob and Fat-Jack watched the incoming rounds ricocheting across the water all around them. The din of battle and the visual panorama were terrifying, yet surrealistic. Peering through the windshield, Bob could scarcely believe his eyes. Could this nightmare really be happening? Bob looked across the cockpit at Fat-Jack and keyed the ICS mike: "JESUS, JACK! THIS IS JUST LIKE THE MOVIES!"

Bob and Fat-Jack weathered the hostile fire and flew the wounded Grunts back to Charlie-Med. The pitched battle at Ban Lanh continued for most of the day, and military records would later reflect 26 Marine casualties. Still, by the late afternoon the Grunts had overrun all of their objectives. Then the demolition specialists plied their perilous trade on the munitions that the Grunts had discovered in Ban Lanh.

1800 Hours: The original twelve helicopters made a final trip to haul the Grunts back to the staging area west of Hoi An. During the extraction, ten of the helicopters took hits. The Grunt company commander, a Captain, was strapped into a web troop seat in an H-46 cabin. An enemy 12.7mm round blasted through the thin fuselage skin and struck the young Captain squarely in the head. The Captain's entire skull exploded and splattered the helicopter cabin and the battle-weary Grunts with brains and blood.

> It is well that war is so terrible; we would grow too fond of it.
> -- (General Robert E. Lee, Confederate States Army; speaking to his victorious army commanders at Fredericksburg, Virginia, on December 13, 1862)

The damaged H-46 followed the rest of the flight back to the staging area, and the Grunts debarked. The flight then returned to Marble Mountain. After his helicopter had refueled and shut down, the young crew chief wept as he cleaned up the gore on the aluminum floor of his helicopter cabin.

The placid Song Ta Trach River meanders upstream from Phu Bai, winding its way southward toward its mountain headwaters. Following the river upstream, one first transverses the coastal flatlands. Farther south the river channel twists its way through rugged mountain passes into a small valley located 22 miles due south of Phu Bai and 31 miles west of Da Nang. Flanked by 2000 foot high peaks on the east and west, the valley is home to a small Vietnamese Montagnard hamlet, a collection of thatched huts. According to our 1:50,000 scale maps, there was no other village, not even a single hootch, within twelve miles.

During the previous decade the French had hacked out a 1600 foot long dirt airstrip and had named it Ruong-Ruong, the same name given to the village. But now the airstrip had been abandoned for many years, and I personally wonder if it had ever been used at all. Two old wooden blockhouses had also been built by the French at the base of Hill 306, a mile south of stone-age Ruong-Ruong. These blockhouses had guarded the river gorge -- against whom I can not imagine. Naturally these structures had been abandoned long ago, and by now they had fallen prey to the jungle-rot that rapidly destroys any wooden structures in the humid Annamese Cordillera.

Here in this remote and Godforsaken wilderness, far from civilization, Marine helicopters inserted a twelve man Recon team. The Recons had come to detect any possible enemy staging areas or troop movements in the narrow valley. Conceivably the NVA could enter the valley from Laos and follow the river downstream toward Hue. Sure enough, the Recons stumbled upon a platoon sized NVA force, and they quickly broke contact. Their presence had been compromised, so they radioed for a rapid extraction.

"Launch Sparrowhawk."

Harpo had pulled section leader duty for the two helicopters on Sparrowhawk standby at Dong Ha. Op's North fragged Harpo to fly down to Phu Bai, the staging area for the emergency Recon extraction. Low fog blanketed the coastal plain, so the flight climbed up into the soup, contacted Phu Bai Approach Control on 315.5 megacycles, and headed down the coast. Less than 20 minutes later they were on the ground at Phu Bai.

Phu Bai, January 16, 1967: After the helicopters had been refueled, the pilots gathered in the HMM-163 ready-room. With Snoopy's famous caricature leering at them, they got the usual detailed briefing, or at least as much information as was known. The Recons were "in close proximity to unfriendly forces at YD-885805," the briefing officer intoned. As was generally the case in such situations, the exact size of the enemy unit was not known, so reinforcing the Recons might be more feasible than extracting them. Accordingly, the plan called for using four H-46s, two of them empty and the remaining two carrying a Sparrowhawk reaction force of 30 Grunts. If possible the two empty helicopters would land and pick up the Recons. If that plan should prove to be impractical, the reaction force would be inserted. Fixed-wing support was out of the question because of the miserable flying weather. Instead, four Huey gunships would escort the four H-46s.

The mini-armada of eight helicopters launched from Phu Bai and headed south. Leading the flight in Bureau Number 151907, Harpo planned to follow the 180 degree radial of the Phu Bai TACAN due south to the extraction coordinates. Unfortunately, once he was airborne he quickly realized that this plan would not work. The cloud base was less than 500 feet above the terrain, and five miles south of Phu Bai the mountains jutted up into the clouds. The flight could not remain VFR over the mountains. True, they could have climbed IFR and flown over the mountains and overcast, but then they would have been unable to find their way down through the clouds into the valley. Foiled, the flight returned to Phu Bai in hopes that the weather would soon improve.

After an hour the Recons radioed an urgent request. They were still in danger, they reported, and they needed help in a hurry. Hearing this, Harpo decided to try another tactic. His helicopter could not go over the mountains, but perhaps it could go through them. Harpo studied his map. From the small village at Ruong-Ruong, the Song Ta Trach twists its way northward through the mountains toward the sea. Joined by tributaries along the way, the river eventually becomes the Song Huong. Known locally as the Perfume River, it flows right past the southern wall of the Citadel in the city of Hue. Since the river twists and snakes its way through the mountain valleys and canyons, maybe the helicopters could do the same thing, Harpo reasoned. Perhaps they could fly upstream in the river gorge and stay below the clouds.

Eight helicopters were obviously too many for such a risky venture, so the reaction force option would have to be scrapped. Leaving two gunships and two of the H-46s behind, Harpo launched and headed west. Reaching the river, he turned south and followed it upstream toward the mountains. The gunship crewmen are unknown, but the two H-46s were crewed as follows:

	Number One	Number Two
Pilot:	Richard O. Harper	R. G. Temte
Copilot:	Gordon R. Jefferson	M. J. "Pep" Pepple
Crew chief:	Theodore Violissi	William P. Goldston
Gunner:	Walter K. Fergus	R. A. Penna

Harpo's copilot, First Lieutenant Gordon R. "Flash" Jefferson, would later describe the weather in a written statement: "The maximum ceiling was 200' [to] 600' AGL [meaning, *above ground level*] with visibility 1/4 mile." With only a quarter mile forward visibility, the helicopters slowed to 65 knots as they followed the winding path of the river. On each side of the river, the mountains rose up into the cloud layer 200 feet above. Single file and groping their way, the helicopters followed the river upstream.

Deeper and deeper into the mountain passes they flew, right over the surface of the river below them. In the lead H-46, Harpo strained to see through the mist ahead. Flash concentrated on his map and followed their progress upriver with his forefinger. They passed the cliffs of Dong Li Hi on the east bank, but the upper half of the rock face was obscured in the clouds. At their slow speed and low altitude they would have made easy targets, but the river gorge was uninhabited.

Suddenly rounding a bend in the shadow of Ma Xoa Mountain, they came to a fork in the river. Almost there! The walls of the canyon fell away, and they flew into a lush and flat quarter mile wide valley. Two miles ahead lay Ruong-Ruong, and a mile farther south were the pickup coordinates, YD-885805.

The FM radio came alive, because the Recons could now hear the helicopters flying up the river toward them. Then, just when success seemed to be so near, they reached the southern end of the valley. Between the helicopters and the Recons lay a four mile long ridge topped by Hill 1094. Over a thousand meters high, the mist-covered ridge blocked further progress to the south. But Harpo and his flight had come too far to turn back now.

> Major Harper told me to orbit in the valley . . . two miles from the pickup zone . . . . Weather was now approximately 150 - 200 feet AGL.
> -- (Captain R. G. Temte; in a written statement)

Alone except for the gunships, Harpo air-taxied up the gorge at the eastern end of Kenine Ridge until he reached Hill 306. Here the Recons manned a defensive perimeter on the south slope, but it was heavily jungled. There was no place to land.

Three hundred meters to the south, Harpo found a clear area where he could land and wait. Could the Recons make their way to it? Yes, they radioed, but they would have to use machetes to hack their way through the nearly impenetrable mass of vines and tangled brambles that covered the slope. It would take them at least two hours.

Impossible! With full fuel tanks, an H-46 carries only 2400 pounds of JP-4 fuel. The twin General Electric turbines burn a total of 1200 pounds per hour, so maximum endurance is only two hours. And now, 45 minutes of that two hours was already gone. Worse yet, the nimble gunship's single T-53 Lycoming turbine sucks up the smaller Huey's fuel supply at an even faster rate.

All aircraft were getting low on fuel, and one UH-1E was below bingo fuel.
-- (Captain R. G. Temte; in a written statement)

Harpo radioed his wingman, who was still orbiting back in Ruong-Ruong Valley. He asked Temte to make his way up the gorge and get in a position to provide suppressive fire, if necessary. Then Harpo keyed the ICS and told his crew chief, Sergeant Theodore J. Violissi, and his gunner, Lance Corporal Walter K. Fergus, of the plan: "We're gonna' use the hoist."

Seventy feet above the ground and ten feet above the tops of the trees, Harpo stabilized the H-46 in a hover over the Recons. Sergeant Violissi quickly rigged the hoist (officially labeled the Integrated Cargo Handling and Rescue System) and used his pistol grip control to lower the steel cable and horse-collar. One by one the Recons were winched up through the trees, through the hell-hole hatch, and into the cabin of Harpo's H-46.

The NVA platoon never seriously challenged the pickup. They cranked off a few rounds, but they evidenced no desire to engage the gunships. They probably failed to realize the tactical advantage they held in the narrow river gorge. Unable to maneuver, speed up, climb, or make sustained gun runs, the gunships were vulnerable to enemy fire.

It took 15-20 minutes to get all the people hoisted into the aircraft.
-- (First Lieutenant Gordon R. Jefferson; in a written statement)

With all of the Recons aboard at last, the helicopters turned and threaded their way down the gorge to Ruong-Ruong Valley. They then sped at treetop level over the flat valley to the river fork. There they slowed and, single file, began to work their way downstream between the cliffs along the riverbank.

The FM radio blared almost nonstop in the earphones of the pilots' flight helmets. The H-46 pilots' transmissions dealt with the obstacles along the river and the cloud base above. The distraught gunship drivers, almost in a state of panic by now, had only one overwhelming concern, their nearly depleted fuel supply. But they all made it back to Phu Bai.

The helicopters refueled, and the Recons were dropped off. The gunships had landed "on fumes," the shaken VMO-2 pilots claimed. They wisely elected to remain at Phu Bai to let their stomachs and nerves settle down.

The H-46 crews fired up their turbines and flew IFR back up to Dong Ha. By now it was late afternoon on January 16. They were destined to remain on Sparrowhawk standby duty throughout the night, they knew, and between flights they would try to stay dry and nap in their H-46 cabins. If all went well, they would be relieved at 0800 Hours the next morning.

Marble Mountain, January 18, 1967: I had not flown as Harpo's copilot since August 8, 1966, five months earlier. As a result of that flight we had both ended up in the hospital. But now on January 18 we were back together again in Bureau Number 152496, and we only logged 1.3 hours of flight time during the day. Time has erased most of the details of that mission from my memory. I recall that the frag was a simple resupply mission west of Hoi An, and we did not attract any ground fire to the best of my recollection. After we landed back at Marble Mountain, we refueled, taxied across the marston-matting, shut down, unstrapped, and started to extricate ourselves from the cockpit. I still remember Harpo's laconic queries as though he had voiced them only yesterday.

"Well, Sturk! What do you think?"

Unsure of what Harpo meant, I grinned and said nothing.

Harpo tried again: "What do you think?"

Still unsure, I shrugged my shoulders and mumbled a noncommittal reply.

Harpo bellowed: "WE BROKE THE JINX!"

Both of us rolled in laughter. We gathered our flight gear and map bags and crawled out of the cramped cockpit of our H-46. We waited for our crew chief and gunner. Then, side by side, the four of us walked across the flight line toward the drab olive-green row of HMM-265 tents. The crew chief and gunner ambled off toward the armory tent to drop off their machineguns while Harpo and I sauntered into the ready-room. Yes, we had broken the jinx, and by now my life had returned to normal.

I looked at the other pilots around me. They were all my friends. The camaraderie, the trust, and the loyalty can never be explained to one who has not experienced the unique bond that is shared by Marine Corps helicopter pilots in combat. Our bond transcended material possessions, military rank, and social status. We shared a brotherly love, a love that no worldly circumstance could ever shatter. War is a cruel game, a brutal game, a deadly game. I knew that this would be the most intense and utopian experience that I would ever have. Although it now sounds insane, right at that moment I would not have traded places with anyone else on earth.

<u>Phu Bai, January 20, 1967</u>: Two days later I had a big event scheduled, my long overdue HAC checkride. I had been delayed by my four months in the hospital, while all of my peers had already been designated HACs and were authorized to fly as pilot-in-command on combat missions. Now it was my turn. Gerry Dooley, the old veteran, grilled me for an hour with questions about possible H-46 systems failures. Then we walked out to our helicopter, lit the fires in the turbines, and took off from the asphalt runway at Phu Bai. After 15 minutes of simulated emergencies, Gerry laughed and opined: "I *guess* you passed." Then with his cigar firmly clenched between his teeth, he took the controls and we headed for YD-755106.

Back in the cabin we had perhaps 600 pounds of cargo consisting of just water and C-Rations. Waiting at our destination was a Grunt platoon atop a gentle hill that overlooks a fork in the Song Huong River. From this vantage point the Grunts could watch the valley leading toward Hue, seven miles to the north. Checking my map, I noted that one mile to the east of the Grunts the ancient Royal Tombs of the Emperors were located at YD-778104. But this was neither the time nor the place for sightseeing. The Grunts popped red smoke, and we zipped down and landed on the hill in the tall elephant grass. After dropping off our meager cargo, we flew back to Phu Bai. The following day I noted with pride that my flight logbook had been inscribed: "Designated HAC - CH-46A - 21 Jan 67."

Later that same week, Vic Vecchitto got fragged for a risky mission. He had been on standby for Sparrowhawk flights, but he got the call to medevac an injured Recon out of the hills. Arriving over the Recon position, Vic found no place to land in the mountainous jungle. Hovering over the high trees, he tried to winch the injured Recon up on the hoist, but the 100 foot long steel cable was not long enough to reach the ground. Vic was hovering only 130 feet above the Recons, but he might as well have been a mile above them. There was nothing he could do to get the injured man into the helicopter.

Vic radioed the men on the ground and told them that he would return. He pulled in collective pitch and headed back to Marble Mountain. There he refueled and got Maintenance to rig up a cable extension for the hoist. Launching for the hills again, Vic found that clouds and fog now blocked his path. He and his copilot climbed above the cloud layer and then made an "IFR penetration," according to squadron records, into a wide valley.

From the valley, Vic flew VFR back to the Recon team, lowered the cable, and hoisted the injured Recon up into the cabin. The remaining uninjured Recons then made their way down to the valley floor. Major Pitman and Gerry Dooley spiraled down, picked them up, and flew them to Marble Mountain.

Despite the terrible flying conditions in January, the Marine Command kept up the military pressure not only near the DMZ, but also down south of Da Nang. Late January saw the start of Operation Tuscaloosa and Operation Cleveland. All types of Marine helicopters except the new H-53s were called upon to support the Grunts in these search and destroy sweeps.

Marble Mountain, January 25, 1967: We had all heard our share of horror stories, and sometimes they were even true. Most of them sounded about the same: "Old what's-his-name, had only two days left in Vietnam, flew a milk run up to Dong Ha, diverted for a medevac, got himself killed."

By the time a pilot had less than a month remaining on his 13 month tour in Vietnam, he was known as a "short-timer." Such men usually began to practice private and superstitious daily rituals designed to ward off everything from evil spirits to NVA bullets. The less time there was remaining, the more intense the rituals became. During a pilot's last two weeks in Vietnam, paranoia often set in, and some men even resorted to earnest prayer. Surely their God would not allow them to die when they were *so close!*

By January 25, Bill Barnes had been a short-timer for a whole month. He had even finished his required attendance at the famous 'Couths Table in the Marble Mountain mess hall. His 13 month combat tour was over, and he now waited for orders to return to the United States. Like others whose tour was over, Bill could be forgiven if he had become jumpy and superstitious.

Only three weeks earlier when flying with Jim Street, combat damage had forced Bill to make an uncontrolled climb with a runaway engine in his H-34. An IFR autorotation followed, but they had survived. Operations had since been tempted to give Bill less hazardous missions when the flight schedule would permit it. After all, he was scheduled to go home. No operations officer wanted to be remembered as the villain who sent a pilot out to die during his last two or three days in Vietnam.

An easy flight out to the hospital ship, the *USS Repose*, was fragged to HMM-263. Bill was chosen for the mission, a real milk run, so he launched in his Powerglide H-34 and flew eastward over the South China Sea. About 20 miles out to sea the ship came into view. Bill started a routine visual approach toward the elevated helicopter landing pad on the hospital ship. He turned onto final approach . . . all lined up . . . tailwheel locked . . . . He had it made now. With a slight flare he slowed his relative motion and intended to stabilize in a high hover over the landing pad.

Then with no sputter or warning, the engine died. Bill would tell me years later: "I pancaked onto the ship."

The H-34 fell onto the small landing pad on the *Repose*, not into the adjacent ocean where they would have sunk like an anvil. Bill and his crew crawled out, unhurt and happy to be alive.

Now a new problem arose. Bill's stricken H-34 blocked the ship's landing pad, and a maintenance crew could not be flown in to make the necessary repairs. Consequently, the stage was now set for the first downed helicopter retrieval in Vietnam by one of the new Sikorsky H-53 Super-Birds.

25 Jan 67: A CH-53A from . . . HMH-463 [lifted] a disabled UH-34 off the landing platform of a Navy hospital ship.
-- (Lieutenant Colonel William R. Fails; in *Marines and Helicopters: 1962-1973*)

The rotor blades on Bill's H-34 were manually folded, and the prescribed sling was attached to the rotor head. Then the powerful new H-53 flew out from Marble Mountain and hovered over the downed helicopter. A crew chief attached the sling, and the H-53 picked up the smaller helicopter. Bill's H-34 got a free ride back to Marble Mountain, where mechanics began the necessary repairs. Shortly thereafter Bill's transfer orders arrived, and within hours he was winging his way back to the United States.

More and more of our flying time was incurred just below the DMZ. Although I only remember one of them, my logbook shows two GCA approaches during the last week of January. Flying with one of my tentmates, Huey Walsh, we slowed to 100 knots and eased down toward Dong Ha, guided only by the controller's voice on the radio. At about 150 feet above the terrain the radar altimeter warning light winked on, but we were still in the clouds and could not see the ground below. I flipped on the windshield wipers to help clear away the rain. We normally did not use the wipers unless we needed them badly, because they would eventually create score marks in the plexiglass. We got visual contact with the ground a few moments later, and Huey jested with a silly laugh: "Well, I guess we're gonna' make it."

I stayed at Dong Ha until January 26. Beginning that afternoon a chain of misfortune would culminate in a night of terror for MAG-16 helicopter pilots, crew chiefs, and gunners. Four H-46s and two Hueys would be destroyed; all would be reduced to smoldering wreckage before the sun rose the next morning. Three of the four downed H-46 crews would spend the night surrounded by the North Vietnamese. It would be a long night in the mountains west of Khe Sanh. In fact, we would call it THE LONGEST NIGHT.

Burnout: I am getting used to this thing called war. It's just like work at home except you get up and go to war and you go to bed late and tired, knowing you will get up and go to war tomorrow. Death is so commonplace it doesn't shock you anymore.
-- (H. Lee Bell; in *1369*)

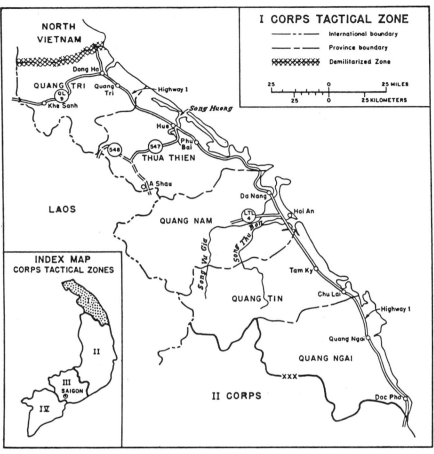

The United States divided South Vietnam into five tactical military zones. American military responsibility for the northernmost zone was assigned to the Marine Corps. The northernmost Vietnamese provinces of Quang Tri, Thua Thien, Quang Nam, Quang Tin, and Quang Ngai fell within this embattled First Corps, or "I-Corps" (pronounced, *eye-core*).

The Marines built their largest helicopter base at Marble Mountain, three miles east of the Da Nang Airfield. They set up another main helicopter base far to the south on the seacoast at Ky Ha, near Chu Lai. In northern I-Corps the Marines also built a base for helicopter operations at Phu Bai, seven miles south of Hue. A temporary helicopter base was later maintained at Quang Tri.

(Adapted from a map originally published in *War in the Northern Provinces*, courtesy of the Department of the Army)

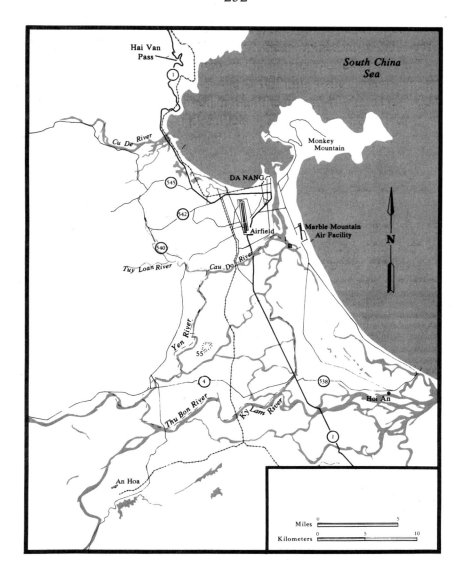

The Marine helicopter base at Marble Mountain lay on the sandy seacoast by the South China Sea, southeast of Da Nang. Below Marble Mountain and Da Nang were the heavily populated and rice-rich coastal flatlands.

(Adapted from a map originally published in *U.S. Marines in Vietnam: An Expanding War, 1966*, courtesy of History & Museums Division, Headquarters USMC)

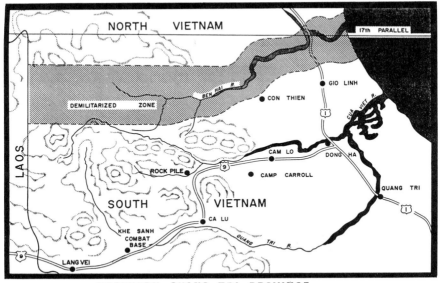

NORTHERN QUANG TRI PROVINCE

In 1966 the North Vietnamese Army 324-B Division marched south across the DMZ into the mountains of Quang Tri Province. On July 15, 1966, the Marines attacked the invading North Vietnamese Army in the mountains and jungles west of Dong Ha. The fighting would continue for three years.

Just below the DMZ the Marines set up artillery bases at Con Thien and at Gio Linh. In 1967 the huge rectangle formed by Marine bases at Con Thien, Gio Linh, Dong Ha, and Cam Lo became a no-man's-land and killing field known as Leatherneck Square. In the mountains to the west, The Rockpile, The Razorback, Mutter Ridge, and Helicopter Valley became focal points in the struggle. For the Marines, "The End of the Line" was their garrison at remote and isolated Khe Sanh.

(Adapted from a map published in *The Battle for Khe Sanh*, courtesy of History & Museums Division, Headquarters USMC)

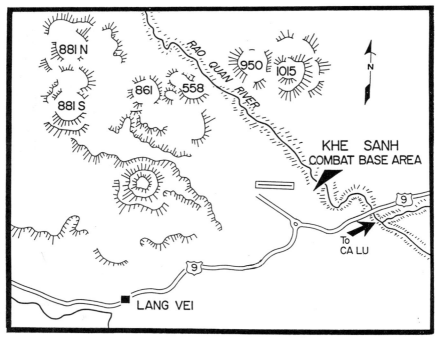

KHE SANH VALLEY

The rugged mountains and jungles in northwest Quang Tri Province concealed a North Vietnamese Army infiltration route into South Vietnam. The Marines set up the garrison at Khe Sanh to monitor and interdict the invading North Vietnamese. North and west of the Khe Sanh airstrip, the Marines manned observation outposts on the peaks of Hill 881 South and Hill 861. They also maintained a radio relay outpost atop lofty Hill 950.

Colonial Route 9, originally built by the French Army, had been a one-lane-wide dirt trail running west from Dong Ha into Laos. The Marines periodically tried to improve the road in an effort to establish a ground route to remote Khe Sanh. However, monsoon rains and hostile enemy action often made the twisting mountain trail impassable west of Razorback Valley.

(Adapted from a map published in *The Battle for Khe Sanh*, courtesy of History & Museums Division, Headquarters USMC)

Cockpit of the CH-46D helicopter (*without* the armored seats).

(Illustration courtesy of Congressional and Public Affairs Office, Naval Air Systems Command)

THUNDERMUG, the HMM-265 squadron mascot. The junior Bonnie-Sue pilots in HMM-265 created *THUNDERMUG* over a year before HMM-265 left the United States for Vietnam. This prized mascot was afforded full military honors and, with the cooperation of the United States Navy, was *piped aboard* ship whenever the squadron deployed. *THUNDERMUG* served a practical as well as aesthetic purpose. At social functions the watertight basin of the toilet would be poured full of an appropriate alcoholic beverage. All Marines present could fill their glasses by dipping them into the basin. The reservoir tank atop the rear of the toilet held batteries that powered the red rotating beacon. *THUNDERMUG* bears the HMM-265 squadron logo and the numerical designation of the first Marine Corps H-46 helicopter, EP-151, Bureau Number 150942.

(Photograph by Marion F. Sturkey)

"Echo-Tango twenty-nine" (ET-29), an H-46 from HMM-262, is on final approach for the flight deck of the *USS Guadalcanal* (LPH-7). This helicopter has not yet been modified for combat operations in Vietnam. Note the visible absence of engine-intake sand and dust filters, and the absence of armor plate over the engines. Also, there is no gunport on the left side of the helicopter. Such an unmodified H-46 would still have the factory installed seats for the pilot and copilot, as opposed to the armored seats that would be installed for combat missions in Vietnam.

The *Guadalcanal* was designed for Marine Corps helicopter assault. These helicopter carriers provided cargo and berthing areas for a battalion of Marine Infantry, plus berthing and maintenance areas for a helicopter squadron. The first ship in this class, the *USS Iwo Jima* (LPH-2), was authorized in January 1958 and was built at the Puget Sound Naval Shipyard in Bremerton, Washington. She was launched on September 17, 1960.

(USMC Photograph A-450439 courtesy of Department of Defense)

William T. "Tee" Holmes Jr. flew H-34s in HMM-263, the "Powerglide" squadron, in Vietnam throughout 1966. Pictured from left to right are Tee and other First Lieutenants H. Ray "Ramjet" Ramsburg, Steve Corrie, and Noel S. Salmon. The four flyers are standing on the south side of the dirt airstrip at Dong Ha in early 1966. Many years after the war, with a mischievous mind, Tee began scribbling several tongue-in-cheek captions for his old wartime photograph:

-- I think they misspelled it. It should be *D-U-N-G* Ha.
-- "The Supremes" before their sex-change operations.
-- Men, that clothesline full of black pajamas is not a good sign.
-- Don't we get one last cigarette?
-- American Mistakes in Vietnam, 1963-1973, Exhibit A.
-- The relief tube is *HOW* far out there?
-- They really expect us to *FLY* those [expletive deleted] things?
-- You reckon if we added some extra fuel tanks, we could fly it
    to Okinawa?

(Photograph and captions courtesy of William T. Holmes)

A Sikorsky H-34 helicopter waits for its next frag. This H-34 squats just outside of the concertina wire at an unidentified outpost in Vietnam.

The H-34 served as the backbone of Marine Corps trooplift capability in Vietnam for years. Until the arrival of the H-46s in 1966, and the H-53s in 1967, the H-34 "carried the load." Even after the arrival of the larger turbine-powered helicopters, the H-34s remained on duty in Vietnam until August 20, 1969. Thereafter, the remaining H-34 helicopters were transferred to Marine Corps Reserve units in the United States. The last known flight of a Marine Corps H-34 took place on October 3, 1973. On that date, Bureau Number 147191 flew from Norfolk, Virginia, to the Marine Corps base at New River, North Carolina. There it was officially removed from Marine Corps records and enshrined at the main-gate entrance to MCAS New River.

(Photograph courtesy of Sikorsky Aircraft)

Two H-46s from HMM-161 land in "Arizona Territory" west of An Hoa. This rolling hill-country drew its nickname from the infamous and hostile badlands of the American West. The Viet Cong R-20 Battalion had controlled the countryside. However, in 1966 the Marines pushed south to An Hoa to safeguard the South Vietnamese industrial complex there. The Marines built the famous Liberty Road that connected An Hoa with Hill 55 and Da Nang. Their construction of the bridge over the Song Thu Bon River was a major engineering feat.

The first mass introduction of main force North Vietnamese Army troops into the An Hoa basin came in 1967. After that, the region was hotly contested for the duration of the war. The daily. life of Marine infantrymen in and around Arizona Territory was eloquently chronicled by Philip Caputo, a former Marine rifle platoon commander. His emotional masterpiece, *A Rumor of War*, first published in 1977, offered readers compassionate insight into the obstacles and frustrations facing the Marine "Grunts."

(USMC Photograph A-422630 courtesy of Department of Defense)

On July 15, 1966, this Bonnie-Sue H-46 helicopter from HMM-265 took hits from enemy AAA fire. Trailing smoke and flames, it is shown just before it crashed in the Song Ngan Valley. Thirteen Marines died in the crash and fire. Three survived.

The helicopter crew: pilot, Captain Thomas C. "Tee-Cee" McAllister; copilot, First Lieutenant George Richey Jr.; crew chief, Sergeant Robert R. Telfer; and gunner, Sergeant Gary A. Lucus. Carrying twelve "Grunts" and heading for Landing Zone Crow, the H-46 (EP-171) was hit repeatedly at about 1500 feet. Pressurized fuel gushed into the cabin and ignited, filling the helicopter with flame and blinding black smoke. The H-46 crashed on a hillside and exploded. Marines on the ground rushed toward the burning wreckage, but were driven away by the intense heat and explosions from the munitions "cooking off" in the blazing inferno.

Over the caption, "Hit by Enemy Ground Fire, a U.S. Helicopter Goes Down in Flames," this photograph headed an article in the August 1, 1966, issue of *Newsweek Magazine*.

(Photograph courtesy of AP/Wide World Photos, Inc.)

(TOP)   On July 25, 1966, wounded Marines from India Company, 3rd Battalion, 5th Marines, are loaded into a Huey. The medevac flight to Dong Ha will take about eight minutes.

(BOTTOM)   An H-46 lands on "Mutter Ridge" to pick up Marines from Mike Company, 3rd Battalion, 4th Marines. The landing zone has been hacked out of the trees and undergrowth.

(USMC Photographs A-190174 [top] and A-193491 [bottom] courtesy of Department of Defense)

Young Vietnamese children crowd around First Lieutenant Marion F. Sturkey at Dong Ha. The lure of free candy, C-Rations, and cigarettes acted like a magnet to attract the young Vietnamese. There was no language barrier, because "Number One!" or "Number Ten!" sufficed to describe anything. Many a Marine was turned into a Pied Piper by carrying a small sack of candy. However, after the massive military buildup in the summer of 1966, civilians were barred from the airfield for security reasons.

(Photograph provided by Marion F. Sturkey)

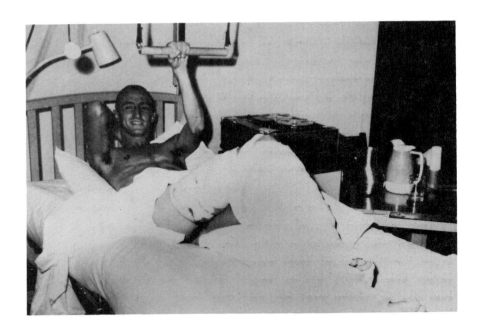

First Lieutenant Marion F. Sturkey convalesces at the United States Naval Hospital in Yokosuka, Japan, in late August 1966.

On the night of August 8, 1966, in the valley east of Razorback Ridge, 24 Marines from Echo Company, 2nd Battalion, 4th Marines, plus four Recon Marines, had been surrounded by North Vietnamese soldiers at XD-986597. Sturkey flew as copilot in the first Bonnie-Sue medevac helicopter from HMM-265. The North Vietnamese opened fire when the helicopter got within 20 to 25 feet of the ground. All four helicopter crewmen were shot.

Pilot	Richard O. Harper	gunshot wounds, hand and chest
Copilot	Marion F. Sturkey	gunshot wound, right foot
Crew chief	Herbert S. Murff	gunshot wound, abdomen
Gunner	Luke A. Stephen	gunshot wound, right forearm

Although wounded, the pilots nursed their helicopter back to the airstrip at Dong Ha. All aboard initially survived, although Herbert Murff later died from medical complications.

(Photograph provided by Marion F. Sturkey)

MY KHE , THURSDAY, AUGUST 18 - 66

DEAR AMERICAN SOLDIER

I HAVE HONOUR To SEND you A FRIEND WHO FROM A FAR COUNTRY FOR tHE love oF IdEAls , Helps MY nATION keep FREEDOM INtHct..

THANK you FOR youR GOOD wIll . J wISH you SWIFt RECOVERY .

WITH love

PHAM THI NE
PHAN CHU TRINH
HiGH SCHOOL

Captain Richard O. "Harpo" Harper was wounded while piloting EP-163 on the night of August 8, 1966.   Ten days later a Vietnamese schoolgirl visited him in the NSA Hospital in Da Nang and gave him this handwritten note.

(Note courtesy of Richard O. Harper)

The Sikorsky H-37 Mohave, the mighty "Deuce." Mechanics and their mascot (the dog) pose by their helicopter in Vietnam.

The Deuce, the name by which the H-37 became known, was born ahead of its time, and it first flew in December 1953. Four decades later the sheer size of this 1950s-vintage helicopter still staggers the senses. The Deuce had two huge supercharged 18-cylinder R-2800 Pratt & Whitney radial engines that pounded out 4,200 shaft horsepower. The five-blade main rotor system spanned 72 feet in diameter. The Deuce incorporated new and advanced features such as an automatic blade fold system for shipboard operations, previously unheard of for helicopters.

Too advanced, to complex, and too cantankerous, the Deuce deserved a better fate. Yet, it pioneered the technology that paved the way for the giant twin-turbine powered Sikorsky H-53.

(Photograph courtesy of Sikorsky Aircraft)

Vietnamese refugees exit the cabin of a Sikorsky H-34. A Vietnamese woman carries a child (by the helicopter door), and a Marine (right foreground) carries another. The H-34 pilot looks down from the cockpit, above.

The Marine Corps H-34 evolved from the HSS-1, a Navy antisubmarine helicopter. The first Marine Corps H-34 flew in January 1957. By the time the "Shu-Fly" Marines of HMM-362 arrived in Vietnam in 1962, the "thirty four" had proved its mettle. The H-34 (it was often called the *Dog*, and its pilots became known as *Dog-Drivers*) had full IFR capability. This tough and reliable Sikorsky helicopter, with a Huey gunship flying chase, became the standard medevac team for the Marines in Vietnam. The goofy-looking eyeballs often painted on the front of the clamshell doors (partially visible in this photograph) added to the mystique of this ungainly-looking but versatile helicopter.

(Photograph courtesy of Sikorsky Aircraft)

(TOP) A downed H-46, with its rotor blades removed, has been recovered by an H-53 from HMH-463.

(BOTTOM) An H-46 from HMM-165, piloted by Captain James F. Pleva, has made a forced landing in a stream. In this photograph, a maintenance crew is removing the rotor blades and rigging the H-46 as a "sling load" to be picked up and flown back to base by an H-53.

(USMC Photographs A-422224 [top] and A-421672 [bottom] courtesy of Department of Defense)

A pilot (right background) examines the charred remains of a Bonnie-Sue H-46 helicopter. This photograph was taken in early February 1967, at the eastern end of the airstrip at Khe Sanh.

This helicopter was among the six that were lost on the night of January 26 and 27, 1967, at or near Khe Sanh. On an emergency extraction attempt, three H-46s were shot down near XD-672529, just across the Laotian border eleven miles northwest of Khe Sanh.

The helicopter in this picture crashed at the Khe Sanh airstrip. Captain Thomas C. "Tee-Cee" McAllister, piloting the helicopter on a GCA approach to Khe Sanh, was attempting an emergency ammunition resupply. In the dense fog at night, forward visibility was less than 25 feet. The H-46 burst into flames when it slammed into a Huey that had been parked on the edge of the runway.

(Photograph by Marion F. Sturkey)

By January 1967 when this picture was taken, new tin roofs had replaced the former canvas tents that had covered the pilots' living quarters at Marble Mountain (we still called them *tents*). Tin shutters, visible on the extreme right of the photograph, are propped open to allow a cooling breeze to enter.

In the background, just over the top of the two-wheel "water buffalo," the western slope of 3000 foot high Son Tra (called, *Monkey Mountain,* but not to be confused with the volcanic-origin *Marble Mountain* two miles to the south) is visible. In the right foreground is the entrance to a heavily sandbagged bunker. The five or six pilots who lived in each tent were responsible for constructing and maintaining their own bunker.

(Photograph by Marion F. Sturkey)

Left to right: Captain Richard H. "Rollo" Langenfeld and First Lieutenants Elliott S. Dix and Marion F. Sturkey relax between combat missions at Dong Ha. These three Bonnie-Sue pilots are lounging on the lowered cargo ramp in the rear of the H-46 helicopter. For Langenfeld and Sturkey, who elected to lie prone in the sunshine, the inflatable air mattresses (called, *rubber ladies*) proved to be useful. When rubber ladies were not available, a shady spot on the grass under the fuselage generally sufficed. If the ground was wet, the aluminum floor inside of the helicopter cabin, or the web troop seats, were the next choices for a spot to rest or to get some sleep.

(Photograph provided by Marion F. Sturkey)

An H-46 from HMM-161 (note the identifying "YR" on the aft pylon) hauls howitzer ammunition to a Marine artillery outpost northwest of Cam Lo. The white cloud of dust and sand, visible in the right background, has been churned aloft by the powerful rotor downwash. The sand filters that covered both jet engine air-intakes prevented sand-erosion of the turbine compressor blades.

Helicopters were the only means of bringing food, water, and ammunition to these hilltop bastions. Empty ammunition crates have been used to *pave* the walkway that runs the length of the outpost. During the monsoon this *paved* walkway allowed the Marines to avoid struggling through a knee-deep quagmire of mud.

(USMC Photograph A-193235 courtesy of Department of Defense)

"Yankee-Romeo thirty-one," an H-46 from HMM-161, eases down to land in a make-shift mountainside landing zone, nothing more than a bomb crater. Note the helicopter crew chief leaning out of the open hatch to help the pilots avoid nearby tree trunks and other obstacles. The whirling rotor blades could chew up small limbs and foliage without major damage, but striking a tree trunk would bring on disaster. At night, even when not under enemy fire, emergency flights into these primitive landing areas challenged all of the skills that the helicopter crews could muster.

In this photograph the special sand filters (the elongated black cylinders on top of the fuselage, just in front of the aft pylon) are clearly visible. These filters prevented sand erosion of the turbine compressor blades. The protective armor plate (bolted to the outside of the fuselage between the sand filters and the jet exhaust port) covering the turbine engines is also visible.

(USMC Photograph A-192732 courtesy of Department of Defense)

-- The Longest Night --

Caesar: Cowards die many times before their deaths;
The valiant never taste of death but once.
-- (William Shakespeare; in *Julius Caesar*)

<u>Khe Sanh, January 26, 1967, 1150 Hours</u>:   The six Recons
tromped up the aluminum helicopter ramp and plopped down in the
red web troop seats in the H-46 helicopter cabin.   Up in the
cockpit, Major Ray F. Smith sucked in collective pitch and took off
from Khe Sanh, heading northwest.   His six passengers, Recon
Team 5-2 from Third Force Recon, were bound for a steep ridge
overlooking two valleys on the Laotian and South Vietnamese
border, where they planned to set up a clandestine observation post.
Concealed and silent, they would watch for enemy troop movement
in the mountains and jungle valleys northwest of Khe Sanh.

Major Smith roared down and dropped off the six Recons in a
narrow valley at map coordinates XD-665527.   Neither he nor
anyone else could have predicted what lay in store for MAG-16
helicopters and crewmen, plus Marine Grunts and the six Marine
Recons, during the next 22 hours.   Enemy fire would swat down
three H-46s.   Two more helicopters would crash during rescue
attempts.   Shot down in Laos, 31 Marines would fight throughout
the night, and the *HMM-265 Command Chronology* for the night
of January 26-27 would later explain:

> Because of the enemy situation and darkness, the downed [H-
> 46 helicopter] crews and troops remained overnight in their
> position, surrounded by the enemy.   [The downed helicopter
> pilots] directed air strikes and artillery fire throughout the night
> to hold their small perimeter from being over-run by the large
> enemy force.

<u>Phou Loutoukou Ridge in Laos, January 26, 1967, 1200 Hours</u>: From the valley where the helicopter had dropped them off, the Recons slowly hacked their way through thick elephant grass toward a nearby ridgeline. Led by Gunnery Sergeant Charles H. Hopkins, they made their way through the undergrowth to the crest in two hours. The Recons had ended up near XD-653526, perched on a 2300 foot high ridge about a quarter mile inside of Laos. Khe Sanh lay slightly over 13 miles to the southeast. The Recons were well hidden in a thin treeline that ran along the rocky spine of the ridge. A steep slope covered with dense and sharp-edged eight foot high elephant grass extended downhill to the southeast, south, and southwest. The jagged Phou Loutoukou Ridge ran farther northwest into the Laotian mountains. To the north was a drop-off, a steep cliff. Below the cliff lay the uninhabited Xe Samou Valley, named after the small stream that winds its way westward along the uninhabited valley floor.

The Marine Command suspected that the North Vietnamese Army was using the valley as a supply route into South Vietnam, and the six Recons had come to the ridge to find out for sure. From the top of the ridge, Team 5-2 had an excellent vantage point from which to watch possible enemy infiltration routes in the lush valley below them. Already the Recons had noted evidence of enemy presence, because numerous foot trails laced the southern slope of the ridge. The six Recons spread out and waited to see what might develop. For four hours they waited.

<u>1745 Hours</u>: A skirmish line of NVA soldiers cautiously moved northeast up the slope of the ridge toward the Recons. Apparently the enemy had seen the helicopter land at midday, and the NVA commander had dispatched a patrol up the ridge to investigate.

The Recons remained motionless and hidden in the tall and thick grass as ten unsuspecting enemy soldiers inched up the hill toward them. The veteran and experienced Recons waited and let the NVA blunder to within 15 feet from them. Then the Recons opened fire with their semiautomatic M-14s, and the surprised North Vietnamese soldiers did not stand a chance.

The patrol . . . opened fire, killing all ten [NVA soldiers]. That turned out to be like kicking a hornet's nest . . . .
-- (John Prados and Ray W. Stubbe; in *Valley of Decision*)

Ten dead NVA soldiers lay sprawled in the grass on the slope in front of Team 5-2. However, several of the enemy had fired a few quick bursts before being cut down. Two of the six Recons had been wounded in this brief but furious exchange of gunfire.

The Recons heard shouting far down below them, and they knew that a larger unit of NVA troops would soon search them out. Before long they spotted a platoon of North Vietnamese soldiers climbing uphill toward them. Within minutes, scores of additional enemy soldiers could be seen as they started to work their way up the slope of the ridge. One group of North Vietnamese moved to the high ground east of the Recons, and another group of enemy soldiers positioned itself on the ridge to the northwest.

The North Vietnamese commander in the valley presumably did not yet know how many Americans he faced, or exactly where they were located on the ridge. With textbook precision the tan-uniformed NVA soldiers cautiously probed the Recons by fire and maneuver. For an hour the six Recons countered periodic incoming hand grenades and rifle fire, and three of the Recons were now seriously wounded. Desperate, they radioed to Khe Sanh for an immediate helicopter extraction.

1820 Hours: Two H-34 helicopters from HMM-163 and two VMO-2 Deadlock gunships flew out to the ridge. The pilot in the lead H-34, Lieutenant Robert J. Hein Jr., radioed the Recons, and they popped a smoke grenade. Hein asked them to use another smoke grenade to mark the location of the closest enemy soldiers. Within moments, Hein easily could see the brilliant smoke from the two smoke grenades -- only 90 feet apart. Still, he decided to try to fly down and snatch the embattled Recons off of the ridge.

Hein circled around to the west and then roared down with the late afternoon sun at his back. Just as he began his landing flare, an NVA machinegun opened fire on the Sikorsky helicopter.

Near Khe Sanh, an H-34 was hit by 20 rounds of 12.7mm fire while attempting an emergency Recon retraction.
-- (*MAG-16 Command Chronology*; January 26, 1967)

The heavy machinegun riddled Hein's H-34. One 12.7mm round tore through the cockpit between his legs. Another smashed through one of the hydraulic lines, spraying the pressurized red fluid throughout the cockpit. Hein instinctively cranked in full power and aborted the landing attempt. Trailing smoke and escorted by his wingman, he limped back toward Khe Sanh. The two VMO-2 gunships stayed on station above the ridge to see what help they could offer to the beleaguered and trapped Recons.

Major Smith and his wingman had already left Khe Sanh and were headed for Marble Mountain, since they had been on standby at Khe Sanh for two days. Two replacement H-46s soon flew to Khe Sanh with new pilots and aircrewmen. These new Bonnie-Sue H-46 helicopters from HMM-265 were crewed as follows:

	EP-171, Bonnie-Sue 20-2	EP-170, Bonnie-Sue 20-3
Pilot:	Joseph G. Roman	Harold J. Campbell
Copilot:	Jim E. Cook	Bill Young
Crew chief:	William B. Motter	James D. Bunker
Gunner:	(unknown)	Walfredo N. Rolon

The new H-46 section leader, Captain Joseph G. "Joe" Roman, was lucky to still be alive. Back on September 14 of the previous year he had suffered an unthinkable calamity, total Inflight Control System Failure. His helicopter had broken into two separate pieces in flight before crashing into the sea. Miraculously, Joe had survived. Now as he arrived at Khe Sanh, he learned of the plight of the Recons 13 miles to the northwest.

Full of enthusiasm, Joe flew out to the ridge to see what help he could offer. He and his Bonnie-Sue wingman, Captain Harold J. "Soupy" Campbell, each had a Sparrowhawk reaction force of 17 Grunts aboard. Orbiting over the ridge and talking to the Recon radioman, Joe decided not to attempt to reinforce the Marines on the ground. Even if reinforced by the 34 Grunts in the two helicopters, the Marines still would be outnumbered.

The enemy seemed to be holding back and waiting for Marine reinforcements and the approaching night. There had been no more incoming fire since the H-34 had been driven away by the 12.7mm machinegun. However, neither of the two H-46s could land and pick up the Recons because they each had a full load of 17 Grunts aboard. Speeding back to Khe Sanh, Joe and Soupy landed and dropped off their load of Grunts. Fifteen minutes later they arrived back over the ridge to try to rescue the Recons down below.

1900 Hours: There was still no incoming fire, the Recon radioman reported. He popped a yellow smoke grenade. Bottoming his collective pitch lever, Joe screamed down toward the ridge and headed for a spot about 20 meters south of the smoke. Just as he flared, he heard the guttural *pop-pop-pop-pop-pop-pop* as the NVA machinegun begin to fire. Then he felt the fuselage shudder as the heavy rounds ripped through the helicopter.

At about 1930 Hours first 46 [meaning, *H-46*] helo came into zone and set down, crew said they were hit and were evac[uating] helo. Chopper was on fire when it landed. Once again they were hit with heavy fire. Helo received most fire from the south.
-- (Debriefing Report, Recon Team 5-2; January 26-27, 1967)

As Joe's big H-46 touched down, the controls shuddered and then froze. Joe's copilot, First Lieutenant Jim E. Cook, was a heavily muscled former football player from Oklahoma. He keyed the ICS: "Let's try to fly it out!" Jim tried to raise the collective, but he would later explain to me: "It [the collective] was like it was set in concrete."

Joe spun around in the cockpit and looked into the cabin to check on his gunner and crew chief. In horror, he saw that the rear of the cabin had become a blazing orange fireball.

Both pilots jettisoned their cockpit escape hatches, unstrapped, and leaped down to the ground. Jim ran back into the burning helicopter cabin and dragged out the crew chief, Corporal William B. Motter. One of the enemy bullets had shattered his right ankle.

Corporal William B. MOTTER, 2079483, received bullet wound in right ankle.
-- (MAG-16 Casualty List; January 26-27, 1967)

Throwing the wounded crew chief over his broad shoulders, Jim ran up the slope toward the Recons in the treeline. Joe grabbed his gunner, and together they dashed toward the tiny perimeter. Halfway there, Joe stopped and emptied his service revolver at four tan-clad soldiers who were crouched on their knees and firing at the

Recons. Then Joe followed Jim toward the Marines atop the ridge. The Recons were blasting away at the North Vietnamese as the four downed flyers reached the treeline.

Quickly the ten Marines (six Recons and the four downed helicopter crewmen) formed a tight perimeter. Joe ran over to the Recon radioman so that he could make radio contact with Soupy, who was still circling high overhead. Joe crawled over the prone torso of the radioman, who had been shot through the calf of his leg. The wounded Recon howled in pain and pleaded: "Lieutenant, get off my leg!"

Joe remembers softly consoling the injured Recon: "You mean, *'Captain*, get off my leg.'"

However, the immediate problem was not radio contact with Soupy, but instead the attacking North Vietnamese soldiers. Seeing that they had downed Joe's helicopter, the enemy soldiers farther down the hill decided to try a frontal assault. Roughly 55 NVA soldiers charged up the hill past the still burning wreckage of Joe's H-46. The enemy soldiers crouched in the grass to fire at the Marines. The Marines fired back, but it was not their rifle fire that blunted the enemy charge. It was Joe's mangled and burning helicopter that saved the day.

A rapid series of explosions shook the ground. The H-46 fuel tanks exploded and sent about 1600 remaining pounds of JP-4 jet fuel skyward in a gigantic fireball. Sixty feet away inside the tiny Marine perimeter, the searing heat was almost unbearable. Then the ammunition and grenades in the wreckage began cooking off in the flames. With the Marines in front of them and the explosions and fire on their flank, the unnerved NVA fled back down the hill to regroup.

Taking advantage of the lull, Joe grabbed the Recon radio and contacted Soupy. The NVA had at least two 12.7mm heavy machineguns, Joe radioed, and that meant the Marines faced at least a company (140 to 190 soldiers) sized unit. By now it was nearly dark, and four of the ten Marines on the hill had suffered serious wounds.

Sergeant Hopkins explained to Joe that the NVA would probably wait until dark to make their next move. Time was on the side of the North Vietnamese. They would likely regroup, gather reinforcements, wait a half hour until it was totally dark, and then charge the perimeter again.

Circling overhead, Soupy had seen his section leader auger in and burn. The NVA clearly were too close for Soupy to land and extract everyone. Perhaps he could return to Khe Sanh, pick up a load of desperately needed reinforcements, and fly them back to the ridge. There was not much twilight left, so Soupy sped back to Khe Sanh, picked up 16 Grunts and a corpsman, and flew back toward the trapped Marines on the ridge.

On the radio, Joe told Soupy that he would have to find a place to land somewhere north of the ridge. The NVA were massed to the south, downslope from the wreckage of Joe's H-46, which was still burning. In the dark, Soupy used the flames as a visual reference point and swooped down toward the ground with a gunship flying cover. Unable to see a place to land, he pulled in power and circled around for another try. On the slope of the ridge, the enemy gunners opened fire on the tandem-rotor helicopter as it neared the ground.

Captain H. J. Campbell, attempting to insert reinforcements, received extremely heavy fire and crashed in the dark . . . .
-- (*HMM-265 Command Chronology*; January 26, 1967)

Hit repeatedly, Soupy's H-46 made it over the crest of the ridge. It then mushed to the ground about 250 meters due east of Joe and the Recons. Horrified, Joe watched his wingman sail over the trees and disappear down behind the slope to the east. Then he heard the impact and saw the ensuing fire.

I saw the glare of the flames from down over the hill where he [Soupy] made his approach. It was obvious then that he had gone down too.
-- (Captain Joseph G. Roman; recorded on USMC Oral History Tape Number 364)

Soupy got everyone out of his burning H-46. His gunner, Corporal Walfredo N. Rolon, had been shot in the right knee. Nobody else even got a scratch from either the enemy fire or the crash. At Soupy's direction, the Grunts managed to retrieve the two .50 caliber machineguns and their ammunition from the burning helicopter.

Atop the ridge, Joe and his contingent began yelling so that Soupy's 21 man group (16 Grunts, the corpsman, and the four helicopter crewmen) could find them. Within 20 minutes, Soupy and his group of Marines groped their way through the dark to the original Recon perimeter.

Now there were 31 Marines on the ridge, and they had a fresh supply of ammunition. Despite their casualties, they were ready to fight. As the senior Marine present, Joe remained the officer-in-charge. Checking those who were wounded, Joe found that one Recon had been hit three times. One enemy round had gone completely through his chest, another round had penetrated his abdomen, and a third bullet had gone through both legs. The gutty Recon still clung to life, but there was little the corpsman could do for him except keep pressure on the wounds and try to stop the bleeding. The corpsman told Joe that unless the man could be flown to a field hospital soon, he would not survive. Two other Recons were seriously wounded, but they would last a while longer. Joe's crew chief, William Motter, had a shattered ankle. He could not stand up, but he could fire and fight.

Meanwhile, Marine F-4 Phantoms and A-4 Skyhawks arrived overhead. Joe could not talk directly to the attack-jet pilots on his FM radio. Instead, Joe radioed target information to a VMO-2 gunship pilot, Captain Michael H. Clemmons, who had both FM and UHF radio capability in his Huey. Clemmons then relayed Joe's instructions to the fixed-wing pilots. Bright moonlight soon illuminated the terrain, and the fast-movers began pounding the slopes below the Marine perimeter near the top of the ridge.

The Marine Command had no friendly artillery in place that could reach the faraway slopes of Phu Loutoukou Ridge in Laos. Consequently, two of the Army's huge "Long Tom" 175mm guns were rushed from Camp Carroll to the base of the Rockpile. By midnight they would be in place and ready to send their shells arcing through the night sky toward the enemy.

Dong Ha, 2000 Hours: Hanging around the Op's North tent at Dong Ha, I knew that our squadron had two crews that had been shot down on the ridge. Listening to the radio traffic, I could not hear Joe's radio transmissions because of the distance involved. But we all could periodically hear the UHF radio transmissions from the gunships and the fixed-wing attack jets. It was patently clear that our squadronmates in Laos were in grave danger.

More reinforcements were on the way. Another H-46 got fragged to fly out to the ridge, drop off reinforcements, and bring back the wounded. HMM-265 had already lost two helicopters on the ridge, so HMM-164 was chosen to provide the needed transportation. With Major J. D. Watson as the HAC, the H-46 crew got ready to launch. I watched the "Northbrook" H-46 from HMM-164 fire up. Fourteen Grunts, all loaded down with extra ammunition, stomped their way up the ramp and into the cabin. Then I saw an extra man climb into the helicopter at the last minute, and I knew him well -- Warrant Officer Duffy DuFriend.

Duffy looked like a miniature modern-day Daniel Boone. He had been assigned to administer logistics chores at Dong Ha, and he relished his life there. Also, Duffy had become fascinated with the off-duty antics of the Bonnie-Sue helicopter pilots and aircrewmen, and he had informally adopted us. Now, Duffy had learned that two of our helicopters had been lost. His friends were trapped somewhere in the mountains far to the west and surrounded by the North Vietnamese. Not one to forsake a friend, Duffy grabbed several bandoliers of ammunition, his pump-action twelve gauge Winchester shotgun, and a shoulder pouch full of zero-zero buckshot shells. Years later my squadronmate Arnie Reiner would explain Duffy's choice of weapons: "He didn't care for the standard Corps-issued M-14 semiautomatic, and instead preferred the spread of heavy gauge buckshot at close range."

Phou Loutoukou Ridge, 2030 Hours: Twenty minutes later, Major Watson arrived over the ridge and radioed Joe in the darkness far down below. After an exchange of information on the known and suspected positions of the North Vietnamese soldiers, Major Watson started a cautious approach. Somehow in the darkness while trying to evade enemy fire, he ended up on the north side of the valley. The *HMM-164 Command Chronology* would later explain his fate:

One squadron aircraft crashed and burned [west of] Khe Sanh while attempting to aid at a previous crash site. The aircraft was called from Dong Ha for the mission and left there after darkness and crashed in the landing zone at approximately 2030 [Hours].

Major Watson's HMM-164 helicopter crashed at XD-676535. The crew and the Grunts in the cabin evacuated the H-46 without serious injury. However, to their chagrin they found out that they were nowhere near the other Marines.

The broad Xe Semou Valley lay between Major Watson and the 31 Marines on Phou Loutoukou Ridge. The two groups of Marines made radio contact with each other, but an attempt to transverse the enemy valley at night would have been akin to suicide. Major Watson wisely elected to remain in place. Always aggressive, Duffy wanted to press the fight, but he was ordered to stay with Major Watson. He would spend the night listening to the battle and the airstrikes across the valley on Phou Loutoukou Ridge.

Phou Loutoukou Ridge: Joe stayed in radio contact with the Huey gunships overhead, but now an ominous new danger arose. Ground fog slowly enveloped the ridge. The fixed-wing attack aircraft would no longer be able to see the terrain below, and no helicopter pilot would be able to find his way down to the stranded Marines. But on the other hand, the NVA would be reluctant to blindly charge through the fog.

Joe kept calling for a medevac helicopter, but there was no way for the medevac pilots to grope their way down to the ridge. Spooky (the nickname for a C-47 gunship) arrived on station, but he also was blinded by the thick night mist. Midnight passed, and the fog held. Marine Corps H-34s, chosen because of their greater loiter-time capability, helplessly circled high overhead while waiting for the fog to dissipate.

January 27, 1967, 0308 Hours: About three hours after midnight the fog slowly began to melt away. As viewed from the air, the crest of the ridge seemed to rise from the surrounding sea of white. Joe knew that a landing attempt still would be a very dangerous task for the circling H-34 medevac pilot. Joe weighed the urgency of the mission against the risks and factored in the obstacles, trees, wind, likely NVA positions, and the high altitude.

Then he radioed the H-34 pilot and asked him to make a downwind landing right in front of the perimeter, near the wreckage of the first H-46 that had been shot down.

Soupy volunteered to stand in the landing area to guide the medevac pilot down with a strobe light. Standing erect and holding the bright light, he would make a perfect target for the NVA soldiers on the slopes below. Soupy knew that, but he also knew that someone had to do it.

> The only men really fit to live are those men who are not afraid to die.
> -- (the motto of Training Squadron VT-5, which qualifies Naval Aviators in Aircraft-Carrier landings in the fixed-wing North American T-28C Trojan)

High overhead, the H-34 pilot flipped off his rotating red anticollision beacons and his red, white, and green running lights. He instantly became invisible to both friend and foe on the ground below. Manning the FM radio, Joe kept talking to a helicopter that he could not see. The metallic whine of the supercharged Wright R-1820 radial engine gradually grew into an ear-shattering roar. Then the dark menacing silhouette of the Sikorsky warhorse materialized out of the night sky as the helicopter got within 100 feet of the ground. Guided by the strobe light held aloft by Soupy, the H-34 pilot safely landed.

The critically wounded Recon -- still alive, but unconscious -- and two others were quickly placed aboard. The medevac pilot evaluated his takeoff path over the trees, downwind, at high altitude, and with almost full fuel tanks. Wary, he stuck his arm out of the hatch and held up only two fingers.

Joe gave the bad news to the Grunts, and they took one of the wounded Recons out of the helicopter. Cranking in full power, the H-34 lurched upward as the turns audibly began to unwind. The pilot dove over the side of the ridge, and Joe held his breath with anticipation. He could almost *feel* the Sikorsky pilot desperately milking the collective pitch lever. He would later describe the takeoff in Marine Corps Oral History Tape Number 364:

He [the H-34 pilot] did an outstanding job. He took off with the wounded [men]. He flew between my rotor blade [from Joe's burned H-46], which was sticking up some fifteen feet into the air, and the trees along the treeline. I saw him take three of four limbs, two inch diameter, off the trees. He lost parts of his [rotor] blades. I thought he had crashed down near Charlie, down near the enemy. Later I talked to him, and he said he found an opening and he staggered out, which is exactly what he did. He got the critical man out. I understand he is still living, and that is the boy that had three gunshot wounds, one through the chest and through the arms, through the legs, and through the abdomen.

The successful evacuation of the two wounded Marines later would be dryly included in the *MAG-16 Command Chronology*. Only the damage to the helicopter was noted: "An H-34 received blade damage after striking foliage lifting from a zone with an emergency medevac."

The fog closed in again, and for the next two hours the Marines on the ridge waited for the NVA to make the next move. Joe knew that tactical air support would be limited until daylight, but the big 175mm guns now at the base of the Rockpile needed only map coordinates to begin firing at the slopes of Phou Loutoukou Ridge. As a team, Joe and Soupy manned the Recon radio. The radio batteries never petered out, and the two downed pilots would call in airstrikes and artillery on the surrounding enemy throughout the long night.

The original Recon team had a four-footed member, a large German Shepherd dog. Between NVA probes when all was quiet, the dog would lie on his belly with his head nestled between his paws. Lying by his handler, Corporal Bolcher, the trained scout dog remained motionless. Yet, Soupy noticed that the dog's eyes never closed, and every 20 minutes or so the dog would stir. The hair on the back of his neck would bristle, and his ears would suddenly pop up, accompanied by an almost inaudible and guttural growl. The experienced handler knew what this meant, and Joe recalls his whispered warnings: "Sir, Charlie's coming."

Sure enough, the dog was never wrong. Within minutes a

squad of NVA soldiers would lob in a grenade or two and then retreat back down the slope. The enemy now appeared content to wait until dawn to make a major assault. On the other hand, perhaps they wanted to use the Marines as bait to lure more helicopters to the ridge. These probes were just their way of insuring that none of the Marines could get any sleep.

Khe Sanh, 0325 Hours: Helicopter crews readied themselves for the struggle that the coming dawn would surely bring. Ammunition was being stockpiled at Khe Sanh, and all of it had to be flown in from Dong Ha, 23 treacherous miles to the east. An infantry company was standing by to fly out to the ridge if helicopters could not extract the trapped Marines at daybreak. Everyone waited for the fog to lift and for dawn to arrive.

Three hours before daylight, Captain Thomas C. "Tee-Cee" McAllister flew IFR toward Khe Sanh in Bureau Number 150272, radio call-sign Bonnie-Sue 20-4. His H-46 was loaded with ammunition for the relief effort to come. Tee-Cee radioed the Khe Sanh GCA controller and began a cautious blind approach through the mountains toward the airstrip. In the copilot's seat sat First Lieutenant Jerry Piatt, and he and Tee-Cee were totally dependent on their cockpit instruments and the controller's voice on the UHF radio. Somewhere ahead and below them, the airstrip was smothered in thick fog. Forward visibility on the ground at the airstrip was reported to be 25 feet at best.

At 100 knots, with their lives depending on the GCA controller, Tee-Cee and Jerry blindly rotored through the fog. Westward through the Riviere de Rao Quan Valley they flew, heading for the unseen runway ahead on the Khe Sanh Plateau. With no visual reference outside of the cockpit, Tee-Cee and Jerry kept their airspeed up as they flew lower and lower along the invisible electronic glideslope. Altitude above the ground meant nothing, for they were flying over a chasm with unseen jagged mountains on each side of them. Only blind and unyielding faith in the electronic glideslope mattered.

Suddenly the runway lights flashed by, only 15 feet below the speeding Boeing helicopter. Easy . . . back cyclic . . . down collective . . . slow it down, the two pilots reasoned. Bleeding off airspeed, they skimmed over the runway. They had it made now, they thought, but sheer disaster lurked just ahead of them.

Tee-Cee and Jerry had no way to know of the danger. One of the Huey gunships, almost out of fuel, had groped its way down the glideslope an hour earlier. The pilot had slowed his gunship and had come to a stationary hover over the runway. However, in the blinding fog he then had been able to see nothing but the runway lights five feet below the skids of his helicopter. He had no idea where he was on the runway. The controller had radioed that he could hear the Huey, but he could not see it because of the fog. The Huey driver had not been able to see well enough to air-taxi his helicopter off of the runway, for he would have had no idea where he would be going, or what he might hit. So in the interest of safety, the controller had agreed that the Huey should be shut down and left right on the runway. No other inbound air traffic had been expected, and the Huey could have been moved if visibility had increased to 100 feet or more.

The stage was set. Now, as Tee-Cee and Jerry skimmed along the runway, the controller suddenly realized the potential danger. The two H-46 pilots heard the controller's frantic last-second query: "You got [meaning, *do you see*?] the Huey on the runway?"

A fourth H-46 crashed . . . on GCA final. This aircraft burned. An H-1 parked [on the runway] suffered overhaul damage.
-- (*MAG-16 Command Chronology*; January 26-27, 1967)

WHHAAAAMM!

In the thick night fog, neither pilot saw the Huey before the impact. Just as they were slowing out of translational lift, Tee-Cee and Jerry slammed into the parked helicopter. The larger and heavier H-46 hit the ground hard, and Tee-Cee would explain the results to me many years later: "Our aircraft hit hard but straight up. The rear pylon collapsed, and it began to burn immediately."

Unhurt, the crew briefly tried to extinguish the fire, but the effort was fruitless. As the flames neared the fuel tanks, Tee-Cee ordered everyone to abandon the helicopter. They all groped their way through the fog blanket to the safety of a bunker, and from this haven they watched the inevitable fiery chain reaction as the flames reached the JP-4 fuel cells. The H-46 and the onboard ammunition exploded in a spectacular pyrotechnic display.

Undaunted, MAG-16 Operations kept helicopters in the air while waiting for the fog to lift. But the fog did not go away. Instead, it claimed another helicopter. VMO-2 had kept gunships orbiting high above the ridge all night. The pilots could talk with Joe Roman down below, but only occasionally would they be able to glimpse the terrain through scattered holes in the fog layer. One gunship crew, trying in vain to penetrate the opaque shroud of mist, sideswiped the side of an unseen mountain.

> An H-1 from VMO-2 crashed in the early morning, fatally injuring the copilot. Weather was the primary factor. The other three crewmembers were injured.
> -- (*MAG-16 Command Chronology*; January 27, 1967)

The crash totally destroyed the Deadlock helicopter. Three of the four crewmembers sustained severe injuries, but they survived and would eventually recover. However, the new copilot, 24 year old Second Lieutenant Jerome J. Ringenberg, from Littleton, Colorado, was killed by the impact.

Marble Mountain, 0330 Hours: Op's North set up a major rescue effort to kick off at dawn and called the squadron duty officers at Marble Mountain. Six H-46s, two from HMM-265 and four more from HMM-164, were ordered to launch immediately and make the night flight up to Dong Ha. Major Charles H. "Chuck" Pitman, a veteran pilot but a relative newcomer to HMM-265, got out of his cot, pulled on his flight suit, and gathered his gear in the dark. Then he rounded up pilots and aircrewmen for the two HMM-265 helicopters.

> Pitman said, "Let's go!" and dragged me out of my hootch.
> -- (Brian W. Rolfe; years later)

Major Pitman had become famous for those two words: "Let's go." It seemed to me that he used them almost daily. He loved to fly, and the more hazardous the mission, the more eager he was to get in on the action. When you flew with Major Pitman on a routine resupply mission, you always knew that he was itching for the chance to drop the resupply frag and get involved in something more exciting. The minute he heard a radio distress call about an emergency extraction, he would turn to his copilot and key the ICS: "Let's go!" (Before he eventually retired from the Marine Corps in the early 1990s, Chuck Pitman would be promoted to Lieutenant General and would be assigned as the highest ranking Marine Corps pilot, Deputy Chief of Staff for Aviation.)

In Bonnie-Sue 30-1, Major Pitman led the six H-46s as they all taxied out onto the dark runway at Marble Mountain. In a kaleidoscope of rotating beacons and running lights, they launched and climbed northward into the night. The two Bonnie-Sue helicopters in the flight of six H-46s were crewed as follows:

	EP-161, Bonnie-Sue 30-1	EP-155, Bonnie-Sue 30-2
Pilot:	Chuck H. Pitman	Brian W. Rolfe
Copilot:	Huey C. Walsh	Gordon R. Jefferson
Crew chief:	Eugene A. Longo	(unknown)
Gunner:	(unknown)	(unknown)

Arnie Reiner recently had been transferred to HMM-164, and he manned the copilot's seat in one of their four "Northbrook" helicopters. Arnie's HAC on this mission was the legendary Captain Vince Tetzloff, commonly called the Mad Russian. This nickname had been prompted by the short-fused temperament and dark brooding behavior for which Vince had become famous in Vietnam. Arnie and Vince settled back in their seats for the night flight up to Dong Ha. Notwithstanding the darkness and foul weather, reaching the runway at Dong Ha did not pose a problem. However, they knew that they would have to wait until dawn to make an attempt to reach their squadronmates on the ridge in the rugged mountains far to the west.

Phou Loutoukou Ridge, 0515 Hours: Down below the crest of the ridge, the shrill jangle of NVA whistles cut through the pre-dawn darkness. Below battalion level, North Vietnamese infantry units used both whistles and radios to communicate. The Recons were quite familiar with the whistles, which were of the type used by athletic event referees.

The Recon team leader, Sergeant Hopkins, told Joe that they were in deep, deep trouble. The NVA had doubtless brought in reinforcements during the long night. Now they were readying an assault, and it likely would come as soon as there was enough light to see. Relief helicopters still would be unable to find their way down through the blanket of white.

With the approaching dawn a new FAC, Captain John D. Holt, arrived in a single-engine Bird Dog, and he joined the Deadlock gunships circling overhead. Two fixed-wing aircraft were on station high above, and Joe radioed target information to the Hueys and the Bird Dog. The FACs worked as radio relays to forward Joe's instructions to the jet pilots. Joe had no visual reference points in the fog, so he resorted to guessing at the direction and distance to the enemy whistles. Seeing the tips of the treetops on top of the ridge sticking up through the white fog blanket, the fixed-wing drivers knew where the Marines were holed up. They began methodically dropping their deadly ordnance down through the fog, based on Joe's verbal guidance.

0710 Hours: Private First Class Steve A. Srsen, one of the Sparrowhawk reaction force Grunts, had crawled about 70 feet down the slope in front of the perimeter. He lay quiet and still, concealed in the tall grass. Srsen had volunteered to be the point man, the listening post, a human trip-wire to warn his comrades of the coming enemy attack.

Srsen yelled: "GRENADES! GRENADES!"

Several hand grenades landed inside of the Marine perimeter. The concussions numbed the senses -- four more casualties. Many Marines jumped to their feet and lofted their own grenades back down the slope to the southwest. Concealed from view in the tall elephant grass below the perimeter, Srsen screamed incoherently, then screamed once again.

> By the screams of our point man, it was obvious that he was either hit or attacked physically.
> -- (Captain Joseph G. Roman; recorded on Marine Corps Oral History Tape Number 364)

Srsen fell quiet, and the corpsman began crawling out toward the area where his screams had come from. Meanwhile, Joe began slowly walking the fixed-wing airstrikes up the treeline toward the Marines' perimeter. Sounding much weaker now, Srsen yelled a final warning to his friends: "Grenades!"

At 270715H Jan 67 [meaning, 0715 Hours on January 27, 1967], friendly unit [was] hit with grenades and SA [small arms] fire, 70 incoming grenades. Most of the fire came from the west. Friendly forces received 1 KIA at this time.
-- (Debriefing Report, Recon Team 5-2; January 27, 1967)

From Srsen's direction came the unmistakable sound of a fierce struggle. After that, no one heard from Srsen again.

0715 Hours: Another shower of grenades landed in and around the perimeter. The chilling rattle of AK-47 fire swept over the ridge. The Marines fired back through the thick vegetation and threw grenades down the incline. Most of the Marines were hit now, mostly by grenade fragments. Neither the Marines nor the North Vietnamese could see each other because of the tall and thick elephant grass.

Hopkins and his assistant patrol leader, Staff Sergeant David A. Woodward, each grabbed a handful of grenades. They ran about 20 feet out through the elephant grass, and from there they hurled their high explosive grenades in the direction of the North Vietnamese. Hopkins got hit in the face and in the hand, but both he and Woodward were able to scamper back into the Marine perimeter.

Now the incoming fire intensified, and the Marines fired back. The only sensation was of chaos, bedlam, and unceasing crescendos of deafening noise.

Joe watched one dazed and bleeding corporal, nearly insane with savage rage, jump to his feet. He began screaming almost incoherently: "COME ON, CHARLIE! COME ON, CHARLIE!" Berserk now, he charged out of the perimeter while firing his M-14 from the hip, ran down the slope, and disappeared in the thick vegetation. Without a word, another bleeding Grunt heroically ran down after him.

Another shower of enemy hand grenades rained down into the

tiny Marine perimeter.

> One grenade landed just a few feet from Roman, wounding him
> in the head.
> -- (John Prados and Ray W. Stubbe; in *Valley of Decision*)

PPOOOWWWW!

Joe reeled under the blow. He was deaf. He could hear nothing, but he felt no pain. What had happened? Had someone kicked him in the head? Exploring with his hand, he found that the left side of his head had been ripped open. Blood covered his hand.

Seeing Joe dazed, Soupy Campbell grabbed the radio. It was now or never, he radioed. In a few moments they would be hand-to-hand. Over the din of gunfire he screamed into the mike: "IT'S MY CALL! MY CALL! DROP IT ALL -- RIGHT NOW!"

The jet pilots salvoed everything they had. The bombs fell too close, a mere 20 to 30 meters west of the perimeter -- unthinkable!

The earth heaved, belched, lurched in protest. The indescribable tooth-rattling concussions numbed the senses. Dirt, rocks, debris, human body parts, and shredded vegetation showered down on the shell-shocked Marines. Many now bled from their ears and noses. Yet, the airstrike had landed right on target. Enemy rifle fire fell silent, and there were no more grenade attacks.

From the south the crazed and wounded corporal staggered back into the perimeter. With him was his friend who had run down after him. Marines do not leave other Marines behind. They brought back the lifeless body of Private Srsen. Originally from San Leandro, California, Srsen had celebrated his twentieth birthday two days earlier on January 25. But today on January 27, he had sacrificed his life in an effort to protect his friends.

> A brave spirit . . . who died a glorious death in his Country's
> cause.
> -- (epitaph of Sergeant Daniel P. Sturkey, Confederate States
>   Army; killed-in-action in Tennessee on January 17, 1864)

For the next hour the Marines could hear the NVA soldiers moving around to the east, and also toward the base of the cliff to

the north. The apparent NVA plan made sense. There were vast
open areas to the south and west as a result of all the airstrikes that
had been going on more or less all night. If the NVA charged
from those directions they would be exposed to Marine rifle fire.
It looked like they planned to lay down a base of fire from the
north and then outflank the Marines to the east, where the slope
was more gradual. The Marines braced for the coming North
Vietnamese attack. They waited as the impenetrable fog finally
burned away in the first early morning rays of the sun.

Dong Ha, 0840 Hours: The FAC radioed the good news to
Dong Ha. The fog had dissipated. The six waiting H-46s powered
skyward, and they were followed by Huey gunships from VMO-2.
High overhead, fixed-wing support had throttled back to maximum
endurance power settings to wait on the helicopters. Now the small
armada headed west.

Two Bonnie-Sue aircraft launched in a flight of six [H-46s]
from Dong Ha . . . .
-- (*HMM-265 Command Chronology*; January 27, 1967)

The plan called for some of the helicopters to swoop down and
extract all of the Marines, if possible. However, that might not
work out. The NVA soldiers were there in at least company
strength, and they had 12.7mm heavy machineguns, deadly against
helicopters. The downed pilots could attest to that. So an alternate
plan called for reinforcing, not extracting, the Marines on the ridge.
Some of the helicopters carried Grunts for this purpose, and all of
the helicopters carried crates of ammunition and grenades.

Phou Loutoukou Ridge, 0900 Hours: In the lead H-46, Major
Pitman radioed his squadronmate, Soupy Campbell, down on the
ridge. Soupy offered his best estimate as to where the NVA were
massing their forces. Their whistles had again started down at the
base of the cliff to the north. Further, Soupy could hear shouted
commands about 80 meters to the southeast on the high ground.
The Vietnamese voices were steadily getting closer and closer, but
no incoming fire was yet being received, he reported.

Major Pitman decided to exercise the extraction option. The H-

46s would approach from the south, and the ridge would shield them from the fire of the North Vietnamese at the base of the steep cliff north of the ridge. The helicopters would have to deal with the enemy on the southeastern spine of the ridge as best they could.

Major Pitman and his copilot, Huey Walsh, would fly down first, followed by one of the HMM-164 helicopters. Back in the cabin the crew chief, Sergeant Eugene A. Longo, and the gunner began heaving the ammunition crates overboard to lighten the load for the rescue.

On the ridge, Soupy organized the Marines into three teams. Each team leader would be responsible for getting all of his men aboard the designated helicopter. The first team included the six Recons (all wounded), their German Shepherd scout dog, and the most critically wounded Sparrowhawk Grunts. Joe Roman and the seriously injured walking-wounded formed the second team. Remaining ammunition and grenades were given to the Marines in the third and last team, headed by Soupy Campbell. Radio in hand, Soupy would wait until all others were safely aboard the helicopters. He would be the last man to leave the landing zone, he shouted to his team.

More whistles, much closer now -- the NVA soldiers were coming!

Major Pitman and his wingman dumped collective pitch and began to spiral down, and Soupy quickly noted the mix-up. Huey Walsh remembers Soupy's Massachusetts brogue coming through loud and clear on the FM radio: "We need *three* helicopters!"

The first two H-46s landed, and the designated Marines all crawled, or were carried, inside. Up in the cockpit, Huey nervously turned to watch the embarkation process. He saw his crew chief, Sergeant Longo, standing on the rear ramp with his .45 caliber pistol drawn. Longo was ready to fight if the enemy tried to rush his helicopter.

Loaded at last, the two H-46s churned skyward. Now Soupy and nine other Marines were left alone, but a third H-46 screamed down toward them. Soupy threw his last three grenades over the cliff to the north -- more whistles and shouts from the east!

0937 Hours: The third helicopter landed, and Soupy rushed his men aboard. There was a brief delay while the crew frantically tossed out the ammunition crates to lighten the load. They quickly abandoned the effort when enemy bullets began ripping through the fuselage.

The Northbrook pilot hovered, turned to the south, and sucked in all of the power the two General Electric turbines could muster. Everyone aboard the helicopter prayed the same simple and silent prayer: "GO! GO!" Six rotor blades chewed into the air as the H-46 clawed for altitude and flying speed. More firing broke out as they cleared the top of the tall grass and vibrated through translational lift. The NVA to the east had closed in.

The port gunner fired back with his hatch mounted .50 caliber heavy machinegun. The Grunts in the cabin bashed out the plexiglass windows and began blasting away with their M-14 rifles.

> Their answering fire of [helicopter] crew-served .50 caliber weapons and the small arms [fire] of the passengers resulted in enemy casualties and suppressed their fire.
> -- (*HMM-265 Command Chronology*; January 27, 1967)

The helicopter weathered the firestorm. Within two minutes it had joined the rest of the flight, safely orbiting 2500 feet above the top of the ridge.

More fast-movers arrived, rolled in, and bombed the remains of the downed H-46s. From the Rockpile far to the east, the 175mm guns opened fire on the location of the former Marine perimeter on the ridge. For 15 minutes the aerial barrage continued, pounding the top of the ridge and the slopes where the enemy troops desperately tried to dig in.

> Part of this firepower was intended to destroy the evidence of American presence in Laos.
> -- (John Prados and Ray W. Stubbe; in *Valley of Decision*)

Meanwhile, across the valley to the northeast, Arnie and Vince searched for the Marines who had been shot down in Major Watson's helicopter. These Marines had never linked up with the Marines on the ridge, and the NVA probably did not know that their helicopter had crashed. Arnie was the first to spot the bright international orange marker that Duffy DuFriend had spread out on the ground. He and Vince swooped down, picked up the stranded

Marines, and headed back up toward safety. Not a shot was fired. As the ground dropped away below the climbing H-46, Duffy stuck his head into the cockpit, and Arnie remembers Duffy's animated ear-to-ear grin and his ecstatic thumbs-up signal.

The six transport helicopters turned to the east. Escorted by the gunships, they sped toward the aid station at Dong Ha.

Dong Ha, 1010 Hours: As the helicopters landed and shut down, the wounded men were carried away for medical treatment. The original Recon Team 5-2 had been decimated. Everyone had been hit. The lone corpsman, HM-3 Cannon, had been shot in one hand. Both Grunt machinegunners, Lance Corporal T. A. Story and Private First Class R. M. Brown, were seriously wounded. The list of the wounded seemed to be endless.

Lieutenant Ringenberg, the Deadlock copilot who died in the Huey crash, was the only Marine aviator who had been killed. However, from just the two HMM-265 helicopters that had been shot down, five of the eight crewmen had been wounded. The squadron Casualty List details their wounds from either enemy rifle fire or enemy hand grenades:

Captain Harold J. CAMPBELL, 085928, received shrapnel wound in left thigh on 27 January . . . .

Captain Joseph G. ROMAN, 083648, received shrapnel wound in [side of head] on 27 January . . . .

Sergeant James D. BUNKER, 2009677, received shrapnel wound in right knee on 27 January . . . .

Corporal William B. MOTTER, 2079483, received bullet wound in right ankle on 26 January . . . .

Corporal Walfredo ROLON, 2104561, received shrapnel wound in right knee on 27 January . . . .

The number of North Vietnamese who were killed and wounded is not known. The original Recon ambush at 1745 Hours on January 26 had left ten enemy soldiers lifeless in the grass in front of the Marine perimeter. At 0715 Hours on January 27, five charging enemy soldiers had been mowed down, and they lay dead within sight of the Marines on the ridge. Exclusive of those 15 who were known to die, official records can not verify further enemy casualties. Out beyond the perimeter and concealed in the elephant grass, the number of NVA killed by Marine rifle fire and grenades is unknown. Also, Marine Air undoubtedly exacted a heavy toll, because the fast-movers and gunships attacked the enemy throughout the night. Further, the final desperate fixed-wing bomb salvo at 0715 Hours had landed amid the main body of the attacking enemy troops. Pieces of their bodies had been blown into the Marine perimeter. In addition, the 175mm Long Tom shells screaming down from the sky likely took a heavy toll. How many North Vietnamese died? No one knows.

Joe Roman got his head bandaged and treated. He was carried back to the Op's North area, where Moose Rolfe was waiting with a quart of bourbon (together, they would soon drink it all). Moose remembers that Joe looked horrible. He stunk, and he was caked with a repugnant combination of grime, gunpowder, blood, and sweat. His ripped and tattered flight suit looked like it had been run through a shredder.

Moose found a clean flight suit and helped his friend peel off the remains of the one in which he had fought throughout the night. As Joe modestly turned away to pull on the clean flight suit, Moose caught a glimpse of the rear of Joe's skivvies. They were covered with blood. Moose's quick glance confirmed that Joe had been hit not only in the head, but also in the buttocks. In the heat of battle, Joe had never even felt the wound.

The night of terror on the ridge in Laos had ended. Most of the Marines involved had survived, although some would later die from the wounds they suffered on the ridge. Others would recover, and most of them eventually would rejoin their units and prepare to fight again another day. Their long night in Laos had ended, but the war remained.

THE AFTERMATH: In a foreign world roughly 14,000 miles away, journalistic voyeurs impatiently waited. They made their livelihood by peddling written and televised accounts of tragedy, misfortune, and hair-raising escapes. Bad news sells newspapers.

Normally an accounting of the harrowing night on the ridge would have been salable news. The international press hungered for stories like this. Reporters and journalists fought each other like rabid dogs in order to be the first to chronicle such stories of men at war. Naturally, the news must not be allowed to become stale. The paying public had consistently shown that it had little appetite for anything other than current up-to-the-minute events.

The international press reporters, safe in their air-conditioned quarters at Da Nang, clamored for the story of the Marines and their battle on the ridge. This story had everything: hand grenade duels, outgunned and surrounded defenders, tracers arcing through the night, airstrikes, six helicopters destroyed, fear, courage, Americans in Laos, and an incredible rescue. Surely this would be front page news all over Europe and America.

Yes, normally it would have been, but not this time. No one outside of Vietnam would get the opportunity to hear about it. That night, January 27, events in the United States would galvanize the attention of the international news media.

Kennedy Space Center in Florida, January 27, 1967, 6:31 PM: High atop the towering Saturn Moon Rocket, the most powerful machine ever built by man, three astronauts lay on their backs in the Apollo capsule. They casually chatted with Mission Control. The astronauts were running through a simulation of the forthcoming Moon Launch that was scheduled for February 21, less than a month away. The sealed and locked capsule atmosphere was pure oxygen, and a faulty electrical circuit generated a spark. There was a single frantic radio transmission from the capsule, then silence. The flash-fire had killed all three men.

ASTRONAUTS WHITE, GRISSOM, [and] CHAFFEE KILLED IN FIRE ON APOLLO LAUNCH PAD
-- (headline, *The State* newspaper, Columbia, South Carolina; January 28, 1967)

The Apollo fire and the deaths of the astronauts preempted all commercially televised news programs in the United States on the night of January 27. The next morning *The State* newspaper in my native South Carolina dedicated all of page A-1 to the Apollo fire. The front page depicted a large photograph of the exterior of the gutted and blackened capsule, still in place on top of the Saturn Moon Rocket. Columns of text detailed the unexpected setback for the United States space program. Also on the front page were large NASA public relations color photographs of the deceased astronauts, each dressed in spiffy business suits, each smiling for the camera.

The American news media devoted all of its resources toward covering the fire, the personal lives of the three dead men, and the State Funeral that followed. The liberal European press became even more inclined toward sensationalism, and it lent non-stop television coverage to every conceivable facet of the personal lives of the three deceased astronauts.

However, after four or five days the fickle paying public grew tired of hearing about the Apollo fire. The funeral had ended, the men had been buried, and the weeping relatives had gone home. The whole issue had become boring, and the public soon clamored for news of more recent events.

By the first week in February 1967, the international media moved on to more current issues. By then the Laotian night of January 26-27 was old news, and old news does not play or pay. The Longest Night had been forgotten.

We are all destined for a place in the legions of the anonymous.
-- (Reverend L. Carroll Pope Jr.; in a sermon on January 21, 1990)

-- The Hill Fights --

Vietnam is a nasty place to fight. But there are no neat and tidy battlefields in the struggle for freedom; there is no "good" place to die.
-- (Hanson Baldwin; in *The New York Magazine*, February 21, 1965)

Since early 1966 the Khe Sanh Plateau had been a major infiltration route into South Vietnam for the North Vietnamese Army. The NVA now used the twin parallel valleys northwest of Khe Sanh to funnel men and supplies into Quang Tri Province from Laos, six miles to the west. Dense jungle cloaked the floor of the valleys and made aerial observation attempts futile, and thick elephant grass and bamboo thickets covered the plateau and limited forward visibility on the ground to about ten feet. Colonial Route 9, running westward from South Vietnam into Laos, was now only a one-lane-wide dirt trail.

I had remained at Dong Ha throughout the harrowing night of January 26 and 27, 1967. Afterwards I returned to Marble Mountain, flew with First Lieutenant Bruce A. "Puzz" Major and Harpo, and then helicoptered back up to Khe Sanh with Captain Temte. In Bureau Number 150270, Temte and I would fly missions out of Khe Sanh until February 6. We would log 19.1 hours in the air during those eight miserable days of rain and fog.

The charred remains of Tee-Cee McAllister's H-46 still lay at the eastern end of the Khe Sanh runway, so I ambled down to take a look. I saw that the aft pylon and most of the fuselage had been consumed by fire. Only the gutted cockpit remained structurally intact, and one rotor blade from the forward rotor head crazily stuck straight up into the air. After poking through the remains, I pulled out my cheap Kodak Instamatic camera and snapped a shot of the ill-fated helicopter, silhouetted against the ridgeline south of Dong Tri Mountain.

HMM-265 now maintained rotating detachments of four H-46s at Khe Sanh, where steel matting covered the former dirt runway. During the monsoon season you could never get completely dry here, it seemed. The rain, fog, and cold nights combined to make our lives miserable. We would spend four to eight days at a time at Khe Sanh, and each of us eagerly looked forward to our return to Marble Mountain for a bath, a clean flight suit, and dry socks.

By February 1967 our squadron had seen many changes. Two newcomers, Colonel Clifford D. Corn and Major H. S. McLellan Jr., became our commanding officer and executive officer, respectively. HMM-265 Captains Duncan B. McLaurin, William F. "Bill" Waterbury, and Timothy "Tim" Dremann, plus First Lieutenant Emmitt E. "Fat-Jack" Exum, had been transferred to other squadrons, and new pilots quickly arrived to fill their shoes. This process continued in February when Captains George W. Cumpston and Wayne A. "Vic" Vecchitto would leave us and transfer to HMM-262 at Ky Ha.

<u>Dong Ha, February 2, 1967</u>: Temte and I pointed EP-150 eastward and joined Harpo at Dong Ha. After a quick briefing, Harpo led our flight of four Bonnie-Sue helicopters into the rolling hills north of Con Thien. The NVA had been zeroing in on our Recon teams there, so we began using a new but dangerous tactic, *feint landings*. The basic premise was nothing new. The famous military strategist, Sun-Tzu, had explained many centuries before that all successful military initiatives should be based on deception.

With a Recon team aboard our lead helicopter, we would launch and head for the hills. Then we would spiral earthward and briefly hover at a likely spot for the Recons to debark, but the Recons would stay in the helicopter. After climbing to 3000 feet again, we would fly to several other spots, all several miles apart, and repeat the procedure. Finally after five or six such feints, the Recon team would be dropped off at a different area. In theory the NVA would have been watching us "land" at multiple locations, and their commanders would be forced to expend a lot of manpower and time trying to locate the Recons. By our feint landings we hoped to induce a degree of paranoia into the North Vietnamese commanders. Hopefully they would think that the Recons were everywhere, watching them from many different locations. This tactic eventually proved to be somewhat successful in keeping the NVA off balance. On the other side of the ledger, our numerous feint landings also subjected our helicopters to more enemy fire than we otherwise would have received.

The following day the "Bullrush" Recon team radioed for an emergency extraction from AT-830648, and the rescue mission proved to be the last flight of EP-160. Flown by First Lieutenants Gordon R. "Flash" Jefferson and Bruce Major, the H-46 swooped down into the mountainside landing zone. The small LZ was surrounded by tall trees, and the rear rotor blades struck a huge boulder on the side of a precipice. The boulder suffered no appreciable damage. However, the helicopter rotor blades shattered, and the resulting centrifugal force imbalance then ripped the helicopter apart. The flight leader, Major D. E. Webb, radioed for help, and soon four more H-46s arrived with 48 Grunts to secure the crash site for the night. The NVA did not press the fight, so Major Pitman led six Bonnie-Sue helicopters back to the location the next morning. The mangled H-46 got externaled back to Marble Mountain by a heavy-hauler, and all of the Marines on the ground were picked up and returned to base.

Most of our flying continued to involve Recon inserts and extractions, because the weather proved to be too foul for the Grunts to mount much of an offensive. On February 8, Major Webb flew an emergency extraction, while Captain Gary L. Young inserted the "Touchdown" Recons at another location. Young had barely climbed up to a safe altitude before the Recon team leader keyed his PRC-25 radio and called for help. Young raced back down, picked up the team members, and flew them back to safety. The NVA were everywhere, it seemed. We knew that as soon as the monsoon ended the NVA and Marine ground units would swing into large scale action, and our helicopter crews then would see almost nonstop duty in the air each day.

Outside of the major cities in Vietnam, there was no electricity to power refrigeration equipment in the rural Vietnamese villages. Since food could not be kept chilled or frozen, the animals raised for food had to be kept alive until just before they were to be eaten. Therefore, we often flew resupply missions to haul live hogs and chickens to civilian distribution centers in the countryside.

The chickens and hogs would be separated and jammed into wooden cages about six feet square and four feet high. The chickens gave us little trouble, but the hogs posed a huge problem. In the heat, the stench from their urine and feces inside of the H-46 cabin would be intolerable. Consequently, we did not carry the hog cages inside of the cabin. Instead, we rigged the hog cages for external sling loads. We flew with the cages dangling from the end of the 14 foot long sling, hanging below the helicopter belly on the external cargo hook.

We flew a unique mission in early February, and the pilots and aircrewmen involved will have to remain anonymous. MAG-16 Operations fragged four Bonnie-Sue H-46s for the flight, and our helicopters were needed to transport chickens and hogs from Hoi An to a distribution center near An Hoa. Our plan called for our four helicopters to pick up the live animal cargo at the small city of Hoi An, and then we would fly westward and follow the Hoi An River inland for about twelve miles. There we would drop off the swine and poultry, and then we would return to Hoi An for many additional loads.

Our flight of four H-46s launched from Marble Mountain around 0900 Hours. The helicopters quickly split up into two groups to avoid bunching up when loading and unloading. At the outset it became obvious that the weather would cause a big problem. The helicopters normally would have flown 3000 feet above the ground, where they would have been out of the effective range of small arms fire. Flying below 1000 feet invited trouble, and flying below 500 feet made the H-46 a tempting bull's-eye. On this dismal February morning the pilots began flying at about 1500 feet, just under a hard overcast. The weather gradually worsened, and after an hour they were forced down to around 1000 feet. To complicate matters, the pilots had to slow down to 85 knots to keep the sling loads from oscillating. At this slower speed and at 1000 feet or less above the countryside, the H-46s became highly inviting targets. The flight route lay inside of the Tactical Area of Responsibility (TAOR) below Da Nang, and in theory this was a "pacified" area. In reality, however, this flat and fertile rice basin was genuine Indian Country where, given half a chance, the local Viet Cong would blast you out of the sky in a heartbeat.

Still, on this mission the H-46 crews were fortunate. So far they were taking fire from only one location. A lone sniper was in the northernmost hootch in the village of Bac Dong Ban. Each time the helicopters flew overhead the sniper cranked off a single round at them, but fortunately the man proved to be a lousy marksman. Unlike the trained NVA soldiers, this amateur sniper was probably aiming directly at the moving H-46, causing his rounds to harmlessly pass behind his target. Still, given enough time, ammunition, and opportunity, he was bound to get lucky sooner or later. This nonsense went on for several trips, and on the helicopter ICS the crewmen all sarcastically cursed both our "Rules of Engagement" and the sniper. This was getting ridiculous, but our H-46 gunners were not supposed to fire into the village.

All pilots will endeavor to minimize non-combatant casualties and civilian property damage. A strike will not be executed where identification of friendly forces is in doubt.
-- (from "Rules of Engagement")

The sniper kept plinking away. One of our Bonnie-Sue H-46s landed at Hoi An and made another sling load pickup of about ten hogs in a cage, around 1200 to 1600 pounds worth of hogs. On climbout the gunner voiced an idea: "Sir, what if the hogs *accidentally* fell on him?"

Why had the pilots not thought of that? Accidents happen. The H-46 cargo hook is electrically actuated and reliable, but in theory it can malfunction. The four man crew fell silent, their mental wheels churning. They were flying in the number two position with no witnesses behind them.

No one made a verbal commitment, but each of the four crewmembers knew what was afoot. The HAC dropped the nose and held the airspeed under 95 knots to keep the bulky cage of hogs from oscillating. Down they went . . . 500 feet . . . 100 feet . . . 50 feet . . . skimming along right over the river. The HAC aimed the H-46 nose right toward the hootch on the riverbank.

The crew chief shouted: "Watch the load! Watch the load!"

The HAC: "Safety Lock."

"Handle down!" shouted the eager copilot.

"Pilot Release."

"You've got it, you're armed!"

The copilot flipped the silver toggle switch forward to the Pilot Release position. The amber Safety Lock light winked off. The HAC now could use his right thumb to depress his "pickle switch" on the cyclic control. The cargo hook would then snap open and drop the sling and the attached cage of hogs.

They raced over the river . . . steady . . . steady . . . .

The red Hook Open light flashed on.

"BOMBS AWAY!"

The HAC climbed, circled around, and made a high speed pass to assess the results of his low-level bombing run. He had not scored a direct hit on the sniper's hootch, but it did not matter. The cage full of hogs had ricocheted into the ground at 95 knots, well over 100 miles per hour. Naturally the wood and bamboo cage disintegrated on impact. The 95-knot-hogs continued, blasting through the hootch, which had literally exploded. The unfortunate hogs evidently had been killed-in-action, because no movement was detected. The hootch had been demolished, and its remnants lay strewn in a line extending 100 feet or so along the riverbank.

The fate of the sniper is unknown, but the pilots flew up the river ten or twelve more times that day. They drew no more ground fire from the village of Bac Dong Ban. Mission accomplished.

Phu Bai, February 10, 1967: I napped in the corner of the ready-room tent at Phu Bai while the afternoon rain sounded out a steady drumbeat on the canvas overhead. The charismatic "Rollo," Captain Richard H. Langenfeld, and I were on standby to fly Bureau Number 152507. We picked up a frag that initially sounded like a milk run, transporting a geologist on a survey mission. "Take him anywhere he wants to go," Rollo was told.

Awakened, I joined Rollo and we met the civilian, a pale, paunchy, balding, bespectacled man dressed in a flowered shirt and khaki trousers. Armed with an imposing briefcase full of papers and a 1:25,000 scale map, he explained that he had flown from Saigon to Phu Bai on a C-130. He needed to check out the flat sandy terrain along the Dam Cau Hai near the coast, he intoned.

The civilian then began a monotone dissertation on the purpose of his task, something about possible dredging of the water to accommodate barges, I gathered.

Rollo intently listened and marked the proper locations on his map. However, I realized that Rollo had not yet grasped exactly what the geologist had in mind. This naive civilian did not merely plan to fly over the survey area and look down at it. He wanted to land, get out, stroll around, and take soil samples and photographs.

The volatile Rollo suddenly understood, and he reacted as though he had been struck by a bolt of lightning. Leaping to his feet, Rollo thundered out a stream of profanity that left the geologist speechless. Flailing the air with his fists to punctuate his message, Rollo vehemently told the civilian that he would not survive five minutes on the ground in the enemy-infested area. Sure, we would land and drop him off if he harbored some secret death wish, Rollo yelled. But we were not crazy enough to risk our helicopter and crew by waiting there in enemy territory while the geologist ambled around dodging bullets.

The geologist stammered something to the effect that he thought the area was "pacified." His meek and ignorant statement triggered yet another verbal barrage from Rollo.

"Well -- I see," the geologist mumbled. Then he shuffled off to look for a airplane ride back to Saigon.

The Marines idolized Bernard B. Fall. Although he harshly criticized their country's foreign policy in Indochina, the Marines nonetheless adopted him. The relationship between Fall and the Marines proved to be one of the great ironies of the Vietnam War.

Born a French citizen in 1926, young Bernard Fall's parents were Austrian Jews and had been killed by the Nazis in the holocaust during World War II. However, teenage Bernard Fall had survived, and he had joined the French Resistance at the tender age of 16. After the war he had become a dedicated and scholarly historian, and in 1953 he had traveled to Vietnam to document the death struggle of the French Army. Vietnam became his private obsession, and over the following years he had made six additional trips to Southeast Asia. Fall's passionate and compelling *Street Without Joy* had become a military classic, and it mirrored the obstacles and frustrations facing the French Army in the flatlands north of Hue. His account of the epic battle of Dien Bien Phu, *Hell in a Very Small Place*, had received worldwide acclaim.

In 1957, Fall had become Professor of International Relations at Howard University, but still he remained fascinated by events in Vietnam. Fall authored insightful books and magazine articles on Indochina. In his writings, Fall never compromised and naturally made many enemies. He quickly pointed out that the Viet Cong could not continue the fight without massive support from Hanoi, but Fall was highly critical of the United States' involvement in South Vietnam. He argued that although the United States could not lose the military war, it could not solve the ideological and political issues that fueled the conflict. Fall lectured at the National War College, once gained a personal interview with Ho Chi Minh, and became the world's best known and most respected international commentator on the conflict in Vietnam.

Although Fall harshly criticized the American government's policy, he praised the American combatants. Fall empathized with the American fighting man, in particular the Marine Grunts. He often lived in the field with them and accompanied them on combat sweeps. In return, the Grunts loved Fall. He understood them, related to them, thrived on their camaraderie, and so they informally adopted him as one of their own. Accordingly, in the early spring of 1967 when the Marines began a search and destroy operation north of Hue, they naturally asked Fall to come along. Fall accepted the opportunity because the region was familiar ground to him. This was the same enemy hotbed that had provided the backdrop for his book, *Street Without Joy*.

That's my area. That's my home ground.
-- (Bernard B. Fall; speaking of the flatlands north of Hue)

In the "Street Without Joy," February 21, 1967: The Grunts of Alpha Company, 1st Battalion, 9th Marines, patrolled roughly 14 miles northwest of Hue and sloshed through the rice paddies interlaced with meandering streams and irrigation canals. Fall tagged along with the Grunts, and like them he was unshaven, exhausted, filthy dirty, and caked with perspiration and dirt. It had been a routine operation, but now it was time to return to base.

Fall knew the routine. The Grunts would secure a landing zone and then radio Battalion for a helicopter extraction. Battalion would forward the request to Air Liaison, and a helicopter squadron would be fragged to fly out to pick up the Grunts. Soon the Marine helicopters would arrive and circle overhead while making radio contact and waiting for the Grunts to pop smoke to mark the landing area. Then the flight leader would dump collective pitch and spiral down earthward for the first pickup.

As they approached the landing zone the Grunts spread out, leery of an ambush. Fall walked along the edge of a dirt trail while talking into his battery powered tape recorder. Walking behind Fall was his close friend, Gunnery Sergeant Byron G. Highland. Maybe Fall just got careless; he should have known better. But he casually stepped into an innocent looking but fresh clump of grass on the dirt path. The grass concealed a booby-trap designed to trigger a buried mine.

WWHHUUUMMPP!

The concussion rocked the paddy and a nearby village. The ear-shattering blast threw Fall's body high into the air.

Corpsmen rushed to the mangled bodies of Fall and Highland, but both men were beyond all mortal attempts to aid them. A Grunt known only as Lance Corporal Leighty took a photograph that would later find its way to Washington D.C. and be filed as "USMC Photo A-188262." It shows two corpsmen bending over the remains of Fall's body. His left leg was gone, severed at the hip, blown away. The twisted right leg was still attached to Fall's torso, but only his combat boot was intact. Not much else was left.

Fall had died in the paddy, and I privately suspect that he would have wanted it no other way. Vietnam was his home, his passion, and his mission in life. From Fall's unfinished notes his final treatise, *Last Reflections on a War*, would be published in book form later that same year.

While the February rains continued night and day, the NVA buildup and the terrible flying weather took their toll on Marine helicopters and crews. On February 22 alone, Marine H-53s retrieved three downed H-34s and one H-46 from MAG-16.

The next day Major Driefer led a flight of four H-46s into the hostile and remote A-Shau Valley, where an Army Special Forces team had come under attack. They had hacked out a small clearing, and Major Driefer took hits from NVA fire and damaged his rotor blades while unsuccessfully trying to squeeze down into the confined landing area. There was no clear place to land. The four helicopters headed back east toward Phu Bai to refuel, and the Special Forces team tried to hack down more trees while under periodic enemy fire.

At 2100 [Hours] the same evening Capt H. H. Clark led the three remaining aircraft to retract the Special Forces [team].
-- (*HMM-265 Command Chronology*; February 23, 1967)

The Bonnie-Sue crews were told that the LZ had been enlarged, so the three undamaged helicopters launched into the night sky and headed back to the valley. Two of the three H-46s took hits, and all three suffered rotor blade damage from impact with the trees. Still, they evacuated all of the Special Forces men and flew them back to Phu Bai.

Five days later on February 28, Major Driefer again got the call to lead an emergency extraction. Frag 28-17A sent him to YC-891994, eight miles south of Dong Ha. His helicopter took five rounds, and his gunner, Corporal T. M. Bastyr, ended up with his buttocks full of shrapnel. Meanwhile, in the mountains west of Dong Ha on Frag 4007, Gerry Lear made an emergency ammunition resupply to the Grunts. His gunner, Corporal E. J. Pendergrass Jr., took a round squarely in his foot. Both H-46s had been peppered with enemy bullets, but the crews completed their assigned missions despite the hostile fire.

March 1967 started off like gangbusters. Lima Company, 3rd Battalion, 3rd Marines, tore into NVA units moving south toward Khe Sanh, and heavy fighting continued into the night. Harpo and his copilot, Gary Young, led a flight of three helicopters that tried to resupply the Grunts and evacuate some of the wounded. With Number Two flown by Rollo and Don McPheron, and Number Three piloted by Tee-Cee McAllister and Lieutenant Bettle, they labored into the following morning to complete the frag. The Grunts captured NVA automated fire direction equipment, stocks of 82mm mortars, and numerous crates of boxed ammunition.

<u>Lang Vei Village, March 2, 1967</u>: One of the greatest non-combatant tragedies of the war took place on March 2. Enemy soldiers in company strength had been spotted while encamped in the lush valley southwest of Khe Sanh. A special bombing mission against the NVA troops was not assigned to Marine Air, but instead to the United States Air Force. Within a few hours two Air Force bombers swept over the valley, relying on the targeting data that had been relayed to them. However, their information proved to be faulty, and the bombers salvoed their lethal loads onto the Montagnard village of Lang Vei.

> USAF aircraft mistakenly bombed the village, killing 112 civilians and wounding 213 . . . .
> -- (Major Gary L. Telfer et al; in *U.S. Marines in Vietnam: Fighting the North Vietnamese, 1967*)

Lying 8000 meters southwest of the Marine outpost at Khe Sanh, Lang Vei was the only village in the vicinity. Montagnards, Bru tribesmen, and several hundred refugees from the fighting in Laos had gathered in Lang Vei to seek protection at the CIDG camp there. A flood of almost 600 indigenous tribesmen had been encamped in huts and makeshift tents in and around Lang Vei on March 2. The bombs fell right on top of them.

Even the hardened Grunts at Khe Sanh were sobered by the news. A Marine relief column pushed southwest along Colonial Route 9 toward the village, and Bonnie-Sue helicopters fired up for the four minute flight from Khe Sanh to Lang Vei. Corpsmen jumped out of the helicopters and did what they could for the wounded. The *HMM-265 Command Chronology* for March 2 would later note: "Major C. H. PITMAN's section of two aircraft carried seventy-three medevacs to Khe Sanh from an area several miles to the southwest." Other Marine helicopters ferried more wounded refugees to Khe Sanh, where a C-130 waited to fly them to South Vietnamese civilian hospitals far from the fighting in the mountains.

The next day the North Vietnamese hit Khe Sanh with scores of 82mm mortar rounds. The entrenched Marines suffered few casualties, but the exposed helicopters sitting by the runway had no place to hide. Two HMM-265 helicopters fell victim to the attack.

A direct mortar hit just behind the forward rotor head destroyed Bureau Number 152498. Another deadly round impacted right by another parked H-46, Bureau Number 152525, and squadron records later reported "approximately 500 shrapnel holes" in the fuselage. The incoming rounds also damaged two Hueys, but none of the helicopter crewmen were injured. North Vietnamese infantrymen probed the base perimeter two nights later, but the Grunts drove the enemy reconnaissance force away. It was becoming clear that the NVA posed a serious threat to the remote Marine outpost in the northwest corner of South Vietnam.

To meet the enemy buildup, the Grunts at Khe Sanh increased their strength to two infantry companies, over 350 men. An artillery detachment, India Battery, 12th Marines, beefed up the arsenal at the outpost with their 105mm and 155mm howitzers, plus 4.2 inch mortars. Giant 175mm Long Tom guns could be moved no farther west than the Rockpile, but a section of light tanks and the potent recoilless-rifled Ontos would arrive by the middle of March. Truck-mounted dual 40mm cannons and quad-fifty machineguns also beefed up the Marine outpost. The coming days would prove the need for this additional firepower at Khe Sanh.

HMM-265 pilots eagerly awaited the end of the monsoon rains. Major Ray Smith had to battle inclement weather as well as enemy fire when he led an emergency mission for the 1st Battalion, 9th Marines, ten miles west of Dong Ha. Bob Mills and First Lieutenant M. J. "Pep" Pepple, flying chase for Major Smith that night, dropped off ammunition and C-Rations while their section leader took the medevacs aboard. Another Bonnie-Sue H-46 swooped down to drop off ammunition for the Grunts on March 11. Mortar rounds screamed down into the landing zone and shrapnel peppered the H-46, but the crew escaped injury and flew the damaged helicopter back to a safe and secure area. However, the next day another crew was not quite so lucky.

Six miles NW of Khe Sanh an HMM-265 H-46 crashed and burned.
-- (*MAG-16 Command Chronology*; March 12, 1967)

The Boeing helicopter cautiously made a power-on approach toward the mile-high peak of Dong Voi Mep, Hill 1739, the rugged mountain that we called Old Tiger Tooth. One engine failed, and the H-46 did not have enough forward speed or altitude to avoid mushing into the side of the mountain. The helicopter overturned on impact and burned, but the wingman raced down, landed, and picked up the unnerved but uninjured pilots and aircrewmen.

Three miles northwest of Khe Sanh, Hill 861 -- in reality, a small mountain -- juts up over a half mile into the sky. Observers or gunners atop Hill 861 would have a grandstand seat from which to view the Grunt bunkers at Khe Sanh. Weather permitting, they could also watch the helicopters and fixed-wing transports shuttle in and out. If the enemy occupied Hill 861 or the nearby twin mountain peaks called Hill 881 North and Hill 881 South, he could lob mortars, rockets, and artillery fire down onto Khe Sanh at will.

Khe Sanh Plateau, March 16, 1967, 1000 Hours: Sergeant Donald Lord led his First Platoon from Echo Company along the lower slope of Hill 861. The night had passed without incident, and now they sweated their way up the steep side of the hill. Passing through a thicket of bamboo, they stumbled into an NVA ambush. Two squads from Second Platoon arrived, and the Grunts fought their way up toward the crest of the hill. The North Vietnamese had withdrawn to the north side of the slope, it appeared. The Grunts planned to call for helicopters in order to evacuate their casualties.

1600 Hours: By late afternoon the Grunts had cleared a landing area, and three H-46s from HMM-164 soon orbited overhead. In the lead H-46, Captain Russell "Russ" Verbael spiraled down and loaded up with Grunt medevacs. He took off and headed for the aid station at Khe Sanh, only two or three minutes flying time to the southeast. Number Two was flown by the HAC, Arnold "Arnie" Reiner, and his copilot, Bob Goodwin. Originally from HMM-265 but now in HMM-164, Arnie had water and ammunition aboard his helicopter. He planned to land, drop off his load, and then pick up more medevacs and fly them back to the aid station just west of the Khe Sanh airstrip.

Arnie roared down while the speedy gunships buzzed around the hill. The improvised landing area was quite small and located on the steep slope of the mountain, and Arnie would later be quoted in a *Sea Tiger* article dated April 12:

> The entire [landing] zone sloped at about a 35 degree angle, and when approaching it from the side, to keep out of the enemy's sight, there wasn't room to set down directly in the zone. I angled in and then backed into the slope . . . and hovered in that position with only the rear wheels and the ramp on the [ground].

Grunts rushed up the inclined ramp and carried about eight medevacs into the helicopter. But before they could exit the cabin and carry out the water and ammunition, the NVA struck.

Two almost simultaneous blasts: BLLAAAMM! BLLAAAMM!

The mortar rounds impacted ten feet from the helicopter.

Arnie had no choice, for no sane pilot sits through a mortar barrage. He snatched in full collective pitch. His damaged H-46 staggered into the air, but Arnie and Bob then found themselves in deep trouble. Eight medevacs were in the cabin, plus the twelve unwounded Grunts who had carried them aboard, plus the water and ammunition crates. Arnie had been caught in a dreaded Triple-H (high, hot, and heavy) nightmare. To make matters worse he was "low and slow" without benefit of translational lift, losing turns only ten feet above the side of the mountain.

Arnie jammed the cyclic forward and frantically milked the collective as his turns audibly began to wind down. Arnie and Bob desperately tried to get into translational lift, desperately tried to get flying speed.

In horror and disbelief, Arnie watched the Triple Tachometer as his lifesaving rotor RPM dropped toward the magic 88 percent redline. Arnie would explain to me many years after the war that he was mushing along ten feet above the tops of the trees and literally falling out of the sky. He could do nothing to stop or slow his descent.

But by chance, Lady Luck rode with Arnie and Bob that day. The steep terrain saved them. With 20 passengers and his cargo still aboard, the overloaded H-46 floundered forward and downward, just over the treetops. Fortunately the helicopter was mushing downward at about a 40 degree angle, the same angle as the slope of the mountain. After skimming the treetops for 80 meters, they came to the edge of a sheer cliff. Arnie dove over the lip of the chasm and into the void below. He eased the collective down and gained airspeed while his twin GE-T-58 turbines struggled to power the rotor RPM back up to 100 percent. With his buttocks tightly puckered together, Arnie nursed the vibrating helicopter back to a safe landing at Khe Sanh.

The Grunts carried the casualties out of the cabin, and Arnie shut down his engines and crawled out of the cockpit. On trembling legs he walked around his helicopter to inspect the battle damage. He could see that the honeycomb sections of all six rotor blades had been holed, and damage to the rotor blade spars remained a matter that he would not allow himself to think about. The fuselage had been shredded with ragged shrapnel holes. Still, aided by a combination of luck, experience, the sloping terrain, the cliff, and flying skill, Arnie had floundered his way home.

He did this in an overloaded aircraft that had damaged rotor-blades and more than 150 shrapnel holes in it.
-- (from a *Sea Tiger* article dated April 12, 1967)

Arnie, his crew, his helicopter, and his passengers had survived the mortar attack on Hill 861, but the Grunts still on the mountainside had not fared as well. Both of their corpsman had been killed by the mortar blasts, and other Grunts had been wounded. Another H-46 spiraled down to pick up the injured Grunts, but a shower of incoming mortars forced the pilots to abandon the attempt. Huey gunships strafed and rocketed the NVA mortar positions north of the hill, and then artillery fire from Khe Sanh hammered the enemy trenches.

Back at the airstrip three miles to the south, Arnie got fragged to fly reinforcements up to the hill. Arnie's H-46 was far too badly damaged to make the trip, so Verbael loaded up his own helicopter with a contingent from Second Platoon, Bravo Company. He churned north with this meager relief force as the sun dipped toward the peaks of the Laotian mountains to the west. Loaded with Grunts, ammunition, and water, Verbael tried to slip down on the back side of the hill where he would be protected from the mortars. However, the terrain, heavy load, high altitude, and enemy fire combined to doom the effort.

At 1705 [Hours] . . . the CH-46 overshot the zone and crashed at the base of the hill.
-- (Major Gary L. Telfer et al; in *U.S. Marines in Vietnam: Fighting the North Vietnamese, 1967*)

Verbael's crash, combined with the previous damage to Arnie's H-46, put the two HMM-164 helicopters out of action. With the Northbrook squadron out of the fight, two HMM-265 crews got ready to launch. "Moose" Rolfe and his wingman, Major T. S. Dunlap, began shuttling the remaining 47 Grunts of Second Platoon from Khe Sanh to Hill 861. Night fell, and the two H-46s were nearly invisible to the NVA mortarmen as they arced down to land near the Grunts. Still, the darkness and the hostile environment made the mission exceptionally hazardous. The squadron command chronology would later report: "Maximum control was required to carry these loads under restrictive altitude and temperature conditions while taking enemy fire." But Moose and Major Dunlap stuck with their task until impenetrable fog blanketed the ridge around 2100 Hours. By then the reinforcements were all in place and entrenched on the hill, and most of the casualties had been helicoptered back to Khe Sanh.

Meanwhile, with his H-46 disabled by battle damage, Arnie had nothing to do but watch the flurry of activity at the Khe Sanh airstrip that night. Always a free spirit, Arnie had never put his surname on his flight suit name-tag, and instead he had informally stenciled just his nickname in the designated spot. He took perverse delight in the fact that the Grunts erroneously referred to him as "Captain Arnie." Without a helicopter to fly, Arnie and his crew spent the night at the edge of the runway. Huey gunships and the two H-46s darted in and out on their way to the fighting north of the outpost, and C-130s flew more Grunts into Khe Sanh and carried the casualties out. Unlike the Marine Corps helicopters, the fixed-wing C-130s always landed uphill, to the west, and took off downhill, to the east, regardless of the wind direction. Years later, Arnie would describe the non-stop chain of nighttime flights to me:

Lots of tagged dead and wounded Marines from the action on the hill were lined up on stretchers, awaiting removal on C-130s which were shuttling in and out. The din of turbines, props, and popping rotorblades filled the night. We had to yell to be heard against the noise. Prop blast and rotor downwash continually swept over everyone on the airstrip. Blowing dust, landing lights, rotating beacons, and the constant movement of personnel around the dead and wounded made the scene a nightmarish ballet of war.

The fighting resumed at dawn the next morning, and the Grunts drove the NVA off of the slopes near the top of Hill 861. In the lull that followed, the Grunts brought in more reinforcements and began searching for the enemy, but the NVA had pulled back to the west and northwest. Still, the Marine Command remained alarmed. What was the large enemy force doing so close to Khe Sanh? Was the Marine outpost itself in grave danger?

Enemy activity obviously had increased throughout I-Corps. The NVA had slipped Russian ground-to-ground rockets into the rice basin south of Da Nang and had scored numerous hits on the airfield. Lieutenant Colonel Clifford D. Corn, the new HMM-265 Commanding Officer, responded to the rocket attack by leading a nighttime counterattack consisting of six Bonnie-Sue helicopters loaded with a total of 100 Grunts. At 0430 Hours, with the LZ lit by descending parachute flares, the H-46s landed and the Grunts began searching for the rocket launchers and the enemy gunners.

Still, the main North Vietnamese threat continued to be in the far north, and nowhere were the Marines in greater peril than at remote Khe Sanh. On March 20 the Special Landing Force (SLF), 2nd Battalion, 4th Marines, pushed inland four miles below the DMZ. Helicopter crews at Khe Sanh stayed busy slipping Recon teams into the mountains near the headwaters of the winding Riviere de Rao Quan. The Marine "eyes and ears" observed alarming enemy troop movements, although the full extent of the buildup was concealed by the monsoon weather. The North Vietnamese seemed to be waiting for the weather to clear before making their move. "What is the NVA plan?" the Marine Command wondered.

When the Grunts and the NVA clashed, the fighting was savage. On the afternoon of March 30, the 35 Grunts of a special weapons platoon from 3rd Battalion, 9th Marines, dug in for the night on Hill 70, north of the Cam Lo River and west of Camp Carroll. Hundreds of NVA soldiers stormed the perimeter that night. Alerted by radio, gunships and medevac helicopters raced toward Hill 70. The gunships rocketed and strafed the attackers, and the medevac helicopters zoomed down to land on the besieged hill. Some wounded Grunts were saved. Lance Corporal Thomas E. Butt took four rounds, one through his abdomen, but a medevac helicopter plucked him off of the hilltop in the midst of the fighting. (Butt would eventually receive the Silver Star 19 years later, and his delayed award would become the subject of a *Reader's Digest* article in November 1988.)

Other Marines were beyond help. Second Lieutenant John P. Bobo, the platoon commander, jammed the stump of his severed right leg into the dirt to try to stem the bleeding. He refused to be evacuated and insisted that he would stay with his Marines. When last seen alive, he was on his knees and firing his shotgun into the ranks of the attackers to cover the withdrawal of his men. (Bobo would be posthumously awarded the Medal Of Honor.) Sixteen of the 35 Grunts died, but helicopter support helped save the rest of the platoon.

April 1, 1967: The beginning of April signaled the imminent end of the dreaded monsoon. Sixteen Purple Hearts had been awarded to Bonnie-Sue crewmembers during the previous month, and better flying weather in April promised to bring more hours in the air. On the first day of the month, Harpo and his copilot, Jim Dalton, safely pulled the "Nettlerash" Recon team out of the bush after an NVA patrol had stumbled onto them. The next day, however, another crew failed to escape the enemy rounds.

Lieutenant Colonel Corn had just taken over as commanding officer of HMM-265 on the first day of February. Now, two months later on April 2, he was leading a flight of five H-46s only three miles from home plate.

> Lt.Col. C. D. Corn 047643/7335 USMC received gunshot wound in right leg . . . .
> -- (*HMM-265 Command Chronology*; April 2, 1967)

Major Gilbert, the H-46 copilot, flew the helicopter back to base, and Colonel Corn got evacuated to CONUS and the Great Lakes Naval Hospital due to the severity of the wound in his leg. Lieutenant Colonel Robert L. Glover Jr. took over command of HMM-265 the very next day.

The following weeks ushered in a whirlwind of activity. The Marines reinforced the garrison at Khe Sanh in the face of clear evidence of a massive North Vietnamese threat to the remote base. Major Pitman and Major Curtis R. Bolscheid extracted the "Eyelet" Recons under fire, but that was becoming almost standard fare, it seemed. Major Driefer, flying out of Khe Sanh, needed a flareship to enable him to rescue another reconnaissance team during an emergency night extraction. And when Captain P. E. Bennett landed to aid yet another besieged team, the Recons shot two NVA soldiers only ten meters behind the helicopter as it took off.

Other missions were more diverse, and helicopter crews sometimes got a chance to help their fixed-wing colleagues. On the night of April 18 a Marine F-4B Phantom fighter-bomber from VFMA-323 took hits from enemy antiaircraft fire. The pilot nursed his crippled jet out to sea, and he and his backseat radar intercept officer (RIO) ejected when the Phantom decided to quit flying. Four H-46s from HMM-265, two H-34s from HMM-161, and four Hueys from VMO-2 launched into the night sky to search for the downed Marine crewmen. The pilot was never found. But at 2100 Hours, 23 miles off the coast, Major T. S. Dunlap peered through the plexiglass windshield of EP-158 and spotted a strobe light in the darkness down below. Within minutes the shaken RIO, bobbing on the waves in his survival raft, was rescued and whisked back to his squadron at Da Nang.

Most flights were more routine, but even logistical troop lifts could become exciting in short order. First Lieutenant "Pep" Pepple cruised along in EP-152 while hauling 15 Grunts in the contested Rockpile area. Without warning he lost one of his two General Electric T-58 turbines. Fortunately he had altitude and airspeed to spare, so his left hand deftly flipped both Fuel Jettison switches to the forward position on the center console to lighten his helicopter. As his JP-4 fuel billowed back into the slipstream at the rate of 600 pounds per minute, Pepple warily headed east toward a secure and flat landing area near Cam Lo. He landed without damage to his helicopter or injury to anyone aboard.

April 20, 1967: HMM-265 moved from Marble Mountain up to Phu Bai in order to be closer to the North Vietnamese threat. Within the same week, HMM-363 also left Marble Mountain and set up operations even farther north at Dong Ha. HMM-262 pulled its H-46s out of Ky Ha and moved north to Marble Mountain to help fill the void. From a broader perspective, April 20 also marked the first time that Haiphong was bombed. Eighty-six warplanes from the *USS Kitty Hawk* and the *USS Ticonderoga* targeted power plants in the industrial North Vietnamese seaport in an obvious escalation of the war.

Notwithstanding the pressure in northern I-Corps, a fierce two day fight sprang up far south of Marble Mountain at Nui Loc Son. Tucked back in the Que Son (not to be confused with *Khe Sanh*) Mountains at BT-022288, Nui Loc Son was a remote and isolated outpost south of An Hoa. Helicopter support at Nui Loc Son usually came from Ky Ha, but I recall landing on one of the elevated helicopter pads and watching the surrounding scenery while my crew chief and the Grunts unloaded our cargo. The rugged region always struck me as the kind of land Rudyard Kipling described when he wrote of British Army battles in India during the 1800s. But on the night of April 21 and 22, there was no time to ponder the natural beauty of this remote region.

NVA mortars began pounding the artillery positions of the 2nd Battalion, 1st Marines, at Nui Loc Son shortly after dark on April 21. Within an hour the enemy kicked off a massive ground attack. Alerted by radio, six H-46s from HMM-265 and six more from other squadrons began flying toward Nui Loc Son to help. Harpo and Captain Abe W. Wolson piloted Bureau Number 150278, the lead helicopter in the second Bonnie-Sue section. Before the night ended their logbooks would show: "Total Pilot time, 7.9 [hours]; Instrument time, 2.0 [hours]." They would log almost eight hours of flight time, and all of it would be at night, in the mountains, in the rain, and under enemy fire.

The first hint of trouble came when Harpo started his first approach toward the landing area. As he cautiously flew below 1000 feet to look for the LZ, his helicopter entered a temperature inversion layer. This caused the interior of the plexiglass windshield in Harpo's H-46 to become opaque with condensation.

Abe saved our lives with his quick thinking . . . .
-- (Richard O. Harper; years later)

Abe popped open the H-46 first aid kit, took out the compress bandages, unstrapped, and began wiping the condensation off of the interior of the plexiglass. Able to see now, Harpo renewed his visual approach while Abe kept wiping away the moisture. All helicopters were "under heavy fire," according to the command chronology, but the H-46s still shuttled Grunt reinforcements to the embattled artillery base. The helicopter crews completed their mission at 2315 Hours, but their long night was not yet over.

Shortly after midnight the Marines at Nui Loc Son again radioed for help. They were running out of small-arms ammunition. Gunships circling on station over Nui Loc Son reported that the ceiling had dropped to around 500 to 800 feet, and that darkness and rain now obscured horizontal visibility. All of the pilots knew that steep mountains, nearly invisible under these nighttime weather conditions, surrounded the landing area.

Only volunteer pilots would fly on this frag.

Harpo and Abe were still in the ready-room tent, and they agreed to give it a try. Major Pitman and Curtis Bolscheid quietly agreed to go along, and Joe Roberts and First Lieutenant R. A. Appel volunteered to join them for copilot duty. The loyal crew chiefs did not have to be asked to volunteer, because a flight in their assigned helicopter without them would have been unthinkable. Each crew chief rounded up a gunner, and together they crawled into the helicopters, took off, and headed south toward the Que Son Mountains. For over three hours the tandem-rotor transports hauled ammunition to the artillery base, and by dawn the mission was complete. No helicopters were lost.

Rain continued to fall throughout the next day, April 22. In the afternoon, Major Pitman and his wingman, P. E. Bennett, began a seven hour mission to stockpile more ammunition and supplies at Nui Loc Son. By sunset the job had been finished, and the North Vietnamese never breached the Grunt perimeter.

The Marines got ready to probe the North Vietnamese positions north of Khe Sanh. Near this remote mountain outpost in the extreme northwest corner of South Vietnam, Major Ray Smith extracted the "Morbid" Recon team, because the Recons had verified the presence of large enemy troop concentrations. Captain Paul M. Nick, leading a flight of two Bonnie-Sue helicopters, took six hits about five miles west of the airstrip. Most of these frags would soon be forgotten, but two other flights would live forever in Marine Corps lore. Further, the young Bonnie-Sue crew chief on these two flights was about to march into modern-day American military history books.

Khe Sanh Plateau, April 24, 1967: MAG-16 helicopters picked up 30 Grunts, including an 81mm mortar detachment, and dropped them atop Hill 700. Five of the Grunts then worked their way toward the crest of nearby Hill 861, where they planned to set up an observation post. They never made it. Three hundred meters from the top of the hill, the five Grunts stumbled into an ambush. Only one of the five escaped alive.

Two more squads worked their way up the steep slope of Hill 861 and linked up with the lone survivor. The enemy was now nowhere to be seen, so the Grunts called for a helicopter to evacuate the bodies. A blunt-nosed H-34, escorted by Deadlock gunships, spiraled down for the pickup. As the helicopter touched down and the pilots bottomed the collective, enemy machinegun fire erupted from concealed bunkers higher up on the slope. The durable H-34 took 35 hits. The pilots' left arms spontaneously acted in concert, yanking in full pitch and cranking in full power. The pilots dove over the side of the hill and made a beeline toward the Khe Sanh airstrip and safety.

Deadlock rolled in to strafe the bunkers and made a startling discovery. The Huey pilots saw that the whole top of Hill 861 was honeycombed with new trenches that linked scores of huge bunkers. Where had the enemy come from?

Two reinforced Marine platoons began working their way up the eastern slope of the hill. These Grunts ran into concentrated mortar attacks and machinegun fire from the entrenched North Vietnamese, and a fierce mortar duel began. Within minutes several wounded Grunts were stranded and lying helpless somewhere in the tall elephant grass between the Marine mortar positions and the NVA trenches and bunkers.

1700 Hours: HMM-265 got the frag: "Emergency medevac!"

Captain J. A. "Jack" House drew the HAC's role. Jim Dalton crawled into the copilot's seat on the left side of the H-46 cockpit. The crew chief, Lance Corporal Daniel D. "Dan" Delude, joined the gunner, G. L. "Red" Logan, back in the cabin. Within two minutes after leaving Khe Sanh they arrived over Hill 861. A Grunt on the slope popped a smoke grenade, and Jack bottomed the collective pitch lever and whistled down toward the Marines below.

> Capt. J. A. House landed in a zone on Hill 861 northwest of Khe Sanh and immediately came under heavy automatic fire. There were seven medevacs in the zone and [they] were under heavy fire.
> -- (*HMM-265 Command Chronology*, April 23 [sic, the date should be *April 24*], 1967)

The Bonnie-Sue helicopter touched down in tall elephant grass, and the first two wounded Grunts soon staggered up the rear ramp. The other casualties would not be able to make it to the helicopter without help, the two Grunts shouted to the crew chief.

Dulude disconnected his long-cord, dashed out of his helicopter, and ran 75 feet to a wounded Grunt. Dulude dragged the man back to the H-46, got him inside, and then he made two more trips to retrieve two more wounded men. NVA machinegun and rifle fire still whipped through the thick elephant grass on the slope of the hill, but Dulude ignored the danger. Red Logan, the H-46 gunner, would describe the mission to me many years later:

> Dan left the aircraft to assist. I don't know how many trips he made. I couldn't see him due to the tall grass. I just remember putting lots of three and four round bursts from the fifty [caliber machinegun] into every place that we drew fire, and I kept firing until all were in and ready to go.

With only one incapacitated Grunt left stranded, mortars suddenly began impacting in the LZ. A Marine Corps citation would later explain: "Undaunted, Lance Corporal DULUDE courageously returned to the last of the injured men and brought him safely back to the aircraft." Corporal Dulude half carried and half dragged the last Grunt up the H-46 ramp, and they collapsed in a jumble of arms and legs onto the metal floor of the cabin.

Logan screamed into his ICS mike that all were aboard. Up in the cockpit, Dalton hit the ramp toggle switch as House pulled in full power. They flew through a hail of enemy fire on takeoff, but they made it back to the medical aid station at Khe Sanh.

Meanwhile, on the southern slope of Hill 861, the Grunts expended all of their mortar rounds and withdrew. Their probe toward the top of the hill had revealed heavy NVA fortifications there, but still the Marine Command had not yet come close to realizing the full scope of the NVA buildup.

The next day; Hill 700, April 25, 1967, 1200 Hours: The eight men of the "Hawk" Recon team had been atop Hill 700 since April 20. They had been flown to their lofty observation point by helicopter, and already they were two days overdue for return to Khe Sanh. But secure and concealed, they radioed numerous enemy troop movement sightings back to base. Perched on Hill 700, Hawk had an excellent lookout point from which to observe enemy activity in the valleys and on nearby Hill 881 North and Hill 881 South. The men of Hawk were concealed in lush elephant grass near the base of a huge dead tree. Thirty meters away a wooded treeline paralleled the top of the ridge. With their position well camouflaged and hidden, Hawk felt safe and secure.

Suddenly the men of Hawk detected movement on the steep slope below their observation point. The Recon team leader, Corporal Robert Walker from Oklahoma, quickly laid out an ambush. Lying motionless in prone firing positions in the thick grass, each of the Recons waited as an unsuspecting NVA patrol inched up the side of the ridge. Each Recon would hold his fire until Walker cranked off the first burst.

Ever so slowly the NVA worked their way up the steep incline. Perhaps they would pass the Recons by without detecting them, the team members hoped. Lance Corporal Fred J. Baker watched as the first six enemy soldiers blindly blundered through the dense undergrowth toward their deaths. Years later he would recall that the NVA were wearing their standard tan uniforms, and their helmets were camouflaged with foliage. The unsuspecting NVA soldiers came within 15 feet -- too close! Walker fired, and the other seven Recons instantly opened up. Baker would later be quoted in a newspaper article.

> The expressions on the North Vietnamese soldiers' faces will never leave my memory. We had surprised them. We killed about six of the regulars, but there were more behind them. The silence that was, was no more. The steady stream of automatic rifle fire was now all that you could hear.

The Recons lay prone and almost invisible in the grass and sprayed the terrain in front of them with their M-16s. Then the men of Hawk got up on their knees and hurled grenades in the direction of the retreating enemy. From the volume of return fire they knew that they had ambushed only the vanguard of a much larger NVA patrol. Why were the NVA soldiers pulling back?

The answer would soon arrive.

A tremendous concussion: BLLAAAMM!

The airburst, most likely an 82mm mortar round, wounded all eight Recons. Four were rendered unconscious. Ray Raymont had his leg ripped open to the bone, and he crawled over to where Terry Burden lay unconscious with gray matter and blood oozing out of a hole in his head. The dazed and bleeding Recon radioman, Private First Class Wells, rolled over and keyed his PRC-25 to call for help. Helicopter support was only minutes away at Khe Sanh.

"Emergency medevac!"

The frag fell to two H-46s from HMM-265, and two Deadlock gunships would tag along to provide covering fire. Quickly the four helicopters launched from Khe Sanh and headed for Hill 700. In the first H-46 the gunner snapped together two belts of .50 caliber ammunition to create a 200 round belt. The plan called for both Number One and Number Two to make a high speed pass and give the helicopter gunners a chance to put suppressive fire into the NVA. Then Number One would land and pick up the Recons while Number Two and the gunships provided covering fire. But things would not work out the way they had been planned.

Number One made a 130 knot pass, and the gunner opened up with his fifty. But the extra linked ammunition slipped off of the ammunition box, twisting the belt. The gun jammed and could not be cleared. Deadlock also reported trouble. The gunship pilots refused to fire because the enemy was too close to the Recons. A Marine Corps report on the mission would later state:

> Hawk had six men seriously wounded and two others slightly wounded, still able to walk. They were so close to the enemy that the gunships were unable to work the area with their rockets or machineguns for fear of hitting the team.

Aboard EP-173, the number two H-46, was the same crew that had made the daring rescue the previous day: House and Dalton in the cockpit, with Dulude and Logan manning the machineguns in the cabin. This time, however, even more risks were involved. The NVA soldiers were a lot closer to the Recons this time, and there were no friendly ground troops nearby in case the helicopter got shot down. Could they possibly succeed again? The fate of the Recons lay in their hands.

The H-46 copilot, Dalton, recalled: "Hawk's voice on the radio was only a harsh whisper . . . ." The men of Hawk were truly desperate. Those still able to walk or crawl had dragged their comrades to a spot where they would all make a final stand. The NVA were slowly and carefully closing in on them. One of the Recons, Fred Baker, would later remember: "We had pulled our K-Bars [fighting knives] out and stuck them in the ground, because it was just a matter of time before we went hand-to-hand."

High overhead in EP-173, the helicopter crew knew that they had no choice. They had to try. Red Logan, the gunner, was still confident. After all, he reasoned, they had done almost the same thing the day before. Although their H-46 had been hit repeatedly, none of the crew had even been nicked by enemy fire. On the ICS the four crewmembers quickly rehearsed the plan. Then House wrapped the helicopter into a shuddering spiral, and the Bonnie-Sue H-46 screamed down toward the men of Hawk on the ridge below.

Swing low, sweet chariot; / Coming for to carry me home.
-- (anonymous; refrain from an old spiritual hymn)

Nothing but tall grass and tree stumps surrounded Hawk, and the pilots could see no clear landing area near the Recons. As the

H-46 flared and bled off airspeed to land, Dalton watched in fascination as one of the enemy soldiers "raised up and threw what appeared to be a grenade at the [Recons]." The men of Hawk were all lying down in the tall grass, but as the H-46 touched down on the spine of the ridge, two Recons stood up and waved their arms. They were 100 feet behind the helicopter and only two of them could move, Wells frantically radioed to the pilots. They could not make it to the H-46 with their critically wounded teammates.

Under increasing rifle fire from the North Vietnamese soldiers, Captain House hovered and tried to back the H-46 toward the Recons. Dulude ran to the rear ramp to give ICS directions to House, who could not see where he was backing the helicopter. Most of the enemy fire came from their nine o'clock position. The port gunner, Logan, tried to conserve his ammunition by ripping off short .50 caliber bursts toward the North Vietnamese.

The whole area was *exploding*, and your gunner was pumping off some heavy rounds.
-- (Fred J. Baker; years later, speaking of the helicopter crew)

Finally the helicopter could move no closer than about 45 feet from the Recons because of the terrain and vegetation. House plopped the H-46 back to the ground, and then he and Dalton began their most difficult task of all. They would have to sit there -- under fire -- until all of the Recons got aboard. They each squeezed back in their armored seats and tried to make as small a target as humanly possible. Their heads, arms, and legs stuck out, but there was nothing they could do about that.

In the H-46 cabin, Dulude did not hesitate. The Marine Corps narrative on the mission would later state: "After moving to within fifteen meters of HAWK, LCPL DULUDE leaped from the ramp to the aid of the wounded, since they were unable to move unassisted."

Logan still fired from his gunner's station, but now incoming enemy rounds from the opposite side ripped into the H-46. Logan grabbed the crew chief's spare M-16, jumped across the cabin, and returned the fire. He could not understand why the NVA bullets kept missing him. Then his luck ran out.

SMMAAACCK!

Something slammed into Logan's arm just above his wrist.

I put my hand down, counted my fingers with my thumb, and
[then] went back to shooting. I was afraid to look at my arm.
-- (G. L. "Red" Logan; years later)

Logan stayed on his feet, and he emptied two or three more M-
16 magazines at the North Vietnamese soldiers. Then, abandoning
the M-16 in favor of something heavier, he manned the crew
chief's .50 caliber machinegun and kept on firing.

Meanwhile, back behind the Boeing helicopter, Dulude dragged
the wounded Recons one by one into the cabin. Wells, the Recon
radioman, weighed over 200 pounds, but Dulude got him aboard.
Fred Baker, although losing strength from loss of blood, was able
to help, and he stuck with Dulude. However, now a new hazard
confronted the Marines. The Marine Corps chronology states: "As
LCPL DULUDE was returning to the aircraft for the second time,
the enemy began to hurl hand grenades into the zone."

Dulude ignored the grenades. With a strength and inner resolve
born of sheer desperation, he kept dragging the wounded Recons
into his waiting H-46. By now NVA rounds had holed the aft
transmission, and hot transmission fluid poured down onto the
metal ramp below. This slippery mess made Dulude's task more
difficult as he pulled the casualties up the inclined ramp and into
the cabin of EP-173. Despite his wounds, Fred Baker still helped
Delude, and Baker would later recall:

I remember going back [to get wounded men] at least three
times, and during one trip I stopped under fire to vomit.

Finally the last of the wounded men was inside of the cabin.
Yet, thinking that someone might be left behind, Dulude ran back
outside to make a final check. According to the Marine Corps
account, "Dulude remained in the zone exposed to the hail of
enemy bullets and grenades until he made sure that all of the
Marines were in the aircraft."

Dulude dashed back into his helicopter, and Logan keyed his
mike and yelled to the pilots that everyone was inside. As Dalton
snapped the ramp switch forward, House snatched in full collective

pitch and sucked in full topping power on the General Electric turbines. The H-46 lurched into the air as Dalton rode the controls with House, and they jammed the cyclic forward. The sturdy helicopter skimmed over the top of the elephant grass, rapidly accelerating. Back in the cabin, one of the wounded Recons bashed out a plexiglass hatch and emptied an M-16 magazine in the direction of the enemy.

With the Recons now airborne, Deadlock rolled in and rocketed the ridgeline. In the H-46, Logan stayed on his fifty and emptied the belt as House and Dalton sped out of range. Logan then turned around to help the injured Recons. Slumped back in a web troop seat, Fred Baker saw that Logan's face was beet-red and totally flushed. Many years later, Baker would remember how Logan excitedly screamed: "IT'S LIKE AN ANT HILL -- I'VE NEVER SEEN SO MANY GOOKS!"

The aerial trip back to Khe Sanh took only three minutes. On the way, those who were conscious began aiding their friends, who were unable to help themselves.

It was a pitiful sight -- four unconscious and everyone bleeding.
-- (Fred J. Baker; describing the flight, years later)

The roar of the battle lay behind them now. The only sounds were the shrill whine of the engines and transmissions and the popping of the rotors. In the cockpit, House and Dalton kept a wary eye on the instrument panel gauges, because they could only guess at the extent of the combat damage to their H-46. As they began a cautious descent toward the Khe Sanh airstrip, a round cooked off in one of the fifties, adding to the tension.

The damaged helicopter landed and was quickly shut down. Those who had been wounded were rapidly bandaged up at the aid station and then carried aboard a waiting C-130. They were flown to Da Nang for treatment at Charlie-Med. Later they would be sent to a more sophisticated hospital to complete their recuperation.

The four HMM-265 crewmembers aboard EP-173 each received decorations for their second daring rescue in two days. Three of these four Marines would eventually survive the war, and two of them would complete their combat tour in Vietnam. (Unfortunately, Jack House would be killed-in-action two months later in June, and Dulude would be severely wounded in October.)

The young crew chief, Dan Dulude, had left his helicopter two days in a row in order to drag wounded Marines to safety. On both occasions he had repeatedly exposed himself to heavy enemy fire, but miraculously he came through totally unscathed. The Grunts and Recons who survived owed their lives to Dulude, and they quickly praised his initiative and courage under fire. Supporting documentation was prepared and forwarded to MAG-16 Headquarters, and the Marine Corps eventually awarded the Silver Star to Dulude -- twice! Lieutenant General Victor H. Krulak signed separate citations that detailed Dulude's heroics on both April 24 and April 25.

Dulude earned his place in modern American military history books. He is reportedly the only member of the Armed Forces of the United States who has been awarded *two* Silver Stars for heroism on *two consecutive days* since the American Civil War in the 1860s. The text on both Silver Star citations begins as follows: "For conspicuous gallantry and intrepidity in action while serving as a Crew Chief with Marine Medium Helicopter Squadron 265 . . . ." (Dan Dulude's incredible luck would run out on October 14. On that day he would be shot twice during a helicopter rescue flight. He would survive, but he would get medevaced to CONUS because of the severity of his wounds.)

While Dulude and his Bonnie-Sue crewmates had been busy on April 24 and April 25, the Marine Command had begun an offensive to drive the NVA off of their hilltop fortresses. The closest peak, Hill 861, became the first objective. Bravo and Kilo Companies, 3rd Battalion, 3rd Marines, had cautiously moved up the rugged slope of the mountain on April 25. This reconnaissance in force ran into heavy machinegun fire when it neared the NVA bunkers. Both companies drew back down the mountainside and dug in for the night.

HMM-164 started a massive troop lift to fly three whole companies from the 2nd Battalion, 3rd Marines, to the base of Hill 861. With this task completed early on April 26, eight of the Northbrook helicopters remained on standby status at the airstrip. The H-46 crewmen knew full well that the outcome of the imminent battle would largely hinge on their ability to shuttle reinforcements and supplies to the Grunts.

The NVA Command was not blind to the coming assault. Over 200 North Vietnamese 82mm mortar rounds screamed down onto the Third Marines command post at Khe Sanh, and scores of NVA recoilless rifle rounds slammed into the remote plateau outpost. Marine artillery at Khe Sanh fired back, and the bloody battle for the hills began. Neither side realized that the fighting would last for twelve grueling days. The international media would later coin a name for this brutal struggle: THE HILL FIGHTS.

The first day provided insight into what lay in store. Drenched by rain and often blinded by fog, the NVA and the Grunts clashed on the slopes of Hill 861. Helicopters started circling down to pick up the casualties. However, the Grunts soon learned to wave them away because the NVA mortar spotters targeted all helicopter landing areas, further endangering the men on the ground.

The most intense fighting involved Bravo Company, commanded by Captain Michael W. Sayers. By 1445 Hours his company had suffered too many casualties to move. Sayers was cut off from the other companies, and he also found that the helicopters could no longer find him through the rain and fog. Under heavy attack on two fronts, he got radioed orders to leave his dead Marines behind and pull back with his wounded men. But even that was no longer possible. Further, Sayers reported that he would not abandon any of his men, dead or alive. He radioed to Khe Sanh that he and his remaining men would form a tight perimeter in the fog and "fight to the very end."

Khe Sanh, April 27, 1967: The Marine Command now realized that even more Grunts, more helicopters, and more firepower were needed. The SLF Grunts, the 2nd Battalion, 3rd Marines, got picked up by the Northbrook H-46s and flown to Khe Sanh. Helicopters also zipped back and forth between the southern slope of Hill 861 and the airstrip to evacuate the wounded from the fighting on the previous day. Major Ray Smith, a native of South Carolina like me, remembers those perilous flights to Hill 861:

April 1967, [I was] trying to get the Marine bodies out. Every time I tried to land, we got mortared. Landing with only the rear wheels on the ground was standard. It was a bad place. The non-wounded hated to see us come, because we attracted the mortars. They would scream [on the radio] at us: "HURRY! GET OUT! GET OUT!"

Marine artillery at Khe Sanh pounded the crest of Hill 861, and fixed-wing jets orbited in a holding pattern high over the hill. Many of the NVA bunkers had reinforced eight-layer log roofs so thick and massive that even a 500 pound bomb would not destroy them. However, Marine Air used snake-eye bombs and napalm to strip away the overhead foliage. The fast-movers then dropped huge 2000 pound bombs onto the bunkers, and no bunker could withstand a direct hit from these larger weapons. But, the Marines wondered, how many other hidden bunker complexes had not yet been located?

Aboard EP-171, piloted by Captain Don A. McPheron and First Lieutenant R. R. Llewellyn, was Recon team "Breaker." They headed for an observation spot eight miles northwest of Khe Sanh near the Laotian border to monitor NVA efforts to reinforce their hilltop fortifications. Luck eluded the crew of EP-171 that day, because an NVA patrol happened to be encamped near the landing area. As McPheron flared to land the enemy opened up on him, shattering his right foot and sending shrapnel into his left eye. The H-46 crashed and burned, and the list of the wounded would later include all four members of the H-46 crew.

CAPT D. A. MCPHERON 090204/7335 USMC received gunshot wound in left foot, shrapnel wound in upper left leg and shrapnel wound of left eye . . . .

1st LT R. R. LLEWELLYN 092389/7335 USMC received shrapnel wound in left arm . . . .

LCpl D. E. ORCUTT 2138515/6332 USMC received a fractured right foot, and missile wound right foot, and shrapnel wounds on both legs . . . .

LCpl C. L. SMITH Jr. 2171257/6351 USMC received multiple

shrapnel wounds on the face, right arm and left leg, and a
fractured right ankle . . . .
-- (from HMM-265 Casualty List; April 27, 1967)

Despite their injuries and the enemy fire, the four downed
crewmen and their Recon passengers helped each other out of the
burning helicopter. They got a safe distance away from the fire,
and there they set up a makeshift perimeter. Meanwhile, First
Lieutenant Thomas P. "Tee-Pee" Berry, the wingman, circled
overhead in EP-163. He had watched his leader auger in and burn,
and now he heard the plea for help from the Recon radioman on
the FM channel. Berry roared down and landed near the burning
helicopter. The downed crewmen and Recons carried each other
up the ramp and into the cabin of Berry's H-46.

Berry pulled in collective pitch halfway to his left armpit, and
EP-163 staggered skyward. In the cabin manning his gunner's
station, Lance Corporal D. E. Wilson took an enemy round in the
left hand. The accelerating H-46 quickly sped out of range of the
NVA patrol, and within minutes the wounded men were deposited
at the Khe Sanh aid station.

Everyone knew the flamboyant Harry R. "Bob" Mills. Although
still only a Captain, Bob was one of the more experienced pilots in
HMM-265. He had been in Vietnam before, flying H-34s in the
delta in the early Shu-Fly days when all Marine Corps pilots flew
out of Soc Trang, below Saigon. Midway through that tour the
United States Army had arrived with their H-21s, which could not
handle high altitude missions like the Marine H-34s. So, Bob and
the Marines had moved up north to Marble Mountain and had left
the lowlands to the Army.

Now Bob was back for his second tour in Vietnam and flying
the much faster, larger, and more powerful H-46. He loved to fly,
and he played the role like he was on a stage, with his red
bandanna around his neck and his .38 caliber revolver carried in a
jaunty shoulder holster. If there was a hot medevac or an
emergency extraction under fire, HMM-265 could count on Bob to
be there. He loved it; he reveled in it.

In the cockpit with cyclic and collective in hand, Bob was

totally in his chosen element, and he was badly needed. On April 20 because of all the fighting in the far north, all HMM-265 Marines, helicopters, and equipment had been moved up to Phu Bai. Here, only seven miles south of Hue, they were located a lot closer to the embattled hills at Khe Sanh.

Phu Bai, April 27, 1967, approximately 2330 Hours: Bob shared a tent with Tom Shea, Joe Roberts, and some other pilots whose names have now been forgotten. Because of all the heavy action up north, Bob and his tentmates had not yet taken the time to build a bunker outside of their tent. Joe, an Annapolis graduate, was exhausted on the night of April 27. He finally wandered back to his tent, crashed onto his cot, and instantly fell asleep. Bob soon peeled off his dirty flight suit and sacked out on his cot ten feet from Joe. He knew that the coming dawn would undoubtedly herald another long day in the cockpit.

> Theirs was a very personal war. They were seldom out of range of enemy fire from the moment of takeoff until the final landing. With rocket and mortar attacks against forward bases, even when they completed a flight, they were subjected to continuing enemy fire.
> -- (Lieutenant Colonel William R. Fails; writing in *Marines and Helicopters: 1962-1973*)

CRRUUUMMPP! CRRUUUMMPP!

Bob instantly bolted upright on his cot. "Incoming or outgoing?" he wondered in the dark, trying to clear away sleep's mental cobwebs.

CRRUUUMMPP!

"Incoming!"

Bob dashed out of his tent clad only in his skivvies with no clothes, no boots, and no weapon. The night was pitch black, and he tried to get his bearings and figure out where the mortar rounds were impacting. Disoriented in the dark, all Bob knew for sure was that the explosions were getting louder. The enemy was walking the mortars from the flight line toward tent city.

Bob took off, ran about ten feet and . . . "AAAARRRRGH!"

Clothes-lined by a tent rope!

Bob was unhurt, but he found himself flat on his back in the soft sand. Well, this was as good a place as any, he reasoned. Like a mad dog he feverishly started digging with his hands, trying to dig a hole big enough to crawl into. Suddenly a human form materialized out of the darkness. Friend or foe? Fortunately it turned out to be Tom Shea, and Tom dropped down on his knees in the sand by Bob. Figuring that the veteran Bob knew what he was doing, Tom also began digging like crazy with his hands.

Bob would explain his mental plight to me many years later. If he had been in the cockpit with his flight suit on, he would have been O.K., he theorized. But in the darkness with no clothes and no weapon, the noise was terrifying. Bob and Tom dug like madmen, making gasping and sucking noises deep in their throats.

CRRUUUMMPP! CRRUUUMMPP! CRRUUUMMPP!

Closer and closer the blasts came. Bob could now hear the booming outgoing Marine counter-battery howitzer and mortar fire. The shrill chatter of Marine M-60s on the base perimeter added to the bedlam. Tracers arced through the night. Bob was defenseless and "naked to the world," as he would later explain. "This is insanity!" he thought to himself.

The only thing I wanted was to get away from the *loud noise*.
-- (Harry R. Mills; years later)

Abandoning his digging, Bob leaped to his feet and began running. Spotting the faint silhouette of a deuce and a half truck, he dove headfirst under the back of it, looking for overhead cover. Then Bob rolled over in the sand and looked up above him. He could not see it in the darkness, but he realized that it was up there somewhere just over his head -- gas tank!

Bob knew that he had to get away. Heart pounding, covered with sand and sweat, he belly-crawled over to a grease rack and hunkered down under it.

Finally the incoming mortars stopped. Next the small arms fire on the base perimeter petered out. After what seemed like an eternity the Marine counter-battery fire fell silent. Bob quietly lay there in the sand, waiting, listening, peering out into the moonless night and seeing absolutely nothing. Slowly he got to his feet. Avoiding the tent ropes this time, Bob groped his way back to his tent and sheepishly slipped inside. Tom was easing back in at the same time, but they did not speak. There was nothing to say. Filthy dirty and now angry at his inability to fight back, Bob dropped down onto his cot and immediately fell into a deep and dreamless sleep.

Sunlight was streaming into the tent as Bob awoke. Everyone was already gone except Joe Roberts, and Bob saw that Joe was in his flight suit and sitting on the edge of his cot, rearranging his maps. Strange, but Bob noticed that Joe looked spiffy and totally refreshed. Bob softly volunteered: "Rough night."

"Uuuuuhhh -- Huh?"

"Pretty rough, pretty rough," Bob self-consciously added.

"Say what?"

"The mortars, the mortars. Where'd you . . . ?"

Bob's question trailed off as reality dawned on him. While Bob and Tom had been groveling in the dark in their skivvies, and while eleven of their squadronmates had been wounded, Joe had been safe in the hands of the angels. He had peacefully slept through the entire mortar attack.

Hill 861, April 28, 1967: Artillery and air attacks on the NVA redoubt had lasted 36 hours. By the afternoon of April 28 the Grunts were ready to mount another ground attack, this time with two full battalions of infantry. The plan called for seizing Hill 861, then Hill 881 South, and finally Hill 881 North.

Gunships and medevac helicopters waited at the Khe Sanh airstrip as the Grunts swarmed up the steep southern slope of Hill 861. By nightfall the former NVA-held hilltop had a new tenant, the 2nd Battalion, 3rd Marines.

The purpose of offensive combat is to destroy the enemy and his will to fight.
-- (from *Guidebook for Marines*)

Helicopters could now land on the very top of the hill, and they brought water, C-Rations, and more ammunition. The odor of decaying NVA bodies, most of them killed by the bombs and artillery during the previous two days, permeated the air. In the heat the stench became nauseating and almost unbearable. Swarms of flies descended on the bloated bodies of the dead, while vultures patiently circled overhead. Over 425 bunkers and individual fighting holes remained as a testament to the size of the defending NVA units. The Grunts realized that even heavier fortifications could be waiting for them on Hill 881 South and Hill 881 North.

April 29, 1967: The Grunts began working their way overland toward Hill 881 South, just under two miles to the west. Skirmishes with small enemy units periodically flared up during the day, and HMM-164 got fragged for the necessary resupply and medevac flights.

The next day, April 30, the Northbrook squadron had a demanding trial by fire. The Grunts tried to maneuver their way between the two North Vietnamese fortresses, Hill 881 South and Hill 881 North, and they ran into murderous and withering fire. Helicopters raced northward to help the Grunts. One of the Northbrook H-46s, YT-22, got drilled with rifle fire at XD-778450, right at the base of the southern slope of Hill 881 North. Huey gunships fired back at the NVA gunners, who were concealed in camouflaged fighting holes only 50 meters from the Grunt ground unit, Mike Company. Other H-46 helicopters somehow managed to slip in and pull out some of the wounded men, but Mike Company paid a horrible price.

> Mike Company ceased to exist on that day; out of 190 men, only 26 were left standing.
> -- (Austin Deuel; in *Vietnam Magazine*, August 1992)

In Mike Company alone, 43 Marines died and over 100 more were seriously wounded on April 30. Decimated by these losses, Mike Company had only about two dozen Grunts who were still able to fight, so HMM-164 helicopters picked up the survivors and flew them to Dong Ha to regroup. But although the NVA had repeatedly targeted the helicopters coming to the aid of the Grunts, none of the Yankee-Tango H-46s got shot down. One of the wounded Grunts, Don Hossack, got medevaced by helicopter to the *USS Repose* by 2200 Hours that night. Years later his heroics on the lower slope of Hill 881 would be immortalized in sculpture on the Vietnam Memorial in San Antonio, Texas.

Hill 881 South, May 1, 1967: Once again the Grunts backed

off to let Air and Artillery blast away at the enemy bunkers. Included in the ordnance fired at or dropped onto the hills were 130 more of the huge 2000 pound bombs. Meanwhile, the helicopters had an easy day, since only resupply and administrative missions were fragged.

The next morning the Grunts surged up the slopes of Hill 881 South, and the NVA did not give up without a fight. Still, by the end of the day the Grunts had triumphed. Yet, their toughest hurdle was still to come, the battle for the last remaining North Vietnamese strongpoint, Hill 881 North.

On May 2 while the main attack on Hill 881 South had been in progress, Echo, Golf, and Hotel Companies had begun climbing up the imposing slope of the northernmost mountain, Hill 881 North. Enemy fire and a freakish and violent squall, with winds approaching 50 miles per hour, stymied the attack and grounded all of the helicopters. The Grunts dug fighting holes on the hillside in hopes that the storm would abate.

<u>Hill 881 North, May 3, 1967, 0415 Hours</u>: The NVA counterattacked. In bitter hand-to-hand fighting in the dark, the North Vietnamese rammed their way through the Grunt lines. A flareship orbited overhead, and soon parachute flares lit up the mountainside. Huey gunships, aided by the artificial mini-suns, angrily buzzed around the hill. However, with many of the Grunt positions overrun the pilots could not determine friend from foe. The pilots eventually had better luck zeroing in on a second wave of about 300 more NVA soldiers who were following the first group of attackers. With guns and rockets, the potent UH-1Es tore into the enemy reinforcement column and stalled its attack.

The eastern sky brightened as the sun crept above mighty Dong Tre Mountain five miles to the east, and the fighting on the slope of Hill 881 North slowly died out. HMM-164 helicopters brought in reinforcements to a secure landing area near the Grunts. Then the Northbrook pilots pulled in power and headed back to Khe Sanh. Many NVA soldiers were still holed up inside of the ragged Marine perimeter, and the helicopter crews wanted to be far away when the Grunts started rooting them out. By 1500 Hours the last of the NVA attackers had been ferreted out of their hiding spots in the Grunt trenches and fighting holes. By the time the shooting had ended, 137 more North Vietnamese bodies littered the hillside.

The Grunts wanted more men and ammunition, but all of the enemy fortifications higher up on the mountainside had not been pinpointed. Consequently, the Marine Command waited until after dark before launching the H-46s of HMM-164. Using the night to shield themselves from enemy observation, the Northbrook pilots hauled C-Rations, ammunition, claymore mines, concertina, trip flares, and more Grunts to the mountainside.

For the helicopter crews, these were risky missions. Flying at night and landing in rugged terrain is hazardous under even the best of conditions, but locating friendly units on Hill 881 North in the dark and under fire created additional perils. Switching from their UHF to their FM radios, the pilots contacted the Grunts down below. Then they attempted to spot the Grunt radioman's flashlight. The pilots knew that the enemy monitored most FM radio transmissions, and at battalion level or above the NVA always had a radioman who was fluent in English. When the pilots called for the Grunt radioman to switch on his flashlight, it was common to look down and see pinpoints of light at several different locations. Which ones belonged to the enemy? Which belonged to the Grunts? For the pilots, it made for a harrowing night.

<u>Lang Vei, May 4, 1967, 0435 Hours</u>: Located five miles southwest of Khe Sanh and two miles from the Laotian border, Lang Vei held no real military significance. The North Vietnamese had ignored the CIDG camp there because it presented no military threat to them. Lang Vei was simply a raggedy Ruff-Puff garrison, commanded by an Army Special Forces team, at the hub of the large refugee village. But two hours before dawn on May 4, the North Vietnamese swept into Lang Vei and routed the defenders. After daylight HMM-164 launched two H-46s for medevac duty at Lang Vei, and many wounded refugees were flown to Khe Sanh for later transfer to South Vietnamese civilian medical facilities far to the south. The NVA soldiers who had overrun Lang Vei had marched back into the surrounding jungle. Could they be heading for Khe Sanh? To guard against a possible enemy attack from the southwest, Marines from the 1st Battalion, 26th Marines, flew into

Khe Sanh from Phu Bai later in the day.

However, while the Grunts worried about the enemy, the helicopter crews knew that their profession carried its own inherent perils. Danger could spring from many factors unrelated to enemy fire. While the Grunts fretted about a possible ground assault from the southwest, a MAG-16 helicopter from HMM-363 fell prey to a less obvious enemy, faulty maintenance. An exhausted and sleep-deprived helicopter mechanic unwittingly vouched for Murphy's Law when he reconnected a hydraulics line -- *backwards*. When the helicopter rotors were engaged, the H-34 overturned on the flight line and whipped itself into an aluminum shambles.

> Flying is not inherently dangerous. But like the sea, it is unforgiving of human error.
> -- (wording on a sign at Whiting Field near Milton, Florida)

Hill 881 North: The assault on Hill 881 North continued, and the battle settled into an almost predictable pattern. The Grunts would maneuver up the hill to pinpoint and engage the enemy. Then they would pull back and let their gunships and artillery pound the NVA while the H-46s or H-34s zipped down to haul out the casualties. Then the Grunts would charge up the hill again, and the cycle would repeat itself.

HMM-164 still drew the lion's share of the H-46 missions at Khe Sanh. As May 5 arrived, the fighting on Hill 881 North raged nonstop. The pilots of YT-21 tried to land at XD-777455, just 400 meters southeast of the crest of the hill. The altitude, heavy load, and sloping terrain drove the H-46 into the trees. The three rotor blades on the forward rotor head ripped into the treetops and "sawed lumber," as we jokingly referred to such accidents. Still, the sturdy Boeing helicopter held together and limped back to Khe Sanh, where the damaged rotor blades were later replaced.

Less than a mile away from the ongoing battle, Major A. B. "Bruce" Colbert piloted his H-46 while scanning the terrain below. Spying a unique opportunity, he landed at XD-784460 and confronted a lone NVA soldier who elected to surrender. Major Colbert aborted his resupply frag and flew the young prisoner straight back to base.

In the trenches and bunkers on top of Hill 881 North, the NVA were taking everything that the Grunts, Air, and Artillery could throw at them. The Marines tried a new tactic when a Northbrook crew flew out to the *USS Princeton* (LPH-5), picked up a psychological warfare team, and rushed it to Khe Sanh. These "psy-ops" teams used a combination of leaflet drops, loudspeaker announcements, radio messages, and other tricks of their trade designed to induce the North Vietnamese to give up the fight. Yet, the NVA continued to defend every foot of ground on the rugged slopes of their fortress. Neither the Marines nor the North Vietnamese had seen fighting as bitter as this since the horrible struggle for Mutter Ridge in September and October of 1966.

Huey Walsh, who had transferred from HMM-265 to HMM-164, manned one of the standby medevac H-46s at Khe Sanh. Huey got a frag from the Operations tent: "Launch immediately." An F-4B Phantom had been hit by North Vietnamese AAA fire while making bombing runs on NVA mortar positions. The pilot had nursed his damaged fast-mover a mile away from Hill 881 North, and then he had ejected. Perhaps the RIO had been incapacitated by the enemy fire. In any event he failed to eject, and he and the doomed Phantom had plunged vertically down into the jungle at 400 knots.

Huey got airborne within two minutes, and in two minutes more he passed over Hill 861 on his way to the crash site. The downed pilot came through loud and clear on Guard Channel on his survival radio, but the unfortunate man had parachuted down through the tall trees with his helmet visor up (it should have been *down*). Limbs had gouged into both of his eyes, blinding him. He could still transmit and receive on his hand-held survival radio, but he was hidden by the vegetation and was unable to give Huey any clue as to his location.

From the jungle floor, a boiling column of dense black smoke from the burning JP-4 jet fuel marked the grave of the Phantom. The RIO was dead, no doubt about it. Huey eased down to treetop level and air-taxied around in an effort to spot the pilot, who still could not see and could only plead for help.

Huey's crew chief leaned out of the open hatch to help with the visual search. Suddenly the Phantom pilot radioed that he could now "hear" the fire and feel the heat. Huey saw that the wind was driving the flames through the tall, dry, and highly combustible elephant grass. He slipped over to the downwind side of the fire, and there he finally glimpsed the downed pilot. The injured man was standing under tall trees by the edge of a small stream.

Huey's hoist cable was not quite long enough, so he let his H-46 fuselage settle into the treetops while he talked the blinded pilot toward the horse-collar. One minute later the Phantom driver got winched up through the hell-hole door in the belly of the helicopter, and he flopped onto the cabin floor. As Huey sucked in collective and accelerated skyward, he watched the wind drive the flames through the treeline where the pilot had been stranded.

On another mission, Huey flew as wingman on a flight to make a routine pickup of a Recon team from the side of a mountain. The standard radio authentication procedures ensued, and then the Northbrook section leader, Captain Arthur C. "Art" Chapman, radioed the Recons: "Pop your smoke." Years later, Huey would chuckle as he explained to me what happened next:

> We asked the Recons to pop smoke. It popped at three different locations that I could see. Art Chapman guessed wrong. He flew to the wrong spot, got shot up, but he made it back to Khe Sanh, trailing smoke.

Sometimes the danger was not a direct result of enemy fire. Circling at 3000 feet, Robert D. "Bob" Porter told his copilot to dump fuel to lighten their load before they spiraled down to pick up a load of wounded Grunts. This was a routine procedure, but the new and inexperienced copilot reached down to the center console with his right hand and meant to flip the two silver Fuel Jettison toggle switches. However, in the excitement of the moment he grasped the nearby Master Fuel Valve switches instead. He raised them over the safety notch and pulled them rearward. Bob's initial warning came within seconds when one of his fuel-starved engines flamed out. On the instrument panel the Gas Generator Tachometer, the Triple Tachometer, and the Torquemeter all began to unwind, and Bob's lifesaving rotor RPM began to die.

Down collective! Back cyclic!

Bob frantically flipped the two Master Fuel Valve switches

forward. After a quick in-flight engine restart, he ordered his errant copilot to sit on his hands for a while. Then he got his own breathing back under control.

After handling the fuel dumping job himself, Bob flew down toward the Grunts and landed. However, after all of the excitement a few minutes before, the crew chief let too many Grunts aboard. When Bob took off, he again heard his turns begin to wind down. Fortunately there was a flat saddleback only 75 feet ahead, and the overloaded H-46 plopped down onto it. Bob ordered some of the walking wounded to get out to lighten the helicopter, and then he flew the more serious casualties to the Khe Sanh aid station.

<u>Hill 881 North, May 5, 1967, 0850 Hours</u>: The Grunts surged forward again, and little by little they inched their way toward the summit. The entrenched enemy fought bravely, but soon the Grunts shot their way across the top of the mountain. By 1445 Hours on May 5 the last of the three peaks, Hill 881 North, was finally in Marine Corps hands.

Electronic news of the battles for the three hills quickly reached the worldwide media. The previous day the *Washington Post* had featured a lengthy news dispatch on the fighting that had taken place on May 3. Detailing the fierce pre-dawn NVA counterattack, the newspaper had reported: "Hand grenades became the main weapons of the brutal battle." The newspaper quoted a wounded Grunt, Private First Class John V. Flannery, a native of Philadelphia, who was being treated at the Khe Sanh field hospital:

They were in front of us and in back of us. When I turned around, one of them was right in back of me . . . . My whole gun team and squad leader were killed.

For a week the *Washington Post* articles described "double canopy jungle, with elephant grass up to 15 feet high, on 3000 foot hills." The newspaper termed the fighting "the most brutal of the war." But newspapers did not confine their coverage to the printed word alone. Photographs of American dead were barred, although discrete photographs of American wounded were allowed. Under the erroneous headline, "Battle for 881 Is in 12th Day," a UPI reporter photographed a Marine casualty sitting on the ground at Khe Sanh. The Grunt had just been medevaced off of Hill 881 North by helicopter. Unclothed from the waist up, the Marine bravely grimaced as corpsmen tended to his wounds.

Pictures of enemy casualties were much more graphic, and photographs of dead North Vietnamese filled the western world's media dispatches. Reporting on the nonstop fighting that had taken place on May 4, the *Washington Post* printed a photograph of a severely wounded NVA soldier under the caption, "Screaming in pain, a wounded North Vietnamese prisoner is carried from a helicopter to medical aid at Khesanh [sic] Marine base." Whether or not the man survived was not reported.

The liberal European media fed its customers a daily diet of sensational radio, television, and newspaper accounts of the battles for the three hills. The communist nations provided their own brand of news. On May 3, China asserted that four United States warplanes had bombed the southern Chinese town of Ninmong, 20 miles north of their border with North Vietnam. And on May 6, North Vietnam paraded three captured American pilots, downed during an air raid on Hanoi, through the streets of the capital.

At the United Nations the following week, Secretary General Thant would publicly express fear that the world was witnessing the initial phase of World War III. He would inform the international press: "I am afraid direct confrontation, first of all between Washington and Peking, is inevitable."

Later that week the *Chicago Daily News* would publish an even more alarming report. Chinese Premier Chou En-lai, the newspaper stated, promised to send Chinese Army troops into North Vietnam if the Marines invaded across the DMZ. Further, the Premier was quoted as saying that China was "ready tomorrow as need be to send a volunteer army into North Vietnam if Hanoi [makes] such a request." Later in the month in New York, noted doctor Benjamin Spock and activists Stokely Carmichael and Martin Luther King Jr. would jointly aid the communist cause by publicly announcing their opposition to United States military policy in Indochina.

Yet, all of this international pacifist hand-wringing and leftist sabre-rattling was widely recognized as a smoke screen, an attempt to divert attention from the central issue. In reality the Chinese-

and Russian-backed North Vietnamese had suffered a crushing battlefield defeat. Two of their finest regiments from the 325-C Division had fortified the three mountains, hoping to use them as a springboard from which to swoop down on the isolated Marines at Khe Sanh. Now these two regiments had been decimated in the bloody process of being driven off of the hills. The North Vietnamese survivors retreated northwest into the impenetrable jungles in the direction of Laos.

By all accounts, the most impartial and factual report on the struggle for the hills would appear in the May 12, 1967, issue of *Time Magazine*. But *Time* pulled no punches. Its editors acknowledged that the Marines "took 1000 casualties." The magazine described the three hills: "So worthless that they have only numbers (representing elevation in meters above sea level), not names." Yet, the magazine pointed out that the North Vietnamese Army had suffered a horrible and humiliating defeat. The photograph preceding the article carried the caption, "Victorious Marines Atop Hill 881 South." The picture confirmed the *Time* writer's characterization: "Hill 881 South was a blasted moonscape of stumps and craters." Without a doubt it had been a vicious and desperate battle.

Time carried other Associated Press pictures that evoked the ghosts of Iwo Jima and Pork Chop Hill from other wars in other times. In the first picture in a poignant sequence of three photographs, a corpsman frantically tried to save a critically wounded Grunt on the denuded slope of Hill 881 South. In the second picture the corpsman stared skyward in helpless anguish as the Grunt died. In the final photograph the corpsman dove for cover as NVA fire whipped all around him.

The Marine strategy had been to take the hills at any cost, and the battle had boiled down to a contest of *will*. The Marines had persevered, but without question the price of their victory was high. However, there had been no other viable choice, for whoever controlled the hills controlled Khe Sanh.

Helicopter pilots and crewmen stayed busy even after the hills fell to the Grunts. Although their regiments had been badly mauled, the NVA soldiers who survived would likely live to fight again another day. Consequently, Recon teams flown in by helicopter kept a wary eye on the retreating North Vietnamese units and called in Air and Artillery on them whenever possible. HMM-164 flew emergency Recon resupply hops to Hill 803, just one mile northwest of Hill 881 North, and also to nearby Hill 802. One of the Northbrook H-46s took heavy fire at XD-746465 in the valley north of Dong Tri Mountain, but the crew escaped injury. From May 6 to May 9, the *HMM-164 Command Chronology* listed a continuing pattern of resupply flights, medevacs, and Recon inserts.

The monsoon had gradually fizzled out, but landing on half mile high mountains kept the risk factor high. HMM-163 lost one of their H-34s when it attempted to take off from Hill 881 South with too heavy a load. Losing turns, the Sikorsky helicopter mushed to the ground and crashed on the side of the hill. At about the same time an H-46 from HMM-265 got holed by NVA rounds while resupplying the Grunts in the same area.

Khe Sanh, May 9, 1967, 1650 Hours: Helicopters engaged their rotors and launched from Khe Sanh with the seven men of Reconnaissance Team "Breaker" aboard. Within minutes the Recons jumped out in a flat valley just north of Lang Phu Trang Ridge, four miles north of Hill 881 North. A half mile east lay the ruins of what once had been the small hamlet of Nguen Rao. The northern skyline was dominated by a mile high mountain, Dong Ta Bang. The Recon mission called for the team to monitor the retreat of the remnants of the NVA 325-C Division. Quickly the seven Marines moved to an observation spot on the northern slope of Hill 665, overlooking the valley. The Recon patrol leader, 21 year old Sergeant James N. Tycz, was a former seminary student from Wisconsin who was known for his habit of leading his men in a brief prayer before each patrol. Second Lieutenant Heinz Ahlmeyer accompanied the patrol, although he was not officially a member of the Breaker Recons.

Hill 665, May 10, 1967, 0030 Hours: Just after midnight the Recons heard movement down below them on the hillside. Then through the moonlight they could see the NVA soldiers, 30 to 50 of them, climbing up the hill. The Recons lay prone and motionless with their M-16s aimed toward the approaching enemy. Perhaps they would not be detected. However, the NVA continued to work their way uphill toward the concealed and silent Recons.

Sergeant Tycz opened fire, and the other Recons followed his lead. In a furious exchange of rifle fire, Lieutenant Ahlmeyer got shot and died almost instantly. Private First Class Steve D. Lopez, the radioman, got hit in the side, the first of four wounds that he would receive during the night. The assistant patrol leader and the corpsman also got hit by NVA rounds in the opening moments of the firefight.

Suddenly a grenade landed among the Recons. Sergeant Tycz grabbed it to hurl it back toward the enemy. Just as the hand-launched bomb left his fingertips, it detonated. The deafening blast flattened Tycz, and he died from multiple wounds and loss of blood within a few moments.

"EMERGENCY EXTRACTION!"

The wounded Lopez rolled over on his back and radioed to Khe Sanh for help. The firing had stopped, he reported, so perhaps a helicopter could fly down and rescue them now.

The frag fell to HMM-164. The Northbrook H-46 squadron was officially assigned to the SLF, but it maintained rotating detachments at Khe Sanh for four days at a time. Two H-46 helicopter crews pulled on their boots, loaded up, lit their turbine engine fires, and headed northeast toward Breaker at XD-758534. The pilots were guided by the rotating beacons on the belly and top of each of the escorting gunships flying 100 meters ahead in the darkness. Although dawn was still about four hours away, bright moonlight illuminated the rolling hills below. On the FM radio the helicopter crews heard Lopez again report that the enemy had apparently pulled back.

"Why?" the pilots wondered. If there really were as many NVA out there in the dark as the Recons had reported, the Recons could easily have been overrun by now. Were there fewer enemy soldiers than the Marines on the hill suspected? Or were the NVA just waiting for the helicopters that they knew would surely come?

With only moonlight to help them see through the night sky, the gunship pilots were unable to offer much visual help, so the H-46 section leader started down alone. Heading for the Recon's flashlight on the hillside, he eased his helicopter earthward. The waiting NVA soldiers let the Marine helicopter get within 25 feet of the ground before firing.

YT-18 received heavy automatic weapons fire entering the landing zone, sustaining 48 hits. Pilot, co-pilot, crew chief, gunner, and corpsman were all WIA.
--(*HMM-164 Command Chronology*; May 10, 1967)

Forty-eight rounds tore through the H-46, wounding the entire crew and the corpsman. Still, the two pilots managed to maintain control of both themselves and their helicopter. With turbines at topping power they climbed, accelerated, and raced toward the aid station at Khe Sanh. YT-1, the wingman, had attracted little fire and took a hit from only one round. He followed his leader as they both sped toward the south and safety.

The NVA soldiers had been patiently waiting near the Recons, and there was no way that a helicopter could snatch the Recons off of the hill. But a basic tenant of Marine Corps doctrine could not be ignored: Marines do not abandon their comrades in combat. Grunts, pilots, officers, and enlisted men of all ranks know this, and this knowledge has sustained them during their nation's wars for the past two centuries. Despite the danger, you know that you will never be abandoned. Your Marine brothers may fail in their effort to save you, and they may even lose their own lives, but they *must* try. They have no choice.

The Marine Air and Recons commanders mulled over the plight of Breaker. An overland rescue attempt was impossible. It would take a Grunt relief force a full day to reach Breaker on foot, even if the NVA did not intervene. Moreover, there was no place near Breaker to land reinforcements by helicopter. The only option remained helicopter extraction. Perhaps the NVA had really pulled back by now, or perhaps a different landing approach direction might be less hazardous.

Two more H-46s were fragged to give it a try. Huey Walsh, my former tentmate at Marble Mountain, had been slated for the HAC's slot in the lead H-46. However, his good friend and squadronmate, Captain Paul T. "Pee-Tee" Looney, had just flown in from the SLF on a relief helicopter to replace Huey and his crew. So, Pee-Tee got the frag instead of Huey, and the last minute switch would save Huey's life. The helicopter extraction force led by Pee-Tee in YT-5 launched northward and disappeared into the Indochinese night.

0235 Hours: Lopez, the Breaker radioman, keyed his FM transmitter and answered Pee-Tee's call. No, they were not taking fire now, Lopez radioed, but the enemy soldiers could periodically be heard scurrying around through the undergrowth on the hillside. Lopez said that he and Lance Corporal Carlson were the only two Recons left alive, and they were both hit. In the darkness, Lopez could offer the pilots little help or directional guidance.

Pee-Tee acknowledged the meager information. He kept talking to Lopez during a cautious power-on approach. And again the disciplined NVA soldiers waited and held their fire until the big Boeing Vertol helicopter flared to land.

> YT-5 received . . . 23 hits. The pilot, Captain P. T. Looney, was fatally wounded.
> -- (*HMM-164 Command Chronology*; May 10, 1967)

Twenty-three rounds tore into the Northbrook H-46. The crew chief and corpsman got hit, but not critically. Light shrapnel caught Pee-Tee in the face and legs, but those injuries alone would not have proved fatal. However, one round got past his bullet-bouncer and struck Pee-Tee squarely in the upper chest.

The uninjured copilot abandoned the landing attempt, sucked in collective, and headed skyward. Although mortally wounded, Pee-Tee managed to unstrap and crawl out of his armored seat. He stumbled back into the cabin as his H-46 rotored through the night toward Khe Sanh. The gunner tried to assist Pee-Tee, who was still alive when they landed five minutes later. Other Marines rushed Pee-Tee into the aid station, but the corpsmen and doctors could not keep his life from slipping away. There was nothing they could do; Pee-Tee drowned in his own blood, the doctors told us. Later, his Casualty Card would read:

> Died 0350H 10 May 67 3rd Medical Battalion Khe Sanh Republic of Vietnam result missile wound of undetermined origin penetrating supraclavicular causing massive uncontrollable hemorrhage and shrapnel wounds face and lower extremities sustained 0300H 10 May in vicinity Khe Sanh Republic of Vietnam when helicopter he was pilot of was

fired upon by hostile forces when about to touch down in landing zone.

Pee-Tee had been killed and others had been wounded, but nothing could be done about that now. The immediate problem remained the wounded Recons still alive on the slope of remote Hill 665. It was now obvious that the NVA wanted to sit back and use the surviving team members as bait and attempt to shoot down any helicopter that tried to get near them. The Recons and the NVA were too close to each other to risk strafing runs in the dark by the gunships. As long as the NVA waited for the helicopters under cover of darkness, the surviving but wounded team members would be safe, Lopez agreed. Consequently, the Marine Command made a calculated tactical gamble. It elected to wait until dawn before making another rescue try.

0520 Hours: Out on the hill, Lopez and Carlson lay bleeding in the tall grass. Nearby the NVA waited for the helicopters, and the helicopters waited for daylight. Low on ammunition, the two wounded Marines crawled among their fallen friends and stripped them of all their remaining grenades and M-16 magazines. During their ammunition stockpiling effort they discovered that the alternate radio operator, although unconscious, was still alive. Pulling him between them, they waited, for there was nothing else that they could do. Wounded four times, Lopez still stayed in radio contact with Khe Sanh throughout the rest of the night.

0630 Hours: Gunships and H-46s launched before the sun peeped over the mountains to the east. But the NVA were not caught napping, and they zeroed in on the first speeding H-46 as it roared down for the pickup.

This attempt . . . failed because of the heavy volume of automatic weapons fire . . . .
-- (from a Marine Corps chronology; May 10, 1967)

Withering machinegun fire drove the H-46 away. In an effort to suppress the fire, Carlson rose to hurl a grenade toward the NVA gunners. The North Vietnamese shot him, and he crumpled to the ground, hit once again.

The night had belonged to the enemy, but the day would belong to the Marines. With the dawn, fixed-wing support arrived from faraway Da Nang, and the Marine pilots could now see the NVA soldiers kneeling in the tall grass only 100 feet from the surviving Recons. The combatants were much too close to each other for risky fixed-wing airstrikes, but there was no other choice.

"Stay down! Flat on the ground!" the gunship pilots radioed a warning to Lopez. Then the fast-movers rolled in hot, and twenty mike-mike ripped into the North Vietnamese, followed by napalm. The NVA had apparently anticipated only helicopters. When the elongated silver napalm canisters began tumbling down and the jellied gasoline ignited, the surviving North Vietnamese soldiers immediately stopped shooting at the helicopters and jets. Under cover of this continuing aerial barrage, a Huey piloted by Major Charles A. Reynolds zipped down, landed, and rescued the Recons who were still alive.

The fixed-wing drivers salvoed the last of their ordnance on the fleeing NVA soldiers, and then they turned and headed southeast toward Da Nang. With the wounded Recons all aboard the Huey, the helicopters climbed above the effective range of ground fire and pointed their noses toward Khe Sanh.

The battered remnants of North Vietnam's 325-C Division marched on northwest into Laos, out of range of Marine artillery. The Marines let them go, for the dense jungles to the northwest totally shielded the NVA from aerial observation attempts. The rescue of the surviving men of Breaker had closed the chapter on the bloody battles for the three mountaintop enemy strongholds. The hills overlooking Khe Sanh now belonged to the Grunts, and the Marine outpost had been saved. This time the NVA had been outgunned, no doubt about it. Air and Artillery had pounded them without mercy, and that deadly pounding proved to be the deciding factor, because the Grunts had been vastly outnumbered.

However, the North Vietnamese learned a costly but valuable lesson. First of all, their timing had been flawed. What, General Giap presumably wondered, would the result have been if he had struck three months earlier? Then the monsoon would have blinded Marine Air and thwarted the Marine artillery spotters. And what if Giap had hauled in his own heavy artillery to blast away at the vulnerable helicopters on the ground at Khe Sanh. In the first days of his battle with the French at Dien Bien Phu, his artillery had put the French airstrip -- the French lifeline -- totally out of business. And what, Giap likely wondered, would the outcome have been if his artillery could have rained down high-explosive shells on the entrenched Khe Sanh defenders for a month? And then, just as was the case during his masterpiece at Dien Bien Phu, what would have happened if his attacking army had held a six-to-one (*eight-to-one*, by some accounts) manpower advantage over the Marines?

Remote Khe Sanh could have been surrounded with no hope of overland relief or resupply. The monsoon would have hamstrung the Marine airplanes and helicopters. Then, would not Giap's loyal People's Army have swept down in human waves of attackers and overwhelmed the Marines, just like they had overwhelmed the French in 1954? And would not such a victory cause the Americans to pull out of all of Indochina, just like the French before them?

Yes, Giap logically theorized, with the monsoon weather in his favor, with proper artillery support, with enough soldiers, he could surround and crush the Marines at Khe Sanh. But to test his theory, Giap would have to wait at least five months for the next monsoon.

To wound all ten fingers of a man is not so effective as to chop one of them off. To rout ten of the enemy's divisions is not so effective as to annihilate one of them.
-- (Mao Tse-tung; December 1936)

-- They Bought the Farm --

During one Medical Evacuation Mission, while the section [a *section* means *two* military aircraft] was enroute to the *USS Tripoli*, the lead aircraft disintegrated in the air. Two pilots, two crewmen, and one passenger were on board. There were no survivors.
-- (*HMM-262 Command Chronology*; August 31, 1967)

Combat pilots develop and nurture an intense love affair with their aircraft. The enemy and aeronautical perils force them to place blind trust in the mechanical reliability of their flying machines, the proud products of American ingenuity and manufacturing excellence. Over the years such trust has inspired honored admonitions that pilots fervently believed, such as "Trust in God and Pratt & Whitney." Among H-46 pilots, myself included, there were few who did not hold absolute faith in the manufacturer's time-honored motto: "Boeing Builds 'Em Better." Yet, for me and all other Boeing H-46 pilots in the spring and summer of 1967, that once rock-solid belief swayed, then cracked, and then completely shattered.

Dong Ha, June 11, 1967: The frag fell to HMM-265, and it called for a routine Recon insertion. The seven Recons of "Summersail-One" crawled into the cabin of EP-158 and strapped themselves into the web troop seats that lined each side of the cabin. Their scout dog, the four-footed member of their team, was already a helicopter insertion veteran and did not need a troop seat, so he curled up on the aluminum floor beside the feet of his handler. The Recons were bound for YD-041681, a saddleback just 900 meters west of the former NVA redoubt on Hill 174.

Up in the cockpit of the Marine H-46 helicopter were the HAC, Major John S. Oldham, and the copilot, Captain Curtis R.

Bolscheid. Ironically, Major Charles H. "Chuck" Pitman had been scheduled to fill the HAC's slot on this flight, but fate delayed him at Phu Bai and left the pilot-in-command slot to Major Oldham. Although I did not know Major Oldham, I knew Bolscheid well. He had been one of my T-28 flight instructors at South Whiting Field in Florida, and his deep booming voice and stinking flight suits had become legendary.

Back in the H-46 cabin the crew chief, Private First Class Thomas M. Hanratty, and the gunner, Lance Corporal Jose J. Gonzales, manned the twin fifties. EP-158 took off and churned northward in the company of another H-46 and two VMO-2 gunships. Approaching the Recons' observation point north of Dong Ha, the SAR H-46 stayed high and dry as Major Oldham spiraled earthward toward the landing area a half mile below.

Hotspur: Doomsday is near; die all, die merrily.
-- (William Shakespeare; in *Henry IV*)

The speeding H-46 suddenly snapped up vertically and then rolled inverted. As Captain Alan H. "Al" Barbour, one of the Deadlock pilots, watched in horror, the doomed H-46 began tumbling earthward end-over-end like a falling anvil (the *HMM-265 Command Chronology* would later dryly note that the falling helicopter exhibited "extremely unusual flight attitudes"). Structural integrity was lost, and the rotor blades snapped off like match-sticks. Still, the Master Battery Switch circuit powered the FM radio, and Bolscheid must have instinctively clamped a death-grip on the cyclic, keying the AN/ARC-44 transmitter. Years later, Barbour would explain to me that he heard Bolscheid's unintelligible and horrible scream all the way to impact.

Barbour dove down toward the crash site, but the hapless crew and passengers of EP-158 were beyond mortal help. The remains of the Boeing Vertol helicopter had slammed into the ground, and roughly 1900 remaining pounds of JP-4 fuel instantly turned the mangled wreckage into a raging inferno. A pillar of dense black smoke mushroomed upward from the fire. All aboard had undoubtedly died on impact, and a report would later simply state: "AIR CRASH / EXPLODED MID-AIR / NO SURVIVORS OBSERVED (CH-46A)." The names of the eleven Marines who died, and their hometowns of record, follow:

Oldham, John S.	Major	Tinne, New Mexico
Bolscheid, Curtis R.	Captain	Pocatello, Idaho
Moshier, Jim E.	Corporal	Bakersfield, California
Gonzales, Jose J.	L/Corporal	El Passo, Texas
Christie, Dennis R.	L/Corporal	Imperial Beach, California
Foley, John J. III	L/Corporal	Plainfield, New Jersey
Havranek, Michael W.	L/Corporal	Missoula, Montana
Kooi, James W.	L/Corporal	Fruitport, Michigan
Chomel, Charles D.	PFC	Columbus, Ohio
Hanratty, Thomas M.	PFC	Beulah, Colorado
Widener, James E.	PFC	Churchville, New York

This crash on June 11 marked the *third time* since May 3 -- just over a month -- that an H-46 had disintegrated in midair. Incredibly, in just under five months a total of eight H-46s would catastrophically self-destruct in similar fashion. The technical history associated with these crashes, and the airframe modifications necessary to make the H-46 airworthy again, would become one of the more intriguing sagas in the annals of civil and military aviation.

The H-46 originally had not been designed as a military helicopter. Instead, it evolved from its civilian cousin, the Boeing Vertol-107, which first flew in April 1958. The Federal Aviation Administration later certified the Vertol-107 as a Commercial Transport Helicopter. Boeing Vertol (*Vertol* is an acronym derived from *Vertical Take-Off & Landing*) then delivered the first airliner-configured helicopter to New York Airways.

Using the same basic civilian design, Boeing Vertol triumphed over Sikorsky in the battle to produce the next generation of assault transport helicopters for the Marine Corps. Greatly modified and designated the CH-46A, the first of the new helicopters rolled off of the assembly line in April 1962. HMM-265 became the first Marine Corps squadron to fly the revolutionary new aircraft.

Generally known simply as the H-46, the new helicopter went to war in 1966 and, despite initial turbine compressor-blade sand erosion problems (soon corrected by new sand-filters), exceeded all expectations. But in 1967 a bewildering series of fatal crashes cast grave doubts on the structural integrity of the helicopter. The H-46s began disintegrating in midair. To understand the problem, a look at civilian aviation history is in order:

September 29, 1959, 10:44 P.M.: A proud Lockheed Electra, Braniff Flight 542, took off from Houston, Texas. Bound for New York, the late-night flight carried a slim load of only 28 passengers in addition to its crew of six, and the Electra's four Allison turboprop engines quickly enabled Flight 542 to reach its cruising speed of just over 400 miles per hour. Flight 542 was passed off to Fort Worth's Air Route Traffic Control Center (ARTCC), and at 11:07 P.M. the flight engineer made a routine radio contact with Braniff Base. No one ever heard from Flight 542 again. The Electra suddenly self-destructed in the air.

On September 30 the rising sun revealed a macabre trail of destruction. Bits and fragments of Flight 542 were strewn over a path almost three miles long across farm fields near Buffalo, Texas. All aboard the airliner had perished.

In the weeks that followed an accident investigation team from the FAA, CAB, Lockheed, Allison, and the airlines flying the Electra tried to piece together the pieces of the puzzle. It soon became obvious that the left wing of the Electra had failed and had ripped off of the fuselage -- but why? In flight tests and in the laboratory the wing was tested, tortured, deliberately warped with hydraulic jacks and then tested again. After six months the investigators had compiled thousands of pages of data and had spent millions of dollars, all without a solid clue. But then *another* Electra fell to its death.

March 6, 1960, 3:50 P.M.: Northwest Airlines Flight 710 was headed for Miami. Indianapolis ARTCC stayed in routine radio contact with the airliner as it leisurely cruised at 18,000 feet, and the 63 passengers aboard could look out of the Electra's windows and see the farmland quickly passing below them. Tragedy struck without warning. Both wings ripped completely off of the fuselage.

People on the ground looked skyward and witnessed the fiery death of Flight 710 and its human cargo. The wingless fuselage vertically dove into a field near Tell City, Indiana.

The impact threw metal debris 1500 feet from the main crash site, and smaller pieces of the missing wings rained down over a much wider area. In aviation lingo, another Electra had "bought the farm."

The technical team still struggling with the first disaster quickly combined both crashes into a single investigation. In both instances the Electra wing had failed and ripped off; that was clear. Nonetheless, the *cause* of the wing failures remained elusive. Yet, 24 hours per day investigation finally identified the sinister culprit -- Whirl Mode Flutter. The assassin of the two Electra airliners had been unmasked, and no Lockheed engineer could have anticipated the deadly combination of events involved.

Whirl Mode Flutter was nothing new, and in aviation circles it had been understood for many years. Most spinning objects (car tires, ceiling fans, aircraft propellers, helicopter rotors) can become imbalanced. In propeller driven aircraft -- or helicopters with a fully articulated rotor system -- a blow, such as turbulence, will cause the spinning propeller or rotor to displace slightly. This is normal. The propeller or rotor, in effect a giant spinning gyroscope, will push back against the displacing force and cause Whirl Mode Flutter. In fixed-wing aircraft, the propeller flutter is easily absorbed (*damped*, in aeronautical terms) and rendered harmless by the huge mass of the wing. Further, all aircraft wings are designed to flex in flight. Anyone can look out of the window of an airliner flying through turbulent air and watch the wing flex as it handles vertical lift imbalances.

However, the Electra accident investigation team stumbled upon a startling sequence of events. On an Electra with (1) a damaged longeron or engine strut, (2) a weakened engine nacelle, and (3) enough turbulence to start the fatal cycle, the entire engine and propeller unit could flutter together. Unfortunately, the *frequency* of this flutter chanced to *match the harmonic frequency* of the Electra's huge wing.

Under the proper circumstances, once the deadly flutter started, it could not be stopped. Whirl Mode Flutter would spread from the engine and propeller unit to the wing. Instead of damping the flutter, the wing would then begin vibrating at the *same* frequency. The wing vibrations would now accelerate the engine and propeller flutter and feed the deadly malignancy. The engine Lord-mounts would snap, and the wobbling engine and propeller, still in harmonic frequency with the wing, would fuel the ever-wilder wing vibrations. In a vicious cycle lasting only seconds, the massive wing would snap like a twig.

Once identified, the vibration problem was quickly corrected. The Electra wing was much more than strong enough, but *stiffeners* were added to damp the deadly Whirl Mode Flutter. There were no more Electra wing failures. However, would a similar sinister malady ever curse another aircraft? YES! -- the Boeing Vertol H-46.

Republic of Vietnam, Spring 1967: Four squadrons of H-46s were now in Vietnam, two at Marble Mountain and two more down at Ky Ha. So far the H-46 had created an unbridled success story. Although enemy fire had downed some of them, the new helicopter had usually proven its ability to absorb heavy battle damage and keep plugging away.

However, there had been two fatal crashes that gave pilots cause for concern. Back on September 14 of the previous year, an H-46 from HMM-265 had suffered a complete in-flight control system failure. However, the cause of that crash had been traced to an over-torqued bolt, and the basic design of the helicopter was not called into question. Another H-46 had lost a rotor blade in flight, but examination of the charred wreckage revealed that a bullet hole through the main spar of the rotor blade had gone undetected for over a month. Metal fatigue from the hairline cracks around the hole had eventually caused the spar to fail, and the integrity of the basic design of the helicopter was not in dispute. Consequently, after a year as a warhorse the H-46 had become the pride of Marine Corps Aviation. But things were about to change.

May 3, 1967: Back at Santa Ana, California, a CH-46D, one of the newer D-Model helicopters, crashed and killed everyone aboard. Wreckage analysis soon showed that the massive attachment brackets on the aft transmission had mysteriously failed. No one knew why.

May 12, 1967: Nine days later in Vietnam, two HMM-262 helicopters were hauling lumber from Ky Ha up to Marble Mountain. If ever there was an easy milk run, this was it. Cruising up the coastline at 3000 feet, the pair of H-46s flew over the mouth of the Hoi An River. Then in the lead H-46, the horrified crew chief watched the entire aft pylon rip off of the number two helicopter. With its rotors gone, the doomed H-46 plummeted a half mile straight down into the ocean, and none of the crew survived the crash.

> The number two aircraft crashed in the ocean at 115 [degrees]/15 miles from channel 37. All 4 crewmembers were killed. The aft pylon was observed to leave the aircraft before it entered the water.
> -- (*HMM-262 Command Chronology*; May 12, 1967)

June 11, 1967: There were some crashes where the cause was subject to question. As previously detailed, on June 11 the helicopter carrying Summersail-One and piloted by Major Oldham and Captain Bolscheid tumbled earthward and crashed north of Dong Ha. No one could be *sure* of the cause.

June 20, 1967: Nine days later another H-46 abruptly snapped out of control and crashed into the sea. There was no possibility of hostile fire, no turbulence, and no distress message. The helicopter simply tore itself apart in the air. The wreckage was never recovered from the ocean floor, but available evidence clearly pointed at the aft pylon as the culprit.

June 30, 1967: For the third time in 19 days, an H-46 suddenly tumbled earthward and crashed. Again, there were no survivors. The Marine Corps, now thoroughly alarmed, grounded all of the newer D-Model helicopters in the United States while an investigative team feverishly worked to pinpoint the cause of the crashes. However, the older A-Model H-46s in Vietnam kept flying.

July 3, 1967: Only four days later an ungrounded CH-46A from HMM-165 crashed in Vietnam, killing everyone in the helicopter. Examination of the wreckage clearly showed a massive structural failure in the main transmission area of the aft pylon.

The H-46 program was now in deep, deep trouble. Teams of

Marine Corps and Boeing Vertol technical experts labored to identify the elusive cause of the crashes. All H-46s in the United States were now grounded, but in Vietnam the H-46s soldiered on because they were desperately needed. Lieutenant General Victor H. Krulak explained in a letter: "We are obligated to keep the CH-46 at work as best we can, since, as you know, it is the backbone of our vertical assault capability in Vietnam."

August 31, 1967: The next month two HMM-262 helicopters in Vietnam drew a medevac frag. After picking up a casualty, they headed for medical facilities aboard the *USS Tripoli* (LPH-10). The aft pylon inexplicably ripped off in midair, and none aboard survived the fiery crash.

> A CH-46A from HMM-262 on the SLF yawed at 3000 feet and lost the tail pylon.
> -- (Lieutenant Colonel William R. Fails; writing in *Marines and Helicopters: 1962-1973)*

September 1, 1967: The very next day an H-46 from HMM-265 returned from a mission and made a routine landing at Marble Mountain. Lucky timing rode with the pilot, Major Charles H. "Chuck" Pitman. Only seconds after touching down on the runway, a horrible vibration consumed the airframe. Within seconds the entire aft pylon ripped completely off of the helicopter.

> At approximately 0930H, EP-153, a Bonnie-Sue aircraft, was involved in an accident while landing at MMAF [meaning, *Marble Mountain Air Facility*]. The aft pylon separated [meaning, *ripped off of the fuselage*] due to a reason or reasons now under investigation by the Accident Board.
> -- (*HMM-265 Command Chronology*; September 1, 1967)

By now I was back at New River and flying as an instructor pilot in the new CH-46D. A patch sewn on my flight suit depicted the world-famous beagle, Snoopy. As he fell earthward in a broken, burning, and doomed H-46, he hurled expletives at Boeing Vertol. Other pilots were more vocal. Captain Ron Rensch vowed to request reassignment back into the older H-34s before his next tour in Vietnam, and Captain James H. "Jim" Street started wearing a parachute on training flights. Our commanding officer finally put an end to the parachute business and explained to Jim that he was demoralizing the newer pilots.

Gradually the investigative team from Boeing Vertol and the Naval Air Systems Command zeroed in on the problem. The H-46 was a highly modified version of the original civilian Boeing Vertol-107. Whether or not those modifications were the culprit, no one knows. In any event, unforeseen and beyond-the-envelop Marine Corps usage had proved too much for the airframe.

Incorporation of automatic blade fold capability had placed extraordinary stress on the rotor mount system. The enlargement of the rear ramp had taken away structural members from the rear fuselage. The rear landing gear, designed initially for civilian operations, had been subjected to full load landings and overload landings, and hard landings when the pilots were under fire in Vietnam. As a result of this abuse the combined weight of the aft pylon, aft rotors, engines, and aft transmission had visibly wrinkled the aluminum skin on the fuselage of many H-46s. More powerful engines in the new D-Model helicopters added still more strain on the transmission and aft pylon area. Further, there was a documented problem with the high frequency vibration level of the twin shafts that connected the two turbine engines to the aft transmission. The H-46, the experts agreed, needed more strength and stiffeners in the aft pylon area.

October 11, 1967: The fix would be neither cheap nor quick. H-46s in Vietnam were shipped to Futema, Okinawa, where repair work began on October 11. Over 1000 man-hours were needed to modify each helicopter. Marine helicopter mechanics conducted the necessary disassembly, Boeing Vertol installed the required stiffeners and structural additions, and then the Marines reassembled the helicopters and prepared them to fly again. H-46s in the United States were modified in a similar manner. Meanwhile, 23 old H-34s from the United States were rushed to Vietnam on October 15 to help fill the void left by the H-46s that were being repaired.

None of the H-46s modified on Okinawa suffered subsequent structural failure. However, back at New River the magnetic transmission chip detector light had given nick-of-time warning to Major Chuck D. Riordan on October 6. He had landed his CH-

46D from HMM-161 in a cornfield only seconds before the forward transmission seized, destroying the helicopter. Later, laboratory examination of the transmission revealed a freak lubrication problem, and there was no deficiency in the area of the aft pylon.

True, there was an in-flight disaster involving a CH-46D from HMM-162 at New River. Piloted by Majors Lynn Ackerman and Hugh Cameron, the H-46 fell prey to a mechanical problem at 1105 Hours on December 1, 1967. Synchronization was lost, the rotors intermeshed, and the fuselage fell like a manhole cover and crashed to earth in the front yard of a local farmer, Caleb Shephard. All aboard died on impact. Part of the rotor system was found in the nearby woods, and remnants of the helicopter were depicted in a color photograph in the Jacksonville, North Carolina, *Daily News* newspaper the following morning. But wreckage analysis pinpointed the unique problem, and there was no deficiency in the aft pylon area.

By February 1968 all H-46 modifications would be completed. The metallurgical surgery would prove to be a complete success, and there would be no more catastrophic in-flight structural failures. The H-46 would eventually go out of production in the United States in 1971. Boeing Vertol would sell the manufacturing rights to Kawasaki Heavy Industries Ltd., which would build 135 more of the durable helicopters for both military and civilian customers.

The H-46A Sea Knight is a twin-turbine-powered, tandem-rotor helicopter, designed by the Boeing Company, Vertol Division. The primary mission of the H-46A is to rapidly disperse combat troops, support equipment, and supplies from amphibious assault landing ships and established airfields to advance bases in underdeveloped areas having limited maintenance and logistic support, under all-weather conditions, day or night . . . .

The H-46D helicopter is a revised version of the H-46A helicopter and is powered by two T58-GE-10 engines. Each engine is rated at 1400 shaft horsepower . . . . A power management system has been added to accomplish load-sharing; a remote topping adjustment allows in-flight topping

adjustments. To accommodate the higher shaft horsepowers of the T58-GE-10 engines, a transmission modification incorporating M-50 steel bearings has been accomplished. In addition, a new droop snoot rotor blade has been added. These modifications improved dual and single engine performance and increased load-bearing capability.
-- (from CH-46A / CH-46D NATOPS Manual)

Over the next two decades the Marine Corps would continue to depend heavily on the now-reliable H-46. Consequently, Boeing would develop a Safety, Reliability, and Maintainability (SS&M) kit for the helicopter and begin delivery of the kit for the venerable warhorse in July 1985. The kit modifications, 26 in all, would be incorporated into the entire H-46 fleet over a four year period. Eventually the Marine Corps would expect the 1962-vintage H-46 to remain on the job well into the Twenty-First Century -- five decades of Marine Corps service.

The Marine Corps H-34 Saga: In the early 1950s the Marine Corps had been shopping for a heavy-lift helicopter. The Sikorsky HR2S, the giant "Deuce," would fit the bill when it became operational, it had been believed. Yet, there still had been a projected need for a few smaller helicopters that could be used for simple logistical flights. The Navy had already been flying the proven Sikorsky HSS-1 as an antisubmarine helicopter. It had been reasoned that, with relatively minor modifications, this same helicopter would be suitable for the Marine Corps. Consequently, in the mid-1950s a decision had been made to procure a limited number of modified HSS-1 helicopters for the Marines. From this modest beginning the H-34 program was born.

Sikorsky had modified the HSS-1 to meet Marine Corps requirements, and the new Marine helicopter, designated the UH-34D, first flew in January 1957. The H-34 or "Dog," as it was affectionately called, had proved to be a sophisticated flying machine. Powered by a supercharged Wright engine that hammered out 1525 horsepower, the H-34 was packed with the latest electronic communications and navigation equipment. Fully stabilized and outfitted with such relative luxuries as a radar altimeter, the "Thirty-Four" was fully IFR capable. Within three years the new H-34, originally viewed as a stepchild for the huge Deuce, had become the darling of Marine aviation -- due greatly to the fact that the cantankerous Deuce had fallen flat on its face.

By the time the Marines of HMM-362 had flown to Soc Trang, Vietnam, in April 1962 on Operation Shu-Fly, the H-34 had become the backbone of the Marine helicopter inventory. Initially lightly armed and lightly armored (the copilot and crew chief had carried grease-guns, nothing more), the H-34 soon got protective armor and twin machineguns for its combat role. Of course, the H-34 had still been looked upon as an interim helicopter as late as the mid-1960s. The Marine Corps had planned to sideline it after the larger and more powerful H-46s and H-53s became operational.

> Such was not the case. The ever-versatile UH-34 simply refused to leave the scene. No one, in 1955 when General Shepherd had first requested that 90 [H-34s] be procured, could have foreseen how this aircraft would become such a seemingly permanent fixture of Marine Corps aviation.
> -- (Lieutenant Colonel William R. Fails; writing in *Marines and Helicopters: 1962-1973*)

It had not worked out that way, because the H-34 had evolved into a reliable workhorse. True, it was ungainly to look at, but it got the job done day after day and night after night. Pilots, crew chiefs, and mechanics loved it and swore by it. And the sweetest sound in the world to a wounded Grunt in Vietnam had been the metallic whine of the radial engine on an inbound H-34. The most beautiful sight had been those gigantic and goofy, yet menacing, eyeballs often painted on the front of the clamshell engine doors.

In the spring of 1966 the new H-46s had begun arriving in Vietnam. In January of the next year the huge H-53s had followed, but still the H-34s soldiered on. They could get in and out of small landing zones that the larger helicopters could not enter, and they became the standard medevac helicopter. When pilots saw an H-34 heading for the hills with a Huey gunship flying chase, nobody had to tell them where the H-34 was going. They knew. And they also knew that while the gunship would orbit above in relative safety, the H-34 was going to spiral down, day or night, into God only knew what. And they knew that if any helicopter could survive the expected hail of incoming rounds and mortars, it would be the wounded Grunt's best friend, the H-34.

The war continued in Vietnam, and finally the days of the Marine Corps H-34 appeared numbered. Hundreds of Hueys and the new D-Model H-46s, plus a full complement of the enormous H-53s, slowly took over the helicopter burden in I-Corps. As the H-34s gradually got destroyed in combat or rotated back to CONUS, they were not replaced.

In early 1968 the Marine Corps would decide to locate the oldest active-duty H-34 so that it could be sent to the aviation museum in Quantico, Virginia. The appropriate helicopter would be found in Vietnam, naturally. However, before it could be sent to Quantico, it would get shot down and destroyed while doing its job along the DMZ. Undaunted, the Marine Corps would locate the next oldest H-34, and it quickly would be spirited out of Vietnam. But before this helicopter could be flown to the museum, operational requirements would require it to be kept in service.

Marine H-34s in Vietnam would continue to fly until August 20, 1969, when the six remaining H-34s would be flown to Da Nang for shipment to CONUS. Two months later the last active duty H-34 squadron would be decommissioned in the United States, but the ageing H-34s still remained in use with Marine Corps Reserve squadrons. Then, three years later in March 1972, a premature announcement in *Naval Aviation News* would proclaim that the "last flight" of a Marine Corps H-34 had taken place at Quantico.

No! Not true! One Marine Corps Reserve squadron would quickly report that its last remaining H-34, Bureau Number 147191, was still flying and doing its job each day, just as it always had done. And HMM-776 would proudly remind Headquarters that it was still flying *six* of its old H-34s. However, the Sikorsky warhorses gradually retired, and by late 1972 it would seem certain that the Marine Corps H-34s existed only in the history books.

Over 500 of these [H-34] helicopters . . . have accomplished every task from space capsule recovery to disaster relief in peacetime, and assault troop lifts to medical evacuations in

war. The UH-34 takes its place in our memories as one of the giants of Marine Aviation.
-- (General Leonard F. Chapman)

On October 3, 1973, the Marines at New River, North Carolina, would hear the strange popping noise of the rotors on the approaching helicopter. But, they would wonder, what was that weird and metallic engine noise? Then the helicopter would roar into view, a battered but proud Sikorsky H-34.

The old warhorse, Bureau Number 147191, would prove to be the *last one*. The helicopter would be stricken from official records and enshrined at the main gate entrance at MCAF New River. An era would come to an end. Old "one-ninety-one" would indeed be the last Marine Corps H-34.

Well, if we ever get into a scrape where we need lots of helicopters in a hurry, I won't be surprised a bit to see someone find some UH-34s and have me flying them again.
-- (Major Dwight L. Bledsoe)

-- Leatherneck Square --

It seemed as though the pilots were trying to twist the fuselage around to escape the rounds. From the ground we could see the tracers converge on the tailpipes. Yet the pilots came around again and again as though it was a training flight. The war seemed to stop. All eyes were fixed on the planes. I don't know what the others felt, but my eyes were glued on the letters M-A-R-I-N-E-S painted on the fuselages. It was good not to be alone.
-- (Major M. P. Caulfield; writing in *Marine Corps Gazette* about the fighting around Con Thien in 1967)

In the Vietnamese language, Nui Con Thien means *Hill of Angels*. In reality, however, nothing could have been farther from the truth. By the late spring of 1967 no angel would have dared set foot anywhere near the muddy and cratered slopes of Con Thien, which was labeled as Hill 158 on our maps. Forsaken by the angels and deserted by the indigenous Vietnamese, Con Thien was now occupied by the United States Marines.

I remember flying to the Grunt outpost at Con Thien during the miserable monsoon in the spring of 1967. Actually, Con Thien was not much of a hill at all. True, the red clay angled upward to a height of 158 meters above sea level, but the slope was almost imperceptible when we looked down at the hill from our cockpits at cruising altitude. The hill did not seem to be a defensible place for the Grunts to set up a forward observation and artillery outpost.

Flying from Dong Ha to Con Thien presented no problem. After two or three trips there we no longer had to resort to our maps, because Hill 158 lay only five minutes northwest on the 310 degree radial of the Dong Ha TACAN. We often made the short trip at low altitude and skimmed along at 125 knots right over the top of the tangled undergrowth that covered the gently rolling hills just inland from the coastal plain. Approaching Con Thien in this manner at low altitude, we got a better appreciation of its value to the Grunts. Although not a steep hill, Con Thien offered the Marines a crucial vantage point. Here they could observe any North Vietnamese troop activity from the South China Sea, nine miles to the east, to the mountains that began just to the west of the outpost. The southern border of the DMZ lay two miles north, well within sight of the Grunt spotters perched on top of Con Thien. But for the Grunts in early 1967, this was a Godforsaken and miserable place. Bob Mills would sum it up years later: "Con Thien was nothing, just big mounds of dirt."

I never got mortared at Con Thien, but others were not as lucky as I. Captain Gerry Dooley crawled into Bureau Number 152497 at Dong Ha to lead a flight of four helicopters on a frag to resupply the Grunts. His crew chief, Sergeant William C. Babbitt, supervised the loading of C-Rations, ammunition, and water, and then they launched. It was almost dark, and rain pelted the plexiglass windshields of the four H-46s as they bored their way northwest. Arriving over Con Thien, two of the H-46s stayed high and dry while Dooley and his wingman raced down and landed at the outpost. The Marines at Con Thien had several Kit Carson scouts and Vietnamese translators with them, and Dooley watched one of these ARVNs peeping at him from behind a bunker as the Grunts unloaded the cargo. Suddenly the ARVN broke into a frantic run away from the helicopter. He had heard the dull *thunnkk* as a North Vietnamese 82mm mortar round left its tube. Both the terrified ARVN soldier and Dooley knew that the deadly explosive projectile was on its way.

At Con Thien, you had nineteen seconds 'till the mortars impacted.
-- (Huey C. Walsh; years later)

Dooley helplessly watched as the first mortar round detonated 80 meters or so in front of his H-46. As the last of the cargo was hurriedly kicked out, another round exploded about 75 feet from the helicopter. Babbitt ran back inside, and Dooley sucked in collective pitch. They felt the vibration as their six rotors bit into the air and their turbines spooled up to full topping power. Just as the helicopter shuddered skyward, a third mortar round exploded 25 feet to the right of the cockpit. The blast splattered the green fuselage with a combination of mud and shrapnel. The armored seat protected most of Dooley's torso, but hot jagged steel tore into his right calf.

Dooley banked hard to the right and skimmed over the bunkers, rapidly accelerating. Sergeant Babbitt had been hit too, but he stayed on his machinegun as Dooley muscled the H-46 southward. The helicopter had suffered little damage, but now a new threat closed in on them -- the weather. Faced with a solid wall of fog and scud south of Con Thien, Dooley blindly climbed IFR and radioed Dong Ha to ask for a GCA approach to the airstrip. He intercepted the invisible electronic glideslope and followed the controller's heading and rate-of-descent directions to a safe landing within ten minutes. Dooley's logbook would later show "0.1 Inst. Time" for the quick IFR approach.

At the aid station north of the Dong Ha runway, Dooley and Babbitt endured the standard but painful cleaning of their minor wounds. Meanwhile, the maintenance crews descended on Dooley's damaged H-46. They covered all of the shrapnel holes with blade tape and began repair and replacement work to make Bureau Number 152497 ready to fly again.

In the early spring of 1967 the NVA mortarmen had begun routinely targeting all helicopters that landed at Con Thien. An inbound helicopter at a normal cruising altitude of 3000 feet could easily be seen by the enemy spotters in the hills to the northwest. Consequently, most pilots elected take off from Dong Ha and fly northward to Con Thien right over the tops of the trees at 125 knots. But regardless of the type of approach used, the helicopter would clearly be visible to the enemy as soon as it landed on the hill. To reduce this threat we started using external sling loads whenever possible to whittle down the amount of time we spent in the landing area. With a sling load dangling on our cargo hook under the belly of our H-46, we could zip down to hover height, quickly pickle the sling as soon as the cargo net touched the ground, and then head skyward for safety.

HMM-265 had been in Vietnam since May 22 of the previous year. Now, one by one, each of the original squadron members was flying on his last combat mission and then leaving for the United States. Two weeks before a pilot's anticipated departure date he could no longer eat at the same table with his squadronmates in the Marble Mountain mess hall. Instead, he would be assigned to a special seat at the infamous "'Couths Table," designed to purge a full year's accumulation of *uncouth* eating habits.

Unlike the rest of the handmade wooden tables, the 'Couths Table was always covered with a plastic tablecloth and adorned with a waterglass full of artificial flowers. The usual profanity, shouting, flatulence, and eating with your hands were strictly outlawed at the 'Couths Table. In lieu of the sleeve of your flight suit, a paper napkin was now required. Here the pilots were expected to regain a semblance of civilized eating habits and table manners to prepare them for their return to western society. "Throw me a [expletive deleted] biscuit!" would soon be replaced with the more acceptable, "Pass the bread, please."

I can not remember my last combat mission in Vietnam. My logbook tells me that on that forgotten flight I strapped myself into Bureau Number 152507 for a brief 0.6 hour frag that involved four landings. However, time has erased my recollection of that final time that I flew helicopters for the Marine Corps in Vietnam. Still, I vividly recall my flight out of Indochina. I sat in one of the extreme right-hand window seats on takeoff from the main Da Nang runway. The big Boeing accelerated northward down the concrete airstrip, rose, and rumbled low out over the city. Three miles off to my right I could see the helicopters on the flight line at Marble Mountain. As the passenger jet climbed northward over Da Nang Bay, Monkey Mountain slowly drifted behind us, and then it was gone. I never saw Vietnam again.

The wound in my right foot had healed, but the hardening scar tissue was making it increasingly difficult to walk. The doctors at the NSA hospital were sending me to the Portsmouth Naval Hospital to have my foot surgically explored. I did not look forward to an encounter with knives and needles again, but the thought of going home greatly lessened my dread.

Another type of final flight took place soon after I left. The mighty Deuce, the giant Sikorsky HR2S, flew its last combat mission on May 14 when one of the twin-engine monsters hauled 20 Grunts and 3000 pounds of cargo on a routine frag. With its two 18 cylinder Pratt & Whitney radial engines, the mighty Deuce cranked out 4200 shaft horsepower to power its massive main rotor, 72 feet in diameter. Too advanced, too complex, too far ahead of its time, the cantankerous Deuce nonetheless had pioneered the technology that paved the way for its successor. Now that the Sikorsky H-53 "Super-Birds" had arrived in Vietnam, the Deuce was ordered to step aside. At the end of the following month the Naval Air Systems Command would order all remaining Deuces to be removed from military records and disposed of in the least expensive manner. Shortly thereafter at Marble Mountain the remaining Deuces made a final fly-over, landed, and then taxied directly into the helicopter junkyard. The Deuce had served well, and it deserved a better fate.

North Vietnam continued to pour soldiers and arms into northern Quang Tri Province. In the remote A-Shau Valley bordering Laos, NVA engineers used bulldozers to carve out a major supply and staging area on the jungle floor. In the latter days of April the enemy boldly had sent 1500 nighttime raiders into the heart of the provincial capital city, Quang Tri, where they had attacked the ARVN jail and freed 250 military prisoners. North Vietnam had marched over 30,000 soldiers into the DMZ and northern Quang Tri Province by early May 1967. To counter this threat, the Marines turned over base security at Chu Lai to the Army and moved all available infantry units northward to block the communist infantry divisions just below the DMZ.

Con Thien, May 8, 1967: Three hours before dawn on the thirteenth anniversary of the fall of Dien Bien Phu, the North Vietnamese stormed the Grunt perimeter at Con Thien. Two NVA battalions armed with rockets and flamethrowers threw themselves at the Grunt defenders, and the attackers soon breached the concertina. Helicopter gunships sped northward in the dark from Dong Ha, but by the time they arrived the ground units were locked in vicious hand-to-hand fighting. Aided by flareships, the pilots were able to target the NVA relief column, but they were unable to fire on the enemy troops who had penetrated the Grunt perimeter. The Marines on the ground had to slug it out without air support until they killed all of the enemy soldiers who had gotten through the tangled concertina and razor ribbon.

Helicopter pilots supporting the Grunts near Con Thien learned of a new threat two days later. The North Vietnamese had moved their mobile Russian SA-2 surface-to-air missile (SAM) launchers and radar vans into the DMZ. Relatively slow helicopters at cruising altitude would be easy prey for the SAMs. To counter this new danger, helicopters would need to fly just over the treetops, but this tactic would make them excellent targets for enemy small arms fire. YZ-78, an H-34 from HMM-363, soon fell victim to the new necessity for low flying. The helicopter took off from Con Thien and skimmed low over the terrain. It promptly got shot down at YD-117692, only 800 meters directly south of the outpost. The copilot and the gunner escaped with serious wounds, but the pilot and crew chief died in the violent crash.

Low flying also brought quick confirmation that the NVA had arrived in great numbers. On May 16, two HMM-265 helicopters tried to drop off a Recon team. A nearby North Vietnamese 12.7mm machinegun targeted the lead H-46, and the HAC, Major T. S. Dunlap, got hit in the arm. While the copilot accelerated skyward, the crew chief, Corporal William P. "Willie-Pete" Goldston, got shot in the side and in both legs. Clearly the NVA had thoroughly infested the rolling hills between the mountains and the sea. The next day fate caught up with a friend of mine. Captain Gary W. Hoglund, like me, had been an enlisted Marine before getting selected for the MARCAD program. Originally from Minnesota, Gary was a MARCAD Class 42-63 graduate, the same class that had produced Tee Holmes and Otto Fritz. Gary had come to Vietnam as a Marine Corps pilot, but he later drew an assignment as a FAC with the Grunts. His Casualty Card contains only a brief narrative:

Died 17 May 67 vicinity Da Nang Republic of Vietnam result fragmentation wounds face chest and right arm from friendly short mortar round while in a defensive position.

Northern Quang Tri Province, May 18, 1967: The Marines

kicked off a massive land, sea, and air offensive. So huge was this effort that three separate names were given to it. The Third Marine Division drive northward from Cam Lo became Operation Hickory. The twin SLF helicopter and amphibious assaults into the DMZ from the sea were called Operation Beau-Charger and Operation Belt-Tight. The goal of this 10,000 man effort was to drive the North Vietnamese Army out of the southern half of the DMZ.

We had been trained to kill anything that moved in the unfriendly environs of the DMZ.
-- (Lewis B. Puller Jr.; in *Fortunate Son*)

Like the indigenous American Indians in the previous century, the Marines attacked at dawn. Swarms of H-46 helicopters launched from the Marine Amphibious Assault Force ships, mainly the *USS Okinawa* (LPH-10). They filled the sky as they swept westward toward the Vietnamese coastline. Two Navy cruisers and seven destroyers began blasting the landing area in the heaviest concentration of naval gunfire since the Korean War. North Vietnamese artillery fired back, and ten enemy salvos bracketed the *USS Point Defiance* (LSD-31).

The helicopters headed for Landing Zone Goose a mile south of the Ben Hai River. As the flight leader radioed, "Feet dry," each pilot cinched his shoulder harness tighter one last time. Many of the Grunt passengers in the web seats in the cabin silently offered up personal prayers for Divine Protection in the hours to come.

Landing Zone Goose was hot. As the first helicopters landed to discharge First Platoon from Alpha Company, the enemy gunners opened up. It would prove to be a long day. Meanwhile, more helicopters launched from Cam Lo to ferry Grunts into the DMZ near the North Vietnamese SAM sites. Leapfrogging past Con Thien, the flight roared down and dropped off the troops. The helicopters then sped back south to Dong Ha and Cam Lo to pick up reinforcements and supplies. Maps became unnecessary for the pilots: "Fly straight north and stop at the river."

Between Con Thien and Dong Ha, a reinforced Grunt company ran into an enemy hornet's nest. Fighting closed to hand grenade range, and the Grunts soon radioed for more ammunition and water. Two Bonnie-Sue H-46 pilots, Gerry Lear and Tee-Cee

McAllister, made sure that the ammunition crates and five gallon water cans were loaded onto pallets at Dong Ha. Because of the expected heavy enemy fire, they planned to make a low speed pass right over the Grunts and roll the pallets off the lowered helicopter ramp without having to land. Once airborne, Gerry radioed the Grunts and asked how the LZ was going to be marked. The answer chilled him: "Look for our two burning tanks."

Roaring in low and fast, Gerry still got drilled by NVA fire. His crew chief took a round in the leg, breaking the bone near the knee. When Gerry landed back at Dong Ha five minutes later, the loyal crew chief vehemently refused to get out of his helicopter. Crippled and bleeding, he wanted to remain with his crewmates, for he thought they were going to make another resupply flight to the embattled Grunts. The stubborn crew chief had to be physically disarmed and carried out of the cabin. Loyalty such as this inspired Major M. P. Caulfield to later write in *Marine Corps Gazette*: "Those young Marines; God, they were magnificent!"

> Yippies, hippies, yahoos, Black Panthers, lions and tigers alike. I would swap the whole damn zoo for the kind of young Americans I saw in Vietnam.
> -- (Spirow Agnew; *before his fall*)

HMM-164, the Northbrook H-46 squadron, had been attached to the Division reserve, SLF Bravo. Because of the heavy fighting around Con Thien and the nearby deserted village of Trung An, HMM-164 flew ashore and came under the control of the Third Marine Division. By noon on May 20 the Northbrook helicopters had carried all elements of the 2nd Battalion, 3rd Marines, into the DMZ northwest of Gio Linh. The pilots then joined the four crews from HMM-165 that had stayed on continuous standby for medevac and resupply missions.

The flying and fighting would continue for the remainder of May. The Marine Command temporarily put an offensive cease-fire into effect on May 23 in honor of Buddha's birthday -- strange war. Otherwise, helicopter crews stayed busy shuttling the Grunts around and hauling the tools of war into the field. Far to the south at Marble Mountain on May 24, the helicopter force was augmented by 22 more of the Super-Birds, the remainder of the H-

53s in the new heavy-hauler squadron, HMH-463. These giant Sikorsky helicopters packed the horsepower to retrieve any downed helicopter except another H-53.

The Bonnie-Sue crews from HMM-265 drew a variety of frags in support of Operation Hickory. On May 24, Major D. E. Schneider flew medevacs out to the *USS Sanctuary* (AH-17). On the return trip while over the sea, one of his engines seized. Instead of 2500 horses driving the main gearbox, he now had only half as many. Major Schneider headed for the beach and made a hasty forced landing. No one got hurt, and all crewmembers and the H-46 were recovered in short order. Two days later on an emergency resupply to the "Grey Rebel" Recon team, Major Pitman took fire on climbout. The crew chief, Private First Class David A. Rice, and the gunner, Sergeant D. H. Randall, caught light shrapnel in the brief exchange of gunfire. However, helicopter crewmen were not the only Marines without immunity to ground fire in helicopters. That same day the NVA zeroed in on a speeding UH-1E Huey on a reconnaissance flight. Among the wounded passengers were Lieutenant Colonel William J. Masterpool of Mutter Ridge fame, his executive officer, and two of their company commanders.

In spite of stiff enemy resistance the Marines kept up the pressure throughout the month. The last major clash took place from May 28 through May 31 on Hill 174, roughly four miles southwest of Con Thien. The NVA tenaciously held on to their fortified hilltop. However, behind Marine Air, rockets, and flamethrowers the Grunts finally burned and blasted the North Vietnamese defenders off of the crest of the hill. With the capture of Hill 174, Operation Hickory came to an end. It had been the first major assault into the DMZ by the United States, and it served notice that the NVA would no longer be able to use the so-called Demilitarized Zone as a protected sanctuary.

Since time immemorial, deception and warfare have gone hand-in-hand. For example, in the early twelfth century B.C. the citizens of Troy believed that the Greek Army had abandoned the ten year siege of their city. The Trojans prematurely celebrated their presumed victory by accepting the Greeks' gift of a large wooden horse (the Trojan Horse), and the rest is history.

In times of war, military and political leaders often deem it appropriate to relate enhanced versions of battlefield events. Most adults recall that after the first day of the most recent Arab-Israeli War, both sides loudly trumpeted their alleged destruction of vast armadas of enemy aircraft. Both sides also reported that their smashing victory had been achieved with the loss of only a few of their own planes. Later, independent verification revealed that the Israelis had lost only two aircraft. The Arabs had lost sixty.

> Appeal to emotion, not to intellect. First, tell the people something that they already know to be true. Next, tell the people that which you would have them believe. Repeat the story many times. The people will soon believe everything that you tell them.
> -- (Adolf Hitler; 1889-1945)

Notwithstanding trumped up claims of military victories, the Vietnam War had its share of heroes. Without question many men, both Asian and American, fervently believed in their cause, and many sacrificed their lives for their beliefs. Some died unheralded and unsung, others gallantly distinguished themselves in death as heroes, and a few died the sacrificial deaths from which legends are born. But the most legendary warrior of all was reputed to be a simple peasant, a young Viet Cong recruit named Nguyen Van Be.

Nguyen Van Be: According to the North Vietnamese he was a "Hero of the Revolution," a martyr, a teenage Vietnamese patriot who joined the revolutionary forces to help free his "oppressed" countrymen. His deeds were likened to "a thousand thunderbolts." The North Vietnamese "Anti-U.S. National Salvation Heroes Emulation and Combatants Congress" paid solemn tribute to Nguyen Be, and the Viet Cong awarded him a posthumous decoration for "indomitable loyalty, resoluteness, and sublime bravery." According to the Viet Cong, Nguyen Be had terrorized his enemies and had achieved immortality in death. His bravery was widely chronicled in poem and song.

Exactly what had Nguyen Be done? According the North Vietnamese press, Nguyen Be had been one of twelve Viet Cong who were transporting ammunition in a sampan along a canal in

May 1966. Suddenly an "entire squadron" of United States amphibious armored vehicles had ambushed Nguyen Be and his comrades. Nguyen Be had bravely stood his ground and, armed only with his rifle, had valiantly fought off his attackers for 30 minutes. Finally his ammunition had run out, his comrades had all been slain, and Nguyen Be had been seriously wounded. "Covered with blood," he had been captured. Despite his wounds, Nguyen Be had feigned cooperation with the "imperialists." Then in an unguarded moment he had seized a claymore mine. Defiantly raising the deadly mine high over his head, Nguyen Be had shouted in triumph: "Long live the National Liberation Front!" Then he had detonated the mine, killing himself and 69 of the Americans.

The news of Nguyen Be's bravery and resourcefulness had quickly spread throughout Vietnam. A photograph of this legendary martyr had been frequently published by the North Vietnamese press. A statue had been erected in Hanoi, showing comrade Nguyen Be proudly holding the mine overhead the instant before he achieved immortality.

Yet, the martyrdom of Nguyen Be became short-lived. Actually, Nguyen Be was alive and well -- in jail.

You should never believe a Vietnamese. He's not like you . . . . What's the point of telling the truth?
-- (Nguyen Cao Ky; quoted in *Life Magazine*, July 23, 1965)

True, Nguyen Be had been a teenager who had joined the Viet Cong. And true, Nguyen Be and his comrades were transporting ammunition by sampan along a canal in May 1966. Nguyen Be and his friends had indeed been ambushed by Americans in armored vehicles. Thereafter, the North Vietnamese and Viet Cong version of events had become imaginative fiction.

In reality, when ambushed by the Americans, one of the Viet Cong had been shot and killed. Except for Nguyen Be, all of the others dove out of the sampan, fled, and escaped. Crying and terrified, young Nguyen Be had cowered in the sampan and had offered no resistance. He had no weapon. He was neither shot at nor wounded. Nguyen Be had been grabbed by the hair, dragged out of the sampan, and turned over to the ARVNs. They had taken him to the town of My Tho and had locked him in the local jail.

Months later an alert South Vietnamese policeman in My Tho had looked at a photograph of the famous "Viet Cong martyr" in an article from the North Vietnamese press. The policeman had immediately realized that the photograph depicted one of his prisoners in the My Tho jail. The police had confronted Nguyen Be, and he sheepishly admitted his identity. He also had agreed to cooperate with the South Vietnamese government in return for a promise of lenient treatment.

In the spring of 1967, Nguyen Be had posed for a photograph to be used on South Vietnamese posters and leaflets. In the picture he was shown holding the North Vietnamese article, complete with his photograph and the story of his "glorious death" ten months earlier. Tongue-in-cheek, *Time Magazine* later printed the new South Vietnamese poster photograph and characterized the miraculously resurrected Nguyen Be: "A better Red when dead."

As June 1967 arrived, the Marines took advantage of the good flying weather and beefed up their positions north of the Cua Viet River. North Vietnamese troops still prowled through much of the countryside. On the second day of the month, Major Pitman drew a routine resupply frag, but he collected eight bullet holes in his H-46 before he finished the mission and returned to Dong Ha. Although no large-scale pitched battles took place in early June, helicopter pilots and aircrewmen risked life and limb each day. On June 3 two "Buffalo City" H-46s from HMM-165 took off on a clandestine across-the-border mission into Laos. Enemy gunners shot down both of the helicopters.

> Aircraft will not cross the demilitarized zone or Cambodian border unless specifically authorized by COMUSMACV.
> -- (from "Rules of Engagement")

A rescue force found and picked up one of the two downed crews, but the other men were lost forever. The very next day, tragedy again struck the Buffalo City squadron. One of their H-46s suffered a sudden and catastrophic in-flight control failure. The stricken helicopter plummeted to the earth, and the impact and fire killed both pilots and both aircrewmen.

HMM-265 got its share of the action on now long-forgotten frags. On June 10, Corporals George L. Bonner and Larry K. Bumgardner crewed a Bonnie-Sue H-46 that headed into the mountains ten miles below the DMZ. Unlike the pilots, Bonner and Bumgardner had no protective armored seats. When enemy rounds tore through the fuselage, Bonner got only light shrapnel injuries, but Bumgardner fared worse. The Marine Corps medevaced him to the hospital on Guam because of the severity of his wounds.

Far to the south, down below Da Nang in Arizona Territory, the Grunts began moving 1650 indigenous refugees into camps at Duc-Duc, the South Vietnamese headquarters of the sprawling An Hoa industrial complex. Most of the helicopter support frags fell to HMM-164, flying from the *USS Tripoli* (LPH-10) on the SLF. Appropriately named Operation Arizona, the project soon pitted the Grunts against NVA units in the rugged hill country west and south of An Hoa. HMM-164 stayed busy shuttling the Grunts from point to point and moving the indigenous refugees, but they lost one of their H-46s on June 20. On takeoff from the *Tripoli*, YT-15 lost power and had to ditch in the ocean. Two crewmen were rescued, but two others were lost.

Most of the flying still took place up near the DMZ, and small-scale missions gradually whittled away at the resources of the helicopter squadrons. At one minute after midnight on June 25, a "Millpoint" H-34 from HMM-363 roared inbound toward Dong Ha on the return trip from an emergency night medevac flight. The Sikorsky warhorse safely landed, but for some unknown reason it overturned and burned while approaching the TAFDS fuel hookup point. The teenage crew chief, Corporal Charlie L. Burney from Smithville, Georgia, died in the resulting fire. The following day another HMM-363 crew manned YZ-75 on a mission to XD-813412. The helicopter flew to a flat plateau only two miles west of the Khe Sanh airstrip, in the eastern shadow of Dong Dang Ridge. The heavily loaded H-34 hit the top of a tree, and the pilots nursed their damaged craft to a small clearing about 300 meters away. The four shaken but unhurt pilots and aircrewmen made their way on foot back to the intended landing area, and their wingman hauled them back to base.

Captain John A. House III, a New York native, had seen his share of close calls during his months with HMM-265. In April he had been the HAC on the two consecutive daring rescue missions for which Corporal Daniel D. "Dan" Dulude, his crew chief, had been awarded two Silver Stars. Now, over two months later on June 30, House strapped himself into his Bonnie-Sue H-46 for what he assumed would be a routine flight. His copilot, First Lieutenant Ted Pittman, took his place on the left side of the cockpit. House had drawn the HAC's slot on a frag to insert the Recons of "Nettlerash Two" at YC-904962, about ten miles south of Phu Bai. House planned to land in a small valley three miles east of the Song Ta Trach River, and according to his map the nearest hamlet was miles away. With the usual aerial escort he took off and headed for the drop point.

As House started his approach, an NVA heavy machinegun took him under fire. The H-46 took numerous hits and caught on fire in the air. House crashed in 80 foot tall trees. Once the rotor blades shattered about 15 feet below the treetops, it was a sheer 65 foot drop to the floor of the jungle below.

In the long run, we are all dead.
-- (John M. Keynes; 1883-1946)

The impact and fire killed House and four of the Recons. Broken and bleeding, the survivors helped drag each other out of the burning wreckage. The wingman, Captain David M. "Delta-Mike" Petteys, raced down, hovered over the treetops, and his crew chief lowered the horse-collar toward the Marines on the ground. One by one the crew chief winched the injured men up through the hell-hole door and into the helicopter cabin. The most critically injured came up first, followed by those who were able to help themselves. As soon as they all were aboard, Petteys sped back to the field hospital at Phu Bai.

The battered copilot, Ted Pittman, and the two aircrewmen, Lance Corporals James A. Michaelson and Gary R. Smith, were in critical condition. All three eventually had their medical status upgraded to "Condition Fair," and they all were medevaced to CONUS as soon as they medically could stand the trip. The bodies of Captain House, the four dead Recons, and the lone corpsman were never recovered from the wreckage on the jungle floor.

<u>Con Thien, July 2, 1967, 0930 Hours</u>:   Alpha and Bravo Companies, 1st Battalion, 9th Marines, slowly swept forward along a winding dirt trail bearing the grandiose name of Route 561. This would prove to be the worst day of 1967 for the Marine Corps in Vietnam. Hidden up ahead, two full battalions from Hanoi's 90th NVA Regiment, 324-B Division, lay in waiting for the Grunts.

> Unwarned, we went to our doom.
> -- (Sergeant H. C. Wall, Confederate States Army; describing
> the Confederate infantry attack at Gettysburg, July 1, 1863)

My former squadron knew nothing of the impending ambush. On this July morning, HMM-265 had regrouped at Phu Bai to stand-down for redeployment to relieve HMM-164 on the SLF. On this bloody day other squadrons would have to bear the brunt of futile efforts to save the Grunts on Route 561.

In the lead, Bravo Company was strung out along the dirt roadbed. The North Vietnamese had dug their trenches and fighting holes on both sides of the trail, which was bordered by thick hedgerows that cut visibility to 20 meters or less. To the north, the NVA artillery was ready and waiting. Nearby, North Vietnamese AAA batteries waited for the Marine jets or helicopters that they knew would respond to their attack. The enemy let the Grunts enter the deadly trap, and then they opened fire.

Machineguns suddenly raked the length of Route 561. In the rear of the column, most of Alpha Company managed to form a tight perimeter. However, the vast majority of the Grunts in Bravo Company were destined to die. One of the few survivors, Corporal Mike Hughes, would later explain:

> We were all wounded, and the men were just lying there, firing. I shouted, "Get up and move back!" and somebody said, "We can't!" I said, "You want to live, you got to move!"

The NVA soldiers closed in and used flamethrowers to ignite the dry hedgerows lining the trail. Forced out into the open by the flames, most of the remaining Grunts gradually fell in a furious exchange of machinegun and rifle fire. Back toward the rear of the column, Sergeant Richard Huff desperately tried to set up his company's mortars. He would later recall the shouted orders from his company commander, 29 year old Captain Sterling K. Coates, when he saw him for the last time. Huff remembers: "He told me to get the mortars firing. Then he ran back up front, and that was the last I saw of him alive."

"Emergency Frag!"

The gunship pilots ran to their waiting Hueys, and the nimble Bell helicopters raced northward from Dong Ha. Arriving over the battlefield in only five minutes, the Hueys circled while the pilots tried to distinguish between the Grunts and the NVA soldiers. In vain they tried to pick out targets for their rockets and M-60s.

The gunships were too late. Down below on Route 561, the Bravo Company FAC was 25 year old Captain Warren O. Keneipp Jr., who until recently had been an F-8 Crusader pilot in VMF-232. Above the crackle of gunfire, Keneipp's last radio transmission was recorded: "I don't think I'll be talking to you again -- we are being overrun!" Within a few minutes, radio contact with all of the platoons of Bravo Company was lost.

> Those Marines who survived had to do what Marines hate most: retreat, leaving their dead behind.
> -- (*Time Magazine*; July 14, 1967)

The North Vietnamese slaughtered the Grunts of Bravo Company. Yet, the gunship pilots still had radio contact with the besieged remnants of Alpha Company, and they wasted little time in targeting the surrounding enemy attackers. Pilots flipped the arming switches on their rockets and guns and rolled in hot. It was easy to pinpoint the enemy, for he was all around the ragged Grunt perimeter. After expending all of their ordnance, the gunships turned to the south and zipped back to Dong Ha to re-arm.

Now the Marine artillery at Con Thien and the big NVA guns in the mountains to the west began a furious duel that would last into the night. A Grunt relief force, spearheaded by four tanks, rushed toward the map coordinates where they expected to find their comrades on Route 561. Charlie Company, the only reserve unit available, boarded helicopters and raced northward. The pilots headed for a spot just behind the makeshift Alpha Company perimeter. Unfortunately they landed amid an artillery barrage that wounded eleven of the Grunt passengers as they ran out of the helicopters. After their human cargo had debarked, the pilots pulled in collective and flew up to where they hoped to reach the men of Bravo Company. They were too late. Turning around and heading back south, the helicopter crews resorted to emergency flights to assist Alpha Company.

While the helicopter gunships made repeated attacks on the enemy, heavier firepower was on the way. Fixed-wing jets from Da Nang began bombing and strafing runs on the enemy soldiers. Bruce Martin piloted one of the F-8E Crusaders from VMF-232, the only F-8 squadron still in Vietnam and the same squadron that Captain Keneipp, the Grunt FAC, had come from. Martin began his letdown southeast of Dong Ha. As he turned to the west he saw a Marine F-4 Phantom that had been hit by one of the 27mm, 37mm, or quad-fifty AAA guns that the NVA had arrayed against the expected onslaught by Marine Air. Martin watched as the damaged F-4 made it as far as the coast. Then it nosed over and dove straight down into the sea. Although Martin did not then know it, the F-4 pilot was an old friend, Major Ray D. Pendergraft.

> Pendergraft R D -- Maj USMC -- Mar 11 30 - Jul 2 67 -- Middletown, OH.
> -- (from *Vietnam KIA's & MIA's*)

Slung under the bombracks on Martin's wings were eight 500 pound snake-eye bombs. The Alpha Company FAC called the shot, and he asked Martin to bring the Crusader in from the west: "Salvo everything you've got." Martin pointed his F-8 down in a 15 degree dive at 450 knots. At 450 feet above the ground he pickled his entire bomb load. As he firewalled the throttle and pulled his jet up into a turning climb, he felt the deadly AAA rounds tear into the fuselage of the Crusader.

Martin's fire warning light flashed on, and his utility hydraulic system failed. He quickly abandoned his original plan to make several 20mm strafing runs, and he headed for the seacoast. On Guard Channel, Martin got off a quick "Mayday" as he manhandled his wounded fast-mover eastward. As he crossed the coast he looked in his rear view mirror and saw a cloud of black smoke billowing out behind his jet.

Martin ejected and parachuted down to a safe landing in the sea. Almost as soon as he crawled into his survival raft, he saw that a rescue helicopter was hovering nearby and waiting for him. The HH-53B helicopter had been searching for the two men from the downed F-4, Major Pendergraft and his RIO, but neither of them had been able to eject. When the helicopter pilots saw Martin punch out of the Crusader, they just flew over about two miles and plucked him out of the water.

Back on Route 561 the four Marine tanks and the Grunts of Charlie Company, who had just flown in by helicopter, linked up with the remnants of Alpha Company. Pushing up Route 561, they discovered a few survivors from the First Platoon of Bravo Company. When asked for directions to the rest of his company, Staff Sergeant Leon R. Burns replied: "Sir, this *is* the company, or what's left of it." (As it later turned out, there were several more Bravo Company survivors that Burns did not know about).

Two of the four Marine tanks got knocked out by the new Soviet RPG-7, which can penetrate eleven inches of steel armor. Still, with the help of the remaining tanks, the gunships, and the fixed-wing support, the Grunts gradually drove the NVA away. The helicopter medevac pilots had been circling to the south, and now they hurried down to pick up the most serious casualties. The dead and the walking wounded could wait. Once loaded, they pulled in power and took off on a beeline for Dong Ha.

When the fighting finally died out, only 27 Grunts from Bravo Company walked away. The men of Alpha Company fared better, but July 2 had been a terrible day for the Marine Corps. In addition to the attacks on the Grunts along Route 561, over 1000 artillery shells had rained down on Con Thien and Gio Linh. And the next day the NVA batteries would pound Dong Ha itself.

July 5, 1967: The Grunts returned to Route 561 on July 5, three days after the ambush, to recover the bodies of their dead. They found that many of their dead Marine brothers had been shot in the back of the head. Captain Keneipp, the FAC, had been staked out and decapitated. The bloated bodies of scores of dead Marines were strewn along the road where they had been killed.

Wearing gas masks because of the stench, the Grunts wrapped their fallen comrades in ponchos and piled them on top of tanks for transport to the rear. It was grisly work. The July 14 issue of *Time Magazine* and the July 17 issue of *Newsweek Magazine* would both print the same macabre photograph. It showed dead Marines stacked like logs on a tank headed for Con Thien.

> None can realize the horrors of war, save those actually engaged. The dead lying all about, unburied to the last. My God, my God! What a scourge is war!
> -- (Samuel Johnson, Sixth Georgia, Confederate States Army)

July 6, 1967: Two speeding Marine Corps A-4 Skyhawk jets from VMA-311 swept inland toward the potent enemy SAM sites near the Ben Hai River in the DMZ. The 5000 pound SA-2 SAM, 35 feet long and carrying a 286 pound warhead, depends on its mobile van and its radar crew for guidance. To knock out the SAM sites, each Skyhawk carried two Shrike air-to-ground missiles (AGMs) under its stubby wings. The sophisticated Shrike has electronic sensors designed to lock in on the SAM radar as it searches the sky for a target. The Shrike then will home in on the radar van and destroy it.

In the lead Skyhawk, Major Ralph E. Brubaker locked in the SAM radar and fired both of his Shrikes. Almost instantly the warning tone blasted through the earphones built into his flight helmet, telling him that the SAM radar had switched from search mode to guidance mode. Brubaker knew that the SAMs had launched. On the ground at nearby Con Thien, the Grunts watched in awe as three SAMs rocketed skyward from their launching rails in the DMZ.

For a fighter pilot or ground-attack pilot, evading a SAM is tricky. You can see the huge missiles coming, and pilots often call them Flying Telephone Poles. You must wait until the SAM gets perilously close to you, but still outside of the 300 foot killing radius of its warhead. Then you snap-roll left or right and dive for the earth below, leaving the SAM guidance radar insufficient time to compensate. However, if you try to evade to early, the SAM guidance system has time to recompute your new flight path and blast you out of the sky. In other words, if you try to evade too early, the SAM wins. And if you try to evade too late, the SAM also wins. Timing is everything.

Major Brubaker waited until the last crucial seconds, and then he threw his Skyhawk out of the trajectory of the onrushing SAM and dove for the ground. The SAM missed. However, in evading the first SAM, Major Brubaker chanced to dive right into the path of one of the other two SAMs. The missile won. Major Brubaker ejected and parachuted to earth. Although injured, he would evade the NVA soldiers and be rescued by a helicopter crew the following day.

Meanwhile on July 6, the 90th NVA Regiment, which had decimated the two Grunt companies on July 2, was about to march into disaster. A Marine observation pilot, radio call-sign "Dream-Hour," spotted the NVA column as it blindly shuffled toward the entrenched Grunts of the 1st Battalion, 3rd Marines. On the FM radio a Grunt company commander, Captain Burrell H. Landes, anxiously queried the pilot about the size of the approaching enemy unit. The pilot radioed back a classic, if nonspecific, reply:

Bravo Six [meaning, *Captain Landes*], I'd hate to tell you -- there's a mess of 'em coming.

Alerted by their eye in the sky, the Grunts locked, loaded, and waited. The NVA regiment stumbled right into prepared and interlocking fields of fire. Then the gunships swooped down and added to the mayhem and carnage. When their ammunition was gone, the pilots backed off to allow artillery a chance to hammer away at the tan-clad troops from the north. Fixed-wing jets from Da Nang then swept in and dropped their gleaming silver napalm canisters. More gunships followed the jets in search of those enemy soldiers who still might have survived. The onslaught continued long into the night.

July 7, 1967: The next morning the rising sun allowed the Marines to see what they had done to an entire enemy regiment. Hundreds upon hundreds of bodies littered the killing field. A fortunate few had died instantly. Most others had been blasted by artillery, and their dismembered arms, legs, and parts of torsos lay helter-skelter in the brush. Still others had been caught by the napalm, and their blackened and charred remains were already under attack by flocks of vultures and millions of black ants.

The grisly carnage was beyond description.
-- (Major Gary L. Telfer et al; writing of the fate of the 90th NVA Regiment in *U.S. Marines in Vietnam: Fighting the North Vietnamese, 1967*)

Most of the dead enemy troops were half buried, lying in pieces, sometimes tangled together, the handiwork of the all night artillery pounding. The Grunts found it impossible to count the enemy bodies or pieces of bodies, so they resorted to counting the enemy canteens in an effort to verify how many of the enemy soldiers had fallen.

For the helicopter pilots at Dong Ha, the news was sweet indeed. They had been unable to offer much assistance to the men of Bravo Company five days before, but now they had helped the Grunts gain a measure of revenge for the debacle on July 2. However, the NVA answered back with their heavy artillery that afternoon. Dong Ha became ground-zero for a merciless NVA artillery barrage, and helicopters and maintenance facilities made prime targets. Ironically, when the first 130mm shell screamed down near a Catholic religious service, the only casualty was the chaplain's assistant.

On July 12 my former squadron finally replaced HMM-164 on the SLF, becoming a part of the Ninth Marine Amphibious Brigade. Pilots and aircrewmen now had hot and cold running water, clean sheets, clean flight suits, and hot meals aboard the *Tripoli*. Yet, although the squadron was now based aboard ship, the flying and fighting still took place ashore. Two days after joining the SLF, EP-160 got riddled when a land mine exploded in an LZ during an emergency medevac. Within a week, EP-158 was lost when it got shot down on takeoff from YD-512486, southeast of Quang Tri and just west of the village of Nha Tho Nhut Tay. The crew chief, Lance Corporal R. C. Kroshus, took a round in the leg, but he and the other three members of the crew were quickly rescued by their wingman.

The Marines prepared for a larger war. The reliable old Huey gunship, the UH-1E, had served well, and it had proved to be the deciding factor in many a firefight. But the Marine Corps envisioned an even deadlier gunship, an armored gunslinger, a faster and more agile tactical helicopter to support the Grunts. In July the Secretary of the Navy approved Marine Corps funding for the Bell AH-1J Huey-Cobra gunship, immediately dubbed the "Snake." This new helicopter had only one purpose, and its "Mission and Description" statement left no doubt about the lethal role it would play in battle:

> The primary mission of this aircraft is that of an armed tactical helicopter capable of delivering weapons fire, low-altitude high speed flight, search and target acquisition, reconnaissance by fire, multiple weapons fire support . . . .

The Snake would be an airborne gun and rocket platform. There would be tandem seating for a pilot and gunner, and their fingertips would control an arsenal. A chin turret would house a three-barrel 20mm gun, a virtual cannon compared to the older M-60s. On short stub-wings the Snake would carry underslung 7.62mm gun pods and a variety of unfaired 2.75 inch rocket pods. With twin engines and ample armor, the Snake would prove to be an aerial force to be reckoned with in the years to come. (The Snake would not arrive in Vietnam until February 1971.)

When the United States upped the stakes, the enemy followed suit. Just after midnight on July 15, Russian 122mm ground-to-ground rockets began raining down on the huge military and civilian airfield at Da Nang. The 45 minute attack destroyed six F-4 Phantoms, two F-8 Crusaders, and three C-130 cargo haulers. Other aircraft were heavily damaged, and one of the ammunition dumps exploded with a mighty roar heard as far south as Hill 55. That same night a team of roughly 60 NVA soldiers staged a commando raid on the South Vietnamese jail at Hoi An. With antitank shells, they blasted through the prison wall and released over 1100 military prisoners.

Late in the month the Marine Command started what would become fancifully known as the "Armored Thrust into the DMZ."

While helicopters waited to rush in a reaction force, a full battalion of Grunts, reinforced with tanks and a few Ontos, stormed northward all the way to the Ben Hai River. Going north was easy, but on July 29 the Grunts of the 2nd Battalion, 9th Marines, found that they had to fight their way back south.

Around midday the helicopters began getting the frags: "Emergency medevac." Marine tanks had carried the wounded to an LZ that supposedly was secure. However, as the helicopters started down, NVA mortars impacted all across the landing area. Fighting raged throughout the afternoon. For the helicopter pilots the trips were short, because it was only about twelve miles from Dong Ha to the Ben Hai River, the border between North Vietnam and South Vietnam. No one needed maps, for the pilots could easily follow Route 1 straight north from Dong Ha to the Second Battalion. All afternoon and into the night the flights continued. By 0900 Hours on July 30 the helicopter crews had evacuated all of the Grunt casualties, so the battalion began to push south and leave the DMZ behind.

<u>August 1, 1967</u>: Intelligence began picking up unsettling information from the A-Shau Valley. The only way to know for sure what was going on there was to fly in Recon teams to take a look. Four Northbrook H-46s from HMM-164 headed toward YC-549828 on the first day of August. Flying as HAC in the lead helicopter, Captain Russ Verbael eased down and dropped off the Recons without any hint of a problem. However, on climbout he took fire from the jungle below, so the other helicopters made feint landings to try to draw the NVA away from the Recons.

They knew there was much anti-aircraft and enemy in the
Valley of the Skull where sure death was lurking about.
-- (H. Lee Bell; in *1369*)

By the late afternoon of the next day the Recons had moved to YC-541823, about 800 meters away. The enemy patrols were all around and too close, so the Recons radioed for an emergency extraction. But it was too late. The pilots tried, but they could not locate the team in the dark. Tracers arced up at them as they searched, and they eventually returned to base to refuel and try again after daylight.

Meanwhile, the *Tripoli* (LPH-10) got set to steam south for refitting at Subic Bay in the Philippines. Before the helicopter carrier left Vietnamese waters, five H-46s and five bitterly disappointed crews from HMM-265 launched from the ship and flew to Marble Mountain. The rest of the squadron sailed south aboard the *Tripoli*, daydreaming of the many delights waiting for them in the city of Alongapoe.

On the third day of the month the NVA would finally down one of the speedy Northbrook H-46s that had been darting in and out of the A-Shau Valley. The helicopter was piloted by First Lieutenants John L. Connolly Jr. and William W. Lindsay. Backing them up in the cabin were the crew chief, Thomas A. Gopp, and the gunner, Sergeant Dexter L. Gorski. On the FM radio, Connolly made contact with the Recons, had them pop smoke, and then he started down. The NVA were close and combing the brush for the team, the Recon radioman warned the pilots. When the helicopter landed, the Recons dashed toward it at full speed and dove inside. As the H-46 rose it was hit by a burst of machinegun fire, and it crashed back to the ground.

The entire crew had been hit. The enemy rounds proved fatal to Corporal Gopp, the young helicopter crew chief. Two of the Recons and the corpsman also died, either from the impact or from the increasing stream of rifle fire that now whistled across the crash site. In all, there were four men dead and four men wounded.

Captain Al Kirk, the wingman, ignored the enemy fire and roared down through a hail of rounds to rescue those still alive. He made the pickup without anyone aboard his H-46 even getting nicked by a bullet or shrapnel. But saving four wounded men carried a tragic price, because the bodies of those who died had to be left behind.

From their quarters at Marble Mountain the five remaining crews from HMM-265 drew their share of the often perilous Recon insert frags. The "Consulate" Recons strapped themselves into one of the Bonnie-Sue H-46s for a flight to the eastern slope of Ba Na Mountain, a 4813 foot high peak southwest of Da Nang. The pilots aborted the frag when .50 caliber fire erupted near their chosen landing area. On the same day the "Brisbane" Recon team, airborne in another HMM-265 helicopter, had planned to debark at ZC-205705, farther to the west. Their plans also changed when NVA troops were encountered near the landing zone. With the helicopter gunners returning the fire, the pilots pulled in pitch and headed for home.

The Medal of Honor is presented by The President in the name of The Congress of the United States. The Medal of Honor is the greatest tribute that can be paid to an American military man. Yet, no sane person willfully initiates conduct designed to win the Medal of Honor. Historically, recipients of this highest honor found themselves merely caught up in events beyond their control. They acted not out of bravery, but instead out of a sincere brotherly love for their friends. Most failed to survive the circumstances for which they were posthumously honored, and the few who did survive tended to shrug off any personal claim of heroism. Gene Atkins, a World War II Medal of Honor recipient from my home state of South Carolina, modestly explained: "I never did a dang thing that nobody else wouldn't have done in my place, no sirree -- just try to stay alive."

Over the past two centuries the Marine Corps has traditionally awarded few Medals of Honor. The elite Marine Corps operates under the presumption that valor and sacrifice under fire is the norm for all Marines. A Marine who is recommended for the Medal of Honor must have made an *exceptional sacrifice* for his Marine brothers, according to tradition.

> Greater love hath no man than this, that a man lay down his life for his friends.
> -- (Jesus Christ; quoted in ST. JOHN 15:13)

Consequently, almost all Marine Corps recipients of this highest honor died in combat during the circumstances for which they later were posthumously honored. Their citations almost inevitably end with the same sentence: "He gallantly gave his life for his country." During the entire year of 1967, only 16 Marines in Vietnam were awarded the Medal of Honor. True to tradition, 15 of these 16 Marines had died as a result of the conduct for which they were later immortalized. But there was one Marine Corps exception in 1967. The lone Medal of Honor survivor was a helicopter pilot, and he had been a former flight instructor of mine -- Captain Stephen Wesley Pless.

Quang Ngai Province, August 19, 1967: Steve Pless piloted a Huey gunship from the "Klondike" squadron, VMO-6. On August 19 he flew chase on a routine medevac flight along the Vietnamese coast near Quang Ngai, far to the south and far from most of the fighting along the DMZ.

On the radio, Pless heard the news that four United States Army soldiers had been captured by about 55 Viet Cong. Although the North Vietnamese valued American prisoners, the Viet Cong did not, but they planned to have a little sporting fun with their captives before killing them. The Viet Cong held the four Americans right on the beach. It was later found that the Americans had been forced to draw straws to determine the order in which they would be killed.

> Some of the enemy [soldiers] were bayoneting and beating the downed Americans.
> -- (from Medal of Honor citation; Stephen W. Pless)

In flight with proper altitude and airspeed, the Huey gunship is a formidable weapons system. However, on the ground it is totally vulnerable. Captain Pless knew the odds against him and his crew. But he also knew that without him the four Americans on the beach were dead men.

Pless dove straight for the beach where the Viet Cong were gathered. He could not fire at the Viet Cong because the American prisoners were in their midst. Instead, he fired at the ocean and sand near them, hoping the Viet Cong would run for cover in the treeline along the beach. But the enemy soldiers did not run. They watched the approaching gunship, knowing that as gunships always do, it would veer away at about 100 meters, circle around, and make another pass at them. They knew that it would not fire on them as long as they stayed with their four prisoners and kept them alive. The Viet Cong stood firm as the gunship kept boring in . . . 200 meters . . . 100 meters . . . it kept coming . . . they raised their rifles to fire.

Pless flared, stood the gunship almost on its tail, and then slammed it onto the beach right among the enemy. Several had to scramble away to avoid being crushed as it dropped into the sand.

Total pandemonium broke out!

Some Viet Cong ran for cover in a nearby treeline. Others fired at the gunship from a distance of only 15 to 45 feet away. The door gunners fired back and frantically swiveled their guns while screaming above the din to the dazed and bleeding Americans: "GET IN! GET IN!" But the four men were too badly wounded to respond. Rounds whipped through the air and ripped through the aluminum skin of the gunship.

The two gunship aircrewmen, Gunnery Sergeant Leroy N. Poulson and Lance Corporal John H. Phelps, abandoned their guns. They leaped out of the helicopter and ran to the aid of the four wounded men. The gunship copilot, Captain Rupert E. Fairfield Jr., crawled back into the cabin. He manned a machinegun, killed three onrushing Viet Cong, and then jumped out of the helicopter to aid Phelps and Poulson.

Pless hovered, turned, and poured burst after burst into the charging ranks of the Viet Cong soldiers. It turned into an Old-West style shootout. The enemy charged from three sides, and Pless fired his guns and rockets into their ranks.

> The enemy directed intense fire at the helicopter and rushed the aircraft again and again, closing to within a few feet before being beaten back.
> -- (from Medal of Honor citation; Stephen W. Pless)

Pless jammed the gunship back into the sand. His crewmen threw the wounded Americans inside and then crawled in after them. Pless sucked in collective, but the small and now overloaded gunship quickly sank back onto the sandy beach.

Sensing that the gunship was in trouble, the Viet Cong charged again. Once more the door gunners beat them back. Pless snatched the gunship into the air, covered about 40 feet, lost turns, and dropped into the edge of the surf.

Again Pless pulled in collective, and again he lost turns and fell. He jettisoned his rockets, and after twice again settling into the water, he finally got into translational lift and headed for the safety of the open sea. Airborne at last, he raced toward the field hospital at Chu Lai.

For "extraordinary heroism" and "gallantry above and beyond the call of duty," Pless later would be awarded the Medal of Honor. Fairfield, Poulson, and Phelps would be awarded the Navy Cross for their participation in the incredible helicopter rescue.

REQUIEM: Of the 16 Marines who had been awarded the Medal of Honor in 1967, Pless had been the only survivor, the only Marine who "lived to tell about it." He would complete his tour as a VMO-6 pilot in Vietnam, return to the United States, and be promoted to the rank of Major. Pless had cheated death in Vietnam, but he would be living on borrowed time.

Died 20 Jul 69 at Pensacola Beach, Florida, as a result of injuries received in a motorcycle accident.
-- (from Casualty Card; Major Stephen W. Pless)

F. Scott Fitzgerald perhaps said it best: "Show me a hero, and I will write you a tragedy." On July 20, 1969, Steve Pless would ride his motorcycle along the Highway 98 causeway crossing Pensacola Bay. As he approached the drawbridge, it would begin to rise. Always the fearless competitor and brave adventurer, Pless apparently would try to outrace the drawbridge. But this time his luck would fail him. He would die instantly.

Each squadron was required to maintain a written chronology detailing the day-to-day essentials, but some of the budding chronology authors provided much more than the bare-bones facts. An abstract from the *HMM-164 Command Chronology* illustrates the type of detailed narratives written by some squadrons:

20 August 1967 . . . Later in the day a recon insert was aborted due to heavy enemy fire in the zone at XD-904498. The aircraft, piloted by 1stLt. J. W. MAHONEY and copiloted by 1st Lt. B. A. McGINLEY, received 16 hits in the aircraft resulting in one recon team member KIA, and the crew chief, Cpl. S. L. DORSSOM, and the aerial gunner, L/Cpl. H. BAUCHIERO, very seriously wounded. The crew chief and

gunner were both returned to Khe Sanh and then medevaced to Phu Bai. The aerial gunner, L/Cpl. H. BAUCHIERO, died of wounds enroute to Phu Bai. One aircraft was sent to Khe Sanh to replace the downed aircraft.

On the same day that Bauchiero died, the *Tripoli* returned from the Philippines and brought the men and helicopters of HMM-265 back to Vietnam. For most of the squadron members, there had been plenty of R&R (meaning, *Rest and Relaxation*, in military lingo) in Alongapoe to divert their minds from the daily horrors of the helicopter war in Vietnam. For many, however, a week of "I&I" (unofficial acronym meaning, *Intoxication and Intercourse*, but not necessarily in that order) would have been a more accurate description of their week in Alongapoe. For months and years afterwards, many a Marine would fondly reflect back on his week in Alongapoe and smile that secret but knowing smile. Alongapoe peddled physical pleasure. For many of the Marines, alcohol provided a temporary refuge and an escape from the reality of the war. Further, nothing had changed since the days of the ancient Roman Army and its female camp followers who met the physical desires of the Roman soldiers. Every imaginable form of sexual pleasure was available in Alongapoe for a price -- a ridiculously *cheap* price. Warfare is horror, pain, and death; but physical gratification is joy, hope, and life.

During the dry season the Marines stayed on the offensive throughout most of I-Corps. Some combat sweeps produced little to show for the effort, like Operation Yazoo in Happy Valley down near Da Nang in late September. On the other hand, heavy contact with the enemy was almost guaranteed up along the DMZ where the North Vietnamese supply lines were shortest. Helicopter pilots knew the enemy was out there, and on every mission the pilots realized they could stumble into deep trouble. For some, superstition began overruling logic. Many pilots adopted a variety of private rituals designed to ward off bad luck and enemy bullets. A few slept in their flak jackets. Others nervously adopted a false and transparent "it won't happen to me" attitude, and a few offered up sincere prayers for Divine Protection. However, most realized that aggressive flying offered them their best hope of making it through the war alive. You had to keep your turns up, your speed up, avoid the deadly Triple-H combination, and make sure you never let yourself get caught low, slow, and stupid. With skill, experience, and a liberal dose of luck you could survive most of the hazards of flying helicopters in a combat environment.

Backed by logistical air support from the transport helicopters, plus tactical weapons support from the gunships and fixed-wing aircraft, the Grunts inflicted horrible losses on the North Vietnamese during the brutal summer of 1967. General Giap had abandoned his hit-and-run tactics in favor of conventional warfare along the DMZ, a war of attrition. Even if he lost eight men for every Marine who died, his seemingly endless manpower pool would enable him to prevail in the end, he reasoned.

Now that General Giap had adopted a war of attrition, he needed a battleground upon which to wear down the Marines. The sandy and flat coastal plain to the east offered no concealment for his troops. The rugged mountains to the west offered concealment, but they prohibited easy movement of his trump card, his deadly heavy artillery. But between the sandy coastal plain on the east and the mountains to the west lay a seven mile wide belt of gently rolling hills covered with tangled undergrowth. Here, Giap easily could resupply his troops by sending vehicles and supplies straight south across the DMZ. He knew that the Marines had no choice but to fight. Their forward staging area, Dong Ha, lay just twelve miles below the Ben Hai River and only nine miles below the southern fringe of the now meaningless DMZ. Giap had assured the Politburo in Hanoi that the Marines would not allow Dong Ha to fall without a fight, a fight that he planned to win.

In addition to their great numerical advantage over the Marines, the NVA had superior artillery. Their Russian D-74 122mm field guns and their feared 130mm howitzers definitely were more accurate than the 105mm and 155mm guns used by the Americans. When the NVA lobbed only a few shells into Dong Ha on August 28, one H-46 was destroyed by a direct hit, and two others were badly damaged by flying shrapnel.

To thwart the North Vietnamese, the Marine Command beefed up its two forward outposts just below the DMZ. Directly north of Dong Ha, seven and a half miles up the now impassable Route 1, was Gio Linh, named after the small hamlet that had once flanked the road. Six miles west of Gio Linh was the Grunt outpost on Hill 158 at Con Thien, almost directly north of Cam Lo. From the geographic square formed by Dong Ha, Cam Lo, Con Thien, and Gio Linh -- called LEATHERNECK SQUARE by the press -- the Marines planned to accommodate General Giap. They planned to meet him head to head and grind it out with him. If the Marines prevailed, Giap's legions would be held at bay along the DMZ. If the Marines failed, the NVA could drive south without opposition and occupy Hue, the former Imperial Capital of Vietnam.

Although the NVA held an overwhelming manpower and artillery advantage, helicopters and fixed-wing jets ruled the sky along the DMZ, and they all belonged to the Marines. True, North Vietnam did have Russian MI-4 Hound and KA-25 Hormone helicopters in its arsenal. Further, their Soviet-built MIG-21 supersonic fighters, which easily could be converted to a ground-attack mode, could have wrecked havoc on the Grunts. But this was a political war, a chess game, a game of unwritten Soviet, Chinese, and American agreements. Hanoi agreed not to use its air power against American troops in South Vietnam, and Washington agreed not to vaporize North Vietnamese military targets with tactical atomic weapons. So in this strange war the Marines, although heavily outnumbered, used their tactical air advantage and their helicopter mobility to kill the NVA soldiers by the thousands.

August 31, 1967: The H-46 squadrons got the bad news on the last day of August. Or, perhaps it was the good news, depending upon your viewpoint. Major General Norman J. Anderson, Commanding General of the First Marine Air Wing, grounded all of the H-46s in Vietnam. The saga had begun back in May after two H-46s inexplicably had disintegrated in midair. After a series of additional fatal crashes, the last straw involved an H-46 from HMM-262. It picked up a single medevac and headed for the *Tripoli* on August 31. Suddenly the aft pylon tore off in flight. All aboard died, and General Anderson reluctantly grounded the entire H-46 fleet in Vietnam.

There was, however, an exception to the grounding order. "Emergency" flights could still be made. One such emergency flight was made in EP-153 the very next day, September 1, by Major Chuck Pitman from HMM-265. As he returned from the mission and landed on the steel runway matting at Marble Mountain, a mysterious imbalance ripped the aft pylon completely off of the fuselage. Eventually the Marine Corps and Boeing Vertol would pinpoint the structural problem that plagued the H-46 fleet, make the necessary airframe modifications, and restore the helicopters to an airworthy status.

Dong Ha, September 3, 1967: The fall monsoon rains, which usually arrive in October, came a month early. By the morning of September 3 the ground had been turned into an ankle deep mire at Dong Ha, where the helicopters of HMM-361 were waiting for the fog and overcast to lift. Then the NVA shells and rockets began whistling down out of the northern sky.

That morning, Dong Ha was transformed into a miniature on-land version of Pearl Harbor. The base ammunition dump exploded, and either the flaming debris or another shell ignited the bladders in the bulk fuel farm.

> The Boeing Technical Rep had his head blown off by one of the rockets, and what was left of him was lying in the street.
> -- (Jon Boulle; quoted by author Philip D. Chinnery in *Life on the Line*)

As the barrage began, one of the luckiest helicopter crews happened to be in a Huey that was already turned up and ready to take off. Brigadier General Louis Metzger dashed to the Huey, dove inside, and planned to help the helicopter crew spot the NVA batteries. The pilots pulled in full power on the T-53 turbine, and the Huey lurched skyward into the path of the falling enemy shells. By chance, one of the incoming projectiles slammed through the thin aluminum skin of the fuselage. Fortunately it struck nothing solid and blasted out through the other side of the helicopter without detonating. General Metzger would later explain:

> We felt the bird shudder and we knew we were hit. After a futile attempt to spot the enemy firing batteries, we finally landed at Camp Evans and examined the [Huey]. There was

a hole about fifteen inches in diameter in the tail. We were fortunate!

Seventeen of the HMM-361 helicopters suffered heavy damage, and most were rendered unflyable. After the shelling stopped, the giant "Dimmer" H-53s flew from Marble Mountain to Dong Ha. The helicopters that had been damaged by the shelling were rigged for external sling loads, and the H-53s began flying them back to Marble Mountain for repairs. With Dong Ha now within range of the potent NVA artillery, helicopter support would have to come from Quang Tri and Phu Bai, farther to the south.

During the coming two months, helicopters became the lifelines to Gio Linh and Con Thien. The monsoon made the dirt roads impassable, and everything was flown in and out by helicopter. Grunts were carried inside of the helicopter cabins, but water, C-Rations, and ammunition were hauled in cargo nets dangling from the external cargo hook under the fuselage. Hover time had to be cut to an absolute minimum because the incoming helicopters became magnets to attract NVA shells and mortars.

The autumn fighting in Leatherneck Square boiled down to a slugfest between the infantry and artillery of the third and fourth largest military machines in the world. The Chinese and Russians had the two largest armies on the planet, and the United States and North Vietnam, in that order, fielded the two next largest military forces. There were no guerrillas, insurgents, or Viet Cong in Leatherneck Square. Instead, the infantry and artillery of the United States and North Vietnam were locked in 24 hour duels that could have been mistaken for the siege of Stalingrad. Those men not manning the howitzers occupied themselves by digging deeper and deeper trenches and piling more mud on top of bunkers.

At Gio Linh the Grunts constructed a huge underground control center for their artillery. Multiple layers of massive twelve inch square beams formed the roof, and these beams were covered with eight feet of dirt. On top of the dirt the Grunt engineers piled ten layers of sandbags. From this underground fortress, automated fire control equipment fed targeting data to the batteries of guns that hammered away at the North Vietnamese.

It is a duel of giant cannon more akin to World War I or Korea than to the rest of the war in Vietnam.
-- (*Time Magazine*; September 22, 1967)

At Gio Linh the Grunts had a mascot, a flea-infested mongrel dog that they named Hardcore. The dog could hear the shrill whistle of incoming shells before the Grunts. He invariably would tuck his tail and scurry for cover whenever he heard an incoming round. The Grunts used Hardcore as an aural trip wire, and when Hardcore ran for cover the Grunts were usually only a step behind him. At night the Grunts hunkered down in their bunkers, but these havens soon became filled with monsoon rainwater and infested with rats. During daylight the Grunts could get food twice a day in a designated bunker that doubled as a C-Ration storage location and an eating shelter out of the rain. But as a precaution, only about a dozen men would enter at one time in order to reduce the number of casualties in the event of a direct hit.

The Grunts at Gio Linh passed the time during lulls in the shelling by engaging in black humor. On top of one bunker, the inhabitants had staked out a tarpaulin that initially had been designed to divert some of the monsoon rainwater. They soon procured some international-orange paint from the helicopter crews and painted a huge bull's-eye on top of the tarpaulin. They wanted something challenging for the NVA artillerymen to aim at, they dryly explained. Another enterprising group of Grunts built a miniature catapult that could hurl a wet sandbag perhaps 15 to 20 feet. Still, there was one device at Gio Linh that was no joke. Near the command bunker the Grunts had mounted a hand-cranked siren to be used only as a last resort. If the base perimeter ever was breached, the siren would send its shrill warning to all of the Grunts, signaling them to burrow down as deep in their bunkers as possible. Then the Marines at Con Thien and Cam Lo would train their heavy artillery on Gio Linh itself, hoping to blast the attackers off of the backs of the Grunts.

Six miles west of Gio Linh, the outpost at Con Thien lay closer to the DMZ, closer to the mountains, and therefore came under even more hostile artillery fire than Gio Linh. In early September the 3rd Battalion, 9th Marines, relieved the previous tenants at Con Thien. The red laterite at Con Thien soon became a knee-deep quagmire. Mortars, artillery shells, and rockets constantly rained down on the Third Battalion Grunts at the remote outpost.

> At best a dismal outpost, Con Thien soon became a very public hell.
> -- (Terrence Maitland et al; in *A Contagion of War*)

The mud at Con Thien proved to be a mixed blessing. Incoming shells usually plunged several feet into the muck before detonating, and the mud shrouded the blast and reduced the amount of deadly flying shrapnel. Many of the incoming rounds were cushioned by the mud and did not detonate at all. But on the other side of the coin, the mud concealed these deadly live rounds, and the outpost quickly became a virtual mine field. A Grunt's life would be snuffed out if he accidentally triggered one of these buried shells in the non-stop process of digging deeper and deeper bunkers and trenches in the deep mud.

The Grunts at Con Thien became known as "The Walking Dead." They slept perhaps a couple of hours each night, holed up in their flooded bunkers with the scurrying rats and listening to the booming of the artillery all night long. The near constant cacophony left them partially deafened. Even during lulls in the shelling they had to shout at each other to be heard. Some of the teenage Marines became deeply embittered, and one would later decry the death of his friend from Georgia:

> He was blown in half for a [expletive deleted] place that had no strategic value, no military value, no sense to it, save to prove to Russia or China or North Vietnam or God or somebody that nineteen year old low- and middle-class Americans would die for their country.

While the Marine and the NVA artillery dueled in the rain, Marine and North Vietnamese infantry units parried in the mud throughout Leatherneck Square. The Grunts used agile M-60 Tiger tanks, usually impervious to the mud, in their drives against the troops from the north.

From safe locations far to the south in Da Nang and Saigon, the worldwide media began reporting on the horrible fighting. The

October 6, 1967, issue of *Time Magazine* featured the see-saw battles in Leatherneck Square and described Con Thien as a "quagmire reminiscent of World War I."

> Everything must be brought into the outpost by helicopter to a landing zone grimly known as "Death Valley."
> -- (*Time Magazine*; October 6, 1967, describing Con Thien)

Time Magazine carried a feature article complete with photographs and maps depicting the entrenched positions of the combatants. According to the *Time* writers, the NVA had 35,000 troops in their 325th, 324-B, and 610th Divisions dug in along the DMZ and waiting for the Marine Grunts to be overrun. As soon as the North Vietnamese defeated the Marines, the magazine editors theorized, the three "Red Divisions" would sweep south along Route 1 to Hue and occupy the city.

Throughout recorded history, walls or barriers have been used to block advancing armies. The Great Wall of China kept the barbarians at bay for centuries, and long sections of that wall still stand today. Hadrian's Wall, the Hindenburg Line, the Siegfried Line, and the Gothic Line were all designed to stop invaders. A few succeeded, but most failed. The mighty Magionot Line was believed to be impregnable. Perhaps it was, but the German Army simply made an end-run around it. Other more simple barriers sometimes met with greater success. During the Algerian War the French built a huge electrified fence across the Algerian and Tunisian border, and it partially achieved its objective. Other walls had been designed not to keep armies out, but instead to keep people in. The infamous Berlin Wall literally sprang up overnight as a barbed wire barrier, but it grew into a masonry and steel monster that kept the citizens of Soviet East Berlin from fleeing into West Germany.

In Indochina in the 1630s, the Nguyen Dynasty had built two 20 foot high walls near the 17th parallel in a vain effort to halt invaders from the north. Now, only 330 years later, could a workable and effective barrier keep North Vietnam's legions from marching south?

In early 1966 a professor at the Harvard Law School had proposed the construction of a static defense line in Indochina. It would stretch from the South China Sea, across South Vietnam and Laos, to the Mekong River on the Thailand border. The idea quickly got rejected because of the billions of dollars it would cost, to say nothing of the troop requirements to man the fortifications along such a lengthy wall. Still, the idea of a protective wall caught on and captured the fancy of many, including Robert S. McNamara, the United States Secretary of Defense.

McNamara envisioned a much shorter barrier, one stretching only from the sea to the western side of the Ho Chi Minh Trail. He planned not a wall, but instead a barrier consisting of concertina, antipersonnel and antitank mines, aural and seismic sensors, lasers, and ground surveillance radar. Roughly 72,000 searchlights would illuminate the barrier, and artillery firebases would be able to pound the entire length of the line. Aviation would play a vital role in "McNamara's Wall," as it would be called. Helicopters would be on standby to rush battalion-sized reaction forces to seal any breach.

The Marine Corps had privately opposed the barrier plan, to no avail. As early as November 26 of the previous year, the Marine Command had been forced to accept a modest plan. A linear barrier would extend from the sea to Dong Ha Mountain, a distance of about 18 miles. Bulldozers would clear a trace 600 to 1000 meters wide. A series of strongpoints would be built along the line, and watchtowers would provide eyeball reconnaissance capability. Then the mines, concertina, sensors, and other obstacles would be emplaced. And, McNamara had decreed, the Marines would construct the barrier.

The plan had been doomed from the very start. Although clearing of the trace had begun after the monsoon ended in the spring of 1967, the Marines never were enthusiastic about the project. To his credit, General Walt had the guts to publicly speak out against it. Yet, orders are orders, and by July 1967 the Marine engineers had cleared a 600 meter wide trace from Con Thien to the sandy plain near the sea. Then the NVA began attacking the construction crews, and more Marines were needed to defend those doing the work. By August the NVA had launched their summer infantry and artillery offensive against the Marines in Leatherneck

Square, so the Marines threw all of their effort into holding back the invading North Vietnamese hordes.

In any event, by late September the start of the monsoon had turned the trace into a sea of mud, and no type of vehicle or bulldozer could make any headway through it. Still, notwith-standing the enemy attacks and the weather, the Marines would complete two of the strongpoints by the end of the year. Nonetheless, the Marines remained skeptical, and one volunteered:

> With these [North Vietnamese] bastards you'd have to build the wall all the way to India, and it would take the whole Marine Corps and half the Army to guard it -- even then [the NVA] would probably burrow under it.

Bob Mills also ridiculed the plan many years later and snickered: "The towers below the DMZ were a farce!" Bob was right, for who in their right mind willingly would have climbed up into one of the wooden towers? If the towers ever had been manned, NVA artillery would have blasted them into splinters.

Success has a thousand advocates, but failure is an orphan. McNamara's Wall, also called McNamara's Folly, may have looked good to McNamara's bean-counters on paper, but it never became operational. The Marines had neither the resources to build it nor the Grunts to staff the necessary reaction force. McNamara never delivered the promised sensors, electronic gadgetry, or artillery, and none of the floodlights or mine fields were ever put into place. The NVA soon blew up the few watchtowers that had been completed, and subtropical vegetation quickly reclaimed the cleared trace. So in the end, before it had even been built, McNamara's Wall already had been breached.

While the infantry slugged it out on the ground, the Marine helicopters kept the Grunts supplied with the tools needed to continue the fight. On September 25, Boeing Vertol presented my former squadron with a plaque recognizing HMM-265 as the first H-46 squadron to log 10,000 combat flight hours. Now based back at Marble Mountain, the squadron members began rebuilding all of their protective bunkers in tent city because of flooding from the monsoon. HMM-265 sent rotating detachments up north and also helped out in the rice basin south of Da Nang.

A new journalist requested a quick helicopter ride to Con Thien, and one of the helicopter crews took him along and dropped him off in the rain and mud at the cratered outpost. The unnerved writer counted 903 incoming shells in less than 24 hours. He quickly hitched a ride south to safety in the next available helicopter. Around Con Thien and Gio Linh, Sikorsky and Boeing helicopter pilots stayed in the air to haul hundreds of external sling loads to the Grunts. Unless human cargo was in the cabin, the pilots would not risk an actual landing. They would swoop down through the rain to hover height and pickle their sling load just as soon as the cargo net touched the ground. But regardless of the risk, a landing was required in order to pick up or discharge troops. Also, when medevacs had to be carried aboard in liters or ponchos, it increased the time of vulnerability sitting there on the ground. Still, there was no other way to haul the wounded men out of Con Thien and Gio Linh.

Few of the wounded Grunts who made it onto a medevac helicopter alive would later die. Lieutenant Donald Shortridge, the Navy surgeon who headed the rag-tag medical team at Con Thien, mused about the survival rate of the casualties flown out by helicopter. In his massive bunker deep underground, he explained how he performed a crude tracheotomy on a Grunt lying on the floor. He proudly described his successful surgery:

> We were holding candles and flashlights. And you know, the kid lived. In fact, of the ones who [were medevaced out on helicopters] alive, we've only lost two that we know of. Out of six-hundred wounded in seventeen days, that's pretty good.

October 14, 1967: Corporal Daniel D. "Dan" Dulude, the now-famous HMM-265 crew chief, twice had been awarded the Silver Star for gallantry and heroism on two consecutive days in April. He had come through that ordeal unscathed, but now the odds were about to catch up with him.

"Launch Sparrowhawk."

Four Bonnie-Sue H-46s loaded up with the Grunt reaction team, called Sparrowhawk, and sped toward ZC-176987. Corporal

Dulude drew the gunner's role for this mission, and he manned the port machinegun aboard EP-156. The "Warcloud" Recons had come under attack, but Sparrowhawk was on the way at 125 knots to join the fight.

Dulude figured this would be just another frag, another two points worth of credit (but only *one* point if none of the helicopters took hits) toward the total of 20 points needed for another Air Medal. Dulude had no way to know that this would be his last mission. As EP-156 roared down toward the Recons, twelve enemy rounds tore through the fuselage. Dulude got hit in the right leg and in the buttocks. The crew chief, Bernie M. O'Donnell, also got wounded in the brief exchange of gunfire.

Dulude made it back to base alive, but his Vietnam tour had come to an end. Three days later on October 17, he was packed aboard a medevac flight headed for the United States. Yet, Dulude was lucky, for many HMM-265 crewmembers would never survive to make that long flight home from Vietnam. On the same day that Dulude got medevaced out of Vietnam, Corporal Howard E. Morse, a young 20 year old HMM-265 crew chief from Detroit, Michigan, climbed into his H-46. Morse's helicopter, EP-158, took heavy damage from enemy gunners at ZC-178978. Critically wounded, Morse still clung to life when his helicopter landed, but he would never leave Vietnam alive.

> Cpl. Howard E Morse 2262077/6320 USMC received wounds on 17 Oct 67 near Quang Nam. Died of wounds 25 Oct 67 at NSA [hospital] Da Nang.
> -- (from *HMM-265 Command Chronology* Casualty List)

Most pilots and aircrewmen realized that blind luck often dictated who got hit and who did not, who lived and who died. On the day that Morse died in the hospital at Da Nang, two H-46s launched on an emergency medevac mission to AT-872880. The "Texas Pete" Recons had a critically wounded man who needed to be flown to the nearest field hospital in a hurry. Luck rode with the pilots and aircrewmen, for the command chronology would later note: "Small arms fire was received with no hits or injuries sustained . . . . The next day EP-162 took twelve rounds while the pilots held the helicopter in a vulnerable hover over the trees in order to hoist up the men of "Petrify," one at a time. When all were aboard they sped to the nearest safe landing area. Luck was an unseen fifth crewmember, for no one had even been nicked by the enemy fire.

Military records list a chain of helicopter fire incidents. Sometimes the records reflect some remote and now long-forgotten location such as ZC-168010, west of Tam Ky. Here at 0730 Hours on October 19, helicopters assisted in the recovery of a downed aircraft. They then picked up nine medevacs from Defend-14 at nearby ZC-167911. But in late 1967 most of the fighting was at a more familiar location, Con Thien and Leatherneck Square.

Leatherneck Square, October 26, 1967, 1500 Hours: The nine cylinder radial Wright engine, the metallic heart and soul of the Sikorsky H-34, hammered away as Bureau Number 148056 crossed the Cua Viet River and headed north into Leatherneck Square. Aboard the helicopter, YZ-66, were two pilots and two aircrewmen from HMM-363, the Millpoint squadron: Captain Ronald D. Bennett, the HAC; Second Lieutenant Vernon J. Sharpless, the copilot; Corporal Edward Clem, the crew chief; and Lance Corporal Howard J. Cones, the gunner. Flying behind them in a loose trail position was their wingman, Captain Frank T. Grassi in YZ-75. They bored on northward toward YD-116654, a small clearing on the eastern slope of a gentle knoll shown on their maps as Hill 48. Several critical medevacs needed to be picked up and flown back to Dong Ha.

Bennett and his crew knew that the LZ would be hot. Their new executive officer, Lieutenant Colonel Frankie E. Allgood, had flown to the same spot just before midnight the previous night to pick up casualties from the 2nd Battalion, 4th Marines. The entire battalion was down to under 400 men. Despite the enemy fire, rain, and fog, Colonel Allgood had flown another frag to assist the besieged battalion around 0300 Hours. After daylight the Grunts had moved about 1000 meters and had come under an NVA 60mm mortar attack. Now, Bennett and the rest of the crew of YZ-66 would try to slip in and pull out the most critically wounded men.

Bennett, who had just celebrated his 26th birthday the previous month, split the needles and wrapped his H-34 into a steep spiral.

The ground rushed up to meet him. As he began to pull the cyclic back to bleed off airspeed, the North Vietnamese opened up on him with machineguns and heavy rifle fire. The Grunt radio operator screamed: "TAKIN' FIRE!"

Bennett and Sharpless did not need the radio warning, for they could see the muzzle flashes and hear the *pop-pop-pop-pop-pop* crackle of gunfire. Twisting on the power and sucking in collective, they jammed the helicopter nose down and accelerated, speeding over the area where they had planned to land just seconds before. The Grunts on the ground watched as enemy tracers reached up for YZ-66.

> Died 26 Oct 67 vicinity Quang Tri Province (01) Republic of Vietnam result injuries sustained when helicopter in which he was pilot crashed and burned as result of hostile automatic weapons and small arms fire.
> -- (from Casualty Card; Captain Ronald D. Bennett)

Exactly where the mortal hit was received, no one will ever know. Those on the ground watched as the tail pylon broke completely off of the Sikorsky helicopter. The H-34 augered in, crashed out beyond the enemy muzzle flashes, rolled over, and caught on fire. Unable to help, the Grunts watched as smoke from the burning 115/145 aviation fuel billowed into the sky.

Flying in YZ-75, Captain Grassi had seen his section leader crash and burn. He did not know if he could help, but he had no choice. He dumped collective and roared down. As he neared the burning wreckage the enemy rounds caught him too. Grassi was hit in the leg and arm, and his gunner and the corpsman in the cabin also had been shot. The uninjured copilot aborted the landing attempt, and the H-34 staggered back skyward. They made it as far as Hidden Charm LZ, and there they zipped down and plopped their damaged helicopter onto the ground.

Back at the original intended landing area, the Grunts watched the dense smoke boil skyward as the remains of Bennett's H-34 burned. Could anyone have survived the crash and fire? Captain James E. Murphy, the battalion air liaison officer, used the thick undergrowth for cover and began crawling out toward the column of smoke. Slithering along the ground with his radio still strapped to his back, he wound his way through the brush around the North Vietnamese soldiers. Reaching the wreckage, Murphy found that Bennett and Clem had been killed by the impact and fire. The copilot, Sharpless, and the gunner, Cones, had managed to get out of the mangled helicopter. Murphy helped the two injured survivors crawl into the nearby brush, where they all concealed themselves. They could hear the NVA soldiers in the distance, but the NVA most likely did not suspect that anyone had lived through the crash.

Murphy radioed an O-1C Bird Dog circling overhead, and the pilot called in an airstrike on the nearby enemy. Then a gray Marine Corps Skyhawk sliced down and laid a smokescreen to partially conceal the position of the three trapped Marines. Under cover of the smokescreen, a Huey slipped down and picked up the stranded men. Hit during the rescue, the pilot sped to Hidden Charm LZ, where he landed and joined the crew of YZ-75.

Later that night, helicopter crews got additional frags for flights to haul medevacs out of the Second Battalion perimeter. The casualties were waiting near the battalion command post, nothing more than a series of fighting holes half full of rainwater. As the first helicopters started down, the pilots could see the twinkling of the muzzle flashes in the darkness. The first several attempts were aborted, and the pilots radioed for the Grunts to lay down a heavy volume of suppressive fire. Under cover of the furious outgoing barrage, the helicopters made it down and picked up the most critically wounded men.

Gradually the fighting and artillery duels in Leatherneck Square died out, and the Marines and North Vietnamese glared at each other across the DMZ. The NVA infantrymen never made the breakthrough General Giap had hoped for, and slowly the Marines knocked out the Russian-built artillery that had caused so much misery during the summer and fall of 1967. Also, the NVA had increasing difficulty in supplying their remaining big guns with ammunition. While the Marines used a daily chain of helicopters to fly in ammunition, the NVA had to move all of their artillery shells overland by truck. Their largest shells weighed 199 pounds each, and all of the roads were now knee-deep quagmires.

The weather had been a major factor in the battles in Leatherneck Square. Helicopters had been forced to fly under the low cloud cover, increasing the risk from enemy fire, but the pilots and aircrewmen had met the challenge and had kept the Grunts supplied with the necessities of warfare. In the end, the helicopter lifeline proved to be the deciding factor for the Marines.

November 14, 1967, 1400 Hours: Two Hueys cruised northward above the Street Without Joy on their way to Dong Ha. Strapped into the rear troop seat aboard the lead Huey was Major General Bruno A. Hochmuth, the commander of the Third Marine Division that had fought so well for so long in Leatherneck Square that summer and fall.

> Died 14 Nov 67 vicinity Thua Thien Province Republic of Vietnam result multiple injuries to the body when the helicopter in which he was a passenger exploded . . . .
> -- (Casualty Card; Major General Bruno A. Hochmuth)

The Huey suddenly exploded in a ball of ugly orange fire and smoke. Then it plunged earthward out of control and crashed. When the accompanying Huey landed nearby on the dike of a rice paddy, flames from the burning JP-4 fuel licked upward from the surface of the water in the paddy. The crushed remains of the Huey were embedded upside down in the mud and muck. The potential rescuers dove under the surface of the water in an effort to get inside of the inverted Huey cabin, but their efforts proved to be fruitless. All six men aboard the Huey had perished upon impact. For the first time in any war, the Marine Corps had lost a division commander.

For the helicopter squadrons, November heralded the arrival of HMM-364 with 32 of their new D-Model H-46s. The D-Model looked exactly like the original A-Model that we had brought to Vietnam in the spring of the previous year. But the new D-Model had more powerful engines, two General Electric T58-GE-10 jet turbines that produced 2800 shaft horsepower to power the new "droop-snoot" rotor blades. The extra power would give the H-46 more lifting ability, more hover-out-of-ground-effect (HOGE) capability for external hoist operations, and an extra margin of safety when operating in Triple-H conditions.

In addition to the new D-Model helicopters, the older A-Model H-46s were rapidly undergoing structural modifications at Futema, Okinawa. By mid-December all 80 of the modified A-Models would be back in Vietnam and ready for service. Even as new life was being injected into the H-46 program, the giant H-53s picked up an increasing share of the cargo hauling frags. But even the mighty H-53 was now looked upon as an interim platform for a yet more powerful helicopter. The Chief of Naval Operations approved Operational Requirement SOR-14-20, calling for a helicopter that could lift 18 tons.

My former squadron stayed busy down at Marble Mountain. Most of the clashes there were relatively small, but those small clashes could get a crew into quick trouble. For example, EP-157 and EP-167 took a total of 22 hits on a mission to support the Grunts on Operation Citrus. With both pilots hit, EP-167 limped back to an emergency landing at An Hoa. Still, the last days of 1967 brought bright spots as well. On December 20, four of the HMM-265 crews were fragged to fly entertainer Bob Hope and his Christmas Show entourage to a variety of safe and secure locations in the Da Nang area -- *rough* duty.

Far to the north, bad news was brewing. Marine Intelligence began picking up a flood of alarming signals from the extreme northwest corner of South Vietnam. Aerial spotters and seismic detectors revealed that thousands of North Vietnamese troops were streaming into the rugged mountains surrounding the remote Marine outpost at Khe Sanh. Also, captured NVA soldiers told their interrogators of imminent plans for what their North Vietnamese commanders had termed "Final Victory."

Intelligence could not identify all of the enemy units, but the information already in hand staggered the Marine Command. The 29th and 95th Regiments of the NVA 325-C Division had dug in all around Hill 881 North, the scene of the brutal battles back in April and May. The entire 304th Division had moved from Laos into the jungle southwest of Khe Sanh. The troops of the 324-B Division had marched west to join their comrades in an apparent effort to surround the Grunt outpost. And other yet unidentified enemy units -- entire NVA divisions! -- were moving into assault positions around the isolated Grunts on the Khe Sanh Plateau.

The Marine Command knew what was coming. Colonial Route 9, running west from Cam Lo through the mountains to Khe Sanh, had been controlled by the NVA for months, and the monsoon rains had made it impassable anyway. Relief or resupply overland was no longer possible. The C-130 and C-123 cargo planes could sometimes grope their way through the clouds and fog and make a successful GCA landing at Khe Sanh, but on other days the weather made such landings impossible. Yet, helicopters could almost always make it to Khe Sanh regardless of the weather. Even in solid fog and clouds, the helicopter pilots could intercept the electronic glideslope east of the Khe Sanh airstrip. They then could zip down to the runway through the Riviere de Rao Quan Valley, which extends east from the plateau. However, as December 1967 drew to a close, the North Vietnamese had ringed that jungle valley with scores of deadly antiaircraft batteries.

> Those who can not remember the past are condemned to repeat it.
> -- (George Santayana; 1863-1952)

Would this be the "Final Victory" that North Vietnam needed, a crushing defeat to drive the United States out of Indochina? As more and more North Vietnamese troops poured into the jungle around the encircled Grunts at Khe Sanh, the Marine Command prepared for the worst. The news of the coming firestorm was relayed to Washington, and President Lyndon B. Johnson bluntly warned his Cabinet: "We face dark days ahead."

At surrounded Khe Sanh, overland reinforcement through the mountains was impossible. Air support would be thwarted by the monsoon that would last until mid-April, four long months away. Trapped and outnumbered over seven-to-one, the Marines dug in and waited. The coming assault promised to be swift and horrible.

> The whole fury and might of the enemy must very soon be turned upon us . . . . Let us therefore brace ourselves to our duties, and so bear ourselves that . . . for a thousand years, men will still say: "This was their finest hour!"
> -- (Winston Churchill; June 18, 1940)

-- The Siege at Khe Sanh --

I saw the battle corpses, myriads of them,
And the white skeletons of young men, I saw them; . . .
But I saw they were not as was thought,
They themselves were fully at rest; they suffered not;
The living remain'd and suffer'd . . . .
-- (Walt Whitman; in "When Lilacs last in the Door-Yard
Bloom'd")

Almost two years earlier in the spring of 1966, Khe Sanh had been majestically beautiful. Here was a secret Shangri-La, hidden away deep in the rugged and jungled Annamese Cordillera in the extreme northwest corner of South Vietnam. This remote and primitive wilderness had once been the royal hunting grounds of the Vietnamese Emperors. Tigers, deer, and wild boar prowled the lush valleys and plateaus. The few indigenous Montagnard natives here bore scant resemblance to their civilized countrymen farther to the east. The natives near Khe Sanh, members of the Bru Tribe, lived in scattered collections of thatched huts nestled along the streams that wound their way along the floor of each valley. These stone-age aborigines worshipped gods of fire and earth, and neither their men nor their women wore clothing above the waist.

I had first flown to Khe Sanh in May 1966 for Search and Rescue North (SAR North) duty. Located six miles from Laos and 15 miles below the DMZ, Khe Sanh was an alternate back-door for rescue flights into North Vietnam. Air Force HH-53 Jolly Green helicopters based at Quang Tri normally rescued the downed United States pilots north of the DMZ. They flew up the eastern coastline and then turned inland, hoping to avoid the North Vietnamese AAA batteries that lined the heavily defended coast. Our Marine Corps H-46s at Khe Sanh were their backup. We could fly straight north over the uninhabited and undefended mountains, and then we would turn east and swoop in from the west. Fixed-wing A-1 Skyraiders, radio call-sign "Sandy," would tag along to provide protective covering fire.

Although the SAR North flights were fraught with peril, Khe Sanh itself seemed to me to be totally removed from the war. Brigadier General Lowell English had summed it up well: "When you're at Khe Sanh, you're not really anywhere." Who in their right mind would ever want to fight here? And fight for what?

Second Lieutenant Richard T. "R-Tee" Harry had arrived in Vietnam with me in May 1966. He also had become fascinated with the awesome and haunting natural beauty surrounding mysterious Khe Sanh. Years later he would write of his first flights into this remote outpost in his blistering political and military critique, *An Alternative to "Peace with Honor."*

> When I first flew into the small marston-matted runway, I was struck by the sheer beauty and enchantment of the place. From the lush green vegetation that surrounded the camp to the small waterfall just visible as the plane made the final approach to the runway, this outpost radiated the timelessness of the Orient.

I fully shared R-Tee's enchantment with mystical Khe Sanh. In early 1966 there had been nothing here except the old dirt French airstrip atop a high plateau, 457 meters above sea level. Two miles to the south at XD-845380 lay the Bru tribal village of Khe Sanh, from which the airstrip drew its name. I remember that while waiting at the airstrip, we had inflated our rubber ladies and had napped on the grass in the shade under the belly of our H-46 fuselages. Half napping and half daydreaming, we had watched the magical "six shades of green" when the sunlight danced across the heavily jungled mountains that surrounded the plateau. To the west lay the ruins of an old French fort. To the north and east, a steep precipice dropped hundreds of feet to the twisting Riviere de Rao Quan. Rugged Dong Tri Mountain, Hill 1015 at XD-855454 on our flying maps, dominated the skyline across the river. Mile high mountains to the northwest guarded the North Vietnamese border. The sheer rock cliffs of mighty Co Roc Mountain, just across the

Laotian border at XD-741317, often glistened and shined like mirrors in the early morning sunlight.

The nearest Marine base, Dong Ha, might as well have been a thousand miles away. In reality, Dong Ha was only 28 miles to the east, only 14 minutes in a speeding 120 knot H-46, but the flight took you over the most rugged terrain imaginable. Khe Sanh was surrounded by a vast rugged wilderness. I had loved it! Beautiful, wild, remote, and unspoiled by man, dreamlike Khe Sanh would remain like this forever, I naively had believed. Unfortunately, military events in 1967 and 1968 would prove me to be an utterly unreliable prophet.

A brief 18-month review is in order. In the summer and fall of 1966 the Marines and the North Vietnamese had clashed in the mountains northwest of Dong Ha. Soon afterwards the Marine Command had put a company of Grunts at Khe Sanh to "monitor" the mountain infiltration routes into South Vietnam. In the spring of the next year, 1967, these Grunts attracted two regiments of NVA soldiers into the hills around the isolated outpost. In April and May of 1967 the Grunts had rushed in reinforcements and had attacked the entrenched enemy northwest of Khe Sanh. After those brutal battles, commonly called The Hill Fights, the North Vietnamese had withdrawn and the Grunts had retained only a token force at the Khe Sanh outpost.

The small airstrip had always been the lifeline to Khe Sanh. In the fall of 1967, engineers had flown into the outpost and had spent almost three months laying crushed rock, asphalt, and steel marston-matting on the airstrip. When it finally reopened in late October, the new 3900 foot long runway could handle VFR and IFR landings by any aircraft up to the size of a C-130 turboprop.

The first new alarm signals began in the late fall of 1967. Helicopters routinely dropped Recon teams into the hills, and the Recons started making startling discoveries. New trails crisscrossed the mountains, and scores of NVA troop columns were spotted as they methodically converged on the plateau. Often the Recons accidentally landed near these NVA units and had to call the helicopter pilots back for an emergency extraction. Looking down from above, pilots saw that new roads had been hacked out of the jungle. The columns of enemy trucks and troops were all headed for Khe Sanh.

In response to the massive enemy buildup, the Grunts raced reinforcements to Khe Sanh. Soon the entire 26th Marine Regiment would be airlifted to the small garrison, marking the first time since Iwo Jima in World War II that all of its battalions had deployed for combat together. More helicopters flew in to bolster the garrison. Huey gunships squatted between new protective revetments, and H-46s stood ready to haul Recon teams into or out of the surrounding hills. Pilots and aircrewmen spent their time digging deeper bunkers and waiting for the enemy onslaught that everyone predicted would surely come.

Somewhere Out There, within artillery range of the Khe Sanh Combat Base, . . . concealed and silent and ominous, lay five full divisions of North Vietnamese Regulars.
-- (Michael Herr; in *Dispatches*)

The news grew worse, day by day. The North Vietnamese 324-B Division had taken up positions to the north of Khe Sanh. The 320th NVA Division had moved to locations to the east near the Rockpile. Around and beyond Hill 881 North were the men of the 325-C NVA Division. To the west toward Co Roc Mountain were the troops of Hanoi's famed 304th Division, the elite "Home Guard," the veterans of Dien Bien Phu, the pride of the North Vietnamese Army. And another yet unidentified division lay in waiting just across the Laotian border. The NVA also had brought along at least two entire artillery regiments, plus an ample number of tanks, trucks, and service vehicles.

Marine pilots flying into Khe Sanh soon would face heavy AAA weaponry. The NVA had trucked in 37mm, 27mm, and 12.7mm guns and had deployed them in the hills overlooking Khe Sanh. Worse yet, many of the deadly batteries had been set up in the valley east of the airstrip, the only available avenue of approach for pilots under IFR flight conditions. Soon the pilots would coin a new name for the instrument glideslope, Flak Alley.

How many NVA soldiers now surrounded Khe Sanh? No one in the United States knows for sure. One noted military historian would later claim that General Giap had massed slightly over

48,000 men for his attack, but records suggest that figure is too high. Another historian would put the number of enemy troops at only 36,800. However, his sources failed to include many NVA units known to have been entrenched in the hills. Most reliable sources would put the initial number of North Vietnamese soldiers at somewhere between 38,400 and 43,100 men, although this figure would rise and fall during the coming siege because of reinforcements and casualties.

Facing the North Vietnamese hordes at Khe Sanh were 5772 Marines, 228 Navy corpsmen and doctors, 30 Army soldiers, and two Air Force liaison officers. Overland relief or resupply was now impossible, for Route 9 had been controlled by the enemy for months. Nothing came in or out of remote and surrounded Khe Sanh except by air. Unfortunately for the Marines, air support would be blinded by the miserable monsoon rain and dense fog that would last until April, four long months away. General Giap had done his homework well. The stage was set.

January 1, 1968: Half a world away, General Leonard F. Chapman Jr. became the 24th Commandant of the Marine Corps on the first day of the new year. The war in Vietnam had stretched his Marine Corps thin. His infantry, artillery, and aviation commands now included over 19,000 draftees who had gone through Marine Corps Boot Camp at Parris Island and San Diego during the past twelve months. The United States now had slightly over a half million servicemen in Vietnam, plus about 90,000 more in the Seventh Fleet and in nearby Thailand. The war had cost the United States 21 billion dollars, and 9353 Americans had been killed during the past year alone.

Now a gigantic showdown loomed at Khe Sanh. Marine helicopters dropped acoustic sensors that detected enemy troops talking, infrared sensors that pinpointed cooking fires, and seismic sensors that picked up vibrations from enemy trucks and tanks. They deployed secret electrochemical analyzers that could detect heavy concentrations of human urine from the NVA soldiers. The intelligence data rocked the Marine Command. There could be no doubt about it. North Vietnam was surrounding Khe Sanh with the largest army that General Giap had fielded since his famous victory over the French at Dien Bien Phu over 14 years before.

Khe Sanh, January 2, 1968, 2030 Hours: Helicopter pilots and aircrewmen had curled up in the helicopters to try to sleep. Dense fog and the darkness rendered the plateau as dark as a cavern at midnight. Then in the eerie glow from a magnesium flare, the Grunts manning a new listening post 400 meters west of the airstrip spotted six men approaching them. The six men failed to respond when challenged. One fled and escaped into the darkness, but the remaining five died in a hail of rifle fire.

The dead all proved to be high-ranking North Vietnamese Army officers, including a regimental commander. One of the men appeared to be Chinese, although medical examination could not confirm this. Why were such men personally checking out the Grunt perimeter? The news quickly spread throughout the base. If any Marines had doubted the warnings from Intelligence, those doubts now should have been erased. The North Vietnamese Army planned to storm down out of the hills and overrun Khe Sanh.

> I can still recall the day we got to Khe Sanh. It was a place
> that God forgot. You knew that death was around.
> -- (Chuck Hoover; quoted by John Prados and Ray W. Stubbe
>   in *Valley of Decision*)

News of the surrounded Marines at Khe Sanh reached the rabid international press. At the Da Nang Press Center, journalists began pouring through *The Battle of Dien Bien Phu*, the British publication by Jules Roy. Frightening and uncanny parallels with Khe Sanh filled Roy's book. Other reporters and correspondents chose to read the more popular book by Dr. Bernard Fall, who had died on a patrol with the Marines only eleven months earlier. Fall's highly acclaimed *Hell in a Very Small Place* took the reader into the trenches and bunkers at Dien Bien Phu. The book eloquently described the death-struggle of the French fortress.

Tragically, Khe Sanh seemed to be a mirror image of Dien Bien Phu. Only 14 years and the nationality of the defenders had changed. In both cases the foreigners held the garrison and the airstrip in the valley, cut off from all hope of overland reinforcement. The monsoon thwarted the foreigners' hope of reinforcement by air. The People's Army held the surrounding mountains and something between a six-to-one and a nine-to-one manpower advantage, depending upon whose troop-count one elected to believe. Artillery and antiaircraft batteries stood ready to swat down any aircraft that penetrated the monsoon cloud cover. Military events appeared inevitably destined to repeat themselves. A brief look backward at 1953 and 1954 is necessary:

<u>Dien Bien Phu Valley, November 20, 1953</u>: The American-made C-119 "Flying Boxcars," C-47s, and other transports took off from Hanoi and headed west. Flying cover were American-made B-26s and Corsair fighters of Flotille 14-F, which had flown ashore from the French aircraft carrier *Arromanches*. Within an hour the flight covered the 200 miles from Hanoi to the skies over Dien Bien Phu. Here the transports slowed to drop speed, and the men of the Sixth Colonial Paras and the First Parachute Light Infantry began jumping down into the wide valley.

The aircraft turned east and headed back toward Hanoi, for there was no airstrip in the remote mountain valley. But here at Dien Bien Phu, only 20 miles east of Laos and surrounded by mountains, the French began building a series of fortresses. Disassembled bulldozers were airdropped into the valley and reassembled by French engineers, and then the French began the formidable task of building an airstrip on the valley floor. Soon the runway was completed, and scores of cargo planes started shuttling in men, arms, and supplies. The French planned to "entice" General Giap to attack Dien Bien Phu. They reasoned that their superior airpower and artillery would allow them to kill the Viet Minh soldiers by the thousands.

Viet Minh artillery was the only major concern of the French. But surely Giap's orientals could not haul their heavy artillery and shells hundreds of miles through the mountains and jungles, the French Command theorized. There were no passable roads, and any organized effort to build them would be met by French AU-1 bombers. French F4U-7 Corsairs would dive-bomb any enemy artillery batteries that might manage to reach the surrounding hills. No, the French reasoned, Giap's siege would be only a series of swarming infantry assaults. Secure behind multiple rows of concertina, tanglefoot, and mines, the French would use their own artillery and airpower to decimate the expected waves of attackers.

The key to French success would be air support. Everything would be flown in by air. The Viet Minh would be able to field a huge attacking force, but the French would control the skies over the valley. C-119s, C-46s, and C-47s would haul in reinforcements, food, and artillery shells for the French 105mm and 155mm howitzers and M-24 tanks. The French field hospital would be supplied each day by flights from Hanoi, and casualties would be flown out on the return leg of these same flights.

Late November 1953: Transport planes now landed in droves each day, flying in supplies and building materials, and the French now had helicopters and Corsairs based at the airstrip. The separate fortresses of Anne-Marie, Gabrielle, Claudine, Elaine, Dominique, Beatrice, and Isabelle had been carved out of the valley floor. In the tradition of French armies on foreign soil, two field brothels staffed by local Vietnamese and Chinese women were set up to service the French soldiers. Soon the valley held 14 battalions of French Legionnaires, infantry, and indigenous allies. By the end of 1953 the French would be ready to fight.

Meanwhile, the Viet Minh also had been busy. General Giap organized the equivalent of 15 battalions of engineers, who constructed a twisting mountain road north to China. Over 400 miles in length, this road allowed trucks to haul in Chinese and Russian artillery and supplies in spite of daily French air attacks. Swarms of coolies pushed reinforced bicycles loaded with antiaircraft shells, while others walked on foot carrying 130 pound backpacks crammed full of small arms ammunition and medical supplies. In the mountains surrounding Dien Bien Phu Valley, artillery was emplaced in protective caves that the Viet Minh soldiers had dug into the sides of the steep slopes.

March 13, 1954: Late in the afternoon, like a thunderclap, the Viet Minh batteries all opened fire in a storm of fire, smoke, and steel. Strongpoint Beatrice became ground-zero. One survivor would later explain: "Shells rained down without stopping like a hailstorm . . . ." The French fired back, but even their howitzers and 120mm mortars could not slow the shelling. Night fell, and human waves of Viet Minh attackers swarmed over the French wire and into the heart of Beatrice.

One by one, the Legion companies at Beatrice ceased to answer radio calls.
-- (Robert B. Smith; in "Battalion Meat Grinder")

By sunrise, Beatrice was gone. Throughout the day the Viet Minh hammered away at the other strongpoints. French fighter planes taking off from the Dien Bien Phu airstrip were met with a withering barrage of AAA fire from hidden batteries in the surrounding hills. By the afternoon the last of the American-made F-8F fighters on the airstrip had been destroyed by either artillery or heavy antiaircraft fire.

March 14, 1954, 1800 Hours: In the afternoon, shells began pounding strongpoint Gabrielle at the northern end of the valley. French bunkers and trenches collapsed under the unrelenting barrage of artillery shells, and by morning it was all over. Gabrielle had fallen. The noose around the neck of Dien Bien Phu had begun to tighten.

By March 17, three days later, the French had also lost strongpoint Anne-Marie, and the enemy now had a toe-hold near the northern end of the vital airstrip. Arriving transport planes would have to brave a gauntlet of fire when landing or taking off. The French lost three cargo planes in two days. So, instead of trying to land, the pilots began parachuting supplies from a relatively secure altitude of 2500 feet. But the flak over the valley was getting steadily thicker.

Soon only medical evacuation planes risked landing on the shell-pocked airstrip. One C-47 packed with critically wounded men took a direct hit from an incoming artillery shell when it tried to take off. The desperate French began turning to American mercenaries, American pilots who parachuted food, medical supplies, and ammunition into Dien Bien Phu. But as the Viet Minh moved closer, the pilots were forced to fly higher, and soon many of their paradrops were landing behind the Viet Minh lines. Many of the American pilots were World War II veterans, and they reported that the flak over

Dien Bien Phu was heavier than anything they had seen over the heartland of Germany in the 1940s.

On the ground the French took a horrible pounding. The worst damage was done by the Viet Minh 351st Heavy Artillery Division, with its huge howitzers and Chinese Army "advisors." Their recoilless rifles, heavy mortars, and feared Russian Katuysha field rockets -- the screeching and howling demons that the World War II Germans had called "Stalin's Organs" -- blasted away at the defenders. One by one the French guns were silenced. Cut off and surrounded, the French still fought on with little hope. Their underground field hospital was now overflowing with wounded men and crawling with thousands of fat white maggots. Doctors worked in knee-deep mud and rainwater from the monsoon.

> King: O God of battles, steel my soldiers' hearts,
> Possess them not with fear! Take from them now
> The sense of reck'ning, or th' opposed numbers.
> Pluck their hearts from them. Not today, O Lord,
> O, not today . . . .
> -- (William Shakespeare; in *Henry V*)

The French appealed for outside help, and the United States tentatively agreed to commit American airpower. The United States military began emergency preparations for "Operation Vulture," the relief of the siege at Dien Bien Phu. Over 200 Navy aircraft from the carriers *USS Boxer* and the *USS Essex*, already in the South China Sea, could bomb and strafe the Viet Minh from dawn until dark each day. President Dwight D. Eisenhower began drumming up public support for the plan. At an April 7 press conference he made his famous "domino theory" assertion: "The loss of Indochina will cause the fall of Southeast Asia like a set of dominoes."

Still, Eisenhower sought an international coalition and congressional approval. Arthur W. Radford, Chairman of the Joint Chiefs of Staff, and Vice President Richard M. Nixon began lining up American political support, because hard decisions lay ahead. The *USS Essex* carried tactical nuclear weapons. Would their use be authorized? Years later,

Radford would acknowledge that the use of nuclear weapons was discussed, and that the use of "Tac-nukes" was not excluded. However, the British refused to go along with Operation Vulture, fearing that it would sabotage the upcoming Geneva Conference. When the British failed to endorse Operation Vulture, Eisenhower backed down, sealing the fate of the French fortress.

Desperation gripped the surviving French by late April. The monsoon thwarted their attempts to resupply the garrison by air, and half of their few paradrops were now landing outside of the shrinking perimeter. Men were fighting with little or no food, surviving on instant coffee and cigarettes, knowing that the only alternative to fighting was death. Ammunition and medical supplies were running out. Each morning the French wire was draped with the bodies of enemy soldiers, but still the Viet Minh pressed their relentless attack.

> A shell burst right in our trench. The Legionnaire next to me disintegrated. Nothing was left of him except little pieces of raw meat. Death was spitting all around us. Men were falling like flies.
> -- (a Dien Bien Phu survivor)

Little was left of Dien Bien Phu by early May. Once 13 miles in circumference, the perimeter had now shrunk to only about two miles in length around the main command post, although separate strongpoint Isabelle still held out three miles to the south. With no hope and little ammunition, the exhausted defenders braced for the final attack. French fighters and bombers from faraway Hanoi braved the flak over the valley, but they were far too few and far too late.

By May 6 the French still clung to the remnants of their fortress, now only about 400 meters in diameter. Then the chilling call of Viet Minh bugles shattered the night, followed by waves of attackers. By early morning it was obvious that the end was near.

May 7, 1954: Viet Minh regiments overran the French fortifications one by one. By the thousands they bayoneted and shot their way through the French redoubts of Juno and

Sparrowhawk (a name that would be reborn twelve years later). When the French commander, Christian de Castries, radioed Hanoi for the last time and was patched through to his wife, he made but one final request: "Have faith for our wounded." Then de Castries spoke with his commanding general. The command bunker and strongpoint Isabelle were about to be overrun. But there would be no surrender, de Castries agreed, and he said goodbye: "Au revoir, mon general; au revoir, mes camarades; Vive la France!"

Once-mighty Dien Bien Phu fell to the victorious Viet Minh, and General Giap at last had the great victory he had sought for so long. The airstrip was cratered and littered with bodies and debris, but Giap allowed French aircraft to fly in and evacuate hundreds of wounded Frenchmen. One pilot would later recall: "We could smell the death around us."

The French Army still controlled the coastal plain and the main cities, but in Europe the French leaders had lost their *will* to continue the struggle. At the Geneva Conference they agreed to withdraw all of their troops and civil administrators from Vietnam. For the French, the war had ended with the fall of Dien Bien Phu.

Khe Sanh, mid-January 1968: The Marine commander at Khe Sanh, Colonel David E. Lownds, had studied the history of the French defeat at Dien Bien Phu in 1954. Now, only 14 years later, he seemed to be faced with a geographic, logistic, political, and military mirror-image of the situation faced by the French before him. In both instances the defenders were surrounded deep in the jungles and mountains, and cut off from overland resupply or reinforcement. In both instances the attackers held the high ground and had hauled in artillery to pound the defenders night and day. The monsoon and scores of antiaircraft batteries would play havoc with attempts to reach the defenders by air. Further, the ratio of attackers to defenders was about the same, something on the order of eight-to-one. Yet, Colonel Lownds emotionally tried to rally his men: "You Marines at Khe Sanh will be remembered in the American history books!"

Around Khe Sanh [General Giap] has ringed 40,000 troops. Northward is grouped his 325-C Division, to the south lies the 304[th Division]. To the east lies the 324-B and another division, and to the southeast there are elements of a fifth division. Across the Laotian border and north of the 17th parallel are Giap's Russian-made howitzers.
-- (*Time Magazine*; February 9, 1968)

The Khe Sanh airstrip! It had to remain open, that much Colonel Lownds knew for sure. The French had lost their airstrip early in the fight, and the Marines had to avoid the same kind of aerial strangulation that had plagued the French. The monsoon, the surrounding mountains, and NVA antiaircraft fire would combine to make fixed-wing landings perilous at best, so helicopters would have to play a major role in keeping Khe Sanh supplied. Furthermore, helicopters would be the only way to reach the Grunts on the hill outposts to the west and north of the garrison. Without helicopters to resupply them, the hill outposts would be overrun. And if the lofty outposts on the hills were lost, Khe Sanh was doomed. Regardless of the cost in helicopters and their crews, Colonel Lownds knew that his vital aerial helicopter lifeline to the hills must not fail.

Khe Sanh, January 20, 1968, 1400 Hours: La Than Tonc, a First Lieutenant in the North Vietnamese Army, nervously waved a white flag tied to a stick as he walked toward the Grunt perimeter at the eastern end of the airstrip. There, with at least 20 M-16 rifles aimed at his chest, he surrendered to a surprised Grunt, Lance Corporal Lou Boria.

Lieutenant Tonc turned out to be the commanding officer of the 14th Antiaircraft Company, a part of the NVA 325-C Division. He had served in the North Vietnamese Army for 14 years, he explained to the Marine interrogator, Gunnery Sergeant Max Friedlander. He had fought for his country, but his superiors had passed him over for promotion and had chosen a less qualified officer, he believed. Disillusioned and unable to get mail from his wife and children, he had eventually decided to defect to the American "imperialists."

Lieutenant Tonc provided a treasure trove of intelligence. The North Vietnamese 68th Artillery Regiment, he related, had emplaced its howitzers in protective caves that had been dug into the rock face of Co Roc Mountain, just across the border in Laos. More howitzers and Russian-made rockets were in hidden firing positions on the northern slope of Hill 881 North. The initial attack would come, he promised, *that night!*

First, according to Tonc, the 6th Battalion, 95-C Regiment, 325-C Division, would storm Hill 861 and overrun the Marine defenders. Then Hill 881 South would become their next objective. The entire 320th Division was assigned to attack and silence the Marine artillery batteries to the east. Then they would turn their attention to the main garrison at Khe Sanh. North Vietnamese AAA fire from the 5th Battalion, 95-C Regiment, would meet any American aircraft that might manage to break through the monsoon cloud cover over Khe Sanh. The Marine helicopters would be destroyed, either on the ground by artillery, or in the air by AAA fire. Then after many days and nights of shelling, after the Marines had been sufficiently battered by artillery, People's Army regiments would gather at the base of the steep precipice to the east of the airstrip. Another regiment would mass to the northwest. Then they would swarm out of a moonless night, charge the perimeter, breach it with explosives, and sweep through the imperialist Marine defenders at Khe Sanh.

Lieutenant Tonc's news was so hot it bubbled . . . .
-- (Robert Pisor; in *The End of the Line*)

The timely revelations by Lieutenant Tonc forewarned the Marines of an attack that very night. Helicopters made last minute trips to the hill outposts to ferry in extra ammunition, and the Marines then waited to see what the coming night would bring.

Hill 861, January 21, 1968, 0030 Hours: At 30 minutes past midnight, just as Lieutenant Tonc had predicted, NVA mortars and shells began whistling down on the Grunts atop Hill 861. Blinded by dense fog and the darkness, the defenders braced for the ground assault. Around 0100 Hours, NVA sapper teams breached the Marine concertina and tanglefoot wire with bangalore torpedoes and satchel charges. Hundreds of enemy soldiers then poured through the gaps in the wire and threw themselves at the Grunts.

Within ten minutes the attackers overran the helicopter landing zone, and in five minutes more they controlled half of the hilltop. Yet, the Grunts fought back. Shoulder to shoulder, they met the attacking waves with grenades, rifle butts, and fists in the dark. No Grunt could see more than ten feet in front of him, and the night was pierced with the pitiful screams of the wounded. Row upon row of North Vietnamese charged into the Grunt lines, but the Grunts finally stiffened and held.

THERE! THERE! THERE IS JACKSON! STANDING LIKE A STONE WALL!
-- (shouted in reference to General Thomas J. "Stonewall" Jackson, Confederate States Army; on July 21, 1861)

The Grunts counterattacked. They charged back down the trenchlines, where the fighting raged hand-to-hand in the flickering light from parachute flares. Meanwhile, the Marine mortarmen on Hill 881 South, a mile and a half to the west, lobbed hundreds of mortar rounds onto the NVA reinforcements. By 0500 Hours the firing diminished, and the Grunts once more owned all of the mountaintop. But although thwarted for the moment on Hill 861, the enemy was about to unleash his firestorm on Khe Sanh itself.

Khe Sanh, January 21, 0530 Hours: With over an hour left before dawn, the helicopter pilots and aircrewmen at Khe Sanh were holed up in their bunkers. No one could sleep, and they listened to the booming of outgoing artillery that was firing in support of the fighting three miles to the north on Hill 861.

Outside of the bunkers, the Marine helicopters had no protection from the hundreds of high-explosive shells that began screaming down onto the garrison. Artillery rounds, 82mm mortars, and rockets from the northwest destroyed trucks, helicopters, tents, and anything above ground that had not been heavily sandbagged. Barrels of aviation fuel exploded. Tear gas canisters ruptured and sent choking clouds of gas across the plateau. However, the worst damage of all would be explained in the Marine Corps publication by Captain Moyers S. Shore II, *The Battle for Khe Sanh*.

One of the first incoming rounds found its mark, scoring a direct hit on the largest ammunition dump . . . . The dump erupted in a series of blinding explosions which rocked the base and belched thousands of burning artillery and mortar rounds into the air. Many of these maverick projectiles exploded on impact and added to the devastation. Thousands of rounds were destroyed and much of this ammunition "cooked off" in the flames for the next 48 hours.

The JP-4 fuel bladders for the turbine-powered helicopters erupted into flames, and many of the helicopters themselves were destroyed. Speaking of the series of deafening explosions, Robert Pisor later would write in *The End of the Line*: "The shock wave tumbled helicopters like toys . . . ." All around the airstrip, Khe Sanh became an inferno of exploding shells and burning aviation fuel, a "blast furnace" according to many. Over a hundred tons of munitions from the ammunition dump exploded or burned.

0630 Hours: The North Vietnamese infantry waited until almost dawn. Then they stormed the Combined Action Company that the Grunts had set up in the Bru village of Khe Sanh at XD-846381, two miles south of the Marine garrison on the plateau. After daylight, helicopters from Quang Tri flew to the village during a lull in the fighting and rescued the remaining Grunts. They were flown back to the garrison to join in the defense of the base.

Throughout the day the shells continued to fall onto the Grunts at Khe Sanh. As the morning fog melted away, Grunt spotters began pinpointing the muzzle flashes of the enemy guns, and the Marine batteries started hammering away at the North Vietnamese. The two adversaries kept up their artillery duel all day and into the night. The next day brought more of the same. And it would continue for days -- and weeks!

Some fixed-wing transports managed to sneak into Khe Sanh through the hail of flak and 12.7mm fire that the NVA threw up at every arriving aircraft. Still, the large transports proved to be highly vulnerable to the AAA fire. The monsoon clouds and rain forced them to fly a predictable straight-in approach right down Flak Alley, as the glideslope quickly got nicknamed. The NVA gunners were ready and waiting for them.

More maneuverable than the fixed-wing transports, the Marine helicopters could more easily vary their approach route and altitude in an effort to avoid the ground fire. Flying a helicopter into Khe Sanh turned out to be a jungle version of the Berlin Airlift, except that the helicopters had to fly through a ring of antiaircraft fire to reach their destination. With the fixed-wing transports limited by monsoon weather and enemy fire, the Marine Command increasingly began relying on its helicopters to keep the garrison at Khe Sanh supplied. Artillery shells, food, fuel, radio batteries, small arms ammunition, medical supplies, and reinforcements all had to come in by air each day. Casualties had to be flown out. Further, helicopters were the *only* way to reach the Grunts high up on the isolated hill outposts to the north and west.

The pilots, aircrewmen, and H-46 helicopters of HMM-262 initially got the job of supporting the Grunts at Khe Sanh. However, because of heavy combat losses suffered by the "Chatterbox" squadron, HMM-364 and its new D-Model H-46s were quickly called in to help. Other squadrons would pitch in to assist as necessary, because NVA gunners put heavy pressure on all flights into the besieged base. To fly supplies into Khe Sanh, the helicopter pilots would launch from the relative safety of Quang Tri and make the quick four minute flight up to Dong Ha. Here they would pick up their external cargo sling loads. With the sling dangling below the helicopter belly, the pilots would pull in collective pitch and head for the mountains to the west. As a pilot neared the end of his 28 mile flight to Khe Sanh, he entered the ring of fire that the North Vietnamese had arrayed against all arriving aircraft. Major David L. Althoff, an H-46 pilot in HMM-262, would later be quoted in *Marine Corps Gazette*:

Khe Sanh was being shelled continually -- anywhere from one to 1300 rounds a day of incoming artillery, rockets, mortars . . . . There were snipers within 25 meters of the [perimeter], and anyone who moved above ground would get shot at. Every inch of the runway was zeroed in, and if an airplane tried to land [the NVA] just walked artillery rounds right up the center line. While our helicopters were on the ground, we'd have eight to ten rounds going off around us.

The monsoon usually covered Khe Sanh with an almost solid blanket of rain, mist, and dense fog that forced helicopter pilots to make an IFR instrument approach through the Riviere de Rao Quan Valley. At first the pilots considered the opaque skies to be a blessing. The AAA gunners down below were also blinded by the fog, the pilots reasoned, and the helicopters would be relatively safe while hidden inside the rainclouds. However, within a week the pilots realized that the enemy gunners had zeroed in on the instrument approach glideslope with 12.7mm machineguns. Although blinded by the fog, the NVA opened up whenever they heard the thud of the helicopter rotors approaching. Major Althoff put it bluntly: "They'd just listen for you and start laying fire down the glideslope. If you were on it, you got drilled."

To counter the threat, helicopter pilots began using a tactic that was not available to their fixed-wing counterparts. They arranged for the controller to bring them down about 500 feet above the prescribed glideslope. The AAA batteries would blindly open fire, but with a little luck most of the rounds would harmlessly pass far under the helicopter.

On the few days when fog and clouds did not shroud Khe Sanh, H-46 pilots flew over the mountains at least 3000 feet above the tops of the peaks. Once directly over the airstrip, they bottomed the collective and screamed down in a tooth-jarring spiral. Without landing, they would stabilize in a brief hover and pickle their external loads just south of the runway. Of course, when they carried human cargo they had to land, drop the ramp, and wait for the Grunts to debark. Under fire, they had to sit there and take the heat while the medevacs were loaded aboard for the return flight to Dong Ha or Quang Tri.

> Helicopters would land on the runway to pick up the dead and wounded. Each time they landed, the NVA gunners would pound the airstrip with incoming rounds.
> -- (Lance Corporal Charlie Thornton; quoted by Eric Hammel in *The Siege of Khe Sanh*)

A Grunt from the 1st Battalion, 9th Marines, remembers his helicopter ride into Khe Sanh. At Camp Evans he climbed into an H-46, strapped himself into one of the web seats, and the helicopter launched and headed west. The skies were clear and sunny as they began the flight, but over the mountains they entered the clouds and flew through what seemed to be an endless aerial sea of white. Unable to see the ground below, the Grunt halfway convinced himself that the clouds and aluminum skin of the helicopter would shield him from enemy fire. But then the helicopter broke out of the base of the overcast. The young Marine tensed every muscle in his body as the H-46 crew chief began ripping off long bursts on the fifty. Between bursts, the Grunt could hear the ground fire below, and he chanced a glance out of the open hatch by his seat. Down below, he saw the twinkling muzzle flashes from the North Vietnamese 12.7mm gunners who were trying to kill him.

The enemy mortarmen on the western slope of Dong Tri Mountain, just north of the airstrip, timed the approach of each H-46 that was headed for Khe Sanh. Roughly 18 seconds before they estimated the helicopter would touch down, they would drop their high-explosive 82mm mortar rounds down the throat of the tube. The rounds would begin impacting on the runway just as the copilot dropped the ramp, and the crew chief would scream above the din to the Grunts: "GET OUT! GET OUT!"

With rifles at high port, the Grunts would run down the ramp and dash for the relative safety of the nearest trench. Through the gray smoke from the exploding rounds, other Grunts carrying wounded men on stretchers would run toward the helicopter to get the casualties aboard. Some H-46 crewmen noted that many of the wide-eyed Grunts had the desperate look of horses caught in a fire during the frantic exchange of reinforcements for casualties. As soon as the last of the wounded men were aboard, the HAC would suck in full collective. The tandem-rotor H-46 would rise and accelerate as it clawed for airspeed and altitude. Years later, Private First Class Lionel Trufant would be quoted by Eric Hammel in *The Siege of Khe Sanh*:

> When the helicopters came in, we had to run out and put the stretchers aboard. It was timed to the second. The helicopters had to judge when to come in because they were going to draw incoming . . . .

Helicopters were not the only aircraft that faced the enemy

gauntlet. On January 22, the second day of the siege, Major William E. Loftus, a Marine Corps A-4 Skyhawk pilot from VMA-311, was one of about ten pilots making bombing and strafing runs on the enemy troops around Khe Sanh. North Vietnamese antiaircraft fire shot down the speeding Skyhawk, but Major Loftus managed to eject directly over the garrison. He parachuted down just outside of the eastern perimeter, where he became hopelessly entangled in the concertina on the lip of the ravine. Second Lieutenant John Dillon, manning the perimeter, helped extricate Major Loftus from the tangle of barbed wire, razor ribbon, and his own parachute shroud lines. Once he was free, an elated Major Loftus hugged Dillon and reportedly exclaimed in front of all the Grunts: "If you weren't so [expletive deleted] ugly, I'd kiss you!"

Another of the attack jets, an F-4B Phantom from VMFA-323, had bored in on the North Vietnamese with napalm and snake-eye bombs. Intense enemy antiaircraft fire ripped into the Phantom, and the pilot and the RIO both ejected and landed in tall elephant grass far to the southwest of the perimeter. On Guard Channel on their survival radios, they pleaded for help.

> Both crewmen hid in the tall elephant grass within earshot of the North Vietnamese who were searching for them. Within minutes, rescue helicopters lumbered on the scene . . . .
> -- (Captain Moyers S. Shore II; in *The Battle for Khe Sanh*)

Two Marine helicopters dropped their resupply frags and sped to assist the downed Phantom flyers. Both men, the VMFA-323 commanding officer and his RIO, Captain Dennis F. Brandon, got picked up and returned to safety.

As the NVA continued to pound Khe Sanh and the surrounding hill outposts, the "Klondike" Huey gunships of VMO-6 stayed busy escorting the H-46 and H-34 transport helicopters. The *VMO-6 Command Chronology* for January 24 dryly noted the hostile flying environment: "Operations at Khe Sanh continued to be seriously hampered by incoming mortars and rockets." Helicopters stayed in the air to haul in tons of artillery shells from Quang Tri and Dong Ha. Most of the ammunition went to the main batteries at Khe Sanh, but some was flown to the 105mm howitzers that the Grunts had set up on Hill 881 South, Hill 861, and Hill 558 (the Marines had never reoccupied Hill 881 *North*, and the North Vietnamese now held it). Gradually the Grunts pinpointed the enemy tubes and concentrated Marine counterbattery fire on them.

Hill 881 South: The Grunts on Hill 881 South, at XD-778438, absorbed more enemy shells than any of the other hill outposts. Jutting over a half mile into the sky, the fortified hilltop was home to about 400 Grunts, who were commanded by Captain William Dabney. The hill would become a graveyard for helicopters, because the NVA targeted each one that tried to land there.

The most dangerous job on Hill 881 South fell to the Grunts assigned to the helicopter support teams. If an inbound helicopter simply wanted to drop off an external sling load, no assistance was needed from the Grunts. However, when an H-46 raced down to *pick up* an external sling load, an unfortunate Grunt had to stand on top of the cargo load and hold up the oval connector so he could slam it into the cargo hook under the H-46 belly. The poor Grunt had to stand there, all alone and silhouetted against the sky, while every 12.7mm machinegun and AK-47 within range blasted away at him. There was no other way to get the job done, and someone had to do it. Worse yet, the NVA mortars were timed to arrive just as the H-46 stabilized in a hover over the pickup point. Dabney lost five of his Grunts to NVA fire during their efforts to marry the sling connector to the helicopter cargo hook.

One morning, Dabney had a pile of cargo nets bundled up to be "externaled" back to Dong Ha by helicopter. The unfortunate Grunt assigned to hook up the sling dutifully climbed on top of the pile and held up the sling connector as the H-46 roared down toward him. He planned to slam the connector into the cargo hook, jump down, and dash for the safety of a nearby bunker. He knew that the mortar rounds would be on their way. But just as the helicopter arrived and the Grunt made the hookup, several NVA rounds shattered the plexiglass windshield as they tore into the H-46 cockpit. The pilots instinctively snatched in full power. Dabney would later recall that the helicopter "launched as if it had been shot from a slingshot." The hapless Grunt tried to leap down, but his feet got entangled in the cargo netting. The pilots flew the H-46 three miles to Khe Sanh with the terrified Grunt dangling by his feet below the cargo net under the fuselage. He survived.

January 25, 1968: An HMM-262 helicopter crew drew a medevac frag to pick up a single casualty on Hill 881 South. The Chatterbox pilot approached the hill at 130 knots, and the copilot keyed his AN/ARC-44 transmitter and radioed the Grunts. The casualty had a serious head wound, the pilots were told. The Grunts would rush him aboard as soon as the H-46 landed. Back in the helicopter cabin the crew chief, Corporal Ernesto Gomez, manned his .50 caliber machinegun as they roared down toward the cratered hilltop.

As the H-46 touched down and the HAC lowered the collective, two Grunts crawled out of a bunker with the wounded man, whose eyes and head were totally swathed with bandages. The Grunts were still 80 feet from the helicopter when the mortars impacted.

BLLAAAMM! BLLAAAMM! BLLAAAMM!

Abandoning the wounded man, the two Grunts dove for cover in a rocket crater. Unable to see and helpless, the injured Grunt staggered around the crater as enemy fire whipped all around him.

Corporal Gomez yanked his electrical long-cord loose and ran out to help. He reached the wounded man and pushed him to the ground. As detailed in his subsequent Navy Cross citation, Gomez "selflessly used his own body to shield his comrade from the hostile fire impacting around them . . . ." He then encouraged another Grunt to help him, and together they carried the blinded man into the waiting H-46. With full topping power on the twin turbines, the helicopter jumped skyward and headed for Charlie-Med at Khe Sanh.

Hill 881 South had become a lethal killing ground. Each night the NVA soldiers would test the Grunt perimeter, and each time the Grunts would throw back the assault. In two instances the enemy engaged in a unique brand of psychological warfare. Under cover of darkness, an NVA soldier crept near the Grunt wire and hurled deadly Bamboo Vipers (poisonous snakes) into the Grunt trenches. Speaking of the trench warfare on the ground, Major Althoff would later explain what he saw during his daily helicopter flights to the hill outpost: "Sometimes in the morning we'd see three or four hundred bodies out along the wire." One Grunt on the hill had a closer view of the carnage, and he would later explain: "We could watch the rats feeding on the enemy dead."

These are the times that try men's souls.
-- (Thomas Paine; December 23, 1776)

Critically wounded Grunts were classified as Priority One medevacs. However, when one of the Grunts got killed on the hill, evacuation of his body back to the main base became a secondary consideration. When body bags were available, the dead Grunts were zipped inside of them to protect their bodies from scavengers until a helicopter landed to pick up or discharge troops. Sometimes this involved waiting several days, because helicopters brought in only external sling loads whenever possible in the interest of safety. During such delays when there were no body bags, the bodies of the dead Grunts were tightly wrapped in ponchos in an attempt to protect them from the rats. This never seemed to work. The rats somehow always won. But since calling a helicopter down for a full landing would inevitably attract a swarm of incoming mortars, some Grunts began using a different tactic. They would load the bodies onto pallets and cover them with piles of cargo nets and slings. The H-46 pilots then could hesitate in a brief hover, a Grunt would slam the sling connector into the cargo hook, and the helicopter would be on its way. This procedure lessened the danger to both those on the ground and the helicopter crews.

As January 1968 drew to a close, the helicopter crews making daily flights into Khe Sanh and the hill outposts had spent ten days in the most hostile aerial environment imaginable. HMM-262 had lost three of its H-46s in the first two days of the battle. Two of them had been destroyed on the ground at Khe Sanh by rockets or artillery shells. Another had been shot down and lost, although the crew had been rescued by an H-34 from HMM-362. Another twelve of the Chatterbox H-46s had taken heavy damage. Major Althoff would later explain the ability of the H-46s to absorb hostile fire and keep flying:

I've [flown] them back with as many as 25 holes in the tail pylon alone -- with one boost shot out, when the aft vertical shaft had six or seven good-sized chunks shot out of it, with no fuel gauges and stuff like this. It continued to fly.

The "Ugly-Angel" H-34s from HMM-362 had handled most of the medevac flights. Mortars proved to be their most formidable adversary, but the reliable old Sikorsky helicopters soldiered on. The H-34 was the oldest and slowest helicopter at Khe Sanh, the last Marine helicopter to be powered by a reciprocating engine. Still, when the Grunts called for a medevac you could count on the trustworthy "Dog," as it was affectionately called (the pilots called themselves *Dog-Drivers*), to get the job done. For example, shrapnel wounded the crew chief and gunner in YL-45, and YL-31 took ten rounds on an emergency medevac, but both H-34s completed their assigned frags.

January 30, 1968: According to the Chinese Zodiac, the "Year of the Monkey" began with the Tet holiday on January 30. That night, North Vietnam launched its Tet Offensive by sending raiders into the heart of South Vietnam's seven largest cities. The NVA attacked 30 provincial capitals, and in I-Corps the capital cities of all five provinces were temporarily overrun. In the city of Hue, the communists routed the South Vietnamese defenders and occupied the walled Citadel, roughly a mile and a half square. The cover of *Life Magazine* would later carry a color photograph of two NVA soldiers manning a fortified barricade they had thrown across a city street in Hue. The accompanying caption would read: "North Vietnamese Soldiers with Chinese AK-47 Automatic Rifles Guard Captured Strongpoint in Hue."

> In my opinion, this is a diversionary effort to take attention away from the north, an attack on Khe Sanh.
> -- (General William C. Westmoreland; the day after Tet)

The Tet Offensive would become the greatest irony of the war in Vietnam. Militarily it would be a resounding defeat for the North Vietnamese, but it spawned a public opinion and political disaster in the United States. President Lyndon B. Johnson, hounded by nightmares of a possible humiliating defeat, became obsessed with Khe Sanh. At his direction a miniature mock-up of the Marine garrison was built in the Situation Room in the White House basement. Here, Johnson spent sleepless nights reading teletypes and studying aerial photographs. Then he made an unprecedented request. Johnson ordered General Earl G. Wheeler,

Chairman of the Joint Chiefs of Staff, to give him *written assurance* that Khe Sanh would not fall. Johnson lamented: "I don't want any damned Dien Bien Phu!"

Such written assurance, of course, was utterly ridiculous on its face -- something akin to a coach giving a baseball player written assurance that he will not strike out. But caught in a political vice, Wheeler complied, and Johnson got assurance to the effect that Khe Sanh would not be overrun. Each member of the Joint Chiefs had endorsed it. Johnson, the ultimate politician, now had his guarantee "signed in blood," he boasted. And if Khe Sanh should fall, the death or capture of thousands of Marines and the guaranteed political fallout would not be on his hands.

In Vietnam, General Westmoreland already had been politically embarrassed by the Tet Offensive, and his military career was on the line. The Marines had told him they could hold on to Khe Sanh; not only hold on to it, but destroy the attackers as well. Westmoreland did not share their confidence, because he knew of the haunting similarities between Dien Bien Phu and Khe Sanh. Faced with intense political pressure from Washington to do *something*, he considered a diversionary amphibious invasion of North Vietnam near Vinh, but soon rejected the plan because of logistical considerations. Without fanfare, Westmoreland and his command staff began plans for the use of tactical nuclear weapons on the North Vietnamese troops massed around Khe Sanh. Tac-nukes were available to him, so why not use them?

What the scientists have in their briefcases is terrifying.
-- (Nikita Khrushchev)

Westmoreland's assistants poured over atomic blast patterns, expected wind direction charts, radiation fallout zones, and even the projected number of civilian casualties. But exclusive of the main Bru village, most of the area around Khe Sanh was wild and uninhabited jungle, so noncombatant blast and radiation injuries and deaths were deemed to be of minimal consequence. The toughest problem would be protecting the Marines on the hill outposts, since some of the prime ground-zero locations were north and west of the base. The tac-nuke plan finally jelled, the delivery aircraft were identified and readied, and Westmoreland now had his trump card. He would be ready if the Marines faltered, and he explained: "I visualize that either tactical nuclear weapons or chemical agents should be active candidates for employment."

By the first week of February, after enduring ten days of siege, Khe Sanh looked like a giant sprawling junkyard. Shredded and flattened tents, empty C-Ration cans, discarded clothing, artillery shell casings, splintered lumber, and jagged chunks of shrapnel littered the ground. Fires burned everywhere. Before the siege had begun, many of the Grunts had doused their sleeping bunkers with fuel oil in an effort to repel the rats. Now the resulting fires were almost impossible to extinguish. Smoke boiled upward from the garbage dump fire and from the diesel fuel fires used to burn human feces. Smoke shrouded the smoldering "burn-pile" of no-longer-needed boots and clothing just outside of the Charlie-Med field hospital. Dense black smoke from pools of aviation fuel set ablaze by enemy shells drifted across the garrison. The gagging odor of feces, urine, rotting food, garbage, Grunts who had not bathed in weeks, and cordite permeated the thick choking smoke.

> Everything I see is blown through with smoke, everything is on fire everywhere. It doesn't matter that memory distorts; every image, every sound comes back out of smoke and the smell of things burning.
> -- (Michael Herr; writing of the Khe Sanh siege in *Dispatches*)

Helicopter pilots flying into Khe Sanh measured their time on the ground in seconds. Any inbound aircraft drew fire, but an aircraft that stopped on the runway invited a virtual hail of incoming shells and mortars. Some fixed-wing transports, the Marine Corps and Air Force C-130s, were still coming in IFR. They slipped down through the clouds to the airstrip, guided by the monotone radar controller's voice. On the south side of the marston-matted runway there was an airstrip control tower, constructed of wooden beams and surrounded by huge piles of sandbags. The sandbags helped, but the control tower remained a bull's-eye. It had been hit time and time again. Michael Herr, the poetic war correspondent for *Esquire Magazine*, wrote that the risk of climbing up into the control tower at Khe Sanh was, in his words: "Worse than having to run in front of a machinegun."

Yet, the Khe Sanh airstrip had to stay open. The Marine howitzers required an endless aerial chain of airplanes or helicopters to haul in the tons of shells needed each day. Everything came in by air: medical supplies, small arms ammunition, C-Rations, fuel, communications wire, grenades, rolls of concertina, and Grunt reinforcements.

Captain Rae H. "Scotty" Scott flew the "Dimmer" H-53s in HMH-463. The enormous H-53s packed 5700 horsepower and could easily carry 38 Grunts or 8000 pounds of internal cargo. But Scotty got a frag to fly a specialized item to Khe Sanh -- toilet tissue. Each C-Ration box came with its own limited supply of tissue, but the near constant diarrhea at Khe Sanh taxed that meager amount. This might create a morale problem, some REMF supply officer evidently decided. The S-4 logistics planners at Quang Tri crammed the cavernous cabin of Scotty's H-53 with untold thousands of rolls of toilet tissue. Scotty braved the enemy ring of fire and made the unique delivery.

> Khe Sanh remains the site of heaviest fighting, with all aircraft being subjected to .50 cal. fire while airborne and mortars and rockets while on the deck.
> -- (*VMO-6 Command Chronology*; February 2, 1968)

Notwithstanding the infamous toilet tissue frag, the more serious flying and fighting continued. On February 4, HMM-362 launched two of its helicopters on an emergency medevac. The lead Sikorsky H-34 got nailed by enemy gunners, went down, and was lost. The wingman picked up the casualties and flew them to the hospital ship in IFR conditions. The following day, pilots were reminded that all of the fighting was not at Khe Sanh. HMM-364 sent one of its new D-Model H-46s on a medevac flight into the ongoing battle to recapture the Citadel in the city of Hue. The H-46 took hits at YD-859176 just east of the village of Thon Than Phu, and the entire crew died in the crash.

Just after midnight on February 7, a mechanized nightmare

would sweep into the CIDG camp at Lang Vei, four miles southwest of Khe Sanh. Eleven Russian PT-76 tanks -- *tanks!* -- would spearhead an infantry assault by units of the North Vietnamese 304th Division.

The Special Forces maintained a 22 man detachment at Lang Vei to shepherd roughly 470 Montagnard CIDG troops. The camp presented no real offensive threat to the NVA. It served mainly as a jumping off point for clandestine raids into Laos, two miles to the west, and small scale intelligence patrols into North Vietnam. Most of the bunkers at Lang Vei were built of three feet thick concrete, reinforced with steel. The large and massive underground command bunker had six feet of reinforced concrete for a roof.

An infantry attack on Long Vei would be something akin to suicide, the defenders reasoned. The Lang Vei commander, Captain Frank C. Willoughby, could count on his 4.2 inch heavy mortars, 106mm and 57mm recoilless rifles, and scores of the potent Light Antitank Weapons, commonly called the LAW rocket. The camp bunkers bristled with .50 caliber and M-60 machineguns, and the perimeter sported claymores and hundreds of reels of concertina and tanglefoot; impregnable, it was thought. Further, supporting artillery fire from Khe Sanh was only a radio call away. Also, the camp contingency plan called for two companies of Grunts from nearby Khe Sanh to reinforce the camp if necessary. Lang Vei seemed secure. Despite the known presence of entire NVA Divisions in the surrounding hills, no one expected an attack here. After all, Khe Sanh was the prize the NVA wanted, not small and insignificant Lang Vei.

Lang Vei, February 7, 1968, 0035 Hours: Sergeant Nicholas Fragos, on duty in the camp observation tower just after midnight, heard a strange mechanical grinding noise. Perhaps the camp's diesel generator was acting up, he initially thought. A magnesium flare then popped overhead and bathed the perimeter in eerie shadows. Fragos could scarcely believe his eyes. The subsequent radio transmissions were recorded:

"They've got tanks!"

"Where?"

"TANKS! TANKS IN THE WIRE!"

Several radio transmissions followed, and then: "WE'VE GOT TANKS INSIDE OUR WIRE! INSIDE OUR WIRE!"

Five North Vietnamese tanks crushed the concertina south of the camp and clanked into the compound. Their searchlights swept back and forth, looking for targets. Four more tanks wheeled in from the west on Route 9. Others lumbered in from the dirt road leading to Khe Sanh village. The tanks were Russian PT-76s, originally built in the Kirov Factory at Leningrad. They rolled forward, firing their 76mm cannons at the bunkers and crushing everything in their path.

The PT-76s handily breached the outer defenses and destroyed one bunker after another at close range.
-- (Jon Guttman; in *Vietnam Magazine,* December 1990)

Behind the tanks came an NVA flamethrower platoon, followed by rows of tan-clad North Vietnamese infantry. Deep in the command bunker, Captain Willoughby radioed to Khe Sanh for help. Marine artillery began firing the Top Secret COFRAM "Firecracker" fragmentation shells at the Lang Vei perimeter. Willoughby then requested Marine helicopters and the two companies of Grunts called for in the contingency plan.

Colonel Lownds refused. It seemed heartless, but it would have been folly to try to send helicopters at night into a compound overrun with enemy tanks and infantry. And, Colonel Lownds reasoned, the NVA probably had a well prepared ambush set up for any Grunt relief column that might try a forced night march down the twisting mountain trail to Lang Vei. (Subsequent events proved that Colonel Lownds was right. Intelligence would later confirm from captured NVA prisoners that a regiment from the 304th NVA Division lay in waiting along Route 9 for the anticipated Grunt relief force. The attack on Lang Vei was mainly a ploy designed to draw out the Marines and enable the NVA to chew them up in a night ambush along Route 9.)

Half of the Americans at Lang Vei survived by holding out in the underground command bunker, because the tanks could not crush six feet of reinforced concrete roof. At daylight the Marine H-46s from HMM-262 and gunships from VMO-6 launched from Quang Tri and made the 20 minute flight to Lang Vei. They slipped down and landed at the "old camp" on the north side of Route 9. Here they picked up 15 Americans and some of the

Montagnards who had managed to evade the North Vietnamese. Only three of the H-46s took hits, for most of the enemy soldiers had already gone. Looking at the ruins of Lang Vei, one Marine helicopter pilot called it a "bleak smoldering shell."

> Jesus, they had tanks . . . . After Lang Vei, how could you look out of your perimeter at night without hearing the treads coming?
> -- (Michael Herr; in *Dispatches*)

Khe Sanh now stood alone. Officially the Marine Command claimed that the fall of Lang Vei would have no effect on the encircled Grunts at Khe Sanh. But each night the NVA dug their trenches ever closer to the Marine wire, and everyone knew that the monsoon would not end until late April.

<u>Khe Sanh, February 10, 1968</u>: Earlier in the day a C-130 had landed, and a critical hit necessitated shutting down the engines for quick repairs. The inevitable rain of mortars began, but emergency repairs were made. The C-130 pilots fired up their four turboprops, roared down the runway, and headed for safety in the clouds. When the airplane landed at Da Nang, incredulous mechanics would count 242 shrapnel and bullet holes in the fuselage and wings.

A flight of helicopters landed at Khe Sanh without incident. Next to try to run the gauntlet was a Marine Corps KC-130 tanker from VMGR-152, piloted by Chief Warrant Officer Henry Wildfang. He piloted a "fuel ship" laden with six bulbous bladders holding tons of fuel for the base. As the huge transport lumbered down and flared to land, bullets riddled the cockpit and cabin. The volatile fuel ignited. Over a thousand gallons of fuel were consumed in a gigantic inferno, and six men perished in the pyre.

> With flames licking at one side, the stricken craft careened off the runway 3,100 feet from the approach end . . . and was rocked by several muffled explosions.
> -- (Captain Moyers S. Shore II; in *The Battle for Khe Sanh*)

The C-130s had been taking a terrible beating from enemy antiaircraft fire. After the fiery crash on February 10, the Air Force C-130s no longer tried to land on the airstrip. However, Marine Corps C-130 pilots still braved the AAA batteries to land and bring supplies and munitions to the besieged garrison.

Air Force C-130s began using a tactic reminiscent of desperate French efforts to resupply Dien Bien Phu. Instead of landing, the Air Force pilots resorted to low passes and parachute drops to supply the Grunts on the ground. The drop zone lay west of the base, and even in IFR weather the fixed-wing transports would make radar controlled approaches and parachute their loads down through the clouds. Loads that landed outside of the drop zone were destroyed by artillery to prevent them from falling into the hands of the NVA.

The smaller and slower twin engine Fairchild C-123s proved to be more resistant to enemy fire, and they also could get airborne in almost half the distance required by the C-130s. So when weather permitted, the C-123s still flew down the glideslope and landed to the west (uphill), regardless of the wind direction. The C-123 pilots could stop their airplane by the time it reached the turn-off ramp, two thirds of the way down the runway on the left. The airplane would whirl around on the ramp, and the cargo would be snatched out as the mortars and shells impacted on the marston-matting. Medevacs would then be rushed aboard. Then the pilots would firewall their throttles and take off to the east. The landing, turnaround, unloading, reloading, and takeoff would take less than two minutes.

Helicopter pilots and aircrewmen flew around the clock to keep Khe Sanh resupplied, now that the fixed-wing aircraft were restricted by the weather and enemy fire. Helicopters were not immune to the danger. An H-34 from HMM-362 had shut down in the protective revetments north of the runway, but it still got destroyed by a direct hit from a 122mm rocket. On a medevac flight, Captain Ed Kufeldt and his copilot, 22 year old Lieutenant George E. Rosental, launched from Khe Sanh in their VMO-6 Klondike gunship. They flew into disaster when they reached the pickup zone. Firing broke out, and 30 rounds tore into the fuselage and cockpit of the Huey. Kufeldt's wounds were not too serious, but his copilot suffered two broken legs and severe injury to his right arm. Despite his wounds, he would eventually survive. Yet, on February 16 another VMO-6 crew fared much worse. The NVA shot down the Huey, and all of the crewmen were lost:

Galbreath B F	Captain	Dec 01 30 - Feb 16 68
Jensen, P A	1st Lieutenant	Mar 27 44 - Feb 16 68
Tolliver J E	Staff Sergeant	Jan 05 40 - Feb 16 68
Schneider H W	Corporal	Nov 21 47 - Feb 16 68

Although the heavy fighting raged around Khe Sanh, small unit battles flared throughout I-Corps. The *HMM-362 Command Chronology* illustrates the dangers faced by the helicopter crews:

HMM-362 was called for an[d] flew an emergency resupply of ammunition and 70 emergency medevacs. Five out of a flight of 6 aircraft were hit while flying the ammunition in and extracting 58 medevacs from BS-486767. YL-40 received 2 hits with little damage. YL-39 received 15 hits wounding 3 ARVN medevacs and the crew chief, and killing one medevac. YL-41 received 20 hits and no injury. The entire flight proceeded to Ky Ha. YL-53 was later called into the same zone and received 2 hits, one wounding the pilot slightly. The crew chief returned fire and reported 2 possible enemy KIA. The aircraft was flown to Ky Ha. YL-51, while on an emergency medevac on Operation "DESOTO," received 5 hits approaching BS-799421, there was no injury to the crew and the mission was completed. YL-34 was hit on an emergency medevac at BS-805423, 4 hits were received on the approach, the mission was aborted and the aircraft was flown to Nui Dang where it remained until it was repaired . . . .

Notwithstanding the small unit action below Da Nang, the real aerial battle was being played out in the skies over Khe Sanh. Helicopter crews encountered the most fire on flights to the hill outposts, mainly Hill 881 South and Hill 861. These hills were well within range of NVA small arms and heavy weapons. The Grunts on the helicopter support teams had dug holes in the landing zones so they could dive for cover when the incoming mortars started. The pilots and aircrewmen had no such protection, but they still had to make the flights. Even water had to be flown to the hill outposts, where each Grunt was rationed to only two canteens of water per day.

There were a few humorous moments. On Hill 881 South a Grunt had developed an impacted and infected wisdom tooth, so Captain Dabney decided to medevac him off of the hill. When the next medevac helicopter landed, the Grunt would help carry a casualty aboard, and the Grunt was supposed to stay in the helicopter for the flight to Quang Tri where he could get medical attention, he was told. As the next H-46 touched down on the hill, the prospective dental patient carried the rear of a litter up the ramp. Suddenly two mortar rounds impacted right beside the helicopter. No sane pilot sits through a mortar barrage if he can help it. With all six rotor blades biting into the air, the H-46 lurched skyward. The Grunt with the bad tooth rolled down the ramp, briefly hung on by his fingertips, and then dropped to the ground as the helicopter raced toward the clouds without him.

An H-34 on an emergency medevac mission was the next helicopter to scream down. The dental patient crawled aboard and hoped for better luck this time. The Wright R-1820 engine roared to full power, and the Sikorsky helicopter took off. However, it would prove to be a short flight.

> This trip covered about 20 feet -- 10 up and 10 down -- because the tail rotor of the UH-34 was literally sawed off by a burst from an enemy machine gun just after the bird became airborne.
> -- (Captain Moyers S. Shore II; in *The Battle for Khe Sanh*)

No tail rotor! The laws of physics and aerodynamics took over. Without antitorque control, with 1525 horses twisting on the main rotor shaft, and with no forward airspeed, the damaged H-34 did not stand a chance. Instinctively the pilots jammed in full left rudder -- nothing! The helicopter slammed to the ground. Everyone crawled out and scrambled for cover in the nearest trenchline or rocket crater.

By now the Grunt with the bad tooth presumably had developed severe misgivings about the reliability of aerial transportation by helicopter. Yet, he was ordered to try again. By the time another H-46 swooped down to the hilltop, there was cargo to be flown out, plus ten medevacs, plus the four men from the downed H-34, plus the dental patient. Everyone got aboard, but the H-46 was now heavily overloaded. The crew chief quickly saw that the Grunt bound for the dentist's chair was not visibly bleeding, and he obviously was ambulatory. "GET OUT!" screamed the crew chief over the metallic whine of the turbines and rear transmission. The frustrated Grunt complied. As the helicopter took off without him, he ran back to his bunker while cursing and shouting that he intended to remain there forever.

Back at Khe Sanh, an H-53 landed, loaded down with huge 155mm "Willie-Pete" shells for the howitzers. The pilots kept the rotors engaged while a crew headed by Corporal William Robertson began offloading the shells by hand. An incoming 122mm rocket shrieked down out of the clouds and exploded behind the Sea Stallion. The blast rolled Robertson up into the cabin of the helicopter and knocked him unconscious. The H-53 lurched skyward, heading for safety in the clouds. When Robertson regained his senses he found himself airborne in the H-53 on his way back to Dong Ha. Partially deafened and bruised but otherwise unhurt, he hitched a helicopter ride back to Khe Sanh the next day. His surprised buddies cheered his arrival and welcomed him back. They erroneously had assumed that the rocket blast had killed him.

Another H-53 flew into Khe Sanh on February 22, and the odds were about to catch up with the two pilots, Captain J. T. "Rex" Riley and his 22 year old copilot, First Lieutenant Carey Smith. The "Dimmer" helicopter took on a full load of medevacs and started to take off. Exactly what happened next is not clear. Eric Hammel would later interview the chaplain of the 1st Battalion, 26th Marines. The chaplain would explain that he heard a "large blast," saw metal and debris fly everywhere, and realized that the H-53 had been hit. Another eyewitness said that a recoilless rifle round struck the helicopter on takeoff, about 50 feet in the air. But while the cause is uncertain, the end result is not in dispute. The H-53 crashed to the ground, and the rotor blades went slashing around with disastrous results.

Years later I would find a color photograph of a downed H-53 at Khe Sanh. I am not positive, but evidence suggests that it is the same Dimmer helicopter that was downed on February 22. Apparently the shell, rocket, or recoilless rifle round impacted right on top of the cockpit, or on one of the spinning rotor blades directly above the front of the helicopter. The blast blew away the entire upper front of the cockpit. The fuselage remained basically intact, although the rotor blades all snapped off ten feet or so from the rotor head. The lower torsos of the two pilots were still in the armored seats, but nothing much was left above their waists. Riley and Smith died in their H-53 at Khe Sanh that day. Most of the medevacs in the cabin survived.

February 22, 1968: Marine Air introduced the "Super-Gaggle." Helicopters supplying the hill outposts had been attracting heavy fire during landings, and casualties among the helicopter crews and the nearby Grunts on the ground were mounting. The Marines had to come up with a way to suppress the fire, or at least a way to prevent the NVA from concentrating all of their guns on just one helicopter. The Super-Gaggle was born.

The plan called for twelve A-4 Skyhawk ground-attack jets from Chu Lai, twelve H-46s loaded with supplies, four Huey gunships, and one tactical air controller in another plane -- 29 aircraft in all. The main problem was the weather. The speedy A-4s could not go zipping around under the overcast with wild abandon, for a mountain hiding in a cloud will persevere every time in a 400 knot collision with an airplane. The overcast had to be high enough to allow the Skyhawks room to operate clear of the rugged terrain. The helicopter pilots did not worry about the clouds like their fixed-wing counterparts. As long as they could eyeball the top of the designated mountain, a landing would present no problem.

When the weather cooperated, at "H" hour the MAG-12 Skyhawks would take off from Chu Lai and head up the coastline. At the same time the H-46s would begin taking cargo aboard at Dong Ha. Then the H-46s and the gunships would launch and head to the west toward the mountains. If all went as planned, all 29 aircraft would arrive over Khe Sanh at the same time. On most days a solid overcast blanketed the mountains, and both the helicopters and the ground-attack jets would make instrument approaches toward the Khe Sanh airstrip. Once they broke out of the cloud base, they would abandon their IFR approach to the runway and fly VFR toward the designated mountain.

No non-flying layman can understand the hazards caused by 29 aircraft swirling about under an overcast in the mountains in a combat environment. The official Marine Corps narrative, *The Battle for Khe Sanh*, explains:

> Only those who have experienced the hazards of monsoon flying can fully appreciate the veritable madhouse that often exists when large numbers of aircraft are confined to the restricted space beneath a low hanging overcast. Coupled with this was the fact that the fluffy looking clouds around Khe Sanh housed mountains which ran up to 3000 feet.

When all was ready, eight Skyhawks armed with napalm, hard bombs, and 20mm cannons would begin making bombing and strafing runs on known enemy positions around the designated hill. Then two more Skyhawks would swoop down to incapacitate the enemy gunners with tear gas. The last two jets would lay down smoke screens across the helicopter approach route.

The H-46s would then roar down to land if they carried Grunt passengers. Otherwise, they would just hesitate at hover height, pickle their external sling loads, and then speed away to safety high above. The A-4s would stay in a racetrack pattern, constantly pelting the NVA with bombs and 20mm cannon fire in order to protect the H-46 transports. The Huey gunship pilots would circle the hill at a lower altitude and attack any observed enemy gun positions. The Hueys also would serve as the SAR ship. Their job called for them to land and pick up the crew of any H-46 that the enemy might shoot down. Speaking of the Super-Gaggle concept years later, William Dabney put it bluntly: "If it weren't for the Gaggle, most of us probably wouldn't be here today."

One NVA sniper worked throughout the night and dug his spider-hole about 120 meters from the Grunt wire. He turned out to be a lousy marksman, but he kept plinking away at the Grunts and inbound helicopters, anything that moved. At night he shot at any light that he could see. Every time the Grunts fired at him, he dropped down in his hole and remained unscathed. The Grunts even tried blasting the sniper with a 106mm recoilless rifle, but the tough North Vietnamese soldier stayed low in his hole. The Grunts called in a Huey gunship with M-60s and 2.75 inch rockets, but the enemy sniper seemed to have a charmed life. The Grunts occasionally caught a glimpse of the Oriental through binoculars. The savvy sniper never raised himself to more than eyeball height above the rim of his spider-hole.

Finally, enough was enough, and the Grunts called in a fixed-wing airstrike. The lethal napalm canister tumbled earthward end over end, ignited, and unleashed an orange and black blast furnace all around the unfortunate sniper, sucking all of the oxygen out of the air. The FAC reported "good coverage" on the target, so the fast-mover pilot headed for home with one killed-by-air (KBA) logged to his credit.

On the hilltop, the Grunts watched in awe for ten minutes while the jellied gasoline finally burned itself out. It had been a horrible way to die, they knew. The gutty little sniper had been a formidable adversary and a tough warrior. He bravely had fought alone, and he undoubtedly had known that he would eventually be killed. Out of the mutual respect that professional military men afford to worthy opponents in death, the Grunts privately and silently mourned his loss. Thirty minutes passed.

To be vanquished and yet not surrender; that is victory.
-- (Konrad Adenauer)

Suddenly the camouflaged cover on the spider hole wiggled . . . wiggled once again . . . and then flopped open. Fifty sets of incredulous eyes strained to see what would happen next. Obviously severely burned and injured, the North Vietnamese sniper stuck his rifle muzzle straight up in the air. In defiance, he cranked off a single round.

To a man, the Grunts all stood and cheered. No one was allowed to shoot at the tough little sniper again. He had *guts*, and the Grunts adopted him as their mascot. They nicknamed him "Luke-the-Gook," and none of the Marines wanted to see any further harm come to him.

Toward the end of February, the Grunts at Khe Sanh and on the hill outposts began to see the tangible results of the horrible toll they were taking on the attacking North Vietnamese. The main garrison had absorbed a monthly high of 1309 incoming shells, rockets, and mortars on February 23. However, the Grunt batteries were now throwing five times that many shells back at the enemy. Grunt patrols outside of the wire turned up clear evidence of terrible enemy casualties. During the day the sky over the Khe Sanh Plateau was filled with the shrieking jet engines of A-4 Skyhawks, F-4B Phantoms, and A-6 Intruders. The Marines on the ground heard the constant thud from the rotors of UH-1E Huey gunships, H-34s, H-46s, and an occasional H-53. And unseen at 35,000 feet high above the plateau, B-52s daily dropped their deadly loads onto known or suspected enemy troop concentrations.

Of course, there had been setbacks as well. On the fifth day of the month, an NVA battalion had stormed Hill 861 and had breached the wire before the Grunt defenders finally drove the attackers back down the mountainside. Lang Vei had fallen two days later, and the next day a small unit from the 1st Battalion, 9th Marines, had gotten overrun. Further, Second Lieutenant Don Jacques, a New Yorker, had led his "Ghost Patrol" from Bravo Company, 1st Battalion, 26th Marines, south of the main base on February 25. Spotting several NVA soldiers in a clearing, Jacques had charged in true Basic School fashion -- right into a carefully laid ambush. Jacques and 25 of his Grunts died when they were cut down by machinegun fire.

<u>February 29, 1968, 2130 Hours</u>: The North Vietnamese mounted a major attack from the east. Units of the 304th NVA Division stormed out of their trenches and headed for the rows of concertina and razor ribbon that ringed Khe Sanh. The enemy never breached the wire. The soldiers in the vanguard of the attack all died with their bangalore torpedoes in hand. Marine Air broke up another charge just before midnight, and yet another attack three hours before dawn. Later, hundreds of decaying North Vietnamese bodies were found along trails leading toward the base perimeter, the victims of a night-long pounding by aircraft and artillery.

Hungry for salable news, the international press zeroed in on the siege. Khe Sanh was the one name with which the American and European public could identify. It conjured up visions of valiant defenders, encircled Marines, human wave attacks, Oriental hordes, and memories of Dien Bien Phu. *Newsweek Magazine* picked up the story of Luke the Gook and his comrades firing at everything that moved. The magazine editors detailed the "37mm flak [and] the hundreds of machine guns that already ring the base." *Newsweek* noted: "Pilots take enormous risks to bring supplies into Khe Sanh." The media painted vivid word pictures of Grunts doing the "Khe Sanh-double-step." It was described as a rapid and half-crouching walk with the head constantly swiveling to make sure there was a trench nearby in case a shell came whistling in. The media published reports of life in the bunkers in the water with the rats and with the numbing cold at night. The rats in the bunkers, *Time Magazine* reported, go berserk during the shelling and "wildly run up to the ceiling made of runway matting and logs.

> We huddled together in the bunker, shoulders high and necks pulled in to leave no space between helmet and flak jacket. There is no describing an artillery barrage. The earth shakes, clods of dirt fall from the ceiling, and shrapnel makes a repulsive singing through the air.
> -- (correspondent John Donnelly; in *Newsweek Magazine*)

Perhaps the most poignant written work about Khe Sanh would come from a then obscure young Syracuse University graduate, Michael Herr, a war correspondent for *Esquire Magazine*. In his spellbinding book, *Dispatches*, he wrote not of the overall grand scope of the war. Instead, Herr captured the emotion, hope, fear, frustration, the putrid stench, the dirt and grime of war, and the trials of the Grunts at Khe Sanh. His book would become "the best book to have been written about the Vietnam War," according to the *New York Times*. Writing of the filth and the horror on the hill outposts, Herr noted:

> Hill 861 was the home of the thousand-yard stare, and I prayed hard for a chopper to come and get me away from there, to fly me over the ground fire and land me in the middle of a mortar

barrage on the Khe Sanh pad -- whatever! Anything was better than this.

March 6, 1968: The monsoon slowly began to abate, and within a month the skies would be clear. But on this foggy day a C-123 winged its way inbound with a load of Grunt replacements. An Air America plane zipped down to land first, and then the C-123 pilots got their chance. As the big transport started its approach, the North Vietnamese AAA gunners laced the fuselage and wings with heavy shells. Crippled and straining for altitude on only one engine now, the pilots tried to turn back toward Dong Ha. They never made it. The C-123 crashed in the inaccessible jungle about four miles east of Khe Sanh. The four crewmen, 43 Marine Grunts, a Navy corpsman from Lima Company, and *Newsweek* photographer Ronald Ellison all died in the crash.

The same day that the C-123 bought the farm, an H-46 from HMM-364, YK-22, got drilled by automatic weapons and shrapnel from mortars. During the same week another H-46 in a Super-Gaggle took hits and suddenly tumbled earthward out of control, carrying 22 Marines to their deaths.

HMM-262 still bore the brunt of the H-46 frags. On March 8, Lieutenant Colonel Mel Steinburg's H-46 was diverted for an emergency medevac mission to Charlie-Med at Khe Sanh. Colonel Steinburg flew his Chatterbox helicopter to the landing pad, and the corpsmen began running toward him with the litters. Colonel Steinburg and his copilot drew themselves back into the metallic folds of their armored seats and tried to make as small a target as possible as the mortars began impacting around them. For a helicopter pilot, there is no worse feeling than sitting on the ground while taking fire. But the two pilots waited until the last of the seven medevacs were carried aboard. Then they sucked in collective pitch and flew out of the barrage of deadly shells.

As the H-46 shuddered through translational lift, shrapnel tore through the aluminum fuselage. In the center of the instrument panel, the large Master Caution Light winked on and drew the pilots' immediate attention. Quickly scanning the twin rows of smaller warning lights below, they spotted the bright amber warning light that no H-46 pilot ever wants to see, "Control Boost." Two sets of buttocks instantly puckered shut.

The admonition in the H-46 NATOPS Manual is clear: "It is impossible to control this helicopter with both boost systems inoperative." A quick glance to the left of the Master Caution Panel revealed that the Number One Boost pressure had dropped to zero. If the Number Two Boost also failed, they were all dead men, they knew. Without the 3000 psi hydraulic fingers to control them, the massive rotor head swashplates would slam to full pitch, flat pitch, left, right, forward, backward, and their helicopter would literally disintegrate in the air. The textbook solution called for an immediate landing.

Colonel Steinburg had just launched from ground-zero in a mortar barrage, and he had no intention of landing there again. He dove over the precipice at the eastern end of the runway and zoomed along eastward right over the treetops. He took fire from the surrounding hills, but 16 minutes later he softly touched down on the grass just south of the airstrip at Dong Ha. All of his medevacs made it into Delta-Med alive.

By the middle of March the clouds over Khe Sanh started melting away, enabling Marine Air to more easily pinpoint the enemy. This did not help Captains Greg Rengel, the HAC, and Steve Stegich, the copilot, when they flew a resupply frag to Hill 861 on March 14. Enemy fire knocked out both of their engines. They autorotated down and lost hydraulic pressure in both systems just as the H-46 slammed into the mountainside. Major Althoff zipped down and picked up all four crewmen, but Rengel and Stegich had been seriously hurt. Both of them later would be medevaced to CONUS.

The official MAG-16 photographer flew into Khe Sanh, but he managed to get himself wounded soon after his arrival. In so doing, he missed one of the greatest false alarms of the siege. Notwithstanding verbal agreements with the Chinese and Russians, the Marine Command had always been worried about a possible air attack on Khe Sanh by North Vietnamese MIGs. So when an airborne early warning controller spotted the telltale blips speeding south over Laos and then turning east -- no response from the IFF black boxes -- the warning signal *rocketed* to the regimental communications center at Khe Sanh. The ground-attack Phantoms,

Skyhawks, and Intruders on station overhead carried napalm and hard bombs that were useless against the supersonic MIG-21s. There was no time to scramble fighters armed with air-to-air missiles from faraway Da Nang. Red Alert! The Grunts hunkered down in their bunkers for protection, but the air attack on Khe Sanh never materialized. Either the MIGs turned tail, or it had been a case of mistaken aerial identity all along.

Meanwhile, 14,000 miles away at Pensacola, Florida, an era came to an end as Second Lieutenant Larry D. Mullins received his Marine Corps commission and Naval Aviator wings on March 22. Mullins was the last Marine to earn his wings under the MARCAD program. And on the same date, while the country that allowed *Life Magazine* to prosper was locked in battle with the North Vietnamese, the *Life* editors elected to put the photograph of Ho Chi Minh on their cover. But in Vietnam, none of this mattered to the helicopter pilots flying into Khe Sanh each day. What mattered to the HMM-262 pilots was enemy bullets, a shortage of helicopters, and the fact that their squadron had been whittled down to only eleven remaining HACs. Four days later they lost yet another helicopter, and they almost lost the entire crew as well:

While resupplying Hill 881 [South], Capt. [Clayton S. "Clay"] SNEAR, with Capt. HAGER as copilot, received battle damage which caused the loss of both engines and the number 1 Boost. Capt. SNEAR autorotated safely to the ground in enemy territory. The crew removed the machine guns and radios and were successfully recovered by an aircraft from HMM-364.
-- (*HMM-262 Command Chronology*; March 28, 1968)

On the last day of the month, three hours before daylight, HMM-362 launched on an emergency night medevac. Somehow up and down lost their meaning in the dark, and the chase helicopter sideswiped the trees and crashed on the side of a mountain. There was no way to reach the crash site before dawn, and by then the crew chief and gunner had died. The pilots, both badly burned, survived and were picked up and flown to safety.

Washington, D.C., March 31, 1968: Looking strangely drawn and tired, President Lyndon B. Johnson delivered a televised address to the nation late in the evening. He read from typewritten text. Johnson declared his willingness to halt the bombing of North Vietnam and "bring this ugly war to an end." Then, Johnson put down his prepared speech and looked directly at the network cameras. With no change in his deadpan facial expression and no change in verbal inflection, Johnson shocked his closest confidants and advisors by stating: "I shall not seek, and I shall not accept, the nomination of my party for another term as your President."

For the past week the Marines had been on the attack. The main garrison had been pounded by 1109 incoming shells on March 23, but the next day the Grunts had charged into the NVA trenches west of the base and had routed the enemy. The gunships of VMO-6 had led the way with their rockets and M-60s. Heavy North Vietnamese fire had downed one of the Hueys. Although all four Huey crewmen were rescued, the pilot later died from burns that he had suffered in the crash. To the south later in the week, the Grunts had gotten helicopter support and had swarmed through fortified North Vietnamese positions.

Near Ca Lu, west of Dong Toan Mountain, the First Marines stockpiled supplies for a ground attack westward toward Khe Sanh. Helicopter support came from two H-46 squadrons, Huey gunships, and H-53s as needed. The written mission for HMM-262 left no doubt about the crucial flying job at hand: "The squadron's mission . . . [is] to provide aircraft, as necessary, for resupply and med-evac to the Marine outposts on Hills 881 [South], 861, 861A, 558, 950, 689, and the Khe Sanh airfield."

Two H-46s stayed at Ca Lu on standby, day and night, with others flying in as needed. With the monsoon rapidly dissipating now, Marine Air could put tremendous pressure on the enemy. Intelligence confirmed that the North Vietnamese 325-C Division was slowly being forced westward into Laos. The 304th Division had pulled back slightly to the southwest. "Hanoi Hanna," the English speaking announcer for Radio Hanoi, had previously been calling on the Grunts at Khe Sanh to surrender to the People's Liberation Army. The Grunts who refused to surrender were "surrounded and doomed," she had boasted. However, now Hanoi Hanna began changing her tune: "Ho Chi Minh would be unhappy if we wasted our time on only six-thousand Marines."

<u>April 1, 1968</u>: On the first day of April, two full battalions of Grunts attacked to the west along Route 9 from Ca Lu. Gunships buzzed overhead to cover the troops on the ground. Behind the attackers came the 11th Engineer Battalion to rebuild the twisting mountain road to Khe Sanh. Elements of the Army Air Cavalry also joined in the offensive. They flew south of Route 9 to Hill 248, which overlooks the Riviere de Quang Tri halfway between Ca Lu and Khe Sanh. The fighting remained fierce. Late on the first night of the attack, two HMM-362 helicopters launched from Phu Bai in miserable weather to fly emergency medical supplies to the small aid station at Ca Lu.

<u>Hill 471, April 4, 1968</u>: The southern tip of Dong Che Dien Ridge, known to the Marines as Hill 471 at XD-846393, lies a mile and a half directly south of the garrison at Khe Sanh. Dug in around the peak of the ridge were the troops of the 304th NVA Division. Behind a furious artillery barrage that was followed by Marine Air, the Grunts charged up the slopes and drove out the enemy. Captain Walter C. Jones, the 26 year old air liaison officer who coordinated the fire of the supporting aircraft, died during the assault when an NVA mortar round landed almost on top of him.

The North Vietnamese intended to reclaim Hill 471. That night their heavy artillery on Co Roc Mountain in Laos hurled shells at the ridge, and their mortars rained high-explosive rounds down on the Grunts. Two hours before dawn the barrage stopped, and the troops of the North Vietnamese 66th Regiment swarmed up the side of the ridge. Most of them died. The battered Grunts still held Hill 471 when the sun peeped above the mountains to the east.

Uncommon valor was a common virtue.
-- (Admiral Chester Nimitz; speaking of the conduct of the Marines who attacked Iwo Jima in March 1945)

Although more fighting lay ahead, the so-called "ring of steel" that the NVA had arrayed around Khe Sanh had been shattered by the Marines. Helicopter crews flew Grunts to hill after hill, valley after valley, where they found incredible stockpiles of supplies and munitions. Huge caches of enemy rockets were discovered, still in their wooden crates from Chinese factories. Boxed AK-47s were still packed in cosmoline. Helicopter pilots stayed busy flying the captured booty back to Dong Ha, although much of it was simply blown up with plastic explosive charges. The Grunts stumbled across thousands of shallow graves and found abandoned PT-76 tanks, medical supplies, food, and all of the essentials of warfare. They discovered hundreds of North Vietnamese field packs laid out in perfect platoon and company formations in the jungle. The North Vietnamese were on the run on all sides of Khe Sanh except for the area around Hill 881 North. That was their fortress, and they showed no inclination to give it up without a fight.

Khe Sanh, April 8, 1968, 0800 Hours: The spick and span command group from the Army's Third Brigade flew into Khe Sanh early in the morning. There was a flurry of obligatory handshaking at Colonel Lownds' command bunker. For the purpose of official entries in history books, those handshakes on April 8 ended the 77 day "Siege of Khe Sanh." The Army soldiers would soon arrive and take over the base, freeing the Marines to go on the offensive to the north and east. Marine helicopters filled the sky as they brought C-Rations, more ammunition, and mail to the garrison. Although HMM-362 had one of its helicopters shot down near the hill outposts, another "Ugly-Angel" crew landed and rescued their downed squadronmates. By now the air corridor between Dong Ha and Khe Sanh seemed to be relatively secure.

Later, when the departing Marine Grunts met an arriving Army column on Route 9, any notion of interservice camaraderie instantly was dashed. The Army marched west toward Khe Sanh. A ragged column of dirty Marines shuffled east in their rotting and tattered utilities. The two columns of men walked by each other and passed within an arm's length on the narrow one-lane-wide dirt road. With eyes focused straight ahead, the Army soldiers and the Marine Grunts did not even look at each other. Not a single word was spoken.

Hill 881 South, April 14, 1968 (Easter Sunday): All of the fighting had not yet ended. In the last four days alone, HMM-362 had medevaced 46 wounded Grunts from the field to the aid stations. Private First Class Lionel Trufant had ridden to Hill 881 South in an H-46, and he remembers hearing the NVA gunners firing at the helicopter during its approach. But most of the large enemy units had pulled back to Hill 881 North by now, and the H-46s began bringing in reinforcements to the Grunts on Hill 881 South. This was to be the Marines' springboard for their assault on the final enemy redoubt, the heavily defended Hill 881 North.

Before dawn on this Easter Sunday morning, the 3rd Battalion, 26th Marines, had moved downslope under cover of darkness. Exactly 2000 meters due north of them, the North Vietnamese on Hill 881 North still held the bastion from which they had lobbed 122mm rockets, mortars, and even 12.7mm fire down on the Grunts. As the first faint rays of the sun appeared over the crest of Dong Tri Mountain, the Grunts pushed northward into the dense fog toward the slope of the NVA-held mountain. Back at the Khe Sanh airstrip, H-46s, gunships, pilots, and aircrewmen waited for the inevitable medevac frags.

Fixed-wing jets shrieked down to drop their lethal loads on the enemy. Then the Grunts on Hill 881 South hammered the southern slopes of Hill 881 North with recoilless rifles, howitzers, and mortars. They even blasted away with .50 caliber machineguns that they had stripped from the broken hulks of the H-46s that had been downed around the outpost during the past three months.

As the attacking Grunts inched forward and upward, they came under withering fire from the enemy bunkers on Hill 881 North. The Grunts in Corporal Bob Saffle's fire team fell as though cut down with a scythe.

Retrieving wounded comrades from the field of fire is a Marine Corps tradition more sacred than life.
-- (Robert Pisor; in *The End of the Line*)

"Emergency medevac!" Back at the airstrip, waiting H-46 copilots reached up to their overhead consoles and flipped the spring-loaded "APP" toggle switches. The shrill whines of the small auxiliary turbines quickly filled the air. Then the main General Electric turbine engines rumbled to life as the Engine Condition Levers were snapped forward on the console to the "Start" position. The Boeing helicopters hovered, then nosed over and accelerated toward the columns of gray smoke rising from the battle five miles to the northwest. On the FM radio the pilots exchanged identification and guidance information with their fellow

Marines on the ground, and then they radioed: "Pop your smoke."

The Grunts on the mountainside braced themselves against the manmade gale as the H-46s landed. As twin hydraulic pistons dropped the ramps, the Grunts carried their casualties aboard. Then they ran back outside and uphill to resume the fight, and the helicopters rotored toward the aid station at Khe Sanh.

As the Grunts neared the crest of the mountaintop, they ran into the main NVA lines of defense. The airborne controller radioed the Grunts and told them to stop their attack. Marine Air and Artillery wanted to pound the peak for an hour to soften-up the defenders. There was no need to needlessly sacrifice the lives of more of the Grunts in a frontal assault against the waiting and entrenched North Vietnamese Army soldiers.

Perhaps the maddening frustration and fury of the past three months overwhelmed the Grunts. They were too close now, and they refused to stop. The Grunts fixed bayonets and swarmed up the slope toward the North Vietnamese. Their battalion operations officer, Major M. P. Caulfield, saw what was happening, and he frantically radioed to his company commanders and told them to stop their men. The radioed reply: "Sir, I can't stop them!"

> We got within a few yards of them, and they broke. In a second they were running for the rear. Their guns were thrown away.
> -- (Private Alex Hunter, Confederate States Army; after he charged enemy fortifications on August 30, 1862)

Hill 881 North, 1428 Hours: With fixed bayonets the Grunts swept through the enemy trenches and bunkers. Within 15 minutes the fighting died out. Most of the tan-uniformed NVA soldiers had been killed, and the rest of them now were fleeing down the north side of the mountain. The Grunts shot a few of them, but they did not pursue the others. They had retaken the last North Vietnamese stronghold, and that was enough. Lieutenant Colonel John Studt explained what happened next:

> I watched the jungle utility-clad Marine shinny-up a shrapnel torn tree, whose limbs had been sheared from the intensive prep fires, and affix the Stars and Stripes.

Helicopters began landing on the mountaintop to evacuate the Grunts who had fallen during the assault. There was no enemy fire. Now the former North Vietnamese fortress had been turned into a barren hill of death. It had been bombed, rocketed, shelled, mortared, blasted, and denuded. One Marine said that it looked just like the surface of the moon.

Their job now over, the ambulatory Grunts started straggling back toward Hill 881 South, roughly one mile away. Their commander proudly described them: "Near exhaustion, filthy, bearded, ragged; some wore bloody battle dressings." Then he quickly added: "They were all grinning."

The Marine Corps helicopters picked up the remaining dead and wounded Grunts and headed for Charlie-Med, three minutes' flying time to the southeast. Like the Grunts, the pilots would not return to this desolate mountain again. As each H-46 took off and clawed its way skyward, the pilots took one final look at the scarred crest of Hill 881 North. Their eyes were drawn to their country's flag, which was still securely tied to the top of the tree trunk. The riveting visual image indelibly burned itself into their memories, never to be forgotten. The red, white, and blue flag of the United States of America triumphantly fluttered in the stiff breeze atop Hill 881 North, deep in the heart of Indochina.

The brave men, living and dead, who struggled here have consecrated it far above our poor power to add or detract. The world will little note nor long remember what we say here, but it can never forget what they did here.
-- (Abraham Lincoln; at Gettysburg on November 19, 1863)

Requiem

**In the final analysis, it's their [South Vietnam's] war. They're the ones who have to win it or lose it. We can help them. But they have to win it.
-- (John F. Kennedy; September 1963)**

The United States and North Vietnam agreed to hold peace talks, and the meetings began in Paris on May 13, 1968. However, the talks quickly stalled over such trivial issues as the *shape* of the conference table. Throughout the world in 1968, the United States confronted a host of new problems and crises. The Soviet Union invaded Czechoslovakia. North Koreans seized the intelligence-gathering ship *Pueblo* and its crew of 83 Americans. France became the fifth member of the international atomic club. Democratic presidential candidate Robert F. Kennedy was assassinated, and college campuses were soon rife with discontent.

The war in Vietnam dragged on. The United States inaugurated Richard M. Nixon as President in January 1969, and he began shifting the war effort to the South Vietnamese and searching for an elusive "peace with honor" for the United States. In Paris after almost four years of little progress, the peace talks finally broke down altogether. In frustration, Nixon ordered an unprecedented and massive B-52 bombing campaign designed to force the North Vietnamese to make concessions. The so-called "Christmas Bombing" raids from December 18 through December 31, 1972, militarily known as Operation Linebacker II, devastated the North Vietnamese heartland between Hanoi and Haiphong. Industrially crippled, North Vietnam agreed to make peace. The following month on January 23, 1973, Nixon announced that a peace agreement had been signed, and a cease-fire went into effect the following day.

Within months the North Vietnamese released 591 American POWs, and the United States pulled its remaining field combat units out of Vietnam. However, the peace would be short-lived. After two years of regrouping, the mechanized North Vietnamese Army ignored the peace treaty and rolled south, and the South Vietnamese retreat soon turned into a humiliating rout, all the way to Saigon. Around midday on April 30, 1975, an NVA Russian-built T-54 tank rumbled unopposed across Cong Ly Boulevard and headed for Independence Palace. The tank battered through the steel gate and churned onto the green palace lawn, and for a moment all was still. Then a young North Vietnamese soldier, Nguyen Van Thieu, leaped from the tank and raced up the steps of the palace. At the top of the steps he turned and unfurled the National Liberation Front flag, blue and red with a bright yellow star. For the United States, the war in Vietnam had ended.

In neighboring Cambodia, the Chinese-backed Khmer Rouge Army captured the capital city of Phnom Penh within two weeks of the fall of Saigon. Insanity set in. The victorious Khmer Rouge, under the leadership of Pol Pot, began an unprecedented genocidal war of vengeance against the people of their own country, lopping off heads, disemboweling young women, and butchering the elderly. Kurt Waldheim, the appalled Secretary General of the United Nations, said there had been "no parallel in history" to the wanton killing in which an estimated two million helpless Cambodians were slaughtered.

Meanwhile in South Vietnam, Saigon was renamed Ho Chi Minh City. Public officials, schoolteachers, former members of the armed forces, and all who had worked with the Americans were herded up and confined in what Hanoi called "reeducation camps." Hundreds of thousands were never heard from again. The new government initially rationed rice to 20 pounds per person per month, but later reduced the ration to only four pounds per month to force the people out of the city and into the rice fields. For two decades afterward, a flood of Vietnamese "boat people" would head out to sea in attempts to escape the killing and anarchy that had engulfed their homeland.

Now that the United States had pulled out of Vietnam, China viewed the Soviet Union as its greatest potential enemy and saw no need to lend further support to the Vietnamese. The Chinese quickly withdrew their military and economic aid. The Soviet Union, increasingly wary of militaristic and now nuclear-capable China, sent military and economic advisors to the destitute Vietnamese. Soviet rubles helped prop up the Vietnamese economy. Soviet military aid helped the Russians and Vietnamese maintain a balance of power against China and the Chinese-backed Khymer Rouge in neighboring Cambodia.

In 1978, Vietnam signed a 25 year "friendship treaty" with the Soviet Union, a pact that China promptly called an armed threat to all of southeast Asia. Then, backed by the Soviet Union, Vietnam's army invaded Chinese-allied Cambodia. By the end of the year the Vietnamese had fought their way into Phnom Penh, the Cambodian capital, where they installed a new government, the "Cambodian National United Front for National Salvation." However, in the Cambodian countryside, hundreds of Khymer Rouge military units, still supplied by China, fought on and tied down the Vietnamese Army in guerilla warfare.

Meanwhile, Vietnam's traditional age-old enemy to the north, China, had seen its military efforts in Cambodia stymied. China had also watched as Vietnam grew increasingly powerful under the guiding hand of Soviet expansionism. Chinese leaders saw their country being geographically trapped between the two militaristic antagonists, the Soviets and the Vietnamese, so on February 17, 1979, they attacked the weaker of the two countries.

China launches an invasion of Vietnam, largely as a retaliation for Vietnam's invasion of Cambodia; 200,000-300,000 Chinese troops supported by aircraft and artillery, strike along the common 480-mile border.
-- (John S. Bowman; in *The Vietnam War: An Almanac*)

The war on two fronts against both China and Cambodia wrecked havoc throughout Vietnam and dealt a fatal blow to the already crippled economy. The average Vietnamese worker earned only $150 per year by 1983. By the following year there were 130,000 refugees from the fighting who were crowded into border camps in Thailand. The United States had already resettled over 600,000 Vietnamese and Cambodian refugees who had fled from their homelands to escape the wanton killing.

The Soviet Union stood by its Vietnamese ally as long as it viewed China as a military threat. However, by the mid-1980s the Chinese became preoccupied with their own internal social and political problems. The Soviets, by now also grappling with internal economic disarray, saw little advantage in pouring more money and arms into Vietnam. Consequently, the Soviets cut Vietnam adrift, and their 25 year treaty became a meaningless scrap of paper.

"We fought for *this*?" many Vietnamese now ask. Economically abandoned by both the Soviets and the Chinese, the Vietnamese are among the most impoverished people on earth. Eighty-five percent of the population ekes out a hand-to-mouth existence in rural hamlets. Outside of the major cities, many of the roads are impassable, and on passable roads roving bands of thugs often stop vehicles and extort "tolls" from travelers.

The drab Vietnamese capital city of Hanoi looks much as it did when the French left in 1954, after allowance is made for the expected deterioration and ravages of over 40 years. Bicycles are the main mode of transportation. Bach Mai Hospital, accidentally bombed on December 22, 1972, by American B-52s during the Christmas Bombing campaign, is still in operation. It still displays photographs of Jane Fonda standing in the rubble. In theory, medical care is free. However, those who are not government functionaries or members of the army have to bribe the hospital staff to prevent waiting for weeks or months before getting treatment. The human misery and bureaucracy are maddening, and electric power at the hospital is lost for an average of two hours per day. Some shops and restaurants are open, but a flourishing black market is the main source of food. The Vietnamese Army still guards all bridges leading into the city 24 hours per day. No one seems to know why.

Always fearful of the Chinese, their powerful traditional enemies to the north, Vietnam maintains the sixth largest army on earth (surpassed only by China, Russia, the United States, North Korea, and India), with the attendant drain on the national economy. General Giap has been put out to pasture with nothing to do, but he has been given the title, Deputy Chairman of the Council of Ministries for Science and Technology. Western journalists who have interviewed him say he expresses no remorse for leading millions of his countrymen into the slaughterhouse.

Old soldiers who fought the French and Americans also ask in disbelief: "We fought for *this*?" Over 300,000 severely disabled veterans are scattered throughout Vietnam. Without government help, most of them have to beg or earn a living as best they can. To its credit, the Vietnamese government does try to help some of them. Some disabled veterans manage to find care in hospitals in the major cities. Also, Than Thanh Institute lies 50 miles from Hanoi, and its 25 bleak masonry buildings are the home for many former soldiers who lost their arms, legs, or minds during the war. There is no heat in the buildings during the winter. There are no glass windows at the institute, and rotting wooden shutters can not keep out the swarms of mosquitoes in the summer. Yet, many of the patients have been fitted with artificial limbs. They feel lucky to have found a home here, but there is no hope for the future.

> We wait until night, and at night we wait until day. And it just goes on that way, like a circle.
> -- (a paraplegic veteran in a Vietnamese hospital; quoted by Michael L. Lanning and Dan Cragg in *Inside the VC and the NVA: the Real Story of North Vietnam's Armed Forces*)

Just below the 17th parallel near the former Marine Corps outpost at Nui Con Thien (translation, *Hill of Angels*), the government maintains Trung Son Cemetery. The Vietnamese people revere spirits and their ancestors, and over 10,000 Vietnamese soldiers are buried beyond an entrance memorial that is inscribed, "The Nation Honors Its Glorious Dead." Each tombstone is constructed of cheap masonry, but the unending rows are perfectly aligned like those at Verdun or Arlington. A small administration building houses a registry of the names of the dead soldiers. The cemetery lies in the most traumatized region of all Vietnam, the former "Leatherneck Square." Marine artillery, tanks, and infantry squared off here against 35,000 North Vietnamese in 1967, and the rolling hills were repeatedly doused with tons of defoliating Agent Orange. Now, no one lives here.

At the former Marine Corps bases and outposts, nothing much is left. The local Vietnamese long ago scavenged through the remains and carried off lumber, tin roofing, screen wire, creosote poles, electrical wiring, and anything conceivably usable. Only piles of rubble and occasional coils of rusty barbed wire remain.

> The place has a postnuclear look to it.
> -- (Morley Safer; describing the former helicopter base at Marble Mountain in *Flashbacks: On Returning to Vietnam*)

With roughly 74 million citizens, Vietnam is now the thirteenth most populous nation on earth. However, although rich in natural resources, Vietnam remains locked in grinding poverty without any industry and with a national economic system unworthy of the name. The French left in the 1950s, the Americans left in the 1970s, and now Vietnam has been abandoned by both the Chinese and the Soviets. Desperate for outside aid, the Vietnamese Politburo knows that the United States pitched in with technology and dollars and pulled its former enemies, Germany and Japan, out of the devastation left in the aftermath of World War II. Consequently, the Vietnamese began making economic overtures to their wartime enemy, the United States.

Vietnam embarked on an intense campaign to normalize relations with America. Recognizing the extreme United States' interest in the fate of servicemen still listed as missing-in-action in Indochina, the Vietnamese government "discovered" the skeletal remains of twelve of these missing men. Amid much ceremony, these remains were returned to United States' custody. Later, there was a *series* of such "discoveries." The Vietnamese government then promised further searches for American remains. In return for their *good faith*, the Vietnamese asked the United States to dissolve its trade barriers, reestablish diplomatic relations, and accept Vietnam as an equal member in the international community of nations. The Vietnamese say that they have always told the United States all they know about the Americans killed or missing during the war. Further, they say they treated American prisoners of war (POWs) humanely and turned all of them over to the United States after the fighting ended.

Those who now accept Hanoi's explanation could profit from a reality check. As late as the 1970s, Hanoi had claimed that none of its soldiers were even fighting in South Vietnam. Of course, the United States was also maintaining that no Americans were fighting in Laos or Cambodia. What -- or who -- can we believe?

With respect to Vietnam's treatment of American POWs, Jeremiah A. Denton Jr. has a story to tell. For those who may not have heard of him, Denton was a United States Navy pilot who flew the A-6 Intruder. On July 18, 1965, Denton was catapulted from the flight deck of the *USS Independence* for a bombing sortie over North Vietnam. He got shot down, captured, and jailed in the infamous "Hanoi Hilton." Almost eight years later Denton was the senior officer among the first group of POWs to be released. On February 13, 1973, at Clark Air Force Base in the Philippines, a C-141 rolled to a stop. Denton was the first POW to exit the aircraft. With hundreds of television cameras recording the moment, he walked to a waiting microphone and announced:

> We are honored to have had the opportunity to serve Our Country under difficult circumstances. We are profoundly grateful to our Commander and Chief and to our Nation for this day. God bless America!

In writing, Denton later told of the interrogations and brutal beatings that lasted for days, lasted until he lost consciousness from the pain. He told of the screaming POWs who were dragged away for interrogation and who were never heard from again, and who were never repatriated. Between senseless torture sessions, Denton himself had been kept in solitary confinement for four of his eight years in Hanoi, and his guards often kept him locked in a coffin for sport. Back in America, Denton would eventually be elected to the United States Senate from his native Alabama. His fellow POWs, including George Coker, a former Pensacola Class 43-63 classmate of mine, vouched for Denton's revelations of torture in Hanoi at the hands of the Vietnamese guards and interrogators.

Dieter Dengler, another pilot, had been captured after being shot down in Laos on February 2, 1966. He escaped and was plucked from the jungle by a helicopter over five months later on July 20. His written account of the subhuman treatment he received at the hands of his Vietnamese captors, first published in 1979, defies all human reason.

Humane treatment of POWs? Be your own judge.

During the war, Hanoi also had maintained that it never failed to disclose the names of the American POWs. As late as 1972, Hanoi stated that it held only 368 American captives. However, North Vietnam repatriated 591 POWs during February of the following year. Almost to the very end, North Vietnam had denied that it held the additional 223 Americans. In view of this eleventh hour disclosure, many wondered if North Vietnam kept additional POWs as "bargaining chips." If not, had other POWs been killed while in captivity?

The answer depends on whom you elect to believe. Hanoi has always maintained that it has given a full accounting with respect to American prisoners. Conversely, based on debriefings of POWs who were released, the United States initially stated that many POWs were left behind. Yet, the United States government later said it believes that the American prisoners in question are now all dead -- case closed. Where does the truth lie?

Bit by bit, the answers seep out. In the early 1990s the Vietnamese government, desperate to curry favor in the United States and gain economic aid, allowed Theodore G. Schweitzer access to previously secret records. The Vietnamese thought Schweitzer was researching a book that would cast a favorable light on their country. However, Schweitzer was actually a covert agent who worked for the United States government. In Hanoi he computer-scanned and photographed North Vietnamese records, war photographs, and the military ID cards of many former American POWs. He also computer-scanned the North Vietnamese "Blue-Book," a chronological registry maintained by the North Vietnamese that listed all Americans captured in North Vietnam. Many of the men listed in the Blue-Book had never been repatriated to the United States. Schweitzer also computer-scanned records and photographs of American airmen who had been killed when they were shot down, or who had died while trying to avoid capture. Knowledge of the fate of many of these men previously had never been acknowledged by Vietnam.

During his months in Hanoi, Schweitzer met and was photographed with General Giap, who is still revered. Schweitzer's aide for the research project was Lieutenant Colonel Nguyen Van Thi, a General Political Directorate (GPD) officer. According to Schweitzer's records, the GPD officer confided to him:

> Our government does not want America to know that our darkest secret is that we killed many Americans in cold blood. They were tortured to death in prison, or simply killed outright from fear they would try to escape. And our leaders are afraid to admit this. They were tortured to death here in Hanoi.

Schweitzer released his photographs, computer records, and interview documents to the United States government. He later contacted technical author Malcolm McConnell, who used Schweitzer's data and published *Inside Hanoi's Secret Archives: Solving the MIA Mystery* in early 1995.

In his book, McConnell also disclosed the results of research work in Moscow in 1993 after the collapse of the Soviet Union. At the "Center for the Preservation of Contemporary Documents," a researcher had stumbled across a transcript of an address to North Vietnam's Politburo on September 15, 1972, during the war. According to the transcript, Lieutenant General Tran Van Quang told the Politburo that there were 1205 American POWs. (Remember that six months later the North Vietnamese would repatriate only 591 POWs.) Quang noted that the United States did not know how many American POWs were held in North Vietnam, and he added: "In accordance with the decree from the Politburo, we keep secret the number of POWs."

After the Quang transcript became public, the American media accepted it as genuine. The Vietnamese government, still pushing for American economic aid, labeled it a forgery (the Vietnamese failed to suggest *why* someone might have forged such a document, and why anyone would want to plant such a document in Moscow, of all places). After a lengthy silence on the issue, the United States government took the position that the transcript was not genuine.

Again, where does the truth lie? Who knows? For many, the only reality that matters is that the American servicemen listed as missing-in-action, just like their comrades on The Wall in our nation's capital, are gone. The long war in Indochina somehow gobbled up all of them.

<u>Washington, D.C., July 11, 1995</u>: In his youth, Bill Clinton had been a fiery opponent of the United States' involvement in the Vietnam War. He also managed to avoid military service there.

Now on July 11, 1995, as the President of the United States, Clinton culminated a 30 month campaign of "preparing the nation" for the resumption of full diplomatic relations with Vietnam. The Vietnamese government had helped Clinton prime the American public opinion pump. The Vietnamese had "discovered" and returned the skeletal remains of 29 more American servicemen during the preceding 17 months. *Bargaining chips*?

> President Clinton turned the page on an ugly chapter in American history [yesterday] by normalizing diplomatic relations with Vietnam.
> -- (*The State* newspaper [South Carolina]; July 12, 1995)

Vietnam got what it wanted: diplomatic recognition, the right to negotiate trade and investment treaties, and a green light for the United States companies which had been waiting to pour dollars into Vietnam. At a press conference in Hanoi, Le Mai, the Vietnamese Deputy Foreign Minister, was ecstatic over the economic windfall. Strange -- he had nothing more to say about further Vietnamese efforts to locate Americans still missing in Indochina.

Here in the United States, fate and a merciful Providence have been kind to me, more kind than I deserve. Exclusive of the surgeon's handiwork on my right foot and the calf of my left leg, I had come through the war physically unscathed. Soon after my return the Marine Corps had promoted me to the rank of Captain. Then, after a year of training new pilots to fly the H-46 in combat, I had made the transition from military helicopter pilot to civilian.

> The following releases from active duty are directed: Capt. Sturkey M.F., HMM-161: Report to HOR Plum Branch, S.C.
> -- (from Original Orders)

Some others never made it. Through a professional acquaintance in Columbia, South Carolina, I met "Robert" (not his real name). Robert had been a Grunt in Vietnam, and it will suffice to state that he had come face-to-face with the darker side of man in

Indochina. For ten years after his return to civilian life, Robert never could put the war behind him and move on. He gradually became obsessed with his wartime experience, and he talked of little else. Robert began drifting from job to job, and then he dropped out of the workforce altogether. After a few years his family left him, but he never expressed bitterness and never complained. Intelligent, yet humble and sincere, Robert relished doing favors for his friends. I once talked to him about my genealogical interests, and the next time I met him he had compiled reams of documentation from the State Archives for me. But Robert mentally crept back into the jungles of Vietnam. He seemed comfortable there. The last time we met we talked at length, and Robert softly told me about Lang Vei. He was *there*, he could *see* it. See, he whispered as he pointed, one of the dead men still sat upright, jaws stretched open and frozen in death. Robert smiled, and I understood. Go in peace, my friend.

In stark contrast to Robert, I knew two men who both should have been named "Benedict." Both lacked, or failed to heed, the inner corrective voice of conscience. These two gutless cowards sold their souls and betrayed the trust and responsibility that had been vested in them. As shameless advocates of deceit, they degenerated into nothing more than ethical prostitutes masquerading in business suits. These two moral weaklings trampled underfoot the principles of honor and integrity. I pity them! Two human lives wasted! A hundred of their shameful ilk could not collectively muster up the worth of an honest man like Robert.

Then I met zealous men like Patrick "Clebe" McClary. A native of South Carolina, Second Lieutenant McClary had commanded the "Texas Pete" Recon team in Vietnam. On March 3, 1968, he and his team had come under attack on Hill 146 down below Da Nang in what we called Arizona Territory. Enemy grenades had blown off his left arm and blasted out one of his eyes. He had severe wounds to all of his extremities. Still, Clebe recovered. Maimed in body, but not in spirit and mind, he returned to civilian life and became a personal inspiration to thousands.

I met quiet but rock-solid men like Sellmore Luckie years after the war. Sellmore had gone to Vietnam as a Lance Corporal in 1967. He got hit in the head by shrapnel at Con Thien, recovered in the hospital at Yokosuka, Japan, and returned to fight at Khe

Sanh and at the Citadel in Hue. Sellmore got hit again in the left arm and in both legs. After the war he became a devoted family man and settled in the community of Lugoff, South Carolina.

Sometimes I think of the fragile and fickle nature of life. My good friend and former MARCAD roommate, William T. "Tee" Holmes, had been shot down on his very first flight in Vietnam on December 8, 1965, but he survived the war. James P. "Crash-Kimo" Andrews, a gunship pilot in VMO-6, got shot down five times, a feat which earned him the infamous nickname, The Black Ace. He also lived through the war. On the other hand, Bonnie-Sue pilots Lynn M. LaPointe and Charles D. "Buzz" Joyner breezed through their tour in Vietnam and returned to the United States. Then, ironically, Lynn soon got killed in an automobile accident, and Buzz succumbed to the ravages of illness.

> The majority of Vietnam veterans are snooping and pooping in the mainstream of American life, lonely guerrillas in company coveralls or three-piece suits.
> -- (Mark Baker; in *NAM*)

My former squadronmate Arnie Reiner now refers to his 13 months in Vietnam as his "other life." I agree. When my thoughts drift back to Vietnam, I remember it like a vivid dream involving someone else, not something that really happened to me. Sometimes my mind wanders back to Marble Mountain, Dong Ha, or Razorback Valley. I see the landing zones and smell the JP-4, and I even wince a little now and then as I hear the gunners open up back in the cabin behind me. I can almost feel the fear and taste the excitement. It is easy for me to remember the details of some of my flights to Hill 55, Con Thien, Khe Sanh, and Laos as though they had taken place only yesterday. Could it really have happened over a quarter-century ago?

Realistically, when I think back on the war, I think of the exhaustion, the stench, the evil, and the fear. I would not want to do it all over again, contrary to the pseudo-romantic notions of those who were far from the flak. The greatest pacifists in the world are those who have seen combat.

Yet, for years I have harbored a secret about Vietnam. My secret is something akin to the *crazy uncle* that none of us are willing to acknowledge. In the English language there are no metaphors to explain the greatest truth of all. The war offered high-tech insanity and the very real possibility of instant death. I did not consider myself to be overly brave. Without question, there were scores of times when I was scared in Vietnam, probably more scared than those around me. No rational man welcomes war. No one wants to die. But now I confess the unthinkable. Deep down inside -- *I loved it!*

In confidence, most of the Marine helicopter pilots who flew in Vietnam agree with me. Looking back, they realize that they also loved the war. Nothing else will ever come close to the raw intensity, the terror, the terrible ecstasy of flying a Marine Corps helicopter down into a hot landing zone. Men pay to skydive, ride roller-coasters, or go to horror movies for the thrill of being scared. The greater the fear, the greater the thrill.

There is no greater horror, and no greater thrill, than combat flying. Dale L. "Papa-Bear" Tinsley has been able to put it behind him, and he suggests: "Let it go, just let it go." But some men became addicted to the thrill of it all. Some evolved into emotionless killer-pawns or mighty warrior-kings. In his literary tribute initially published in Great Britain under the title, *The Invisible Air Force: The True Story of the CIA's Secret Airline*, and later republished in the United States as *Air America*, author Christopher Robbins quotes Mike Barksdale, a former Marine Corps helicopter pilot who flew in Vietnam:

> People who are used to living for excitement, like flying in a war, have got nothing to live for when the war is over.

Flying a Marine Corps helicopter in combat is a game played for the highest stakes of all -- your life. Men love competitive games. And although the mechanics of flying are complex, the *clarity* of combat negates the need for bothersome rules. Life is simple. You crash, or you make it back to base. You get hit, or you come through unscathed. You live, or you die. You bask in the simple glory of being alive when so many others around you are dead. For the moment in the game of combat flying, you know that you are winning, and all competitive men love to win.

The game of war is dirty and ugly, yet somehow beautiful. At night, watching red tracers arcing up to kill me was often terrifying. Still, no other experience on earth could have created the raw power of those moments. Nothing else can compare to the spooky dancing shadows cast by a descending parachute flare at night. Flying during the day, my eyes saw many terrible things that would have been better left unseen. Conversely, I still recall the morning when I flew west along the Cam Lo River and first glimpsed the primitive splendor of the mist-shrouded Rockpile and Razorback. If Rudyard Kipling had used remote Razorback Valley as an inspiration for his mystic *KIM*, he would have been right: "Surely the Gods live here!"

But overshadowing all else, above all other emotions, I miss the trust and the camaraderie. Marines in Vietnam shared a common bond, a brotherhood, a proud tradition forged at Parris Island, San Diego, Pensacola, or Quantico. Our bond was honed and refined by years of tradition and tempered in the fire of combat. In the final analysis, we did not fight in Vietnam for the nebulous concept called freedom. We did not fight for the South Vietnamese people. Instead, we fought for the Marine Corps and for our friends.

> We fought for each other, or to uphold the honor of the Corps. That was what mattered.
> -- (Angus Deming; in *Newsweek Magazine*, August 7, 1995)

We placed an almost holy trust in our fellow Marines. We entrusted each other with our lives, our most precious possessions. I knew that my friends would risk their own lives to save mine. They might fail in the attempt, but I knew that they would try. No man can ask for more than that. All for one; one for all. Pride in our *unity* sustained us, and Don Steigman would later recall:

> There is no greater accomplishment of which I am prouder than [of] having flown helicopters through the hail of gunfire, rain, blood, and mud that was Vietnam. . . . The stovepipe jocks and fixed-wingers will never know what that was like: exhilaration, fear, pride, and camaraderie beyond belief. Pity the poor souls who never had the opportunity to excel for Corps and Country as we did!

Years after the war, Bonnie-Sue pilot George Diacont laughed and reminded me: "Remember, we almost got killed twice a month." George was right, but despite the danger and hardships it became a grand adventure, a utopian experience never again to be equalled. It can not be explained to someone who has not stepped through the magic looking-glass into the crucible of modern warfare. Vietnam evolved into a horrible nightmare, a trip into the bowels of a mechanized and insane neverland that stopped time. Yet, we were secretly drawn to it, attracted to it without reason or logic, galvanized by the *challenge*. Gerry Dooley came close to pinpointing the lunacy. He mused years later about flying a mission, getting shot up, making it back alive, and then joking about the whole affair. He had reveled in the unparalleled thrill of victory over death, he exclaimed with a throaty laugh.

Gerry was right, because I remember one of my two SAR North missions from Quang Tri. One of the Jolly Greens had gone down, and we got the frag. I strapped myself into the armored seat on the left, and we launched from the soccer field and headed north over the ocean in our Bonnie-Sue H-46. I scanned my map, and we planned to make our desperate dash past the North Vietnamese radar controlled antiaircraft batteries just south of Le Thuy.

The excitement became tangible, alive, almost unbearable. The earphones in my flight helmet blared out a constant cacophony from the UHF radio and our helicopter ICS. Four "Sandy" Skyraiders waited for us up ahead with hard bombs, napalm, and 20mm cannons, while "Red Crown" tracked us on radar and fed us a steady stream of vectors. A pair of F-4 Phantoms circled high overhead so that they could dive down on any MIGs that might try to shoot us down with Atoll air-to-air heat-seeking missiles. It seemed to me that 20 people were all trying to talk on Guard Channel at the same time. Most were too excited or too scared, and some talked too fast and several octaves too high. In the cabin behind our cockpit, our crew chief and gunner kept up a nervous chatter with us on the ICS. We turned to the west. My HAC radioed "Feet dry" as our helicopter raced over the coastline and flew into the hostile skies over North Vietnam.

Puffs of lethal gray flak blossomed in the sky around us. "SHOOT 'EM! SHOOT 'EM!" we screamed into the ICS, but our crew chief and gunner had already opened up with their fifties. I *prayed* for covering fire from Sandy. My eyeballs strained to locate each telltale twinkling of the AAA muzzle flashes down below. Hearts pounding, we forged ahead. I cheered as I watched the Skyraiders dive earthward to attack the enemy batteries. Strange, but the visual panorama seemed like a vivid movie to me, somehow unlike reality.

Fifty minutes later we made it back to Quang Tri alive. On rubbery legs we crawled out of our H-46, lapsed into inane boyish laughter, and collapsed onto the soft green grass. The thrill, the ecstasy, surpassed human description. We rolled in the grass, laughed, and congratulated ourselves on nothing more than our survival, our ultimate victory, our greatest joy of all. Life truly is an *incredible* gift.

Military rank, social status, and financial standing meant nothing. We were all equal, all brothers, all proud professionals, all Marines. We gloried in our tradition, in our brotherhood, and in our sacred trust that can be broken by nothing other than death itself. Together we shared the passion, the love, the horror, the incommunicable experience of Marines at war. We lived and flew in the presence of death, but we were never more alive.

All of us were young, with hearts and spirits touched by fire. Years later, our survival would become our victory.

King: But we . . . shall be remembered --
We few, we happy few, we band of brothers;
For he today that sheds his blood with me
Shall be my brother . . . .
-- (William Shakespeare; in *Henry V*)

Only guard yourself, and guard your soul carefully.
Lest you forget the things your eyes saw. And lest
these things depart your heart all the days of your
life. And you shall make them known to your
children, and to your children's children.

-- (DEUTERONOMY 4:9)

Glossary

<u>AAA</u>: Antiaircraft Artillery. Also called "Triple-A." Refers to either the weapon or the fire from such a weapon.

<u>ADF</u>: Automatic Direction Finder. Sometimes called a "Bird-Dog." An aircraft *homing* radio that provides direction to low frequency ground stations.

<u>AH-1J</u>: Bell AH-1J Huey Cobra. Generally called the "Cobra" or the "Snake." (Also called a "gunship," but should not be confused with the less-heavily armed UH-1E gunship.) An armed attack helicopter specifically designed for close air support for Marine Corps infantry.

<u>Air America</u>: The private air arm of the Central Intelligence Agency. Air America pilots flew their fixed-wing aircraft and helicopters throughout Indochina from the 1950s to the 1970s.

<u>Air Medal</u>: Awarded by the United States to recognize acts of heroism or meritorious service by pilots and aircrewmen.

<u>AK-47</u>: Russian- or Chinese-manufactured Avtomat Kalashnikova, Model 1947, 7.62mm assault rifle. The standard rifle used by the North Vietnamese Army.

<u>Arc-Light</u>: Also called "Rolling Thunder." Usually called "Heavy Artillery" in warnings to other pilots. A bombing mission by B-52 heavy bombers.

<u>Arizona Territory</u>: The name used by the Marines to describe the hostile region southwest of An Hoa near the Que Son Mountains. This enemy-infested region drew its nickname from the late 1800s badlands of the American West.

<u>ARVN</u>: Spoken: "rr-vinn." Army of the Republic of Vietnam. The army of South Vietnam. Singular or plural, can indicate a military unit, or a single South Vietnamese soldier.

<u>Atoll</u>: Soviet-built air-to-air missile. An infrared homing missile used by North Vietnamese Air Force pilots.

ATS: Automatic Trim System.

Autorotation: A rapid descending glide without engine power in a helicopter. In cruising flight in a helicopter, a loss of engine power requires *immediate* action by the pilot. The collective pitch lever, controlling the aerodynamic angle-of-attack of the rotor blades, must be *bottomed* immediately, and the helicopter will begin a *very rapid descent*. The upward flow of air through the rotor system will then *power* the rotor system and keep the rotor RPM above the minimum required for gliding descending flight. Without adequate rotor RPM, the rotor blades would *cone*, and the helicopter would take on the aerodynamic characteristics of a falling manhole cover.

A-1: Douglas A-1 Skyraider. A Korean War-vintage land or carrier based ground-attack aircraft. Its reciprocating engine gives it excellent loiter time. Usually called "Sandy" because of its radio call-sign.

A-4: Douglas A-4 Skyhawk. A light ground-attack jet aircraft used as a tactical bomber, or to support ground troops.

A-6: Grumman A-6 Intruder. A twin-jet attack bomber designed for low altitude bombing missions day or night, and in inclement weather.

A-7: Vought A-7 Corsair. A carrier based jet attack aircraft.

Bangalore Torpedo: An elongated explosive charge designed to blast a footpath through enemy concertina and wire defenses.

BLT: Battalion Landing Team.

Bullet Bouncer: A nickname for the "Pilot's Armored Chest Protector." Sometimes called a "Chicken-Plate." The Bullet Bouncer is a thick plate of steel alloy body-armor worn in a cloth harness over a helicopter pilot's chest and abdomen. It will deflect frontal small arms fire and shrapnel. The Bullet Bouncer is to a helicopter pilot what the ancient Breast Plate was to a medieval knight.

B-52: Boeing B-52 Stratofortress. An eight-engine heavy jet aircraft designed as a nuclear bomber, but used as a tactical conventional bomber in Vietnam.

CIA: Central Intelligence Agency.

CIDG: Civilian Irregular Defense Group. A South Vietnamese paramilitary force of dubious fighting ability and inclination. Often called "Ruff-Puffs."

Claymore: A United States-built directional and electrically detonated mine.

Collective Pitch: Usually called "the collective" or simply "collective." Refers to the control arm, held in a helicopter pilot's *left* hand, that *simultaneously* changes the pitch -- the aerodynamic angle-of-attack -- on *all of the rotor blades* on a helicopter. An increase in "collective" creates more vertical lift, but it requires more engine power because of the increased aerodynamic drag on the rotors. Basically, pulling the "collective" up increases aerodynamic lift and makes the helicopter rise, or climb. Lowering the "collective" decreases aerodynamic lift and makes the helicopter descend.

Concertina: Loose vertical coils of barbed wire. Often called "tanglefoot." Used as a barrier against infantry attacks.

CONUS: Spoken: "co-nuss." Continental United States.

C-Rations: Factory-manufactured military pre-packaged meals.

Cyclic Pitch: Usually called "the cyclic" or simply "cyclic." Also refers to the control stick, held in a helicopter pilot's *right* hand. Cyclic Pitch is *independent* of Collective Pitch. By moving the Cyclic, a pilot tilts the vertical axis of the helicopter rotor system. The helicopter then moves in the direction that the top of the vertical axis is pointed, because the aerodynamic lift generated by the rotor blades *pulls* the helicopter upward along the vertical axis of the rotor system. Pilots change the *direction* of movement of the helicopter with the Cyclic: forward, backward, left, or right.

C-47: Douglas C-47 Skytrain. A World War II-vintage twin-engine cargo aircraft. When fitted with three General Electric SUU-11 7.62mm miniguns that can fire an incredible 6000 rounds per minute, the ungainly C-47 became "Spooky" or the "Magic Dragon." It provided fire support for ground troops.

C-130: Lockheed C-130 Hercules. A four engine turboprop transport aircraft, used as a cargo hauler or as an aerial tanker.

Deck: Navy and Marine Corps lingo for the *floor* or the *ground.*

Dixie Station: The name given to the location of United States aircraft carrier operations off the coast of South Vietnam.

DME: Distance Measuring Equipment. An integral part of an aircraft's TACAN navigation radio transmitter-receiver. DME continually digitally displays the distance, in nautical miles, from the aircraft to the ground station to which the pilots tune the TACAN.

DMZ: Demilitarized Zone.

FAC: Spoken: "fack." Forward Air Controller.

Fast-Mover: A slang term used by helicopter pilots and infantry-men to refer to a speeding fixed-wing jet aircraft.

Feet Dry: A verbal radio report: "Feet Dry." It is used by Marine Corps and Navy fixed-wing aircraft and helicopters. All pilots radio "Feet Dry" to their aircraft carrier (or to other aircraft, or to controlling ground stations) as they cross over the seacoast and head inland toward their target or landing area. This radio report means that the pilot is no longer flying over the ocean; he is flying over land (his feet are now *dry*) and continuing to fly farther inland.

Feet Wet: A verbal radio report: "Feet Wet." (Also see *Feet Dry*, above.) Marine Corps and Navy pilots radio "Feet Wet" as they cross over the seacoast and head out to sea toward their aircraft carrier. This report means that the pilot is now over the ocean (his feet are now *wet*) and continuing to fly out to sea.

Frag: The common contraction for "Fragmentary Order." A flight assignment.

F-4: McDonnell Douglas F-4 Phantom. A twin-jet fighter and interceptor, also used as a ground-attack aircraft by the Marines, the Navy, and the Air Force.

F-8: Chance Vought F-8 Crusader. A jet fighter and interceptor flown by the Marines and the Navy. Mainly used in Vietnam as a dive bomber.

GCA: Ground Controlled Approach. A ground-based radar system that allows a controller to "talk" a pilot down an electronic glideslope in inclement weather.

Ground Effect: An aerodynamic condition that gives a helicopter rotor system more *lift* when hovering very close to the ground. Ground Effect is extremely valuable to pilots. Hovering *just above the ground*, (roughly within a half-rotor-system-diameter distance of the ground) the spinning rotor system compresses the air between the rotors and the ground. This compressed air acts as a buoyant cushion, and *less engine power is needed* to turn the rotor system. A helicopter Hovering In Ground Effect (HIGE) can lift much more weight than a helicopter Hovering

Out of Ground Effect (HOGE).

Grunt: An infantryman.

Guard Channel: The military emergency radio frequency, 243.0 megacycles. All military aircraft automatically *receive* or *monitor* Guard Channel at all times. In an emergency a pilot can manually select Guard Channel and *transmit* on "Guard." The distress message will be heard by all military aircraft within radio range, regardless of the UHF radio frequency to which they are tuned.

Gunship: A heavily armed version of the Bell UH-1E "Huey." Also, the standard AH-1J "Cobra" armed helicopter. These helicopter gunships are designed to be used as offensive weapons against enemy ground troops.

Helicopter Valley: The Song Ngan River Valley in northwest Quang Tri Province.

Hill Fights, The: The common term for the battles just north of Khe Sanh for control of Hill 861, Hill 881 North, and Hill 881 South in April and May of 1967.

H-1: Bell UH-1E "Huey." A single-turbine light helicopter used by the Marines for both observation and ground-attack roles.

H-34: Sikorsky UH-34D Sea Horse. Often called the "Dog." The first Marine Corps helicopter used in Vietnam. It is powered by a radial Wright engine.

H-37: Originally known as the HR2S. Entered Marine Corps service as the Sikorsky CH-37 Mohave. Called the "Deuce" because of the engine pods mounted on each side of the fuselage (the metal cowling around the engine air intakes was invariably painted to make the engine pods look like they had a set of giant eyeballs). The first Marine Corps *heavy* helicopter.

H-46: Boeing Vertol CH-46 Sea Knight. Often called the "Frog" or the "Flying Frog" because of its appearance when viewed from the front. A twin-turbine tandem-rotor helicopter used to carry troops or cargo.

H-53: Sikorsky CH-53 Sea Stallion. A twin-turbine heavy transport helicopter, the largest helicopter used by the Marine Corps.

HAC: Spoken: "hack." Helicopter Aircraft Commander.

Hatch: Navy and Marine Corps lingo for a *door* or a *window*.

HMH-(xxx): Marine Corps heavy helicopter squadron.

HMM-(xxx): Marine Corps medium helicopter squadron.

Hootch: Slang military terminology for a *thatched hut*, a *primitive house*.

ICS: Internal Communications System. Called "Intercom System" by civilians. In Marine Corps fixed-wing aircraft and helicopters, all members of the crew are electrically connected by the ICS. By talking into the microphones built into their flight helmets and listening to the built-in earphones, all members of the crew can communicate.

IFF: Identification, Friend or Foe. A military radar transponder for helicopters and fixed-wing aircraft. The IFF identifies aircraft as hostile, or friendly.

IFR: Instrument Flight Rules. Also refers to inclement weather to the extent that a pilot must fly under Instrument Flight Rules.

Indian Country: Enemy territory. An area where an ambush or attack is likely.

JP-4: Jet fuel. Essentially kerosene, JP-4 is the fuel used by all jet aircraft and turbine powered helicopters.

Ka-25: Ka-25 Hormone. Soviet-built light helicopter flown by the North Vietnamese Air Force.

KIA: Killed-in-action. A servicemen killed by hostile forces in wartime.

Knots: The speed of aircraft or ships, expressed in nautical miles per hour.

Laterite: A powdery, red, sandy soil often found in many areas on the coastal plain in Vietnam.

Leatherneck Square: The common name used to describe a bloody killing ground in northern Quang Tri Province. Roughly the shape of a square, it was bounded by Dong Ha on the southeast, Gio Linh on the northeast, Con Thien on the northwest, and Cam Lo on the southwest.

LZ: A helicopter *Landing Zone*.

MARCAD: Spoken: "marr-cadd." Marine Aviation Cadet.

Marston-matting: Interlocking metal panels designed to be laid on the ground and used as a tactical airfield runway or aircraft parking area.

Meatball: Also called "The Meatball" or simply "The Ball." The Meatball is the bright orange "ball" visible on a gyrostabilized fresnal lens, the optical landing system used by fixed-wing pilots, day or night, to land on an aircraft carrier. To land, a pilot rolls into the *groove* behind the ship and lines up on the angled deck. When he vertically nears the invisible glideslope, the Meatball becomes visible on the fresnal lens on the edge of the flight deck. If the Meatball is centered on the lens, the pilot knows that his aircraft is on the glideslope. If the Meatball is high on the lens, the pilot knows that his aircraft is above the glideslope. If the Meatball is low, the aircraft is low.

Medevac: A contraction for *Medical Evacuation*. The aerial transportation of a sick or wounded military man. The term is also used to refer to the man who is being evacuated, or to the aircraft used for the evacuation flight.

MIA: Missing-in-action. A serviceman whose location is unknown after a ground battle or an aerial mission in wartime.

MIG: Spoken: "migg." The common name given to the series of Soviet-built Mikoyan/Gurevich jet fighter aircraft.

Milk Run: A non-hazardous flight. A flight with no anticipated problems.

Mi-4: Mi-4 Hound. Soviet-built medium helicopter flown by the North Vietnamese Air Force.

Mi-6: Mi-6 Hook. A giant Soviet-built helicopter capable of carrying 65 combat equipped troops.

Montagnard: A Stone-age Vietnamese mountain tribesman.

MPC: Military Payment Certificate. Often called "funny-money."

Mutter Ridge: The common name used by the Marines to refer to the Nui Cay Tri Ridge in northern Quang Tri Province.

M-14: United States-built 7.62mm rifle. The Marines used the M-14 rifle until 1968, when they replaced it with the newer and lighter M-16 rifle.

M-16: United States-built .223 caliber lightweight rifle used by the Marine Corps since 1968.

M-60: United States-built 7.62mm machinegun used by Marine Corps infantry units. Also can be mounted in a fixed gunmount in helicopters.

M-79: United States-built 40mm grenade launcher. It looks like a huge caliber sawed-off shotgun. The M-79 replaced the outdated rifle grenade.

NATOPS: Spoken: "naa-tops." Naval Air Training and Operating Procedures. There is a NATOPS manual, a giant operating instructions manual, for each Navy and Marine Corps aircraft.

NLF: National Liberation Front.

No Joy: A pilot's in-flight radio report: "No Joy." It means that the pilot *can not see* another aircraft that he is looking for. Also used by a pilot to report that he *can not hear* radio transmissions from another aircraft or ground station.

Nung: A Chinese mercenary. In Vietnam, Nungs were paid by the American CIA.

NVA: North Vietnamese Army. Can be either singular or plural. Indicates either a North Vietnamese Army unit, or a single North Vietnamese soldier.

O-1: Cessna O-1. A light observation aircraft. Also called a "Bird Dog."

Pri-Fly: The fixed-wing or helicopter flight operations center on an aircraft carrier. Pri-Fly is a glass-enclosed communications and control center located on the inboard side of the "island" superstructure of the ship, overlooking the flight deck. Pri-Fly is roughly 40 feet above the deck. It is the home of the "Air-Boss" during launch or recovery flight operations.

PT-76: Soviet-built amphibious tank, originally manufactured in the Kirov factory in Leningrad, Russia. The PT-76 was first used in South Vietnam during the North Vietnamese attack against the Lang Vei outpost in February 1968.

Punji Stake: A hardened strip of wood or bamboo, embedded vertically in the ground and sharpened at the top. Punji Stakes are generally camouflaged and placed along foot-trails or likely avenues of attack. They are intended to impale the foot or torso of the unwary person who steps or falls on them.

Razorback, The: A three mile long, 1000 foot high, ridge of volcanic rock north of the Cam Lo River. The Razorback is honeycombed with caves, and it is a natural defensive fortress.

Recon: Marine Force Reconnaissance. Also used to refer to an individual member of Marine Force Reconnaissance, a "Recon."

REMF: Spoken: "ree-miff." An unofficial acronym for "Rear-Echelon-Mother-Fu[remainder of expletive deleted]." A derogatory and contemptuous term used by combat troops and airmen to describe all military personnel in safe locations far from the fighting in wartime, especially those in administrative roles.

RIO: Spoken: "ree-oh." Radar Intercept Officer.

Rockpile, The: A strategic 700 foot high granite outcropping in Quang Tri Province at map coordinates XD-979558.

R & R: Military acronym for "Rest and Relaxation," a vacation from the war.

Rubber Lady: Inflatable air mattress.

SAM: Spoken: "samm." Surface-to-air missile.

SAR: Spoken: "sarr." Search and Rescue. A mission to search for, locate, and rescue a downed airman.

SAR North: A search and rescue mission into North Vietnam.

SAS: Spoken: "sass." Stability Argumentation System.

Slick: A helicopter that has been stripped of all nonessential weight so that it can lift heavier cargo loads, either internally or on an external cargo hook.

SOG: Spoken: "sogg." Studies and Observation Group. A military task force that was assigned clandestine missions in Laos, Cambodia, and North Vietnam.

Sparrowhawk: A small reaction force of Marine infantrymen. Also refers to the helicopters transporting the reaction force.

Spatial Disorientation: Vertigo. A condition caused when a pilot, because of poor visibility, can not see the surface of the earth or sea and becomes disoriented because of vestibular illusions of the inner ear.

Strike: An assault involving a helicopter landing and the discharge of Marine infantrymen for the purpose of attacking the enemy.

S-1: Military Administration.

S-2: Military Intelligence.

S-3: Military Operations.

S-4: Military Logistics and Supply.

TACAN: Spoken: "tack-ann." Tactical Air Navigation. An aircraft UHF navigation receiver-transmitter that displays both distance (in nautical miles) and bearing to a given ground station. The primary air navigation radio.

TAFDS: Spoken: "taff-dass." Tactical Airfield Fuel Dispensing System. Used by the Marine Corps in Vietnam and commonly called the "fuel pits."

TAOR: Tactical Area of Responsibility.

Translational Lift: The increased lifting power available as a helicopter transitions from hovering flight to forward flight. A hovering helicopter is held aloft by the *lift* generated by its spinning rotor system. The rotor blades *bite* into the air, forcing the air downward and pulling the helicopter upward. Yet, without forward airspeed, a low-pressure area is created above the spinning rotors (the rotors are *sucking* the air downward), and the rotor blades can not get a solid *bite* of air. However, as the helicopter laterally *accelerates forward through the air*, the low pressure area is eliminated because the helicopter is continually moving into undisturbed air. This allows the rotors to get a solid *bite* of undisturbed air, and lifting power is increased. This increased lifting power is called Translational Lift.

Triple-H Condition: High, Hot, and Heavy. *High* altitude equates to less dense air, making a helicopter rotor system less efficient. *Hot* ambient air temperature makes a turbine engine less efficient. *Heavy* cargo loads demand more engine power. In a Triple-H (high, hot, and heavy) situation, helicopter pilots must exercise extreme caution and adhere to strict weight, temperature, and altitude limitations. Otherwise, the unwary pilot may find that he has simultaneously run out of airspeed, altitude, engine power, and rotor RPM.

Turns: Slang expression for the *rotor RPM* of a helicopter.

T-28: North American T-28 Trojan. A high-performance fixed-wing training aircraft used by Marine Corps and Navy pilots for aerial gunnery and aircraft carrier landing qualification prior to transitioning into helicopter training.

UHF: Ultra High Frequency. A long distance, line-of-sight, radio frequency used for both communication and navigation radios in military aircraft.

VFR: Visual Flight Rules. Also refers to clear visibility conditions that allow a pilot to fly under Visual Flight Rules.

Viet Cong: An unofficial contraction derived from "Vietnamese Communist." Commonly used to identify military *guerrillas* in South Vietnam, as opposed to invading soldiers of the North Vietnamese Army. Either singular or plural; can refer to a military unit, or to a single guerrilla fighter. Often verbally shortened to "VC" and sometimes spoken as "Victor Charlie" or simply "Charlie."

Viet Minh: The common contraction for "Vietnam Doc Lap Nong Minh Hoi," the communist coalition of Vietnamese who fought the Japanese in World War II. They later fought the French in the late 1940s and early 1950s.

VMA-(xxx): Marine Corps fixed-wing attack squadron.

VMF-(xxx): Marine Corps fixed-wing fighter squadron.

VMO-(xxx): Marine Corps observation squadron.

Wave Off: An aborted landing. Can be used as a noun or a verb.

WIA: Wounded-in-action.

Willie-Pete: White phosphorus.

Yankee Station: The name given to the location of United States aircraft carrier operations off the coast of North Vietnam.

115/145: High octane aviation fuel used by aircraft and helicopters which have reciprocating engines.

Bibliography

BOOKS:

Baker, Mark. <u>NAM</u>. New York, NY: Berkley Books, 1981.

Bell, H. Lee. <u>1369</u>. Little Rock, AR: Halo Press, 1992.

Bowman, John S. <u>The Vietnam War: An Almanac</u>. New York, NY: Random House, 1985.

Camp, R. D. <u>LIMA-6</u>. New York, NY: Berkley Books, 1985.

Caputo, Philip. <u>A Rumor of War</u>. New York, NY: Ballentine Books, 1977.

Cash, John A., et al. <u>Seven Firefights in Vietnam</u>. New York, NY: Bantam Books, 1988.

Chinnery, Philip D. <u>Life on the Line</u>. New York, NY: St. Martin's Press, 1988.

Dengler, Dieter. <u>Escape from Laos</u>. New York, NY: Kensington Publishing Co., 1979.

Denton, Jeremiah A. Jr. <u>When Hell Was in Session</u>. Clover, SC: Commission Press, 1976.

Dougan, Clark, et al. <u>Nineteen Sixty-Eight</u>. Boston, MA: Boston Publishing Co., 1983.

Doyle, Edward, et al. <u>Setting the Stage</u>. Boston, MA: Boston Publishing Co., 1981.

Doyle, Edward, et al. <u>Passing the Torch</u>. Boston, MA: Boston Publishing Co., 1981.

Doyle, Edward, et al. <u>America Takes Over</u>. Boston, MA: Boston Publishing Co., 1982.

Doyle, Edward. <u>The Aftermath</u>. Boston, MA: Boston Publishing Co., 1985.

Eschmann, Karl J. <u>Linebacker: The Untold Story of the Air Raids over North Vietnam</u>. New York, NY: Ballentine Books, 1989.

Fails, William R. <u>Marines and Helicopters: 1962-1973</u>. Washington, D.C.: U.S. Marine Corps, 1978.

Fall, Bernard B. Street Without Joy. Harrisburg, PA: The Telegraph Press, 1964.

Fall, Bernard B. Last Reflections on a War. Garden City, NY: Doubleday & Company, 1967.

Fremantle, Anne. Mao Tse-tung: An Anthology of His Writings. New York, NY: Mentor, 1962.

Gettleman, Marvin E. Vietnam: History, Documents, and Opinions on a Major World Crisis. New York, NY: Fawcett World Library, 1963.

Hammel, Eric. The Assault on Khe Sanh: An Oral History. New York, NY: Warner Books, 1989.

Hammel, Eric. The Siege of Khe Sanh: An Oral History. New York, NY: Warner Books, 1989.

Harry, Richard T. An Alternative to "Peace with Honor". Washington, D.C.: U.S. Marine Corps, 1976.

Herr, Michael. Dispatches. New York, NY: Avon/Discus, 1980.

Lake, Bruce R. 1500 Feet Over Vietnam. Haverhill, NH: Almine Library, 1990.

Lanning, Michael Lee, et al. Inside Force Recon: Recon Marines in Vietnam. New York, NY: Ballentine Books, 1989.

Lanning, Michael Lee, et al. Inside the VC and the NVA: The Real Story of North Vietnam's Armed Forces. New York, NY: Ivy Books, 1992.

Lowry, Timothy S. And Brave Men, Too. New York, NY: Berkley Books, 1985.

Lowry, Timothy S. Valor. New York, NY: Berkley Books, 1989.

McClary, Clebe. Living Proof. Atlanta, GA: Cross Roads Books, 1978.

McConnell, Malcolm. Inside Hanoi's Secret Archives: Solving the MIA Mystery. New York, NY: Simon & Schuster, 1995.

McDonald, Peter. Giap. New York, NY: W.W. Norton & Co., 1993.

Melton, William R., et al. U.S. Marines in Vietnam: Vietnamization and Redeployment, 1970-1971. Washington, D.C.: U.S. Marine Corps, 1986.

Morocco, John, et al. Thunder from Above: Air War, 1941-1968. Boston, MA: Boston Publishing Co., 1984.

Parker, Gary W. A History of Marine Medium Helicopter Squadron 161. Washington, D.C.: U.S. Marine Corps, 1978.

Pearson, Willard. The War in the Northern Provinces, 1966-1968. Washington, D.C.: U.S. Army, 1991.

Pisor, Robert. The End of the Line: The Siege of Khe Sanh. New York, NY: W.W. Norton & Company, 1982.

Puller, Lewis B. Jr. Fortunate Son. New York, NY: Grove Press, 1991.

Robbins, Christopher. Air America. New York, NY: Avon Books, 1979.

Safer, Morley. Flashbacks: On Returning to Vietnam. New York, NY: St. Martin's Paperbacks, 1990.

Schell, Jonathan. The Real War. New York, NY: Pantheon Books, 1988.

Sterling, Robert J. Loud & Clear. New York, NY: Dell, 1970.

Shore, Moyers S. II. The Battle for Khe Sanh. Washington, D.C.: U.S. Marine Corps, 1977.

Shulimson, Jack. U.S. Marines in Vietnam: An Expanding War, 1966. Washington, D.C.: U.S. Marine Corps, 1982.

Simmons, Edwin H., et al. The Marines in Vietnam: 1954-1973, An Anthology & Annotated Bibliography. Washington, D.C.: U.S. Marine Corps, 1985.

Stockwell, David B. Tanks in the Wire!. New York, NY: Jove Books, 1989.

Telfer, Gary L., et al. U.S. Marines in Vietnam: Fighting the North Vietnamese, 1967. Washington, D.C.: U.S. Marine Corps, 1984.

Weiss, Stephen, et al. A War Remembered. Boston, MA: Boston Publishing Co., 1986.

West, Francis J. Jr. Small Unit Action in Vietnam: Summer, 1966. Washington, D.C.: U.S. Marine Corps, 1977.

Winter, Ronald. Masters of the Art. New York, NY: Carlton Press, 1989.

N.A. Guidebook for Marines. Washington, D.C.: Leatherneck Assn., 1962.

N.A. The Flight Jacket. Montgomery, AL: Paragon Press, 1963.

NEWSPAPER ARTICLES:

Bledsoe, Debra-Lynn. "Welcome Home". The State (Columbia, SC), Nov. 9, 1986. pp. 1A & 13-14A.

Brinkley-Rogers, Paul. "Vietnam Goes to War to Win U.S. Support". The State (Columbia, SC), Apr. 14, 1991, pp. 1D & 6D.

Brinkley-Rogers, Paul. "Breathing new life into old Battlefield". The State (Columbia, SC), Apr. 14, 1991, pp. 1D & 6D.

Butts, Jack, et al. "10 Hours of Fierce Battle Makes for a Long Night". Pacific Stars & Stripes, Unk, Unk.

Hopkins, Art. "Chopper Crash Kills Three". Daily News (Jacksonville, NC), Dec. 2, 1967, pp. 1 & 8.

McAllister, J. F. "Fearless Flying Skill Saves Marines from Mortar Attack". Sea Tiger (USMC publication in Republic of Vietnam), Apr. 12, 1967, p. 6.

Trainor, Bernard E. "Troop's Love Makes the Man in Combat". Wilmington Morning Star (Wilmington, NC), Mar. 6, 1991, p. 1A.

Unk. (multiple articles). The Washington Post (Washington, D.C.), May 3, 6, 7, 9, & 10, 1967, N.A.

Unk. "Wounded Marines Lifted from Jungle". Pacific Stars & Stripes, Jul. 27, 1966, pp. 1 & 24.

Unk. (multiple articles). The State (Columbia, SC), Numerous dates from Jul. 1, 1966, through Jan. 28, 1967, N.A.

Unk. (multiple articles). The State (Columbia, SC), Jul. 11-12, 1995, N.A.

VIDEO & AUDIO RECORDINGS:

Diacont, George H. Jr. (Untitled videotape depicting four helicopter crashes in the Song Ngan Valley). Quang Tri Province, Republic of Vietnam, Jul. 15, 1966.

Roman, Joseph G. (Untitled videotape depicting a helicopter crash in the ocean near Marble Mountain). Quang Nam Province, Republic of Vietnam, Sept. 14, 1966.

Roman, Joseph G., and Campbell, Harold J. Jr., et al. U.S. Marine Corps Oral History Tape No. 364. Da Nang, Republic of Vietnam, Jan. 27, 1967.

SPECIAL PUBLICATIONS:

Ellis, F. B. Aircraft Accident Report 5-67A. Republic of Vietnam: U.S. Marine Corps, 1967.

Roman, Joseph G. <u>Commendations</u> (for PFC J. Srsen, Cpl. R. E. Jones, and HM3 Cannon). Republic of Vietnam: U.S. Marine Corps, 1967.

N.A. <u>Command Chronologies</u> (1st MAW, MAG-16, MAG-36, HMM-363, HMM-364, HMM-164, HMM-163, HMM-362, HMM-263, HMM-161, HMM-265, VMO-2, HMM-262, VMO-6, 2nd Battalion/4th Marines, First Force Recon, Third Force Recon). Republic of Vietnam: U.S. Marine Corps, 1966-1968.

N.A. <u>After Action Reports</u> (same military units as above). Republic of Vietnam: U.S. Marine Corps, 1966-1968.

N.A. <u>Unit Diary, HMM-265</u>. Republic of Vietnam: Jul. and Aug. 1966.

N.A. <u>Radio Frequency Card, 1st MAW</u>. Republic of Vietnam: U.S. Marine Corps, 1967.

N.A. <u>Casualty Cards</u> (Paul T. Looney, William Emerson, Robert R. Telfer, Dean W. Reiter, Herbert S. Murff, Frederick C. Fracker, Lynn M. LaPointe, Marion F. Sturkey, Gary A. Lucus, Stephen W. Pless, Augusto M. Xavier, Howard E. Morse, Jack E. Muisener, John S. Oldham, Ronald E. Pfeifer, John A. Prombo, Phillip A. Ducat, Thomas A. Gopp, William T. Hale, John A. House, Ronald L. Belknap, James J. Carroll, Lonnie W. Clark, Charlie L. Burney, Ronald D. Bennett, Gary W. Hoglund, John T. Corle, Francis E. Visconti, and Bruno A. Hochmuth). Washington, D.C.: U.S. Marine Corps, (various dates).

N.A. <u>NATOPS Flight Manual, CH-46A & CH-46D Helicopters</u>. Washington, D.C.: Dept. of the Navy, 1966.

N.A. <u>NATOPS Flight Manual, UH-34D, G, & J Helicopters</u>. Washington, D.C.: Dept. of the Navy, 1965.

N.A. <u>NATOPS Checklist, CH-46D/UH-46D Helicopter</u>. Washington, D.C.: Dept. of the Navy, 1966.

N.A. <u>Aviator's Flight Log Book</u> (for Richard Harper, William Holmes, Duane Jensen, Otto Fritz, Marion Sturkey, Arnie Reiner, Gerry Dooley, Jack Exum, John Maxwell, Bob Mills, and Ray Smith). Republic of Vietnam: U.S. Marine Corps, 1966 & 1967.

N.A. <u>Vietnam, 1:50,000 Series Maps</u>. Washington, D.C.: Army Map Service, courtesy of Library of Congress, 1960-1966.

Unk. <u>Vietnam KIAs & MIAs</u>. Humble, TX: TME Publishing, 1988.

MAGAZINE ARTICLES:

Althoff, David L. "Helicopter Operations at Khe Sanh". <u>Marine Corps Gazette</u>, May 1969, pp. 47-49.

Borchgrave, Arnaud. "The Battle for Hill 400". <u>Newsweek</u>, Oct. 10, 1966, pp. 46-48.

Burrows, Larry. (Untitled article and photographs of casualties on Mutter Ridge). <u>Life</u>, Dec. 23, 1966, pp. 152-153.

Burrows, Larry. (Untitled article and photograph of casualty on Mutter Ridge). <u>Life</u>, Oct. 28, 1966, p. 39.

Burrows, Larry. "One Ride with Yankee Papa 13". <u>Life</u>, Apr. 16, 1965, pp. 24-unk.

Caulfield, M. P. "India Six". <u>Marine Corps Gazette</u>, Jul, 1969, pp. 27-31.

Cloud, Stanley W. "Still a Killing Field". <u>Time</u>, Apr. 30, 1990, pp. 26-28.

Deming, Angus. "The Remembered War". <u>Newsweek</u>, Aug. 7, 1995, p. 68.

Greenberg, Lawrence M. "'Spooky': Dragon in the Sky". <u>Vietnam</u>, Apr. 1990, pp. 22-28.

Greenberg, Lawrence M. "Arsenal". <u>Vietnam</u>, Feb. 1990, pp. 16 & 58-60.

Guttman, Jon. "Book Reviews". <u>Vietnam</u>, Apr. 1990, pp. 54-55.

Guttman, Jon. "Arsenal". <u>Vietnam</u>, Dec. 1990, p. 8.

Hammond, J. W. Jr. "Combat Journal". <u>Marine Corps Gazette</u>, Jul. 1968, pp. 20-29.

Hammond, J. W. Jr. "Combat Journal". <u>Marine Corps Gazette</u>, Aug. 1968, pp. 46-51.

Hemmingway, Al. "A Place of Angels". <u>Vietnam</u>, Feb. 1991, pp. 27-32.

Hemmingway, Albert. "Fighting Forces". <u>Vietnam</u>, Dec. 1992, pp. 10-20.

Hemmingway, Albert. "Fighting forces". <u>Vietnam</u>. Oct. 1990, pp. 12 & 64.

Hemmingway, Albert. "Seventy-Seven Days in Hell". <u>Vietnam</u>, June 1990, pp. 30-37.

Isby, David C. "Arsenal". <u>Vietnam</u>, Dec. 1989, pp. 10-14.

Kirkpatrick, Charles E. "Terrible Swift Sword". Vietnam, Apr. 1991, pp. 19-24.

Leroy, Catherine. (Untitled article and photograph of a casualty on Hill 881 North). Life, May 19, 1967, p. 42.

Luehrs, R. E. "Marine Medical Evacuations". Marine Corps Gazette, May 1969, pp. 56-57.

McConnell, Malcolm. "Forever Proud". Reader's Digest, Nov. 1988, pp. 65-70.

Perry, Merton. "The Dusty Agony of Khe Sanh". Newsweek, Mar. 18, 1968, pp. 28-unk.

Rider, J. W. "Helicopters in Vietnam: Use and Misuse". Marine Corps Gazette, Oct. 1967, pp. 30-32.

Shulimson, Jack, et al. "First In, First Out". Marine Corps Gazette, Jan. 1984, pp. 36-46.

Sider, Don. "Khe Sanh: Ready to Fight". Time, Feb. 16, 1968, pp. 38-39.

Steele, Richard. "Siege at Con Thien". Newsweek, Oct. 9, 1967, pp. 49-50.

Stewart, William. "Vietnam; A War on Poverty". Time, Apr. 30, 1990, pp. 22-25.

Stokes, Robert. "A Day at Dong Ha". Newsweek, Mar. 25, 1968, pp. 40-41.

Stokes, Robert. "Dark Clouds". Newsweek, Mar 4, 1968, pp. 29-unk.

Truby, David J. "Arsenal". Vietnam, Aug. 1989, pp. 8 & 64-66.

Wharton, Donald. "Invasion Repelled". Vietnam, Dec. 1989, pp. 38-44.

Witteman, Paul A. "Vietnam 15 Years Later". Time, Apr. 30, 1990, pp. 18-21.

Unk. "Americans at War". Newsweek, Aug. 1, 1966, pp. 28-33.

Unk. "The Roughest Yet". Newsweek, Aug. 8, 1966, p. 30.

Unk. "Slogging It Out". Newsweek, Aug. 15, 1966, pp. 34-35.

Unk. "In Repose". Newsweek, Aug. 15, 1966, pp. 35-36.

Unk. "'Great to be Alive'". Newsweek, Sept. 26, 1966, p. 65.

Unk. "Where's Charlie". Newsweek, Oct. 17, 1966, p. 40.

Unk. "The Semifinals". Newsweek, Oct. 31, 1966, p. 48.

Unk. "Hugging The Belt". Newsweek, Nov. 7, 1966, p. 49.

Unk. "Transition". Newsweek, Nov. 21, 1966, p. 86.

Unk. "Death of a Scholar". Newsweek, Mar. 6, 1967, p. 25.

Unk. "Credibility Gap". Newsweek, Mar. 13, 1967, p. 50.

Unk. "Bombs and Mortars". Newsweek, Mar. 20, 1967, p. 40.

Unk. "Casualty Figures". Newsweek, Mar. 20, 1967, p. 41.

Unk. "The Price of War: A Missing Limb, An Aching Heart". Newsweek, Jul. 10, 1967, pp. 24-25.

Unk. "Ambush at Con Thien". Newsweek, Jul. 17, 1967, p. 45.

Unk. "The Attack on Da Nang". Newsweek, Jul. 24, 1967, p. 43.

Unk. "When They Call, Go!". Newsweek, Aug. 7, 1967, p. 37.

Unk. "Turning the Tables". Newsweek, Aug. 21, 1967, pp. 40-41.

Unk. "Barring the Way: McNamara's Line". Newsweek, Sept 18, 1967, p. 29.

Unk. "Waiting: Khe Sanh and Saigon". Newsweek, Mar. 11, 1968, p. 58.

Unk. "After Khe Sanh". Newsweek, Apr. 29, 1968, p. 36.

Unk. "Division from the North". Time, Jul. 29, 1966, p. 21.

Unk. "Buildup on the Border". Time, Sept. 30, 1966, p. 29.

Unk. "The Rockpile". Time, Oct. 7, 1966, pp. 40-41.

Unk. "Waiting for the Bugles". Time, Oct. 21, 1966, p. 46.

Unk. "On the Street Without Joy". Time, Mar. 3, 1967, p. 31.

Unk. "The Hero". Time, Mar. 10, 1967, pp. 30-31.

Unk. "Arrow of Death". Time, May 12, 1967, pp. 24-25.

Unk. "Gnat of Hill 881". Time, May 12, 1967, p. 42.

Unk. "Province in Trouble". Time, Apr. 21, 1967, p. 43.

Unk. "Escalation from Hanoi". Time, May 19, 1967, pp. 32-33.

Unk. "Demilitarizing the Zone". Time, May 26, 1967, pp. 24-25.

Unk. "Under Fire". Time, Jun. 9, 1967, p. 31.

Unk. "Taking Stock". Time, Jul. 4, 1967, pp. 20-21.

Unk. "The Versatile Enemy". Time, Jul. 21, 1967, pp. 28-31.

Unk. "Band of Heroes". Time, Sept. 1, 1967, p. 16.

Unk. "The Bitterest Battlefield". Time, Sept. 22, 1967, p. 28.

Unk. "Thunder from a Distant Hill". Time, Oct. 6, 1967, pp. 21-24.

Unk. "The 13[cent] Killers". Time, Oct. 27, 1967, pp. 36-39.

Unk. "Fallen Stars". Time, Nov. 24, 1967, pp. 27-28.

Unk. "Showdown at Khe Sanh". Time, Feb. 2, 1968, pp. 25-26.

Unk. "The General's Gamble". Time, Feb. 9, 1968, pp. 22-32.

Unk. "Waiting for the Thrust". Time, Feb. 23, 1968, pp. 31-32.

Unk. "On the Defensive". Time, Mar. 1, 1968, pp. 18-19.

Unk. "Living on Air: How Khe Sanh Is Sustained". Time, Mar. 1, 1968, p. 19.

Unk. "Period of Adjustment". Time, Mar. 15, 1968, p. 21.

Unk. (Untitled article, consisting of text and photographs, which detailed the surgical removal of an undetonated mortar round from the body of Nguyen Van Luong). Life, Oct. 14, 1966, pp. 98A & 98B.

Unk. "Victory or Rain-Out". Newsweek, Oct. 16, 1967, p. 42.

Unk. "Drawing the Noose". Newsweek, Feb. 5, 1968, pp. 39-40.

Unk. "How the U.S. Lost Lang Vei". Newsweek, Feb. 19, 1968, pp. 42-43.

Unk. "Waiting for the Second Wave". Newsweek, Mar. 4, 1968, pp. 28-29.

Unk. (Untitled article detailing a fatal fire in the Apollo space capsule). Life, Feb. 10, 1967, pp. 30-31.

Unk. (Untitled article about Con Thien). Life, Oct. 27, 1967, p. 43.

Unk. "An Alumnus in Vietnam". St Vincent College Magazine, Unk, pp. 13-14.

Index

About The Author

Marion Sturkey enlisted in the Marine Corps in April 1961. After boot camp at Parris Island he received the Leatherneck Magazine Award. Three years later the Marine Corps selected then-Corporal Sturkey for the MARCAD flight training program. Marion graduated from Pre-Flight Class 43-63 as Cadet Regimental Commander in April 1964. After completion of flight training, he became Naval Aviator number T-9219 in April 1965 and received his commission as a Second Lieutenant.

Marion joined HMM-265, the first Marine Corps squadron to fly the new Boeing H-46 helicopters. After training for another year in North Carolina and the Caribbean, Lieutenant Sturkey and his "Bonnie-Sue" squadronmates landed in Vietnam in May 1966. Marion flew combat missions until he was wounded during an emergency medevac flight in August 1966. After four months in the Naval hospital in Yokosuka, Japan, he went back to Vietnam, rejoined his squadron, and returned to duty in the cockpit. From the Boeing Company, Marion received the Boeing Rescue Award. His military decorations include the Purple Heart, multiple Air Medals including the Single Mission Air Medal, the Vietnamese Cross of Gallantry, and the Presidential Unit Citation.

The Marine Corps promoted Marion to the rank of Captain when he returned to the United States in 1967. He spent a year at MCAF New River, North Carolina, training new pilots to fly the H-46 in combat. Piloting Bureau Number 154007 (full of ferry tanks for an assault on the record books) on March 1, 1968, Marion set the unrefueled endurance record (9.1 hours) for the CH-46D series of Marine Corps helicopters. After seven years of service, he was released from active duty in April 1968.

Marion now lives in his original hometown, his beloved rural community of Plum Branch, South Carolina. *Bonnie-Sue'* is his second book.

To Order This Book:

Books are $24.00 each . . . . _____

Add $3.00 for shipping and handling . . . . _____
   (no additional charge for more than one book)

TOTAL . . . . _____
   (South Carolina residents, add sales tax)

Do you want the author
to autograph your book?

Yes_____ No_____

<u>Print</u> or <u>type</u> your name and address. Make your <u>check payable</u> to
Heritage Press International. Books are shipped Fourth Class
Book Rate. Mail your order to the address below. Please allow 30
days for delivery:

Heritage Press International
204 Jefferson Street
P. O. Box 333
Plum Branch, SC 29845
(Phone: 864-443-5081)